the Forties Gals

By James Robert Parish

As Author

The Fox Girls*
The Paramount Pretties*
The RKO Gals*
The Slapstick Queens
Good Dames
Hollywood's Great Love Teams*
Elvis! and Supplement
Great Movie Heroes
Great Child Stars
Great Western Stars
Film Directors Guide: Western Europe
Film Actors Guide: Western Europe
The Jeanette MacDonald Story
The Tough Guys*
Hollywood Character Actors*

As Co-author

The Emmy Awards: A Pictorial History
The Cinema of Edward G. Robinson
The MGM Stock Company: The Golden Era*
The Great Spy Pictures
The George Raft File
The Glamour Girls*
Liza!
The Debonairs*
Hollywood Players: The Forties*
The Swashbucklers*
The All-Americans*
The Great Gangster Pictures
The Great Western Pictures
Hollywood Players: The Thirties*
Film Directors Guide: The U.S.
The Great Science Fiction Pictures
Hollywood on Hollywood
The Leading Ladies*
The Hollywood Beauties*
The Funsters*

As Editor

The Great Movie Series
Actors' Television Credits: 1950–1972 and Supplement

As Associate Editor

The American Movies Reference Book
TV Movies

By Don E. Stanke

As Co-author

The Glamour Girls*
The Debonairs*
The Swashbucklers*
The All-Americans*
The Leading Ladies*
The Hollywood Beauties*

*Published by Arlington House

the Forties Gals

**JAMES ROBERT PARISH
AND DON E. STANKE**

with Roger Greene and Thomas Nocerino

Research Associates:
John Robert Cocchi and Florence Solomon

 Arlington House
333 Post Road West, Westport, Connecticut 06880

Copyright © 1980 by James Robert Parish and Don E. Stanke

All rights reserved. No portion of this book may be reproduced without the written permission of the publisher except by a reviewer who may quote brief passages in connection with a review.

Library of Congress Cataloging in Publication Data

Parish, James Robert.
   The Forties gals.

   Includes index.
   1. Moving picture actors and actresses—United States—Biography. I. Stanke, Don E., joint author.
II. Title.
PN1998.A2P3895   791.43'028'0922 [B]   79-18602
ISBN 0-87000-428-X

Manufactured in the United States of America

For BETTY GRABLE
(1916–1973)

Acknowledgments

Research Material
Consultant:

DOUG McCLELLAND

Research Verifier:

EARL ANDERSON

Jack Barnich
Richard E. Braff
Kingsley Canham
Howard Davis
Morris Everett, Jr.
Film Favorites (Bob Smith, Charles Smith)
Films in Review
Focus on Film
Connie Gilchrist
Alex Gildzen
Pierre Guinle
Tim R. Hinch
Charles Hoyt
Mary Catherine Johnston
Ken D. Jones
Miles Kreuger
William T. Leonard
David McGillivray
Albert B. Manski

Alvin H. Marill
Virginia Mayo
Jim Meyer
Mrs. Earl Meisinger
Peter Miglierini
Richard Picchiarini
Michael R. Pitts
Screen Facts (Alan G. Barbour)
Anthony Slide
Bea Smith
Irene Solomon
Madolin Stanke
Charles K. Stumpf
T. Allan Taylor
Evelyn Thomson
Lou Valentino
Rich Wentzler
Moya Wharton

And special thanks to Paul Myers, curator of the Theatre Collection at the Lincoln Center Library for the Performing Arts (New York City), and his staff: Monty Arnold, David Bartholomew, Rod Bladel, Donald Fowle, Maxwell Silverman, Dorothy Swerdlove, Betty Wharton, and Don Madison of Photo Services.

Contents

Lauren Bacall 11
Susan Hayward 67
Ida Lupino 131
Virginia Mayo 195
Ann Sheridan 255
Esther Williams 323
Jane Wyman 367
Index 441

With Humphrey Bogart in *The Big Sleep* ('46).

1

LAUREN BACALL

> 5′ 8½″   119 pounds
> Tawny blonde hair   Blue-green eyes
> Virgo

ALTHOUGH SHE IS very much a chic "with it" lady of today, Lauren Bacall ironically is firmly tied to the past in the public's eye. She achieved her greatest film successes in the Forties opposite her offscreen husband, Humphrey Bogart, and it is through his enduring legend that she managed to sustain a high degree of public recognition after her movie career foundered in the Fifties. Later she made a spectacular comeback onstage in a series of starring theatrical vehicles: *Goodbye, Charlie*; *Cactus Flower*; and *Applause!*

But to the mature moviegoer, and even to today's generation of TV watchers, Lauren is still that special Forties Gal with the distinctive "Look." It is difficult, three decades after the fact, for her to escape the stereotyped image engendered by her early cinema popularity. Obviously her unique impact was forceful. Years ago she admitted, "Sometimes I've thought that if the public didn't stop taking these trips down Memory Lane about me, I was going to lose my mind...." Thankfully, Lauren has proceeded on her own special level.

In a cover story on Bacall, *Time* magazine once assessed: "What is fascinating about Bacall is not so much her kinetic sea-green eyes or her svelte-as-sin 129-lb. body, but the distillation of glamour into poise, inner amusement, and enriched femininity that no twenty-year-old sex kitten has lived long enough to acquire. [Onstage] playgoers can sense the discipline that shapes her performance, the reliable professionalism of the middle years, so that in her deft command of her craft as an actress-comedienne she is an authentic as well as beguilingly lovely symbol of the generation." Perhaps critic James Agee best described the special allure of Lauren Bacall when he noted of the then screen newcomer, ". . . [she] has cinema personality to burn, and she burns both ends against an unusually little middle. . . . She has a javelinlike vitality, a born dancer's eloquence in movement, a fierce female shrewdness, and a special sweet sourness. With these faculties, plus a stone-crushing self-confidence and a trombone voice, she manages to get across the toughest girl a piously regenerate Hollywood has dreamed of in a long while. . . ."

This is the mettle that has made Bacall a very distinctive Forties Gal.

Betty Joan Perske was born in New York City on Tuesday, September 16, 1924, the only child of William and Natalie Weinstein Perske. Her father, an Alsatian immigrant, was a salesman of medical instruments. Her mother, of German-Rumanian background, was a native New Yorker. The family of three lived in less than comfortable circumstances on 103rd Street where Betty's parents regarded quarreling with one another as a way of life. When Betty was six years old her parents separated, and they were divorced in 1932. The last time Betty was to ever see her father was in 1934 when he left New York to live near Washington, D.C.*

After the divorce Natalie Perske adopted the surname of Bacal, which is the Rumanian version of Weinstein (meaning "wine glass" in German). She found a job as a private secretary to the head of a large corporation and set herself the personal goal of raising her daughter. Many years later in a *Saturday Evening Post* interview with Thomas Meehan, Betty would say, "When I was a kid, it was me and my mother against the world, and she was awfully good to me." Natalie Bacal was ambitious for her daughter, and with the financial help of her brothers she managed to send Betty to a private boarding school called Highland Manor in Tarrytown, New York.

From the time she was three years old, Betty had taken dancing lessons. When she reached her eighth year, her dream was to become a ballerina. She fervently studied ballet until she was thirteen, when her teacher informed her that she could never attain proficiency in the art because she lacked the correct foot formation to stand *en pointe*. She was simply unable to hold the requisite position for very long because it hurt her toes. With the demise of this dream career she turned to acting as a secondary outlet, and her mother enrolled her in Saturday afternoon drama classes. From these, Betty determined that she wanted to be a stage actress. She thought of motion pictures as a "second-rate medium" that was "strictly for Priscilla Lane and Kay Francis." She had to admit, though, that her favorite actress was Bette Davis.

While a student at Julia Richman High School in Manhattan, Betty managed to wangle some Seventh Avenue modeling jobs, using any extra dollars to buy tickets for theatre balcony seats from where she would idolize Broadway actresses such as Helen Hayes, Katharine Cornell, Jane Cowl, and Tallulah Bankhead. On her graduation at fifteen from high school in 1940, her mother enrolled her at the American Academy of Dramatic Arts where she studied with, among others, Marilyn Cantor, Eddie's daughter. However, Betty was too impatient to tolerate the regimen of the Academy, and she withdrew after less than a year.

Armed with pushy self-confidence, she joined the parade of stage hopefuls by making the rounds of producers' offices. She

*Over the years Bacall has been understandably bitter about her father's "treatment" of his family. Recently, a *Los Angeles Times* staff writer interviewed ninety-year-old William Perske in his Chevy Chase, Maryland, luxury apartment, where he lives with his second wife, Sally. Of his daughter's attitude toward him, he comments, "Everything that Betty wrote in her book about me is what her mother told her happened. Not having seen me for forty-nine years, she didn't know anything except what her mother put into her head. . . . I've sent her letters. I've sent her telegrams. Never once did I have a response." Of his wishes for the future: "I'd like to see the grandchildren, but I don't want to see her—after what she wrote about me! I went through forty-nine years of the devil. I don't want a repetition of it. I've suffered enough."

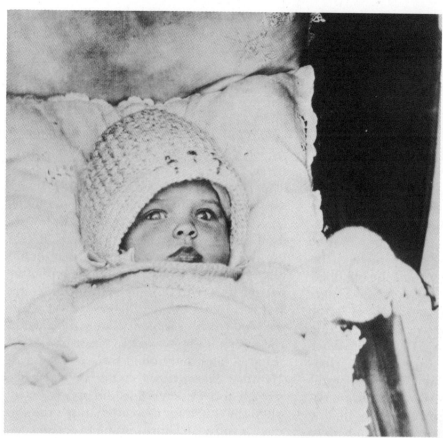

At age seven months.

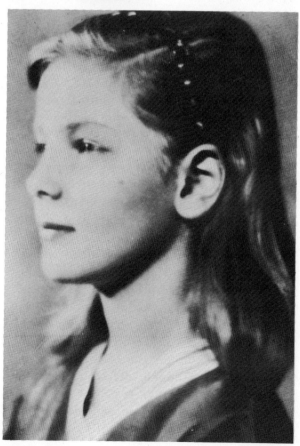

At age ten.

also added another "l" to the name of Bacal (which she had assumed as her own after her mother's divorce) so that her surname would *not* rhyme with cackle or tackle.

Among her acquaintances and competitors along Producers' Row, Betty became tagged as "The Windmill" because of her long-strided walk and her gangling limbs. Modeling assignments continued to keep her in pocket money, but her ambition was still set on the theatre.

When modeling proved to be a bore for Betty, she quit in order to take an usherette's job at the St. James Theatre. This at least allowed her to be closer to her true professional love. At this point she obtained publicity (although nameless) in *Esquire* magazine through the auspices of critic George Jean Nathan who picked her as one of the "Bests of the Year." He described her as "the prettiest theatre usher: the tall, slender blonde in the St. James Theatre, right aisle, during the Gilbert and Sullivan engagement—by rapt agreement among the critics, but the bums are too dignified to admit it."

During her free hours Betty "hung out" at Walgreen's Drug Store at 44th Street and Broadway, hoping that someone of importance might spot her. She also acted as a hostess at the Stage Door Canteen where Broadway producers often alternated as top host. To supplement her usherette's salary, she hawked *Actor's Cues*, a mimeographed sheet containing newsy items about Broadway. Her news beat was outside Sardi's Restaurant, where again she nurtured hopes of being discovered. Her stomach was often filled at Schrafft's at 83rd Street and Broadway where a friend named Issur Danielovitch worked the soda counter. A student at the American Academy of Dramatic Arts, Danielovitch also dreamed of show business success, and he sympathized with Betty's plight to the point of "forgetting" to present her with a tab for some of her repasts. A few years later Danielovitch would change his name to Kirk Douglas.

Betty's friends were amazed at but respectful of her bold approach to big-time producers. She would frequently plunk herself in front of them, blocking their paths, and say: "I'm Betty Bacall and I'd be a really great asset to your production." There is no known record of the detained producers' reactions and remarks to her. However, producer Max Gordon took her at her word and gave her a walk-on part in his staging of *Johnny Two by Four*, written by Rowland Brown. The play opened at the Longacre Theatre on a drizzly March 16, 1942. It was a murder melodrama set in a Greenwich Village speakeasy, circa 1925, in which bodies tumbled left and right and trumpet solos set the tone of the period. Betty's part (62nd billing in a cast of 66) was that of a speakeasy patron. The critics trounced the production, and it closed a few days later. "It was a rotten play," Betty recalled, "but rotten or not, I was terrifically excited to be in it."

Bacall later auditioned for a road tour of *My Sister Eileen*; however her inexperience was all too evident. She did much better when she tested for the understudy's role (to star Dorothy McGuire) in the proposed national touring company of the hit play *Claudia*. Betty won the role, but then she decided that it might be damaging to her career to be away from Broadway for so long a period. She rejected the job offer.

Although Bacall's "acting debut" had gone unnoticed by New York's theatre critics, Baron Niki de Gunzberg, an executive at *Harper's Bazaar* magazine, took particular notice of her when they met at a New York City club. He in turn introduced her to ace photographer Louise Dahl-Wolfe and *Harper's Bazaar* fashion editor Diana Vreeland. Beginning with the February 1943 issue, photographs of Betty appeared in nearly every issue of the prestigious magazine. Nevertheless, she took a leave from that promising job when George S. Kaufman offered her a role in the play *Franklin Street*. The show, authored by Ruth Goetz, required the ingenue to portray a girl who wanted to become an actress. Kaufman visualized Betty as that young woman, and she grabbed the opportunity. However the production, which opened in Wilmington, Delaware, in the fall of 1942, folded in Washington, D.C.

Betty Bacall then returned to the salary-paying job of a *Harper's Bazaar* model and found herself as the cover girl for the March 1943 issue "in a getup that made her look like a teen-age Mata Hari" (*Saturday Evening Post*). Wearing a high-collared, wide-shouldered coat and a white beanie-type hat, she was photographed standing patriotically outside the door of the American Red Cross Blood Donor Service. Not long after this photograph appeared, she won a contest sponsored by a modeling agency and was named "Miss Greenwich Village of 1943."

Meanwhile, out in Hollywood, producer/director Howard Hawks was seeking a sultry dame to act the part of Marie in his film version of Ernest Hemingway's *To Have and Have Not* (1944). Luckily for all concerned, Hawks' wife always read *Harper's Bazaar*. She handed her husband a copy of the March issue and pointed to the girl on the cover. Hawks telephoned his New York contact, agent Charles Feldman, who got in touch with Betty through the magazine. A few days later, Betty, accompanied by her mother, arrived in Los Angeles by train.

The new Warner Bros. contractee ('44).

At Warner Bros., the studio to which Hawks was then committed, Betty was screen-tested in a scene from the script of *Claudia* (the play which had been made into a film in 1943 by Twentieth Century-Fox and had catapulted Dorothy McGuire to movie fame). Bacall was not pleased about having to rehash a scene from *Claudia* after her New York stage test in the role, nor was she willing to fathom the movie industry's habit of trying to change every newcomer into a stereotype of the acceptable "look." "I don't get it," she once protested. "When you go into a store to buy something, you buy it because you like it and can use it. You don't take a potato masher home and carve it into a spoon."

Hawks liked Betty's test well enough to put her under personal contract (at $250 a week). Soon Jack L. Warner, the studio head, saw Bacall's audition and asked Hawks to share her contract with the studio. Meanwhile Columbia Pictures offered the fledgling a decorative bit in their planned tribute-with-plot honoring America's magazine cover girls, appropriately enough entitled *Cover Girl* (1944). Betty rejected that deal.

All of this occurred in May 1943, at which time the Hawks-Warner Bros. team changed her first name to Lauren (over her protests) and ordered their publicity department to begin exploiting the new girl. Most of the information handed to fan magazines was true with the exception of that regarding the lineage of her parents who were now purported to "trace their American ancestry back several generations." Not given to admitting to phony information, Lauren Bacall simply told anyone who asked that she was part-Rumanian, part-French, and possibly part-Russian. At nineteen, her height was 5'8½", her weight was 119 pounds, and she had blue-green eyes and long, tawny blonde hair. Her figure measured: 34-23½-35. "My sex is in my face," she was to purr.

Hawks did nothing to alter her physical appearance, since he wanted her to remain as he had discovered her on the magazine cover. He did, however, order her to the remote sound stages and open fields of the

Warner Bros. lot where she developed her trademark voice and diction. For months she recited lines under every possible condition until she went, according to Hawks, from "a high nasal pipe to a low guttural wheeze." He instructed her to speak slowly and softly.

Six months passed before he was ready to start the cameras rolling on *To Have and Have Not*, with Humphrey Bogart as the star. Betty—everyone continued to call her by her given name—was to receive third billing, following Bogart and Walter Brennan. When the 43-year-old Bogart met his new leading lady, having already viewed her test, he told her, "I think we're going to have a lot of fun making this picture together, kid."

Hawks had warned Bogart of his directorial intentions, saying: "You are about the most insolent man on the screen, and I'm going to make this girl a little more insolent than you are." The director worked hard with his feminine lead to make her one of the most self-willed characters that ever appeared on the silver screen. A few times he permitted her to project her own interpretation of a gesture or a line while Bogart patiently stood on the sidelines waiting. Because he liked the newcomer, Bogart even went so far as to allow her to steal a few scenes from him. Hawks was to say later, "Without his help, I couldn't have done what I did with Bacall. The average leading man would have gotten sick and tired of the rehearsal and the fussing around."

The plot of *To Have and Have Not* has Betty as Marie Browning (nicknamed "Slim"), a tough-as-nails thief who is buying her way from Trinidad to the United States after the fall of France in 1940. She arrives at the island of Martinique where she encounters Harry Morgan (Bogart), the skipper of the cabin cruiser "Quan Conch." She applies the name of "Steve" to the skipper only because he reminds her of a Steve. Oblivious to the war, Morgan hires himself out to wealthy clients who want to fish. When his funds are impounded by the Vichy police, he undertakes the job of rescuing the local French underground leader (Walter Molnar) and his wife (Dolores Moran) from a nearby inlet. Morgan needs the money for his own needs and to buy "Slim" a plane ticket to the States.

Further along in the film, Steve returns to Martinique to find "Slim" singing in a cafe to the accompaniment of Cricket (Hoagy Carmichael). Expecting a visit from the Vichy police, Morgan instructs her to pack for a quick departure. But when he learns that his alcoholic sidekick Eddie (Brennan) has been arrested, he whips the Vichy police representatives (Dan Seymour and Sheldon Leonard) into submission, having the former call for the release of Eddie. Together, Morgan, Marie, and Eddie leave the intrigue-ridden island of Martinique.

Betty "sang" two songs in the film: "How Little We Know" and "Am I Blue?" There is still much speculation as to who actually performed the soundtrack singing for her, with some film historians crediting teenaged Andy Williams with the feat.

The dialogue (written by Jules Furthman, William Faulkner, and Hawks) between Bogart and Betty is sexy and loaded with double-entendres. At the start the girl figures the toughened skipper to be a pushover for her physical charms, but when he stoically waits it out, she tries to antagonize him into bedding her. In one scene she takes a bottle of liquor to his room and asks: "Who's the girl, the one who left you with a high opinion of women? She must have been some girl." When she kisses him, she adds, "It's even better when you help." Then she exits, leaving him seated in a chair. However, she reappears a few scenes later, to further arouse him. This time her exit line had male members of movie audiences whistling. Standing seductively at the door, she says: "You know you don't have to act with me, Steve. You don't have to say anything, and you don't have to do anything. Not a thing. Oh, maybe just whistle. You know how to whistle, don't ya, Steve? You just put your lips together and—blow." She slams the door shut behind her and Bogart gives a low wolf-call whistle. The sultry scene has become a classic of erotic cinema.

With Humphrey Bogart in *To Have and Have Not* ('44).

With Dan Seymour, Aldo Naldi, Humphrey Bogart, and Sheldon Leonard in *To Have and Have Not*.

The film was sneak-previewed at Huntington Park, California, in the early summer of 1944. When Jack L. Warner read some of the audience comment cards and discovered the highly favorable reaction to Bacall, he decided to first launch a widespread publicity campaign on the young actress. Thus the film was held from general release until October.

When *To Have and Have Not* did open, the critics quickly displayed their intrigue over Lauren. James Agee in *The Nation* called her a "very entertaining, nervy, adolescent new blonde" and added: "It has been years since I have seen such amusing pseudo-toughness on the screen." *Variety* judged her "an arresting personality in whom Warner Bros. has what the scouts would call a find." The *Variety* critic then became all male with, "She can slink, brother, and no fooling!"

The name of Lauren Bacall became an overnight household reference point throughout America. Her face appeared on the cover of *Life* magazine in 1945 and she was dubbed "The Look" by columnist Walter Winchell. She was most often compared with Marlene Dietrich and Katharine Hepburn, while her voice was measured to be somewhere between Ann Sheridan's and Veronica Lake's. For fan consumption it was written that she did not drink much but was a cigarette chain smoker. She loved coffee and artichokes, and her favorite off-screen costume was reported to be slacks with a sweater over a blouse, offset with "outrageous" shoulder bags. Her culinary abilities were non-existent and she liked to dance. The studio photo department found that she appeared more glamorous by slightly blurring her pictures, yet she was purportedly scornful of insincerity. Her own description of herself was "bittersweet chocolate."

She received further worldwide fame in February 1945 when she was photographed in a half-sitting, half-reclining position atop an upright piano with Vice-President Harry S. Truman at the keyboard. Taken at the National Press Club, the photograph became as widely circulated as the kneeling in-bed shot of Rita Hayworth garbed in a lacy, black negligee. For her piano music appreciation shot, Betty wore a wide-shouldered, wide-lapeled gray suit with the skirt at her kneecaps. Framed by her shoulder-length hair, her exotic eyes and full, pouty mouth ("The Look") appeared to be beckoning the seemingly asexual Mr. Truman to abandon the keyboard and politics and to take her into his arms.

In response to the sexual image that was building up around her, Betty once confessed, "I was not what you'd call a woman of the world. I'd lived with mother all my life."

Photoplay magazine's editor, Fred R. Sammis, selected Lauren as one of ten screen newcomers who would "make movie history in 1945." The other nine were: June Haver, William Eythe, Richard Crane, Gloria DeHaven, Diana Lynn, Jeanne Crain, Turhan Bey, Van Johnson, and Esther Williams. Sammis described Lauren Bacall as "a slim American girl of twenty-one who is groping her way in an alien star world."

It would be a reasonable assumption that Bacall and Bogart fell in love with one another at their initial meeting. Columnists insisted upon referring to them as "in love," although Bogart was then still enmeshed in a love/hate relationship with his third wife, actress Mayo Methot. After earlier, unsuccessful, and childless marriages to actresses Helen Mencken and Mary Phillips, Bogart met Methot in 1936 during the filming of *Marked Woman* (1937). For years after their wedding they were known as "The Battling Bogarts" because of their outlandishly knock-down, drag-out quarrels, many of which resulted from alcoholic binges.

On May 10, 1945, Bogart obtained a divorce from Mayo Methot, and on Monday, May 21, he married Betty Joan Perske Weinstein Bacall near Mansfield, Ohio, at Malabar Farm, the home of his friend, novelist Louis Bromfield. Betty was twenty; Bogart was forty-five. Caustic observers gave little chance for the union to be a successful one, but Bogart explained, "Career girls especially don't want to go through the strug-

The rising star performing publicity modeling ('45).

On her wedding day to Humphrey Bogart, with Judge Herb Schettler (May 2, 1945).

gle of marrying a young man who's searching for a job. That's what Betty told me before we got married. She liked the idea of moving into an established home. Most girls today aren't the covered-wagon type. They prefer older husbands."

The newlyweds moved into Bogart's residence on Benedict Canyon Road, later bought a mansion on Mapleton Drive in Holmby Hills,* and derived pleasure from the $55,000 Bogart yacht *Santana*. In the Bogart garage were parked two Jaguars, a Mark VII for Betty (whom he nicknamed "Baby") and an XK 120 for good measure. Bogart considered himself anti-social and shunned nightclubs and most Hollywood parties (though he thrived on knowing all the latest industry gossip). Said Betty, "I married an old-fashioned man—eighteenth century. He's a prude. This surprises you. These are not the terms in which you think of him. But let me tell you something. Bogie, because he is not a secure man, is a very deceptive one." Betty was to later recall the early years of her marriage to Bogart with the assertion: "When I was away from Bogie for even three or four hours, I couldn't wait for the moment I saw him again, and he felt the same way about me."

It was not until a year after the release of *To Have and Have Not* that Betty was seen in her second film, Warner Bros.' *Confidential Agent* (1945), this time co-starred with Charles Boyer. She has referred to this soundstage excursion into international intrigue as "a terrible movie in which I was dreadful too." Based on a Graham Greene novel, the story is set in London during October 1937. She is Rose Cullen, an English (!) girl who befriends Denard (Boyer), an agent of Loyalist Spain who hopes to squelch the English sale of coal to the Fascists. They meet on a channel crossing where she tells him: "I don't like melodrama." Nevertheless, the 118-minute film is loaded with it. Their chief opponents, among many, are two Spanish traitors to the

---

*The house had been built by Joan Bennett. It was later to be inhabited by Judy Garland and Sid Luft, and still later would become the property of Hal Wallis and Martha Hyer.

With Charles Boyer in *Confidential Agent* ('45).

Republican cause, Peter Lorre and Katina Paxinou, both of whom are artfully done away with before the optimistic finale.

Contrary to Betty's opinion of the Robert Buckner production, James Agee (*The Nation*) found it "a surprisingly serious translation of Graham Greene's thriller." Agee agreed with Betty in stating that she was not very good by calling her "still amateurish" and noting that "she is about as English as Pocahontas." However, he excused her performance with mention of "her very individual vitality [which] more than makes up for her deficiencies." Bosley Crowther (*New York Times*) was less gallant, labeling her performance as "close to being an unmitigated bore," and he chose to add: "The noise that she makes in this picture is that of a bubble going 'poof.'"

The failure of *Confidential Agent* to establish Lauren as a top screen name did a great deal to erode her self-confidence. The situation was not helped by tyrannical Jack L. Warner. Lauren would admit later, "I was always insecure about my career because Jack Warner convinced me very early that I was no good, worthless, rotten to the core. He was very good at that. I knew they would have no respect for me as an actress, a talent, a potential, and I was right. I was a commodity, a piece of meat." Fortunately for Bacall, Bogart was on hand to instill his wife with a sense of professional and personal confidence.

In early 1946 Warner Bros. scheduled *Stallion Road* (1947) as a contemporary Western drama co-starring Bogart and Bacall, but they both refused the assignment. After a short suspension period, Jack L. Warner assumed that they would agree to make the picture, and he announced on February 12, 1946, that they would be its stars after all. The couple continued to hold out, however, and Ronald Reagan and Alexis Smith received the assignments as, respectively, a veterinarian and a rancher.

In *Two Guys from Milwaukee* (1946) Bacall and Bogart "guest starred" as themselves. In the stilted plot Prince Henry (Dennis Morgan) of the Balkans regards Lauren Bacall as his dream girl. He is further convinced of that fact when he attends a movie and watches her sing "And Her Tears Flowed Like Wine." Later, on a plane, he finds himself seated next to his dream girl. As he settles down for a pleasant trip with her, he is jolted back to reality when a hand taps him on the shoulder. It is Humphrey Bogart, giving him the high sign to move away. Finis.

The Big Sleep (1946), the next feature co-starring the team of Bogart and Bacall, was actually completed prior to *Confidential Agent* and *Two Guys from Milwaukee,* but it was not released in the United States until August 1946. (Warner Bros.' rationale was that the delay would allow word-of-mouth to build about the Bogart-Bacall romance; moreover, Jack L. Warner had ordered new scenes filmed to bolster the sexual relationship between the movie's co-stars. The most notable addition was the repartee bounced back and forth between the two, dealing on the surface with horse racing, but in actuality connoting the sensual rapport between the two.)

In a promotional trailer advertising *The Big Sleep,* Bogart is seen browsing in a book store for "a good mystery . . . something off the beaten track like *The Maltese Falcon.*" He is handed Raymond Chandler's best seller *The Big Sleep* which, the salesgirl points out, "has everything the *Falcon* had and more."

Certainly *The Big Sleep* has more major characters (twenty-two as compared to *Falcon*'s thirteen) which makes for confusion in any synopsis of the film. Whereas Betty was featured in her debut film with Bogart, in *The Big Sleep* she received co-star billing as Vivian Sternwood Rutledge, one of two spoiled daughters of General Sternwood (Charles Waldron). She hires private eye Philip Marlowe (Bogart) to vanquish a dealer in smut (Theodore Von Eltz) who has some nude photographs of Carmen Sternwood (Martha Vickers), the general's younger daughter.

In this picture the love team of Bogart and Bacall continued their oncamera battle of supremacy, each trying to top the other in aggressive toughness. At their first meeting Bacall's character tells the detective, "So you're a private detective. I didn't know they existed except in books or else they were greasy little men snooping around hotel corridors. My, you're a mess, aren't you?" She also advises him, "I don't like your manners." He sarcastically grants that his manners are not the best and adds: "I grieve over them on long winter evenings." She resents his talking back to her and asks, "Do you always think you can handle people like —trained seals?" He replies, "Unnha . . . and I usually get away with it, too."

When the smut dealer is murdered, all evidence of guilt points to thumb-sucking Carmen, and Vivian (who has now become his pal) asks Marlowe to quit the case. By this time he is too enmeshed in the intricate proceedings and wants to see old General Sternwood pacified before he dies (referred to by Marlowe as "The Big Sleep"). Several other bodies pile up along the route of Marlowe's investigation until he focuses on Eddie Mars (John Ridgely), a big-time gambler and owner of a casino where Vivian whiles away her time at the gaming tables. In a confrontation with Mars, Marlowe gets a confession from him and manages to extricate himself from the situation in one piece. Later Marlowe agrees to help Vivian avoid implication in the series of crimes.

It was in this film that Betty sang "And Her Tears Flowed Like Wine" which had been used in *Two Guys from Milwaukee.* Again the consensus of opinion is that Andy Williams supplied the soundtrack singing for Lauren.

Directed by Howard Hawks and playing opposite Bogart, Bacall was back on familiar ground in *The Big Sleep,* and she fared much better than she did in *Confidential Agent.* Kate Cameron (*New York Daily News*) observed, "When Baby has Howard Hawks, who discovered her, as her director and husband Humphrey Bogart to back her up in every scene, she can do anything any other pretty Hollywood starlet can do on the screen. She has confidence and poise." The *New York Times*' Bosley Crowther insisted, "Miss Ba-

In 1947.

With Humphrey Bogart in *Dark Passage* ('47).

call is a dangerous looking female, but she still hasn't learned to act." On the other hand, the public, not as demanding as the *New York Times*, accepted Bacall as a major Hollywood personality,* and within the industry the search was well under way to find Lauren Bacall types. (One of the most proficient to emerge in post-World War II Hollywood was Lizbeth Scott, a fetching combination of Bacall and Veronica Lake.)

In 1947 Bogart, abetted by Sam Jaffe and Mary Baker, established his own production company called Santana Pictures Corporation (named after his yacht). This was accomplished through an alleged secret liaison with Columbia, the studio that would release the Santana productions. Although Warner Bros. was furious over the business deal, there was little that the studio could do about it. When Bogart went to Columbia for *Dead Reckoning* (1947) it was originally planned that his leading lady would be Lauren. However, that deal did not work out, and it was Lizbeth Scott who had the opportunity to show her mettle opposite Bogart in this taut thriller.

Betty's fourth film with her husband was Warner Bros.' *Dark Passage* (1947), rated by *Photoplay* as "nothing to get steamed-up about." Set in San Francisco, the film has Betty appearing as Irene Jansen who encounters Vincent Parry (Bogart) after his escape from San Quentin. She sympathizes

*In 1978 United Artists released the remake of *The Big Sleep* starring Robert Mitchum and Sarah Miles, with the setting changed to London. *Variety* labeled it a "so-so but handsome re-make," and the *New York Times* found Miles, in the old Bacall role, "at least twice as lewd as the screenplay requires her to be, and nowhere near as electrifying." When the new version was in production Bacall snapped, "I think they're fools to do it. The first one was absolutely perfect. I don't believe in doing anything again when it was perfect the first time. . . ."

With Humphrey Bogart in a publicity pose for *Dark Passage*.

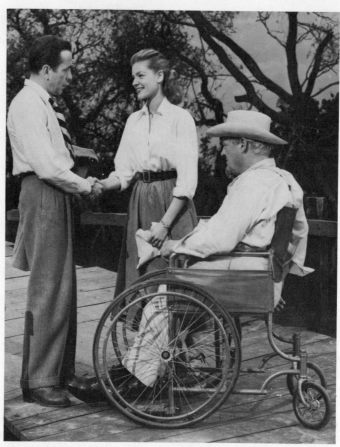
With Humphrey Bogart and Lionel Barrymore in *Key Largo* ('48).

with the escapee and takes him to her apartment. He suspects her motives, however, when he discovers that she is also acquainted with Madge Rapf (Agnes Moorehead), the star prosecution witness at his homicide trial. Meanwhile he undergoes plastic surgery to disguise his looks. Eventually Parry pressures Madge into admitting her guilt in the case, but she falls to her death from her apartment window and the truth-proving evidence is now lost. He decides to flee to the safety of South America and makes a telephone call to Irene who agrees to join him there. This was a different type of role for Betty, one in which she was not asked to slink or to act cheap or neurotic. Although she accomplished the characterization well, the role was undemanding.

On October 26, 1947, Bogart and Bacall led a delegation of twenty-five celebrities who flew to Washington, D.C., to protest alleged violations of personal freedom by the House Committee on Un-American Activities in hearings on Communist infiltration in Hollywood. Among the personalities who accompanied the Bogarts were John Huston, Evelyn Keyes, June Havoc, Richard Conte, William Wyler, and Paul Henreid. Later John Huston was to say, "It didn't do much good, but it gave us a secure feeling to be in there fighting for what we believed was justice."

Warner Bros. suspended Betty a few more times during the late Forties, once when she rejected *Romance on the High Seas* (1948), to be replaced by Janis Paige, and again when she refused *The Girl from Jones Beach* (1949) which was ultimately played by Virginia Mayo. Of her studio difficulties, Betty once said, "The parts I was offered just didn't give me any opportunity to learn anything. I was thrown into terrible pictures just so they could use a name that clicked and take advantage of the fact that I was married to Bogie, a very famous man who also hap-

Aboard the *Santana* with Humphrey Bogart in the late Forties.

pened to be a top-rate actor."

Her only film of 1948 marked the last time she would act on the screen opposite her husband. *Key Largo,* updated from the Maxwell Anderson verse drama of 1939, was directed by John Huston on a 78-day schedule. Although exteriors were filmed in Flordia, the indoor scenes were shot at the Warner Bros. studio.

Betty played Nora Temple, the widowed daughter-in-law of elderly, wheelchair-confined James Temple (Lionel Barrymore), the proprietor of an out-of-the-way Key Largo hotel. It is off-season when the hotel has few guests. When Frank McCloud (Bogart) arrives to visit the Temples (he had been in the Army with Nora's late husband), he finds that they are being held prisoner by gangster Johnny Rocco (Edward G. Robinson) and his men. It takes some time before the disillusioned Frank summons the interest or courage to combat Rocco and his cronies, after which the path is clear for Nora and Frank to create their own joint future.

Newsweek magazine applauded Betty's performance: "The surprise of *Key Largo* is Miss Bacall, who forgets her curves to play Nora straight and comes off with a forthright credible characterization." On the other hand, *Motion Picture* magazine termed her "a disappointment—she's so wonderful to look at, but so empty." (Actually the female who stole the limelight in *Key Largo* was veteran actress Claire Trevor. As the aging lush of a mistress who cowers at Rocco's brutality, she won a Best Supporting Actress Academy Award for her work.)

On Thursday, January 6, 1949, the Bogarts became parents for the first time with the birth of their six-pound, six-ounce son, Stephen Humphrey. Louis Bromfield was appointed the boy's godfather. The 48-year-old father told an interviewer, "I may not strike people as a family man, but, by God, I am one."

Later in 1949 Betty was again suspended for refusing the lead in *Storm Warning* (1950), a part eventually played by Ginger Rogers. During that same year she was also named by the National Academy of Vocal Arts as having one of the world's ten outstanding speaking voices.

Her first bitchy screen role came with Jerry Wald's film interpretation of Dorothy Baker's novel, *Young Man with a Horn* (1950). Told in flashback by narrator Hoagy Carmichael, it is the story of the rise and fall of a jazz trumpeter named Rick Martin (Kirk Douglas) who dreams of hitting the unattainable high note. The two women in his life are singer Jo Jordan (Doris Day) and wealthy dabbler Amy North (Lauren). When Rick and Amy marry, her non-musical influence upon him causes the trumpeter to forsake his music and his old friends. Eventually he starts a downhill course, ending up in a hospital for alcoholics with Jo lending support. The movie ended up being a very bowdlerized version of Miss Baker's trenchant work.

According to *Motion Picture,* Betty "has been handed an endless line of babble that makes her about as mysterious as a high school girl playing Marlene Dietrich."* Nevertheless, she enacted the role of the neurotic with insight. She also took second-billing to Douglas, her buddy of New York days. (She had recommended his dramatic talents to producer Hal B. Wallis who signed him for pictures in 1946.) Hair stylist Betty Lou Delmont shortened the famed Bacall tresses from shoulder length to above the collar and gave them waves and curls. Milo Anderson created her costumes which consisted largely of tailored suits with skirts a few inches above the ankles (popular for 1950 wear).

---

*The dialogue given Bacall to deliver was no credit to Hollywood.

Bacall: You don't like me, do you?
Douglas: No . . . you're very charming.

Bacall (about Doris Day): She's so simple and uncomplicated. It must be wonderful to wake up in the morning and know just what door you're going through.

Bacall: I don't have much respect for myself.
Douglas: I thought you were something wonderful, but now you're acting like a child.
Bacall: Don't stop now—you're just getting interesting.

Bacall (after a big fight with Douglas, is seen exiting the scene): Call me sometime.
Douglas: Call you what?

With Kirk Douglas in *Young Man with a Horn* ('50).

With Jack Carson in *Bright Leaf* ('50).

In 1950 Betty took the role of Sonia Kovac in Warner Bros.' *Bright Leaf,* replacing the originally assigned Ruth Roman when the latter's schedule became too full. In Ranald MacDougall's heavy-handed script, Lauren wore a nineteenth-century wardrobe for the first time and hair stylist Myrl Stoltz gave her the unflattering (for her) upsweep of the period.

Sonia Kovac is a woman of the world in a southern town noted for its tobacco wealth. She is the well-off proprietress of a house of ill repute whose financial aid enables Brant Royle (Gary Cooper), her first love, to produce a cigarette-making machine. Their partnership is a mammoth success until Margaret Jane (Patricia Neal), a competitor's daughter, flutters her eyelashes at him and he weds her. Later in the chronicle he is financially ruined and leaves town alone, bidding farewell to Sonia, his one remaining friend. *Bright Leaf* turned out to be production-line filmmaking at its more bland. Professionally it did nothing for anyone involved, although it allowed Gary Cooper and Patricia Neal to carry on their offcamera romance on the sound stages.

Fed up with the treatment she had received at Warner Bros., Bacall bought her way out of her studio contract. "After he'd grossed millions on pictures I'd been in," she said later, *"I had to pay money to that s.o.b. Jack Warner."* As she exited the Warner gates she vowed that she would never again return. Ironically, six months after she made the payoff to the studio, the company released, free-of-charge, any contract player who wished to terminate his or her pact. Television was making its impact felt. Bacall enunciated her philosophy of filmmaking at this time:

"What I want is a chance really to say something in pictures . . . to find out what I can really do. I'm frank enough to admit that I have a special and definite field: I'm no Duse, and I don't want to run the gamut of emotions. Nor do I feel that I'll ever get an Academy Award.

"Like Bogie, I believe that motion pictures were founded on colorful, exciting personalities, rather than on superb acting. I believe that most movie fans would rather see Bing Crosby being Bing, Gable being himself, and Danny Kaye and Gloria Swanson just being Kaye and Swanson, instead of some weighty problem play in which these personalities—or others like them—are anything but their well-loved selves.

"Personally, I don't think it matters very much if you're off the screen even five years —if you're a personality movie-goers really want to see. Maybe I'm wrong, but I'm willing to find out. I can't act with sincerity in a picture I don't think is right for the kind of screen personality that I believe Lauren Bacall should be. In pictures, people either like me or hate me; there's no middle ground— and I'm happy it's that way."

In 1951 the Bogarts did a syndicated radio series, "Bold Venture," produced by the Santana firm. Set in the West Indies and trying to capture the flavor of *To Have and Have Not,* it was an action show that had Betty as Bogart's ward. The program lasted one radio season.

On Wednesday, August 22, 1951, a few months after moving to the Holmby Hills mansion, the Bogarts became parents for a second time with the birth of a daughter, Leslie Howard Bogart. Bogart's surroundings now seemed complete with a wife who could outargue him and a son and a daughter. Although he had lost his argument against moving to the new residence, the place soon became the watering hole for what was to be known as the Holmby Hills Rat Pack. Betty would tell the press, "We had kind of an endless open house. There was a light above the front door, and, when we switched it on, that meant that we were up, drinking, and not averse to having friends join us. So maybe five nights a week, we'd have a crowd in— people like Judy Garland, Betty Comden, Adolph Green, Mike Romanoff, David Niven, Nunnally Johnson, Jimmy Van Heusen, and 'Swifty' Lazar, the agent. And, of course, Frank Sinatra was around almost every night."

The Rat Pack appointed Betty the official Den Mother, and her duties included mixing

With Ralph Reed in *How to Marry a Millionaire* ('53).

With Fred MacMurray in *Woman's World* ('54).

In *The Cobweb* ('55).

drinks, emptying ashtrays, and keeping fights under control. One of the "Rats" reported: "Bogie had a remarkable talent for goading people into fighting each other. And Bogie could be difficult to handle when he'd been drinking. But Betty could always handle him, no matter how drunk he got—she was the one person who could."

It was also in 1951 that Betty journeyed to the Belgian Congo with her husband while he starred with Katharine Hepburn in John Huston's *The African Queen* (1951). Despite the discomfort of the intense African sun and a battle against man-eating ants and dysentery, Betty and Miss Hepburn became good friends during the filming. The grueling location trek was worth the effort, for Bogart won an Academy Award as Best Actor of 1951.

After three and a half years off the screen (she rejected the lead opposite Gary Cooper in *Blowing Wild,* 1953), Betty came back in *How to Marry a Millionaire* (1953) at Twentieth Century-Fox. Her co-stars were on-the-wane Betty Grable and her studio successor Marilyn Monroe. The film's plotline had been used many times before by Fox—that of three working girls who seek wealthy husbands. The trio rent an expensive New York penthouse, but although each chooses an older, rich man as a target, each ends up with a younger, more attractive man. Lauren's mate proves to be Cameron Mitchell, who, it turns out, is a millionaire after all. Filmed in CinemaScope, it was Betty's first color movie. It is also her first screen comedy. Alton Cook *(New York World-Telegram)* noted the occasion with the comment: "First honors in spreading mirth go to Miss Bacall. She takes complete control of every scene with her acid delivery of viciously witty lines." Cook went on to label her as "a champion at rowdy comedy."

After making her television debut on Ed Sullivan's "Toast of the Town," in which she read "Casey at the Bat," Betty returned to

Twentieth Century-Fox. There she co-starred in *Woman's World* (1954)* as Fred MacMurray's wife. The screenplay is another look at the human chess game involved with big business (here the auto industry). Clifton Webb is the car mogul who must select a new general manager from among three top candidates. Bacall and MacMurray are on the verge of getting a divorce because she is tired of all the time that he devotes to his work. As it works out, the couple is pleased that MacMurray loses the promotion to Van Heflin.

At MGM, the following year, Betty played a widow who consoles mental sanitarium doctor Richard Widmark in *The Cobweb* (1955), a role originally slated for Lana Turner. During that same year she broke her vow and returned to Warner Bros. for the onlocation (at China Camp, California) CinemaScope, color film, *Blood Alley*. As the daughter of an American doctor in Communist-occupied China, she is among the passengers on a ship filled with refugees that is being guided to Hong Kong by John Wayne (who was a last-minute casting replacement for truculent Robert Mitchum). The British magazine *Picturegoer* referred to her as "the ever-fascinating Lauren Bacall."

In May 1955 as the Bogarts celebrated their tenth wedding anniversary, Bogart told friends and relations why he thought their marriage in Hollywood had survived: "We're old-fashioned. We believe in double beds. It's pretty hard to sulk over something if you share the same bed."

On May 30, 1955, Betty portrayed on television the role created at Warner Bros. by Bette Davis in *The Petrified Forest*. In the NBC-TV offering on "Producers Showcase," she co-starred with Bogart (repeating his stage and film role as Duke Mantee) and Henry Fonda. The expensive production was well received. There were plans for the acting couple to star in a video version of F. Scott Fitzgerald's *The Last Tycoon*, but nothing materialized.

Eight months later she starred on CBS-TV as the dead wife's specter in *Blithe Spirit*, wearing flowing gowns and with her face whitened. Her co-stars were effervescent Claudette Colbert and Noël Coward. These two video outings did much to bolster Bacall's standing in her profession.

Meanwhile, the Bogarts were coping with their private grief. On March 4, 1956, Bogart underwent surgery for cancer of the esophagus. The nine-hour ordeal was only partially successful. At home Betty remained by his side in the evenings, but he insisted that she continue working at her craft.

At Universal-International she was Lucy Moore in *Written on the Wind* (1956), playing a cool-headed New York career girl. She is beguiled by visiting Texan Kyle Hadley (Robert Stack) who holds back none of the family oil riches in wooing her. With him is his less-than-rich friend and protector Mitch Wayne (Rock Hudson) who demonstrates a detached interest in Lucy. In Texas, after Lucy and Kyle are wed, Kyle and his nymphomaniac sister Marylee (Dorothy Malone) suspect Mitch and Lucy of having an affair. Lucy is drawn to Mitch because it has become increasingly difficult for her to communicate with her neurotic husband. When Lucy announces that she is pregnant, the film rises to high melodrama. A drunken Kyle threatens to shoot Mitch, and in the struggle Kyle is killed. Marylee then becomes the family head and clearly indicates that there is no room for Lucy, who wants to clear out as quickly as she can anyway.

Written on the Wind is a highly polished production directed by Douglas Sirk. While Betty was excellent as the befuddled Lucy, the acting honors went to Stack and Malone, with the latter earning an Oscar as Best Supporting Actress of 1956.

Warner Bros. had originally purchased John P. Marquand's novel *Melville Goodwin, U.S.A.* with Bogart and Bacall in mind, but because of Bogart's continuing illness, the leads were given to Kirk Douglas and Susan

---

*Also in 1954 Lauren appeared on the October 24 multi-network telecast of *Light's Diamond Jubilee* produced by David O. Selznick. In the playlet *The Girls in Their Summer Dresses*, written by Irwin Shaw, she co-starred with David Niven. Bacall and Bogart were teamed that year on an outing of Edward R. Murrow's TV show, "Person to Person."

With John Wayne and Mike Mazurki in *Blood Alley* ('55).

Advertisement for *Blood Alley*.

With children, Stephen and Leslie, and Humphrey Bogart on the set of *The Left Hand of God* ('55).

With Kim Novak and Frank Sinatra at the premiere of *The Desperate Hours* (October 1955).

Caricature of Noël Coward, Mildred Natwick, Lauren Bacall, and Claudette Colbert for the CBS-TV production of *Blithe Spirit* (January 14, 1956).

Hayward. The film emerged in January 1957 as *Top Secret Affair.*

In the ten months following Bogart's serious operation, he continued to lose weight and was confined to a wheelchair in which he was transported downstairs from his bedroom by means of a service elevator. Eventually his daily trips downstairs had to be discontinued, and out of necessity he had to be limited to his room. On Sunday, January 13, 1957, he fell into a coma from which he did not recover, and he died the next morning. He was fifty-eight years old.

In March 1957 Betty was seen on motion picture screens opposite Gregory Peck in *Designing Woman,* in a role originally intended for Grace Kelly. Labeled "sophisticated comedy" the glossy MGM picture—Dore Schary's last personal production at the studio—tells what happens when a chic dress designer (Lauren) weds a diamond-in-the-rough sportswriter (Peck). They have problems adjusting to each other's life-style, but eventually they overcome their difficulties. At best the film can be rated as merely amusing. (More astute filmgoers noted that this entry was a thickly disguised remake of 1942's *Woman of the Year* which had starred Katharine Hepburn and Spencer Tracy.) *Films in Review* decided, "Unintentionally, . . . *Designing Woman* reveals several significant things: Gregory Peck cannot do comedy; Lauren Bacall's looks are not aging too well; Jack Cole does not prove the masculinity of chorus boys by flitting about the set and kicking gangsterish boobies in the behind."

Frank Sinatra, who had consoled Betty in her grief over Bogart's death, now became her steady companion.* Their friendship deepened into a romance in the summer of 1957, with Bacall telling Louella Parsons, "We're going to get married before long." Miss Parsons rushed to her typewriter to reveal this exclusive item to the syndicated world, but when her column was printed,

---

*Bacall had almost co-starred with Sinatra in his *The Man with the Golden Arm* (1955), but for financial reasons turned down the role. Years later she would admit, "I think I was wrong."

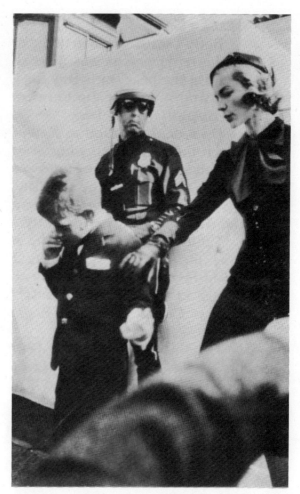

With son Stephen at Humphrey Bogart's funeral (January 1957).

the crooner immediately stopped seeing Lauren. In *Tell It to Louella* (1961) Miss Parsons wrote, "The only solace I had was that if my story could cause Frank to take off in all directions, except that one where Lauren was, then the romance could not have had any great depth or meaning for him." Miss Parsons stated of Betty, "She never blamed me, never tried to deny the story or equivocate. What is more, she accepted the knowing leers with her head high."

Betty's last Hollywood-made film for a period of six years was *The Gift of Love* (1958), Twentieth Century-Fox's remake of *Sentimental Journey* (1946), in which she and Robert Stack play a married couple (Julie and Bill) who have no children. They adopt an orphan girl (Evelyn Rudie), to whom Julie readily adjusts and vice versa, but Bill is unable to cope with the child's fantasies. After

With
Gregory Peck in
Designing Woman ('57).

In *Designing Woman*.

With Robert Stack and Evelyn Rudie in a pose for *The Gift of Love* ('58).

Julie dies her spirit returns to bring Bill and the child together in love. This would be Lauren's second and final ethereal role. She still was much too sultry and earthly at this time to portray such whimsical characterizations.

In October 1958 the actress went to Europe for a six-week holiday, returning to Hollywood in December. Then she received an offer to star in an English-made film. As she recalled in a *McCall's* magazine story in 1966, "I wanted to work, but I also had a terrible desire to get away from Hollywood, from that whole life. I couldn't have it back, you know, ever, and I found it painfully tough to make the adjustment."

In January 1959 she and her children flew to London. "I came back to life in London," she would say in 1966. "I was there for nine months and I had a wonderful time. I have a number of close friends in London, people like Noël Coward, Laurence Olivier, John Gielgud, and Vivien Leigh, and they were all marvelous to me." In London she was TV-interviewed by Edward R. Murrow for his "Small World" CBS network series.

The J. Lee Thompson-directed film, *North West Frontier* (1959), took her to India for onlocation shooting, then back to England. On completion of the movie she journeyed to France and Spain, but she planned to return to London to make a home for the children. While in Spain, she received a telephone call from Leland Hayward asking if she would be interested in starring in a Broadway play. She later recalled: "Suddenly I thought, 'My gosh, I'd better find out.' I've always believed you should find out if you really are as good as you tell yourself you are, and that involves taking chances. I'd sooner fall on my face, but at least try something, rather than never do anything."

Thus once again she packed her bags and set out with her children, this time to New York to undertake the role. Called "an un-

Rehearsing her role in the Broadway show *Goodbye, Charlie* (October 1959).

With Ursula Jeans in *Flame over India* ('60).

even comedy" by *Theatre Arts* magazine, *Goodbye, Charlie* opened at the Lyceum Theatre on December 16, 1959, to lukewarm reviews. In a wardrobe designed by Mainbocher, Betty was in the lead role as a beautiful woman who is the reincarnation of a modern crude Don Juan. She/he is sent back to earth to experience the romantic hurts he himself inflicted upon the fairer sex in his previous life. The play was written and directed by George Axelrod, also responsible for *The Seven Year Itch* and *Will Success Spoil Rock Hunter?* "It was no picnic," Betty has admitted, "but in one sense it was good for my ego which was plenty low. I discovered that I was a Broadway box-office draw.* People kept buying tickets, mainly to see me . . . and that was nice." After 109 performances, the show closed on March 19, 1960. (Twentieth Century-Fox made a diluted film version of the property in 1964 with Debbie Reynolds as the reincarnated soul.)

Betty's English film debut was released in the United States as *Flame over India* in 1960. She plays an American widow, Mrs. Catherine Wyatt, who is caught up in the turn-of-the-century Moslem uprising in India. Filmed in Technicolor against an exotic background, it is an exciting if minor adventure with Betty as her "personable and workmanlike" *(New York Times)* self. This film revealed that Betty could no longer physically play younger leading ladies and that she would have to forge a new career portraying more mature women oncamera.

In New York, at a party hosted by Roddy McDowall, Betty was introduced to Jason Robards, Jr., then on Broadway in *Toys in the Attic.* "We hit it off immediately," Betty has said, "and then a few days later I ran into Jason again at Lee Strasberg's annual New Year's Eve bash. And from that night on, well—one thing led to another." Unfortunately at the time Robards was married. Only a few weeks prior to meeting Bacall, he had wed his second wife, Rachel Taylor. He thereafter managed to obtain a divorce, but only after "a hell of a fight." Betty married Robards, who in many ways resembled Bogart, in Ensenada, Mexico, on July 4, 1961. On Saturday, December 16, 1961, a boy, Sam Prideaux Robards, was born.

Betty allegedly told a friend, "I've had all the babies I'm going to have, and I can't wait to get back to work." But publicly she took great pride in her third child, stating, "He's an absolute smash. I'm afraid I'm very besotted about him." The Robards moved to the fashionable apartment called The Dakota on Central Park West in New York. Unlike her union to Bogart in which Betty was seldom separated from her husband, she and Robards were very often apart, due to career commitments.

Her down-to-earth husband, she claimed, was "honest, irritating, demanding, unpredictable, vulnerable, impatient, funny, egocentric, extravagant, exhausting and exciting." Due to the inevitable comparisons with Bogart, Robards rejoined, "I don't feel at all resentful or competitive toward Bogie. . . . He helped to make her the kind of woman I was attracted to in the first place. With her patience and strong will, Betty makes our marriage work. So I thank Bogie for that."

Lauren returned to moviemaking in 1964 with *Shock Treatment* at Twentieth Century-Fox. It was a grade B-plus affair that shared double-bill showings in New York with *The Seven Faces of Dr. Lao.* This return to the new Hollywood, after six years, was an inauspicious one, and we can only assume that she was indeed anxious to return to work. Like *The Cobweb*, this entry deals with mental illness. An actor (Stuart Whitman) is hired to feign insanity so that he can gain information within the institution from one of the patients (Roddy McDowall), a dangerous killer. Bacall is Dr. Edwina Beighley, a psychiatrist who is none too sympathetic or eth-

---

*Bacall received generally glowing reviews: "Miss Bacall, one of the most radiant young ladies of our time, is here given the chance to speak mostly like a man (which is her natural manner) and to perform the almost impossible task of transmitting her femininity through a trench coat, which she achieves with brilliance" *(New York Journal-American)*. "As the untutored female, Miss Bacall gives a good, slam-bang performance—broad and subtle by turns, full of horseplay and guile. If this is the kind of part she wants to play, she can take satisfaction in realizing that she is playing it as well as anyone could, Lon Chaney and Mae West not excepted" *(New York Times)*.

With groom Jason Robards, Jr., cutting their wedding cake at Twentieth Century-Fox (July 5, 1961).

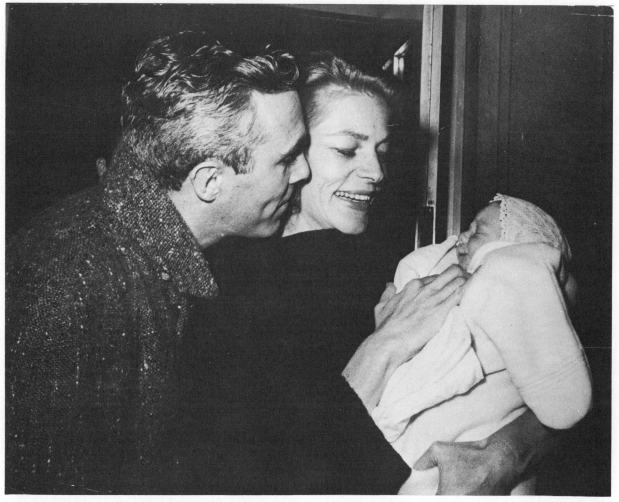

With Jason Robards, Jr., and their son Sam ('61).

ical. It was a toss-up whether the script was more strident than the forced emoting.

Also in 1964 Lauren had one of the two meaty roles in *Sex and the Single Girl* at her alma mater, Warner Bros. Supposedly "based" on the infamous book by Helen Gurley Brown, only the title remained in the much-altered farcical scenario. With fourth billing, Lauren plays the role of Sylvia, who is long-married to Frank (Henry Fonda). They argue a lot, insult each other, find fault with one another, but like every bit of it. They are neighbors to Bob Weston (Tony Curtis), a magazine writer. His immediate goal is to expose as a fraud Helen Gurley Brown (Natalie Wood), a 23-year-old virgin with a best-selling book of advice to single girls on the subject of sex. He employs his argumentative neighbors as a prime example of why a girl should not marry.

Although roundly denounced by the critics—"[It] is enough to put one off sex, single girls, and movies" (Judith Crist); "Fooey. Three cheers for the old folks at home" (Howard Thompson)—the Technicolor film has grossed $4.35 million in distributors' domestic rentals.

In July 1965, Bacall was deeply saddened by the death of her good friend Adlai Stevenson, for whose presidential candidacy she had twice campaigned. "I saw a great deal of him while he was ambassador to the U.N.," she reflected a few months later. "He could always make me laugh and feel good again."

In late 1965 she was taken out of the doldrums by Abe Burrows, the author of a new Broadway-bound play called *Cactus Flower*

With
Roddy McDowall
and Stuart Whitman
in *Shock Treatment* ('64).

In the episode
Double Jeopardy on
"The Bob Hope
Chrysler Theatre"
(NBC-TV,
January 8, 1965).

With Natalie Wood in *Sex and the Single Girl* ('65).

which he also planned to direct. Betty agreed to star as the well-starched nurse of a dentist (Barry Nelson) who finds that her life, after all, can be a bundle of laughs. As she discovers love and excitement, the cactus plant on her office desk sprouts a flower.

The production opened at the Royale Theatre on December 8, 1965, and was a hit. By now there was no surprise that Bacall could be beguiling onstage. Her glowing performance led Richard L. Coe to editorialize in the *Washington Post*: "Casting Lauren Bacall, everyman's 20th Century Athena, in a French farce turns out to have been a brilliant idea. . . . Now for Miss Bacall. Is there a wiser woman living? Is there a face more patient of male conceit, juvenility, absurdity, stupidity? With the composure of a computer determined to ignore its sex, Miss Bacall pleases demanding patients and mortal idiots. Her eyes firmly on Olympus, determined to ignore human trivia, her voice dry as vodka, her slim legs planted properly under her desk, Miss Bacall deals with all comers and contretemps."

In May 1966 the toast of Broadway told the *Saturday Evening Post*: "I live for now, and with *Cactus Flower* now is a lot of fun. This is the year that I'm the star of a Broadway hit, and dammit, I'm loving it while it lasts." The play would run for more than two years, closing in 1967 after over 1,000 performances.*

Prior to committing herself to *Cactus Flower*, Betty co-starred with Paul Newman in *Harper* (1966). The Warner Bros. movie was designed to present a more clean-cut, smoother private eye in comparison with Bogart's interpretations of that profession in the Forties. The casting of Bogart's widow was considered a coup by the producers, but in another way it was actually a dig at Bacall's veteran standing in the industry. This

---

*When Columbia filmed the play in 1969, Ingrid Bergman won the coveted role as the nurse. One of Bacall's less acidulous remarks regarding her losing the movie part was, "These things happen in films all the time. They never think you're right for the role you created. Their idea is to improve on something—their way . . . oh, it's infuriating."

As a *Time* magazine cover subject (July 29, 1966).

film sought to grab some nostalgia appeal by suggesting that the appearance of Lauren, a holdover from the Forties, was a bid to return to the good old days of classic detective filmmaking.

In *Harper,* as the crippled, wealthy Mrs. Elaine Sampson, she hires Lew Harper (Newman) to find her rich husband who has been kidnapped for ransom. In his investigation Harper encounters a variety of individuals, all with unique hang-ups and each portrayed by name players (Julie Harris, Robert Wagner, and Shelley Winters, among others). Smartly directed by Jack Smight, the feature was a popular one with audiences as well as with critics. Although Lauren received a good deal more publicity than many of her co-players, the performances by Miss Harris and Miss Winters in offbeat assignments were far more diverting.

There had been rumors for years that the Bacall-Robards marriage was not a successful one. Some felt that Lauren's insistence on remolding Robards' professional career (particularly trying to transform him into a Bogart-style movie star) was the basis for their disharmony. At any event, on Thursday, September 11, 1969, after eight years of marriage, Betty divorced Jason in Juarez, Mexico. She commented later, "There is nothing to say about *that* except that it's over. *Period.*"

As for the growing anti-establishment cult

As Stephanie in *Cactus Flower* ('67).

Playbill for *Cactus Flower*.

emerging around Bogart, she was more communicative. "The whole thing of commercializing dead people—I don't know how to deal with it. . . . His children and I have no weapon. Not only doesn't the money go to the estate, but some jerk is making a fortune from it."

Betty's mother had died in August 1969, thereby missing what would prove to be the triumph of her daughter's career. In November, Betty began training under the guidance of vocal coach David Craig for the role of Margo Channing in *Applause!*, the musical version of *All About Eve* (1950) which had starred Bette Davis as the age-conscious stage star. (Anne Baxter had been an earlier choice for the stage role.) During the rehearsal period columnist Earl Wilson asked Lauren, "And you're going to sing, not talk?" Her reply, "My dear, I'm going to sing, God help me. I've always been the most frustrated piano-bench-sitter listener who wanted to sing. But I always had to get drunk to do it. But this is not singing in somebody's living room. This is onstage and I *love* it. I sing about nine songs."

In eight weeks of pre-Broadway tryouts, *Applause!* came close to folding in Baltimore, but the February 1970 engagement in Detroit was a sellout. The $750,000 musical opened at New York's famed Palace Theatre on March 30, 1970. The next day in the *Newark Evening News,* critic Edward Sothern Hipp reflected the critical consensus when he reported, "For the first time this season, Fun City has a musical in which book and score are top drawer, the choreography exciting, and the cast, from Lauren Bacall down to a talented young chorus, something to tell the world about." (The musical, co-produced by Lawrence Kasha and Joseph Kipness, was choreographed by Ron Field and scripted by Betty Comden and Adolph Green, with music and lyrics by Charles Strouse and Lee Adams.) *Time* magazine cheered, "Lauren Bacall is the pearl in a half-good, half-not-so-good oyster of a musical called *Applause!* Star quality is supposed to be indefinable, but Bacall helps to define it. Just as one does not have to search for Picasso's signature to recognize a Picasso, so Bacall's work bears the indelible marks of style and self. She owns the stage but wants the earth. A bundle of past struggles, future aspirations and present tensions, she is never in true repose. Her presence is a demand—a lot from others and even more from herself. It is also a gift, not of the best acting, singing, and dancing, but of the distilled essence of a full life experience poured through those modes of expression. Like her friend Katharine Hepburn, she welds character and personality. Thanks to nature's potter, she also happens to be a striking beauty."

Vivacious Lauren, who proved a better dancer than singer, received an Antoinette Perry (Tony) Award in April 1970 as Best Actress in a Musical. Her closest competition was her friend Katharine Hepburn who starred in the ill-conceived musical *Coco*. Betty confided to Ralph Blumenfeld of the *New York Post,* "It meant a great deal to me, because at this particular juncture in my life,

The toast of Broadway ('68).

it seems to me for the first time I've really felt that I've earned something on my own, that I've done something that has to do with my ability."

In August 1971, Betty, the toast of Broadway, left the New York company of *Applause!* to be replaced by Anne Baxter who had co-starred with Bette Davis in the movie version. Miss Baxter was chosen over Rita Hayworth and Lizabeth Scott. Bacall went on the road for several months of touring in *Applause!* She was particularly anxious to perform the West Coast engagements to demonstrate to the film/television industry just what she could accomplish on the stage. In 1973 she headed the London company of the musical. While there, an abridged version of *Applause!* was videotaped by CBS-TV for a March 25, 1973, showing in which John J. O'Connor of the *New York Times* found her to be "viciously, exuberantly, desperately alive."

In 1974 Bacall was one of fourteen international big-name stars in Paramount's *Murder on the Orient Express*. The blockbuster mystery was based on an Agatha Christie

With Lee Roy Reams in the Broadway musical *Applause!* (March 1970).

With Wendy Hiller, Rachel Roberts, Sean Connery, Tony Perkins, and Martin Balsam in *Murder on the Orient Express* ('74).

On the ABC-TV special *Happy Endings* (April 10, 1975) with Robert Preston.

novel in which master sleuth Hercule Poirot (Albert Finney) ingeniously solved the complex caper. Filmed in London and Paris, the production reportedly cost $2.5 million, but during its first five weeks of release it grossed some $4,499,719.

In the Sidney Lumet-directed production, Betty has the role of Mrs. Hubbard, a beautifully garbed (costumes designed by Tony Walton) but gabby American widow. She, along with the other suspects, is aboard the Orient Express train, and each has had more than ample reason to murder a nasty American millionaire (Richard Widmark). Poirot interrogates each suspect, thus providing interesting cameo performances by Ingrid Bergman, Sean Connery, Wendy Hiller, Anthony Perkins, Michael York, Rachel Roberts, Jean-Pierre Cassel, Vanessa Redgrave, and Martin Balsam. Since most of the performers opted for "hamminess" rather than subtlety, it is difficult to rate the acting beyond commenting on the amount of scene-stealing and caricaturing.

When Wildwood Productions undertook the filming of *All the President's Men* (1976), based on the noted book by newsmen Carl Bernstein and Bob Woodward, it was announced that Betty and Patricia Neal were the top choices to play the role of Katherine Graham, publisher of the *Washington Post.* (Jason Robards, Jr., would play *Post* editor Ben Bradlee.) In the final script, however, the character of publisher Graham was omitted.

On April 10, 1975, Betty was seen on ABC-TV in *Happy Endings,* a comedy special consisting of four short plays. With Robert Preston she was in *A Commercial Break,* authored by Peter Stone. The appearance marked her return to New York after an absence of two years. To Kay Gardella of the *New York Daily News* she said: "I'm not sure where I ought to be. I'm not sure there's any place I should be." (Acquaintances of the star claimed that the actress was rather piqued about her single domestic status.)

Lauren was in California and Carson City, Nevada, in January 1976 when she went to work in *The Shootist* (1976), opposite John Wayne and James Stewart. As directed by Don Siegel, the film emerged a tribute to Wayne's screen career as the Iron Duke, and for many astute critics proved to be the best Wayne vehicle in years.* He played a deadly gunfighter—a legend in his own time—now a feisty old man who is dying of cancer. He arrives in Carson City of 1901 and decides to spend his remaining days at the boarding house of the Widow Rogers (Bacall). But his past catches up with him and a deadly gun duel is inevitable. James Stewart is the uncompromising elder doctor who has no comforting words for the terminally ill gunslinger. David McGillivray reported in *Films and Filming:* "It is in his scenes with Lauren Bacall as Mrs. Rogers, in which two lonely old people make diffident attempts to offer each other companionship, that Wayne excels himself." Despite solid reviews from many quarters, *The Shootist* did not fare well at the box office. Too many potential filmgoers decided the picture would be depressing and life was morbid enough without sitting through, as the *New York Times* termed it, a "geriatric Western."

Meanwhile Lauren taped an appearance for ABC-TV's "Wide World of Entertainment" on which Henry Fonda was honored with film clips and comments from his various co-workers. It was also at this time that Bacall and Frank Sinatra (a few months before he wed Barbara Marx) patched up their long-time disagreement.

On the romantic front, in recent years Bacall has been rumored to be in love with or on the verge of wedding playwright Peter Stone, British businessman Henry Stewart, French designer Ungaro, English actor Basil Hoskins, and Hollywood legend John Wayne. However, she admits, "The only man who never let me down, who never disappointed me, was Bogie. I just have not been lucky with men." She further states, "I'm not worried about being alone. I've faced life alone for so long now that I'm not bothered anymore."

*It also proved to be Wayne's final film; he died of cancer on June 12, 1979.

With John Wayne in *The Shootist* ('76).

Bacall did not accept a role in the film project *Lydia*, to be filmed in the Okefenokee swamps of Georgia, but she did co-hostess NBC-TV's *Big Event* (September 26, 1976). In the summer of 1977 she starred in a strawhat tour of the musical *Wonderful Town*. The production received poor reviews: "Bacall . . . is an explosion looking for a place to happen and *Wonderful Town*, unfortunately, is not that place. She is too confined in the role, too overshadowed by the orchestra, the better singing voices of other cast members, and the demands of a book that places her in a world that seems alien. An innocent from Ohio? Never. Bacall exudes cosmopolitan chic, always three jumps ahead of the rest of the crowd." The show toured New York, Philadelphia, Dallas, Miami, etc., generating good box-office receipts because of the Bacall marquee allure.

Her arrival in each new town was cause for a fresh onslaught of interviews. To Rex Polier of the *Philadelphia Bulletin* she confessed, "I'm in good shape. I jog and exercise a lot. I keep in shape. I like to function . . . to feel that I am using myself well, physically as well as mentally. Work for me is very important." As for Bogart, she stated, "He has lasted so long and will last forever. . . . I guess it was when I did *Applause!* that I finally was free of him and of being just a widow. But I cannot forget. He gave me much too much as a person. And I don't want to forget."

October 16, 1977, found Lauren as the subject of a Film Festival tribute at the Palace of Fine Arts Theatre in San Francisco. Thirteen movie clips were shown, starting and concluding with *To Have and Have Not*. In the question-and-answer period, she mentioned that Howard Hawks was unsure

Playbill for the 1977 tour of *Wonderful Town*.

—when he brought Lauren to Hollywood—whether to put her in a film with Bogart or Cary Grant. "I've often wondered what would have happened if he had chosen Grant." When asked if her stage hits had revitalized her movie career, she admitted, "Not at all. I created the part in *Cactus Flower*, but was not considered right for the film version.... When we opened *Applause!* in L.A. I was more nervous than for the Broadway opening. I figured I'd show 'em what they'd missed. Well, they couldn't have cared less. A few of my friends came, and a few people in the industry made the effort to show up. My L.A. opening proved nothing, except that nobody cared."

Asked for her comments on awards, she shot forth: "I hate awards. They give them for standing up and sitting down, turning left and turning right. The only reason they're given is to put more money into someone's pocket or boost TV ratings. Awards only contribute to the commercial aspect of the industry, and not to the quality. Awards are terrific—you get them if you're living or dead. Acting never began as competition. As someone once said, if it had, it would have been Lunt vs. Fontanne." (When later queried about whether she would appear if she were nominated for an Academy Award, the actress laughed, "You're damn right I would.")

Bacall was one of the hosts on the "American Film Institute 10th Anniversary" (CBS-TV, November 21, 1977), and then on March 14, 1978, she starred in a CBS-TV telefeature, *Perfect Gentlemen*. The twist to the crime drama was that it is a gang of women (Bacall, Ruth Gordon, Sandy Dennis, and Lisa Pelikan) who commit the crime. The TV movie was not well received, although the *Hollywood Reporter* acknowledged, "Bacall [married to a labor union leader!] lends her highly resourceful presence and no-nonsense maturity which holds the film together when it threatens to dissipate; she acquits herself admirably." On March 31, 1978, Bacall joined with Eve Arden, Bert Convy, Richard Crenna, Mary Tyler Moore, and others in a salute to the CBS-TV network; thereafter she could be seen on TV in a charge card commercial. (In 1978 she would participate in a billboard advertising campaign for a whiskey.) Subsequently she became professionally involved with a Public Broadcasting System TV documentary on the life of William Faulkner, and signed to join with Glenda Jackson, Carol Burnett,

Advertisement for *Perfect Gentlemen* (CBS-TV, March 14, 1978).

Promoting products in 1978.

and James Garner in Robert Altman's film *Health*. The $5.2 million feature was shot largely in St. Petersburg Beach, Florida, in the spring of 1979. Lauren was cast in this seriocomic film as Esther Brill, the eighty-three-year-old grand lady of health foods who becomes a candidate for the presidency of the United States. When asked to portray the octogenarian virgin, Lauren wryly commented, "I guess you don't have to be one to play one." Thereafter, she was a presenter at both the 51st Annual Academy Awards (April 9, 1979) and at the 32nd Tony Awards (June 4, 1979). To keep professionally active, she accepted a guest starring role in James Garner's NBC-TV detective series, "The Rockford Files," and was then signed to star in *The Fan,* a Robert Stigwood-produced feature film to be written by Norman Wexler and shot in New York in the fall of 1979.

It has been no secret over the years that while Bacall approves of the adoration of Bogart, she abhors the commercialism that has been involved in merchandising products revolving around the late star. No less annoying to her were the several late Seventies biographies of her (and Bogart) which appeared. These led the saucy star to pen her own memoirs, *Lauren Bacall—By Myself,* which appeared in early 1979, published by Alfred A. Knopf. One London newspaper paid a reputed $300,000 for the serial rights to the book. Of her literary project, Bacall would say, "It's one of my life's great accomplishments. I wrote every day. I dug out all the old letters and scrapbooks, taped conversations with all my old friends, and then got down to it. Of course, I overwrote to a ridiculous degree — 1,000 pages. But there was a lot to say." The final results, a 377-page tome, soon became the number-one bestseller on the nonfiction list, aided by Bacall's cross-country promotional tour. Two prime reasons for reader interest in her writing were that she wrote the book herself ("I would never do an 'as told to' because I think it is a totally boring, uninteresting idea."), and she was so very candid ("I knew when I agreed to do it that I would have to tell the truth—that's the only valid reason for writing an autobiography. It's easy when it's about people who are not living. With people who are still with us, it becomes difficult. I certainly didn't set out to hurt anyone or do anyone in. It just had to be a straightforward, very honest autobiography, and there is no way I could ever pass over anyone who was important to me, who changed me. Even if I would like to, I couldn't").

These days the still very iconoclastic Bacall, who recently bought a home in Amagansett, New York, has a great deal to say on a variety of subjects:

Aging and plastic surgery: "Have I had a face lift? Can't you see I haven't? I'm never going to have one. I don't have the guts, I suppose. What if they made a mistake, cut a nerve? This is my face and I'm going to live with this face. It's me, Betty Bacall — by myself and part of myself, wrinkles and all."

Remarriage: ". . . if love is going to come along in your life, it comes along. I don't think you can look for it. A new man? I'm not waiting for that. There's a good chance it won't happen now, at my age. It would be nice to have some terrific relationship, but

The star, 1970s style.

more than that I think I'd rather have a terrific new play."

Being a career woman: "My total insanity drives me, gives me the motivation to go in the race. The terrifying secret of the movie business is that each time you work you have to prove yourself all over again. . . . I still intend to work in films. I don't have that much to choose from. It's not that easy to find parts now that I'm over twenty-two."

The film business: "I think the whole motion picture industry is in some difficulty because the whole product is so small. . . . All that wheeler-dealer atmosphere in Hollywood . . . I really hate it. I suppose I'm sour grapes to a degree, but anyone would resent being passed over. . . . I don't understand actually. I thought the old Hollywood was very productive. And it seemed there were more stars who lasted longer. The studio setup was much better for the industry as a whole, if not always for the individual actors."

Contentment: "Luxury for me would be to have a flat in London and a nice little suite in a hotel in Paris so I could leave things in one cupboard and not have to carry the makeup and hair rollers. The utmost luxury is not having to think about money. I have had a great deal hardly ever, never. The only time I never had to think about it was when working in the theatre in a hit show."

Work: "I think I've hung in there for quite a while, and I do think I am a good actress. I hope I have contributed some hours of pleasure for some people, but I do not think I am a great actress. Great is a word misused all the time.

"I think I have value and worth as a human being. I've tried to be a good mother and a good wife. I feel I'm a better friend more than anything. . . . What is very important in life is to do things that are really important to your own being. You must not spend life doing things other people expect you to do. Everyone has his own route. I've got one time around and I am not planning to waste it. . . . Not to dismiss one's family, children,* husband, or lovers, I really believe in work. One's life should be concentrated on work and everything else should be fringe. Work is the most rewarding and lasting thing. Sure I dream of the right part in a film, to find a play to do in London and to meet the prince on a white horse. I know I was lucky. I am not a has-been. I'm a will-be."

*Her son Stephen resides in Connecticut with his wife Daletrend Gemelle; they have a son named James Stephen Humphrey Bogart. Stephen has no ambition for acting, nor does daughter Leslie, who in her mid-twenties is quite attractive and is a registered nurse. Son Sam lives with Bacall.

FILMOGRAPHY

TO HAVE AND HAVE NOT (*Warner Bros., 1944*) 100 min.

Producer/director, Howard Hawks; based on the novel by Ernest Hemingway; screenplay, Jules Furthman, William Faulkner; music, Franz Waxman; orchestrator, Leonid Raab; songs, Hoagy Carmichael and Johnny Mercer, Carmichael and Stanley Adams, Harry Akst and Grant Clarke; technical advisor, Louis Comien; art director, Charles Novi; set decorator, Casey Roberts; gowns, Milo Anderson; assistant director, Jack Sullivan; makeup, Perc Westmore; sound, Oliver S. Garretson; special effects, E. Roy Davidson, Rex Wimpy; camera, Sid Hickox; editor, Christian Nyby.

Humphrey Bogart (Harry Morgan); Walter Brennan (Eddie); Lauren Bacall (Marie Browning); Dolores Moran (Helene De Bursac); Hoagy Carmichael (Cricket); Walter Molnar (Paul De Bursac); Sheldon Leonard (Lieutenant Coyo); Marcel Dalio (Gerard); Walter Sande (Johnson); Dan Seymour (Captain M. Renard); Aldo Nadi (Bodyguard); Paul Marion (Beauclerc); Pat West (Bartender); Sir Lancelot (Horatio); Eugene Borden (Quartermaster); Harold Garrison, Elzie Emanuel (Black Urchins); Major Fred Farrell (Headwaiter); Adrienne d'Ambricourt, Marguerita Sylva (Cashiers); Margaret Hathaway, Louise Clark, Suzette Harbin, Gussie Morris, Kanza Omar, Margaret Savage (Waitresses); Emmett Smith (Emil, the Bartender); Hal Kelly (Detective); Chef Joseph Milani (Chef); Ron Rondell (Naval Ensign); Marcel de la Brosse (Sailor).

CONFIDENTIAL AGENT (*Warner Bros., 1945*) 118 min.

Producer, Robert Buckner; director, Herman Shumlin; based on the novel by Graham Greene; screenplay, Buckner; dialogue director, Jack Daniels; assistant director, Arthur Kueker; art director, Leo K. Kuter; set decorator, William Kuehl; music, Franz Waxman; music director, Leo F. Forbstein; sound, Oliver S. Garretson; camera, James Wong Howe; editor, George Amy.

Charles Boyer (Denard); Lauren Bacall (Rose Cullen); Katina Paxinou (Mrs. Melandez); Peter Lorre (Contreras); George Coulouris (Captain Currie); Wanda Hendrix (Else); John Warburton (Forbes); Dan Seymour (Mr. Muckerji); George Zucco (Inspector Geddes); Miles Mander (Brigstock); Lawrence Grant (Lord Fetting); Holmes Herbert (Lord Benditch); Art Foster (Chauffeur); Olaf Hytten (Harry Bates); Herbert Wyndham (Fortescue); William Stack (Butler); Herbert Clifton (Jarvis); D. Martin Jones (Detective); Bill Ellfeldt, Leighton Noble (Piano Players); Jack Carter, Stanley Mann (Singers); Arthur Gould Porter (Passenger Flirt); Alec Harford (Bartender); Gordon Richards (Immigration Officer); Keith Hitchcock (Plainclothesman); Charles Knight, Montague Shaw (Customs Officers); Lynne Baggett (Singer); Grayce Hampton (Woman on Road); Gilbert Allen (London Bobby); Brandon Hurst (Lancashire Man on Train); Cyril Delavanti, Bobby Hale, George Broughton (Mining Group); Geoffrey Steele (Hotel Clerk); Henry Mowbray (Radigan); John Rogers (Seaman); Leyland Hodgson (Freight Officer).

TWO GUYS FROM MILWAUKEE (*Warner Bros., 1946*) 90 min. (British release title: *Royal Flush*)

Producer, Alex Gottlieb; director, David Butler; screenplay, Charles Hoffman, I. A. L. Diamond; assistant director, Jesse Hibbs; art director, Leo K. Kuter; set decorator, Jack McConaghy; gowns, Leah Rhodes; music, Frederick Hollander; orchestrator, Leonid Raab; song, Charles Lawrence, Joe Greene, and Stan Kenton; dialogue director, Felix Jacoves; makeup, Perc Westmore; sound, Stanley Jones; montages, James Leicester; special effects, Harry Barndollar, Edwin B. DuPar; camera, Arthur Edeson; editor, Irene Morra.

Dennis Morgan (Prince Henry); Joan Leslie (Connie Reed); Jack Carson (Buzz Williams); Janis Paige (Polly); S. Z. Sakall (Count Oswald); Patti Brady (Peggy); Tom D'Andrea (Happy); Rosemary DeCamp (Nan); John Ridgely (Mike Collins); Pat McVey (Johnson); Franklin Pangborn (Theatre Manager); Humphrey Bogart, Lauren Bacall (Themselves); Joel Fluellen (Porter); Philo McCullough (Passenger); George Reed (Clarence, the Porter); Creighton Hale (Committee Member); Marilyn Reiss and Doris Fulton (Bobby Soxers); Lottie Williams (Old Lady); Russ Clark, Jack Mower (Cops); Chester Clute (Mr. Carruthers, the Customer); Tristram Coffin (Polly's Customer); Cosmo Sardo (Henry's Barber); Frank Marlowe (Cabby); Jody Gilbert (Large Woman); Douglas Carter, Lex Barker (Ushers); Charles Williams (Man at Microphone); Monte Blue, Ross Ford (Technicians); Charles Coleman (Valet); Patricia White [Barry] (Nurse); Janet Barrett (Stewardess); Peggy Knudsen (Juke Box Voice).

THE BIG SLEEP (*Warner Bros., 1946*) 114 min.

Producer/director, Howard Hawks; based on the novel by Raymond Chandler; screenplay,

William Faulkner, Leigh Brackett, Jules Furthman; music, Max Steiner; orchestrator, Simon Bucharoff; assistant director, Robert Vreeland; art director, Carl Jules Weyl; set decorator, Fred M. MacLean; gowns, Leah Rhodes; sound, Robert B. Lee; special effects, E. Roy Davidson, Warren E. Lynch, William McGann, Robert Burks, Willard Van Enger; camera, Sid Hickox; editor, Christian Nyby.

Humphrey Bogart (Philip Marlowe); Lauren Bacall (Vivian Sternwood Rutledge); John Ridgely (Eddie Mars); Martha Vickers (Carmen Sternwood); Dorothy Malone (Bookshop Proprietress); Peggy Knudsen (Mrs. Eddie Mars); Regis Toomey (Bernie Ohls); Charles Waldron (General Sternwood); Charles D. Brown (Norris); Bob Steele (Canino); Elisha Cook, Jr. (Harry Jones); Louis Jean Heydt (Joe Brody); Sonia Darrin (Agnes); James Flavin (Captain Cronjager); Thomas Jackson (District Attorney Wilde); Dan Wallace (Carol Lundgren); Theodore Von Eltz (Arthur Gwynn Geiger); Joy Barlowe (Taxicab Driver); Tom Fadden (Sidney); Ben Welden (Pete); Trevor Bardette (Art Huck); Joseph Crehan (Medical Examiner); Emmett Vogan (Ed).

DARK PASSAGE (*Warner Bros., 1947*) 106 min.

Producer, Jerry Wald; director, Delmer Daves; based on the novel by David Goodis; assistant director, Dick Mayberry; art director, Charles H. Clarke; set decorator, William Kuehl; music, Franz Waxman; orchestrator, Leonid Raab; wardrobe, Bernard Newman; makeup, Perc Westmore; sound, Dolph Thomas; special effects, H. D. Koenekamp; camera, Sid Hickox; editor, David Weisbart.

Humphrey Bogart (Vincent Parry); Lauren Bacall (Irene Jansen); Bruce Bennett (Bob Rapf); Agnes Moorehead (Madge Rapf); Tom D'Andrea (Sam, the Taxi Driver); Clifton Young (Baker); Douglas Kennedy (Detective); Rory Mallinson (George Fellsinger); Houseley Stevenson (Dr. Walter Coley); Bob Farber, Richard Walsh (Policemen); Clancy Cooper (Man on Street); Pat McVey (Taxi Driver); Dude Maschemeyer (Man on Street); Tom Fadden (Waiter in Cafe); Shimen Ruskin (Driver/Watchman); Tom Reynolds (Hotel Clerk); Lennie Bremen (Ticket Clerk); Mary Field (Mary, the Lonely Woman); Michael Daves, Deborah Daves (Children); John Arledge (Lonely Man); Ross Ford (Ross, the Bus Driver); Ian MacDonald (Cop); Ramon Ros (Waiter); Craig Lawrence (Bartender).

KEY LARGO (*Warner Bros., 1948*) 101 min.

Producer, Jerry Wald; director, John Huston; based on the play by Maxwell Anderson; screenplay, Richard Brooks, Huston; art director, Leo K. Kuter; set decorator, Fred M. MacLean; wardrobe, Leah Rhodes; makeup, Perc Westmore; music, Max Steiner; orchestrator, Murray Cutter; song, Ralph Rainger and Howard Dietz; sound, Dolph Thomas; special effects, William McGann, Robert Burks; camera, Karl Freund; editor, Rudi Fehr.

Humphrey Bogart (Frank McCloud); Edward G. Robinson [Johnny Rocco (Howard Brown)]; Lauren Bacall (Nora Temple); Lionel Barrymore (James Temple); Claire Trevor [Gaye Dawn (Maggie Mooney)]; Thomas Gomez [Curley (Richard Hoff)]; John Rodney (Deputy Clyde Sawyer); Marc Lawrence (Ziggy); Dan Seymour (Angel Garcia); Monte Blue (Sheriff Ben Wade); Jay Silverheels, Rodric Redwing (Osceola Brothers); William Haade (Ralph Feeney); Joe P. Smith (Bus Driver); Alberto Morin (Skipper); Pat Flaherty, Jerry Jerome, John Phillips, Lute Crockett (Ziggy's Henchmen); Felipa Gomez (Old Indian Woman).

YOUNG MAN WITH A HORN (*Warner Bros., 1950*) 111 min. (British release title: *Young Man of Music*)

Producer, Jerry Wald; director, Michael Curtiz; based on the novel by Dorothy Baker; screenplay, Carl Foreman, Edmund H. North; art director, Edward Carrere; music director, Ray Heindorf; song, Sammy Cahn and Ray Heindorf; camera, Ted McCord; editor, Alan Crosland, Jr.

Kirk Douglas (Rick Martin); Lauren Bacall (Amy North); Doris Day (Jo Jordan); Hoagy Carmichael (Smoke Willoughby); Juano Hernandez (Art Hazzard); Jerome Cowan (Phil Morrison); Mary Beth Hughes (Marge Martin); Nestor Paiva (Louis Galba); Orley Lindgren (Rick as a Boy); Walter Reed (Jack Chandler); Jack Kruschen (Cab Driver); Alex Gerry (Dr. Weaver); Jack Shea (Male Nurse); James Griffith (Walt); Dean Reisner (Joe); Everett Glass (Man Leading Song); Dave Dunbar (Alcoholic Bum); Robert O'Neill (Bum); Paul Burns (Pawnbroker); Julius Wechter (Boy Drummer); Ivor James (Boy Banjoist); Hugo Charles, Sid Kane (Men); Vivian Mallah, Lorna Jordan, Lewell Enge (Molls); Paul Dubov (Maxie); Ted Eckelberry (Elevator Boy); Keye Luke (Hamundo); Dick Cogan (Interne); Hugh Murray (Doctor); Helene Heigh (Tweedy Woman); Bill Walker (Black Minister).

BRIGHT LEAF (*Warner Bros., 1950*) 110 min.

Producer, Henry Blanke; director, Michael Curtiz; based on the novel by Foster FitzSimons; screenplay, Ranald MacDougall; art director, Stanley Fleisher; set decorator, Ben Bone; music, Victor Young; orchestrators, Sidney Cutner, Leo Shuken; dialogue director, Norman Stuart; costumes, Leah Rhodes, Marjorie

Best; assistant director, Sherry Shourds; makeup, Perc Westmore, Ray Romero, John Wallace; sound, Stanley Jones; montages, David Jones; camera, Karl Freund; editor, Owen Marks.

Gary Cooper (Brant Royle); Lauren Bacall (Sonia Kovac); Patricia Neal (Margaret Jane); Jack Carson (Chris Malley); Donald Crisp (Major Singleton); Gladys George (Rose); Elizabeth Patterson (Tabitha Jackson); Jeff Corey (John Barton); Taylor Holmes (Lawyer Calhoun); Thurston Hall (Phillips); James Griffith (Ellery); Marietta Canty (Queenie); William Walker (Simon); Charles Meredith (Pendleton); Leslie Kimmel (Hokins); John Pickard (Devers); Elzie Emanuel (Black Boy); James Adamson, Ira Buck Woods (Black Peddlers); Paul "Tiny" Newland (Blacksmith); J. Lewis Johnson (Black Grandpa); Eddie Parkes (Hotel Clerk); Shelby Bacon (Fauntleroy); Pat Flaherty (Farmer); Peter Kellett, Hubert Kerns (Farmer's Sons); Rene De Voux (Cousin Emily); Eileen Coughlan (Cousin Pearl); Cleo Moore (Cousin Louise); Nita Talbot (Cousin Theodora); Pat Goldin (Cousin Arthur); Chalky Williams (Sheriff); Marshall Bradford (Farmer); Ed Peil, Sr. (Conductor); Kermit Whitfield (Detective Curson); Charles Conrad (Edwards); Sam Flint (Johnson).

HOW TO MARRY A MILLIONAIRE *(Twentieth Century-Fox, 1953)* C-95 min.

Producer, Nunnally Johnson; director, Jean Negulesco; based on plays by Zoë Akins, Dale Eunson, and Katherine Albert; screenplay, Johnson; art directors, Lyle Wheeler, Leland Fuller; music directors, Alfred Newman, Cyril Mockridge; camera, Joe MacDonald; editor, Louis Loeffler.

Betty Grable (Loco); Marilyn Monroe (Pola); Lauren Bacall (Schatze Page); David Wayne (Freddie Denmark); Rory Calhoun (Eben); Cameron Mitchell (Tom Brookman); Alex D'Arcy (J. Stewart Merrill); Fred Clark (Waldo Brewster); William Powell (J. D. Hanley); George Dunn (Mike, the Elevator Man); Harry Carter (Elevator Operator); Robert Adler (Cabby); Tudor Owen (Mr. Otis); Maurice Marsac (Antoine); Emmett Vogan (Man at Bridge); Hermione Sterler (Madame); Abney Mott (Secretary); Ralph Reid (Jewelry Salesman); Ivan Triesault (Captain of Waiters); Herbert Deans (Stewart); Tom Greenway (Motorcycle Cop); Charlotte Austin, Merry Anders, Ruth Hall, Lida Thomas, Beryl McCutheon (Models); James Stone, Tom Martin (Doormen); Eve Finnell (Stewardess); Benny Burt (Reporter); Richard Shackleton (Bellboy).

WOMAN'S WORLD *(Twentieth Century-Fox, 1954)* C-94 min.

Producer, Charles Brackett; director, Jean Negulesco; story, Mona Williams; screenplay, Claude Binyon, Mary Loos, Richard Sale; additional dialogue, Howard Lindsay, Russel Crouse; art director, Lyle Wheeler; music, Cyril J. Mockridge; assistant director, Henry Weinberger; camera, Joe MacDonald; editor, Louis Loeffler.

Clifton Webb (Gifford); June Allyson (Katie); Van Heflin (Jerry); Lauren Bacall (Elizabeth); Fred MacMurray (Sid); Arlene Dahl (Carol); Cornel Wilde (Bill Baxter); Elliott Reid (Tony); Margalo Gillmore (Evelyn); Alan Reed (Tomaso); David Hoffman (Jerecki); George Melford (Worker at Auto Assembly Plant); George E. Stone, George Eldredge, Paul Power, William Tannen, Jonathan Hale, Rodney Bell, Carleton Young (Executives); Virginia Maples, Beverly Thompson, Eileen Maxwell (Models); Joyce Newhard, Virginia Carroll, Fritzi Dugan, Jarma Lewis, Marcoreta Hellman, Billie Bird, Janet Stewart, Mary Carroll, Louise Robinson, Jean Walters, Ann Kunde, Kathryn Card (Women in Bargain Basement).

THE COBWEB *(MGM, 1955)* C-124 min.

Producer, John Houseman; associate producer, Jud Kinberg; director, Vincente Minnelli; based on the novel by William Gibson; screenplay, John Paxton; music, Leonard Rosenman; art directors, Cedric Gibbons, Preston Ames; set decorators, Edwin B. Willis, Keogh Gleason; camera, George Folsey; editor, Harold F. Kress.

Richard Widmark (Dr. Stewart McIver); Lauren Bacall (Meg Paversen Rinehart); Charles Boyer (Dr. Douglas N. Devanal); Gloria Grahame (Karen McIver); Lillian Gish (Victoria Inch); John Kerr (Steven W. Holte); Susan Strasberg (Sue Brett); Oscar Levant (Mr. Capp); Tommy Rettig (Mark); Paul Stewart (Dr. Otto Wolff); Jarma Lewis (Lois Y. Demuth); Adele Jergens (Miss Cobb); Edgar Stehli (Mr. Holcomb); Sandra Descher (Rosemary); Bert Freed (Abe Irwin); Fay Wray (Edna Devanal); Mabel Albertson (Regina Mitchell-Smythe); Oliver Blake (Curly); Olive Carey (Mrs. O'Brien); Eve McVeagh (Shirley); Virginia Christine (Sally); Jan Arvan (Mr. Appleton); Ruth Clifford (Mrs. Jenkins); Myra Marsh (Miss Gavney); James Westerfield (James Petlee); Marjorie Bennett (Sadie); Stuart Holmes (Mr. Wictz); Roy Barcroft (Lieutenant Ferguson); Ed Agresti (Barber); Lenore Kingston (Switchboard Operator); Dayton Lummis (Dr. Chase); Norman Ollestad (Usher); John McKee (Deputy Sheriff); Kay Kuter, Henry Sylvester, Moria Turner, Alvin Greenman (Patients).

BLOOD ALLEY *(Warner Bros., 1955)* C-115 min.

Director, William A. Wellman; based on the

novel by A. S. Fleischman; screenplay, Fleischman; music, Roy Webb; orchestrators, Maurice de Packh, Gus Levene; assistant director, Andrew V. McLaglen; costumes, Gwen Wakeling, Carl Walker; camera, William H. Clothier; editor, Fred MacDowell.

John Wayne (Wilder); Lauren Bacall (Cathy); Paul Fix (Mr. Tso); Joy Kim (Susu); Berry Kroeger (Old Feng); Mike Mazurki (Big Han); Anita Ekberg (Wei Long); Henry Nakamura (Tack); W. T. Chang (Mr. Han); George Chan (Mr. Sing).

WRITTEN ON THE WIND (*Universal, 1956*) C-99 min.

Producer, Albert Zugsmith; director, Douglas Sirk; based on the novel by Robert Wilder; screenplay, George Zuckerman; art directors, Alexander Golitzen, Robert Clatworthy; music, Frank Skinner; music supervisor, Joseph Gershenson; song, Victor Young and Sammy Cahn; costumes, Jay Morley, Jr.; gowns, Bill Thomas; assistant directors, William Holland, Wilson Shyer; special camera, Clifford Stine; camera, Russell Metty; editor, Russell Schoengarth.

Rock Hudson (Mitch Wayne); Lauren Bacall (Lucy Moore Hadley); Robert Stack (Kyle Hadley); Dorothy Malone (Marylee Hadley); Robert Keith (Jasper Hadley); Grant Williams (Biff Miley); Robert J. Wilke (Dan Willis); Edward C. Platt (Dr. Paul Cochrane); Harry Shannon (Hoak Wayne); John Larch (Roy Carter); Roy Glenn (Sam); Maidie Norman (Bertha); Dani Crayne (Blonde); Jane Howard, Floyd Simmons (Beer Drinkers); Glen Kramer, Phil Harvey, Colleen McClatchey, Carlene King Johnson (College Students); Carl Christian (Bartender); Don Harvey (Taxi Starter); Robert Malcolm (Hotel Proprietor); Robert Lyden (Kyle as a Boy); Robert Winans (Mitch as a Boy); Kevin Corcoran (Boy in Drugstore); June Valentine, Hedi Duval, George DeNormand (Bits).

DESIGNING WOMAN (*MGM, 1957*) C-118 min.

Producer, Dore Schary; associate producer, George Wells; director, Vincente Minnelli; story idea, Helen Rose; screenplay, Wells; art directors, William A. Horning, Preston Ames; set decorators, Edwin B. Willis, Henry Grace; costumes, Helen Rose; music, Andre Previn; song, Overstreet, Higgins, and Edwards; choreography, Jack Cole; gowns, Rose; assistant director, William Shanks; camera, John Alton; editor, Adrienne Fazan.

Gregory Peck (Mike Hagen); Lauren Bacall (Marilla Hagen); Dolores Gray (Lori Shannon); Sam Levene (Ned Hammerstein); Tom Helmore (Zachary Wilde); Mickey Shaughnessy (Maxie Stulz); Jesse White (Charlie Arneg); Chuck Connors (Johnny O); Edward Platt (Martin J. Daylor); Alvy Moore (Luke Coslow); Carol Veazie (Gwen); Jack Cole (Randy Owen); Richard Deacon (Larry Musso); Casey Adams (Musical Director); George Cisar (Fred Seixas); Syl Lamont (Danziger); Eddie Simms (Joey Yustik); Rodney Bell (Drunk Reporter); Chuck Webster, Gene O'Donnell, Jack Daly, Reid Hammond, Wilson Wood, Jack Shea (Reporters); Don Orlando (Italian Waiter); Jan Arvan (TV Director); Mario Siletti (Andrucci); Paul Power (Sheldon Stevens); Nora Marlowe (Jennifer Deane); Kay Mansfield (Assistant Fitter); Dean Jones (Assistant Stage Manager); Sammy White (Bewildered Man); Matt Moore (Stage Door Man); May McAvoy (Wardrobe Woman); Harriett Brest, Eva Pearson (Women); Mushy Callahan (Referee).

THE GIFT OF LOVE (*Twentieth Century-Fox, 1958*) C-105 min.

Producer, Charles Brackett; director, Jean Negulesco; based on a story by Nelia Gardner White; screenplay, Luther Davis; music, Cyril J. Mockridge; music director, Lionel Newman; orchestrator, Edward B. Powell; song, Sammy Fain and Paul Francis Webster; art directors, Lyle Wheeler, Mark-Lee Kirk; set decorators, Walter M. Scott, Eli Benneche; wardrobe, Charles LeMaire; assistant director, Jack Gertsman; makeup, Ben Nye; color consultant, Leonard Doss; sound, Charles Peck, Warren De Laplain; special camera effects, L. B. Abbott, Emile Kosa, Jr.; camera, Milton Krasner; editor, Hugh S. Fowler.

Lauren Bacall (Julie Beck); Robert Stack (Bill Beck); Evelyn Rudie (Hitty); Lorne Greene (Grant Allan); Anne Seymour (McMasters); Edward Platt (Dr. Miller); Joseph Kearns (Mr. Rynicker); Benjamin Sherman "Scatman" Crothers (Sam, the Gardener); Charity Grace (Sarah, the Housekeeper); Alena Murray (Nurse); Sean Meany, Joe Devlin (Waiters); Kay Cole (Girl); Rosemary Ace (Secretary); Kurt Katch (Professor); Myna Cunand (Wife); Paul Kruger (Justice of Peace); Robert Brubaker (State Trooper); George Chester (Driver); John Bradford (Air Force Lieutenant); Theresa Harris (Sam's Wife).

FLAME OVER INDIA (*Twentieth Century-Fox, 1959*) C-130 min. (British release title: *North West Frontier*)

Producer, Marcel Hellman; director, J. Lee Thompson; screenplay, Robin Estridge; music, Mischa Spoliansky; music director, Muir Mathieson; art director, Alex Vetchinsky; assistant director, Stanley Hosgood; costumes, Yvonne Caffin; Miss Bacall's costumes, Julie Harris; sound, E. R. Daniels, Gordon K. McCallum, Roy

Fry; special effects, Syd Pearson; camera, Geoffrey Unsworth; second unit camera, H. A. R. Thomson; editor, Frederick Wilson.

Lauren Bacall (Catherine Wyatt); Kenneth More (Captain Scott); Herbert Lom (Van Leyden); Wilfrid Hyde-White (Bridie); I. S. Johar (Gupta); Ursula Jeans (Lady Windham); Eugene Deckers (Peters); Ian Hunter (Sir John Windham); John Gwillim (Brigadier Ames); Govind Raja Ross (Prince Kishan); Basil Hoskins (A. D. C.); S. M. Asgaralli (Havidar, the Indian Soldier); S. S. Chowdhary (Indian Soldier); Moultrie Kelsall (British Correspondent); Lionel Murton (American Correspondent); Homi Bode (Indian Correspondent); Ronald Cardew (Colonel at Kalapur Station); Frank Olegario (Maharaja).

SHOCK TREATMENT (*Twentieth Century-Fox, 1964*) 94 min.

Producer, Aaron Rosenberg; director, Denis Sanders; based on the novel by Winifred Van Atta; screenplay, Sydney Boehm; music, Jerry Goldsmith; assistant director, Joseph E. Rickards; costumes, Moss Mabry; art directors, Jack Martin Smith, Hilyard Brown; set decorators, Walter M. Scott, Paul S. Fox; makeup, Ben Nye; sound, Robert O'Brien, Elmer Raguse; special camera effects, L. B. Abbott, Emil Kosa, Jr.; camera, Sam Leavitt; editor, Louis Loeffler.

Stuart Whitman (Dale Nelson); Lauren Bacall (Dr. Edwina Beighley); Carol Lynley (Cynthia); Roddy McDowall (Martin Ashley); Olive Deering (Mrs. Mellon); Ossie Davis (Capshaw); Donald Buka (Psychologist); Pauline Myers (Dr. Walden); Evadne Baker (Interne); Robert Wilke (Technician Newton); Bert Freed (Josephson); Judith De Hart (Matron); Judson Laire (Harley Manning); Lili Clark (Alice); Douglass Dumbrille (Judge); Timothy Carey (Hulking Patient); Jack Braddock (Jim, the Technician); Roy Gordon (Butler); Olan Soule (Hugo Paige); Paul Denton (Uniformed Guard); Leonard Stone (Psychiatrist); John Lawrence (Nurse); Sheila Rogers (Miss Gould).

SEX AND THE SINGLE GIRL (*Warner Bros., 1964*) C-114 min.

Producer, William T. Orr; director, Richard Quine; based on the book by Helen Gurley Brown; screen story, Joseph Hoffman; screenplay, Joseph Heller, David R. Schwartz; art director, Cary Odell; music/music director, Neal Hefti; song, Hefti and Quine; orchestrator, Arthur Morton; costumes, Edith Head, Norman Norell; assistant directors, Charles L. Hansen, Mickey McCardle; camera, Charles Lang; editor, David Wages.

Tony Curtis (Bob Weston); Natalie Wood (Helen Gurley Brown); Henry Fonda (Frank); Lauren Bacall (Sylvia); Mel Ferrer (Rudy); Fran Jeffries (Gretchen); Leslie Parrish (Susan); Edward Everett Horton (The Chief); Larry Storch (Motorcycle Cop); Stubby Kaye (Helen's Cabby); Howard St. John (Randall); Otto Kruger (Dr. Anderson); Max Showalter (Holmes); William Lanteau (Sylvester); Helen Kleeb (Hilda); Count Basie and His Orchestra (Themselves); Barbara Bouchet (Frannie); William Fawcett (Bum); Cheerio Meredith (Elderly Woman); Claire Carleton, Yvonne White, Mary Kovacs (Women); Philip Garris (Young Man); Taggart Casey (Guard); Charles Morton, Irving Steinberg, Tom Harkness, Jerry Martin, Sheila Stephenson, George Carey, Tom Quine (Board Members); Fredd Wayne (Production Man).

HARPER (*Warner Bros., 1966*) C-121 min. (British release title: *The Moving Target*)

Producers, Jerry Gershwin and Elliott Kastner; director, Jack Smight; based on the novel *The Moving Target* by Ross MacDonald; screenplay, William Goldman; art director, Alfred Sweeney; set decorator, Claude Carpenter; music, Johnny Mandel; song, Dory and Andre Previn; assistant director, James H. Brown; makeup, Gordon Bau; sound, Stanley Jones; camera, Gordon Hall; editor, Stefan Arnsten.

Paul Newman (Lew Harper); Lauren Bacall (Mrs. Elaine Sampson); Julie Harris (Betty Fraley); Arthur Hill (Albert Graves); Janet Leigh (Susan Harper); Pamela Tiffin (Miranda Sampson); Robert Wagner (Alan Traggert); Shelley Winters (Fay Estabrook); Robert Webber (Dwight Troy); Harold Gould (Sheriff Spanner); Strother Martin (Claude); Roy Jensen (Peddler); Martin West (Deputy); Jacqueline De Wit (Mrs. Kronberg); Eugene Iglesias (Felix); Richard Carlyle (Fred Platt); Tom Steele (Eddie); Horace Brown (Bartender); James McHale (Cab Driver); Mary Gregory (Waitress); Andres Oropeza (Piano Player); China Lee, Rosanne Williams (Bunny Dancers); Harvey Parry, Joe Pronte, John D. Saenz, Billy Shannon, James Sheppard, Fred Stromsoe, Jerry Summers, Morton C. Thompson, Ronald Veto, James Turley, Herb Pacheco, Ann Pat Kelly, Saul Gorss, Paul Baxley, Jerry Brutsche, John D. Cadiente, Gene Coogan, Richard Crockett, Robert Herron, Sam Mides (Stunts).

MURDER ON THE ORIENT EXPRESS (*Paramount, 1974*) C-131 min.

Producers, John Brabourne, Richard Goodwin; director, Sidney Lumet; based on the novel by Agatha Christie; screenplay, Paul Dehn; production designer, Tony Walton; art director, Jack Stephens; music, Richard Rodney Bennett; music director, Marcus Dods; costumes, Walton;

makeup, Charles Parker, Stuart Freeborn, John O'Gorman; titles/montage, Richard Williams Studios; sound, Peter Handford, Bill Rowe; sound editor, Jonathan Bates; process camera, Charles Staffell; camera, Geoffrey Unsworth; editor, Anne V. Coates.

Albert Finney (Hercule Poirot); Lauren Bacall (Mrs. Hubbard); Martin Balsam (Bianchi); Ingrid Bergman (Greta Ohlsson); Jacqueline Bisset (Countess Andrenyi); Jean-Pierre Cassel (Pierre Paul Michel); Sean Connery (Colonel Arbuthnot); John Gielgud (Beddoes); Wendy Hiller (Princess Dragomiroff); Anthony Perkins (Hector McQueen); Vanessa Redgrave (Mary Debenham); Rachel Roberts (Hildegarde Schmidt); Richard Widmark (Ratchett); Michael York (Count Andrenyi); Colin Blakely (Hardman); George Coulouris (Dr. Constantine); Denis Quilley (Foscarelli); Vernon Dobtcheff (Concierge); Jeremy Lloyd (A. D. C.); John Moffatt (Chief Attendant); George Silver (Chef).

THE SHOOTIST *(Paramount, 1976)* C-100 min.

Producers, M. J. Frankovich, William Self; director, Don Siegel; based on the novel by Glendon Swarthout; screenplay, Miles Hood Swarthout, Scott Hale; music, Elmer Bernstein; production designer, Robert Boyle; set decorator, Arthur Parker; makeup, Dave Grayson, Joe Di Bella; Miss Bacall's costumes, Moss Mabry; men's costumes, Luster Bayless; ladies' costumes, Edna Taylor; assistant directors, Joe Cavalier, Joe Florence; special effects, Augie Lohman; sound re-recording, Arthur Plantadosi, Lee Fresholtz, Michael Minkler; camera, Bruce Surtees; editor, Douglas Stewart.

John Wayne (J.B. Books); Lauren Bacall (Bond Rogers); Ron Howard (Gillom Rogers); James Stewart (Dr. Hostetler); Richard Boone (Sweeney); Hugh O'Brian (Pulford); Bill McKinney (Cobb); Harry Morgan (Marshall Thibido); John Carradine (Beckum); Sheree North (Serepta); Richard Lenz (Dobkins); Scatman Crothers (Moses); Gregg Palmer (Burly Man); Alfred Dennis (Barber); Dick Winslow (Streetcar Driver); Melody Thomas (Girl on Streetcar); Kathleen O'Malley (School Teacher).

PERFECT GENTLEMEN *(CBS-TV, 1978)* C-106 min.

Executive producer, Bud Austin; producer/director, Jackie Cooper; teleplay, Nora Ephron; art director, Jim Claytor; set decorator, Rick Gentz; music, Dominic Frontiere; camera, William K. Jurgensen.

Lauren Bacall (Lizzie Martin); Ruth Gordon (Mama Cavagnaro); Sandy Dennis (Sophie Rosenman); Lisa Pelikan (Annie Cavagnaro); Robert Alda (Ed Martin); Stephen Pearlman (Murray Rosenman); Steve Allie Collura (Vinnie Cavagnaro); Dick O'Neill (Mr. Appleton); Rick Garia (Nick Auletta); Robert Kya-Hill (Johnson); Ken Olfson (Desk Clerk); Ralph Manza (Frankie Fox).

HEALTH *(20th Century-Fox, 1980)* C-

Executive producer, Tommy Thompson; producer/director, Robert Altman; screenplay, Frank Barhydt, Altman, Paul Dooley; art director, Bob Quinn; set director, Jacques Price; costumes, Beth Alexander; assistant directors, Thompson, Bob Dahlin; sound, Bob Gravenor; camera, Edmond Koons; editor, Dennis Hill.

With: James Garner, Carol Burnett, Glenda Jackson, Lauren Bacall, Paul Dooley, Henry Gibson, Dick Cavett, Donald Moffat, Diane Stillwell, McIntyre Dixon, Alfred Woodard, Ann Ryerson, Allan Nicholls, Margery Bond, Mina Kolb, Georgann Johnson, Bob Fortier, Nancy Foster, the Steinettes.

With Dana Andrews in *My Foolish Heart* ('49).

2

SUSAN HAYWARD

> 5' 3½"   112 pounds
> Red hair   Hazel eyes
> Cancer

"Lots of actresses came from Brooklyn. Barbara Stanwyck, Susan Hayward—of course, they're just movie stars."—from All About Eve

LIKE STANWYCK, her cinema superior, Susan Hayward was always a fighter, and a tough one at that. It was this pugnacious chemistry that gave the pert redhead her dynamic individuality oncamera and off. (For some, however, this trademark of inner strength made Hayward's screen interpretations all too predictable, her gestures a bit too familiar.) Robert Wise, who directed Susan in her Academy Award-winning performance *I Want to Live!* (1958), would explain at the time, "In motion pictures, Susan Hayward is as important a figure as Sarah Bernhardt was to the stage. Somewhere within her is a chemical combination that can excite and hold audiences as surely as Garbo and very few other greats of the screen. Susan is one of two or three actresses who can hold up a picture all by herself."

Hayward was an aggressive, exciting battler in everything she attempted and she usually arose the winner. This victor's quality continued to intrigue moviegoers for decades, allowing Susan to rise above her ingenue status of the early Forties to become a top box-office attraction and Oscar winner in the Fifties. She proved herself a triumphant champ in almost all arenas.

Doug McClelland, the prime biographer of Susan Hayward, would acknowledge in his 1975 book on the late star, "There was something almost majestically gallant about Susan Hayward. A moment comes to mind from *Valley of the Dolls* in which the white-haired veteran star Helen Lawson (Hayward) had her red wig destroyed in a powder-room hairpull at a party. Told she could leave via the kitchen, Lawson took a long, hard look at herself in the mirror and, tying her neckerchief around her head, said, 'No, I'll go out the way I came in.' And she did."

Edith Marrener was born on Saturday, June 30, 1917, in a third-floor, walk-up tenement flat at Church Avenue and East 35th Street in Brooklyn, New York. Her father, Walter, was a red-haired Irishman whose assorted jobs had included being a Coney Island barker and a subway guard. Her mother, Ellen, was Swedish. Edith had been preceded in birth by a sister, Florence, and a brother, Walter, Jr. However, she was her father's favorite, especially because of her resemblance to his mother, Kate Harrigan.

"I learned at a very early age that life is a battle," she would later admit. "My family was poor; the neighborhood was poor. I knew that if I got my dress dirty, there was no money to have it cleaned. . . . When the soles of our shoes wore out, we stuffed paper in them." It was a case of the survival of the fittest in a rough neighborhood, and Edith soon learned how to fight for what she wanted.

When she was about six years old, she was hit by an automobile when she ran pell-mell into the street after a parachute she had fashioned from paper. Her injuries included fractures of both legs and a dislocated hip. The doctors at the free clinic forecast that she might never walk again, and they placed her in a body cast. For six months she was confined to bed, and then she was pulled in a red wagon to school at P.S. 181 until she was able to graduate to crutches. She used those crutches into the second grade when, through determination and strong will, she was able to walk on her own.

She grew up loving movies, for they provided her with an escape from her drab surroundings. She once said, "I used to go very early and stay very late. The vaudeville performers got to recognize me as I sat in the front row, and they always asked me up on the stage to help the magician get his rabbit out of a hat. She loved those moments, along with paying a dime to swim at Erasmus Hall High School where she donned a gray swimsuit and "felt like a bathing beauty."

She grew up a loner, with few friends, but she seemed to prefer it that way. When she was twelve, she had the distinction of being the only girl hired by the *Brooklyn Eagle* to deliver its newspapers. At P.S. 181 she received her first sample of acting, always performing as the fairy princess or the pretty little heroine. But at Girls Commercial High School she joined the drama club and let it

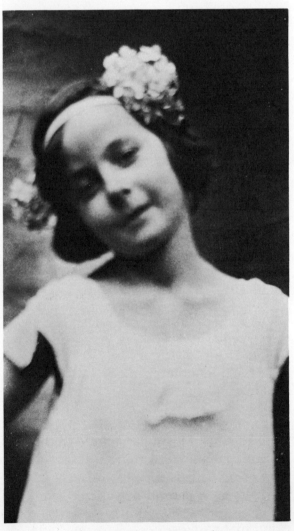

The young Susan Hayward.

be known that she preferred to take character parts. Good acting roles, not pretty costumes, were her criterion. As the future actress would later recall, "I decided [at this time] that my big aim was to get out of school and make money.... I became a very determined person."

While still in school she did some modeling which provided funds for a semblance of independence. In the meantime, her father, who suffered from a weak heart, was confined to bed and unable to work. Upon graduation she embarked briefly on a dress designing career. It was during this period that she changed the spelling of her first name to Edythe, undoubtedly believing that it added class. However, uppermost in her thoughts was getting a job as an actress. She enrolled for one term at the Feagan Drama School in Manhattan and was featured in a "Pictorial Short" made by Vitaphone in 1936, appearing as a fashion model.

It was as a professional fashion model that Edythe earned her livelihood. The *Saturday Evening Post* carried a layout of the upcoming 1937 fashions, featuring Edythe in a series of modeling poses. Katharine Brown, David O. Selznick's New York story editor, saw the magazine spread and contacted Edythe through the Walter Thornton Agency. The members of the Selznick staff were pledged to aid their boss in locating an unknown to play the lead role of Scarlett O'Hara in *Gone with the Wind* (1939), and Miss Brown thought that Edythe was a likely candidate.

Edythe was elated at the possibility of a chance to portray the heroine in a giant screen epic, but her father was less jubilant, feeling that Hollywood wouldn't be a proper place for his little girl. However, Edythe's mother and sister thought differently, and they urged her to grab the opportunity if it were offered.

As a result of her interview with Katharine Brown, Edythe was given two round-trip train tickets to Hollywood for a screen test. Accompanied by sister Florence she arrived in Los Angeles in mid-1937. At the Selznick studio, she screen-tested for the part of Scarlett O'Hara. Alan Marshal stood in as Ashley Wilkes for the audition. As has been often recalled over the years, the competition for the coveted role of Scarlett was tremendous, with such cinema veterans as Joan Bennett, Paulette Goddard, Katharine Hepburn, and Jean Arthur under consideration.

Edythe's screen test did not satisfy the demanding Mr. Selznick. Her inexperience and faulty diction were chiefly responsible. Selznick informed her personally that she had failed, and he recommended that she return to New York. "I like oranges; I think I'll stay," she told him. He then suggested that she turn in the return train tickets to his secretary, but she replied, "I've already cashed them in to live on." Since she had used his money, Selznick told her that he might use her as a stand-in for whoever was selected to play Scarlett.

With no income, the Marrener girls were forced to wire an aunt for money. According to the legend surrounding the Brooklyn redhead, she was bicycling one day when she accidentally toppled onto the lawn of agent Benny Medford. Not only did Medford pick her up bodily, but he also volunteered to take her as a client. He changed her name to Susan Hayward* and took her *Gone with the Wind* screen test to Warner Bros. where she was given a six-month contract as a starlet.

Warners' new employee—age twenty, with hazel eyes and 112 pounds of well-distributed flesh on a 5'3½" frame—was put to work posing in bathing suits and evening dresses, and was also ordered to enroll in the studio's acting classes. Her initial feature film credit was Warner Bros.' *Hollywood Hotel* (1937), a film inspired by Louella Parsons' weekly radio show of the same name. Susan Hayward was seen briefly in the finale with other newcomers, including Ronald Reagan.

Soon after completion of the picture, Miss Parsons took the neophytes on a nine-week, coast-to-coast vaudeville tour across the

---

*It has been written that the surname Hayward was chosen due to its similarity to that of Rita Hayworth, another Hollywood redhead, but the theory remains unconfirmed.

United States. Also in the group was Jane Wyman with whom Ronald Reagan was having a romance. Susan's onstage bit was opposite Reagan (whom she disliked), and it involved a slap which she administered with gusto. An immediate clash with Miss Wyman resulted from Susan's firm application of her hand to Reagan's face.

It was reported that in the course of the tour Susan had met a midwesterner with whom she fell in love, but his name has never been divulged. During the tour her initial greeting as she would sweep onstage was, "Anyone here from Brooklyn?" The query, especially in the northeast area, briefly stopped the show. Louella Parsons at the time described Susan in a column as "ultra-moral and conventional—a real Miss Prim, easily shocked by backstage stories, even when they were mild. And her feelings were so easily hurt she dissolved into tears if anyone even looked at her crossly. She seldom went out, even when we hit such big towns as Philadelphia and New York. If she did go, it was usually with a relative or friend from Brooklyn."

Susan returned to California at the end of the Parsons tour, accompanied by her mother and brother. (Her father had died in 1937 soon after she went to Hollywood for the first time.) Within a few months of her return to the Warner Bros. lot, she was cast —without billing—as a telephone operator in *The Sisters* (1938), which showcased a prettified Bette Davis and the charming, devil-may-care Errol Flynn. After that, an eighteen-minute short subject called *Campus Cinderella* (1938), starring Penny Singleton, had Susan as a college coed, and Kay Francis' *Comet over Broadway* (1938) found Hayward onscreen briefly as a fledgling actress.

Her best early role at Warner Bros. was in *Girls on Probation* (1938), which was completed after *Comet over Broadway*, although released first. In this minor film of gangsterism, Susan played a socialite whose evening gown is borrowed by Jane Bryan, an employee of a dry cleaning shop. When the gown's owner discovers that the garment is damaged, she arranges for the worker's dismissal and arrest. The film's male co-star was Susan's former antagonist, Ronald Reagan.

These assorted screen appearances ended Susan's six-month contract with Warner Bros. and the studio decided to let her go.* With a family to support, she had to borrow money while she looked for work. Finally, Artie Jacobs, the newly appointed head of Paramount's talent department, signed her to a $200-a-week contract. As he would recall, "Susan Hayward walked in here one day, picked up a cold script and read it like a veteran. She was a natural, a neglected Scarlett girl, and we signed her pronto."

Paramount then had what the studio termed the "Golden Circle," comprised of young contract players who were tutored in all phases of movie-making. One of the goals was to enrich Susan's accent, and this was accomplished with the aid of a voice coach.

Her initial job at Paramount was in the thankless role of Isobel Rivers in a remake of *Beau Geste* (1939). She was a replacement for temperamental Frances Farmer. Based on the P. C. Wren novel about the French Foreign Legion, the 1939 rendition was adapted by Robert Carson which prompted *Liberty* magazine to observe, "Because the 1939 edition in treatment and setting so closely resembles the earlier version, it graphically demonstrates the great strides made in screen techniques since the advent of sound."

Isobel is the ward of Lady Patricia Brandon (Heather Thatcher), the adopted "aunt" of the Geste brothers: Beau (Gary Cooper), John (Ray Milland), and Digby (Robert Preston). She is romantically attracted to John and waits for his return after he follows Beau into the Foreign Legion. John is the only one of the brothers to survive the battle of Fort Zinderneuf. In this obvious man's action picture of desert heroics, there is not much room for amplifica-

---

*Max Arnow, a Warner Bros. executive in charge of talent at the time of Susan's tenure, would say years later, "She had a wonderful mind, but no heart. It took too long to teach her to cry."

Peggy Moran (third from left), Johnnie Davis, Dorothy Comingore (behind chair), and Susan Hayward in the short subject *Campus Cinderella* ('38).

With Ronald Reagan, Joseph Crehan, and Jane Bryan in *Girls on Probation* ('38).

With Ray Milland, Gary Cooper, and Robert Preston in *Beau Geste* ('39).

With Richard Denning in *Adam Had Four Sons* ('41).

tion of Isobel's characterization. Susan once described the part in these words: "I waved goodbye to the boys at the beginning and hello to them [sic] at the end."

A month after the release of *Beau Geste*, Susan was seen in *Our Leading Citizen* (1939) as the daughter of Bob Burns, the latter playing a folksy, Main Street lawyer. Their small-town bliss is temporarily disrupted by a dash of communism. Next she was in *$1,000 a Touchdown* (1939) which starred wide-mouthed comics Joe E. Brown and Martha Raye. The latter plays an heiress who turns a financially depressed university into a drama school and hires Susan as a faculty member. Hayward's character asserts, "I teach romance," and goes on to substantiate her claim by organizing the football squad to neck by moonlight with the female members of the student roster.

During 1940 Susan was not seen in any motion pictures, but she dated Jon Whitcomb, a commercial artist she had known in her New York days. A navy lieutenant stationed in California, he was later to recall: "Susan had a kind of self-confidence that made you remember her."

That same year she was borrowed by Columbia to play her first celluloid "bitch" role, appearing in *Adam Had Four Sons* (1941). The feature starred Warner Baxter and Swedish import Ingrid Bergman and was directed by Gregory Ratoff. (Susan always expressed her appreciation for the director's treatment of her in this career-making picture.) In the third-billed position, Susan, as Hester, makes her first appearance when the narrative is about one-third completed. She is the wife of David (Johnny Downs), one of the four sons of widowed Warner Baxter. It is not long before malicious and sex-hungry Hester becomes enmeshed with another son, Jack (Richard Denning). Soon brother turns against brother, with David eventually coming to realize that his wife is no good. He sends her away and becomes friends again with brother Jack. Although Howard Barnes of the *New York Herald-Tribune* thought the picture "inferior" and the story "silly," it garnered favorable comments for both Miss Bergman (as the governess) and Susan. *Newsweek* observed, "Susan Hayward is effective in the film's only vital role."

In March 1941, after viewing *Adam Had Four Sons* in Los Angeles, illustrator Joseph St. Amand announced the formation of a "Perfect Legs Institute of America." Backed by a task force of press agents, St. Amand demanded that Susan Hayward be drafted as the Institute's president. In taking notice of the Institute, *Time* magazine pictured a barefoot Susan, with her skirt pulled far up her thighs, standing at the edge of the vast Pacific Ocean. With her back to the camera, she looked over her left shoulder with pursed lips to indicate, perhaps, that the beating surf was a bit chilly.

Republic then borrowed Susan to menace her unsuspecting, onscreen country cousin, Judy Canova, in *Sis Hopkins* (1941). As the daughter of a rich plumbing manufacturer (Charles Butterworth), Susan is a coed forced to share quarters with the hillbilly cousin. To show her contempt, she manages to have the cousin arrested for indecent exposure by fixing the threads on the girl's burlesque outfit when the cousin goes onstage as a part of a sorority initiation exercise. Later Susan gets her just comeuppance in the form of a bucket of water in the face.

Hayward implored Paramount to cast her in *Hold Back the Dawn* (1941), as the worldly-wise, ex-girl friend of the immigrant hero (Charles Boyer), but the role went to more popular Paulette Goddard. Instead, the studio placed her in a B-mystery, *Among the Living* (1941). With second billing, after Albert Dekker who plays a dual role (one good and one bad), she is the flirtatious Millie Pickens who acquires the bankroll of the murderous Dekker before turning him in to the police for the $5,000 reward offered for his capture. She also incites a mob to kill the culprit, with little, if any, remorse. Although the *New York Times* labeled *Among the Living* as "the dreariest film of the year," the *New York Herald-Tribune* called it a "superior psychological melodrama" and found Susan to be "especially good."

With Bob Crosby in *Sis Hopkins* ('41).

In the annals of Hollywood's creation of stars, very frequently it was the persistence, ingenuity, and daring of the individual performers that maneuvered them into a position of prominence and wealth. Such was the case with the determined Susan Hayward who seemingly never accepted the word "no" or understood the meaning of defeat. At a 1941 Paramount Pictures sales convention in Los Angeles, Susan was at the tail end of a roster of stars and technicians to be introduced from the stage by studio production chief William LeBaron. "Now I want you to meet one of our most promising new actresses," he announced. Susan glided onto the stage and shouted into the microphone, "Did anybody in the house ever hear of me before?" When the audience shouted "No!" she exclaimed, "You said it! But I'm drawing my salary every week. Is that economics? Do any of you boys out there get paid if you don't deliver?" Again the collective answer was an enthusiastic "No!" She then yelled: "Anybody in the house like to see me in a picture?" The replies came back as "Yes!" with substantial applause for the gutsy girl. She thereupon whipped her head around and asked a bemused LeBaron, "Well, how about it?" and strode off the stage without waiting for his answer. The applause and shouts from the salesmen were thunderous.

As a direct result of her unprecedented sales pitch at the convention, she was given a supporting role in Cecil B. DeMille's *Reap the Wild Wind* (1942). The color production was based on a *Saturday Evening Post* serial and heralded as Hollywood's most lavish production since *Gone with the Wind*. Budgeted at $1,650,000, and with a 222-day shooting schedule, the film boasted 153 speaking parts. The completed feature premiered on March 18, 1942, at the new Hollywood Paramount Theatre on Holly-

With John Wayne in *Reap the Wild Wind* ('42).

wood Boulevard, in what was described as the "first wartime gala."

In sixth billing, Susan is Drusilla Alston, the refined cousin of tomboy Loxi Claiborne (Paulette Goddard) who owns a Key West salvage schooner. While Loxi endeavors to prove that rival salvager King Cutler (Raymond Massey) is responsible for the demise of many of the ships, Drusilla falls in love with Cutler's brother Dan (Robert Preston). As she tells him, "When I'm in your arms I don't care what they say about you. I'll love you always." Meanwhile Loxi recruits the help of dandy Stephen Tolliver (Ray Milland) and Captain Jack Stuart (John Wayne) in her efforts to rightfully discredit King Cutler. Later in the involved plot Drusilla stows away aboard a ship which is sunk in a heavy fog and she loses her life. Before the film winds to a "happy climax," Stuart is killed by a giant squid, and Tolliver kills Cutler, the latter having shot his brother Dan. At the finish Tolliver and Loxi realize that they love one another.

This important feature represented Susan's first film in Technicolor and the first in which she wore a lavish wardrobe (circa 1840), here designed by Natalie Visart. There are many who feel that the casting would have been greatly aided if Susan and Paulette Goddard had switched roles, since Hayward was suited temperamentally to portraying the "sea-going Scarlett O'Hara" called Loxi.

In *The Forest Rangers* (1942), also in Technicolor, Susan was third-billed as Tana Mason, the hoydenish, long-time friend and admirer of Ranger Don Stuart (Fred MacMurray). She fully believes that she will one day become his wife, but when he takes a trip to New York and returns with a bride, Celia (Paulette Goddard), she is resentful and predicts, "I'll drive that society deb number one right back to the nightclub circuit." She strives to accomplish just that and almost succeeds while Ranger Stuart is away hunting a pyromaniac responsible for igniting several forest fires. In a tremendous final conflagration, Celia and Tana are surrounded by flames. When Tana is overcome with fright, it is Celia who rescues her.

Continuing her very active production schedule, Susan was then in the cast of *I Married a Witch* (1942), filmed at Paramount but sold to United Artists for distribution rights. Based on Thorne Smith's unfinished novel *The Passionate Witch,* the film offered Veronica Lake as a reincarnated early-day witch in search of a descendant of the man who had her burned at the stake. Such a person is Wallace Wooley (Fredric March), a candidate for governor who is engaged to marry Estelle Masterson (Susan), a publisher's daughter. In her nearly thankless role, Susan walks out on her fiancé when she finds him in the arms of the blonde witch.

Star Spangled Rhythm (1942) was one of those Paramount all-star offerings filled with revue sketches in which top as well as lesser box-office names performed offbeat musical and/or comedic material. Susan was seen in a sketch concerned with the wartime rubber shortage. She complains to her boyfriend (Ernest Truex), "I want something to bring out the woman in me. You don't even bring out the gypsy in me." But when he brings her a "trinket" which turns out to be a hard-to-get girdle, she embraces him. Susan's accent in this skit wavered between hard-crusted Brooklynese and refinement of the uptown quality.

She was then seen in a fifteen-minute short subject, *A Letter from Bataan* (1942), in which her boyfriend soldier (Richard Arlen) writes to the folks at home to save such war-shortage ingredients as "kitchen fat," etc. At the conclusion of the letter, it is revealed by telegram that the soldier has been killed in action.

Susan was again borrowed by Republic to co-star opposite John Carroll in *Hit Parade of 1943* as a midwestern girl whose mind is filled with musical words and tunes. Arriving in New York to pursue a career in song writing, she bunks-in with her city cousin (acidulous Eve Arden) and meets a singer (Carroll) who begins blithely stealing her songs. However, it isn't long before he repents and permits her to rightfully receive credit for the songs she has authored. For the first

With Eve Arden and Grandon Rhodes in *Hit Parade of 1943* ('43).

time onscreen, it was revealed that Susan possessed a passable singing voice when she sang portions of several songs in this modest picture.

Young and Willing (1943) was one of several films shot at Paramount but sold to United Artists. Directed by Edward H. Griffith from a Virginia Van Upp scenario, the story deals with stagestruck young people. Susan plays Katie Benson, the serious actress of a group who aspire to stage stardom. They (Barbara Britton, Martha O'Driscoll, William Holden, Eddie Bracken, and James Brown) share an apartment from which they venture forth in search of jobs and fame. Katie, along with being the serious-minded type, is also sarcastic.

In November 1943, while entertaining soldiers at the Hollywood Canteen, Susan met Jeffrey "Jess" Barker* who was the master of ceremonies. When he asked her for a date, she reportedly told him, "I won't go out with you. I've been reading about you in the columns, Mr. Barker, and I just don't want to add my name to that long list of dates." She weakened eventually and dated him. It has been said that she slapped his face on their first date when he attempted to kiss her. (Barker, under contract to Columbia, had gone to Hollywood from the New York stage where he had played the juvenile lead in *You Can't Take It with You*.)

Susan was then borrowed by producer Samuel Bronston for *Jack London* (1943), released through United Artists. Directed by Alfred Santell, the movie biography of the

*Not to be confused with Lex Barker, one of Lana Turner's husbands and a screen Tarzan.

Cheesecake, 1943 style.

adventurer-writer (1876–1916) was based on *The Book of Jack London,* written by his widow, Charmian Kittredge London. Susan plays Charmian, the manuscript reader who takes an interest in the novice writer (Michael O'Shea) and is responsible for the publication of *The Call of the Wild.* She later becomes his wife. The *New York Times* praised Susan for playing London's sweetheart "with charm and vivacity," but it noted that the film strayed from the truth in several instances (for example, by completely ignoring his first wife). The *Times'* Bosley Crowther concluded his comments by asserting: "Frankly, it must be admitted that the proper film biography of London has not yet been made."

Republic borrowed Susan for a third time —on this occasion for the John Wayne vehicle *The Fighting Seabees* (1944), a wartime tribute to that organization of fighting men. Wayne (as Wedge Donovan) and Dennis O'Keefe (as Navy Lieutenant Commander Robert Yarrow) are the two leaders responsible for fashioning the Seabees, with Susan as the newspaper reporter semi-engaged to O'Keefe but later in love with Wayne. The latter is killed in the Pacific Theatre of War, and Susan is left with a wounded O'Keefe. Most of the attention in this patriotic action yarn was focused on star Wayne and the battle scenes. Peppery Susan had to struggle for screen notice in this picture, especially when she was camouflaged so often in a wardrobe of regulation helmets and functional togs. Nevertheless her beauty and vitality managed to shine through.

She next aided the war effort by co-starring with Alan Ladd, Betty Hutton, and William Bendix in a thirteen-minute Paramount short, *Skirmish on the Home Front* (1944). It was made for the Office of War Information and illustrated the folly of one married couple (Susan and Bendix) who cash in their war bonds, while a second couple (Ladd and Hutton) keep their bonds and find future financial happiness.

There is a certain amount of prestige at-

In *The Hairy Ape* ('44).

tached to any screen version of a Eugene O'Neill Broadway drama, but *The Hairy Ape* (1944), made by Paramount for United Artists release, provided only a minimum of class entertainment. Susan as Mildred Douglas is an attractive passenger aboard the ship on which burly stoker Hank Smith (William Bendix) toils. He is a half-demented individual with an immense hairy body. The society girl finds her way below deck to the furnace room where she encounters the sweating Hank. She is repelled by him, but at the same time is perversely attracted to the animalistic person. She calls him "the filthy beast," and that sends his mind into real turmoil. Later, on shore, he goes to her penthouse and makes love to her. Thereafter he has countless moments of self-hatred and realizes that he will never be able to attain status at any level of society. He finally enters a gorilla cage at a zoo and is crushed to death by an actual hairy ape.

In the estimation of James Agee, writing for *The Nation,* Susan was "of the wrong social wave length to carry this particular role, but there are roles, not yet invented so far as I know, in which she could do a paralyzingly good job on one important kind of vicious American woman." *Time* magazine referred to her as "Hollywood's ablest bitch-player."

After nine months of an off-again, on-again romance, Susan married Jess Barker on July 23, 1944, at St. Thomas Episcopal Church in Los Angeles. Susan was 27; Barker was 30. Prior to exchanging vows in the presence of witnesses Jean Pettebone and Henry Rogers (Susan's press agent), Susan had her lawyers draw up an agreement, which Barker signed, separating her income from his. This action on Susan's part is clear indication that she had little hope for their marriage.

In fact, two months after they married, they threatened to terminate the union, but after a brief, two-week separation they went back together and purchased a house at 3737 Longridge Avenue, Van Nuys, California, in the San Fernando Valley. Never one for parties or nightclubs, Susan became even more of a stay-at-home in marriage. She was given to spells of laziness, followed by periods of furious activity. Her living room, for example, remained partially unfurnished for many months.

Benny Medford, Susan's first agent, once said of her, "She's smart, but cold as a polar bear's foot." In her search for professional recognition, she became short-tempered and bored with small talk. Because she had no time for the pleasant amenities enjoyed by others, she was considered determinedly aloof. Yet she was dependable in her work, always on time at the studio, and never late for an appointment. Even so, she was turned down by Paramount for the role of Phyllis Dietrichson in that studio's production of *Double Indemnity* (1944), and star Barbara Stanwyck was handed the role. In addition, Hayward's company boss, Buddy DeSylva, refused to loan her to United Artists for *Dark Waters* (1944) for the role of Leslie Calvin (played by Merle Oberon). DeSylva's reasoning for refusing to loan her was strictly personal. "You've been rude, snippy, and uncooperative with stars and directors," he told her. "Maybe this will teach you."

Instead, she was assigned to play the third-billed role of the spoiled, bitchy sister to Loretta Young in *And Now Tomorrow* (1944). In this film Alan Ladd is the physician who cures and romances the deaf Miss Young, while Hayward maneuvers in the background to woo away Loretta's one-time beau, Barry Sullivan.

And Now Tomorrow was far from distinguished film fare, and it certainly provided Susan with scant dramatic range. It was also a flat finale to her tenure at Paramount, for she refused to renew her contract with the studio. She decided, independent soul that she was, to take her chances with free-lancing.

On February 19, 1945, Susan gave birth to twin sons, Timothy, a blond, and Gregory, a redhead. The boys were born two months prematurely, but they responded to incubator life and were soon taken home. After motherhood, Susan became more of a homebody than ever, doting on her sons. While Jess Barker believed that children

With Grant Mitchell, Beulah Bondi, Loretta Young, and Barry Sullivan in *And Now Tomorrow* ('44).

With husband Jess Barker and twin sons Timothy and Gregory in Hollywood (February 1946).

should be disciplined rigidly, Susan tended to be more lenient. As a result this married couple, maladjusted from the beginning, had a new cause for disagreement. Then, too, they often clashed over money, inasmuch as Susan was thrifty, while Jess loved to spend.

When she was able to return to film work (she had already guested on such radio shows as the Edgar Bergen and Charlie McCarthy program in late 1945), producer Adrian Scott contracted her for the starring role—with billing over the title for the first time in her career—in *Deadline at Dawn* (1946) at RKO. In this rather turgid mystery drama, Susan plays a dancehall girl who is just a bit on the jaded side. When a young and apparently innocent sailor (Bill Williams) is accused of murdering a whore, she comes to his aid because she knows that he is incapable of such a deed. The sailor has six hours to prove his innocence—hence the meaning of the title. The young man is saved when the murderer (Paul Lukas) is apprehended and proved guilty.

In 1946 Susan was approached by distinguished stage actress Eva LeGallienne to join her American Repertory Theatre which would be based in New York. However, Susan had other career ideas, and Miss LeGallienne hired June Duprez instead—a fortunate decision for Susan, because the repertory venture proved to be a short-lived operation.

Independent producer Walter Wanger took a strong liking to Susan and signed her to a personal contract in 1946. Her first assignment for Wanger was at a $200,000 salary in Universal's *Canyon Passage* (1946). It was Susan's first Western film, directed on location in Oregon by Jacques Tourneur. As the daughter of a small-town lawyer (Stanley Ridges), she is engaged to banker Brian Donlevy until businessman Dana Andrews rides into town. She then has affection only for him. Hers was a thankless role in this male-oriented action film, but it did provide her with a change of pace from the conniving rich girl roles she had endured of late.

Wanger's next job for her was as Angie Evans in *Smash-Up, The Story of a Woman* (1947). It was this Universal release that established Susan's dramatic reputation within the film industry. In the John Howard Lawson scenario, adapted from an original story by Dorothy Parker and Frank Cavett, the narrative tells of Angie's plight in coping with neglect and boredom as the ex-singer wife of popular crooner Ken Conway (Lee Bowman). It is revealed that in her singing days Angie required a few stiff drinks before she could perform. When she retires to become a homemaker and finds that she is alone most of the time, she once again turns to alcohol for refuge. In the course of the drama she loses her husband and child and returns to singing for a living. (Susan's voice was dubbed by Peg LaCentra.)

Because this film came so close in release to *The Lost Weekend* (1945), the male version of the alcoholic's story, *Smash-Up* was inevitably compared with it. The former garnered an Oscar for star Ray Milland and it was a much more harrowing film experience than its successor.

It has been written that Susan was more relaxed during the 96-day shooting schedule of *Smash-Up* than at any prior time. The reasons given were her faith in director Stuart Heisler and her general affection for the cast members who, along with Bowman, included Eddie Albert and Marsha Hunt.

Three days before the film's official release (on February 6, 1947), Hollywood insiders were predicting that Susan would be a top contender for the next season's Academy Awards. At the same time, Wanger announced that he had purchased, for $200,000, the Henry James novel *The Aspern Papers* and that he would film it as *The Lost Love,* with Susan as his star.

Two months later, *Newsweek* magazine, in reviewing *Smash-Up,* observed, "Miss Hayward's bouts with demon rum are more to be censored than pitied, considering that she is attractive drunk or sober and is apparently immune to hangovers." At the same time the national magazine dubbed the film "a psychological phony."

Producer Joan Harrison borrowed Susan

With Lee Bowman in *Smash-Up, The Story of a Woman* ('47).

With Robert Young and Lovyss Bradley in *They Won't Believe Me* ('47).

for RKO's *They Won't Believe Me* (1947) in which she has a strong but brief appearance as Verna Carlson, the gold-digging girl friend of broker Larry Ballantine (Robert Young). He leaves his shrewish wife (Rita Johnson) to run off with Verna to Reno. On the way, Verna is killed in an automobile accident and the broker tells the police that it is his wife. When he returns home to find that his wife has committed suicide, he is charged with Verna's murder. A trial follows these events. When the broker is certain that the jury will not believe his story and tries to leap from a courtroom window, he is shot dead. The climax of the drama is that the jury had found him not guilty.

The *New York Times* called the movie "an impressive nugget out of the film Gold Coast" and gave Susan the accolade of "first-rate." In *Time* magazine, James Agee noted that Susan "proficiently sells her special brand of sexiness."

It was a surprise to few when on October 1, 1947, Susan sued Jess Barker for divorce on the grounds of "cruelty and grievous mental anguish." She asked for custody and support of their two sons. The action was dropped a few weeks later when Susan informed the press: "I have come to the conclusion, as has Jess, that marriage is a contract that should be lived up to, and there really isn't much in life for you when you reach sixty, say, unless you have lived up to it. . . . Working out my marriage problems made me realize that I was growing up and maturing."

The Henry James novel *The Aspern Papers* reached the screen as *The Lost Moment* (1947). In the murky dramatization, Susan plays Tina Bordereau, a Venetian girl who is wasting away her youth as the housekeeper of a very old and very dusky mansion whose owner is Tina's 105-year-old aunt (Agnes Moorehead). "Miss Tina," as the old-young housekeeper-niece is called, is a schizoid who, as a child, reveled in hearing her aunt read love letters from famous poet Jeffrey Ashton. Ashton has long since died, but the aunt carries his letters in a box. As Tina grew older, she imagined that she was Jeffrey's lover, and she stole the letters and a ring from her aunt who had grown near blind and was confined to her chair.

Into this gloomy setting comes an enthusiastic American (Robert Cummings) who hopes to take the poet's letters home with him and publish them. The aunt eventually reveals that she murdered her lover and that Tina has stolen the letters. He persuades the repressed Tina to dine with him, and they soon realize that their initial antipathy has turned to romance. Nevertheless, he is still determined to get the correspondence, but, just as they are within his grasp, the old house burns down, consuming both the aunt and her valuable letters. Suddenly "Miss Tina" becomes normal and flings herself into the arms of the compassionate American.

Susan once referred to the film as "The Lost Hour and Thirty-Five Minutes" [actually the picture was pruned to 88-minutes for general release], while Wanger later admitted, "We missed badly on that one." During the filming, director Martin Gabel, according to Susan, "went around telling everybody not to talk to me. Yes, even warned the crew not to speak to me because he said I had to maintain a mood for the part." Susan got so angry with Gabel that she broke a lamp over his head and never once regretted the action.

As predicted, Susan was Oscar-nominated for Best Actress of 1947 for *Smash-Up,* but at the Shrine Auditorium in Los Angeles on the evening of March 20, 1948, it was Loretta Young who won for her accented performance as the Swedish housekeeper in *The Farmer's Daughter.* This win was considered an upset, since the award had been expected to go to Rosalind Russell for *Mourning Becomes Electra.*

There are those individuals who declare that *Tap Roots* (1948) should have died "a slow, lingering death" *(New York Times),* but the film version of James Street's novel

Advertisement for *The Lost Moment* ('47).

proved that had *Gone with the Wind* been produced in 1948 rather than in 1939, Susan would have been ready to play Scarlett O'Hara. Under the direction of George Marshall and photographed in striking color, the Civil War story emerges in many aspects as similar to the David O. Selznick masterpiece. It falls short in its dialogue (screenplay by Alan LeMay, with additional dialogue by Lionel Wiggam) and in its stodgy choice of leading man Van Heflin, who was hardly in the Rhett Butler-Clark Gable category. In costumes designed by Yvonne Wood, the southern belles of the picture, and Susan in particular, sashay with as much grace as any of the Margaret Mitchell ladies of Georgia.

The setting for *Tap Roots* is Mississippi, where a community declares itself neutral in the War Between the States and intends to remain independent of state rule. The leader of this rebellion is strong-bodied Hoab Dabney (Ward Bond), the father of Morna (Susan), Aven (Julie London), and Bruce (Richard Long). Morna has survived one romantic upset with Clay MacIvor (Whitfield Connor) but comes to life again in the arms of a tough-nosed newspaper editor named Keith Alexander (Heflin). They are both strong-willed and determined. The inhabitants of the Mississippi community known as Lebanon Valley lose their rebellious fight to be apart from the state, but not before a great deal of blood is shed. In viewing the film, the *New York Times* critic noted that Susan was "generously endowed by nature and further enhanced by Technicolor," but he added that she was "defeated at almost every turn by the script."

Wanger loaned Susan to producer Joseph Sistrom for *The Saxon Charm* (1948) as a costar to Robert Montgomery and John Payne. Thirty-year-old Susan received second billing as Janet Busch, the faithful, understanding wife of Eric (Payne) who strives to receive recognition as a playwright with a biographical study of Molière. All along the line the couple is sidetracked by megalomaniacal producer Matt Saxon (Montgomery), who may be charming and beguiling, but who is also utterly ruthless. It was an offbeat casting assignment for Susan,

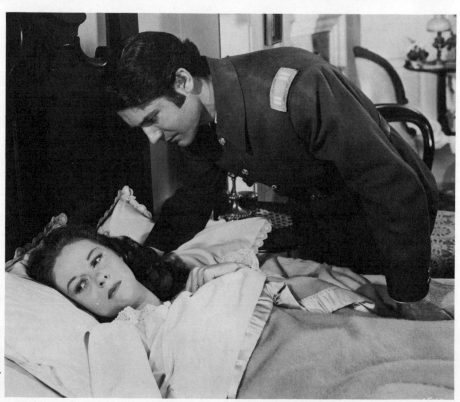

With Whitfield Connor in. *Tap Roots* ('48).

With Chill Wills (at piano) in *Tulsa* ('49).

and her fans were disappointed to find her giving such a subdued characterization.

Susan was another Scarlett O'Hara type of character—named Cherokee Lansing—in Walter Wanger's *Tulsa* (1949), released through Eagle-Lion. Unlike Scarlett, however, Cherokee is a twentieth-century gal, a half-Indian who owns most of the oil fields around Tulsa, Oklahoma. With the death of her cattleman father (Harry Shannon) she turns to oil-leasing with an almost unscrupulous vengeance. Her fiancé (Robert Preston) breaks their engagement because of her consuming ambition, but a climactic oil fire (one of the best filmed up until then) brings her to her senses.

During the 59-day filming schedule, Susan wore costumes designed by Herschel, many of which unavoidably became oil-smeared due to the oncamera action. Susan kept many of these costumes as mementos, exhibiting them in a glass trophy-type case. (They were stolen by burglars in 1960.)

Although Darryl F. Zanuck, the mercurial head of Twentieth Century-Fox, turned down Wanger's bid to have Susan portray Virginia Cunningham in *The Snake Pit* (1949) —the role was played by Olivia de Havilland —he arranged to buy Susan's contract for $200,000. This transaction would serve to bolster Hayward's industry status, for with the financial and promotional backing of a major studio, she would be in a far better position to make her name more important to the moviegoing public. Few Hollywood observers doubted that firebrand Susan would soon make her mark at the lot where the major female attractions were Betty Grable, June Haver, Gene Tierney, Linda Darnell, Anne Baxter, and Jeanne Crain.

Her first production under the Fox banner was *House of Strangers* (1949), adapted from the Jerome Weidman novel *I'll Never Go There Anymore*.* Gloomily lensed by cinematographer Milton Krasner to set just the right perspective, the dramatic story offers the account of an Italian banker (Edward G. Robinson) and his four sons (Richard Conte, Luther Adler, Paul Valentine, and Efrem Zimbalist, Jr.) and the familial difficulties incurred. The second son (Conte), a lawyer, is encouraged to marry an Italian girl (Debra Paget), but he falls in love with a very smart, very American miss named Irene Bennett (Susan). When the brothers overthrow their father and take over his bank, Conte bribes a juror and is turned over to the police by his brother, Adler. The attorney is sent to jail while the remaining three sons control the banking enterprise. The father dies heartbroken, but Conte gets out of jail and refuses to join his brothers. Their attempts to murder him fail, and at the finale he leaves with Susan to start life anew.

Smartly gowned by Charles Le Maire, Susan's role was subordinate to those of Robinson and Conte. However, her presence in the cast gave her box-office prestige.

Samuel Goldwyn then borrowed Susan for *My Foolish Heart* (1950), taken from the J. D. Salinger short story, "Uncle Wiggily in Connecticut." At boarding school, Susan as Eloise Winters falls in love with a party crasher (Dana Andrews). He is later killed in the war and she is left pregnant. In desperation she persuades the boyfriend (Kent Smith) of her chum (Lois Wheeler) to marry her. Her unhappy life causes her to drink heavily and ignore her growing daughter (Gigi Perreau). Eloise finally straightens out after re-evaluating her life (in flashback form) and discovers that hers has been a "foolish heart."

The picture, although overly soap operaish, had many attributes: gowns by Edith Head and Mary Wills, direction by Mark Robson, and a title song composed by Victor Young and Ned Washington. According to *Look* magazine, "In her best screen job to date, Miss Hayward makes the tragedy of a girl in love in wartime very real indeed." *Variety* joined in: "Her performance is a gem, displaying a positive talent for capturing reality."

Susan justly received her second Academy Award nomination as Best Actress for her performance in *My Foolish Heart*. The competition that year was Jeanne Crain *(Pinky)*, Olivia de Havilland *(The Heiress)*, Deborah Kerr *(Edward, My Son)*, and Loretta Young *(Come to the Stable)*. The winner, announced on March 23, 1950, was Miss de Havilland, who had been expected to be victorious. The Best Song Oscar was awarded to Frank Loesser for "Baby, It's Cold Outside" from MGM's *Neptune's Daughter*, beating out the also-nominated title tune from *My Foolish Heart*.

At the conclusion of 1949 Hedda Hopper picked Susan as the prospect she considered most likely to achieve stardom. Miss Hopper explained, "I've watched Susan Hayward for a good many seasons now, and always I've thought 'If that girl ever gets the right part —watch her go!' All the time Susan was ripe as a pink-skinned peach for her big break— and now she has it. Her sad-sweet triumph in *My Foolish Heart* will, I predict, set her off toward a top-notch starring career at long last and someday an Academy Award."

In 1950, Susan, who usually had a sharp eye for the type of film that would help or stymie her career, was placed on studio suspension for refusing to star in *Stella*, a Sol C. Siegel production for which she did not feel well-suited. She was replaced by Ann Sheridan. Instead, Hayward journeyed to Georgia to replace the pregnant Jeanne Crain in *I'd Climb the Highest Mountain* (1951). As Mary Elizabeth Eden, an urban miss around the turn of the century who weds a country parson (William Lundigan), Susan has to learn to "make do" with the inconveniences of rural living and even has to face a competitor (Lynn Bari) for the affections of her soft-spoken husband. Again, Susan's devotees were disappointed

---

*When Fox remade *House of Strangers* as the Western *Broken Lance* (1954), Jean Peters would inherit Susan's role; in yet another Fox remake, the circus-set *The Big Show* (1961), Esther Williams would play the revamped Hayward part.

Placing her footprints at Grauman's Chinese Theatre in Hollywood (August 28, 1951).

With William Lundigan in *I'd Climb the Highest Mountain* ('51).

With Jayne Meadows, Gregory Peck, and James Robertson Justice in *David and Bathsheba* ('51).

to discover that she was not swilling alcohol or being nasty oncamera.

Susan next starred with Tyrone Power, the uncrowned king of the Twentieth Century-Fox lot, in *Rawhide* (1951). She plays an entertainer heading west with her niece (Judy Ann Dunn) when they stop at a remote relay station run by Power. A gang of outlaws soon take over the station and imprison Power, Susan, and her niece. They attempt to dig their way out and make a hole large enough for the child to escape. When this bit of daring is noted by the outlaw leader (Jack Elam), he and his men treat the prisoners cruelly. In the end, of course, Susan and Power subdue their captors and admit their mutual love.

Hayward was fast becoming the busiest major personality on the Twentieth Century-Fox lot. The studio refashioned Jerome Weidman's novel *I Can Get It for You Wholesale* into a vehicle for Susan. Her co-stars in this 1951 melodrama were Dan Dailey and George Sanders, with Susan in the role of tough Manhattan fashion designer Harriet Boyd who schemes to claw her way to the top of her profession. She gave a far tougher, more memorable interpretation to Weidman's focal figure than Elliott Gould who starred in the 1962 Broadway musical version of the novel. However, in the expensively-mounted color epic *David and Bathsheba* (1951), Susan played second-fiddle to Gregory Peck as David, the hero who slew Goliath. She is the married woman of biblical fame who tempts the great David to commit adultery. Neither the very twentieth-century Susan nor the extremely stiff Peck was properly cast in this historical claptrap. The film boasted some cornball dialogue and the two leads could do little to disguise the forced prose.

Peck: You are not eating.
Hayward: I ate earlier. It is my custom when I am alone.

Peck: When I looked upon you from my terrace tonight, I knew every moment away from you would be a moment lost.

Hayward: Think not of this one night, but of all the days and nights to come.

Hayward: A woman is interested in everything about her man, especially [of those things] before she met him.

While Susan's popularity with film audiences was surging, her husband's career was continuing downward. He had now been relegated to featured roles, and in 1950 he had only one movie job (in *The Milkman*). His reported salary for 1951 was $665, resulting from TV work. Susan's income for the same year was a healthy $175,000. He remained at home most of the time, shopping in supermarkets, bathing the twins, watering fruit trees, and supervising the household. Once, when he was under consideration for a job, he was asked: "What do you need a job for? Your wife's making plenty of money."

In December 1951, *Photoplay* magazine named the twelve most beautiful women in Hollywood and listed, "in the order of our experts' selections," Susan in number ten spot (preceded by Ava Gardner, Ann Blyth, Elizabeth Taylor, Arlene Dahl, Linda Darnell, Joan Crawford, Mona Freeman, Loretta Young, and Marlene Dietrich, and followed by Rita Hayworth and Deborah Kerr). The magazine's "experts" listed their reasons for choosing her: "An exotic type, crowned with the most beautiful golden red hair." The magazine article pointed out that her beauty consisted of an "oval-shaped face, blue-green eyes, red-gold hair, fair skin, few freckles."

By 1952 Susan was the acclaimed queen of Twentieth Century-Fox, a spot previously enjoyed by such blonde songbirds as Alice Faye and Betty Grable. The year began with her portrayal of singer Jane Froman in *With a Song in My Heart*. Shot in Technicolor and with Susan wearing Charles Le Maire-designed gowns, the film is a masterpiece of the biography genre. It follows Miss Froman's career from the day when as a young hopeful she meets a fellow musician (David Wayne) who aids her until her career surpasses his. They marry, but he is filled with self-pity. World War II breaks out and she embarks on an overseas tour to entertain the troops. En route the plane carrying her is forced into a crash landing in the sea. Jane suffers multiple leg injuries which require several operations. However, the legs do not properly mend. A plucky girl, she takes to crutches and continues with her tour. Thereafter she meets the pilot (Rory Calhoun) of the plane that had crashed, and before long the two of them have fallen in love. She also encounters a hospital nurse (Thelma Ritter) who becomes her friend and companion. Back in the United States, her husband steps aside—finally—to permit her to marry the ex-pilot.

In preparation for her demanding role of a singer and dancer, a role for which she allowed her full-styled hair to be shorn, Susan took preliminary lessons from Elsie Janis who had entertained troops during World War I. Hayward proved to be adept at dancing, but it was decided to only have her mouth the words to the songs sung off-camera by Miss Froman. Shortly after the film's release, Capitol Records issued an LP recording of the Froman songs from the film, with Susan on the cover, dressed in the shoulderless, red gown worn in the sequence where she sings the title tune.

Susan and Gregory Peck were reunited with Fox director Henry King for *The Snows of Kilimanjaro* (1952), derived from Ernest Hemingway's famous story. Also in the cast was Ava Gardner as Peck's true love. Although Susan received billing above Gardner, her role is smaller as the woman Peck marries after Gardner dies. She is far more visible in RKO's *The Lusty Men* (1952), made

With Selmer Jackson (center), Charlton Heston, and George Melford in *The President's Lady* ('53).

on loan to producer Jerry Wald. It is a rugged story of rodeo performers, with Robert Mitchum as the veteran rider who undertakes to train a novice (Arthur Kennedy). Susan, as Kennedy's wife, is unhappy about the arrangement, since she would prefer to settle down on a ranch—somewhere or anywhere. Director Nicholas Ray gave the offering a toughness that was satisfying and believable, and there was an exciting chemistry between Mitchum and Susan.

In *The President's Lady* (1953), one of Susan's favorite films, she plays Rachel Jackson, the wife of President Andrew Jackson (Charlton Heston). The young Rachel weds Jackson before her divorce is final from Lewis Robards (Whitfield Connor) and is then charged with adultery. Although she remarries Jackson after the divorce is properly finalized, she is forever ostracized from polite society. As the 96-minute chronicle moves toward a conclusion, she grows to become a pipe-smoking, white-haired old lady (the only time Susan played an oldster).

Susan received a third Oscar nomination, this time for *With a Song in My Heart*, but once again she was a loser. At the Pantages Theatre on March 19, 1953, the winner was announced as Shirley Booth *(Come Back, Little Sheba)*.

In *White Witch Doctor* (1953) Twentieth Century-Fox cast Susan in the title role as a nurse who dutifully carries out her pledge to heal. With her on the safari is manly Robert Mitchum whose goal is the rich gold fields of the dark continent. The backgrounds for the Henry Hathaway-directed feature were filmed in Africa, but stars Mitchum and Susan never left the Fox lot. The picture itself was a lot of contrived nonsense, geared to display the vitality of the two contrasting magnetic personalities.

On February 14, 1953, it was announced by the Foreign Press Association of Hollywood that, according to polls of fans in fifty countries, the most popular stars of 1952 were Susan and John Wayne. Both personalities received the Henrietta Award (later to be known as the Golden Globes).

Five months later, Hollywood wags noted that Jess Barker had moved out of the house he shared with his wife. It was learned that on Sunday, July 12, there had been a violent quarrel at the Barker residence while both allegedly had been drinking. Jess reportedly chased the nude Susan through their grounds, dunked her in the swimming pool and even paddled her backside. On July 23, when the couple was due to celebrate their ninth wedding anniversary, Susan announced that she intended to file for divorce, which she finally did in September in a Burbank, California, court. On November 17, the Barkers spent two hours with a children's court conciliation commissioner in an attempt to resolve their difficulties. After the meeting, Susan voiced her determination to proceed with the divorce action.

During the making of *Demetrius and the Gladiators* (1954), Susan's beefy co-star, Victor Mature, commented, "Susan acts like someone a hundred years old. We're practically on a Mister and Miss basis. We all wish we could help her, but we just don't know how to go about trying." The trouble in her personal life made her moody and withdrawn, which was not too unusual for Susan who generally kept to herself. However, this time it was clear that she was not happy.

Advertised with the slogan "It Begins Where *The Robe* Left Off" and having been filmed in "the Wonder of Four-Track High Fidelity Stereophonic Sound" and in CinemaScope, *Demetrius and the Gladiators* has Susan as Messalina, the young wife of Claudius (Barry Jones). She entices the somber-faced but muscular ex-slave Demetrius (Mature) to her villa for an amorous fling. He remains with her until the call of Christianity overcomes him and he returns to the righteous path. In summing up the film, the *New York Times'* Bosley Crowther wrote: "This one is no more like *The Robe* than either of them is like nature or Roman history." There were few kind words for Susan's overly broad interpretation of the aristocratic temptress.

Despite the vapidity of her screen assignments, Susan remained a top-drawing box-office attraction. Next to Twentieth Century-Fox's own Marilyn Monroe, she was the most potent female personality on the studio's performer payroll, and she was soon paired with the very mature Gary Cooper in *Garden of Evil* (1954). In this film she gallops into the sleepy Mexican town of Puerto Miguel (circa 1850) to seek help in rescuing her husband (Hugh Marlowe) who is lying under a log in a caved-in gold mine back in the hills. She solicits help from three men (Cooper, Richard Widmark, and Cameron Mitchell) who are en route to the California gold fields. After a harrowing three-day trip, they find Marlowe alive, but he points out that Apache Indians have been prowling about and seem anxious to kill white men. He proves to be right, with only stalwart Cooper and vital Susan surviving the Indian arrows to continue a journey northward.

Filmed in Mexico, this feature, in Technicolor and CinemaScope, boasted a memorable Bernard Herrmann music score. Beyond this, the entry demonstrated that all-American Cooper was too old to play romantic leads.

On August 17, 1954, Susan was awarded a divorce from Jess Barker in a Burbank Superior Court. Her income was declared as $17,000 monthly, with assets totaling $1,293,319. She received custody of the twins and the right to retain all of her real and personal property. Barker was awarded a Ford station wagon and the right to visit the boys on alternate weekends. During the divorce proceedings it was revealed that Susan had once ground out a cigarette in Barker's face. In recounting the particulars of the quarrel which sparked the divorce, Susan testified, "As I recall, I said to Mr. Barker that if he loved me he'd go to work. I don't recall what happened next, but I remember asking my husband 'Do you love me' and he said, 'To me, you're a good meal ticket.' "

Susan's escorts before and after her divorce were varied, but she seemed to concentrate on Richard Egan and Jeff Chandler. Columnist Mike Connolly reported, "Jeff Chandler keeps phoning Susan Hayward. It looks serious for these two, who were kids together in Brooklyn." Fellow columnist Cal York discovered, "Jeff Chandler and Susan Hayward won't be seeing each other, unless they happen to meet at the same party. Although friends since high school days with so much in common, their mutual advisors feel that Jess Barker's attitude toward his ex-wife is too unpredictable to risk possible misunderstanding." Furthermore, columnist Erskine Johnson announced that Susan would not take her twins onlocation with her to Africa for *Untamed* (1955) due to the visitation rights given Barker by the Superior Court and because Barker had "some damaging evidence to uncork against his famous wife if his demands aren't met." Naturally, Johnson did not divulge to his readers just what was meant by the "damaging evidence."

Untamed, directed by Henry King, is a Western-style film about the colonization of Africa and the establishment of a new Boer settlement. Susan is Katie O'Neill (shades of Scarlett O'Hara again), in Africa with her staid Irish husband (John Justin). On their initial wagon train ride, the spouse is killed in a Zulu attack. The surviving settlers are rescued by Paul Van Riebeck (Tyrone Power), a Boer commander. Katie soon falls in love with the swashbuckling figure, and he helps her to build a home in the wilderness. However, promptly thereafter he departs to establish a Dutch Free State within Africa. He leaves her pregnant and in the care of Kurt (Richard Egan), a burly fellow who wants her as his very own. She beds down with him but then locates a large diamond which makes her rich. A shift in situations makes her poor again, but she is once more saved by Paul who returns to claim her as his mate. The use of color and CinemaScope did not manage to salvage this film from being "heavily and obviously done." (Robert Mitchum had been Susan's first choice for co-star in this picture.)

Susan was then co-starred with the all-time king, Clark Gable. Clark wanted Grace Kelly for *Soldier of Fortune* (1955), but Twentieth Century-Fox assigned Susan to assume the role of Jane Hoyt when Miss Kelly became too busy with international wedding plans. Despite rumors that Gable and Hayward did not enjoy a rapport during the making of the adventure film, it does not show onscreen. Once again Susan is a wife in search of a missing husband. Here she travels to Hong Kong to find her mate (Gene Barry) who has disappeared into Red China during a photographic expedition. She requests the help of Hank Lee (Gable), an American adventurer who operates a smuggling business as a sideline. In a rather unconvincing plot twist, after Hoyt is found and rescued by Lee, he suggests that his wife and Lee remain together. Hoyt knows that they are in love, and he bows out of the picture gracefully. Thereafter manly Lee swears that he will abandon his smuggling and other adventures in order to remain close at hand to the desirable Jane. *The Hollywood Reporter* wrote of Susan in this slickly made potboiler, "[She] is far better than she has been in most of her recent pictures and seems potentially to be a perfect running mate for the dynamic and ruggedly handsome Gable."

Once again, volatile Susan made national headlines. On April 26, 1955, she was hospitalized after consuming an overdose of sleeping tablets. She had placed an hysterical phone call to her mother who telephoned the police, and they in turn broke down the door of Susan's Sherman Oaks home. It was reported that the death attempt had been made after a meeting with Barker turned into a heated argument. At Cedars of Lebanon Hospital her stomach was pumped out and she was bombarded with news reporters taking pictures and asking a range of personal questions. At his next sermon—devoted to the evils of Hollywood—evangelist Billy Graham asserted that Susan tried to kill herself because "movie stars are miserable, unhappy people."

On November 4, 1955, Susan was again in

With John Justin in *Untamed* ('55).

the news when starlet Jill Jarmyn charged that Susan beat her with a hair brush in the bedroom of actor Don "Red" Barry. Miss Jarmyn claimed that she walked into Barry's house, unannounced, to find Susan clad in polka-dot pajamas, in the bedroom presence of Barry.

Stage, screen, recording, and nightclub star Lillian Roth had authored a successful biography, *I'll Cry Tomorrow*, which was considered in the mid-Fifties to be the ultimate in daring confessional prose. It was inevitable that a major Hollywood studio would buy the screen rights, and the winner in the bidding was MGM where Susan had never worked. The Roth story (written by the subject in collaboration with Gerold Frank and Mike Connolly) was a compelling one, telling of the rise of a vaudeville-Broadway-Hollywood singing star and her fall and thorough degradation due to acute alcoholism. It was made to order for Susan's dynamic array of intense dramatics, and she wrote a letter to Dore Schary, then head of MGM, pointing out that she ought to play the part. (According to Doug McClelland in his Pinnacle Book biography of Susan, June Allyson and Jane Russell had been under studio consideration.) Susan's main ally in her quest for the role was Miss Roth herself who believed that Hayward embodied all the requisite physical and emotional qualities, demonstrated in such past performances as *With a Song in My Heart*. Finally Susan won the much sought-after part.

The movie version of *I'll Cry Tomorrow* (1955) is just as frank as the revealing autobiography. It depicts a little girl (Carole Ann Campbell) who is thrust into show business by her fame-hungry mama (Jo Van Fleet) and who grows to become one of New York's most-in-demand talents. Life at the

With Eddie Albert, Peter Leeds, Jo Van Fleet (seated), Donald Barry, and Margo in *I'll Cry Tomorrow* ('55).

top is more than the entertainer can handle, however, and she slowly turns to alcohol for consolation. On a drunken spree she weds a young man (Don Taylor), divorces him, marries another (Richard Conte)—who proves to be a sadist—and then contracts to sing in Hollywood pictures. Later she returns to New York where she evolves into a pathetically heavy drinker. She lies and cheats to wheedle money for booze, and in a fit of desperation she decides to leap from a hotel window—but she doesn't have the fortitude to carry out her plan. She then finds her way to an Alcoholics Anonymous headquarters where she is rescued by heavy doses of coffee and the kindness of Eddie Albert and Margo. Cured of her propensity for strong drink, the narrative concludes with her touching appearance on TV's "This Is Your Life."

Susan gave her emotional all in depicting the tormented Miss Roth, doing onlocation research at Alcoholics Anonymous offices and Los Angeles jails and observing "life" in that city's skid row area. The result, under Daniel Mann's direction, is one of Susan's best acting jobs. (There are some who felt Susan, as always, was too strident in tone, too jerky in movement, and too plastic in emotion.) Shot in black-and-white and minus the gimmick that was expected to save Hollywood—CinemaScope—the film was to garner $6,004,000 in domestic and Canadian theatre rentals. Susan performed her own singing for the soundtrack of *I'll Cry Tomorrow,* and it proved to be an effective job of vocalizing. Later the MGM recording company released an LP album with Susan performing several of the songs from the feature.

At the Hollywood premiere of *I'll Cry Tomorrow* with Lillian Roth and producer Lawrence Weingarten.

With John Wayne in *The Conqueror* ('56).

This personal success for Susan was followed in release by *The Conqueror* (1956), presented by RKO-Howard Hughes and produced/directed by Dick Powell. Reportedly shot in Utah at a cost of $6,000,000 (during 1954–55), it is one of Susan's and John Wayne's less remembered outings. The viewer is asked to believe that she is Bortai the proud daughter of a Tartar ruler who is kidnapped by a dark-skinned Mongol (Wayne) and forced into marriage although she claims to hate him and at one point in the proceedings attempts to lop off his head. In the end, her feelings change from hate to lust to love. The film consumes 110 minutes of multi-hued Utah scenery and fiery redheaded Susan, but it is sheer boredom (unless one obtains a perverse delight in mocking the incongruities of casting, dialogue, and situations). Susan once recalled this embarrassing film with these words: "I had hysteria all through that one. Every time we did a scene, I dissolved in laughter. Me, a red-haired Tartar princess! It looked like some wild Irishman had stopped off on the road to Old Cathay."

A few of Susan's recurring escorts during this period were producer John Beck and the fickle billionaire Howard Hughes, but both men, if they were romantic interests at all, counted as only brief episodes in Hayward's life. She was too strong and demanding for either one of them to survive the courting.

Susan won her fourth Oscar nomination for *I'll Cry Tomorrow*. Her competition this time included Katharine Hepburn (*Summertime*), Jennifer Jones (*Love Is a Many Splendored Thing*), Anna Magnani (*The Rose Tattoo*), and Eleanor Parker (*Interrupted Melody*). At the Pantages Theatre on March 21, 1956, Miss Magnani was announced as the winner of the Best Actress Academy Award. "That was my favorite role, and one I really wanted to win the Oscar for," Susan admitted years later. "I probably showed my disappointment when it went to Anna Magnani, but I managed not to shed any tears until everything was over and my company had gone home, and then I sat down and had a good cry and decided that losing was just part of the game." Win or lose, she had planned a post-Oscar show party at her home, and at this gathering was a tall, handsome Georgia lawyer named Floyd Eaton Chalkley.

In May 1956 Susan was awarded the Cannes Festival honor as Best Actress of 1955, a year when no male actor was named, thus making her prize a "Grand Presentation." *The Hollywood Reporter* interpreted this award presentation situation to mean that Susan's *I'll Cry Tomorrow* performance was "head and shoulders above any actor, male or female, and explains why there was no male award."

Susan refused Twentieth Century-Fox's offer to star in the psychological study *The Three Faces of Eve* (1956). That role was given to a youngish newcomer named Joanne Woodward and garnered her the Oscar. Also, Fox and Cole Porter wanted Hayward to headline the screen version of *Can-Can* in 1956, but due to an assortment of production problems, that musical would not be filmed until 1960, at which time another redhead, Shirley MacLaine, would play the lead. When she rejected Fox's demand that she star in *Hilda Crane* (1956) she was placed on suspension and Jean Simmons substituted in the role.*

Hayward returned to her alma mater, Warner Bros., for *Top Secret Affair* (1957), based on the John P. Marquand novel *Melville Goodwin, U.S.A.* (The property had been originally slated by the studio for Humphrey Bogart and Lauren Bacall, but those plans were altered due to Bogart's illness.) Susan plays Dottie Peale, a powerful magazine

---

*On the other hand, there were many roles over the years that Susan had been suggested or touted for, but had not played: *Gold Diggers in Paris* (1938), *Three Cheers for the Irish* (1940), *For Whom the Bell Tolls* (1943), *Murder, He Says* (1945), *Duel in the Sun* (1946), *Forever Amber* (1947), *Anna Lucasta* (1949), *My Cousin Rachel* (1952), *Band of Angels* (1956), *The Painted Veil* (1957), *The Wayward Bus* (1957), *The Sun Also Rises* (1957), *Sweet Bird of Youth* (1962), *Night of the Iguana* (1964), etc. Instead, the following actresses played in those respective films: Rosemary Lane, Priscilla Lane, Ingrid Bergman, Helen Walker, Jennifer Jones, Linda Darnell, Paulette Goddard, Olivia de Havilland, Yvonne De Carlo, Eleanor Parker, Jayne Mansfield, Ava Gardner, Geraldine Page, Gardner, *et al.*

With Kirk Douglas in *Top Secret Affair* ('57).

publisher (Clare Boothe Luce?) who sets out to discredit hard-nosed Major General Goodwin (Kirk Douglas) of the U.S. Army when he receives a government appointment which she wanted to be given to another man. In the course of events she becomes romantically entangled with the virile man, but she is even more intent on squashing his pride when he later leaves her. A senatorial investigation follows, and he is revealed to be a very fit candidate. Humbled, Susan's heroine admits that she has been wrong in her estimation of him. It is then that the two find each other irresistible. Although Susan's dialogue is sparkling and she has one engaging comedic drunk scene, it is clear that she was not suited for the role.

Whatever speculation existed concerning Susan's romantic inclinations ended on February 8, 1957, when she eloped to Phoenix, Arizona, with Floyd Eaton Chalkley. Chalkley was a former FBI agent who had turned to law and who had also become a successful automobile dealer. His home was in Carrollton, Georgia, about fifty miles from Atlanta. It was the second marriage for both. Susan's age was "given" as 37 and Chalkley's was listed as 47. They were married in an Episcopalian ceremony, although Chalkley was a Roman Catholic.

Then there was talk that Susan Hayward would star in *Peyton Place* (1957) for Twentieth Century-Fox, but it was Lana Turner who accepted the Oscar-nomination role. When Fox was preparing the movie version of *South Pacific* (1958), Susan was interested in winning the important screen assignment; she even studied with song coach Bobby Tucker. But then one evening she encountered producer-director Joshua Logan at a party. She informed him she would do *anything* to play Nellie Forbush in *South Pacific*. He said, "Anything?" She replied, "Absolutely ANYTHING." He responded, "Will you test for it?" Susan shot back, "Absolutely NOT!" And so Mitzi Gaynor won the starring part.

Back in 1952–53, condemned murderess Barbara Graham was the talk of California and most of the nation. *San Francisco Examiner* reporter Ed Montgomery believed in the woman's innocence throughout the

With Lorna Thayer in *I Want to Live!* ('58).

Winning her Oscar for *I Want to Live!*

highly publicized trial and up until the moment of the woman's death in the gas chamber at San Quentin prison. Sparked by producer Walter Wanger, a screenplay of the woman's plight was created from Montgomery's copious notes and articles and from Barbara Graham's letters to various individuals. Wanger could conceive of no other actress but Susan to play the heady lead role. He had pressure applied from several sources to drop such a controversial project as one dealing with capital punishment, but he was determined to tell the dramatic story, and Susan was eager for the opportunity to work for and with Wanger again.

The stark screen drama was released on October 28, 1958, as *I Want to Live!* It follows Miss Graham through her days as a B-girl and on to her association with a seedy group of minor crooks who murder an old lady in southern California. Her cohorts link her to the killing, and after a complex trial she is convicted, remaining on Death Row for months before she is led to the gas chamber. Throughout her imprisonment she carried a stuffed animal, a beloved possession of her late child, the only thing the youngster had ever loved in her short lifetime.

After completing the grueling work in the film, Susan returned to the Chalkley home in Georgia where she was accepted as one of the natives. She was content to be a housewife for the man she loved, but from the moment she had arrived in Hollywood in 1937, it had been her prime intent to win an Academy Award. She flew from Georgia with her husband to attend the ceremonies at the Pantages Theatre on April 6, 1959, having been given her fifth Best Actress nomination. Wearing a black satin gown with shoulder straps that revealed her bare shoulders, she sat in the audience with her husband, holding his hand. When presenters James Cagney and Kim Novak announced that Susan had won,* she bounded

---
*The other nominees were Rosalind Russell (*Auntie Mame*), Shirley MacLaine (*Some Came Running*), Deborah Kerr (*Separate Tables*), and Elizabeth Taylor (*Cat on a Hot Tin Roof*).

to the stage while 67,851,000 at-home viewers watched on television. A triumphant Susan held the statuette thoughtfully as she thanked the industry and Wanger in particular. Later she commented, "I've wanted an Oscar for so long. Winning him means so much to me." Wanger would say, "Thank God, now we can all relax. Susie finally got what she's been chasing for twenty years." Immediately following the ceremonies, Susan and her husband returned to Georgia.

In the year following her Oscar victory, Susan made two films. The first, *Woman Obsessed* (1959), has her in the role of a Canadian farm widow with a son (Dennis Holmes) and a stiff-chinned handyman (Stephen Boyd) whom she finally weds. It is a laborious outing (shot in Colorado) with Susan doing her best, *but. . . .*

Thunder in the Sun (1959), her first Paramount film since 1944, was a laughable excursion into fantasy with Susan as a French-accented Basque lady who, with friends, carries native grape seedlings across the continent to California. She is unhappily married to Carl Esmond, and when he succumbs to Indian arrows, she relaxes in the muscular arms of Jeff Chandler. All of the Basques, except Susan, perform by leaping into the air and hitting their adversaries with their strong feet.

In late 1959 it was announced that Susan was to star in Universal's *Elephant Hill,* but this project was abandoned. She was also Walter Wanger's first choice to assume the role of *Cleopatra* when it was planned as a 1960 extravaganza. However, since she did not want to be separated from her husband for the length of time it would require to shoot such an undertaking abroad, she turned down the offer. (Elizabeth Taylor eventually accepted the project—released in 1963—which would change the course of her life.)

Susan's film commitments to Twentieth Century-Fox were concluded with *The Marriage-Go-Round* (1960), the movie version of the 1958 hit Broadway comedy that had starred Claudette Colbert and Charles Boyer. This attempt at froth paired Susan as

With husband
Floyd Eaton Chalkley
in Hollywood ('59).

With Jeff Chandler in *Thunder in the Sun* ('59).

dean of women at a university with, of all people, stern-faced James Mason as her professor husband. Their mature connubial bliss is disrupted by the presence of amazon sex object Julie Newmar (of the Broadway cast). Out of necessity, the scenario of the original play had to be laundered, thereby deleting much of the bubble from the proceedings, but it was again evident that Susan should veer away from comedy.

She was back to the hard-boiled type of woman as *Ada* (1961), a self-educated ex-whore married to the governor (Dean Martin) of an unspecified southern state. When the governor is beaten up by henchmen of political boss Wilfrid Hyde-White and is hospitalized, Ada takes over the reins as the state's chief. Her ruthless attack on her husband's enemies is relentless, and she barks out orders like an army top sergeant. The story is unbelievable, but Susan is in rare fighting form.

Back Street (1961) had been made twice before by Universal, but never in so glossy a fashion as accomplished by producer Ross Hunter. Opulence is the word that best describes this tearjerking remake. As Rae, a midwestern beauty, she goes to the big city to make her way in the competitive fashion world. Within two years she has reached the top and has fallen in love with Paul Saxon (John Gavin), a married man and heir to a department store chain. She tries to break her emotional ties with the man, but she later encounters him in Paris where she has self-exiled herself. Their affair begins anew and he stakes her to a love cottage in the countryside where she waits patiently for him to join her for an occasional brief rendezvous. When his alcoholic wife (Vera Miles) finds out about them, she threatens to commit suicide, which fails to move him a great deal (Gavin appears unshaken by many things). Angry and half drunk, the wife

With Wilfred Hyde-White, Martin Balsam, and Dean Martin in *Ada* ('61).

With Virginia Grey in *Back Street* ('61).

drives her husband to a party. Their car is wrecked and she is killed. Paul is hospitalized with major injuries and dies, but he is able to tell his son (Robert Eyer) about Rae. The ending of the picture finds the son with his young sister (Tammy Marihugh) going to the cottage to console the grief-stricken Rae.

Susan defended the soap-and-suds film with the following comment: "These days unless you have incest and a couple of rapings, the critics are not impressed, but there are many people who want to see a decent picture. *Back Street* is a love story. It's simply love, old-fashioned love. And I think audiences have liked it. You don't feel dirty when you come out of the theatre."

Of her marriage versus career, Susan observed, "I've solved the problem of working in Hollywood by living as far away from it as I possibly can. We have a comfortable home in the Deep South. It's surprising how happy one can be once you've made the break from the treadmill. I fly in only when a movie I'm signed to do is ready to roll." Her advice to young movie hopefuls included, "I would advise any young girl not to make Hollywood her career. If she proves herself a good enough actress elsewhere, she'll be asked to work in Hollywood soon enough. But it's hell if you start here as an unknown, simply as a very minor studio property. No girl in her right mind would want that. Funny, though I wouldn't recommend it to any young girl, yet I'm not sorry I went through it all. It may be hell, yet it's better than working in the five-and-dime store."

The *Harvard Lampoon* named Susan the worst actress of 1961 for her performances in *Ada* and *Back Street*.

Susan, with Chalkley, traveled to England and Ireland for the making of *I Thank a Fool* (1962), her first joint American-English film, co-starring Peter Finch. She plays a Canadian physician who again falls in love with a married man (Finch) and becomes his mistress in England. When he becomes incurably ill, she takes care of him and is finally

With Michael Craig in *Stolen Hours* ('63).

forced to mercy-kill the poor devil by means of a deadly injection.

Susan then returned to England for the remake of Bette Davis' *Dark Victory*, newly entitled *Stolen Hours* (1963). The storyline remained largely intact. She is an international playgirl who suffers from horrendous headaches. At the same time she is having an affair with a Harley Street doctor (Michael Craig) who diagnoses her case. She later finds her file in his office cabinet and notes that her case is terminal. Like Davis' heroine in the 1939 edition, she comes to terms with the ordeal and marries the doctor. She eventually goes totally blind, a development that is immediately followed by death. Several of Susan's scenes were deleted from the release print, giving the product a rather choppy continuity. In 1976, a third rendition of *Dark Victory* would be produced as a three-hour telefilm starring Elizabeth Montgomery. It proved to be inferior to the Davis and Hayward renderings.

In 1964 Susan traveled back to California (Los Angeles and San Francisco) to star in the Harold Robbins story *Where Love Has Gone* (1964). Her co-stars were Michael Connors, in an obligatory, thankless role, and Bette Davis. As with the book original, it is an obvious commercial attempt to capitalize on the scandal engendered by the Lana Turner-Johnny Stompanato affair wherein Lana's daughter Cheryl was thought to have killed underworld figure Stompanato, Lana's lover. It was generally known that Susan and Miss Davis were grinning and bearing it throughout the filming. Whereas Susan had had a bit in the Davis feature *The Sisters,* she was now top-billed over Davis, and this did not sit well with the aging Bette. In spite of the film's shabby theme, it found its audience.

Susan was in Venice in late 1965 for the Joseph L. Mankiewicz-directed *The Honey Pot* (1967), adapted from *Volpone*, Ben Jonson's play of 1606. Filming stopped when Floyd Eaton Chalkley took sick back in Georgia with hepatitis resulting from an untreated

With Bette Davis in *Where Love Has Gone* ('64).

World War II blood infection. He was taken to Holy Cross Hospital in Fort Lauderdale, Florida, where his condition worsened. He asked to be returned home to Carrollton, a wish that Susan obeyed. On January 9, 1966, Chalkley died there. According to Ron Nelson, a close friend of Susan's, she "locked herself in the bathroom and yelled her lungs out," and then faced her responsibilities bravely.

Afterward Susan flew back to Venice to complete her work on *The Honey Pot,* in which she received second billing to Rex Harrison. The sophisticated tale is centered about Cecil Fox, an eccentric millionaire who calls together his three ex-loves, claiming that he is dying. The trio (Edie Adams, Capucine, and Susan) attend the "wake" while Fox, abetted by his accomplice (Cliff Robertson), watches their reactions to his demise. Susan is Mrs. "Lone-Star" Crockett Sheridan, a wealthy Texan who is killed off too early in the proceedings because, of the three ladies, she is the one most likely to remain near and dear to Fox. Due to editing of the generally unsuccessful film, Susan's role in the finished product is no more than a cameo.

Returning to Georgia, Susan sold the Chalkley holdings which included their own private lake, a guest house for friends, 450 acres with cows, and the main family residence. She then moved to Fort Lauderdale, Florida, where she had spent happy times with her husband who had a boat and who loved to fish. Six months after Chalkley's death, Susan traveled incognito to Pennsylvania where she was received into the Catholic Church by Reverend Daniel J. McGuire, the pastor of Saints Peter and Paul Church

With Tony Scotti and Barbara Parkins in *Valley of the Dolls* ('67).

in the Pittsburgh suburb of East Liberty. "I hope to Christ there is something to reincarnation," she told a friend, "because I want to see Eaton again."

In 1967 she emerged from her Florida seclusion to enact the part of Helen Lawson, an aging musical stage star in Twentieth Century-Fox's *Valley of the Dolls* (1967), adapted from the Jacqueline Susann bestselling novel. Susan was called in when the originally assigned Judy Garland was removed from the project. Her part is small compared to the others, but she received special billing ("Susan Hayward as Helen Lawson") and larger-sized billing than her neophyte "co-stars" Patty Duke, Sharon Tate, and Barbara Parkins. True to the novel, Lawson's oversized character is a stereotype of the theatrical institution, a performer who has forgotten more than the newer crop has learned. She is redhaired, but in a confrontation with Neely O'Hara (Duke), a beginning singer, she is snatched wigless to reveal a patch of white hair. The wig is tossed into the toilet of the ladies' bathroom and Miss Lawson is forced to leave the party with a bandana over her head. Susan's song in this movie was dubbed by Eileen Wilson.

In conjunction with *Valley of the Dolls* and other Fox releases during 1967–1968, Susan was seen in excerpts from the film in a 30-minute short subject called *Think 20th*.

In 1968 film producer Martin Rackin telephoned Susan in Florida to ask her for a favor. That request was to perform the taxing musical *Mame* in Las Vegas at Caesar's Palace. After 96 grueling performances—often with two shows nightly—she was forced to quit because her voice gave out. At her final press conference, she confessed that she had "never copped out on a job in [her] life." Susan was replaced in the role by Celeste Holm.

On January 22, 1971, Susan awakened in her Fort Lauderdale apartment on the ninth floor to find it engulfed in flames. When the firemen arrived she was found knotting together blankets for an expected retreat, but she registered calm throughout the ordeal.

It was in 1972 that Susan returned to filmmaking for her friend Rackin at the Screen Actors' Guild minimum fee of $487* for a cameo-type role in Cinerama's *The Revengers* with her co-star of 1943, William Holden. She was a last-minute replacement for Mary Ure. The post-Civil War Western was directed by another of Hayward's pals, Daniel Mann. She plays a lonely Irish-born nurse who fleetingly meets Holden in his vengeful search for the killers of his family. She begs him to give up his quest, but he will not.

Also in 1972, Susan starred in two television series pilots/telefeatures. In the first, for CBS, she replaced an ailing Barbara Stanwyck in *Heat of Anger*, playing a stalwart woman attorney who has a young associate (James Stacy). The series, if it had sold, would have been called "Fitzgerald and Pride." The second was *Say Goodbye, Maggie Cole* for ABC in which she was a female physician who found herself involved in a personal struggle with death. *Variety* found the latter to possess too many "soap opera-like overtones." In a *TV Guide* interview in February 1972, she described her venture into television: "In TV, there's no more fooling around and taking it easy. I was frenzied when I had to learn ten pages of dialogue every day, instead of the three pages we used to do in films, but I soon found out I was able to handle it. Fortunately, my brain is in good shape."

It was also in 1972 that she began experiencing severe headaches. She was hospitalized at Century City Hospital in Los Angeles under the name of Margaret Redding. When she was released from the hospital in May 1973, she weighed a slight 85 pounds and wore a wig. (Her hair had fallen out from chemotherapy and radiation treatments.) By December 1973 she was partially paralyzed on her right side, except for her arm. A fighter through and through, she de-

---

*She had been paid $50,000 for two weeks' work in *Valley of the Dolls*, during which her relatively brief four scenes were shot.

In the Las Vegas edition of the musical *Mame* ('68).

With William Holden in *The Revengers* ('72).

With Darren McGavin in the ABC-TV telefeature *Say Goodbye, Maggie Cole* ('72).

With James Stacy in the CBS-TV telefeature *Heat of Anger* ('72).

cided that she wanted to make an appearance at the forthcoming Academy Award presentations and she did so in April 1974. Supported by Charlton Heston as she walked to the podium, Susan received a resounding ovation.

It was not generally revealed until a few weeks later that she was suffering from a brain tumor. She was bedridden in a home she had bought in Culver City, California, and was allowed only a few visitors, such as Barbara Stanwyck, Katharine Hepburn, and Greta Garbo (who had heard that Susan was a great admirer of hers). On March 14, 1975, Susan Hayward died at two in the afternoon.* Her body was flown to Carrollton, Georgia, to be buried next to her husband. A pink marble tombstone was placed on her grave.

A month later it was revealed that Susan's estate was estimated at $950,000. Of this, $200,000 was left to her brother Walter, with the remainder going to her sons Greg-

*In August 1979, there was speculation in the press about the coincidence of the cancer deaths of John Wayne, Susan Hayward, Dick Powell, and Agnes Moorehead, all of whom were connected with *The Conqueror*, a film made in 1954 on location in St. George, Utah. According to reports, the explosion of an atomic bomb in the Nevada desert in 1953 had created an atomic cloud known as "Dirty Harry" which was blown across the Nevada and Utah deserts leaving a radioactive atmosphere over St. George.

ory and Timothy.* Excluded from the bequest was her sister Florence, from whom she had been alienated for many years. In the early summer of 1976, "the complete furnishings, wardrobe, art properties, and personal effects of the late Susan Hayward" were sold at auction in Los Angeles.

Not too many years before, when Susan had been asked about her motion picture tenure, she had said, "I've enjoyed every minute of my career. It isn't art to me, it's work, and darn good work, but it's never been my life. There are other things vastly more important to me."

---

*Gregory is a veterinarian in Florida and Timothy is a Hollywood press agent.

FILMOGRAPHY

HOLLYWOOD HOTEL (*Warner Bros., 1937*) 109 min.

Producer, Hal B. Wallis; associate producer, Sam Bischoff; director, Busby Berkeley; story, Jerry Wald, Maurice Leo; screenplay, Wald, Leo, Richard Macaulay; dialogue director, Gene Lewis; art director, Robert Haas; songs, Richard Whiting and Johnny Mercer; orchestrator, Ray Heindorf; music director, Leo F. Forbstein; camera, Charles Rosher, George Barnes.

Dick Powell (Henry Bowers); Rosemary Lane (Virginia Stanton); Lola Lane (Mona Marshall); Hugh Herbert (Chester Marshall); Ted Healy (Fuzzy); Glenda Farrell (Jonesey); Johnny Davis (Georgia); Frances Langford (Alice); Benny Goodman and His Orchestra, Louella Parsons, Ken Niles, Jerry Cooper, Duane Thompson, Raymond Paige and His Orchestra (Themselves); Alan Mowbray (Alexander Dupre); Mabel Todd (Dot Marshall); Allyn Joslyn (Bernie Walton); Grant Mitchell (B. L. Faulken); Edgar Kennedy (Callaghan); Fritz Feld (The Russian); Curt Bois (Dress Designer); Eddie Acuff (Cameraman); Sarah Edwards (Mrs. Marshall); William B. Davidson (Director Melton); Wally Maher (Drew, the Assistant Director); Paul Irving (Bragwell); Lilly Taylor (Cleo); Joseph Romantini (Headwaiter); Jerry Fletcher (Bellboy); Jack Mower (Airport Guard); Jeffrey Sayre (Co-Pilot); Billy Wayne (Photographer); John Harron (Radio Representative); Jean Haddox (Hotel Maid); Betty Farrington, Helen Dickson (Onlookers); Carole Landis (Hatcheck Girl); Alan Davis (Assistant at the Imperial); Lester Dorr, Allen Fox, Owen King, Bobby Watson, George O'Hanlon (Casting Assistants); Clinton Rosemond, Pearl Adams (Black Couple); Susan Hayward (Starlet at Table); Ronald Reagan (Master of Ceremonies).

THE SISTERS (*Warner Bros., 1938*) 99 min.

Producer, Hal B. Wallis; associate producer, David Lewis; director, Anatole Litvak; based on the novel by Myron Brinig; screenplay, Milton Krims; music, Max Steiner; music director, Leo F. Forbstein; orchestrator, Hugo Friedhofer; assistant director, Jack Sullivan; dialogue director, Irving Rapper; costumes, Orry-Kelly; art director, Carl Jules Weyl; sound, C. A. Riggs; camera, Tony Gaudio; editor, Warren Low.

Bette Davis (Louise Elliot); Errol Flynn (Frank Medlin); Anita Louise (Helen Elliot); Jane Bryan (Grace Elliot); Ian Hunter (William Benson); Henry Travers (Ned Elliot); Beulah Bondi (Rose Elliot); Donald Crisp (Tim Hazleton); Dick Foran (Tom Knivel); Patric Knowles (Norman French); Alan Hale (Sam Johnson); Janet Shaw (Stella Johnson); Lee Patrick (Flora Gibbon); Laura Hope Crews (Flora's Mother); Harry Davenport (Doc Moore); Irving Bacon (Norman Forbes); Mayo Methot (Blonde); Paul Harvey (Caleb Ammen); Arthur Hoyt (Tom Selig); John Warburton (Lord Anthony Bittick); Stanley Fields (Ship's Captain); Ruth Garland (Lora Bennett); Larry Williams (Young Man); Vera Lewis, Lottie Williams, Bessie Wade, Mira McKinney, Georgie Cooper (Women); Lee Phelps, Granville Bates (Announcers); Bob Perry (Referee); Rosella Towne, Susan Hayward, Paulette Evans, Frances Morris (Telephone Operators); Edgar Edwards (Soldier); Mildred Gover (Black Maid); Jang Lim (Chinese Man); Loia Cheaney (Maid).

GIRLS ON PROBATION (*Warner Bros., 1938*) 63 min.

Director, William McGann; story/screenplay, Crane Wilbur; camera, Arthur Todd.

Jane Bryan (Connie Heath); Ronald Reagan (Neil Dillon); Sheila Bromley (Hilda Engstrom); Anthony Averill (Tony Hand); Henry O'Neill (Judge); Elisabeth Risdon (Kate Heath); Sig Rumann (Roger Heath); Dorothy Peterson (Jane Lennox); Susan Hayward (Gloria Adams); Larry Williams (Terry Mason); James Nolan (Dave Warren); Esther Dale (Mrs. Engstrom); Arthur Hoyt (Mr. Engstrom); Lenita Lane (Marge); Peggy Shannon (Ruth); Janet Shaw (Inmate); Kate Lawson, Maud Lambert (Matrons); Brenda Fowler (Head Matron); Joseph Crehan (Todd); James Spottswood (Public Defender); Pierre Watkin (Prosecuting Attorney); Jan Holm (Girl Clerk); Ed Keane (Mr. Brice); Art Miles (Bus Announcer); Dickie Jones (Magazine Boy); Emory Parnell, Dick Rich, Max Hoffman, Jr., Glen Cavender (Policemen); Stuart Holmes (Foreman); Cliff Saum (Patrolman); John Hamilton (Police Chief); Ed Stanley (Sutton); George Offerman, Jr. (Elevator Operator); Jack Mower (Police Sergeant).

COMET OVER BROADWAY (*Warner Bros., 1938*) 69 min.

Associate producer, Bryan Foy; director, Busby Berkeley; based on the story by Faith Baldwin; screenplay, Mark Hellinger, Robert Buckner; music, Heinz Roemheld; camera, James Wong Howe.

Kay Francis (Eve Appleton); Ian Hunter (Bert Ballin); John Litel (Bill Appleton); Donald Crisp (Joe Grant); Minna Gombell (Tim Adams); Sybil Jason (Jacqueline Appleton); Melville Cooper (Emerson); Ian Keith (Wilton Banks); Leona

Maricle (Janet Eaton); Ray Mayer (Tim Brogan); Vera Lewis (Mrs. Appleton); Nat Carr (Burlesque Manager); Chester Clute (Willis); Edward McWade (Harvey); Clem Bevans (Lem); Dorothy Comingore (Miss McDermott); Jack Mower (Hotel Manager); Edgar Edwards (Walter); Lester Dorr (Performer); Alice Connor, Fern Barry, Susan Hayward (Amateur Actors); Owen King (Actor); Jan Holm (Ticket Booth Girl); Jerry Fletcher (Bellhop); Ed Stanley (Doctor); Emmett Vogan (Prosecutor); Raymond Brown (Judge); Howard Mitchell (Court Officer); Charles Seel (Jury Foreman); Loia Cheaney, Janet Shaw (Women); Kay Gordon, Jessie Jackson (Chorus Girls); Jimmy Conlin (Comic); Sidney Bracy (English Porter).

BEAU GESTE (*Paramount, 1939*) 114 min.

Producer/director, William A. Wellman; based on the novel by Percival Christopher Wren; screenplay, Robert Carson; art directors, Hans Dreier, Robert Odell; technical advisor, Louis Van Der Ecker; music, Alfred Newman; orchestrator, Edward Powell; sound, Hugo Grenzbach, Walter Oberst; camera, Theodor Sparkuhl, Archie Stout; editor, Thomas Scott.

Gary Cooper (Beau Geste); Ray Milland (John Geste); Robert Preston (Digby Geste); Brian Donlevy (Sergeant Markoff); Susan Hayward (Isobel Rivers); J. Carroll Naish (Rasinoff); Albert Dekker (Schwartz); Broderick Crawford (Hank Miller); Charles Barton (Buddy McMonigal); James Stephenson (Major Henri de Beaujolais); Heather Thatcher (Lady Patricia Brandon); James Burke (Lieutenant Dufour); George F. Huntley (Augustus Brandon); Harold Huber (Voisin); Donald O'Connor (Beau as a Child); Billy Cook (John as a Child); Martin Spellman (Digby as a Child); Ann Gillis (Isobel as a Child); David Holt (Augustus as a Child); Harvey Stephens (Lieutenant Martin); Stanley Andrews (Maris); Harry Woods (Renoir); Arthur Aylsworth (Renault—a Deserter); Henry Brandon (Renour—Another Deserter); Barry Macollum (Krenke); Ronnie Rondell (Bugler); Frank Dawson (Burdon, the Butler); George Chandler (Cordier); Duke Green (Glock); Thomas Jackson (Colonel in Recruiting Office); Harry Worth (Corporal); Nestor Paiva (Corporal Golas); George Regas, Francis McDonald (Arab Scouts); Larry Lawson (Legionnaire N. Fenton); Joe Colling (Trumpeter O. Leo); Gladys Jeans (Girl in Port Said Cafe).

OUR LEADING CITIZEN (*Paramount, 1939*) 89 min.

Producer, George Arthur; director, Al Santell; story, Irvin S. Cobb; screenplay, John C. Moffitt; camera, Victor Milner.

Bob Burns (Lem Schofield); Gene Lockhart (J. T. Tapley); Susan Hayward (Judith Schofield); Joseph Allen, Jr. (Clay Clinton); Charles Bickford (Shep Muir); Elizabeth Patterson (Aunt Tillie); Clarence Kolb (Jim Hanna); Paul Guilfoyle (Jerry Peters); Fay Helm (Tonia); Kathleen Lockhart (Mrs. Barker); Otto Hoffman (Stony); Kathryn Sheldon (Miss Swan); Hattie Noel (Drusilla); James Kelso (Chief of Police Donovan); Russell Hicks (Chairman); Gus Glassmire (Doctor); Thomas Louden (Frederick, the Butler); Olaf Hytten (Charles, the Butler); Harry C. Bradley (Director); Harry Smiley, Jack H. Richardson, Thomas A. Curran, Hayden Stevenson, Broderick O'Farrell, Frank O'Connor, Harry B. Stafford, Helen Dickson, Ethel May Halls (Members); Sid D'Albrook, Harry Tenbrook, Galan Galt, Oscar G. "Dutch" Hendrian, Paul Kruger, George Magrill (Workmen); Ruth Robinson (Mrs. Hanna); Nell Craig, Peggy Leon, Lillian West (Bridge Players); Heinie Conklin, C. L. Sherwood (Porters); Syd Saylor (Sam, the Porter); Gertrude Messinger, Florence A. Dudley, Jane Webb (Telephone Operators); Wally Maher (Convention Clerk); Cyril Ring, Larry Steers, Arthur Arlington (Delegates).

$1,000 A TOUCHDOWN (*Paramount, 1939*) 71 min.

Associate producer, William C. Thomas; director, James Hogan; screenplay, Delmer Daves; art directors, Hans Dreier, William Flannery; song, Leo Robin and Ralph Rainger; camera, William Mellor; editor, Chandler House.

Joe E. Brown (Marlowe Mansfield Booth); Martha Raye (Martha Madison); Eric Blore (Henry); Susan Hayward (Betty McGlen); John Hartley (Bill Anders); Syd Saylor (Bangs); Joyce Mathews (Lorelei); Tom Dugan (Popcorn Vendor); Matt McHugh (Brick Benson); Josef Swickard (Hamilton McGlen, Sr.); Hugh Sothern (King Richard); George McKay (Mr. Fishbeck); Adrian Morris (Two Ton Terry); Edward Gargan (Ironmansky); William Haade (Guard); Grace Goodall (Nurse); Frank M. Thomas (Dr. Black); Bob Milasch (Tramp); Jimmy Conlin (Sheriff); Emmett Vogan (Coach); Johnny Morris (Newsboy); George Barton (Truck Driver); Jack Perrin, Phil Dunham (McGlen's Sons); Fritzi Brunette, Gertrude Astor (McGlen's Sons' Wives); D'Arcy Corrigan (Cecil); Constantine Romanoff (Duke); Charles Middleton (Stage Manager); Dot Farley (Hysterical Woman); *Madison College Football Team:* Jack Shea (Dimples); Jolly Rowlings (Harry); Harry Templeton (Hank); Jack Chapin (Red); James F. Hogan (Spud); Don Evan Brown (Jack); Arthur Bernard (Dick); Bob Layne (Irish); Wayne "Tiny" Whitt (Big Boy); John Hart (Buck); *Madison College Coeds:* Linda Brent (Bertie); Maxine Conrad (Sally); Cheryl Walker (Blondie); Mary Ray (Toots); Dorothy Dayton (Gen); Paula De Cardo (Dora); Judy King (Honey); Patsy Mace (Ginger); Wanda McKay (Babe); Jane Webb (Billie).

ADAM HAD FOUR SONS (*Columbia, 1941*) 81 min.

Producer, Robert Sherwood; associate producer, Gordon S. Griffith; director, Gregory Ratoff; based on the novel *Legacy* by Charles Bonner; screenplay, William Hurlbutt, Michael Blankfort; production designer, David Hall; art director, Rudolph Sternad; set decorator, Howard Bristol; gowns, David Kidd; assistant director, Norman Deming; camera, Peverell Marley; editor, Francis D. Lyon.

Ingrid Bergman (Emilie Gallatin); Warner Baxter (Adam Stoddard); Susan Hayward (Hester Stoddard); Fay Wray (Molly Stoddard); Richard Denning (Jack Stoddard); Johnny Downs (David Stoddard); Robert Shaw (Chris Stoddard); Charles Lind (Philip Stoddard); Billy Ray (Jack as a Boy); Steven Muller (David as a Boy); Wallace Chadwell (Chris as a Boy); Bobby Walberg (Philip as a Boy); Helen Westley (Cousin Philippa); June Lockhart (Vance); Pietro Sosso (Otto); Gilbert Emery (Dr. Lane); Renie Riano (Photographer); Clarence Muse (Sam).

SIS HOPKINS (*Republic, 1941*) 99 min.

Associate producer, Robert North; director, Joseph Santley; based on the play by F. McGrew Willis; screenplay, Jack Townley, Milt Gross, Ed Eliscu; art director, John Victor Mackay; music director, Cy Feuer; songs, Frank Loesser and Jule Styne; camera, Jack Marta; editor, Ernest Nims.

Judy Canova (Sis Hopkins); Bob Crosby (Jeff Farnsworth); Charles Butterworth (Horace Hopkins); Jerry Colonna (Professor); Susan Hayward (Carol Hopkins); Katharine Alexander (Clara Hopkins); Evia Allman (Ripple); Carol Adams (Cynthia); Lynn Merrick (Phyllis); Mary Ainslee (Vera de Vere); Charles Coleman (Butler); Andrew Tombes (Mayor); Charles Lane (Rollo); Byron Foulger (Joe); Betty Blythe (Mrs. Farnsworth); Frank Darrien (Jud).

AMONG THE LIVING (*Paramount, 1941*) 68 min.

Producer, Sol C. Siegel; associate producer, Colbert Clark; director, Stuart Heisler; story, Brian Marlowe, Lester Cole; screenplay, Cole, Garrett Fort; camera, Theodor Sparkuhl; editor, Everett Douglas.

Albert Dekker (John Raden/Paul Raden); Susan Hayward (Millie Pickens); Harry Carey (Dr. Ben Saunders); Frances Farmer (Elaine Raden); Gordon Jones (Bill Oakley); Jean Phillips (Peggy Nolan); Ernest Whitman (Pompey); Maude Eburne (Mrs. Pickens); Frank J. Thomas (Sheriff); Harlan Briggs (Judge); Archie Twitchell (Tom Reilly); Dorothy Sebastian (Woman in Cafe); William Stack (Minister); Ella Neal, Catherine Craig (Mill Girls); George Turner, Harry Tenbrook (Mill Workers); Patti Lacey, Roy Lester, Ray Hirsch, Jane Allen (Jitterbug Dancers); Delmar Watson (Newsboy); Eddy Chandler (Motorcycle Cop); Richard Webb (Hotel Clerk); Mimi Doyle (Telephone Operator); Ethan Laidlaw, Charles Hamilton (Guards); Bessie Wade (Woman); Rod Cameron, Keith Richards, Abe Dinovitch, Jack Curtis, Chris Frank (Men); Lane Chandler, Frank S. Hagney (Neighbors).

REAP THE WILD WIND (*Paramount, 1942*) C-123 min.

Producer, Cecil B. DeMille; associate producer, William Pine; director, DeMille; story, Thelma Strabel; screenplay, Alan LeMay, Charles Bennett, Jesse Lasky, Jr.; music, Victor Young; art directors, Hans Dreier, Roland Anderson; process camera, Farciot Edouart; special effects, Gordon Jennings; camera, Victor Milner; editor, Anne Bauchens.

Ray Milland (Stephen Tolliver); John Wayne (Captain Jack Stuart); Paulette Goddard (Loxi Claiborne); Raymond Massey (King Cutler); Robert Preston (Dan Cutler); Susan Hayward (Drusilla Alston); Lynne Overman (Captain Phillip Philpott); Charles Bickford (Mate of the "Tyfib"); Walter Hampden (Commodore Devereaux); Louise Beavers (Maum Maria); Martha O'Driscoll (Ivy Devereaux); Elisabeth Risdon (Mrs. Claiborne); Hedda Hopper (Aunt Henrietta); Victor Kilian (Widgeon); Oscar Polk (Salt Meat); Janet Beecher (Mrs. Mottram); Ben Carter (Chinkapin); Wee Willie Davis (The Lamb); Lane Chandler (Sam); Davison Clark (Judge Marvin); Lou Merrill (Captain of the "Pelican"); Frank M. Thomas (Dr. Jepson); Keith Richards (Captain Carruthers); Victor Varconi (Lubbock); J. Farrell MacDonald (Port Captain); Harry Woods (Mace); Raymond Hatton (Master Shipwright); Milburn Stone (Lieutenant Farragut); Barbara Britton, Julia Faye, Amada Lambert (Charleston Ladies); D'Arcy Miller, Bruce Warren (Charleston Beaus); Constantine Romanoff (Pete on the Sponge Boat); Jimmie Dundee (Galley Growler); J. W. Johnson (Clerk of Devereaux Company); Stanhope Wheatcroft (Secretary of Devereaux Company); Sam Flint (Surgeon); Oscar G. "Dutch" Hendrian (Mate of Charleston Packet); Nestor Paiva (Man with Suspenders); Frank Lackteen, Alan Bridge, Frank Richards, Al Ferguson, Frank Hagney (Cutler Men in Barrel Room); Byron Foulger (Devereaux Courier); Stanley Andrews (Bailiff); Dale Van Sickel (Roy—Member of "Falcon"); Helen Dickson, Dorothy Sebastian (Ad Lib Women in Ballroom); Frank Ferguson (Snaith).

THE FOREST RANGERS *(Paramount, 1942)* C-87 min.

Associate producer, Robert Sisk; director, George Marshall; story, Thelma Strabel; screenplay, Harold Shumate; art directors, Hans Dreier, Earl Hedrick; music, Victor Young; songs, Frank Loesser and Frederick Hollander; Joseph J. Lilley; camera, Charles Lang; editor, Paul Weatherwax.

Fred MacMurray (Don Stuart); Paulette Goddard (Celia Huston); Susan Hayward (Tana Mason); Lynne Overman (Jammer Jones); Albert Dekker (Twig Dawson); Eugene Pallette (Mr. Huston); Regis Toomey (Frank Hatfield); Rod Cameron (Jim Lawrence); Clem Bevans (Terry McCabe); James Brown (George Tracy); Kenneth Griffith, Keith Richards, William Cabanne, George Barton, Clint Dorrington, Ronnie Rondell, Bert Stevens, Nick Vehr (Rangers); Jimmy Conlin (Mr. Hansen); Arthur Loft (John Arnold); Chester Clute (Judge); George Chandler, Tim Ryan, Lee Phelps, Edwin J. Brady (Keystone Cops); Pat West (Bartender); Monte Blue (Hotel Clerk); Buddy Bowles, Janet Dempsey (Hansen Kids); Sarah Edwards (Mrs. Hansen); Harry Woods, Robert Homans (Lumbermen); Katharine Booth, Louise LaPlanche (Girls); Ethan Laidlaw, Karl Voss, Bob Kortman, Al Thompson, Myron Geiger, George Bruggeman, Carl Saxe, Harry Templeton, Perc Launders (Lumberjacks).

I MARRIED A WITCH *(United Artists, 1942)* 98 min.

Producer/director, Rene Clair; based on the novel *The Passionate Witch* by Thorne Smith and Norman Matson; adaptors, Robert Pirosh, Marc Connelly; costumes, Edith Head; art directors, Hans Dreier, Ernst Fegte; music director, Roy Webb; special effects, Gordon Jennings; camera, Ted Tetzlaff; editor, Eda Warren.

Fredric March (Wallace Wooley); Veronica Lake (Jennifer); Robert Benchley (Dr. Dudley White); Susan Hayward (Estelle Masterson); Cecil Kellaway (Daniel); Elizabeth Patterson (Margaret); Robert Warwick (J. B. Masterson); Eily Malyon (Tabitha Wooley); Robert Greig (Town Crier); Viola Moore (Martha); Mary Field (Nancy Wooley); Nora Cecil (Harriet); Emory Parnell (Allen); Helen St. Rayner (Vocalist); Aldrich Bowker (Henry, the Justice of the Peace); Emma Dunn (Wife of the Justice of the Peace); Harry Tyler, Ralph Peters (Prisoners); Kathryn Sheldon (Elderly Wife); Charles Moore (Rufus); Ann Carter (Jennifer, Jr.); Charles Bates (Wooley Son); George Guhl (Fred, the Policeman); William Haade (Policeman); Wade Boteler (Policeman Who Arrests Daniel); Eddy Chandler (Motorcycle Cop); Ralph Dunn, Alan Bridge (Prison Guards); Frank Mills (Joe, the Cabby); Jack Gardner (Radio Voice); Jack Luden (Ambulance Driver); Billy Bletcher (Photographer); Ernie Shields (Waiter); Beverly Andre, Mickey Rentschler (Young Folks at Country Club); Lee Shumway (Fireman); Monte Blue (Doorman); Gordon DeMain (Man with Masterson); Reed Hadley (Young Man); Georgia Backus (Older Woman); Marie Blake (Purity); Billy Bevan (Puritan Vendor).

STAR SPANGLED RHYTHM *(Paramount, 1942)* 99 min.

Associate producer, Joseph Sistrom; director, George Marshall; screenplay, Harry Tugend; music, Robert Emmett Dolan; songs, Johnny Mercer and Harold Arlen; art directors, Hans Dreier, Ernst Fegte; camera, Leo Tover, Theodor Sparkuhl; editor, Paul Weatherwax.

Betty Hutton (Polly Judson); Eddie Bracken (Jimmy Webster); Victor Moore (Pop Webster); Anne Revere (Sarah); Walter Abel (Frisbee); Cass Daley (Mimi); Macdonald Carey (Louie the Lug); Gil Lamb (Hi-Pockets); William Haade (Duffy); Bob Hope (Master of Ceremonies); Fred MacMurray, Franchot Tone, Ray Milland, Lynne Overman (Men Playing Cards Skit); Dorothy Lamour, Veronica Lake, Paulette Goddard, Arthur Treacher, Walter Catlett, Sterling Holloway (Sweater, Sarong, and Peekaboo Bang Number); Tom Dugan (Hitler); Paul Porcasi (Mussolini); Richard Loo (Hirohito); Alan Ladd (Scarface); Mary Martin, Dick Powell, Golden Gate Quartet (Dreamland Number); William Bendix, Jerry Colonna, Maxine Ardell, Marjorie Deanne, Lorraine Miller, Marion Martin, Chester Clute (Bob Hope Skit); Vera Zorina, Johnnie Johnston, Frank Faylen (Black Magic Number); Eddie "Rochester" Anderson, Katherine Dunham, Slim and Slam, Woody Strode (Smart as a Tack Number); Susan Hayward (Genevieve—Priorities Number); Ernest Truex (Murgatroyd—Priorities Number); Marjorie Reynolds, Betty Rhodes, Dona Drake, Louise LaPlanche, Lorraine Miller, Donivee Lee, Don Castle, Frederic Henry, Sherman Sanders (Swing Shift Number); Bing Crosby (Old Glory Number); Virginia Brissac (Lady from Iowa—Old Glory Number); Irving Bacon (New Hampshire Farmer—Old Glory Number); Matt McHugh (Man from Brooklyn—Old Glory Number); Peter Potter (Georgia Boy—Old Glory Number); Edward J. Marr (Heavy—Old Glory Number); Gary Crosby (Himself); Albert Dekker, Cecil Kellaway, Ellen

Drew, Jimmy Lydon, Charles Smith, Frances Gifford, Susanna Foster, Robert Preston, Christopher King, Alice Kirby, Marcella Phillips (Finale); Walter Dare Wahl and Company (Specialty Act); Cecil B. DeMille, Preston Sturges, Ralph Murphy (Themselves); Dorothy Granger, Barbara Pepper, Jean Phillips, Lynda Grey (Girls); Karin Booth (Kate); Gladys Blake (Liz); Eddie Dew, Rod Cameron (Petty Officers).

YOUNG AND WILLING *(United Artists, 1943)* 82 min.

Producer/director, Edward H. Griffith; based on the play *Out of the Frying Pan* by Francis Swann; screenplay, Virginia Van Upp; art directors, Hans Dreier, Ernst Fegte; camera, Leo Tover; editor, Eda Warren.

William Holden (Norman Reese); Eddie Bracken (George Bodell); Robert Benchley (Arthur Kenny); Susan Hayward (Kate Benson); Martha O'Driscoll (Dottie Coburn); Barbara Britton (Marge Benson); Mabel Paige (Mrs. Garnet); Florence MacMichael (Muriel Foster); James Brown (Tony Dennison); Jay Fassett (Mr. Coburn); Paul Hurst, Olin Howlin (Cops); Billy Bevan (Phillips); Barbara Slater, Laurie Douglas, Blanche Grady, Lynda Grey, Louise LaPlanche, Judith Gibson, Cheryl Walker, Kenneth Griffith (Performers); Fay Helm (Miss Harris); William Cabanne (Soda Jerk); Betty Farrington (Woman).

JACK LONDON *(United Artists, 1943)* 94 min.

Producer, Samuel Bronston; associate producer, Joseph K. Nadel; director, Alfred Santell; based on *The Book of Jack London* by Charmian Kittredge London; screenplay, Ernest Pascal; art director, Bernard Herzbrun; set decorator, Earl Wooden; dialogue director, Edward Padula; assistant director, Sam Nelson; music director, Fred Rich; sound, Ben Winkler; special effects, Harry Redmond; camera, John W. Boyle; editor, William Ziegler.

Michael O'Shea (Jack London); Susan Hayward (Charmian Kittredge); Osa Massen (Freda Maloof); Harry Davenport (Professor Hilliard); Frank Craven (Old Tom); Virginia Mayo (Mamie); Ralph Morgan (George Brett); Louise Beavers (Mammy Jenny); Jonathan Hale (Kerwin Maxwell); Leonard Strong (Captain Tonaka); Paul Hurst ("Lucky Luke" Lanigan); Regis Toomey (Scratch Nelson); Hobart Cavanaugh (Mike); Olin Howlin (Mailman); Albert Van Antwerp (French Frank); Ernie Adams (Whiskey Bob); John Kelly (Red John); Robert Homans (Captain Allen); Morgan Conway (Richard Harding Davis); Edward Earle (James Hare); Lumsden Hare (English Correspondent); Paul Fung (Japanese General); Pierre Watkin (American Consul); Arthur Loft (Fred Palmer); Sven Hugo Borg (Victor); Edmund Cobb (Father); Charlene Newman (Child); Wallis Clark (Theodore Roosevelt); Richard Loo (Japanese Ambassador); Sarah Padden (Cannery Woman).

HIT PARADE OF 1943 *(Republic, 1943)* 82 min. (TV title: *Change of Heart*)

Associate producer, Albert J. Cohen; director, Albert S. Rogell; screenplay, Frank Gill, Jr.; additional dialogue, Frances Hyland; music director, Walter Scharf; songs, Harold Adamson and Jule Styne; J. C. Johnson and Andy Razaf; orchestrator, Marlin Skiles; choreography, Nick Castle; art director, Russell Kimball; set decorator, Otto Siegel; assistant director, Phil Ford; sound, Thomas Carman; camera, Jack Marta; editor, Thomas Richards.

John Carroll (Rick Farrell); Susan Hayward (Jill Wright); Gail Patrick (Toni Jarrett); Walter Catlett (J. MacClellan Davis); Eve Arden (Belinda Wright); Melville Cooper (Bradley Cole); Albert Whitman, Louis Williams (Pops and Louie); Mary Treen (Janie); Count Basie and His Orchestra with Dorothy Dandridge, Freddie Martin and His Orchestra, Ray McKinley and His Band, Golden Gate Quartet, Three Cheers, The Music Maids (Themselves); Jack Williams (Harlem Sandman); Chinita Marin (Tam-Boom-Ba Number); Wally Vernon (Vaudeville Actor); Warren Ashe (Master of Ceremonies); Tom Kennedy (Westinghouse); Addison Richards (Producer); Gary Breckner, Ken Niles (Announcers); Bud Jamison, Grandon Rhodes (Escorts); Astrid Allwyn (Joyce); Paul "Tiny" Newlan (Doorman); Milton Kibbee (Pastry Man); Olaf Hytten (Waiter); Hooper Atchley (Man in Cab); Ernest "Sunshine Sammy" Morrison (Heaven Air Pilot).

THE FIGHTING SEABEES *(Republic, 1944)* 100 min.

Associate producer, Albert J. Cohen; director, Edward Ludwig; story, Borden Chase; screenplay, Chase, Aeneas MacKenzie; music, Walter Scharf; song, Peter DeRose and Sam M. Lewis; art director, Duncan Cramer; set decorator, Otto Siegel; assistant director, Phil Ford; special effects, Howard and Theodore Lydecker; camera, William Bradford; editor, Richard Van Enger.

John Wayne (Wedge Donovan); Dennis O'Keefe (Lieutenant Commander Robert Yarrow); Susan Hayward (Constance Chesley); William Frawley (Eddie Powers); Addison Richards (Captain Joyce); Leonid Kinskey (Johnny Novasky); Paul Fix (Ding Jacobs); J. M. Kerrigan (Sawyer Collins); Ben Welden (Yump Lumkin); Grant Withers (Whanger Spreckles); Jay Norris

(Joe Brick); William Forrest (Lieutenant Tom Kerrick); Duncan Renaldo (Juan); Joey Ray, Al Murphy, Roy Barcroft, Abdullah Abbas, Charles Sullivan (Men); Chief Thundercloud (Indian); William Hall (Swede); Jean Fenwick (Secretary to Captain Joyce); LeRoy Mason (Jonesey); Adele Mara (Twinkles Tucker); Forbes Murray (Navy Surgeon); Bud Geary (Workman); Ben Taggart (Aircraft Carrier Captain); Hal Taliaferro (Lieutenant Commander Hood); Crane Whitley (Lieutenant Commander Hunter).

THE HAIRY APE (*United Artists, 1944*) 91 min.

Producer, Jules Levy; associate producer, Joseph Nadel; director, Al Santell; based on the play by Eugene O'Neill; screenplay, Robert D. Andrews, Decla Dunning; art director, James Sullivan; assistant director, Sam Nelson; music, Michael E. Michlet; music director, Eddie Paul; sound, Corson Jowett; special effects, Harry Redmond; camera, Lucien Andriot; editor, William Ziegler.

William Bendix (Hank Smith); Susan Hayward (Mildred Douglas); John Loder (Lazar); Dorothy Comingore (Helen); Roman Bohnen (Paddy); Tom Fadden (Long); Alan Napier (MacDougald); Charles Cane (Gantry); Rafael Storm (Aldo); Charles La Torre (Portuguese Proprietor); Don Zelaya (Concertina Player); Mary Zavian (Waitress); George Sorel (Police Captain); Paul Weigel (Doc); Egon Brecher (Musician); Gisela Werbisek (Refugee Woman); Carmen Rachel (Young Girl); Jonathan Lee (Water Tender); Dick Baldwin (Third Engineer); Bob Perry (Bartender).

AND NOW TOMORROW (*Paramount, 1944*) 85 min.

Associate producer, Fred Kohlmar; director, Irving Pichel; based on the novel by Rachel Field; screenplay, Frank Partos, Raymond Chandler; art directors, Hans Dreier, Hal Pereira; set decorator, Ted von Hemert; assistant director, Oscar Rudolph; music, Victor Young; sound, Earl Hayman; process camera, Farciot Edouart; camera, Daniel L. Fapp; editor, Duncan Mansfield.

Alan Ladd (Dr. Merek Vance); Loretta Young (Emily Blair); Susan Hayward (Janice Blair); Barry Sullivan (Jeff Stoddard); Beulah Bondi (Aunt Em); Cecil Kellaway (Dr. Weeks); Grant Mitchell (Uncle Wallace); Helen Mack (Angeletta Gallo); Darryl Hickman (Joe); Anthony Caruso (Peter Gallo); Jonathan Hale (Dr. Sloane); Conrad Binyon (Bobby); Connie Leon (Hester); Minerva Urecal, Frank Mayo, Russ Clark, Joseph Granby (Patients); Betty Farrington (Mrs. Blodgett); Harry Holman (Santa Claus); Ann Carter (Emily at Seven); Merrill Rodin (Merek Vance at Twelve); Eleanor Donahue (Janice at Four); Byron Foulger (Clerk); Doris Dowling (Maid of Honor); Doodles Weaver (Charlie); Mae Clarke (Receptionist).

DEADLINE AT DAWN (*RKO, 1946*) 82 min.

Executive producer, Sid Rogell; producer, Adrian Scott; director, Harold Clurman; based on the novel by William Irish; screenplay, Clifford Odets; assistant director, William Dorfman; art directors, Albert S. D'Agostino, Jack Okey; set decorator, Darrell Silvera; gowns, Renie; music, Hanns Eisler; music director, C. Bakaleinikoff; sound, Earl A. Wolcott, James G. Stewart; special effects, Vernon L. Walker; camera, Nicholas Musuraca; editor, Roland Gross.

Susan Hayward (June Goff); Paul Lukas (Gus Offman); Bill Williams (Alex Winkley); Joseph Calleia (Val Bartelli); Osa Massen (Helen Robinson); Lola Lane (Edna Bartelli); Jerome Cowan (Lester Brady); Marvin Miller (Sleepy Parsons); Roman Bohnen (Collarless Man); Steven Geray (Edward Homick—Man with Gloves); Joe Sawyer (Babe Dooley); Constance Worth (Mrs. Nan Raymond); Joseph Crehan (Lieutenant Kane); Jason Robards, Sr., Philip Morris (Cops); Emory Parnell (Captain Bender); Lee Phelps (Philosophical Cop); Ernie Adams (Waiter); Dorothy Curtis (Giddy Woman); Pearl Varvelle (Bit with Whispering Man); Annelle Hayes (Society Woman); Myrna Dell (Hatcheck Girl); Ed Gargan (Bouncer); Byron Foulger (Night Attendant); Isabel Withers (Nurse).

CANYON PASSAGE (*Universal, 1946*) C-90 min.

Producer, Walter Wanger; associate producer, Alexander Golitzen; director, Jacques Tourneur; based on the serialized novel by Ernest Haycox; screenplay, Ernest Pascal; art directors, John B. Goodman, Richard H. Riedel; set decorators, Russell A. Gausman, Leigh Smith; music director, Frank Skinner; songs, Hoagy Carmichael; assistant director, Fred Frank; dialogue director, Anthony Jowitt; sound, Bernard B. Brown; special camera, D. S. Horsley; camera, Edward Cronjager; editor, Milton Carruth.

Dana Andrews (Logan Stuart); Susan Hayward (Lucy Overmire); Brian Donlevy (George Camrose); Patricia Roc (Caroline Dance Marsh); Hoagy Carmichael (Hi Linnet); Ward Bond (Honey Bragg); Andy Devine (Ben Dance); Stanley Ridges (Jonas Overmire); Lloyd Bridges (Johnny Steele); Fay Holden (Mrs. Overmire); Victor Cutler (Vane Blazier); Tad Devine (Asa Dance); Denny Devine (Bushrod Dance); Onslow Stevens (Lestrade); Rose Hobart (Marta Lestrade); Dorothy Peterson (Mrs. Dance); Halliwell Hobbes (Clenchfield); James Cardwell (Gray

Barlett); Ray Teal (Neil Howison); Virginia Patton (Liza Stone); Francis McDonald (Cobb); Erville Alderson (Judge); Ralph Peters (Stutchell); Jack Rockwell (Teamster); Joseph P. Mack, Gene Stutenroth, Karl Hackett, Jack Clifford, Darrel Hudson, Dick Alexander (Miners); Chief Yowlachie (Indian Spokesman); Harry Shannon (McLane); Frank Ferguson (Minister); Rex Lease, Will Kaufman (Players); Sherry Hall (Clerk).

SMASH-UP, THE STORY OF A WOMAN (*Universal, 1947*) 103 min. (British release title: *A Woman Destroyed*)

Producer, Walter Wanger; associate producer, Martin Gabel; director, Stuart Heisler; story, Dorothy Parker, Frank Cavett; screenplay, John Howard Lawson; additional dialogue, Lionel Wiggam; art director, Alexander Golitzen; set decorators, Russell Gausman, Ruby R. Levitt; music/music director, Daniel Amfitheatrof; songs, Jimmy McHugh and Harold Adamson; Jack Brooks and Edgar Fairchild; assistant director, Fred Frank; sound, Joe Lapis; special camera, David Horsley; camera, Stanley Cortez; editor, Milton Carruth.

Susan Hayward (Angie Evans); Lee Bowman (Ken Conway); Marsha Hunt (Martha Gray); Eddie Albert (Steve); Carl Esmond (Dr. Lorenz); Carleton Young (Mr. Elliott); Charles D. Brown (Mike Dawson); Janet Murdoch (Miss Kirk); Tom Chatterton (Edwards); Sharyn Payne (Angelica); Robert Shayne (Mr. Gordon); Larry Blake (M.C.); George Meeker (Wolf); Erville Alderson (Farmer); George Meader (Attorney); Ruth Sanderson (Maggie); Steve Olsen, Fred Browne (Bartenders); Virginia Carroll, Nanette Vallon, Dorothy Christy (Women); Al Hill, Richard Kipling, Clarence Straight (Men); William Gould (Judge); Connie Leon (Mary); Vivien Oakland (Woman at Bar); Robert Verdaine (Maitre d'); Laurie Douglas (Singer); Ernie Adams (Waiter); Ethel Wales (Farmer's Wife); Ralph Montgomery (Doorman); Noel Neill (Girl at Party); Lee Shumway (Benson); Joan Shawlee, Peg LaCentra, Matt Dennis (Offstage Voices).

THEY WON'T BELIEVE ME (*RKO, 1947*) 95 min.

Executive producer, Jack J. Gross; producer, Joan Harrison; director, Irving Pichel; story, Gordon McDonell; screenplay, Jonathan Latimer; art directors, Albert S. D'Agostino, Robert Boyle; set decorators, Darrell Silvera, William Magginetti; music, Roy Webb; music director, C. Bakaleinikoff; assistant director, Harry D'Arcy; sound, John Tribby, Clem Portman; special effects, Russell A. Cully; camera, Harry J. Wild; editor, Elmo Williams.

Robert Young (Larry Ballantine); Susan Hayward (Verna Carlson); Jane Greer (Janice Bell); Rita Johnson (Greta Ballantine); Tom Powers (Trenton); George Tyne (Lieutenant Carr); Don Beddoe (Thomason); Frank Ferguson (Cahill); Harry Harvey (Judge Fletcher); Wilton Graff (Patrick Gold, the Prosecutor); Janet Shaw (Susan Haines); Glen Knight (Parking Lot Attendant); Anthony Caruso (Tough Patient); George Sherwood (Highway Cop); Perc Launders (Police Stenographer); Byron Foulger (Mortician); Hector Sarno (Nick); Carl Kent (Chauffeur); Lee Frederick (Detective); Elena Warren (Mrs. Bowman); Herbert Heywood (Sheriff); Lillian Bronson (Mrs. Martha Hines); Paul Maxey (Mr. Speed Bowman); Jean Andren (Maid); Martin Wilkins (Black Sailor); Dot Farley (Emma); Milton Parsons (Court Clerk); Lee Phelps (Bailiff); Frank Pharr (Patrick Collins); Ellen Corby (Screaming Woman); Matthew McHugh (Tiny Old Man); Lida Durova (Girl at Newsstand); Netta Packer (Spinster); Bud Wolfe (Driver); Sol Gorss (Gus); Harry D'Arcy (Fisherman); Lovyss Bradley (Miss Jorday).

THE LOST MOMENT (*Universal, 1947*) 88 min.

Producer, Walter Wanger; director, Martin Gabel; based on the novel *The Aspern Papers* by Henry James; screenplay, Leonardo Bercovici; art director, Alexander Golitzen; set decorators, Russell A. Gausman, Kenneth Swartz; music, Daniele Amfitheatrof; music arranger/orchestrator, David Tamkin; assistant director, Horace Hough; sound, Charles Felstead, Jesse Moulin; camera, Hal Mohr; editor, Milton Carruth.

Robert Cummings (Lewis); Susan Hayward (Tina Bordereau); Agnes Moorehead (Juliana); Joan Lorring (Amelia); Eduardo Ciannelli (Father Rinaldo); John Archer (Charles); Frank Puglia (Pietro); Minerva Urecal (Maria); William Edmunds (Vittorio); Martin Garralaga (Waiter); Eugene Borden (Proprietor); Nicholas Khadarik (Singer); Julian Rivero (Story Teller); Lillian Molieri, Donna De Mario (Pretty Girls); Robert Verdaine (Young Man); Wallace Stark (Sketch Artist); Saverio Lo Medico (Waiter).

TAP ROOTS (*Universal, 1948*) C-109 min.

Producer, Walter Wanger; director, George Marshall; based on the novel by James Street; screenplay, Alan LeMay; additional dialogue, Lionel Wiggam; production designer, Alexander Golitzen; art director, Frank A. Richards; set decorators, Russell A. Gausman, Ruby R. Levitt; music, Frank Skinner; orchestrator, David Tamkin; assistant director, Aaron Rosenberg; makeup, Bud Westmore; costumes, Yvonne Wood; sound, Leslie I. Carey, Glenn E. Anderson; camera, Lionel Lindon, Winton C. Hoch;

editor, Milton Carruth.

Van Heflin (Keith Alexander); Susan Hayward (Morna Dabney); Boris Karloff (Tishomingo); Julie London (Aven Dabney); Whitfield Connor (Clay MacIvor); Ward Bond (Hoab Dabney); Richard Long (Bruce Dabney); Arthur Shields (Reverend Kirkland); Griff Barnett (Dr. MacIntosh); Sondra Rodgers (Shellie); Ruby Dandridge (Dabby); Russell Simpson (Sam Dabney); Jack Davis (Militia Captain); Gregg Barton (Captain); George Hamilton (Quint); Jonathan Hale (General Johnston); Arthur Space, Kay Medford (Callers); William Haade (Mob Leader); Harry Cording (Leader); Bill Neff, Keith Richards (Lieutenants); Dick Dickinson (Field Hand); Elmo Lincoln (Sergeant).

THE SAXON CHARM (*Universal, 1948*) 88 min.

Producer, Joseph Sistrom; director, Claude Binyon; based on the novel by Frederick Wakeman; screenplay, Binyon; art director, Alexander Golitzen; set decorators, Russell A. Gausman, Ted Offenbacker; music, Walter Scharf; orchestrator, David Tamkin; assistant director, Frank Shaw; makeup, Bud Westmore; costumes, Mary K. Dodson; choreography, Nick Castle; sound, Leslie I. Carey, Glenn E. Anderson; special effects, David S. Horsley; camera, Milton Krasner; editor, Paul Weatherwax.

Robert Montgomery (Matt Saxon); Susan Hayward (Janet Busch); John Payne (Eric Busch); Henry "Harry" Morgan (Hermy); Harry Von Zell (Zack Humber); Cara Williams (Dolly Humber); Chill Wills (Captain Chatham); Heather Angel (Vivian Saxon); John Baragrey (Peter Stanhope); Addison Richards (Abel Richman); Barbara Challis (Ingenue); Curt Conway (Jack Bernard); Fay Baker (Mrs. Noble); Philip Van Zandt (Chris); Martin Garralaga (Manager); Max Willenz (Proprietor); Fred Nurney (Headwaiter); Archie Twitchell (Mr. Maddox); Barbara Billingsley (Mrs. Maddox); Eula Guy (Harassed Secretary); Al Murphy (Bald Man); Clarence Straight (Mr. McCarthy); Bert Davidson (Mr. Noble); Maris Wrixon (Mrs. McCarthy); Peter Brocco (Cyril Leatham); Kathleen Freeman (Nurse); Robert Spencer (Leading Man).

TULSA (*Eagle Lion, 1949*) C-90 min.

Producer, Walter Wanger; associate producer, Edward Lasker; director, Stuart Heisler; story, Richard Wormser; screenplay, Frank S. Nugent, Curtis Kenyon; art director, Nathan Juran; set decorators, Armor Marlowe, Al Orenbach; music, Frank Skinner; music conductor, Charles Previn; orchestrator, David Tamkin; music director, Irving Friedman; song, Allie Wrubel and Mort Greene; costumes, Herschel; assistant director, Howard W. Koch; makeup, Ern Westmore, Del Armstrong; sound, Howard Fogetti; special effects, John Fulton; camera, Winton Hoch; editor, Terrell Morse.

Susan Hayward (Cherokee Lansing); Robert Preston (Brad Brady); Pedro Armendariz (Jim Redbird); Chill Wills (Pinky Jimpson); Harry Shannon (Nelse Lansing); Ed Begley (Johnny Brady); Jimmy Conlin (Homer); Paul E. Burns (Tooley); Lloyd Gough (Bruce Tanner); Roland Jack (Steve); Chief Yowlachie (Charlie Lightfoot); Pierre Watkin (Winters); Lane Chandler (Mr. Kelly); Tom Dugan (Taxi Driver); Lola Albright (Candy Williams); Iron Eyes Cody (The Osage Indian); Dick Wessel (Joker); John Dehner, Selmer Jackson (Oilmen); Larry Keating (Governor); Joseph Crehan (Judge McKay).

HOUSE OF STRANGERS (*Twentieth Century-Fox, 1949*) 101 min.

Producer, Sol C. Siegel; director, Joseph L. Mankiewicz; based on the novel *I'll Never Go There Any More* by Jerome Weidman; screenplay, Philip Yordan; art directors, Lyle Wheeler, George W. Davis; set decorators, Thomas Little, Walter M. Scott; music/music director, Daniele Amfitheatrof; orchestrator, Maurice de Packh; assistant director, William Eckhart; makeup, Ben Nye, Dick Smith; costumes, Charles Le Maire; sound, W. D. Flick, Roger Heman; special effects, Fred Sersen; camera, Milton Krasner; editor, Herman Jones.

Edward G. Robinson (Gino Monetti); Susan Hayward (Irene Bennett); Richard Conte (Max Monetti); Luther Adler (Joe Monetti); Paul Valentine (Pietro Monetti); Efrem Zimbalist, Jr. (Tony Monetti); Debra Paget (Marie Domenico); Hope Emerson (Helene Domenico); Esther Minciotti (Theresa Monetti); Diana Douglas (Elaine Monetti); Tito Vuolo (Lucca); Albert Morin (Victorio); Sid Tomack (Waiter); Thomas Browne Henry (Judge); David Wolfe (Prosecutor); John Kellogg (Danny); Ann Morrison (Woman Juror); Dolores Parker (Nightclub Singer); Tommy Garland (Pietro's Opponent); Mushy Callahan (Referee); Herbert Vigran (Neighbor); Sally Yarnell, Jeri Jordan, Marjorie Holliday, Donna La Tour, Maxine Ardell (Chorus Girls); Lawrence Tibbett (Voice on Recording).

MY FOOLISH HEART (*RKO, 1949*) 98 min.

Producer, Samuel Goldwyn; director, Mark Robson; based on the story "Uncle Wiggily in Connecticut" by J. D. Salinger; screenplay, Julius J. and Philip G. Epstein; art director, Richard Day; set decorator, Julia Heron; music, Victor Young; orchestrators, Leo Shuken, Sidney Cutner; music director, Emil Newman; song, Young and Ned Washington; assistant director, Ivan

Volkman; makeup, Blagoe Stephanoff; costumes, Mary Wills, Edith Head; sound, Fred Lau; special effects, John Fulton; camera, Lee Garmes; editor, Daniel Mandell.

Dana Andrews (Walt Dreiser); Susan Hayward (Eloise Winters); Kent Smith (Lew Wengler); Lois Wheeler (Mary Jane); Jessie Royce Landis (Martha Winters); Robert Keith (Henry Winters); Gigi Perreau (Ramona); Karin Booth (Miriam Ball); Tod Karns (Her Escort); Philip Pine (Sergeant Lucey); Martha Mears (Nightclub Singer); Edna Holland (Dean Whiting); Marietta Canty (Grace); Barbara Woodell (Red Cross Receptionist); Regina Wallace (Mrs. Crandell); Jerry Paris (Usher); Phyllis Coates (Girl on Phone); Bud Stark (Elevator Operator); Ed Peil, Sr. (Conductor).

I'D CLIMB THE HIGHEST MOUNTAIN *(Twentieth Century-Fox, 1951)* C-87 min.

Producer, Lamar Trotti; director, Henry King; based on the novel by Cora Harris; screenplay, Trotti; music, Sol Kaplan; music director, Lionel Newman; art directors, Lyle Wheeler, Maurice Ransford; camera, Edward Cronjager; editor, Barbara McLean.

Susan Hayward (Mary Elizabeth Eden Thompson/Narrator); William Lundigan (William Asbury Thompson); Rory Calhoun (Jack Stark); Barbara Bates (Jenny Brock); Gene Lockhart (Dr. Brock); Lynn Bari (Mrs. Billywith); Ruth Donnelly (Glory White); Kathleen Lockhart (Mrs. Brock); Alexander Knox (Salter); Jean Inness (Mrs. Salter); Dorothea Carolyn Sims (Martha Salter); Fay and Kay Fogg (Martin Twins); Claude Stowers (Station Master); Dr. Wallace Roger (Minister); Myrtle Stovall (Minister's Wife); Bobby C. Canup (Two-Headed Boy); Nina G. Brown, Arispah Palmer, Caroline White (Women).

RAWHIDE *(Twentieth Century-Fox, 1951)* 86 min. (TV title: *Desperate Siege*)

Producer, Samuel G. Engel; director, Henry Hathaway; story/screenplay, Dudley Nichols; art directors, Lyle Wheeler, George W. Davis; music, Lionel Newman; camera, Milton Krasner; editor, Robert Simpson.

Tyrone Power (Tom Owens); Susan Hayward (Vinnie Holt); Hugh Marlowe (Zimmerman); Dean Jagger (Yancy); Edgar Buchanan (Sam Todd); Jack Elam (Tevis); George Tobias (Gratz); Jeff Corey (Luke Davis); James Millican (Tex Squires); Louis Jean Heydt (Fickert); William Haade (Gil Scott); Milton Corey, Sr. (Dr. Tucker); Ken Tobey (Wingate); Dan White (Gilchrist); Max Terhune (Miner); Robert Adler (Billy Dent); Edith Evanson (Mrs. Hickman); Vincent Neptune (Mr. Hickman); Si Jenks (Oldtimer).

I CAN GET IT FOR YOU WHOLESALE *(Twentieth Century-Fox, 1951)* 90 min. (British release title: *This Is My Affair*)

Producer, Sol C. Siegel; director, Michael Gordon; based on the novel by Jerome Weidman; adaptor, Vera Caspary; screenplay, Abraham Polonsky; art directors, Lyle Wheeler, John De Cuir; music director, Lionel Newman; camera, Milton Krasner; editor, Robert Simpson.

Susan Hayward (Harriet Boyd); Dan Dailey (Teddy Sherman); George Sanders (Noble); Sam Jaffe (Cooper); Randy Stuart (Marge); Marvin Kaplan (Four Eyes); Harry Von Zell (Savage); Barbara Whiting (Ellie); Vicki Cummings (Hermione Griggs); Ross Elliott (Ray); Richard Lane (Kelley); Mary Philips (Mrs. Boyd); Steve Geray (Bettini); Charles Lane (Pulvermacher); Marion Marshall (Terry); Marjorie Hoselle (Louise); Jack P. Carr (Bartender); Tamara Shayne (Mrs. Cooper); Michael Hogan (Ship's Officer); Jan Kayne (Ida); Bess Flowers (Saleswoman).

DAVID AND BATHSHEBA *(Twentieth Century-Fox, 1951)* C-116 min.

Producer, Darryl F. Zanuck; director, Henry King; screenplay, Philip Dunne; music, Alfred Newman; art directors, Lyle Wheeler, George Davis; camera, Leon Shamroy; editor, Barbara McLean.

Gregory Peck (David); Susan Hayward (Bathsheba); Raymond Massey (Nathan); Kieron Moore (Uriah); James Robertson Justice (Abishai); Jayne Meadows (Michal); John Sutton (Ira); Dennis Hoey (Joab); Walter Talun (Goliath); Paula Morgan (Adultress); Francis X. Bushman (King Saul); Teddy Infuhr (Jonathan); Leo Pessin (David as a Boy); Gwen Verdon (Specialty Dancer); Gilbert Barnett (Absalom); John Burton (Priest); Lumsden Hare (Old Shepherd); George Zucco (Egyptian Ambassador); Allan Stone (Amnon); Paul "Tiny" Newlan (Samuel); Holmes Herbert (Jesse); Robert Stephenson, Harry Carter (Executioners); Cecil Weston (Woman); Carmen Lopez, Mary Ellen Gleason, Shirley Karnes, Ann Cameron, Mildred Brown, Anne Molinari (Wives); Arthur Loeb, Anthony Natale (Men).

WITH A SONG IN MY HEART *(Twentieth Century-Fox, 1952)* C-117 min.

Producer, Lamar Trotti; director, Walter Lang; story/screenplay, Trotti; music director, Alfred Newman; choreography, Billy Daniel; songs, Lorenz Hart and Richard Rodgers; Lew Brown and Sammy Fain; Arthur Freed and Nacio Herb Brown; Irving Caesar and Vincent Youmans; June Hershey and Don Swander; James Bland; Dan Emmett; Frank Loesser and Arthur

Schwartz; Peggy Lee and Dave Barbour; Sammy Cahn and Jule Styne; George M. Cohan; Bud Green, B. G. De Sylva, and Ray Henderson; De Sylva, Al Jolson, and Joseph Meyer; Fred Fisher; Katherine Lee Bates and Samuel A. Ward; Gus Kahn, Fud Livingston, and Matty Malneck; Ira and George Gershwin; Leo Robin and Ralph Rainger; Don George and Charles Henderson; Newman and Eliot Daniel; E. A. Fenstad and Lincoln Colcord; Ballard MacDonald and James F. Hanley; Ted Koehler and Harold Arlen; Max Showalter and Jack Woodford; Ken Darby; art directors, Lyle Wheeler, Earle Hagen; costumes, Charles Le Maire; camera, Leon Shamroy; editor, J. Watson Webb.

Susan Hayward (Jane Froman); Rory Calhoun (John Burns); David Wayne (Don Ross); Thelma Ritter (Clancy); Robert Wagner (G.I. Paratrooper); Helen Westcott (Jennifer March); Una Merkel (Sister Marie); Richard Allan (Dancer); Max Showalter (Guild); Lyle Talbot (Radio Director); Leif Erickson (General); Stanley Logan (Diplomat); Jane Froman (The Singing Voice of Jane Froman); Frank Sully (Texas); George Offerman (Muleface); Ernest Newton (Specialty); William Baldwin (Announcer); Carlos Molina, Nestor Paiva, Emmett Vogan (Doctors); Maude Wallace (Sister Margaret); Dick Ryan (Officer); Douglas Evans (Colonel).

THE SNOWS OF KILIMANJARO *(Twentieth Century-Fox, 1952)* C-117 min.

Producer, Darryl F. Zanuck; director, Henry King; based on the story by Ernest Hemingway; screenplay, Casey Robinson; music, Bernard Herrmann; art directors, Lyle Wheeler, John De Cuir; set decorators, Thomas Little, Paul S. Fox; special camera effects, Ray Kellogg; camera, Leon Shamroy; editor, Barbara McLean.

Gregory Peck (Harry); Susan Hayward (Helen); Ava Gardner (Cynthia); Hildegarde Neff (Countess Liz); Leo G. Carroll (Uncle Bill); Torin Thatcher (Johnson); Ava Norring (Beatrice); Helene Stanley (Connie); Marcel Dalio (Emile); Vincente Gomez (Guitarist); Richard Allan (Spanish Dancer); Leonard Carey (Dr. Simmons); Paul Thompson (Witch Doctor); Emmett Smith (Molo); Victor Wood (Charles); Bert Freed (American Soldier); Agnes Laury (Margot); Janine Grandel (Annette); John Dodsworth (Compton); Charles Bates (Harry at Seventeen); Lisa Ferraday (Vendeuse); Maya Van Horn (Princess); Ivan Lebedeff (Marquis); Martin Garralaga (Spanish Officer); Julian Rivero (Old Waiter).

THE LUSTY MEN *(RKO, 1952)* 113 min.

Producers, Jerry Wald, Norman Krasna; director, Nicholas Ray; suggested by the story by Claude Stanush; screenplay, Horace McCoy, David Dortort; art directors, Albert S. D'Agostino, Alfred Herman; set decorators, Darrell Silvera, Jack Mills; music, Roy Webb; sound, Phil Brigandi, Clem Portman; camera, Lee Garmes; editor, Ralph Dawson.

Susan Hayward (Louise Merritt); Robert Mitchum (Jeff McCloud); Arthur Kennedy (Wes Merritt); Arthur Hunnicutt (Booker Davis); Frank Faylen (Al Dawson); Walter Coy (Buster Burgess); Carol Nugent (Rusty Davis); Maria Hart (Rosemary Maddox); Lorna Thayer (Grace Burgess); Burt Mustin (Jeremiah); Karen King (Ginny Logan); Jimmy Dodd (Red Logan); Eleanor Todd (Babs); Riley Hill (Hoag, the Ranch-Hand); Bob Bray (Fritz); Sheb Wooley (Slim); Marshall Reed (Jim-Bob); Paul E. Burns (Travis Waite); Sally Yarnell, Jean Stratton, Nancy Moore, Louise Saraydar, Mary Jane Carey, Alice Kirby (Girls); Chuck Roberson (Tall Cowboy); Lane Bradford (Jim-Bob Tyler); Chili Williams, Hazel Boyne, Barbara Blaine (Women); Sam Flint (Doctor); Emmett Lynn (Travis White); Glenn Strange (Rig Ferris, the Foreman); Denver Pyle (Niko); Dan White, Lane Chandler (Announcers).

THE PRESIDENT'S LADY *(Twentieth Century-Fox, 1953)* 96 min.

Producer, Sol C. Siegel; associate producer/director, Henry Levin; based on the novel by Irving Stone; screenplay, John Patrick; art directors, Lyle Wheeler, Leland Fuller; music, Alfred Newman; camera, Leo Tover; editor, William B. Murphy.

Susan Hayward (Rachel Donelson Robards); Charlton Heston (Andrew Jackson); John McIntire (Jack Overton); Fay Bainter (Mrs. Donelson); Whitfield Connor (Lewis Robards); Carl Betz (Charles Dickinson); Gladys Hurlbut (Mrs. Phariss); Ruth Attaway (Moll); Charles Dingle (Captain Irwin); Nina Varela (Mrs. Stark); Margaret Wycherly (Mrs. Robards); Ralph Dumke (Colonel Stark); Jim Davis (Jason); Robert B. Williams (William); Trudy Marshall (Jane); Howard Negley (Cruthers); Dayton Lummis (Dr. May); Harris Brown (Clark); Zon Murray (Jacob); James Best (Samuel); Selmer Jackson (Colonel Green); Juanita Evers (Mrs. Green); George Melford (Minister); George Hamilton (House Servant); Vera Francis (Slave Girl); Leo Curley (Innkeeper); Ann Morrison (Mary); William Walker (Uncle Alfred); Sherman Sanders (Square Dance Caller); Rene Beard (Black Boy); Sam McDaniel (Henry—Phariss' Driver); George Spaulding (Chief Justice Marshall); Willis Bouchey (Judge McNairy); Mervyn Williams (Young Senator).

WHITE WITCH DOCTOR *(Twentieth Century-Fox, 1953)* C-96 min.

Producer, Otto Lang; director, Henry Hathaway; based on the novel by Louise A. Stinetorf; screenplay, Ivan Goff, Ben Roberts; art directors, Lyle Wheeler, Mark-Lee Kirk; music, Bernard Herrmann; camera, Leon Shamroy; editor, James B. Clark.

Susan Hayward (Ellen Burton); Robert Mitchum (Lonni Douglas); Walter Slezak (Huysman); Mashood Ajala (Jacques); Joseph C. Narcisse (Utembo); Elzie Emanuel (Kapuka); Timothy Carey (Jarrett); Otis Greene (Bakuba Boy); Charles Gemora (Gorilla); Paul Thompson, Naaman Brown (Witch Doctors); Myrtle Anderson (Aganza); Everett Brown (Bakuba King); Dorothy Harris (Chief's Wife); Michael Ansara (De Gama); Michael Granger (Paal); Leo C. Aldridge-Milas (Council Member); Louis Polliman Brown (Councilman); Floyd Shackelford (Chief); Henry Hastings, John Iboko (Men).

DEMETRIUS AND THE GLADIATORS *(Twentieth Century-Fox, 1954)* C-101 min.

Producer, Frank Ross; director, Delmer Daves; based on characters in the novel *The Robe* by Lloyd C. Douglas; screenplay, Philip Dunne; assistant director, William Eckhardt; choreography, Stephen Papich; music, Franz Waxman and Alfred Newman; makeup, Ben Nye; wardrobe, Charles Le Maire; art directors, Lyle Wheeler, George W. Davis; set decorators, Walter M. Scott, Paul S. Fix; sound, Arthur L. Kirbach; special camera effects, Ray Kellogg; camera, Milton Krasner; editors, Dorothy Spencer, Robert Fritch.

Victor Mature (Demetrius); Susan Hayward (Messalina); Michael Rennie (Peter); Debra Paget (Lucia); Anne Bancroft (Paula); Jay Robinson (Caligula); Barry Jones (Claudius); William Marshall (Glydon); Richard Egan (Dardanius); Ernest Borgnine (Strabo); Charles Evans (Cassius Chaerea); Everett Glass (Kaeso); Karl Davis (Macro); Jeff York (Albus); Carmen de Lavallade (Slave Girl); John Cliff (Varus); Barbara James, Willetta Smith (Specialty Dancers); Selmer Jackson (Senator); Douglas Brooks (Cousin); Fred Graham (Decurion); George Eldredge (Chamberlain); Paul Richards (Prisoner); Paul Kruger (Courtier); Paul "Tiny" Newlan (Potter); Peter Mamakos, Shepard Menken (Physicians); Ray Spiker, Gilbert Perkins, Mickey Simpson, George Barrows, Paul Stader, Fortune Gordien, Jim Winkler, Lyle Fox, Dick Sands, George Bruggeman, Jack Finlay, Woody Strode (Gladiators).

GARDEN OF EVIL *(Twentieth Century-Fox, 1954)* C-100 min.

Producer, Charles Brackett; director, Henry Hathaway; based on a story by Fred Freiberger and William Tunberg; screenplay, Frank Fenton; music, Bernard Herrmann; songs, Emilio D. Uranga; Ken Darby and Lionel Newman; art directors, Lyle Wheeler, Edward Fitzgerald; set decorator, Pablo Galvan; assistant director, Stanley Hough; makeup, Ben Nye; wardrobe, Charles Le Maire; sound, Nicholas De La Rosa, Jr., Roger Heman; special camera effects, Ray Kellogg; camera, Milton Krasner, Jorge Stahl, Jr.; editor, James B. Clark.

Gary Cooper (Hooker); Susan Hayward (Leah Fuller); Richard Widmark (Fiske); Hugh Marlowe (John Fuller); Cameron Mitchell (Luke Daly); Rita Moreno (Singer); Victor Manuel Mendoza (Vicente Madariaga); Fernando Wagner (Captain); Arturo Soto Rangel (Priest); Manuel Donde (Waiter); Antonio Bribiesca (Bartender); Salvador Terroba (Victim).

UNTAMED *(Twentieth Century-Fox, 1955)* C-111 min.

Producers, Bert E. Friedlob, William A. Bacher; director, Henry King; based on the story by Helga Moray; adaptors, Talbot Jennings, William A. Bacher; screenplay, Jennings, Frank Fenton, Michael Blankfort; art directors, Lyle Wheeler, Addison Hehr; music, Franz Waxman; orchestrator, Edward B. Powell; camera, Leo Tover; editor, Barbara McLean.

Tyrone Power (Paul Van Riebeck); Susan Hayward (Katie O'Neill); Richard Egan (Kurt); John Justin (Shawn Kildare); Agnes Moorehead (Aggie); Rita Moreno (Julia); Hope Emerson (Maria De Groot); Brad Dexter (Christian); Henry O'Neill (Squire O'Neill); Paul Thompson (Tschaka); Alexander D. Havemann (Jan); Louis Mercier (Joubert); Emmett Smith (Jantsie); Jack Macy (Simon); Trude Wyler (Madame Joubert); Louis Polliman Brown (Bani); Tina Thompson, Linda Lowell, Bobby Diamond, Gary Diamond, Brian Corcoran (Maria's Children); Christian Pasques (Young Joubert); Edward Mundy (Grandfather Joubert); John Dodsworth (Captain Richard Eaton); Kevin Corcoran (Young Paul); Eleanor Audley (Lady Vernon); Cecil Weston, Myra Cunard, Ann Cornwall (Women); Kem Dibbs, Michael Ross (Outlaws).

SOLDIER OF FORTUNE *(Twentieth Century-Fox, 1955)* C-96 min.

Producer, Buddy Adler; director, Edward Dmytryk; based on the novel by Ernest K. Gann; screenplay, Gann; art directors, Lyle Wheeler, Jack Martin Smith; set decorators, Walter M. Scott, Stuart A. Reiss; music, Hugo Friedhofer; music conductor, Lionel Newman; orchestrator, Edward B. Powell; costumes, Charles Le Maire; assistant director, Hal Herman; sound, Eugene Grossman, Harry M. Leonard; special camera effects, Ray Kellogg; camera, Leo Tover; editor, Dorothy Spencer.

Clark Gable (Hank Lee); Susan Hayward (Jane Hoyt); Michael Rennie (Inspector Merryweather); Gene Barry (Louis Hoyt); Tom Tully (Tweedie); Alex D'Arcy (Rene); Anna Sten (Madame Dupree); Russell Collins (Icky); Leo Gordon (Big Matt); Richard Loo (Poilin); Soo Yong (Daklai); Frank Tang (Yink Fai); Jack Kruschen (Austin Stoker); Mel Welles (Rocha); Jack Raine (Major Leith-Phipps); George Wallace (Gunner); Alex Finlayson (Australian Airman); Noel Toy (Luan); Beal Wong (Chinese Clerk); Robert Burton (Father Xavier); Robert Quarry (Frank Stewart); Charles Davis (Hotel Desk Clerk); Victor Sen Yung (Goldie); Frances Fong (Maxine); Ivis Goulding, Barry Bernard (English People); Kam Tong (Needle); George Chan (Cheap Hotel Clerk); William Yip (Bartender).

I'LL CRY TOMORROW *(MGM, 1955)* 117 min.

Producer, Lawrence Weingarten; director, Daniel Mann; based on the biography by Lillian Roth, Mike Connolly, and Gerold Frank; screenplay, Helen Deutsch, Jay Richard Kennedy; music director, Charles Henderson; background music, Alex North; assistant director, Al Jennings; costumes, Helen Rose; art directors, Cedric Gibbons, Malcolm Brown; camera, Arthur E. Arling; editor, Harold F. Kress.

Susan Hayward (Lillian Roth); Richard Conte (Tony Bardeman); Eddie Albert (Burt McGuire); Jo Van Fleet (Katie); Don Taylor (Wallie); Ray Danton (David Tredman); Margo (Selma); Virginia Gregg (Ellen); Don Barry (Jerry); David Kasday (David as a Child); Carole Ann Campbell (Lillian as a Child); Peter Leeds (Richard); Tol Avery (Fat Man); Ralph Edwards (Himself); Charles Tannen, Harlan Warde (Stage Managers); Ken Patterson, Stanley Farrar (Directors); Voltaire Perkins (Mr. Byrd); George Lloyd (Messenger); Nora Marlowe (Nurse); Peter Brocco (Doctor); Bob Dix (Henry); Anthony Jochim (Paul, the Butler); Kay English (Dress Designer); Eve McVeagh (Ethel); Jack Gargan (Drug Clerk); Veda Ann Borg (Waitress); Robert R. Stephenson, Joe DuVal (Bartenders); Gail Ganley (Lillian at Fifteen); Vernon Rich (Club Manager); George Pembroke, Mary Bear (Couple); Jack Daly (Taxi Driver); Guy Wilkerson, Marc Krah, Henry Kulky (Men); Ruth Storey (Marge Belney); James Ogg (Usher); Bernadette Withers Kathy Garner (Girls).

THE CONQUEROR *(RKO, 1956)* C-111 min.

Presenter, Howard Hughes; producer, Dick Powell; associate producer, Richard Sokolove; director, Powell; screenplay, Oscar Millard; music, Victor Young; music director, Constantin Bakaleinikoff; choreography, Robert Sidney; assistant director, Edward Killy; costumes, Michael Woulfe, Yvonne Wood; art directors, Albert D'Agostino, Carroll Clark; set decorators, Darrell Silvera, Al Grenbach; makeup, Mel Berns; second unit director, Cliff Lyons; sound, Bernard Fredericks; camera, Joseph LaShelle, Leo Tover, Harry J. Wild; editor, Stuart Gilmore.

John Wayne (Temujin); Susan Hayward (Bortai); Pedro Armendariz (Jamuga); Agnes Moorehead (Hunlun); Thomas Gomez (Wang Kahn); John Hoyt (Shaman); William Conrad (Kasar); Ted de Corsia (Kumlek); Leslie Bradley (Targutai); Lee Van Cleef (Chepei); Peter Mamakos (Bogurchi); Leo Gordon (Tartar Captain); Richard Loo (Captain of Wang's Guard); Richard Keane, Grace Lem (Customers); David Hoffman (Potter); Bob Lugo (Wang Kahn's Guard); Ray Spiker, Charles Horvath (Thugs); Alberto Morin (Drunken Soldier); Henry Escalente, Max Wagner, Bernie Gozier (Tartar Generals); Larry Chance (Tartar); Billy Curtis, George Spotts, Harry Monty, Irving Fulton (Midget Tumblers); Sylvia Lewis (Solo Dancer); Jarma Lewis, Pat McMahon (Girls in Bath); George E. Stone (Sibilant John); Torben Meyer (Scribe); Ken Terrell (Sorgan); Charles Lung (Vendor).

TOP SECRET AFFAIR *(Warner Bros., 1957)* 100 min. (British release title: *Their Secret Affair*)

Producer, Martin Rackin; supervising producer, Milton Sperling; director, H. C. Potter; based on characters in the novel *Melville Goodwin, U.S.A.* by John P. Marquand; screenplay, Roland Kibbee, Allan Scott; art director, Malcolm Bert; music, Roy Webb; orchestrators, Gus Levene, Maurice de Packh; camera, Stanley Cortez; editor, Folmar Blangsted.

Kirk Douglas (Melville Goodwin); Susan Hayward (Dottie Peale); Paul Stewart (Bentley); Jim Backus (Colonel Gooch); John Cromwell (General Grimshaw); Michael Fox (Lotzie); Frank Gerstle (Sergeant Kruger); Roland Winters (Senator Burwick); A. E. Gould-Porter (Butler); Charles Lane (Bill Hadley); Edna Holland (Myrna Maynard); Ivan Triesault (German Field Marshal); Lee Choon Wha (Korean Dignitary); Franco Corsaro (Armande); Lyn Gaborn (Stumpy); Patti Gallagher (Girl); Sid Chatton (Drunk at Table); Jonathan Hale (Mr. Jones); Charles Meredith (Personage); James Flavin (Man); Hal Dawson, Hugh Lawrence, Richard Cutting (Reporters).

I WANT TO LIVE! *(United Artists, 1958)* 120 min.

Producer, Walter Wanger; director, Robert

Wise; based on newspaper articles by Ed Montgomery and the letters of Barbara Graham; screenplay, Nelson Gidding, Don Mankiewicz; music/music conductor, John Mandel; art director, Edward Haworth; set decorator, Victor Gangelin; assistant director, George Vieria; sound, Fred Lau; camera, Lionel Lindon; editor, William Hornbeck.

Susan Hayward (Barbara Graham); Simon Oakland (Ed Montgomery); Virginia Vincent (Peg); Theodore Bikel (Carl Palmberg); Wesley Lau (Henry Graham); Philip Coolidge (Emmett Perkins); Lou Krugman (Jack Santo); James Philbrook (Bruce King); Bartlett Robinson (District Attorney); Gage Clark (Richard G. Tibrow); Joe De Santis (Al Matthews); John Marley (Father Devers); Raymond Bailey (San Quentin Warden); Alice Backes (San Quentin Nurse); Gertrude Flynn (San Quentin Matron); Russell Thorson (San Quentin Sergeant); Dabbs Greer (San Quentin Captain); Stafford Repp (Sergeant); Gavin MacLeod (Lieutenant).

WOMAN OBSESSED (*Twentieth Century-Fox, 1959*) C-103 min.

Producer, Sydney Boehm; director, Henry Hathaway; based on the novel *The Snow Birch* by John Mantley; screenplay, Boehm; music, Hugo Friedhofer; music conductor, Lionel Newman; orchestrator, Earle Hagen; art directors, Lyle R. Wheeler, Jack Martin Smith; set decorators, Walter M. Scott, Stuart A. Reiss; wardrobe designer, Charles Le Maire; makeup, Ben Nye; assistant director, David Hall; sound, W. D. Flick; special camera effects, L. B. Abbott; camera, William C. Mellor; editor, Robert Simpson.

Susan Hayward (Mary Sharron); Stephen Boyd (Fred Carter); Barbara Nichols (Mayme Radzevitch); Dennis Holmes (Robbie Sharron); Theodore Bikel (Dr. Gibbs); Ken Scott (Sergeant Le Moyne); Arthur Franz (Tom Sharron); James Philbrook (Henri); Florence MacMichael (Mrs. Gibbs); Jack Raine (Ian Campbell); Mary Carroll (Mrs. Campbell); Fred Graham (Officer Follette); Mike Lally (Ticket Taker); Richard Monahan (Store Clerk); Dainty Doris (Fat Woman); Harry "Duke" Johnson (Juggler); Lou Manley (Fire Eater); Tommy Farrell, Freeman Morse, Jimmy Ames (Carnival Spielers); Al Hustin (Fire Warden).

THUNDER IN THE SUN (*Paramount, 1959*) C-81 min.

Producer, Clarence Greene; director, Russell Rouse; story, Guy Trosper; adaptor, Stewart Stern; screenplay, Rouse; art director, Boris Leven; music, Cyril Mockridge; song, Mockridge and Ned Washington; choreography, Pedro de Cordoba; Miss Hayward's costumes, Charles Le Maire; second unit director, Winston Jones; camera, Stanley Cortez; editor, Chester Schaeffer.

Susan Hayward (Gabrielle Dauphin); Jeff Chandler (Lon Bennett); Jacques Bergerac (Pepe Dauphin); Blanche Yurka (Louise Dauphin); Carl Esmond (Andre Dauphin); Fortunio Bonanova (Fernando); Felix Locher (Danielle); Bertrand Castelli (Duquette); Veda Ann Borg (Marie); Pedro de Cordoba (Gabrielle's Dance Partner).

THE MARRIAGE-GO-ROUND (*Twentieth Century-Fox, 1960*) C-98 min.

Producer, Leslie Stevens; director, Walter Lang; based on the play by Stevens; screenplay, Stevens; music, Dominic Frontiere; song, Alan Bergman, Marilyn Keith, and Lew Space; art directors, Duncan Cramer, Maurice Ransford; set decorators, Walter M. Scott, Paul S. Fox; costumes, Charles Le Maire; makeup, Ben Nye; assistant director, Eli Dunn; sound, E. Clayton Ward, Frank W. Moran; camera, Leo Tover; editor, Jack W. Holmes.

Susan Hayward (Content Delville); James Mason (Paul Delville); Julie Newmar (Katrin Sveg); Robert Paige (Dr. Ross Barnett); June Clayworth (Flo Granger); Mary Patton (Mamie); Everett Glass (Professor); Ben Astar (Sultan); Bruce Tegner (Judo Man at Pool); Mark Bailey (Boy); Ann Benton (Girl); John Bryant (Young Professor).

ADA (*MGM, 1961*) C-108 min.

Producer, Lawrence Weingarten; director, Daniel Mann; based on the novel *Ada Dallas* by Wirt Williams; screenplay, Arthur Sheekman, William Driskill; music, Bronislau Kaper; music conductor, Robert Armbruster; song, Warren Roberts and Wally Fowler; art directors, George W. Davis, Edward Carfagno; set decorators, Henry Grace, Jack Mills; costumes, Helen Rose; assistant director, Al Jennings; makeup, William Tuttle; sound, Franklin Milton; special camera effects, Lee LeBlanc; camera, Joseph Ruttenberg; editor, Ralph E. Winters.

Susan Hayward (Ada Dallas); Dean Martin (Bo Gillis); Wilfrid Hyde-White (Sylvester Marin); Ralph Meeker (Colonel Yancey); Martin Balsam (Steve Jackson); Frank Maxwell (Ronnie Hallerton); Connie Sawyer (Alice Sweet); Ford Rainey (Speaker); Charles Watts (Al Winslow); Larry Gates (Joe Adams); Robert F. Simon (Warren Natfield); William Zuckert (Harry Davers); Mary Treen (Club Woman); William Quinn, Mack Williams, Merrit Bohn, Robert Burton, Jon Lormer (Committeemen); Helen Beverly (Mrs. Stauton); Amy Douglass (Mrs. Bradville); Helen Kleeb (Mrs. Smith); Peg LaCentra (Maude Penmore); Ray Teal (Kearney Smith); Kathryn Card (Mrs. Betty Mae Dunston); Louise Lorimer (Mrs. Dan-ford); Jack Carr, Dick Ryan, Kathryn Hart, Shirley Cytron, Richard Benedict, John Hart, Mike Mahoney, Joe McGuinn, Robert Reiner, Ann Staunton, Lucile Curtis (Bits); William A. Ritchie (Jed Helker); Emory Parnell (Guard); Ann Seaton (Sylvester's Secretary); Mary Benoit, Carol Forman (Newswomen).

BACK STREET (*Universal, 1961*) C-107 min.

Producer, Ross Hunter; director, David Miller; based on the novel by Fannie Hurst; screenplay, Eleanore Griffin; music, Frank Skinner; song, Skinner and Ken Darby; music supervisor, Joseph Gershenson; art director, Alexander Golitzen; set decorator, Howard Bristol; costumes, Jean Louis; makeup, Bud Westmore; assistant director, Phil Bowles; sound, Waldon O. Watson, Frank H. Wilkinson; camera, Stanley Cortez; editor, Milton Carruth.

Susan Hayward (Rae Smith); John Gavin (Paul Saxon); Vera Miles (Liz Saxon); Virginia Grey (Janie); Charles Drake (Curt Stanton); Reginald Gardiner (Dalian); Tammy Marihugh (Caroline Saxon); Robert Eyer (Paul Saxon, Jr.); Natalie Schafer (Mrs. Evans); Doreen McLean (Miss Hatfield); Alex Gerry (Mr. Venner); Karen Norris (Mrs. Penworth); Hayden Rorke (Charley Claypole); Mary Lawrence (Marge Claypole); Joe Cronin (Airport Clerk); Ted Thorpe (Hotel Clerk); Joseph Mell (Proprietor); Dick Kallman (Sailor); Joyce Meadows (Showroom Model); Lilyan Chauvin (Paris Airport Employee); Joanne Betay, Vivianne Porte, Isabelle Felders, Melissa Weston, Bea Ammidown (*Harper's Bazaar* Models); Iphigenie Castiglioni (Signora Vitaliano); Jeanne Manet (Paris Secretary); Dick Kallman (Sailor); Ruthie Robinson (Marilyn at Ten); Betsy Robinson (Marilyn at Six); Victor Ronito (Maitre d'); Barbara Banning (Woman); Jeno Mate (Ex-King Jodek).

I THANK A FOOL (*MGM, 1962*) C-100 min.

Producer, Anatole De Grunwald; associate producer, Roy Parkinson; director, Robert Stevens; based on the novel by Audrey Erskine Lindop; screenplay, Karl Tunberg; art director, Sean Kenny; dress designer, Elizabeth Haffenden; music, Ron Goodwin; makeup, Tony Sforzini; assistant director, Dave Tomblin; special effects, Tom Howard; sound, Gordon Daniel, A. W. Watkins, Cyril Swern; camera, Harry Waxman; editor, Frank Clarke.

Susan Hayward (Christine Allison); Peter Finch (Stephen Dane); Diane Cilento (Liane Dane); Cyril Cusack (Captain Ferris); Kieron Moore (Roscoe); Athene Seyler (Aunt Heather); Richard Wattis (Ebblington); Brenda De Banzie (Nurse Drew); Miriam Karlin (Woman in the Black Maria); Laurence Naismith (O'Grady); Clive Morton (Judge); J. G. Devlin (Coroner); Richard Leech (Irish Doctor); Yolande Turner (Polly); Edwin Apps (Junior Counsel); Judith Furse, Grace Arnold (Waitresses); Peter Sallis (Sleazy Doctor).

STOLEN HOURS (*United Artists, 1963*) C-100 min.

Executive producers, Stuart Millar, Lawrence Turman; producer, Denis Holt; director, Daniel Petrie; based on the play *Dark Victory* by George Brewer, Jr. and Bertram Block; adaptor, Joseph Hayes; screenplay, Jessamyn West; music, Mort Lindsey; song, Lindsey, Marilyn Keith, and Alan Bergman; art director, Wilfred Shingleton; set decorator, Joan Hoesli; Miss Hayward's costumes, Fabiani; wardrobe, Evelyn Gibbs; titles, Maurice Binder; makeup, George Partleton; assistant director, Colin Brewer; sound, C. T. Mason; camera, Harry Waxman; editor, Geoffrey Foote.

Susan Hayward (Laura Pember); Michael Craig (John Carmody); Diane Baker (Ellen Pember); Edward Judd (Mike Bannerman); Paul Rogers (Eric McKenzie); Robert Bacon (Peter); Paul Stassino (Dalporto); Jerry Desmonde (The Colonel); Ellen McIntosh (Miss Kendall); Gwen Nelson (Hospital Sister); Peter Madden (Reynolds); Joan Newell (Mrs. Hewitt); Chet Baker (Himself).

WHERE LOVE HAS GONE (*Paramount, 1964*) C-114 min.

Producer, Joseph E. Levine; director, Edward Dmytryk; based on the novel by Harold Robbins; screenplay, John Michael Hayes; art directors, Hal Pereira, Walter Tyler; set decorators, Sam Comer, Arthur Krams; costumes, Edith Head; assistant director, D. Michael Moore; dialogue director, Frank London; title song, Sammy Cahn and James Van Heusen; music, Walter Scharf; makeup, Wally Westmore, Gene Hibbs; sound, John Carter, Charles Grenzbach; special camera effects, Paul K. Lerpae; process camera, Farciot Edouart; camera, Joseph MacDonald; editor, Frank Bracht.

Susan Hayward (Valerie Hayden); Bette Davis (Mrs. Gerald Hayden); Michael Connors (Luke Miller); Joey Heatherton (Dani); Jane Greer (Marion Spicer); DeForest Kelley (Sam Corwin); George Macready (Gordon Harris); Anne Seymour (Dr. Sally Jennings); Willis Bouchey (Judge Murphy); Walter Reed (George Babson); Ann Doran (Mrs. Geraghty); Bartlett Robinson (Mr. Coleman); Whit Bissell (Professor Bell); Anthony Caruso (Rafael).

THE HONEY POT (*United Artists, 1967*) C-150 min.

Producers, Charles K. Feldman, Joseph L. Mankiewicz; director, Mankiewicz; based on the play *Mr. Fox of Venice* by Frederick Knott; adapted from the novel *The Evil of the Day* by Thomas Sterling; based on the play *Volpone* by Ben Jonson; production designer, John De Cuir; art director, Boris Juraga; assistant director, Gus Agosti; choreography, Lee Theodore; music, John Addison; sound, David Hildyard; camera, Gianni Di Venanzo; editor, David Bretherton.

Rex Harrison (Cecil Fox); Susan Hayward (Mrs. "Lone-Star" Crockett Sheridan); Cliff Robertson (William McFly); Capucine (Princess Dominique); Edie Adams (Merle McGill); Maggie Smith (Sarah Watkins); Adolfo Celi (Inspector Rizzi); Herschel Bernardi (Oscar Ludwig); Cy Grant, Frank Latimore (Revenue Agents); Luigi Scavran (Massimo); Mimmo Poli (Cook); Antonio Corevi (Tailor); Carlos Valles (Assistant Tailor); Performance of *Volpone:* Hugh Manning (Volpone); David Dodimead (Mosca).

VALLEY OF THE DOLLS (*Twentieth Century-Fox, 1967*) C-123 min.

Producer, David Weisbart; director, Mark Robson; based on the novel by Jacqueline Susann; screenplay, Helen Deutsch, Dorothy Kingsley; art directors, Jack Martin Smith, Richard Day; set decorators, Walter M. Scott, Raphael G. Bretton; gowns, Travilla; makeup, Ben Nye; assistant director, Eli Dunn; music adaptor/conductor, Johnny Williams; songs, Andre and Dory Previn; orchestrator, Herbert Spencer; choreography, Robert Sidney; sound, Don J. Bassman, David Dockendorf; special effects, L. B. Abbott, Art Cruickshank, Emil Kosa, Jr.; camera, William H. Clothier; editor, Dorothy Spencer.

Barbara Parkins (Anne Welles); Patty Duke (Neely O'Hara); Paul Burke (Lyon Burke); Sharon Tate (Jennifer North); Tony Scotti (Tony Polar); Martin Milner (Mel Anderson); Charles Drake (Kevin Gillmore); Alex Davion (Ted Casablanca); Lee Grant (Miriam); Naomi Stevens (Miss Steinberg); Robert H. Harris (Henry Bellamy); Jacqueline Susann (Reporter); Robert Viharo (Director); Mike Angel (Man in Hotel Room); Barry Cahill (Man in Bar); Richard Angarola (Claude Chardot); *with:* Joey Bishop (Master of Ceremonies at Telethon); George Jessel (Master of Ceremonies at Grammy Awards); *and:* Susan Hayward (Helen Lawson); Judith Lowry (Aunt Amy); Jeanne Gerson (Neely's Maid); Linda Peck, Pat Becker, Corinna Tsopei (Telephone Girls); Robert Street (Choreographer); Robert Gibbons (Desk Clerk at Hotel in Lawrenceville); Leona Powers (Woman at Martha Washington Hotel); Barry O'Hara (Assistant Stage Manager); Norman Burton (Neely's Director in Hollywood); Margot Stevenson (Anne's Mother); Jonathan Hawke (Sanitarium Doctor); Marvin Hamlisch (Pianist); Billy Beck (Man Sleeping in Movie House); Dorothy Neumann, Charlotte Knight (Neely's Maids); Robert McCord (Bartender at New York Theatre); Peggy Rea (Neely's Voice Coach); Gertrude Flynn (Ladies' Room Attendant).

HEAT OF ANGER (*CBS-TV, 1972*) C-75 min.

Executive producer, Dick Berg; producer, Ron Roth; director, Don Taylor; teleplay, Fay Kanin; camera, Robert C. Moreno; editor, John Link.

Susan Hayward (Jessie Fitzgerald); Lee J. Cobb (Frank Galvin); James Stacy (Gus Pride); Fritz Weaver (Vincent Kagel); Bettye Ackerman (Stella Gavin); Jennifer Penny (Chris Gavin); Mills Watson (Obie); Tyne Daly (Jean Carson); Ray Simms (Ray Carson); Jack Somack (Stoller); Lynette Mettey (Fran); and: Lucille Benson, Arnold Mesches, Noah Keen.

THE REVENGERS (*National General, 1972*) C-108 min.

Producer, Martin Rackin; director, Daniel Mann; story, Steven W. Carabatsos; screenplay, Wendell Mayes; art director, Jorge Fernandez; set decorator, Carlos Grandjean; music/music director, Pino Calvi; assistant directors, Robert Goodstein, Felippe Palamino; sound, Jesus Gonzalez Gancy, Angel Trejo; special effects, Frank Brendell, Jesus Doran, Laurencio Bordero; camera, Gabriel Torres; editor, Walter Hannemann.

William Holden (John Benedict); Ernest Borgnine (Hoop); Susan Hayward (Elizabeth Reilly); Woody Strode (Job); Roger Hanin (Quilberon); Rene Koldehoff (Zweig); Jorge Luke (Chamaco); Jorge Martinez De Hoyos (Cholo); Arthur Hunnicutt (Free State); Warren Vanders (Tarp); Larry Pennell (Arny); John Kelly (Whitcomb); Scott Holden (Lieutenant Mercer); James Daughton (Morgan Benedict); Lorraine Chanel (Mrs. Benedict); Raul Prieto (Warden).

SAY GOODBYE, MAGGIE COLE (*ABC-TV, 1972*) C-75 min.

Producers, Aaron Spelling and Leonard Goldberg; director, Jud Taylor; teleplay, Sandor Stern; music, Hugo Montenegro; camera, Tim Southcott; editor, Bill Mosher.

Susan Hayward (Dr. Maggie Cole); Darren McGavin (Dr. Lou Grazzo); Michael Constantine (Dr. Sweeney); Michele Nichols (Lisa Downey); Dane Clark (Hank Cooper); Beverly Garland (Mrs. Myrna Anderson); Jeanette Nolan (Mrs. Downey); Maidie Norman (Fergy); Richard Anderson (Dr. Ben Cole); Frank Puglia (Mr. Alessandro); Richard Carlyle (Anderson); Peter Hobbs (Pathologist); Harry Basch (Isadore Glass); Leigh Adams (Night Nurse); Jan Peters (Ivan Dvorsky); Robert Cleavers (Brig).

In 1945.

3

IDA LUPINO

> 5′ 3″   105 pounds
> Brown hair   Blue eyes
> Aquarius

IF WARNER BROS. fostered such female superstars of the Thirties as Ruth Chatterton, Bette Davis, Olivia de Havilland, and Kay Francis, it also sponsored many appealing actresses of the Forties: Lauren Bacall, Joan Leslie, Virginia Mayo, Eleanor Parker, Ann Sheridan, Jane Wyman, and Ida Lupino. Of the determined ladies who rose to fame on Warner Bros. celluloid during the World War II years, few exceeded the versatility of British-born Miss Lupino. She could range from comedy *(Pillow to Post,* 1945) to stark drama *(The Hard Way,* 1942), to historical drama *(Devotion,* 1946), or romp through a song-and-dance variety outing *(Thank Your Lucky Stars,* 1945). She seemed destined for top-of-the-rung fame.

In his book, *Ida Lupino* (1977), Jerry Vermilye suggests several reasons why legendary status has eluded this extremely talented, gutsy cinema star. She had not wanted to be an actress; composing and writing were her major interests. When she did sign on at Warner Bros., she was constantly in the shadow of the lot's reigning queen—Bette Davis. Ida's scope of acting ability emerged oncamera as all too pure and simple; she was taken for granted. Looking back on Ida's career to date, Vermilye explains that her wrongfully dimmed popularity today can be attributed "as much to her performing versatility as to her avoidance of the publicity pursued by more extroverted types. Lupino has never known fame as a cover girl, partygoer, or gimmick-seeker. Nor did she ever develop, despite her obvious nervous intensity in highly dramatic roles, the type of mannerisms and larger-than-life screen persona that might have made her ripe for imitation—and thereby greater immortality—à la Bette Davis."

Then, too, Lupino was not content to remain merely in front of the camera. She branched out into film directing/producing in 1949, becoming one of the few women to enter the still male-dominated field. How did she become intrigued with film directing? "I had to do something to fill up my time. When you're under contract at Warners, you either are between pictures or on suspension. I learned a lot from the late George Barnes, a marvelous cameraman."

Jack Edmund Nolan in a *Film Fan Monthly* article would judge, "Uniquely among woman directors, she had a *successful* acting career behind her (and ahead of her) when, in 1949 at age thirty-one, she first obtained her director's 'ticket.' Uniquely, she's held her own in the toughest kind of man's world . . . and has in fact shot more exhibited film (albeit most of it for TV series) than any woman director in film history. And (though she insists she was never 'a beauty') she's a lot prettier than the other lady directors."

In short, Ida Lupino is an extremely talented maverick—a situation which has frustrated stereotype-demanding Hollywood. In turn, the movie industry has subtly lashed back at the star: no Oscar nominations, despite years of consistently fine performances oncamera; and the biggest insult of all—few filmmaking jobs in recent years.

Ida Lupino was born in London, England, on Friday, February 4, 1916, during a dramatic episode in England's history.* Kaiser Wilhelm of Germany chose that moment to wage a Zeppelin attack on the British.

She was the first-born daughter (sister Rita arrived two years later in 1918) of Stanley and Connie Emerald Lupino, comedy players on the British stage. The Lupino name had been recognized in European theatres since the sixteenth century. It was then in Naples, Italy, that Alfredo Lupino, the first of the clan, set the precedent by entertaining audiences with his acrobatic ballet dancing and singing. Since stage actors were ill thought of in those days, the authorities soon confiscated the Lupino belongings, and Alfredo and his followers were forced to become vagabonds, surreptitiously clowning their way through Italy until emigrating to England. There the players were accepted, and thus began the Lupinos' legendary connection with the theatre. Ida's great-uncles, Mark and Harry, were stage headliners, as was her grandfather, George Lupino. It was the latter who probably most influenced Ida's life.

During her early years, both Ida's mother and father (whom she called "Weenie" and "Stanley") were active onstage, and consequently they were not at home very much of the time. Thus it was grandfather George, made an invalid by a stroke in his sixtieth year, who babysat with Ida. Confined to a wheelchair, George spent the last ten years of his life painting and composing symphonies. He taught Ida to paint, which led to her winning a prize at the Royal Academy of Art's child competition. George also taught her to sing and to recite Shakespearean passages.

When Ida was seven years old, her grandfather died and she was packed off to school at Clarence House at Hove. There she wrote and produced a play called *Mademoiselle.* The creative effort convinced her that she should become a writer. Meanwhile, to please her father, who assumed automatically that a Lupino would choose no other field but that of the theatre, she acted in self-improvised scenes with her little sister Rita. Her par-

*Some sources say she was born in Brixton, England, on January 1, 1914; other references list 1917 or 1918 as her birth year.

ents, as well as visiting actors and newspaper worker friends, were delighted by these presentations.

The Lupino household, when Stanley and "Weenie" were there, was once described by Ida as "goofy" because it was the headquarters for their theatrical associates. In the summer of Ida's tenth year, Stanley constructed a theatre at the foot of the garden behind the Lupino home. It included modern lighting equipment, a callboard, a pit, and seating accommodations for one hundred people. On that stage Ida performed her interpretations of Camille, Hamlet, and Juliet. Never did the fledgling performer portray children onstage; she was much too precocious for that.

At the age of twelve Ida made her first professional stage appearance at London's Tom Thumb Theatre. There she and the offspring of other actors performed parodies of Shakespeare and enacted segments from the current musical comedies.

By the time she was thirteen Ida had left school because, as she recalled, "I could spout Shakespeare by the yard, and that proved to Stanley that I was a great kid. He never cared whether I could add or subtract anyhow." She auditioned for the Royal Academy of Dramatic Art that same year and received a recommendation of "fair" which qualified her for admittance. At thirteen she physically looked like eighteen, and she lied to the Academy's directors by telling them that she was fifteen (the minimum age for beginning students).

After working in student productions of *Pygmalion* and *Julius Caesar,* among others, in which she played adult roles, she decided to give the movies a try. With her auburn hair bleached blonde, and with dramatically penciled eyebrows, she went to British International Studios. There her cousin, comedy actor Lupino Lane, helped her to obtain jobs as a cinema extra. "It was terrible work," she recalled to Kyle Crichton of *Collier's* magazine in 1937. "The equipment was poor and nobody knew too much about pictures, which meant that we worked all the time. For weeks we would work from nine in the morning till six the next morning, twenty-one hours straight."

Since she had no time to travel from the studio to her home, Ida took a room over a butcher shop not far from British International at Elstree, where she recalled, "I tried to get a few hours' rest, but it was a noisy neighborhood and I'd still be stirred up by the excitement of the work, and many times I wouldn't have any sleep at all." During her film apprenticeship in which she did what she calls "crowd work," she went by the name of Ida Ray.

Through the Royal Academy of Dramatic Art and her Cockney agent, Ida continued to seek more important film work. Her ten percenter made the prediction that he would elevate her to the position of the Janet Gaynor of the English cinema by finding sweet, young roles for his client. However, her first important screen assignment was that of a young girl who embarks on an adult romance. The job came about in a most unique fashion. The film was *Her First Affaire* (1932) and the director was American Allan Dwan. The latter has recalled, "I went up to an agent's office to get some actors. I wanted a girl about fourteen years old who, in the story, was going to have her first affair. And the woman they brought in for that part was around thirty-five years old, though still a girlish type. And she had her daughter with her, just because she didn't want to leave her home. And she and the agent went on with their spiel about why she'd be good in it, and I'm looking at the kid. I said, 'What about her—can she act?' 'Well, our family have been actors, but no, she's not an actress.' 'Well,' I said, 'That's whom I want—I want her.' Well, they were shocked—*everybody* was when the word went out I was insisting on this girl whose mother had come for the job. Finally they bent over my way and I got her. She was Ida Lupino. And she was great. But it was unknown in England for a little girl to play a little girl."

In the plot of the Sterling Films release, Ida's character becomes involved with a married author (George Curzon). Her notices were respectable, and immediately she

With Harry Tate in *Her First Affaire* ('32).

was publicized as the "English Jean Harlow." All intentions of transforming her into another Janet Gaynor were tossed aside.

Her movie career was thus launched, and director Bernard Vorhaus then chose her for a role in the United Artists-British production, *Money for Speed* (1933). In this she was a heartless gold digger. *Picturegoer* magazine found Ida "sound as the girl who, by pretending to fall in love with [Cyril] McLaglen, causes him, when disillusioned, to take to drink."

For the First National-British production of *High Finance* (1933) Ida was again a selfish, money-grabbing blonde. After this trio of featured roles, she found herself typecast. Thus at the age of fifteen, when most girls were experiencing daydreams involving men, romance, and the vast unknown, Ida—mature and sophisticated—was living onscreen the life of the reckless, daring adventuress. She was allowed to emerge briefly from the mold to make with the wisecracks in *The Ghost Camera* (1933) as the sister of a detective (John Mills) who searches for a camera that has recorded on film a killing and the killer. But she was back to seductive roles in *I Lived with You* (1933) in which she vamps Ivor Novello, one of England's movie matinee idols who also happened to be her godfather. "So, there I was ... lying on a couch on top of my godfather playing an eighteen-year-old hooker," she recalled to David Galligan in *Andy Warhol's Interview*, in February 1976. Because of Novello's status in the British entertainment industry, *I Lived with You* is considered to be Ida's first "prestige" film. (*Picturegoer* magazine reported, "The girls are Ursula Jeans and Ida Lupino, the latter showing remarkable talent. . . .")

She made one more British film, *Prince of Arcadia* (1933) opposite the international favorite, Carl Brisson, before she was to hearken to a call from Hollywood.

Paramount Pictures, in its search for a demure youngster to portray the title role in *Alice in Wonderland,* had been cabled by their British scout, Donovan Pedelty, to stop looking. He had found *the* girl. What Pedelty had seen was the good-girl portion of *Money for Speed,* and he assumed that Ida could and would want to fulfill the role of Lewis Carroll's Alice. On his recommendation, Pedelty was authorized to sign the English teenager to a six-month contract at the astronomical figure of $650 a week. The contract was signed in London in July 1933, and the following month Ida and her mother set sail for America. Mr. Lupino and sister Rita were left behind. "I didn't want to leave home," Ida has admitted. "It was frightening going to a place with the terrifying name of Hollywood."

In the smog-free Hollywood of 1933, she and her mother rented a house in the hills, with a swimming pool. She then reported to Paramount for testing. One glance at the mature blonde with the penciled eyebrows told the Paramount executives that a mistake had been made. She was definitely not the type to play Wonderland's sweet little Alice. The title role was later given to Charlotte Henry, while Ida was given the starlet treatment. She posed in bathing suits and began making the accustomed rounds of Hollywood nightclubs in the presence of studio-selected escorts.

The studio biography sheets stated that the new contractee preferred to sleep without a pillow and gave her the nickname of "Loopy." Her hobbies were listed as tennis, golf, swimming, and dancing. She liked grapefruit juice, loved George Bernard Shaw's works, hated picnics, and had total command of the French language. It was revealed that she enjoyed wearing sneakers and that she could whistle through her teeth "like a boy." Of her constant companion, her mother, Ida publicly announced that she had "the loveliest legs on the stage" and that "Weenie" had been "the fastest tap dancer of her day."

For six months she played the movie publicity game and then came to the conclusion that she did not like Hollywood or its world premieres or its nightclubs. She wanted to get to work. In the meantime, one of her frequent escorts was Howard Hughes who took her dancing at Hollywood night spots. "Very proper, of course," she remembered years later. "My mum went along." When Hughes asked her what she wanted for her sixteenth birthday she requested a pair of binoculars. He offered her a telescope and a bottle of Chanel Cinq perfume, but she stood firm on her request for the binoculars because, as she said, "I didn't want a telescope, and I didn't give a damn about Chanel Cinq." He gifted her with the binoculars and the tribute: "Ida, you're not a phony."

After turning down the initial assignment of waving a fan over the head of Claudette Colbert in *Cleopatra* (1934) and saying one line of dialogue, Ida's American film debut came about on February 10, 1934, with the release of Paramount's *Search for Beauty.* The picture was based on an obscure play called *Love Your Body* and was geared to promote a variety of studio contractees. Co-starred with Larry "Buster" Crabbe, she plays an Olympic champion, and they become innocent victims of exploitation by a health magazine. When the magazine sponsors a nationwide contest in search of beauty and brawn, Buster and Ida help to put an end to the publication's cheap and dishonest policies.

The *New York Times* labeled the modest film "depressing," but Ida has described *Search for Beauty* as "a darling little thing." She adds, "The greatest thing about it was that I met my best girlfriend, Ann Sheridan. . . . We were both so homesick. We didn't want to be stars, we just wanted to meet some nice guy and settle down." Ann Sheridan, some years later, would say about Ida: "She's a dear, close friend. I adore her. And she's a damn fine actress, too."

Ida's second Paramount film was *Come On Marines!* (1934), filmed in mid-winter at Malibu Lake, and also with Miss Sheridan in the cast. Along with several other girls, they are debutantes from a Parisian finishing school who are shipwrecked off the Philippine Islands. "We were either in satin pajamas," Ida has recalled, "dancing on tabletops, or wearing those undies with the lace that were all in one." Even Malibu Lake in winter can be cold, and Ida has recalled that she and Ann Sheridan "were both freezing to death." The debutantes in the tale are rescued by a small contingent of U.S. Marines, led by fun-loving Sergeant Lucky Davis (Richard Arlen). Naturally the military man succumbs to the beauteous charms of the leader of the blue-bloods, Esther Smith-Hamilton (Ida). In *Variety*'s review of the energetic if slight comedy, it noted: "Miss Lupino, while not getting much of an opportunity so far at Paramount, still suggests fine possibilities."

Again opposite Richard Arlen in *Ready for Love* (1934), Ida played a stagestruck miss in love with a newspaperman (Arlen) who in turn mistakes her for another girl. Pal Ann Sheridan had a tiny bit in the seventy-seven-minute proceedings. This comedy was followed by a farce called *Paris in Spring* (1935), lavishly produced and directed by Lewis Milestone. Ida had the second feminine lead as Mignon De Charelle, a French miss who contemplates suicide atop the Eiffel Tower because she thinks that her betrothed (James Blakeley) has stopped loving her. After a switch of partners and bedrooms, the four lead players (including Mary Ellis and Tullio Carminati) eventually pair off as intended, and no one is obliged to commit suicide.

With Tullio Carminati in *Paris in Spring* ('35).

With Kent Taylor and Gail Patrick in *Smart Girl* ('35).

Ida's professional path continued to be strewn with disappointments which Paramount, in no real way, attempted to assuage with juicy parts. After losing the lead to Carole Lombard in the prestige musical *We're Not Dressing* (1934), Ida was also pushed aside to make way for Loretta Young to star with Charles Boyer in *Shanghai* in 1935. MGM tested Miss Lupino for *The Bishop Misbehaves* (1935), which required that the female lead have a strong British accent. However, Ida's diction, by this time, was considered too American, and that role went to Metro's own Maureen O'Sullivan.

Instead Ida obediently took the assignment in Paramount's *Smart Girl* (1935) as a rich girl who loses her wealth and is forced to go to work. She becomes a designer of women's hats and wins the affections of Kent Taylor. After the completion of this pseudo-comedy, her fourth in a row, Ida complained, "I'm not funny. I'll never be funny. If I can't get a part I can get my teeth into, I'm going back home." She was aware that her option was due to expire in November 1935, and she hoped to get Paramount assignments that were more suited to her talents.

On May 23, 1935, *The Hollywood Reporter* announced, "Ida Lupino gets her best role to date in *Peter Ibbetson,* having been assigned to the second feminine lead by Paramount." Although it was a smaller role than those she had been recently undertaking, the production was on a far grander scale. Adapted from the novel by George du Maurier and the play by John Nathaniel Raphael, the black-and-white feature was directed by Henry Hathaway and starred Gary Cooper in the title role of an architect in nineteenth-century England who encounters his childhood sweetheart Mary (Ann Harding). Although she is now married to the Duke of Towers (John Halliday) Ibbetson and Mary cannot control their mutual love. When Ibbetson accidentally kills

Mary's husband, he is sent to prison for the remainder of his life, but in the midst of his incarceration he finds a strange sort of contentment in dreaming about his beloved Mary. At the end of this fantasy romance Mary dies, and soon thereafter so does the prisoner. Finally they are reunited in a heavenly garden, now able to enjoy an ethereal bliss. In the midst of this teary love tale, Ida appeared as Agnes, an earthy Cockney girl who has her feathered straw hat set for Ibbetson. Yet she loses him to his dream of recapturing the love of his youth.

Ida appeared in only two scenes in *Peter Ibbetson,* causing Andre Sennwald to observe in the *New York Times*, "[She] is excellent in a brief part." For the role of Agnes, Ida wore a dark wig.

Based on her solid performance in *Peter Ibbetson,* in November 1935 Paramount negotiated a new pact with Ida. She was signed for a fifty-two week deal at a reported weekly salary of $1,750.

In the midst of her professional rise, there was some personal turmoil. Ida's father, Stanley Lupino, paid a visit to Hollywood in the autumn of 1935. On December 14 he gave a party at the Trocadero Club, with Ida acting as his hostess. His guest of honor was actress Thelma Todd with whom he had worked in the British-made film *You Made Me Love You* (1934). That same evening, following the party, Miss Todd was found dead in her garage. The death was considered "mysterious," and a grand jury hearing was held. Ida was among those summoned to provide testimony. The case was never solved, and it remains to this day one of Hollywood's so-called love mysteries. (Miss Todd was living at the time with director Roland West.)

In spite of Paramount's renewed interest in her, Ida found herself shunted to yet another comedy role, this time in *Anything Goes* (1936), a loose adaptation of Cole Porter's Broadway musical hit. In support of Bing Crosby, Ethel Merman, and Charles Ruggles, Ida provided a few comedic moments and was the recipient of a Crosby tune as she lay against a pile of pillows in a rowboat while it floated through placid waters.

She was given her initial loan-out by Paramount to the producing team of Mary Pickford and Jesse Lasky for their rendition of an original story by Arnold Pressburger and Rene Pujal entitled "Monsieur Sans Gene." The Americanized version registered on

With Francis Lederer and Erik Rhodes in *One Rainy Afternoon* ('36).

motion picture screens as *One Rainy Afternoon* (1936). The idea of the story had a promise of top comedy, but somewhere along the way its potential fizzled. Ida was seen as Monique Pelerin, an ice skating instructress who decides to see a motion picture one rainy afternoon. It is a reserved seat type of theatre in which Philippe Martin (Francis Lederer) is ushered to the wrong seat. His intent was to sit next to his married lady friend (Countess Liev de Maigret). Instead he is placed in the seat adjacent to Monique. Of course it is dark in the theatre, and, when he kisses the lady next to him, he receives a forceful slap across the face. The "victim's" scream brings forth a vengeful crowd, and the masher is arrested. Monique is forced to testify against him in court, much to her consternation since she secretly enjoyed his ardent attentions. The mixup ends well when the two principals fall in love.

Ida was back at Paramount as the threat in *Yours for the Asking* (1936), an inconsequential tale of gamblers. Third-billed, she plays Gert Malloy who is employed by three stalwart gamblers (James Gleason, Lynne Overman and Edgar Kennedy) to turn their partner's (George Raft) affections away from a society matron (Dolores Costello Barrymore) who, they fear, is causing him to go legitimate. With the help of her "uncle"—actually another con artist (Reginald Owen)—Gert nearly succeeds in diverting Raft's attentions, but the devious trio who employed her soon realize that she seeks a great deal more than what they have paid her to accomplish. They fire her, leaving the way clear for Raft to rekindle his interest in Dolores. As the feisty yet enticing Gert Malloy, Ida was asked to employ an east side of New York accent, which she did capably, without a trace of the British in her enunciation.

A brief illness resulting from nervous tension forced Ida to relinquish a role in *Rose Bowl* (1936) opposite Buster Crabbe, and she was replaced by Eleanore Whitney. However, she recovered in time to be loaned to the team of Mary Pickford-Jesse Lasky a second time for *The Gay Desperado* (1936). Her co-stars were Metropolitan Opera tenor Nino Martini and ethnic character actor Leo Carrillo. Carrillo portrays a Mexican bandit ("the worst bad man in this whole country") who first kidnaps Martini as his singing mascot and then attempts to kidnap a tempestuous, spoiled rich girl (Ida) as his amorata. Frank S. Nugent of the *New York Times* ranked the movie as a "first-rate musical comedy," while the *New York Herald-Tribune* found Ida "comically effective." Director Rouben Mamoulian did his best to make the proceedings into an uplifting outing, but the plot premise and the limitations of Martini's screen personality were somewhat self-defeating.

Ida was next loaned to RKO for Edward Small's economy production, *Sea Devils* (1937). It was a time-worn variation on the theme of two wild and woolly servicemen (this time in the Coast Guard) who fight a lot à la *What Price Glory* and *Here Comes the Navy*. This time around it was Victor McLaglen and Preston Foster who hate each other. Ida is McLaglen's daughter and he wants her to wed the man of his choice (Donald Woods) and not the rowdy Foster. To muddy the situation, Ida prefers Foster. In the estimation of the *New York Times*' Frank S. Nugent, "Ida Lupino sparkles whenever an essentially dull role gives her a chance."

That movie was followed by yet another loan-out, this time to Columbia for *Let's Get Married* (1937) opposite Ralph Bellamy. Definitely in the B-minus class of film, the story has Ida as the heiress apparent to father Walter Connolly's fortune, most of which has been gathered through political machinations. She is engaged to marry a snobbish society figure (Reginald Denny) but prefers the strong arms of weatherman Ralph Bellamy. Lupino tried her best to enliven her assignment as the nouveau riche ex-10th Avenue girl, but the film still sank.

Offscreen and offcamera, Ida's multiple talents were made manifest with her composition of a musical score called "Aladdin's Lamp." The composition was performed by the Los Angeles Philharmonic under the direction of Maury Rubene in the summer of

With Preston Foster in *Sea Devils* ('37).

With Ralph Bellamy in *Let's Get Married* ('37).

With Jack Benny, the Yacht Club Boys, and Alexander Pollard in *Artists and Models* ('37).

1937. She admitted that she preferred music to acting and that one day she hoped to be able to devote all her energies to it.

Ida was then directed by Raoul Walsh* in what turned out to be an extremely popular film called *Artists and Models* (1937). With Jack Benny as its star, the film boasted not only forty of America's most beautiful models, but the musical and comedy talents of Louis Armstrong, Martha Raye, Andre Kostelanetz, Judy Canova, Connie Boswell, and a host of others. In the loosely constructed plot, Benny runs an advertising agency which launches a campaign on behalf of the million-dollar Townsend Silver account to find a model to fit the image of the Townsend Silver Girl. Ida is Paula Sewell, a professional model who falls in love with the agency's big account chief (Richard Arlen).

*Walsh would say of Ida, "Her willingness to cooperate reminded me of Theda Bara."

Clearly there in support of both Benny and Arlen—not to mention the attention-grabbing specialty performers—Ida loudly voiced her dissatisfaction with such a role and demanded something more dramatic in her casting assignments. "I don't care a fig about being pretty-pretty on the screen," she said, and asked Paramount to release her from the contract. The company obliged and told the gateman that she was never again to be allowed entrance to the Paramount lot.

Hedda Hopper, who was also in the cast of *Artists and Models,* advised her, "Listen, you're either going to be a very fine actress or you're going to blow the whole thing. Why don't you let your hair grow natural, let your eyebrows grow in, and take that junk off your face." Ida took her advice, but not before going back to RKO for *Fight for Your Lady* (1937) opposite John Boles and Jack

Oakie. In this candidate for Hollywood's list of forgotten films, Ida, as a Hungarian cafe entertainer in Budapest, consoles an American singer (John Boles) who is contemplating suicide, although she is engaged to marry Budapest's top swordsman (Erik Rhodes). The proceedings were extremely silly, but many of the bits were funny. It did not deserve the rank reviews it received (causing RKO to pull it from release). Ida is quite deft—in her Marlene Dietrichesque tuxedo outfit—doing a ventriloquist club number. The scene has Lupino throwing her vocal to the lips of the dummy while she herself is being dubbed!

With money she had saved, Ida then went home to England to visit with her father and to escort her sister Rita back to America. "He wanted her to come back with me," she has said, "since my mother was in Hollywood. It was a bad separation for my mother and father." There were rumors that Ida sought film work in her homeland, but no deals materialized.

The unemployed actress returned to California in late 1937 where her agent obtained radio work for her in such offerings as Cecil B. DeMille's "Lux Radio Theatre." For DeMille she was heard, with Robert Montgomery, in an abridged version of *The Thirty-Nine Steps* in the part created on film in 1935 by Madeleine Carroll.

Ida was professionally idle throughout much of 1938. Then on November 17, 1938, in Los Angeles, she wed actor Louis Hayward.* Hayward was twenty-nine; Ida was twenty. At least in her public remarks, Ida insisted that she would now be content to be "simply" a housewife. "But," explained Ida at a later date, "Louis wasn't the kind who liked to paint houses and that sort of thing. He thought I should have a career, so he talked me into getting back into harness again."

After an absence of some sixteen months from motion picture screens, Ida returned in Columbia's *The Lone Wolf Spy Hunt* (1939).

*He was born Charles Louis Hayward in Johannesburg, South Africa, on March 19, 1909.

She was Val, the outspoken, brassy girlfriend of Michael Lanyard (Warren William), also known as the notorious Lone Wolf. She accomplished little within the plot to aid Lanyard in his attempt to bring to justice a ring of international spies, led by Ralph Morgan and Rita Hayworth. Many thought that Virginia Weidler, as the gentleman sleuth/crook's daughter, gave the film its main interest point. *Variety* found Ida "at times, ridiculous."

She remained at Columbia for *The Lady and the Mob* (1939) in which she plays a girl who hopes to marry Lee Bowman. He is the son of an aristocratic rich lady (Fay Bainter in the title role) who hires a gangster mob to help investigate a crooked dry cleaning establishment and in the process uncovers her city's racketeers. It was Miss Bainter's picture all the way, leaving Ida to stand unceremoniously on the sidelines.

The fog machines worked overtime at Twentieth Century-Fox to simulate a mysteriously dismal London for *The Adventures of Sherlock Holmes* (1939), the second of two Fox films that year to star Basil Rathbone (Holmes) and Nigel Bruce (Dr. Watson). Ida obtained the feminine lead role of Ann Brandon whose boyfriend (Alan Marshal) becomes embroiled in the devilish attempts by master fiend Professor Moriarty (George Zucco) to steal Britain's crown jewels. Lupino was more than competent as a worrisome miss, but she was forced to give way to Rathbone and Bruce, the focal points of the Arthur Conan Doyle story.

On September 18, 1939, Ida was heard again over "Lux Radio Theatre," this time joining Barbara Stanwyck and Brian Aherne in a condensation of *Wuthering Heights*. She played Isabella, the role handled by Geraldine Fitzgerald in the United Artists 1939 release. (Ida would return to "Lux Radio Theatre" on November 4, 1950, in a repeat of *Wuthering Heights* but would enact the role of Cathy, while upcoming Jeff Chandler would act as Heathcliff.)

Meanwhile, Paramount was preparing a third rendition of Rudyard Kipling's *The Light That Failed* (1939), with Ronald Col-

With Fay Bainter (seated), Joseph Caits, Tom Dugan, Harold Huber (seated), Warren Hymer, Joseph Sawyer, Tommy Mack, and Jim Toney in *The Lady and the Mob* ('39).

man set as the star. The supporting but dramatically viable role of Bessie Broke was uncast, although Colman was insistent that Vivien Leigh was the proper actress to play the pivotal part. On the other hand, Ida believed that she was capable of fulfilling the role's needs, but she realized that Paramount's edict barring her from the lot was still in effect. Therefore, she telephoned the film's director, William A. Wellman, and asked if she might go to his house for a reading. "He told me to get my ass over there. Over I went, read, and he told me I had the part."* The major hurdle to overcome thereafter was Colman who resented her in the

*Years later Ida would relate that Wellman said re *The Light That Failed* job, " 'I'm not going to test you. You have the role. And I have a .22. If you don't come through for me, I'll shoot out every arc light on the set and maybe you too.' " Lupino added, "He brought me back to Paramount at three times my former salary and got me a dressing room on the first floor. Nothing could have been sweeter. It wasn't such a large role, but it was colorful."

Bessie role for which he so desperately wanted Vivien Leigh, and for a time on the set he displayed some ungentlemanly behavior. However, when Wellman alerted him that Ida was effectively stealing the picture, Colman adjusted his demeanor. Eventually he and Ida became friends, and he later regretted his show of bad manners.

In *The Light That Failed* Colman plays Dick Heldar, an artist who picks Bessie Broke (Ida) off the streets of London. In her face he perceives the bone structure and skin texture that will result in a masterpiece of portraiture. Although she is surly and not the least bit enthusiastic about the prospect of modeling for a portrait, she finally agrees to do so, reasoning that it will net her a few easy coins. When completed, Heldar's painting—which he entitles "Melancholy"— is a masterful work of art. Later the artist loses his eyesight, and vicious Bessie, in a

With Ronald Colman in *The Light That Failed* ('39).

highly charged dramatic scene, rubs out the canvas impressions made by his brush. It is her revenge for his intent to return her to the streets from which she came.

Frank S. Nugent *(New York Times)* adjudged the feature a "letter-perfect edition" of the Kipling story and praised Ida: "[Her] Bessie is another of the surprises we get when a little ingenue suddenly bursts forth as a great actress." Howard Barnes wrote in the *New York Herald-Tribune,* "Ida Lupino, who I never have thought had much talent, is extremely fine as Bessie, the street walker who poses for the hero and destroys his masterpiece in a moment of pique. . . ."

Ironically, a brief period of film inactivity followed her dramatic success as Bessie Broke and Ida returned to radio work. But then Warner Bros., seeking a possible backstop to their highly dramatic Bette Davis, signed Ida to a long-term studio contract. For her first assignment at the Burbank lot, she was cast in a secondary role to that of stars George Raft and Ann Sheridan in *They Drive by Night* (1940). Raoul Walsh, who had great faith in Ida's talents, cast her as Lana, the shrewish wife of Ed Carlsen (Alan Hale), a gruff ex-truck driver who now owns his own fleet of vans. She had wed Ed seven years before the story commences, obviously a practical union on her part to gain a wealthy status and to divert herself on the rebound from an abortive romance with Joe Fabrini (Raft).

In this well-remembered feature, Ida is first seen in Ed's office, wearing a loud print dress with a swag and a black hat. She arranges to meet Joe at night in front of a restaurant, but he never appears. "I waited so long in front of that restaurant," she tells him later, "they thought I was a picket." In spite of Joe's indifference toward her, she firmly believes that he has a yen for her, and she persuades Ed to give him the job of company traffic manager. Later the frustrated Lana becomes more so when she discovers that Joe is enamored of ex-waitress Cassie Hartley (Sheridan).

A few evenings later, Ed becomes drunk at a nightclub and Lana drives him home. "Come on, sit up, you drunken pig," she spits at him, but he is too far gone to hear. She drives into the garage, leaves the ignition on and closes the entrance door by exiting between the electric eyes. The next morning Ed is found dead, and the case is proclaimed an accident. Lana thinks that Joe will now desert Cassie and join forces with her in running the Carlsen Trucking Company. Joe is businesslike with her, but not friendly. In a moment of utter frustration, she yells at him, "I committed murder to get you. Do you understand? Murder!" Joe is aghast at her confession and displays his contempt. Now Lana comes to the realization that she will never have him, but she decides to make sure that no one else will either. Therefore she goes to the district attorney (Henry O'Neill) and informs him that Joe forced her to kill Ed. At the trial, on the witness stand, an unkempt Lana makes an appearance. Her wild eyes darting to and fro indicate that she has lost her reason. She stares at Joe at the defense table and screams, "I didn't want to kill anyone. He made me kill him. Yes, he made me do it. He made me do it." It is obvious that Lana is now completely insane and she is led from the courtroom. The case is dismissed and Joe is free, able to dash into the arms of his waiting Cassie.

Lana Carlsen was to represent Ida's true moment of cinematic triumph. For the young woman who had been ready to permanently return to England a few months before her dramatic "discovery" it was a time of great personal victory. Warner Bros. heralded Ida as another Bette Davis. (In fact the role of Lana and the murder of her spouse by locking him inside a garage were both borrowed from Miss Davis' sinister character and deeds as performed in Warner Bros.' *Bordertown* in 1935.)

The critics now took substantial notice of Miss Lupino, some seven years after she began her Hollywood career. Suddenly everyone was interested in the intense actress with the large luminous eyes and captivating husky voice. *Newsweek* magazine thought that in *They Drive by Night* she "stole the show" with her "arresting performance" and noted: "Every so often Hollywood discovers Ida Lupino. . . . This time she will undoubtedly stay discovered." The New York newspaper *PM* declared, "Everybody seemed a little surprised that Ida Lupino, the puck-cheeked fun girl, should be able to do this sort of Ophelia stuff."

At Warner Bros. as at all the major studios, there was a ranking hierarchy of contract lead players. In the male division the top contenders were James Cagney, Errol Flynn, the soon to depart Paul Muni, Edward G. Robinson, George Raft, John Garfield, Pat O'Brien, George Brent, and such *then* lesser lights as Jeffrey Lynn, Humphrey Bogart, Ronald Reagan, Wayne Morris, Dennis Morgan, James Stephenson, and Eddie Albert. Prime roles were offered to the male actors in order of their box-office importance. The same procedure was followed with the distaff performers: Bette Davis, Ann Sheridan, Olivia de Havilland, Ida, Priscilla Lane, Jane Bryan, Brenda Marshall, Joan Leslie, Jane Wyman, Gloria Dickson, and Gale Page. Just as Miriam Hopkins had been employed recently at the studio as a threat against protean Miss Davis, so Ida was considered now a performer with sufficient mettle and creativity to accept the castoff roles that the Queen of the Lot did not care to undertake.

One of the second-hand casting offers tossed at Ida was the role of Marie Garson, the dancehall girl turned gun moll in Raoul Walsh's *High Sierra* (1941). It proved to be a boon to her career.* Her co-star was Hum-

---

*In the book *Here's Looking at You, Kid* (1976), Ida told author James R. Silke that in the early Forties she was noted for her publicity poses wearing a five-inch-high pompadour, flower-print dresses, and a thick smear of red lipstick, and fluttering her big round eyes. "I loved having people put me in good clothes," she admitted. However, just as *The Light That Failed* typed her as a British cockney, so *High Sierra* led to her being pegged as a gun moll. "My fan mail used to come from Brooklyn saying, 'You're one of us, baby.' It all became impossibly and beautifully Brooklyn and I loved that . . . oh, God, I did!"

With Humphrey Bogart in *High Sierra* ('41).

phrey Bogart, who had had a featured role in *They Drive by Night* as George Raft's truck-driving brother. Bogart appears as "Mad Dog" Roy Earle, an aging gangster who would like to retire and settle down. Earle is maneuvered out of prison through the auspices of Big Mac (Donald MacBride) who wants him on the outside to accomplish the heist of jewels from the safe of the posh Tampico Inn in California. It required a strong personality to match the integrity of a Bogart screen characterization, and Ida filled the demands admirably. Throughout the action-filled melodrama she is continually contrasted with innocent, crippled Velma (Joan Leslie), the young girl who also attracts the gangster's interest. But while Velma remains starry-eyed about Mad Dog's constant benevolence toward her, it is Ida's Marie who sizes up the full potential as well as the weaknesses of her lover.

When Earle has his reunion with Marie in the course of *High Sierra*, she promptly asks him about his time in prison. "How was it? I mean, knowin' you're in for life, I should think you'd go crazy." After he explains his reaction to jail, she smartly sums it up: "Yeah, I get it. You always hope ya can get out, that sort of keeps ya goin'." Later when the police are on their trail after the Inn holdup, Marie has a chance to flee on a bus with her dog Pard, but when she learns that Mad Dog is trapped atop a mountain by the police, she goes to find him. Although she is unable to get behind police lines, Earle hears the dog bark and comes out into the open where he is shot to death. In a rather strange finale, Marie, carrying her dog, is led away from the mountain as she smiles into the camera and declares that now Earle is "free . . . free." It took someone of Ida's special flintiness to make this off-kilter, liberated character come alive plausibly. (The film would be remade by Warner Bros. as a 1949 Western, *Colorado Territory*, with Joel McCrea and Virginia Mayo, and then as *I Died a Thousand Times*, 1955, with Jack Palance and Shelley Winters. Neither remake enjoyed the popularity of the original.)

The Sea Wolf (1941) came next on Ida's agenda. She plays Ruth Webster, a drab and sickly girl plucked out of San Francisco Bay on a foggy night when the ferry on which she was a passenger sinks. Her rescuer is Captain Wolf Larsen (Edward G. Robinson), the satanic sea captain of the scavenger ship *Ghost*. Also aboard is a young drifter named George Leach (John Garfield), who signed on as a crewman, and Humphrey Van Weyden (Alexander Knox), a self-ordained psychologist who figures Larsen to be a psychotic sadist. There develops between Ruth and Leach a meeting of the minds akin to romance, although there is no verbal communication involving sentiment or emotions. They are both too busy avoiding the hatred of Larsen. Larsen eventually loses his eyesight and is abandoned by his crew aboard his sinking ship with Van Weyden. Ruth and Leach successfully escape.

Based on the Jack London tale, this version, the sixth to be screened, was adapted by Robert Rossen and directed by Michael Curtiz. The role of George Leach was especially written into the script for Garfield who had become one of Warner Bros.' top leading men. The film, boasting exceptional mood photography by Sol Polito, had the magic of Erich Wolfgang Korngold's eerie musical score which helped to make *The Sea Wolf* one of the studio's more memorable films of 1941.

Ida was hastily reunited with Garfield in the film version of Irwin Shaw's play, *The Gentle People*, which had a Broadway run in 1939 with Sylvia Sidney and Franchot Tone in the leads. The screen adaptation emerged as *Out of the Fog* (1941), a menacing title for a story involving innocent, ordinary people who are victimized by a small-time crook. The victims are Stella Goodwin (Ida) and her father Jonah (Thomas Mitchell). She has a dream of going to Cuba where she hopes to find adventure and romance, but she soon comes to consider Harold Goff (Garfield)—a petty chiseler—as something special. The father is unable to change her mind, and he plots to get rid of Goff so that she will return to ordinary but gentle George Watkins (Eddie Albert).

With Edward G. Robinson and John Garfield in *The Sea Wolf* ('41).

According to Bosley Crowther of the *New York Times*, "It doesn't even come close to being a really good film, and, if you want the honest truth, it is literally as old-fashioned as sin." Crowther claimed that Ida's performance was "much too rigid and dour." Howard Barnes *(New York Herald-Tribune)*, on the other hand, singled her out: "Ida Lupino, as I have said so many times in the past, is one of the great actresses of the screen, and she does not fall down in this instance."

Ida had exercised her rights as a star when it came to the casting of the con man in *Out of the Fog*. Humphrey Bogart was the first choice for the role, but she and Bogart had not been on good terms since their initial meeting on the set of *They Drive by Night* when he had accidentally kicked her script across the sound-stage floor. Their feud was furthered during the making of *High Sierra* when they got into a political argument at the Warner Bros. commissary. Thus she rejected Bogart for the Harold Goff role and agreed to the substitution of Garfield.

Ladies in Retirement, a play by Reginald Denham and Edward Percy, was seen on Broadway in 1940, with Flora Robson making her American debut in the role of the 60-year-old housekeeper with two younger, batty sisters. When Columbia purchased the screen rights, executive producer Lester Cowan asked studio head Harry Cohn to borrow Ida for the role. "You're out of your mind choosing this child to play that role," Cohn screamed. However, Cowan, with the help of director Charles Vidor, convinced Cohn that Ida could do it by changing the age of the oldest sister to forty-five and making the two daffy ones more mature. "I must admit," Ida has said, "that it was difficult for me at that age to play a role in which I would give the illusion of being forty-five. The fact that it was a period picture helped somewhat because I could wear period hair-dos which made me look older. They pulled my hair back in a very severe hair-do." Cinematographer George Barnes suggested that the aging makeup consist only of "running red under the eyes in the circle area" without adding gray to the hair or phony facial lines. "I will do what I can with my camera," he told Ida, "but nearly everything depends on your performance." To appease the star and to make her feel more at ease, her husband Louis Hayward (whose career was floundering) was assigned to the cast.

In *Ladies in Retirement* (1941), Ellen Creed (Ida) is housekeeper to one-time music hall actress Leonora Fiske (Isobel Elsom) in her home on the English moors. Into this tranquil scene Ellen is forced to bring her two sisters, despite the objections of her employer. The sisters (Elsa Lanchester and Edith Barrett) are obviously not of sound mind, but Ellen does not want to place them in an asylum, and besides she has promised them that they will always be with her. Miss Fiske objects when the sisters bring into the house bits of driftwood, sea shells, and dead animals. When she orders Ellen to rid the household of the uninvited guests, this demand becomes the lady's death warrant. Ellen soon thereafter kills Miss Fiske by strangling her. Ellen tells Lucy (Evelyn Keyes) the maid and two nuns (Emma Dunn and Queenie Leonard) from the nearby convent that Miss Fiske has departed on an extended trip. Then along comes Ellen's nephew (Hayward) who ultimately unravels the mystery and promises to keep silent in return for a payment of money.

Critics praised Ida for this, her favorite film, and the picture proved commercially sound. The *New York Times* offered this praise: "Give Ida Lupino the largest measure of credit, for her role is the clue to the suspense. Perhaps she is too slight to portray the stolid threat that lay in Flora Robson's original performance, but she is nonetheless the thin ribbon of intensity that makes the film hair-raising."

Ida, who continually found herself being passed over at Warner Bros. for showcasing roles, was next loaned to Twentieth Century-Fox for *Moontide* (1942), cast opposite

With Elsa Lanchester, Edith Barrett, and Louis Hayward in *Ladies in Retirement* ('41).

With Jean Gabin in *Moontide* ('42).

Jean Gabin in his American film debut. Again she is a waif with not much to live for, but Gabin, a dockworker in San Pablo, California, saves her from drowning and eventually marries her. Because of his sincere, mature love which is displayed offhandedly, she develops into a pretty girl who is then pursued by Gabin's friend (Thomas Mitchell). Although Fox thought that Gabin might have the box-office impact of another Charles Boyer, American audiences were not attracted to his continental charisma. It was Ida who provided whatever commercial allure the low-keyed film possessed.

In 1942 Ida was commissioned a lieutenant by the American Ambulance Corps and was placed in charge of dispatching emergency air-raid ambulances in the Los Angeles area. She was required to wear a uniform at all times, except when in front of the cameras, of course. Through a special switchboard installed in her home, she was able to reach every emergency ambulance post in Los Angeles. She took her special assignment seriously, feeling that it was the least she could do while her husband was serving with the U.S. Marine Corps. Ida lived with her mother and sister in a country-style home near Santa Monica, California. (On July 12, 1942, in London, Stanley Lupino died, and his deeply saddened wife and daughters were unable to attend the last rites due to wartime travel restrictions.)

In September 1942, Warner Bros. sneak-previewed a moderately budgeted production entitled *The Hard Way*.* However, when the audience reaction cards were read praising Ida's work in the Jerry Wald production, it was decided to hold it from general release

*MGM had offered Warner Bros. $100,000 for the screen rights to *The Hard Way*, planning to team Joan Crawford, Clark Gable, and Lana Turner in the venture.

until December when it would be eligible for the next Academy Awards. The Daniel Fuchs and Peter Viertel scenario presented Ida as Helen Chernen, whose ambitions are thwarted by a loveless marriage (to Roman Bohnen) in a bleak industrial town named Greenhill. Since she hates her drab life, she transfers all her frustrated hopes to her younger sister Katherine (Joan Leslie). When the girl shows some talent as a singer-dancer, Helen uses these attributes to get her into show business. She pushes Katherine into a vaudeville act with Paul Collins (Dennis Morgan) and Albert Runkel (Jack Carson). The two men genuinely like the gentle girl and accept her as one of them. Runkel especially takes a shine to the girl, and Helen rushes her into marrying him. Soon Collins is out of the act and the Runkels go it alone, successfully.

Further into the picture, Helen decides that Katherine is experienced enough to perform as a single. When the young performer leaves her husband behind, he commits suicide. Later Katherine reaches Broadway. This time when Helen once more tries to interfere with her love life (Collins is now again on the scene), Katherine rejects her sister. Thus Helen is left alone and still as miserable as she was at the beginning.

Ida has admitted, "Though *The Hard Way* did a great deal for my career as an actress, when I saw the picture at a preview I couldn't stand looking at my own scenes. I thought the other actors in it were magnificent but that my own performance was incredibly bad. I walked out in the middle of the picture." However, the critics, for the most part, did not agree. *Time* magazine adjudged her to have captured the "top acting honors" and noted that she "plays the most hateful jade since Bette Davis in *The Little Foxes.*" The *New York World-Telegram* asserted: "Miss Lupino joins Ruth Chatterton and Bette Davis in the right to be a Great American Actress," while the *New York Herald-Tribune* commented: "The chief asset of the film is the acting of Ida Lupino as the

With Joan Woodbury and Dennis Morgan in *The Hard Way* ('42).

ambitious sister.... Her portrayal is grim and bitter. She relentlessly holds to the characterization of being a single-minded witch. Without her, *The Hard Way* would be a tough row to hoe, indeed."

Ida was next seen on loan-out to Twentieth Century-Fox in *Life Begins at 8:30* (1942). She plays Kathi Thomas, the crippled daughter of a one-time actor (Monty Woolley) turned drunkard. Based on Emlyn Williams' play *The Light of Heart,* it hovers between comedy and drama. Woolley provides the comedic touches during his wild scenes of inebriety, while Ida comes close to stark melodrama in her interpretation of the love-starved girl whose sole cause for living is the care and loyalty of her father. Into her drab existence comes a handsome suitor (Cornel Wilde). Thereafter the father has an opportunity to return to the stage as *King Lear.* However, when he learns that the suitor is serious about marrying his daughter, he embarks on a drunken binge and forsakes the stage. The emotionally confused Kathi finds it difficult to choose between her beau and her father, but the tale ends happily with the actor finally gaining some mature insight and the daughter getting wed. *Photoplay* magazine stated: "Performances glitter like jewels," and it gave the film a rating of "outstanding." Bosley Crowther *(New York Times)* endorsed Ida's performance, reporting that she "plays the crippled daughter with compassion and simplicity."

In 1943, while her husband Louis Hayward was serving in New Zealand as a marine captain, Ida appeared onscreen in two films. *Forever and a Day* was RKO's feature-length film derived from the pens of twenty-one writers as a tribute to British-Americans. Seven directors and producers were involved in the multi-episode story which utilized the acting talents of seventy-nine name actors. It was an independently produced venture which related the chronicle of a London house, built in 1804 by Admiral Eustace Trimble (C. Aubrey Smith). The viewer follows the narrative of the house's

With Monty Woolley in *Life Begins at 8:30* ('42).

Advertisement for *Thank Your Lucky Stars* ('43).

inhabitants through the nineteenth century right up into World War II. Ida appeared in episode number three, along with Brian Aherne. She is the maid Jenny while he is her admirer. Because of what the *New York Times* termed a "lively performance," Ida's episode came through as the most entertaining of the lot.

In the spring of 1943 Ida was awarded the New York Film Critics' Award as Best Actress of 1943 for her acting job in *The Hard Way*. "It's the only thing I've ever won outside the dime jackpot at Lake Tahoe," she was to say later. The New York critics had quite a time choosing between Ida and Katina Paxinou (of *For Whom the Bell Tolls*), but Ida was the victor on the final ballot by a vote of eleven to six. Meanwhile, on the West Coast, her peers chose to ignore her histrionics in *The Hard Way* by *not* nominating her for an Academy Award. (Screen newcomer Jennifer Jones won the Oscar that year as Best Actress for her performance in *The Song of Bernadette*.)

Thank Your Lucky Stars was a Warner Bros. 1943 release which utilized just about everyone on the studio lot, and those good people were, for the most part, used in costumes and routines other than those for which they were known onscreen. With Olivia de Havilland, another cinema sob sister, Ida did a flouncy-skirted song-and-dance number entitled "The Dreamer." George Tobias, anything but limber-legged, joined them in the amusing jive takeoff. Other in-the-spirit segments included Bette Davis "singing" "They're Either Too Young or Too Old" and Errol Flynn performing a barroom ballad. Bosley Crowther (*New York Times*) referred to the product as "amateur night" but

With Nazimova and Paul Henreid in *In Our Time* ('44).

added: "It is lovely and genial."

Crowther's opinion of Ida's next film in release, *In Our Time* (1944), was sour enough to include calling it "an early talkie tragedy which was out to set a record running-time" (110 minutes), and he concluded: "[The film] is almost as stale in its methods as the things about which it tells." The Ellis St. Joseph and Howard Koch setting is pre–World War II Poland where a traveling English lass named Jennifer Whittredge (Ida) meets and falls in love with Count Stephan Orvid (Paul Henreid), a Polish nobleman. His clan (including Victor Francen, Nazimova, and Nancy Coleman) is against the love affair, but the Nazi invasion comes along to occupy their minds with more important tasks. Directed by Vincent Sherman, the film staggers on to transplant Jennifer to London where she loses her memory during a German air attack. Despite sincere performances by the entire cast and a well-mounted setting, the black-and-white picture simply does not impress the more discriminating viewer.

In 1944 Ida hinted that she would like to abandon moviemaking and concentrate her energies on a musical comedy for which she was writing the music, lyrics, and book. Her tentative title was *Make Up Your Mind*. Ida continued to be a frequent guest on radio. In 1944 she was heard on "Duffy's Tavern," playing the lead in the movie version of Archie's life; on Eddie Cantor's "March of Dimes Special" she joined with Monty Woolley, Dick Powell, Edward G. Robinson, Cass Daley, and Harry Von Zell in some hijinks.

Warner Bros.' all-star offering of 1944 was *Hollywood Canteen*, a tribute to that organization. Many of the Warner contract players were seen briefly as themselves, including Ida. The thin plot is honorable enough: two G.I.'s spend three nights at the Canteen before taking assignments in the Pacific war. Joan Leslie was *the* girl in the storyline.

With the end of the European portion of World War II, Louis Hayward returned home to California. He was as restless about his private life as he was regarding his uncertain professional future in films, and he told Ida that he "didn't want to be tied to one woman." As a result she and Hayward were divorced on May 11, 1945. Soon thereafter she suffered a nervous breakdown and was ordered by her physician to rest. For the next year she lived aboard a forty-two-foot yawl at Newport Beach, California, some thirty miles from Los Angeles. The craft was owned by a friend, Sandra Perry. Years after her divorce from Hayward, Ida was to say, "There was nothing bitter when we parted. . . . He's a darling, wonderful man. It was just that he was more mature than I. I was too young and full of life to have married then."

Prior to her hiatus from working before the cameras, Ida had completed *Pillow to Post* (1945). It was her first comedy in more than six years. During the filming she admitted that she was glad to be doing farce again after all the suffering she had been enduring onscreen since *The Adventures of Sherlock Holmes*. Adapted for the screen by Charles Hoffman from a play by Rose Simon Kohn, *Pillow to Post* was directed by Vincent Sherman, the third time he had supervised a Lupino vehicle.

In the comedy Ida is a traveling saleslady who winds up for the night in an auto court that admits married couples only. She persuades an unwilling Army lieutenant (William Prince) to pose as her husband so that they can obtain a night's sleep. The deception leads to several near-slapstick situations, many of which were classified by critic James Agee (*Time* magazine) as "corn." Mr. Agee went on to add, "Fortunately, however, corn is edible, and the serious thinkers (Miss Lupino, for that matter, started in comedy) turn out to have a nice knack for foolishness." *Newsweek*, on the other hand was unimpressed: "Although Miss Lupino clowns courageously to invigorate a shopworn theme, the spontaneous laughs are few and far between."

Ida's next film in evidence was *Devotion*, which had been completed in late 1943 but was not released until April 1946. The reason for the long delay was that the costume drama was not very satisfying film fare. Warner Bros. chose to release *Devotion* a month after Paramount's *To Each His Own* in order to capitalize on the success of Olivia de Havilland's performance in the latter. Miss de Havilland was Ida's feminine co-star in *Devotion*.

Written for the screen by Keith Winter and directed by Curtis Bernhardt, it is an untrue, soap opera-ish account of the lives of the Brontës: Charlotte (de Havilland), Emily (Ida), Anne (Nancy Coleman), and Branwell (Arthur Kennedy). It seems obvious that the authors (Theodore Reeves wrote the "original story") didn't do their homework with regard to the talented, complex Brontës. In the 107-minute telling, a friend of the Brontë patriarch (Montagu Love) is sandwiched into the story as a triangular love object of both Emily and Charlotte. According to the film, this explains the lifelong rift between the two sisters. The man in the mawkish plot is Arthur Nichols, played by grimacing Paul Henreid. Charlotte is later romantically involved with Professor Heger (Victor Francen) which is anything but historically accurate. The best elements of the production are Erich Wolfgang Korngold's score, Casey Roberts' Yorkshire sets, and Ernest Haller's cinematography. As Bosley Crowther summed up the net results in the *New York Times*, "It is a ridiculous tax upon reason and an insult to plain intelligence."*

By May 1946 Ida was well enough to make an appearance at a lavish dinner dance given at the Clover Club by Cary Grant, James Stewart, Eddy Duchin, and Johnny McLain. With Bing Crosby she performed a rumba which, according to columnist Cal York, "was really something."

*Film enthusiasts have a field day with one unintended mood breaker in *Devotion*. In the scene where Ida's character is dying, de Havilland quietly enters her screen sister's bedroom. Filmgoers can easily spot a hand sneaking out on the bottom left of the screen to shut the door behind Olivia.

In October 1946, more than a year after it was completed, Warner Bros. found occasion to release *The Man I Love,* starring an especially appealing and vulnerable Ida as Petey Brown,* a torch-carrying blues singer. The cause of her mental torment is piano player Sam Thomas (Bruce Bennett) who is allegedly in love with a society lady and has sought release from onshore problems by becoming a sailor. Petey has a couple of sisters (Andrea King and Martha Vickers) who are also plagued by domestic problems, while a neighbor (Dolores Moran) is two-timing her husband (Don McGuire). Lurking inside the atmospheric nightclub where Petey sings is her boss and professional skirt chaser, Nicky Toresca (Robert Alda), who means nothing but trouble.

*The character of Petey sang "Bill," "The Man I Love," "Body and Soul," and "Why Was I Born?" but the soundtrack was dubbed by Peg LaCentra.

Another emotional film, *Deep Valley* (1947), permitted Ida to suffer as never before. She plays Libby, the daughter of the Sauls (Henry Hull and Fay Bainter) who have not spoken to one another in seven years. Libby has a speech defect which provides Pa with a reason to poke fun at her. Into this strange household comes a work crew composed largely of convicts who are to construct a road through the mountains near the Saul home. It is instantaneous love between Libby and Barry Burnett (Dane Clark), one of the prisoners. Through her strong feelings for him, she regains faultless speech. Although Ma and Pa later make up, Barry and Libby run away to a mountain shack while a posse searches for them. The *New York Times* asserted: "The film is very well acted," adding: "Miss Lupino displays nice shadings of emotion and, in the early part, when she is required to speak haltingly, she manages to be quite convincing."

With Nancy Coleman, Olivia de Havilland, and Paul Henreid in *Devotion* ('46).

156

With Bruce Bennett in *The Man I Love* ('46).

With Dane Clark in *Deep Valley* ('47).

With Eleanor Parker in *Escape Me Never* ('47).

Escape Me Never (1947) is again one of the Warner Bros. pictures which was completed a year prior to its release. Set in the Alps, it is a remake of the 1935 British film which starred Elisabeth Bergner and Hugh Sinclair. This time around it is Ida who plays Gemma Smith, the unfortunate waif with a fatherless child who meets musician and ladies' man Sebastian Dubrok (Errol Flynn).* He is actually in love with his brother's (Gig Young) fiancée (Eleanor Parker), but he weds the waif in order to provide something of a home for the child. As he prepares to desert them and flee to the arms of his brother's girl, Gemma's baby dies, so he decides to stick around after all.

With Flynn "accompanying" her on an accordion, Ida in *Escape Me Never* "sang" an Erich Wolfgang Korngold composition called "Love for Love," but again it was Peg LaCentra's voice which was heard onscreen. Bosley Crowther *(New York Times),* among others, detested the film, judging it "something harsh and unbelievable, like a terrible faux pas in a grade-school play." He furthermore thought Ida to be "downright embarrassing, the way she bounces and kitty-cats around, alternately clutching an infant and Mr. Flynn to her heaving breast."

On June 25, 1948, Ida became an American citizen in Los Angeles. Giving her allegiance to a new country was some recompense for having withdrawn her loyalty to her studio in 1947. As Ida recounted to James R. Silke in *Here's Looking at You, Kid* (1976):

> One night towards the end of my contract, there was Hal Wallis and Jack [Warner] coming out of his office. Jack saw me and said, "Ida, why are you here?"
>
> "I'm about to be chewed out."
>
> "Oh, Ida, Ida, Ida sweet as apple cida . . ." he sang and we went into a soft-shoe routine.
>
> Then he asked me to sign a four-year exclusive contract and I said, "No, no, no! I want a home, a husband, a child and I don't want to be told someday that I will be replaced by some starlet as I was told I would replace Bette [Davis]."
>
> He told me, "If you don't sign, you'll never work for Warners again." And I didn't.
>
> The beautiful thing about Warner Bros. when I was there was I only worked with great people, actors, directors, producers. But when I left, nobody said goodbye.

Holding true to her wish not to be single, on August 5, 1948, Ida married Collier H. Young, a Columbia Pictures film executive, who had been Louis Hayward's best friend. They were wed in La Jolla, California, each for the second time. Ida was thirty; Young was thirty-nine.

Prior to her marriage, Ida had gone to Twentieth Century-Fox for *Road House* (1948). Her co-star was Cornel Wilde, who by this time was a star in comparison to his small part in *High Sierra.* The other two principals of the tale were Richard Widmark (menacing) and Celeste Holm (loyal). Ida is Lily Stevens, the singer in the road house operated by Jefty Robbins (Richard Widmark) who is in love with her. He brings his old Army buddy Pete Morgan (Wilde) into the business as manager. Pete soon falls for Lily's charms and she is attracted to him.

Meanwhile, within and at the road house, Susie (Holm), the club's cashier, likes Pete but does not push her luck. When Lily and Pete inform Jefty that they are in love, the latter fakes a robbery of the establishment's safe, leaving clues that implicate Pete in the alleged crime. A courtroom trial is held where Jefty asks the judge to permit Pete to be paroled in his care, an offer that the judge

---

*Ida has always had kind things to say of her Warner Bros. confrere, Errol Flynn. (He called her "Lupe" and "Mad Idea.") "I only know one thing," says Ida. "He never raped anyone. They all raped him. He'd call and say, 'Lupe, come up here. There's a daughter and her mother and a deputy here, come help!' And I'd go up and throw them out. Can you imagine him having to rape anyone?"

With husband-to-be Collier Young in 1947.

(Grandon Rhodes) considers to be an unselfish gesture.

At this point Jefty turns more malicious by keeping both Pete and Lily under close scrutiny. Lily convinces Pete not to run away because it would jeopardize his parole. Still later Susie finds evidence that proves Pete was innocent of the robbery. During a subsequent fight, Lily picks up Jefty's gun and shoots him as he walks toward her with a boulder raised above his head.

It was Ida's voice heard coming from the screen in the singing rendition of three songs in *Road House,* the most memorable of which was "Again." This song gained nationwide popularity, although it was not Oscar-nominated. Kay Nelson's costumes helped Ida to create the role of the unhappy chanteuse. This film also helped to solidify Ida's screen image with moviegoers. She might be on the wrong side of the law as in *High Sierra,* or unusually selfish as in *The Hard Way,* but she would do nearly anything for her man, as in *The Man I Love.* In all these films, and especially in *Road House,* she displayed a tough-as-nails veneer that concealed an impressive femininity—a personality combination used to more exaggerated effect by Susan Hayward.

For Columbia, Ida starred with Glenn Ford in *Lust for Gold* (1949) as the woman who leaves her husband to run off with miner Ford to seek gold in the famous lost Dutchman Mine in Arizona. Most of the narrative was related via flashback. There were some sturdy performances in this modestly produced entry, but it was *not* a major box-office release, and it represented the beginning of the downward slant of Lupino's theatrical film career.

In 1949 there were one million television sets in America. Capitalizing on this, enterprising Ida joined with Anson Bond (of the Bond Clothing firms) in writing and producing a film for television. That same year, she and husband Young formed Emerald Productions, named after Ida's mother. Their first screen effort was *Not Wanted* (1949), which was directed and co-written by the star, although she did not appear in the feature. The film dealt with the subject of unwed motherhood and showcased two young actors discovered by Ida and Young, Sally Forrest and Keefe Brasselle.

With Richard Widmark in *Road House* ('48).

With Gig Young in *Lust for Gold* ('49).

With Howard Duff in *Woman in Hiding* ('49).

Ida returned to acting in Universal's *Woman in Hiding* (1949) opposite a radio ("Dear John" and "Sam Spade") and stage actor who turned to movies in 1946. His name was Howard Duff. (He was a replacement for Ronald Reagan who had fractured his thigh.) In this highly melodramatic offering Ida discovers that her spouse (Stephen McNally) is out to murder her for her money. She flees, to be saved by a man (Duff) who had befriended her.

Emerald Productions underwent a name change to Filmmakers and, in 1950, presented *Never Fear* which Ida directed and co-authored with Collier Young. Again their stars were Sally Forrest and Keefe Brasselle, and they introduced to the screen a Los Angeles gardener named Hugh O'Brian. This film dealt with the adjustment problems that a young dancer (Forrest) must face when she contracts polio.

On the set of the pictures directed by Ida, she was known as "Grandma" or "Loopy." Although she and Young had separated in September 1949 when Ida moved to a Malibu Beach cottage with her aunt Mrs. Charles Beatty (a former English stage comedienne), they remained friendly. Young once commented, "Things aren't normal unless Ida resigns three times on every picture—once before it starts, and twice during production."

One-time Lupino beau Howard Hughes was now head of the RKO studios. He was so impressed with the tightly budgeted Lupino-Young films that he asked them to affiliate their production company with his corporation. They accepted, since it would

In 1950 at a Hollywood Foreign Press Association dinner with correspondent Bert Reisfeld, Jane Wyman, and journalist group president, Ram Bagai.

With husband Collier Young in Hollywood in 1950, dancing at Ciro's.

mean RKO financing, production facilities, and distribution. In exchange for these benefits, Hughes' outfit would be entitled to one-half the profits of their films.

The next, *Outrage* (1950), released through RKO, was about a rape victim and starred their discovery Mala Powers. Of the actors they had found, Ida has said, "Of course we'd like to keep our finds, but that would mean contracts, and soon we'd be just like all the other producers who have to make pictures they aren't excited about because they have a lot of actors eating up overhead."

Hard, Fast and Beautiful (1951), which was also directed by Ida, was their next for RKO. The story concerned an amateur tennis champ (Sally Forrest) who is driven to success by an unscrupulous mother (Claire Trevor).*

On October 20, 1951, Ida divorced Collier Young in Minden, Nevada, using the

---

*Ida recalls of *Hard, Fast and Beautiful,* her third directorial effort, "We were barely making ends meet, and had hocked our life insurance policies. Just as shooting started, the assistant director rushed to me and said our money men went broke! We had a $65,000 payroll to meet in two weeks. I kept smiling and lining up shots until 5 P.M.

"Then I called my agent, Charlie Feldman, and told him all about it. He said to send the script over. If he liked it, there'd be $65,000 in the bank. Two hours later the money was there."

standard charge of "mental cruelty." The next day, October 21, she was wed to Howard Duff in Glenbrook, Nevada. Ida was 33; Duff was 36. It was her third marriage and his first. They spent a short honeymoon in San Francisco before returning to Hollywood.

At this time Ida was established as Hollywood's only active woman producer-director, which caused her to say, "You feel like something in a cage that people are peering at." Still, she wanted to keep active in front of the camera, too, where she commanded $75,000 per picture. From their four produced features, Filmmakers' executives had yet to earn any sizable fortune. They estimated that their take-home pay amounted to less than $100,000.

In 1950 Ida had starred with Robert Ryan in RKO's *On Dangerous Ground*. In typical Howard Hughes fashion, the product was not released until some fourteen months later. In this Nicholas Ray-directed drama, Ida plays Mary Malden, a blind woman who comes into contact with New York law enforcer Robert Ryan. He has been sent to the country to help the local sheriff track down the murderer of a schoolgirl. In the snow-covered rural area Ryan and Ida slowly fall in love. As she explains to him, "Sometimes people who are never alone are the loneliest people of all." The suspect in the case proves to be her mentally defective brother (Sumner Williams) who falls to his death when cornered. *Newsweek* said of this offbeat film: "The resolution is plausible enough, and the acting throughout is effective, but the film never achieves the dramatic intensity to match its good purposes."

Another Filmmakers production was *Beware, My Lovely* (1952) in which Ida again starred with Robert Ryan. It was adapted from the Mel Dinelli play *The Man* which was produced on Broadway in 1950 with Dorothy Gish and Don Hanmer. While the stage version was limited to one set wherein a

With Robert Ryan in *Beware, My Lovely* ('52).

With Crane Whitley (right) in *Jennifer* ('53).

widow is set upon by a homicidal killer, the film's camera brought more than the one room into focus and caught reflections from mirrors and edged around corners for effect. Director Harry Horner managed to shift filmgoers to the edge of their seats with a shocking opening, but after that the film was reduced to no more than routine melodrama. As *Saturday Review* explained: "Just too many things keep happening at the wrong time, and the final explanation of the hero's mental aberration is altogether too naive for belief."

On April 23, 1952, in Hollywood, a four-pound, three-ounce baby girl was born to Ida Lupino Duff. She was named Bridget.

Ida's next directorial effort produced a box-office "sleeper" called *The Hitch-Hiker* (1953), which she also partially scripted. It told of two businessmen (Edmond O'Brien and Frank Lovejoy) who take a fishing vacation and pick up a hitch-hiker (William Talman) whose intents are murderous.

With Duff, she then starred in *Jennifer* (1953) for Allied Artists. In this low-budget feature, filmed in Santa Barbara, California, Lupino is employed at a lonely mansion where she discovers a murder. The ingenue (Mary Shipp) of the story is befriended and protected by Ida.

In 1953 Ida and Duff separated for a short time, but they were soon back together. It was rumored that their careers caused the rift in their marriage. Shortly after reconciling with Ida, Duff signed a contract with Universal-International.

Ida co-starred in and directed *The Bigamist* for Filmmakers in 1953. Her co-stars were Edmond O'Brien in the title role and Joan Fontaine. The latter, who was then the wife of Ida's ex-husband, Collier Young, was a last-minute replacement for actress Jane

In *The Bigamist* ('53).

With Jack Palance in a pose for *The Big Knife* ('55).

Greer. Ida took third billing in this venture. The low-cost feature has O'Brien wed to Fontaine who is more helpful to him in his business career than as a wife. He travels a great deal, and on one such trip he meets a middle-class waitress (Ida) with whom he falls in love. He marries her, meanwhile returning home occasionally to his first wife who does not suspect his double-life situation. The waitress later has his child. At almost the same time Fontaine decides that she wants to adopt a child. The bigamist's tale is unraveled by an adoption agency official (Edmund Gwenn). The man is taken to court but the judge (John Maxwell) is unable to pass sentence, and that is where the film concludes. (Also in the cast were Lilian Fontaine, Joan's mother, and Collier Young in a bit part as a barfly.)

Photoplay thought that the film was made with "disarming simplicity and earnestness," adding: "Good acting gives life to a matter-of-fact plot."* When the film was sneak-previewed in San Francisco, with Ida and Edmund Gwenn in attendance, the hit of the evening was Ida's very, very red hair.

Ever anxious to reach into new directions that would insure her participation in show business, Ida joined with actors Dick Powell, Charles Boyer, and David Niven in 1953 to form Four Star Productions. The company produced "Four Star Theatre" for CBS-TV. The anthology program debuted on December 31, 1953, and ran through 1955. During the span of the show, Ida appeared in some twenty-four episodes.

Filmmakers' final feature film proved to be *Private Hell 36* (1954), co-authored by Ida. (As with *The Bigamist*, this film was distributed by Filmmakers.) Don Siegel directed this taut screen exercise, with Ida starring as a nightclub entertainer. Along with police detectives Howard Duff and Steve Cochran she becomes greedy when they uncover stolen loot. It was a suspenseful film, but with no major studio release it suffered in the waning distribution marketplace.

With Duff, Ida starred as the cruel superintendent of *Women's Prison* (1955) for Columbia. Her rough treatment of convicts (such as Audrey Totter and Phyllis Thaxter) leads to revolt and eventually to prison reform. Duff plays the prison doctor who sides with the prisoners in their rebellion against the ruthless woman. If Columbia executives hoped to match the excellent job that Warner Bros. had done in 1950 with *Caged*, they must have been badly disappointed.

When producer-director Robert Aldrich decided to put onto film the Clifford Odets play about a disillusioned Hollywood film star (Jack Palance) who wants to give up acting, he signed Ida to play the actor's wife. *The Big Knife* (1955), which was clearly anti-Hollywood in its bias, was released on November 9, 1955, with what has been termed "star-studded" casting. Behind-the-scenes Hollywood morals came into play in this interesting offering. As Marion Castle, Ida's character displays an intriguing array of bitter and disillusioned feelings that equal those of her spouse. In the course of the offering, Palance is driven to suicide by blackmail and threats from a ruthless studio head (Rod Steiger) and his hatchet man (Wendell Corey). Also in the cast were Shelley Winters as a studio call girl, Everett Sloane as the actor's agent, and Jean Hagen as a nymphomaniac. The film garnered third prize at the Venice Film Festival in late 1955. However, its approach was too unrelentingly morbid to appeal to a sizable viewing audience.

For RKO, Ida co-starred in another name-filled cast in *While the City Sleeps* (1956). Set for the most part at a newspaper office, it relates the story of the search by the fourth estate and police for a psychopathic killer (John Barrymore, Jr.) who derives satisfaction from murdering women. In a lineup that includes Dana Andrews, Rhonda Fleming, George Sanders, Vincent Price, Thomas Mitchell, and Sally Forrest, Ida plays the newspaper's sob sister.

That same year Lupino accepted a cameo

---

*That same year, 1953, a British-produced farce *The Captain's Paradise* dealt with a seaman (Alec Guinness) who enjoyed the pleasures of wives (Yvonne De Carlo and Celia Johnson) in two different ports.

With Jan Sterling and Cleo Moore (center) in *Women's Prison* ('55).

role as the widow of a dead Korean veteran in *Strange Intruder*. The film's star was Edmund Purdom, he of the handsome face but stolid acting presence.

Also in 1956 Ida took on her first television directorial job for NBC's "On Trial" series, produced by Joseph Cotten. With her direction of the segment *The Trial of Mary Surratt*, she began an active behind-the-camera career in the video medium.

Meanwhile on January 4, 1957, Ida and Duff were seen for the first time in their CBS-TV situation comedy series, "Mr. Adams and Eve." They played Hollywood actors who strive to maintain a semblance of normal domestic living, most of the time with little success. Although inside sources insisted that the series would not be a winner because the series' leads "would not be identified with the next-door neighbors," the program lasted for two television seasons. In fact, Ida was nominated for an Emmy in 1957 for Best Continuing Performance by an Actress in a Leading Role in a Dramatic or Comedy Series. (She lost to Jane Wyatt of "Father Knows Best.")

During the next nine years, Ida was involved strictly with television. When not directing segments for such series as "Have Gun, Will Travel," "Sam Benedict," "The Untouchables," and "Alfred Hitchcock Presents," she was seen in acting assignments on shows like "Bonanza," "The Virginian," "Burke's Law," and "The Rogues." In 1963, *Newsweek* magazine estimated that she had directed "more than fifty television shows." By this time the Duffs had had their domestic ups and downs, resulting in at least four known separations and reconciliations. She told *Newsweek*, "We call ourselves the Guttersnipes, as opposed to the Rat Pack. We don't wear Italian shoes and we don't drive foreign cars. We rarely talk about show business. I'm sure there's something much more interesting in this world." The actors whom she directed for television affectionately

With Thomas Mitchell, Vincent Price, and James Craig in *While the City Sleeps* ('56).

With Edmund Purdom and Ann Harding in *Strange Intruder* ('56).

With husband Howard Duff and daughter Bridget in 1958.

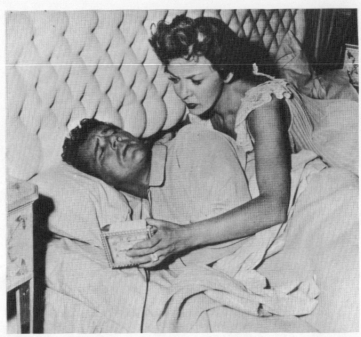
With Howard Duff in their CBS-TV series "Mr. Adams and Eve."

called her "Mother," while husband Duff referred to her as "the ex-Limey broad."

Ida returned to theatre-released films in 1966, directing *The Trouble with Angels* for producer William Frye for Columbia release. It is based (by Blanche Hanalis) on Jane Trahey's novel *Life with Mother Superior.* The Mother Superior of the piece, played by Rosalind Russell, has her hands full at St. Francis Academy, a convent school, when mischief-maker Mary Clancy (Hayley Mills) enrolls. Quietly, and with compassion, Mother Superior prepares the scamp to be a devoted nun. The film is winsome but, according to Bosley Crowther *(New York Times),* "Under Ida Lupino's direction . . . it has the quality of hit-or-miss contrivance, rather than homely, schoolgirl truth." (When the more vapid sequel *Where Angels Go . . . Trouble Follows* was produced in 1968, it would be James Neilson who directed Rosalind Russell and the other cast members.)

Three years later, in 1969, Ida was back on the motion picture screens in *Backtrack.* This entry was merely a bastardized cut-and-paste blending of TV episodes from the "Laredo" and "The Virginian" series, with Ida seen as Mama Dolores.

Ida suffered the same plight as other middle-aged actresses: she was too old to play convincingly a typical screen heroine and unable to find many character lead assignments that would allow her to retain her dignity and professional standing. However, in June 1972 she was seen as Steve McQueen's salty mother in *Junior Bonner,* directed by Sam Peckinpah. With Robert Preston as her dream-laden husband, they represent one of the prime reasons why son Junior left home to become a rodeo rider. After traveling the countryside in search of himself, Junior returns to his Arizona home to find his parents separated, his dad in a hospital, and his brother (Joe Don Baker) swindling both parents. Kathleen Carroll wrote in the *New York Daily News,* "What a joy it is to watch seasoned pros like Preston and Miss Lupino at work." Unfortunately the well-intentioned feature received scant bookings. (During the first days of filming, Lupino and Peckinpah were at artistic odds; Ida threatened to leave the shooting in Arizona. Eventually they patched up their differences.)

Also in 1972 Ida took a cameo role with George Raft in Paramount's *Deadhead Miles.* The gimmick of their appearance in this film starring Alan Arkin was to present them in

Directing an episode of "The Donna Reed Show" with Donna Reed and Ann Rutherford (ABC-TV, December 10, 1959).

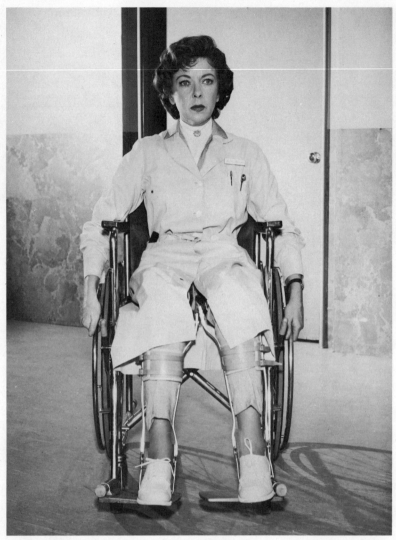

Starring in *Image of a Doctor* episode of "The General Electric Theatre" (CBS-TV, February 26, 1961).

a takeoff of *They Drive by Night* as they are seen stranded in an automobile, vintage 1940. The Tony Bill-produced feature has yet to be officially released.

In September 1972, a few weeks after Ida had told columnist Pat Campbell, "I love that old man of mine. We've been married for twenty-one years, and I'm still crazy about him," Howard Duff walked out of their Brentwood home and moved to the Bel Air Sands Hotel. Ida sobbed, "I've been dropped like a lump of ice." She later confided to Al Coombes of *The National Enquirer,* "I feel so cheated. Everyone knew he was going out with other girls—everyone except me. Now all I have left is my black cat Dollybird." A few months later, columnist John J. Miller reported: "Lupino has her next groom picked out already—businessman Tom Foley." (Foley, an auto dealer, and Ida never did wed.) Meanwhile, Howard Duff had met a young girl named Judy with whom he was reportedly sharing living quarters in a Malibu cottage.

Professionally the pickings were slim for Ida in the mid-Seventies. She continued appearing in telefeatures: *Women in Chains* (1972), another distaff prison yarn; *The Strangers in 7A* (1972) with Andy Griffith; *Female Artillery* (1973), dealing with a wagon train of women involved with a man (Dennis Weaver) on the run; *I Love a Mystery* (1973),

With Howard Duff in the *A Distant Fury* episode of "The Virginian" (NBC-TV, March 20, 1963).

In *A Distant Fury* episode of "The Virginian."

With Peter Brown and Neville Brand in *Backtrack* ('69).

a 1967-filmed takeoff on the old radio whodunit show; and *The Letters* (1973), a tri-episode story with Ida playing Pamela Franklin's mother.

When further work failed to materialize (she was mentioned in 1974 to possibly direct a film version of Frances Farmer's autobiography, *Will There Really Be a Morning?*), in January 1975 she traveled to Durango, Mexico, to co-star with Ernest Borgnine, Eddie Albert, William Shatner, and John Travolta in the low-budget thriller, *The Devil's Rain*. As Emma Preston, she becomes a satanic slave of Corbis (Borgnine), he being the leader of a coven of witches. All of Corbis' followers have wax-like forms without eyes and melt when shot or stabbed. She unsuccessfully tries to torture her son Mark (Shatner) into becoming one of them and dies a tragic death.

According to John Stark of the *San Francisco Examiner*, "Not even a talented, veteran cast saves this movie about the occult from being anything but pure hell." Frances Herridge of the *New York Post* wrote, "I've seen a lot of bad horror films in my time, but never one as inept and foolish. . . . Such participating actors as Eddie Albert, William Shatner, and Ida Lupino ought to pay to have the prints burned." In spite of such devastating reviews, the film grossed $530,311 in the first five days of its showing in the St. Louis and Kansas City areas, and it was a big domestic rental hit of 1975 earning $1,800,000. Ida was "honored" at the third annual Golden Scroll Awards presentation in February 1976 when she was named best supporting actress for her work in *The Devil's Rain*. She was also honored by The Count Dracula Society for her efforts in the horror genre.

At the "Star Spangled Hollywood" revue held in Hollywood in November 1975, the proceeds of which went to the Motion Picture and TV Relief Fund, Ida was one of three performers to receive awards. (The

With Andy Griffith on the CBS-TV telefeature *The Strangers in 7A* ('72).

With Charles Martin Smith in the *Blockade* episode (ABC-TV, January 24, 1973) of "The Streets of San Francisco."

With Nina Foch, Lee H. Montgomery, Linda Evans, Anna Navaroo, Dennis Weaver, and Sally Anne Howes in *Female Artillery* (ABC-TV, January 17, 1973).

Before and after in *The Devil's Rain* ('75).

other two were Glenn Ford and Beulah Bondi.) Ida was not present to receive the honor, which was accepted for her by Edie Adams.

Ida continued to appear on television in segments of "Pete and Mac" and "Ellery Queen" and did three recorded radio spots for the California Avocado Advisory Board. In between these commitments, she took a role in the low-budget thriller *The Food of the Gods*. Loosely derived from H. G. Wells' novel, producer/director/scripter Bert I. Gordon concocted a crass product for the action market dealing with a rash of oversized insects, rodents, and animals who go on a killing spree. Ida, looking very blowsy, was Mrs. Skinner, the farmer's wife who is eventually killed by marauding giant rats. *The Food of the Gods* certainly did not please the critics ("Atrocious," claimed *Variety*), but it made a sizable bundle at the box office.

Ida's career was supposed to take a turn toward stage work in 1976 when it was reported that she would tour in *Ladies in Retirement*, recreating her film role of the sane sister. It was also rumored that she might make her Broadway stage debut as Laurette Taylor in *The Answer*, an original biographical play.

While neither of those two stage ventures came to pass, Ida did appear in a two-hour television special of Tennessee Williams' play *Eccentricities of a Nightingale*, with Frank Langella and Blythe Danner. The TV special was syndicated on the PBS network.

In June 1976, work-hungry Miss Lupino made another independent suspense film. It was called *Kid Stuff*, and she co-starred with Ralph Meeker (also the executive producer)

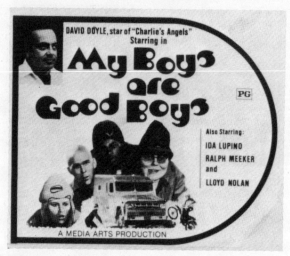

Advertisement for *My Boys Are Good Boys* ('78).

and Lloyd Nolan. When Peter Perry Pictures released the 90-minute exploitation entry in February 1978, it was retitled *My Boys Are Good Boys*. It dealt with three youths who break out of a maximum security prison, rob Meeker's armored truck, and return to jail without being detected. At the finale it is revealed that it is Meeker's spouse (Lupino) who planned the caper.

More important for Ida's latter-day career have been her recent television appearances. She played the exploitative (and soon murdered) wife of Johnny Cash on *The Swan Song* episode of "Columbo" (NBC-TV, February 23, 1977) and then was especially effective as an aging movie star in the *I Will Be Remembered* segment of "Charlie's Angels" (ABC-TV, March 9, 1977). In the course of the drama, which finds an unknown assailant trying to drive her crazy, Ida's character snarls, "You don't know Hollywood. You don't climb your way to the top, you claw your way."

These days Ida is very much a loner,* who remains above pretense or game-playing. Her daughter Bridget, according to Ida, "... has no desire to be an actress. She also swears that she will not marry until her early thirties." Presently, Bridget specializes in interior design.

Outspoken as always, Ida has recently discussed a variety of subjects with the press.

Her personal life: I am happier now, leading more of a peaceful existence. . . . I am very suspicious of my fellow humans. I have retreated from the whole Hollywood scene."

Her casual garb: "I don't feel I have to dress as though I am twenty years old. I don't live in the past."

Her weathered looks: "You could pack the bags under my eyes and go off to Las Vegas for a holiday."

Howard Duff: ". . . [he] may be one of the reasons I have retreated into myself. . . . He will occasionally write one lousy check to buy food—not a regular thing. . . . I have to earn a living."

Her status as one of the rare female film directors: ". . . I didn't see myself as any advance guard or feminist. . . . I have not too many women friends. I'm not particularly a woman's woman. I'm not a group type. In fact, there are very few women I really like. I don't like to see women behaving in a masculine manner and ordering men around. That's why I don't have too many women friends, because my sex is inclined to go through the back door to get to the front door."

Her iconoclastic nature: "If people think I'm eccentric—that's too damned bad!"

---

*She did make an appearance at the National Film Society banquet at the Beverly Hilton Hotel in May 1979 to accept their Artistry in Cinema Award. Other recipients of the tribute that night were Glenn Ford and Janet Leigh.

FILMOGRAPHY

HER FIRST AFFAIRE (*Sterling Films, 1932*) 72 min.

Producer, Frank Richardson; director, Allan Dwan; based on the play by Frederick Jackson and Merrill Rogers; screenplay, Dion Titheradge, Brock Williams; art director, James Elder Willis; costumes, Gilbert Clark; camera, Geoffrey Faithfull; editor, Dr. Seabourne.

Ida Lupino (Anne); George Curzon (Carey Merton); Diana Napier (Mrs. Merton); Harry Tate (Major Gore); Muriel Aked (Agatha Brent); Arnold Riches (Brian); Kenneth Kove (Professor Hotspur); Helen Haye (Lady Bragden); Roland Culver (Drunk); Melville Gideon (Himself).

MONEY FOR SPEED (*United Artists-British, 1933*) 72 min.

Director/story, Bernard Vorhaus; screenplay, Vera Allison, Lionel Hale, Monica Ewer.

John Loder (Mitch); Ida Lupino (Jane); Cyril McLaglen (Bill); Moore Marriott (Shorty); Marie Ault (Ma); and: John Hoskins, Ginger Lees, Cyclone Davis, Lionel Van Praag.

HIGH FINANCE (*First National-British, 1933*) 67 min.

Producer, Irving Asher; director, George King.

Gibb McLaughlin (Sir Grant Rayburn); Ida Lupino (Jill); John Batten (Tom); John H. Roberts (Ladcock); D. A. Clarke-Smith (Dodman); Abraham Sofaer (Myers).

THE GHOST CAMERA (*Radio, 1933*) 68 min.

Producer, Julius Hagen; director, Bernard Vorhaus; story, J. Jefferson Farjeon; screenplay, H. Fowler Mear; art director, James A. Carter; music, W. L. Trytel.

Henry Kendall (John Grey); Ida Lupino (Mary Elton); John Mills (Ernest Elton); S. Victor Stanley (Albert Sims); George Merritt (Inspector); Felix Aylmer (Coroner).

I LIVED WITH YOU (*Woolf and Freedman Film Service, 1933*) 100 min.

Producer, Julius Hagen; director, Maurice Elvey; based on the play by Ivor Novello; screenplay, H. Fowler Mear.

Ivor Novello (Prince Felix Lenieff); Ursula Jeans (Gladys Wallis); Ida Lupino (Ada Wallis); Minnie Rayner (Mrs. Wallis); Eliot Makeham (Mr. Wallis); Jack Hawkins (Mort); Cicely Oates (Flossie Williams); Davina Craig (Maggie); Douglas Beaumont (Albert Wallis).

PRINCE OF ARCADIA (*Woolf and Freedman Film Service, 1933*) 80 min.

Producers, Archibald Nettlefold, Reginald Fogwell; director, Hans Schwartz; based on the play *Der Prinz Von Arkadien* by Walter Reisch; screenplay, Fogwell; music, Robert Stolz.

Carl Brisson (Prince Peter); Margot Grahame (Mirana); Ida Lupino (Princess); Annie Esmond (Queen); Peter Gawthorne (Equerry); C. Denier Warren (Detective).

SEARCH FOR BEAUTY (*Paramount, 1934*) 78 min.

Director, Erle Kenton; based on the play *Love Your Body* by Schuyler E. Grey and Paul R. Milton; screen story, David Boehm, Maurine Watkins; screenplay, Frank Butler, Claude Binyon, Sam Hellman; songs, Ralph Rainger and Leo Robin; sound, Joel Butler; camera, Harry Fischbeck; editor, James Smith.

Larry "Buster" Crabbe (Don Jackson); Ida Lupino (Barbara Hilton); Toby Wing (Sally); James Gleason (Dan Healey); Robert Armstrong (Larry Williams); Gertrude Michael (Jean Strange); Roscoe Karns (Newspaper Reporter); Verna Hillie (Susie); Pop Kenton (Caretaker); Frank McGlynn, Sr. (Reverend Rankin); Clara Lou Sheridan [Ann Sheridan] (Beauty Contestant).

COME ON MARINES! (*Paramount, 1934*) 68 min.

Director, Henry Hathaway; story, Philip Wylie; screenplay, Byron Morgan, Joel Sayre; music, Ralph Rainger; song, Rainger and Leo Robin; art directors, Hans Dreier, Earl Hedrick; sound, Jack Goodrich; camera, Ben Reynolds; editor, James Smith.

Richard Arlen (Sergeant Lucky Davis); Ida Lupino (Esther Smith-Hamilton); Roscoe Karns (Terence V. "Spud" McGurk); Grace Bradley (Jo-Jo LaVerne); Edmund Breese (General Cabot); Monte Blue (Lieutenant Allen); Virginia Hammond (Susie Raybourn); Roger Gray (Celeano); Julian Madison (Brick); Emile Chautard (Priest); Clara Lou Sheridan [Ann Sheridan] (Shirley); Toby Wing [Dolly (Dorothy Barclay)]; Lona Andre (Loretta); Leo Chalzel (Bumpy); Pat Flaherty (Peewee Martin); Fuzzy Knight (Mike); Jean Chatburn, Jennifer Gray, Kay McCoy, Mary Blackwood (Girls); Brooks Benedict (Marine Orderly); Harry Strang (Radio Operator); Kit Guard (The Cook); Jack Pennick (Corporal Spike); James Bradbury, Jr., Harry Tenbrook, Charles Sullivan, Eddie Baker, Colin Tapley, Yancey Lane, Eldred Tidbury (Marines); Anna Demetrio (Fat Cantina Woman); Billy Franey (Henderson, the Street Cleaner); Boyd Irwin (Officer).

READY FOR LOVE *(Paramount, 1934)* 77 min.
Director, Marion Gering; story, Roy Flanagan; screenplay, J. P. McEvoy, William Slavens McNutt; camera, Leon Shamroy.

Ida Lupino (Marigold Tate); Richard Arlen (Julian Barrow); Marjorie Rambeau (Goldy Tate); Trent [Junior] Durkin (Joey Burke); Beulah Bondi (Mrs. Burke); Henry Travers (Judge Pickett); Esther Howard (Aunt Ida); Ralph Remley (Chester Burke); Charles E. Arnt (Sam Gardner); Charles Sellon (Caleb Hooker); Irving Bacon (Milkman); Oscar Smith (Pullman Porter); Ben Taggart (Pullman Conductor); Franklyn Ardell (Dean); Fredric Santley (Farnum); James C. Burtis (Blaine); David Loring (Skyscraper); Wilbur Mack (Davis); Louise Carter (Mrs. Thompson); Eleanor Wesselhoeft (Mrs. Black); Clara Lou Sheridan [Ann Sheridan] (Bit); Ralph Lewis (Mr. Thompson).

PARIS IN SPRING *(Paramount, 1935)* 80 min.
Producer, Benjamin Glazer; director, Lewis Milestone; story, Dwight Taylor; screenplay, Samuel Hoffenstein, Franz Shulz, Keene Thompson; songs, Harry Revel and Mack Gordon; camera, Ted Tetzlaff; editor, Eda Warren.

Mary Ellis (Simone); Tullio Carminati (Paul d'Orlando); Ida Lupino (Mignon De Charelle); Lynne Overman (Dupont); James Blakeley (Albert De Charelle); Jessie Ralph (Countess De Charelle); Dorothea Wolbert (Francine); Harold Entwistle (Charles, the Butler); Arnold Korff (Doctor); Hugh Enfield [Craig Reynolds] (Alphonse); Joe North (Etienne); Sam Ash (Clerk); Jack Raymond (Elevator Man); Akim Tamiroff (Cafe Manager); David Worth, Charles Martin, Jerry Miley, Fred Kohler, Jr. (Collegians); Elsa Peterson (Hairdresser); Arthur Housman (Interviewer); Michael Mark (Bartender); Nanette Lafayette, Alice Ardell (Manicurists).

SMART GIRL *(Paramount, 1935)* 69 min.
Producer, Walter Wanger; director, Aubrey Scott; story/screenplay, Frances Hyland; camera, John Mescall; editor, Tom Persons.

Ida Lupino (Pat Reynolds); Kent Taylor (Nick Graham); Gail Patrick (Kay Reynolds); Joseph Cawthorn (Karl Krausemeyer); Pinky Tomlin (Hans Krausemeyer); Sydney Blackmer (Harry Courtland); Greta Meyers (Mrs. Krausemeyer); Claude King (James Reynolds); Fern Emmett (Miss Brown); Perry Ivins (Auctioneer); Harold Minjir (Nelson); Charles Wilson (Morgan); Boothe Howard (Donovan); Kernan Cripps (O'Brien); Louise Brien (Helen Barton); Theodore Von Eltz (Fred Barton); Monte Vandergrift (Smith); Ernest Hilliard (Waiter); Broderick O'Farrell (Minister).

PETER IBBETSON *(Paramount, 1935)* 88 min.
Producer, Louis D. Lighton; director, Henry Hathaway; based on the novel by George du Maurier and the play by John Nathaniel Raphael; adaptor, Constance Collier; screenplay, Vincent Lawrence, Waldemar Young; additional scenes, John Meehan, Edwin Justus Mayer; music, Ernst Toch; art directors, Hans Dreier, Robert Usher; music supervisor, Nat W. Finston; sound, Harry D. Mills; special effects, Gordon Jennings; camera, Charles Lang; editor, Stuart Heisler.

Gary Cooper (Peter Ibbetson); Ann Harding (Mary, Duchess of Towers); John Halliday (Duke of Towers); Ida Lupino (Agnes); Douglass Dumbrille (Colonel Forsythe); Virginia Weidler (Mimsey); Dickie Moore (Gogo); Doris Lloyd (Mrs. Dorian); Elsa Buchanan (Madame Pasquier); Christian Rub (Major Duquesnois); Donald Meek (Mr. Slade); Gilbert Emery (Wilkins); Marguerite Namara (Madame Ginghi); Elsa Prescott (Katherine); Marcelle Corday (Maid); Adrienne D'Ambricourt (Nun); Blanche Craig (Countess); Stanley Andrews (Judge).

ANYTHING GOES *(Paramount, 1936)* 97 min. (TV title: *Tops Is the Limit*)
Producer, Benjamin Glazer; director, Lewis Milestone; based on the play by Howard Lindsay and Russel Crouse; songs, Cole Porter; additional songs, Leo Robin and Richard A. Whiting; Frederick Hollander; Hoagy Carmichael and Edward Heyman; camera, Karl Struss; editor, Eda Warren.

Bing Crosby (Billy Crocker); Ethel Merman (Reno Sweeney); Charles Ruggles (Reverend Dr. Moon); Ida Lupino (Hope Harcourt); Grace Bradley (Bonnie Le Tour); Arthur Treacher (Sir Evelyn Oakleigh); Robert McWade (Elisha J. Whitney); Richard Carle (Bishop Dobson); Margaret Dumont (Mrs. Wentworth); Jerry Tucker (Junior); Edward Gargan (Detective); Matt Moore (Ship's Captain); Rolfe Sedan (Bearded Man); G. Pat Collins (Purser); Harry Wilson, Bud Fine, Matt McHugh (Pug Uglies); Billy Dooley (Ship's Photographer); Jane Wyman (Bit).

ONE RAINY AFTERNOON *(United Artists, 1936)* 80 min. (Reissue title: *Matinee Scandal*)
Producers, Mary Pickford, Jesse Lasky; director, Rowland V. Lee; based on the story "Monsieur Sans Gene" by Arnold Pressburger and Rene Pujal; screenplay, Stephen Morehouse Avery; additional dialogue, Maurice Hanline; music, Ralph Irwin; songs, Irwin and Preston Sturges; Irwin, Jack Stern and Harry Tobias; music directors, Alfred Newman, Merritt Gerstad; assistant director, Percy Ikerd; art director, Richard Day; wardrobe, Omar Kiam; camera, Peverell Marley; editor, Margaret Clancy.

Francis Lederer (Philippe Martin); Ida Lupino (Monique Pelerin); Hugh Herbert (Toto); Roland Young (Maillot); Erik Rhodes (Count Alfredo Donstelli); Joseph Cawthorn (Monsieur Pelerin); Countess Liev de Maigret (Yvonne); Donald Meek (Judge); Georgia Caine (Cecile); Murray Kinnell (Theatre Manager); Mischa Auer (Leading Man); Eily Malyon (President of Purity League); Richard Carle (Minister of Justice); Phyllis Barry (Pelerin's Secretary); Lois January (Felice—Maillot's Secretary); Seger Ellis, Margaret Warner (Singers on Screen); Iris Adrian (Cashier); Jack Mulhall (Ice Rink Announcer); Billy Gilbert (Court Clerk); Florence Lawrence, Florence Turner, Eric Mayne, Donald Reed, Alfred Valentino, Francis Powers, Edward Bibby (Bits).

YOURS FOR THE ASKING *(Paramount, 1936)* 68 min.

Producer, Lewis E. Gensler; director, Alexander Hall; story, William R. Lipman, William H. Wright; screenplay, Even Green, Harlan Ware; Philip MacDonald; art directors, Hans Dreier, Roland Anderson; camera, Theodore Sparkuhl.

George Raft (Johnny Lamb); Dolores Costello Barrymore (Lucille Sutton); Ida Lupino (Gert Malloy); Reginald Owen [Dictionary McKinney (Colonel Evelyn Carstairs)]; James Gleason (Saratoga); Edgar Kennedy (Bicarbonate); Lynne Overman (Honeysuckle); Skeets Gallagher (Perry Barnes); Walter Walker (Mr. Crenshaw); Robert Gleckler (Slick Doran); Richard Powell (Benedict); Louis Natheaux (Dealer); Keith Daniels (Henchman); Florence Wix, Bess Flowers, Olive Tell (Women); Dennis O'Keefe (Man); Harry C. Bradley, Jack Byron (Chauffeurs); Max Barwyn, Francis Sayles, Edward Peil, Sr. (Waiters); Groucho Marx, Charles Ruggles (Sunbathers on Beach).

THE GAY DESPERADO *(United Artists, 1936)* 85 min.

Producers, Mary Pickford, Jesse L. Lasky; director, Rouben Mamoulian; story, Leo Birinski; screenplay, Wallace Smith; art director, Richard Day; music director, Alfred Newman; songs, George Posford; Giuseppi Verdi; Miguel Sandoval; costumes, Omar Kiam; sound, Paul Neal; camera, Lucien Andriot; editor, Margaret Clancy.

Ida Lupino (Jane); Nino Martini (Chivo); Leo Carrillo (Pablo Braganza); Harold Huber (Campo); Mischa Auer (Diego); Stanley Fields (Butch); James Blakeley (Bill); Paul Hurst (American Detective); Adrian Rosley (Radio Station Manager); Allan Garcia (Police Captain); Frank Puglia (Lopez); Michael Visaroff (Theatre Manager); Chris-Pin Martin (Pancho); Harry Semels (Manuel); George Du Count (Salvador); Alphonso Pedroza (Coloso); Len Brixton (Nick); Trovadores Chinacos (Guitar Trio); M. Alvarez Maciste (Guitar Soloist).

SEA DEVILS *(RKO, 1937)* 88 min.

Producer, Edward Small; director, Ben Stoloff; screenplay, Frank Wead, John Twist, P. J. Wolfson; art director, Van Nest Polglase; music director, Roy Webb; special effects, Vernon Walker; camera, J. Roy Hunt, Joseph August; editor, Arthur Roberts.

Victor McLaglen (Medals Malone); Preston Foster (Mike O'Shay); Ida Lupino (Doris Malone); Donald Woods (Steve Webb); Helen Flint (Sadie); Gordon Jones (Puggy); Pierre Watkin (Commander); Murray Alper (Seaman); Billy Gilbert (Cop).

LET'S GET MARRIED *(Columbia, 1937)* 69 min.

Director, Alfred E. Green; story, A. H. Z. Carr; screenplay, Ethel Hill; camera, Henry Freulich; editor, Al Clark.

Ida Lupino (Paula Quinn); Walter Connolly (Joe Quinn); Ralph Bellamy (Kirk Duncan); Raymond Walburn (Harrington); Robert Allen (Charles); Nana Bryant (Mrs. Willoughby); Reginald Denny (George Willoughby); Edward McWade (Tom); Emmett Vogan (Dick); Will Morgan (Harry); Granville Bates (Hank Keith); Charles Irwin (Mike); Arthur Hoyt (Minister); George Ernest (Billy Norris); James Flavin (Dolan); Vesey O'Davoren (Butler); Ted Oliver (Cop); Clyde Davis (Waiter); Ed Cook (Boy); Sherry Hall (Reporter).

ARTISTS AND MODELS *(Paramount, 1937)* 97 min.

Producer, Lewis E. Gensler; director, Raoul Walsh; story, Sig Herzig, Gene Thackrey; adaptors, Eve Greene, Harlan Ware; screenplay, Walter DeLeon, Francis Martin; songs, Ted Koehler and Victor Young; Frederick Hollander and Leo Robin; Harold Arlen and Burton Lane; art director, Hans Dreier; camera, Victor Milner; editor, Ellsworth Hoagland.

Jack Benny (Mac Brewster); Ida Lupino (Paula); Richard Arlen (Ian Townsend); Gail Patrick (Cynthia); Ben Blue (Jupiter Pluvius); Judy Canova (Toots); Yacht Club Boys (Themselves); Cecil Cunningham (Stella); Donald Meek (Dr. Zimmer); Hedda Hopper (Mrs. Townsend); Martha Raye, Andre Kostelanetz and His Orchestra, Russell Patterson's Personettes, Louis Armstrong, Connie Boswell, Anne and Zeke Canova (Specialties); Peter Arno, McClelland Barclay, Arthur William Brown, Rube Goldberg, John La Gatta, Russell Patterson (Artists); Sandra Storme

(Model); Edward Earle (Flunkey); Nick Lukats (Photographer); Rex Moore (Attendant); Dale Armstrong, Arthur Shank (Radio Announcers); Antrim Short (Prop Man); Harry Hayden (Lord); Mary Shepherd, Gloria Wheeden (Water Waltzers); Pat Moran (Tumbler); Jack Stary (Cycling Star).

FIGHT FOR YOUR LADY (*RKO, 1937*) 67 min.

Producer, Albert Lewis; director, Ben Stoloff; story, Jean Negulesco, Isabel Leighton; screenplay, Ernest Pagano, Harry Segall, Harold Kusell; art director, Van Nest Polglase; music director, Frank Tours; songs, Harry Akst and Frank Loesser; camera, Jack MacKenzie; editor, George Crone.

John Boles (Robert Densmore); Jack Oakie (Ham Hamilton); Ida Lupino (Marietta); Margot Grahame (Marcia Trent); Gordon Jones (Mike Scanlon); Erik Rhodes (Spadissimo); Billy Gilbert (Boris); Paul Guilfoyle (Jimmy Trask); Georges Renavent (Joris); Charles Judels (Felix Janos); Maude Eburne (Nadya); Charles Coleman (Butler).

THE LONE WOLF SPY HUNT (*Columbia, 1939*) 71 min.

Associate producer, Joseph Sistrom; director, Peter Godfrey; based on the novel *The Lone Wolf's Daughter* by Louis Joseph Vance; screenplay, Jonathan Latimer; music director, Morris Stoloff; art director, Lionel Banks; gowns, Kalloch; camera, Allen G. Siegler; editor, Otto Meyer.

Warren William (Michael Lanyard); Ida Lupino (Val Carson); Rita Hayworth (Karen); Virginia Weidler (Patricia Lanyard); Ralph Morgan (Gregory); Tom Dugan (Sergeant Devan); Don Beddoe (Inspector Thomas); Leonard Carey (Jameson); Ben Welden (Jenks); Brandon Tynan (Senator Carson); Helen Lynd (Marie Templeton); Irving Bacon (Sergeant); Marek Windheim (Waiter); Jack Norton (Charlie Fenton, the Drunk); Dick Elliott (Little Cop); Marc Lawrence (Heavy Leader); James Craig (Guest); Adrian Booth (Girl Whom Lanyard Meets in Club); I. Stanford Jolley (Doorman); Edmund Cobb (Police Clerk); Eddie Hearn (Police Sergeant).

THE LADY AND THE MOB (*Columbia, 1939*) 65 min.

Producer, Fred Kohlmar; director, Ben Stoloff; based on a story by George Bradshaw and Price Day; screenplay, Richard Maibaum, Gertrude Purcell; camera, John Stumar; editor, Otto Meyer.

Fay Bainter (Hattie Leonard); Ida Lupino (Lila Thorne); Lee Bowman (Fred Leonard); Henry Armetta (Zambrogio); Warren Hymer (Frankie O'Fallon); Harold Huber (Harry the Lug); Forbes Murray (District Attorney); Joe Sawyer (Blinky Mack); Tom Dugan (Brains Logan); Joseph Caits (Bert the Beetle); Jim Toney (Big Time Tim); Tommy Mack (The Canary); George Meeler (George Watson).

THE ADVENTURES OF SHERLOCK HOLMES (*Twentieth Century-Fox, 1939*) 82 min.

Associate producer, Gene Markey; director, Alfred Werker; based on the play *Sherlock Holmes* by William Gillette; screenplay, Edwin Blum, William Drake; art directors, Richard Day, Hans Peters; music director, Cyril J. Mockridge; camera, Leon Shamroy; editor, Robert Bischoff.

Basil Rathbone (Sherlock Holmes); Nigel Bruce (Dr. Watson); Ida Lupino (Ann Brandon); Alan Marshal (Jerrold Hunter); Terry Kilburn (Billy); George Zucco (Professor Moriarty); Henry Stephenson (Sir Ronald Ramsgate); E. E. Clive (Inspector Bristol); May Beatty (Mrs. Jamison); Peter Willes (Lloyd Brandon); Mary Gordon (Mrs. Hudson); Holmes Herbert (Justice); George Regas (Mateso); Mary Forbes (Lady Conyngham); Frank Dawson (Dawes, the Butler); Arthur Hohl (Bassick); Leonard Mudie (Barrows); Ivan Simpson (Gates); Eric Wilton (Butler); Anthony Kemble-Cooper (Tony Conyngham); Denis Green (Sergeant of Guard); Robert Noble (Jury Foreman); Neil Fitzgerald (Court Clerk).

THE LIGHT THAT FAILED (*Paramount, 1939*) 97 min.

Producer/director, William A. Wellman; based on the novel by Rudyard Kipling; screenplay, Robert Carson; art directors, Hans Dreier, Robert Odell; music, Victor Young; camera, Theodor Sparkuhl; editor, Thomas Scott.

Ronald Colman (Dick Heldar); Walter Huston (Torpenhow); Muriel Angelus (Maisie); Ida Lupino (Bessie Broke); Dudley Digges (Thenilghai); Ernest Cossart (Beeton); Ferike Boros (Madame Binat); Pedro de Cordoba (Monsieur Binat); Colin Tapley (Gardner); Fay Helm (Red-Haired Girl); Ronald Sinclair (Dick as a Boy); Sarita Wooten (Maisie as a Girl); Halliwell Hobbes (Doctor); Charles Irwin (Soldier Model); Francis McDonald (George); George Regas (Cassavetti); Wilfred Roberts (Barton); Colin Kenny (Doctor); Joe Collings (Thackeray); Major Sam Harris (Wells); Carl Voss (Chops, the Officer); Barbara Denny (Waitress); Pat O'Malley (Bullock); George Chandler, George Melford (Voices); Cyril Ring, Hayden Stevenson (War Correspondents); Clara Blore (Mother); Gerald Rogers (Sick Man).

THEY DRIVE BY NIGHT (Warner Bros., 1940) 93 min.

Executive producer, Hal B. Wallis; associate producer, Mark Hellinger; director, Raoul Walsh; based on the novel *Long Haul* by A. I. Bezzerides; screenplay, Jerry Wald, Richard Macaulay; music, Adolph Deutsch; orchestrator, Arthur Lange; dialogue director, Hugh MacMullen; assistant director, Elmer Decker; art director, John Hughes; gowns, Milo Anderson; makeup, Perc Westmore; sound, Oliver S. Garretson; special effects, Byron Haskin, H. F. Koenekamp, James Gibbons, John Holden, Edwin B. DuPar; camera, Arthur Edeson; editor, Thomas Richards.

George Raft (Joe Fabrini); Ann Sheridan (Cassie Hartley); Ida Lupino (Lana Carlsen); Humphrey Bogart (Paul Fabrini); Gale Page (Pearl Fabrini); Alan Hale (Ed J. Carlsen); Roscoe Karns (Irish McGurn); John Litel (Harry McNamara); Henry O'Neill (District Attorney); George Tobias (George Rondolos); Charles Halton (Farnsworth); Joyce Compton (Sue Carter); John Ridgely (Hank Dawson); Paul Hurst (Pete Haig); Charles Wilson (Mike Williams); Norman Willis (Neves); George Lloyd (Barney); Lillian Yarbo (Chloe); Eddy Chandler, Frank Faylen, Ralph Sanford, Sol Gorss, Michael Harvey, Eddie Fetherston, Alan Davis, Dick Wessel, Al Hill, Charles Sullivan, Eddie Acuff, Pat Flaherty, Mike Lally, Dutch Hendrian, Frank Mayo, Charles Sherlock, Don Turner, Ralph Lynn (Drivers); Marie Blake (Waitress); Frank Wilcox, J. Anthony Hughes (Reporters); Mack Gray (Mike); Demetris Emanuel (Waiter); Brenda Fowler, Dorothy Vaughan (Matrons); Howard Hickman (Judge); John Hamilton (Defense Attorney); William Haade (Tough Driver); Joe Devlin (Fatso); Phyllis Hamilton (Stenographer).

HIGH SIERRA (Warner Bros., 1941) 100 min.

Executive producer, Hal B. Wallis; associate producer, Mark Hellinger; director, Raoul Walsh; based on the novel by W. R. Burnett; screenplay, John Huston, Burnett; music, Adolph Deutsch; orchestrator, Arthur Lange; art director, Ted Smith; gowns, Milo Anderson; makeup, Perc Westmore; sound, Dolph Thomas; special effects, Byron Haskin, H. F. Koenekamp; camera, Tony Gaudio; editor, Jack Killifer.

Humphrey Bogart (Roy Earle); Ida Lupino (Marie Garson); Alan Curtis (Babe Kozak); Arthur Kennedy (Red Hattery); Joan Leslie (Velma); Henry Hull ("Doc" Banton); Barton MacLane (Jake Kranmer); Henry Travers (Pa); Elisabeth Risdon (Ma); Cornel Wilde (Louis Mendoza); Minna Gombell (Mrs. Baughman); Paul Harvey (Mr. Baughman); Donald MacBride (Big Mac); Jerome Cowan (Healy); John Eldredge (Lou Preiser); Isabel Jewell (Blonde); Willie Best (Algernon); Arthur Aylesworth (Auto Court Owner); Sam Hayes (Radio Commentator); Wade Boteler (Sheriff); Cliff Saum (Shaw); Eddy Chandler (Policeman); Louis Jean Heydt, William Hopper, Robert Emmett Keane (Men); Maris Wrixon (Another Blonde); Zero the Dog (Pard the Dog).

THE SEA WOLF (Warner Bros., 1941) 100 min.

Producers, Jack L. Warner, Hal B. Wallis; associate producer, Henry Blanke; director, Michael Curtiz; based on the novel by Jack London; screenplay, Robert Rossen; art director, Anton Grot; music, Erich Wolfgang Korngold; special effects, Byron Haskin, H. F. Koenekamp; camera, Sol Polito; editor, George Amy.

Edward G. Robinson (Wolf Larsen); John Garfield (George Leach); Ida Lupino (Ruth Webster); Alexander Knox (Humphrey Van Weyden); Gene Lockhart (Dr. Louie Prescott); Barry Fitzgerald (Cooky); Stanley Ridges (Johnson); Francis McDonald (Svenson); David Bruce (Young Sailor); Howard da Silva (Harrison); Frank Lackteen (Agent); Louis Mason, Dutch Hendrian (Crew Members); Cliff Clark, William Gould (Detectives); Ernie Adams (Pickpocket); Jeanne Cowan (Singer); Wilfred Lucas (Helmsman); Ethan Laidlaw, George Magrill (Sailors).

OUT OF THE FOG (Warner Bros., 1941) 93 min.

Producer, Hal B. Wallis; associate producer, Henry Blanke; director, Anatole Litvak; based on the play *The Gentle People* by Irwin Shaw; screenplay, Robert Rossen, Jerry Wald, Richard Macaulay; art director, Carl Jules Weyl; music director, Leo F. Forbstein; special effects, Rex Wimpy; camera, James Wong Howe; editor, Warren Low.

Ida Lupino (Stella Goodwin); John Garfield (Harold Goff); Eddie Albert (George Watkins); Thomas Mitchell (Jonah Goodwin); John Qualen (Olaf Johnson); George Tobias (Igor Propotkin); Aline MacMahon (Florence Goodwin); Jerome Cowan (District Attorney); Odette Myrtil (Caroline Pomponette); Leo Gorcey (Eddie); Paul Harvey (Judge Moriarity); Charles Wilson, Jack Mower (Detectives); Konstantin Sankar (Bublitchki); Ben Welden (Boss); Murray Alper (Clerk); Barbara Pepper (Cigarette Girl); Frank Coghlan, Jr. (Newspaper Vendor); Charles Drake, Richard Kipling, Eddie Graham, Jack Wise, Alexander Leftwich (Reporters).

LADIES IN RETIREMENT (Columbia, 1941) 92 min.

Producers, Lester Cowan, Gilbert Miller; director, Charles Vidor; based on the play by Reginald Denham and Edward Percy; screenplay,

Garrett Fort, Denham; art director, Lionel Banks; music director, Morris Stoloff; music, Ernest Toch; camera, George Barnes; editor, Al Clark.

Ida Lupino (Ellen Creed); Louis Hayward (Albert Feather); Evelyn Keyes (Lucy); Elsa Lanchester (Emily Creed); Edith Barrett (Louisa Creed); Isobel Elsom (Leonora Fiske); Emma Dunn (Sister Theresa); Queenie Leonard (Sister Agatha); Clyde Cook (Bates).

MOONTIDE *(Twentieth Century-Fox, 1942)* 94 min.

Producer, Mark Hellinger; director, Archie Mayo; based on the novel by Willard Robertson; screenplay, John O'Hara; art directors, Richard Day, James Basevi; music, Cyril J. Mockridge, David Buttolph; camera, Charles Clarke; editor, William Reynolds.

Jean Gabin (Bobo); Ida Lupino (Ada); Thomas Mitchell (Tiny); Claude Rains (Nutsy); Jerome Cowan (Dr. Brothers); Helene Reynolds (Woman on the Boat); Ralph Byrd (Father Price); William Halligan (Bartender); Sen Yung (Takeo); Chester Gan (Hirota); Robin Raymond (Mildred); Arthur Aylesworth (Pop Kelly); Arthur Hohl (Jennings, the Hotel Clerk); John Kelly (Mac); Tully Marshall (Mr. Simpson); Vera Lewis (Mrs. Simpson); Bruce Edwards (Man); Gertrude Astor (Woman); Marion Rosamond, Roseanne Murray (Girls at Beach); Tom Dugan (Waiter).

THE HARD WAY *(Warner Bros., 1942)* 109 min.

Producer, Jerry Wald; director, Vincent Sherman; screenplay, Daniel Fuchs, Peter Viertel; art director, Max Parker; choreography, LeRoy Prinz; music director, Leo F. Forbstein; songs, Jack Scholl and M. K. Jerome; special effects, Willard Van Enger; camera, James Wong Howe; editor, Thomas Pratt.

Ida Lupino (Helen Chernen); Dennis Morgan (Paul Collins); Joan Leslie (Katherine Chernen); Jack Carson (Albert Runkel); Gladys George (Lily Emery); Faye Emerson (Blonde Waitress); Paul Cavanagh (John Shagrue); Leona Maricle (Laura Bithorn); Roman Bohnen (Sam Chernen); Ray Montgomery (Johnny Gilpin); Julie Bishop (Chorine); Nestor Paiva (Max Wade); Joan Woodbury (Maria); Ann Doran (Dershka); Thurston Hall (Motion Picture Exhibitor); Lou Lubin (Frenchy); Jody Gilbert (Anderson); Emory Parnell, Edgar Dearing (Police Officers); Lew Harvey, C. Harry Clark (Working Men); Jean Ames (Pudgy Girl); Dolores Moran (Young Girl); Frank Mayo (Guard); Edward McWade (Doorman); Libby Taylor (Essie); Murray Alper (Duglatz); Frank Faylen (Policeman); Joel Davis (Jimmy at Six); Lon McCallister (Callboy); Dick French (Playboy); Frances Morris (Telephone Operator).

LIFE BEGINS AT 8:30 *(Twentieth Century-Fox, 1942)* 95 min.

Producer, Nunnally Johnson; director, Irving Pichel; based on the play *Light of Heart* by Emlyn Williams; screenplay, Johnson; music, Alfred Newman; art directors, Richard Day, Boris Leven; camera, Edward Cronjager; editor, Fred Allen.

Monty Woolley (Thomas); Ida Lupino (Kathi Thomas); Cornel Wilde (Robert); Sara Allgood (Mrs. Lothian); Melville Cooper (Marty); J. Edward Bromberg (Gordon); William Demarest (Cop); Hal K. Dawson (Producer); William Halligan (Sergeant McNamara); Milton Parsons (Announcer); Inez Palange (Mrs. Spano); Charles La Torre (Mr. Spano); James Flavin (Policeman); Fay Helm (Ruthie); George Holmes (Jerry); Wheaton Chambers (Floorwalker); Alec Craig (Santa Claus); Cyril Ring (Box-Office Man).

FOREVER AND A DAY *(RKO, 1943)* 105 min.

Producers/directors, Rene Clair, Edmund Goulding, Cedric Hardwicke, Frank Lloyd, Victor Saville, Robert Stevenson, Herbert Wilcox; screenplay, Charles Bennett, C. S. Forrester, Lawrence Hazard, Michael Hogan, W. O. Lipscomb, Alice Duer Miller, John Van Druten, Alan Campbell, Peter Godfrey, S. M. Herzig, Christopher Isherwood, Gene Lockhart, R. C. Sheriff, Claudine West, Norman Corwin, Jack Hartfield, James Hilton, Emmett Lavery, Frederick Lonsdale, Donald Ogden Stewart, Keith Winters; art directors, Albert S. D'Agostino, Lawrence P. Williams, Al Hermans; music director, Anthony Collins; special effects, Vernon L. Walker; camera, Robert de Grasse, Lee Garmes, Russell Metty, Nicholas Musuraca; editors, Elmo J. Williams, George Crone.

Anna Neagle [Miriam (Susan)]; Ray Milland (Bill Trimble); Claude Rains (Pomfret); C. Aubrey Smith (Admiral Trimble); Dame May Whitty (Mrs. Trimble); Gene Lockhart (Cobblewick); Ray Bolger (Sentry); Edmund Gwenn (Stubbs); Lumsden Hare (Fitts); Stuart Robertson (Lawyer); Claude Allister (Barstow); Ben Webster (Vicar); Alan Edmiston (Tripp); Patric Knowles (Courier); Bernie Sell (Naval Officer); Halliwell Hobbes (Doctor); Clifford Severn (Nelson Trimble); Charles Coburn (Sir William); Jessie Matthews (Mildred); Charles Laughton (Bellamy); Montagu Love (Sir John Bunn); Reginald Owen (Mr. Simpsen); Sir Cedric Hardwicke (Dabb); Ernest Cossart (Mr. Blinkinsop); Peter Godfrey (Mr. Pepperdish); Buster Keaton (Dabb's Assistant); Wendy Barrie (Edith); Ida Lupino (Jenny); Brian Aherne (Jim Trimble); Edward Everett Horton (Sir Anthony); Isobel Elsom (Lady Trimble-Pomfret); Eric Blore (Selsby); June Duprez (Julia); May Beatty (Cook); Merle Oberon (Marjorie); Una O'Connor (Mrs. Ismay); Nigel Bruce (Major Garrow); Roland Young (Mr. Barringer); Richard Haydn (Mr. Fulcher); Elsa Lanchester (Mamie); Sara Allgood (Cook in 1917); Ruth Warrick (Leslie); Donald Crisp (Captain Martin); Kent Smith (Gates Pomfret); June Lockhart (Daughter); Billy Bevan (Cabby); Herbert Marshall (Curate); Victor McLaglen (Spavin); Reginald Gardiner (Man); Walter Kingford (Man); Ethel Griffies, Harry Allen (Cockney Couple); Joy Harrington (Bus Conductoress); Daphne Moore (Nurse); Arthur Treacher, Anna Lee, Cecil Kellaway, Mary Gordon, Evelyn Beresford, Moyna MacGill (Bits).

THANK YOUR LUCKY STARS (*Warner Bros., 1943*) 127 min.

Producer, Mark Hellinger; director, David Butler; story, Everett Freeman, Arthur Schwartz; screenplay, Norman Panama, Melvin Frank, James V. Kern; songs, Schwartz and Frank Loesser; vocal arranger, Dudley Chambers; orchestral arrangements, Ray Heindorf; music adaptor, Heinz Roemhold; orchestrator, Maurice de Packh; choreography/dance stager, LeRoy Prinz; dialogue director, Herbert Farjean; art directors, Anton Grot, Leo K. Kuter; set decorator, Walter F. Tilford; gowns, Milo Anderson; makeup, Perc Westmore; assistant director, Phil Quinn; sound, Francis J. Scheid, Charles David Forrest; special effects, H. D. Koenekamp; camera, Arthur Edeson; editor, Irene Morra.

Eddie Cantor (Joe Sampson/Himself); Joan Leslie (Pat Dixon); Dennis Morgan (Tommy Randolph); Dinah Shore (Herself); S. Z. Sakall (Dr. Schlenna); Edward Everett Horton (Farnsworth); Ruth Donnelly (Nurse Hamilton); Joyce Reynolds (Girl with Book); Richard Lane (Barney Jackson); Don Wilson (Himself); Henry Armetta (Angelo); Willie Best (Soldier); Humphrey Bogart, Jack Carson, Bette Davis, Olivia de Havilland, Errol Flynn, John Garfield, Alan Hale, Ida Lupino, Ann Sheridan, Alexis Smith, George Tobias, Spike Jones and His City Slickers (Specialties); Jack Mower, Creighton Hale (Engineers); Don Barclay (Pete); Stanley Clements, James Copedge (Boys); Leah Baird, Joan Matthews, Phyllis Godfrey, Lillian West, Morgan Brown, George French (Bus Passengers); Joe De Rita (Milquetoast Type); Frank Faylen (Sailor); Eleanor Counts (Sailor's Girl Friend); Charles Soldani, J. W. Cody (Indians); Noble Johnson (Charlie, the Indian); Harry Pilcer (Man in Broadcasting Station); Mike Mazurki (Olaf); Bennie Bartlett (Page Boy); Marjorie Hoshelle, Anne O'Neal (Maids); Jerry Mandy (Chef); Betty Farrington (Assistant Chef); William Haade (Butler); Lou Marcelle (Commentator); Mary Treen (Fan); Ed Gargan (Doorman); Billy Benedict (Bus Boy); Juanita Stark (Secretary); *Ice Cold Katie Number:* Hattie McDaniel (Gossip); Rita Christiani (Ice Cold Katie); Jess Lee Brooks (Justice); Ford, Harris, and Jones (Trio); Matthew Jones (Gambler); *Errol Flynn Number:* Monte Blue, Art Foster, Fred Kelsey, Elmer Ballard, Buster Wiles, Howard Davies, Tudor Williams, Alan Cook, Fred McEvoy, Bobby Hale, Will Stanton, Charles Irwin, David Thursby, Henry Ibling, Earl Hunsaker, Hubert Hend, Dudley Kuzello, Ted Billings (Pub Characters); *Bette Davis Number*: Jack Norton (Drunk); Henri DeSoto (Maitre d'); Dick Elliott, Dick Earle (Customers); Harry Adams (Doorman); Sam Adams (Bartender); Conrad Wiedell (Jitterbug); Charles Francis, Harry Bailey (Bald-Headed Men); Joan Winfield (Cigarette Girl); Sylvia Opert, Nancy Worth (Hatcheck Girls); *The Lucky Stars:* Harriette Haddon, Harriett Olsen, Nancy Worth, Joy Barlowe, Janet Barrett, Dorothy Schoemer, Dorothy Dayton, Lucille LaMarr, Sylvia Opert, Mary Landa; *Humphrey Bogart Sequence:* Matt McHugh (Fireman); *Ann Sheridan Number:* Georgia Lee Settle, Virginia Patton (Girls); *Good Night, Good Neighbor Number:* Igor DeNavrotsky (Dancer); Brandon Hurst (Cab Driver); Angelita Mari (Duenna); Lynne Baggett (Miss Latin America); Mary Landa (Miss Spain).

IN OUR TIME (*Warner Bros., 1944*) 110 min.

Producer, Jerry Wald; director, Vincent Sherman; screenplay, Ellis St. Joseph, Howard Koch; art director, Hugh Reticker; set decorator, Casey Roberts; technical advisor, Stephen Barasch; music, Franz Waxman; music director, Leo F. Forbstein; assistant director, William Kissel; sound, C. A. Riggs; montages, James Leicester; camera, Carl Guthrie; editor, Rudi Fehr.

Ida Lupino (Jennifer Whittredge); Paul Henreid (Count Stephan Orvid); Nancy Coleman (Janine Orvid); Mary Boland (Mrs. Bromley); Victor Francen (Count Paval Orvid); Nazimova (Zofya Orvid); Michael Chekhov (Uncle Leopold); Ivan Triesault (Bujanski); Leonid Snegoff (Conductor); Marek Windhelm (Antique Dealer); Shimen Ruskin (Bartender); Faye Emerson, Lynne Baggett (Friends of Count Orvid); Walter Palm, William Gymes (German Aristocrats); Max Willenz (Headwaiter); Mary Landa (Flower Girl); Alex Akimoff (Wine Seller); Frank Reicher (Count Jarsky); Michael Visaroff (Dr. Kowalik); John Bleifer (Wladek); Sylvia Arslan (Nanetchka); Sonia Levkova (Graffina's Daughter); Mici Goty (Graffina); Wolfgang Zilzer (Father Joseph).

HOLLYWOOD CANTEEN *(Warner Bros., 1944)* 124 min.

Producer, Alex Gottlieb; director/screenplay, Delmer Daves; music numbers staged by LeRoy Prinz; art director, Leo Kuter; set decorator, Casey Roberts; assistant director, Art Lucker; makeup, Perc Westmore; wardrobe, Milo Anderson; music director, Leo F. Forbstein; music adaptor, Ray Heindorf; songs, Cole Porter; E. Y. Harburg and Burton Lane; Ted Koehler and Lane; Harold Adamson and Vernon Duke; Koehler and M. K. Jerome; Marian Sunshine, Julio Blanco, and Obdulio Morales; Larry Neal and Jimmy Mundy; Bob Nolan; Heindorf; Koehler, Heindorf, and Jerome; Jean Barry, Leah Worth, and Dick Charles; camera, Bert Glennon; editor, Christian Nyby.

Joan Leslie (Herself); Robert Hutton (Slim); Dane Clark (Sergeant); Janis Paige (Angela); Andrews Sisters, Jack Benny, Joe E. Brown, Eddie Cantor, Kitty Carlisle, Jack Carson, Joan Crawford, Helmut Dantine, Bette Davis, Faye Emerson, Victor Francen, John Garfield, Sydney Greenstreet, Alan Hale, Paul Henreid, Andrea King, Peter Lorre, Ida Lupino, Irene Manning, Nora Martin, Joan McCracken, Dolores Moran, Dennis Morgan, Eleanor Parker, William Prince, Joyce Reynolds, John Ridgely, Roy Rogers and Trigger, S. Z. Sakall, Alexis Smith, Zachary Scott, Barbara Stanwyck, Craig Stevens, Joseph Szigeti, Donald Woods, Jane Wyman, Jimmy Dorsey and His Band, Carmen Cavallaro and His Orchestra, Golden Gate Quartet, Rosario and Antonio, Sons of the Pioneers, Virginia Patton, Lynne Baggett, Betty Alexander, Julie Bishop, Robert Shayne, Johnny Mitchell, John Sheridan, Colleen Townsend, Angela Green, Paul Brooke, Marianne O'Brien, Dorothy Malone, Bill Kennedy, Mary Gordon, Chef Joseph Milani (Themselves); Jonathan Hale (Mr. Brodel); Barbara Brown (Mrs. Brodel); Betty Brodel (Herself); Steve Richards [Mark Stevens], Dick Erdman (Soldiers on Deck); James Flavin (Marine Sergeant); Eddie Marr (Dance Director); Ray Teal (Captain); Rudolph Friml, Jr. (Orchestra Leader); George Turner (Tough Marine); Betty Bryson, Willard Van Simons, William Alcorn, Jack Mattis, Jack Coffey (Dance Specialty).

PILLOW TO POST *(Warner Bros., 1945)* 94 min.

Producer, Alex Gottlieb; director, Vincent Sherman; based on the play by Rose Simon Kohn; screenplay, Charles Hoffman; art director, Leo Kuter; set decorator, Walter F. Tilford; music, Frederick Hollander; orchestrator, Jerome Moross; music director, Leo F. Forbstein; assistant director, Jesse Hibbs; sound, Charles Lang; special effects, Warren Lynch; camera, Wesley Anderson; editor, Alan Crosland, Jr.

Ida Lupino (Jean Howard); Sydney Greenstreet (Colonel Michael Otley); William Prince (Lieutenant Don Mallory); Stuart Erwin (Captain Jack Ross); Johnny Mitchell (Slim Clarke); Ruth Donnelly (Mrs. Wingate); Barbara Brown (Kate Otley); Regina Wallace (Mrs. Mallory); Willie Best (Lucille); Paul Harvey (J. R. Howard); Louis Armstrong and His Orchestra (Themselves); Grady Sutton (Alex); Don McGuire (Sailor on Bus); Leah Baird (Sailor's Mother); Joyce Compton (Gertrude Wilson); Bob Crosby (Clarence Wilson); Charles Jordan (Corporal Corliss); Anne Loos (Pudge Corliss); Bunny Sunshine (Celeste Corliss); Ferdinand Munier (Traveling Salesman); Diane Dorsey (Young Girl); Bobby Blake (Wilbur); Marie Blake (Wilbur's Mother); Dorothy Dandridge (Herself); Carol Hughes (Loolie Fisher); Ann O'Neal (Mrs. Bromley); Johnny Miles (Marine).

DEVOTION *(Warner Bros., 1946)* 107 min.

Producer, Robert Buckner; director, Curtis Bernhardt; story, Theodore Reeves; screenplay, Keith Winter; assistant director, Jesse Hibbs; art director, Robert M. Haas; set decorator, Casey Roberts; dialogue director, James Vincent; music, Erich Wolfgang Korngold; music director, Leo F. Forbstein; sound, Stanley Jones; special effects, Jack Holden, Jack Okey, Rex Wimpy; camera, Ernest Haller; editor, Rudi Fehr.

Olivia de Havilland (Charlotte Brontë); Ida Lupino (Emily Brontë); Nancy Coleman (Anne Brontë); Paul Henreid (Arthur Nichols); Sydney Greenstreet (William Makepeace Thackeray); Arthur Kennedy (Branwell Brontë); Dame May Whitty (Lady Thornton); Victor Francen (Monsieur Heger); Montagu Love (Reverend Brontë); Ethel Griffies (Aunt Branwell); Odette Myrtil (Madame Heger); Edmond Breon (Sir John Thornton); Marie de Becker (Tabby); Donald Stuart (Butcher); Forrester Harvey (Hoggs); Doris Lloyd (Mrs. Ingham); Hilda Plowright (Elderly Woman); Rita Lupino (Giselle); Sonia Lefkova (Marie); Elyane Lima, Sylvia Opert, Anne Goldthwaite, Irina Somochenko (French Girl Students); Micheline Cheirel (Mlle. Blanche); Hartney Arthur (Man); Edgar Norton, Crauford Kent, Frank Dawson (Club Members); Flo Wix (Englishwoman); Brandon Hurst (Duke of Wellington); Reginald Sheffield (Charles Dickens).

THE MAN I LOVE *(Warner Bros., 1946)* 97 min.

Producer, Arnold Albert; director, Raoul Walsh; based on the novel by Maritta Wolff; adaptors, Jo Pagano, Catherine Turney; screenplay, Turney; dialogue director, John Maxwell; art director, Stanley Fleischer; set decorator,

Eddie Edwards; music, Max Steiner; orchestrator, Hugo Friedhofer; music director, Leo F. Forbstein; songs, Ira and George Gershwin; Oscar Hammerstein II and Jerome Kern; P. G. Wodehouse, Hammerstein II, and Kern; Henry Creamer and Jimmy Johnson; Edward Heymann and Johnny Green; assistant director, Reggie Callow; sound, Dolph Thomas, David Forrest; special effects, Henry Barndollar, Edwin DuPar; camera, Sid Hickox; editor, Owen Marks.

Ida Lupino (Petey Brown); Robert Alda (Nicky Toresca); Andrea King (Sally Otis); Martha Vickers (Virginia Brown); Bruce Bennett (Sam Thomas); Alan Hale (Riley); Dolores Moran (Gloria O'Connor); John Ridgely (Roy Otis); Don McGuire (Johnny O'Connor); Warren Douglas (Joe Brown); Craig Stevens (Johnson); Florence Bates (Mrs. Thorpe); Patrick Griffin (Buddy Otis); Eddie Bruce, Tom Quinn (Drunks); Barbara Brown (Maggie); Janet Barrett (Cashier); Robin Raymond (Lee, the Waitress); Frank Ferguson (Army Doctor); Jack Wise (Waiter); Jack Mower (Desk Sergeant); Monte Blue (Cop); Jack Daley (Flynn, the Bartender); Ben Welden (Jack Atlas); John Vosper (Man with Gloria).

DEEP VALLEY *(Warner Bros., 1947)* 104 min.

Producer, Henry Blanke; director, Jean Negulesco; based on the novel by Dan Totheroh; screenplay, Salka Viertel, Stephen Morehouse Avery; art directors, Max Parker, Frank Durlauf; set decorator, Howard Winterbottom; music, Max Steiner; music arranger/orchestrator, Murray Cutter; music director, Leo F. Forbstein; assistant director, Art Lueker; sound, C. A. Riggs; special camera effects, William McGann, H. F. Koenekamp; camera, Ted McCord; editor, Owen Marks.

Ida Lupino (Libby); Dane Clark (Barry); Wayne Morris (Barker); Fay Bainter (Mrs. Saul); Henry Hull (Mr. Saul); Willard Robertson (Sheriff); Rory Mallinson (Foreman); Jack Mower (Supervisor); Harry Strang, Eddie Dunn (Possemen); Ralph Dunn (Deputy); Ray Teal (Prison Official); William Haade, Clancy Cooper (Guards); Bob Lowell, Lennie Bremen, Ross Ford, John Alvin (Convicts); Ian MacDonald (Blast Foreman).

ESCAPE ME NEVER *(Warner Bros., 1947)* 104 min.

Producer, Henry Blanke; director, Peter Godfrey; based on the novel and play by Margaret Kennedy; screenplay, Thames Williamson, Lenore Coffee; dialogue director, Robert Stevens; art director, Carl Weyl; set decorator, Fred M. MacLean; music, Erich Wolfgang Korngold; music arranger/orchestrator, Hugo Friedhofer; ballet sequence staged by LeRoy Prinz; music director, Leo F. Forbstein; assistant director, Claude Archer; sound, Dolph Thomas; special effects, Harry Barndollar, Willard Van Enger; camera, Sol Polito; editor, Clarence Kolster.

Errol Flynn (Sebastian Dubrok); Ida Lupino (Gemma Smith); Eleanor Parker (Penella MacLean); Gig Young (Caryl Dubrok); Reginald Denny (Ivor MacLean); Isobel Elsom (Mrs. MacLean); Albert Basserman (Heinrich); Ludwig Stossel (Steinach); George Zoritch, Corps de Ballet (Ballet Performers); Frank Puglia (Guide); Hector Sarno (Waiter); George Humbert (Vendor); Robert St. Angelo (Burly Servant); Alfredo Sabato, Mario Siletti (Gondoliers); Leon Lenoir (Butler); Angela Greene (Girl); Helene Thimig (Landlady); Helen Pender, Joan Winfield (Girls); Frank Reicher (Priest); Milada Mladova (Natrova); Ivan Triesault (Choreographer); Leonard Mudie (Doctor); Doris Lloyd (Mrs. Cooper); Jack Ford (Double for Albert Basserman).

ROAD HOUSE *(Twentieth Century-Fox, 1948)* 95 min.

Producer, Edward Chodorov; director, Jean Negulesco; story, Margaret Gruen, Oscar Saul; screenplay, Chodorov; art directors, Lyle Wheeler, Maurice Ransford; set decorator, Thomas Little; music, Cyril Mockridge; orchestrators, Herbert Spencer, Earle Hagen; songs, Dorcas Cochrane and Lionel Newman; Johnny Mercer and Harold Arlen; Don George, Charles Henderson, and Newman; assistant director, Tom Dudley; makeup, Ben Nye, Tom Tuttle, Bill Riddle; costumes, Kay Nelson; special effects, Fred Sersen; camera, Joseph LaShelle; editor, James B. Clark.

Ida Lupino (Lily Stevens); Cornel Wilde (Pete Morgan); Celeste Holm (Susie Smith); Richard Widmark (Jefty Robbins); O. Z. Whitehead (Arthur); Robert Karnes (Mike); George Beranger (Lefty); Ian MacDonald (Police Captain); Grandon Rhodes (Judge); Jack G. Lee (Sam); Marion Marshall (Millie); Tom Moore (Foreman); Ray Teal (Cop at Depot); James Metcalf (Mr. Green); Harry Seymour (Desk Clerk); Heinie Conklin (Court Clerk).

LUST FOR GOLD *(Columbia, 1949)* 90 min.

Producer/director, S. Sylvan Simon; based on the novel *Thunder God's Gold* by Barry Storm; screenplay, Ted Sherdeman, Richard English; art director, Carl Anderson; set decorator, Sidney Clifford; music, George Duning; music director, Morris Stoloff; assistant director, James Nicholson; makeup, Clay Campbell; costumes, Jean Louis; sound, Lodge Cunningham; camera, Archie Stout; editor, Gene Havlick.

Ida Lupino (Julia Thomas); Glenn Ford (Jacob

Waltz); Gig Young (Pete Thomas); William Prince (Barry Storm); Edgar Buchanan (Wiser); Will Geer (Deputy Ray Covin); Jay Silverheels (Walter); Paul Ford (Sheriff Lynn Early); Will Wright (Parsons); Eddy Waller (Coroner); Virginia Mullen (Matron); Antonio Moreno (Ramon Peralta); Arthur Hunnicutt (Ludi); Myrna Dell (Lucille); Tom Tyler (Luke); Elspeth Dudgeon (Mrs. Bannister); Paul Burns (Bill Bates); Hayden Rorke (Floyd Buckley); Fred Sears (Hotel Clerk); Kermit Maynard (Man in Lobby); William J. Tannen (Eager Fellow); Edmund Cobb, Richard Alexander, George Chesebro (Men); Arthur Space (Old Man); Percy Helton (Barber).

WOMAN IN HIDING (*Universal, 1949*) 92 min.

Producer, Michel Kraike; director, Michael Gordon; based on the magazine serial "Fugitive from Terror" by James R. Webb; screenplay, Oscar Saul; adaptor, Roy Huggins; art directors, Bernard Herzbrun, Robert Clatworthy; set decorators, Russell A. Gausman, Ruby R. Levitt; music, Frank Skinner; music director, Milton Schwarzwald; assistant director, Frank Shaw; makeup, Bud Westmore, Del Armstrong, John Holden; sound, Leslie I. Carey, Robert Pritchard; special camera, David S. Horsley; camera, William Daniels; editor, Milton Carruth.

Ida Lupino (Deborah Chandler Clark); Howard Duff (Keith Ramsey); Stephen McNally (Seldon Clark); John Litel (John Chandler); Taylor Holmes (Lucius Maury); Irving Bacon (Link); Don Beddoe (Fat Salesman); Joe Besser (Salesman); Peggy Dow (Patricia Monahan).

ON DANGEROUS GROUND (*RKO, 1951*) 82 min.

Producer, John Houseman; director, Nicholas Ray; based on the novel *Mad with Much Heart* by Gerald Butler; adaptors, A. I. Bezzerides, Ray; screenplay, Bezzerides; art directors, Albert S. D'Agostino, Ralph Berger; music director, C. Bakaleinikoff; camera, George E. Diskant; editor, Roland Gross.

Ida Lupino (Mary Malden); Robert Ryan (Jim Wilson); Ward Bond (Walter Brent); Charles Kemper (Bill Daly); Anthony Ross (Pete Santos); Ed Begley (Captain Brawley); Ian Wolfe (Carey); Sumner Williams (Danny Malden); Gus Schilling (Lucky); Frank Ferguson (Willows); Cleo Moore (Myrna); Olive Carey (Mrs. Brent); Richard Irving (Bernie); Pat Prest (Julie); Bill Hammond (Fred); Tommy Gosser (Crying Boy); Kate Lawson (Woman); Eddie Borden (Old Man); Joan Taylor (Hazel); Vince Barnett (Sergeant Wendell).

BEWARE, MY LOVELY (*RKO, 1952*) 77 min.

Producer, Collier Young; director, Harry Horner; based on the story and the play *The Man* by Mel Dinelli; screenplay, Dinelli; art directors, Albert S. D'Agostino, Alfred Herman; set decorators, Darrell Silvera, Al Orenback; music, Leith Stevens; music director, C. Bakaleinikoff; camera, George E. Diskant; editor, Paul Weatherwax.

Ida Lupino (Mrs. Gordon); Robert Ryan (Howard); Taylor Holmes (Mr. Armstrong); Barbara Whiting (Ruth Williams); James Willmas (Mr. Stevens); O. Z. Whitehead (Mr. Franks); Dee Pollack (Grocery Boy); Brad Morrow, Jimmy Mobley, Shelley Lynn Anderson, Ronnie Patterson (Boys); Jeanne Eggenweiler (Girl).

JENNIFER (*Allied Artists, 1953*) 73 min.

Producer, Berman Swartz; director, Joel Newton; story, Virginia Myers; camera, James Wong Howe; editor, Everett Douglas.

Ida Lupino (Agnes); Howard Duff (Jim); Robert Nichols (Orin); Mary Shipp (Lorna); Matt Dennis (Himself); Ned Glass (Grocery Clerk); Kitty McHugh (Landlady); Russ Conway (Gardener); Lorna Thayer (Grocery Clerk).

THE BIGAMIST (*Filmmakers, 1953*) 80 min.

Producer, Collier Young; director, Ida Lupino; story, Larry Marcus, Lou Schor; screenplay, Young; music, Leith Stevens; song, Matt Dennis and Dave Gillan; camera, George Diskant; editor, Stanford Tischler.

Joan Fontaine (Eve Graham); Edmond O'Brien (Harry Graham); Ida Lupino (Phyllis Martin); Edmund Gwenn (Mr. Jordan); Jane Darwell (Mrs. Connelley); Kenneth Tobey (Tom Morgan); John Maxwell (Judge); Peggy Maley (Phone Operator); Mack Williams (Prosecuting Attorney); James Todd (Mr. Forbes); James Young (Executive); Lilian Fontaine (Miss Higgins); John Brown (Dr. Wallace); Matt Dennis (Himself); Jerry Hausner (Ray); Kem Dibbs (Tanner Driver); Mac McKim (Boy on Street); Collier Young (Barfly).

PRIVATE HELL 36 (*Filmmakers, 1954*) 81 min.

Producer, Collier Young; associate producer, Robert Eggenweiler; director, Don Siegel; screenplay, Young, Ida Lupino; art director, Walter Keller; set director, Edward Boyle; music, Leith Stevens; assistant directors, James Anderson, Leonard Kunody; makeup, David Newell; dialogue coach, David Peckenpah; sound, Thomas Carmen, Howard Wilson; camera, Burnett Guffey; editor, Stanford Tischler.

Ida Lupino (Lilli Marlowe); Steve Cochran (Detective Sergeant Calvin Brimer); Howard Duff (Jack Farnham); Dean Jagger (Captain Michaels); Dorothy Malone (Francey Farnham); Bridget Duff (Farnham's Child); Jerry Hausner

(Nightclub Boss); Dabbs Greer (Bartender); Chris O'Brien (Coroner); Kenneth Patterson (Superior Officer); George Dockstader (Fugitive); Jimmy Hawkins (Delivery Boy); King Donovan (Burglar).

WOMEN'S PRISON *(Columbia, 1955)* 80 min.

Producer, Bryan Foy; director, Lewis Seiler; screenplay, Crane Wilbur, Jack DeWitt; art director, Gary Odell; set decorator, Louis Diabe; assistant director, Carter De Haven, Jr.; music director, Mischa Bakaleinikoff; sound, George Cooper; camera, Lester H. White; editor, Henry Batista.

Ida Lupino (Amelia Van Zant); Jan Sterling (Brenda Martin); Cleo Moore (Mae); Audrey Totter (Joan Burton); Phyllis Thaxter (Helene Jensen); Howard Duff (Dr. Clark); Warren Stevens (Glen Burton); Barry Kelley (Warden Blackburn); Gertrude Michael (Sturgess); Vivian Marshall (Dottie); Ross Elliott (Don Jensen); Mae Clarke (Saunders); Adelle August (Grace); Don C. Harvey (Captain Tierney); Edna Holland (Sarah); Lynne Millan (Carol); Mira McKinney (Burke); Mary Newton (Enright); Diane DeLaire (Head Nurse); Jana Mason (Josie); Lorna Thayer (Woman Deputy); Murray Alper (Mug); Ruth Vann, Mary Lou Devore (Girl Patients); Eddie Foy III (Warden's Secretary).

THE BIG KNIFE *(United Artists, 1955)* 111 min.

Producer/director, Robert Aldrich; based on the play by Clifford Odets; screenplay, James Poe; art director, William Glasgow; music director, Frank DeVol; assistant director, Nate Slott; camera, Ernest Laszlo; editor, Michael Luciano.

Jack Palance (Charles Castle); Ida Lupino (Marion Castle); Shelley Winters (Dixie Evans); Wendell Corey (Smiley Coy); Jean Hagen (Connie Bliss); Rod Steiger (Stanley Hoff); Ilka Chase (Patty Benedict); Everett Sloane (Nat Danziger); Wesley Addy (Hank Teagle); Paul Langton (Buddy Bliss); Nick Dennis (Nick); Bill Walker (Russell); Mike Winkelman (Billy Castle); Mel Welles (Bearded Man); Robert Sherman (Bongo Player); Strother Martin (Stillman); Ralph Volkie (Referee); Michael Fox (Announcer).

WHILE THE CITY SLEEPS *(RKO, 1956)* 100 min.

Producer, Bert E. Friedlob; director, Fritz Lang; based on the novel *The Bloody Spur* by Charles Einstein; screenplay, Casey Robinson; art director, Carroll Clark; set decorator, Jack Mills; costumes, Norma; music, Herschel Burke Gilbert; assistant director, Ronnie Rondell; sound editor, Verna Fields; camera, Ernest Laszlo; editor, Gene Fowler, Jr.

Dana Andrews (Edward Mobley); Rhonda Fleming (Dorothy Kyne); Sally Forrest (Nancy Liggett); Thomas Mitchell (Griffith); Vincent Price (Walter Kyne, Jr.); Howard Duff (Lieutenant Kaufman); Ida Lupino (Mildred); George Sanders (Mark Loving); James Craig (Harry Kritzer); John Barrymore, Jr. (Robert Manners); Vladimir Sokoloff (George Palsky); Robert Warwick (Amos Kyne); Ralph Peters (Meade); Mae Marsh (Mrs. Manners); Pit Herbert (Bartender); Andrew Lupino (Bit); Celia Lovsky (Miss Dodd).

STRANGE INTRUDER *(Allied Artists, 1956)* 82 min.

Producer, Lindsley Parsons; associate producer, John H. Burrows; director, Irving Rapper; based on the novel *The Intruder* by Helen Fowler; screenplay, David Evans, Warren Douglas; assistant director, Kenneth Walters; music, Paul Dunlap; song, Carroll Coates; camera, Ernest Haller; editor, Maurice Wright.

Edmund Purdom (Paul Quentin); Ida Lupino (Alice); Ann Harding (Mary Carmichael); Jacques Bergerac (Howard); Gloria Talbott (Meg); Carl Benton Reid (James Carmichael); Douglas Kennedy (Parry); Donald Murphy (Adrian); Ruby Goodwin (Violet); Mimi Gibson (Libby); Eric Anderson (Johnny); Marjorie Bennett (Joady).

BACKTRACK *(Universal, 1969)* C-95 min.

Producer, David J. O'Connell; director, Earl Bellamy; screenplay, Borden Chase; music, Jack Marshall; assistant directors, Henry Kline, Carter DeHaven III, James M. Walters, Jr.; art directors, George Patrick, Howard E. Johnson; set decorators, John McCarthy, James M. Walters, Perry Murdock, Ollie Emmett; makeup, Bud Westmore; sound, Waldon O. Watson, Frank H. Wilkinson, Earl Crane, Jr., Robert Bertrand; camera, Benjamin H. Kline, John L. Russell, Andrew Jackson; editor, Michael R. McAdam.

Neville Brand (Reese); James Drury (Ramrod); Doug McClure (Trampas); Peter Brown (Chad); William Smith (Riley); Philip Carey (Captain Parmalee); Ida Lupino (Mama Delores); Rhonda Fleming (Carmelita Flanagan); Fernando Lamas (Captain Estrada); Ross Elliott (Sheriff Abbott); George Savalas (Turnkey); Randy Boone (Randy); Gary Clarke (Steve); Priscilla Garcia (Gaviota); Ruben Moreno (Yaqui Chief).

JUNIOR BONNER *(Cinerama, 1972)* C-100 min.

Producer, Joe Wizan; director, Sam Peckinpah; screenplay, Jeb Rosebrook; second unit director, Frank Kowalski; assistant directors, Frank Baur, Michael Messinger, William Sheehan; music, Jerry Fielding; songs, Rod Hart; art director, Edward S. Haworth; set designer, Angelo

Graham; set decorator, Jerry Wunderlick; technical advisor/coordinator, Casey Tibbs; costumes, Eddie Armand; makeup, Donald W. Roberson; sound, Charles Wilborn, Richard Portman, Larry Hooberry; camera, Lucien Ballard; editor, Robert Wolf.

Steve McQueen (Junior Bonner); Robert Preston (Ace Bonner); Ida Lupino (Elvira Bonner); Ben Johnson (Buck Roan); Joe Don Baker (Curly Bonner); Barbara Leigh (Charmagne); Mary Murphy (Ruth Bonner); Bill McKinney (Red Terwiliger); Sandra Deel (Nurse Arliss); Donald Red Barry (Homer Rutledge); Dub Taylor (Bartender); Charles Gray (Burt); Matthew Peckinpah (Tim Bonner); Sundown Spencer (Nick Bonner); Rita Garrison (Flashie); Rod Hart, Casey Tibbs (Rodeo Riders).

DEADHEAD MILES *(Paramount, 1972)* C-92 min.

Producers, Tony Bill, Vernon Zimmerman; associate producer, John Prizer; director, Zimmerman; screenplay, Terry Malick; assistant directors, Russell Vreeland, Fred Brost; technical advisor, Joe Madrid; wardrobe, Dick Brunno; sound, Charles Knight; camera, Ralph Woolsey; editor, Bud Smith.

Alan Arkin (Cooper); Paul Benedict (Hitchhiker); Avery Schreiber (The Boss); Oliver Clark (Duranzo); Hector Elizondo (Bad Character); Charles Durning (Red Ball); Larry Wolf (Pineapple); Barnard Hughes (Old Man); Diane Shalet (Donna James); William Duell (Auto Parts Salesman); Madison Arnold (Hostler); Donna Anderson (Waitress); Allen Garfield (Juicey Brucey); Patrick Dennis-Leigh (Loader); Dan Resin (Foreman); Bruce Bennett (Johnny Mesquitero); Phil Kenneally, John Milius (Cops); Bill Littleton (Chicken Farmer); John Steadman (Old Sam); and: George Raft (Himself); Ida Lupino (Herself).

WOMEN IN CHAINS *(ABC-TV, 1972)* C-73 min.

Producer, Edward K. Milkis; director, Bernard L. Kowalski; teleplay, Rita Larkin; music director, Kenyon Hopkins; music, Charles Fox; camera, Howard Schwartz; editor, Argyle Nelson.

Ida Lupino (Tyson); Lois Nettleton (Sandra Parker/Sally Porter); Jessica Walter (Dee Dee); Belinda Montgomery (Melinda); Penny Fuller (Helen Anderson); John Larch (Barney); Barbara Luna (Leila); Neile Adams (Connie); Hazel Medina (Althea); Kathy Cannon (Alice); Lucille Benson (Billie); Joyce Jameson (Simpson).

THE STRANGERS IN 7A *(CBS-TV, 1972)* C-73 min.

Producer, Mark Carliner; director, Paul Wendkos; based on the novel by Fielden Farrington; teleplay, Eric Roth; music, Morton Stevens; camera, Robert Hauser; editor, Bud S. Isaacs.

Andy Griffith (Artie Sawyer); Ida Lupino (Iris Sawyer); Michael Brandon (Billy); James A. Watson, Jr. (Riff); Tim McIntire (Virgil); Susanne Hildur (Claudine); Connie Sawyer (Mrs. Layton); Joe Mell (Danny); Victoria Carroll (Miss Simpson); Squire Fridell (Pete); Virginia Vincent (Woman); Charlotte Knight (Old Woman); Marc Hannibal (Policeman).

FEMALE ARTILLERY *(ABC-TV, 1973)* C-73 min.

Producer, Winston Miller; director, Marvin Chomsky; story, Jack Sher, Bud Freeman; teleplay, Freeman; music, Frank DeVol.

Dennis Weaver (Deke Chambers); Ida Lupino (Martha Lindstrom); Sally Ann Howes (Sybil Townsend); Linda Evans (Charlotte Paxton); Lee Harcount Montgomery (Brian Townsend); Albert Salmi (Frank Taggert); Anna Navarro (Sarah Gallado); Nina Foch (Amelia Craig); Charles Dierkop (Sam); Nate Esformes (Johnny); Lee de Broux (Squat); Robert Sorrells (Scotto).

I LOVE A MYSTERY *(NBC-TV, 1973)* 113 min.

Producer, Frank Price; director, Leslie Stevens; created by Carlton E. Morse from his radio series; teleplay, Stevens; music, Oliver Nelson; camera, Ray Rennahan.

Ida Lupino (Randolph Cheyne); Les Crane (Jack Packard); David Hartman (Doc Long); Hagan Beggs (Reggie York); Jack Weston (Job Cheyne); Melodie Johnson (Charity); Karen Jensen (Faith); Deanna Lund (Hope); Don Knotts (Alexander Archer); Terry-Thomas (Gordon Elliott); and: Peter Mamakos, Andre Philippe, Lewis Charles, Francine York.

THE LETTERS *(ABC-TV, 1973)* C-73 min.

Executive producers, Aaron Spelling, Leonard Goldberg; producer, Paul Junger Witt; associate producer, Tony Thomas; director for episode three, Paul Krasny; teleplay (episode three), James G. Kirsch; art director, Tracy Borman; music supervisor, Rocky Moriana; camera, Leonard J. Smith; editor, Robert L. Swanson.

Episode: *Dear Karen:*

Pamela Franklin (Karen Forrester); Ida Lupino (Mrs. Forrester); Ben Murphy (Joe Randolph); Shelley Novack (Sonny); Frederick Merrick (Billy); Ann Noland (Sally); Brick Huston (Officer); Charles Picerni (Man); Henry Jones (Postman).

THE DEVIL'S RAIN *(Bryanston, 1975)* C-85 min.

Executive producer, Sandy Howard; producers, James V. Cullem, Michael S. Glick; director, Robert Fuest; screenplay, Gabe Essoe, James Ashton, Gerald Hopman; production designer, Nikita Knatz; music, Al De Lory; camera, Alex Phillips, Jr.; editor, Michael Kahn.

Ernest Borgnine (Corbis); Eddie Albert (Dr. Richards); Ida Lupino (Mrs. Preston); William Shatner (Mark Preston); Keenan Wynn (Sheriff Owens); Tom Skerritt (Tom Preston); Joan Prather (Julie Preston); Woodrow Chambliss (John); John Travolta (Danny); Claudio Brooks (Preacher); Lisa Todd (Lilith); George Sawaya (Steve Preston); Erika Carlson (Aaronessa Fyffe).

THE FOOD OF THE GODS *(American International, 1976)* C-88 min.

Executive producer, Samuel Z. Arkoff; producer/director, Bert I. Gordon; based on the novel by H. G. Wells; screenplay, Gordon; art director, Graeme Murray; set decorator, John Stark; music, Elliot Kaplan; makeup, Phyllis Newman; assistant director, Flora Gordon; special effects, John Thomas; sound, George Mulholland; camera, Reg Morris; editor, Corky Ehlers.

Marjoe Gortner (Morgan); Pamela Franklin (Lorna Scott); Ralph Meeker (Bensington); Ida Lupino (Mrs. Skinner); John Cypher (Brian); John McLiam (Mr. Skinner); Belinda Balaski (Rita); Tom Stovall (Thomas).

MY BOYS ARE GOOD BOYS *(Peter Perry, 1978)* C-90 min.

Executive producer, Ralph Meeker; producers, Colleen Meeker, Bethel Buckalew; director, Buckalew; screenplay, Buckalew, Fred F. Finkleoffe.

With: Ralph Meeker, Ida Lupino, Lloyd Nolan, Robert Cokjlat, Brice Coefield, Sean T. Roche, Kerry Lynn.

With Burt Lancaster in *The Flame and the Arrow* ('50).

4

VIRGINIA MAYO

> 5' 4"   115 pounds
> Ash blonde hair   Hazel eyes
> Sagittarius

IN HIS *The Filmgoer's Companion* (1977), Leslie Halliwell describes Virginia Mayo as "American 'peaches and cream' leading lady of the forties; played a few bit parts before being cast as decoration in colour extravaganzas."

However, for many filmgoers of the era, Virginia was far more. She represented a pleasing combination of attractiveness and jaunty personality. While studio bosses Samuel Goldwyn and Jack L. Warner would cast her as merely a beautiful onscreen distraction, she continually demonstrated a capacity for versatility and astuteness of performance. She could caper with Danny Kaye (*Wonder Man,* 1945, *The Secret Life of Walter Mitty,* 1947, etc.), match barbs with Bob Hope *(The Princess and the Pirate,* 1944), snarl back at James Cagney *(White Heat,* 1949), or parade as a vicious hedonist *(The Best Years of Our Lives,* 1946). In fact, no less a judge than Bette Davis insisted in 1948 that a role assigned to the Queen of Warner Bros. was much more suited to the younger and quite talented Miss Mayo.

In her cinema career Virginia was typical of the emerging actress stars of the Forties: she displayed a unique sense of self which made her a multi-dimensional character onscreen, no matter what the scope of the assignment.

She was born Virginia Clara Jones in St. Louis, Missouri, at 5:30 A.M. on Tuesday, November 30, 1920. She registered an even eight pounds on the doctor's scale. Her father, Luke Ward Jones, employed as a display advertising salesman with the *St. Louis Globe-Democrat,* was a popular man in the community who served several terms as president of the local Parent-Teacher Association. The sole occupation of her mother, Martha Henrietta Rautenstrauch Jones, was the raising of Virginia and Virginia's older brother (by two years), Lee Lake. Not long after Virginia's birth she was given the nickname of "Sis" by the family.

One family ancestor was Captain James Piggott who, after serving with General Washington's armies in the battles of Brandywine and Saratoga (both in 1777), went west to Illinois where he founded the city of East St. Louis. "He was quite a doer," Virginia says, because he also opened the push to the far western frontier by establishing the first ferry boat system across the Mississippi River. Another forebear, Joseph Fenton, joined the American Revolutionary Army as a private in New York State at the age of seventeen. Having survived the war, he was pensioned off and quietly spent the remainder of his days in "leisure" ("He lived to be a very old man," Virginia says) on the monthly check received from the government. Because of Private Fenton's patriotic adventures, Virginia is entitled to be designated as a Daughter of the American Revolution.

When Virginia was six years old she was enrolled in the drama school operated by her father's older sister, Alice Wientge. There, for ten years, she learned how to properly use her body, hands, and voice onstage. Mrs. Wientge's staff included dance teachers who gave Virginia an early education in all forms of dance expression. The students were given recitations to memorize, commensurate with their ages. As time went by, Virginia was requested to teach the younger students, but she found this assignment boring. Aunt Alice's scholastic schedule also included Shakespeare. Today Virginia admits that she often did not understand the writings of the Bard and that she much preferred comedies or dancing.

During her grammar school years, because of her background, Virginia became the star actress in plays. She was also commissioned by her aunt to perform, as donated talent, at out-of-the-city churches and Masonic lodges. Consequently her education suffered, and she even now bemoans the fact that she never really learned to add figures. "I was always out," she remembers. However, there was never a question in her mind that she wanted to be an actress when she grew up. When the other kids would suggest playing ball, she would respond with a loud "No! Let's play show." She recently admitted to this book's co-author Don E. Stanke, "I was very lucky to fall under my aunt's teaching and professional guidance because all I ever wanted to do was 'show business.'"

With brother Lee.

Through the auspices of Aunt Alice, at the age of twelve Virginia was chosen to participate as an "extra" dancer with the Stratford-on-Avon British Touring Company when it played St. Louis in 1933. "I was paid a dollar a night," she says. "I'll never forget that." She also remembers that the dancers were required to frolic in bare feet and that it was mid-winter. This, her professional stage debut, occurred at the American Theatre in "flimsy costumes." She shivers at the remembrance: "It was c-o-l-d as ice." Two of the British productions in which she either did a walk-on or danced were *A Midsummer Night's Dream* and *The Merry Wives of Windsor.*

At Soldan High School, Virginia became a member of the drama club and took a course in public speaking. She recalls "gliding" through that one like "duck soup." She was also chosen to star in all of the school's stage productions, but she continued to improve upon her dancing after class hours.

Following graduation from high school in January 1938, Virginia joined a dancing group which performed in floor shows at the Chase Hotel in St. Louis. This was followed, in the summer of 1938, by a job dancing (ballet, tap) with the chorus of the famous St. Louis Municipal Opera which specialized (and still does) in outdoor stage musicals. This work represented the realization of her "first big goal" and she looks back on it as one of the most beautiful summers of her life when everything seemed to be happening according to plan. At no time did her parents protest her stage work, because, as she says, "It was at the end of the Depression, and the fact that I could use my talents and get paid for them impressed them very much."

With the end of the summer came the seasonal closing of the Municipal Opera Theatre. Thereafter, Virginia and six of the other girls took jobs as dancers at the Jefferson Hotel. About a month after Virginia began work at the club, a specialty act called "Pansy-the-Horse" was booked, along with headliner Rudy Vallee. One afternoon the two men who had created the "Pansy" act, Andy Mayo and Nomi Morton, stopped Virginia in a hallway and inquired if she would consider joining their act. It was explained that they would soon need a replacement inasmuch as Andy's wife, Florence, was pregnant.

The act consisted of Mayo and Morton as the front and rear of the horse "Pansy," while the girl member of the trio, clad in a brief, colorful costume, sang, danced, and acted as the ringmistress who commanded the horse to do its tricks. The humor of the piece lay in the cloth animal's inability to perform each stipulated trick and in its adoration of its trainer.

A few days after meeting Mayo and Morton, Virginia agreed to take the job of ringmistress, but to avoid confusion with booking agents, she was asked to change her name to Mayo. Thus the credits continued to read "Mayo and Morton." For the next four and a half years the team played vaudeville dates in theatres east of the Mississippi River. (There was one exception when the troupe was booked for a date in Texas.) The act was frequently used in movie houses as an intermission relief and in theatres which featured the big bands of the era.

In the winter of 1940 Virginia was forced to leave the show for a few days to attend the funeral of her father in St. Louis, but she returned to the act in time to perform at the Radio City Music Hall in New York for the seven-week run of *The Philadelphia Story.* "We did six or seven shows a day," Virginia relates. "I would get into the theatre at ten in the morning to get ready for the show—I was always late because I came by subway. The Music Hall was quite a place to work, with big dressing rooms and all great facilities." She was not alone in the big city during this extended run, since several of her St. Louis dancing friends were members of The Rockettes.

In the autumn of 1941 "Pansy" was hired as an act for Eddie Cantor's Broadway revue, *Banjo Eyes.* At the outset it was decided that Virginia would probably not be needed because Cantor intended to enact her part. When the show opened on December 25, 1941, at the Hollywood Theatre,

197

however, it was Virginia who filled the ringmistress' uniform. It happened that during the New Haven tryouts Cantor had been unable to milk as many laughs as anticipated. Along with her position as ringmistress, Virginia had a small speaking part and filled in as a dancer. In retrospect, Virginia admits that she was ambitious in those days, "I was voted the one most likely to succeed from the cast of *Banjo Eyes*."

Unfortunately, *Banjo Eyes* received unkind reviews and closed on April 15, 1942, allegedly due to Cantor's "illness." The "Pansy" team then went on the road again and was hired, in October 1942, by showman Billy Rose as an attraction at his famed Diamond Horseshoe. Here again it was decided that Virginia would not be needed. This time the act was to be worked into the theme of the show as "Mrs. Astor's Pet Horse," with a black footman doing the honors of the horse's trainer. Mayo and Morton interceded on Virginia's behalf and persuaded Rose to at least interview her. When he did, he was so taken with her that he not only kept her in the act but also created special numbers for her. She was used as the show's mistress of ceremonies and had several specialty dance sequences. "It was a real showcase," she remembers.

Dressed in elaborate costume, she was seen at her best in the John Murray Anderson-choreographed numbers which attracted the attention of, among others, movie mogul David O. Selznick. Selznick screen-tested her with a young actor named Kevin O'Shea and placed her on an optional type of contract, with *no* salary. In the meantime, she made her motion picture debut in *Follies Girl* (1943) for Producers Releasing Corporation. In this quickie film shot in a New Jersey studio, starring Wendy Barrie and Doris Nolan, she was seen briefly, but not heard, as one of the models in the employ of dress designer Barrie.

Then, one night at the Diamond Horseshoe, word spread backstage that movie producer Sam Goldwyn was in the audience. The next day Virginia was invited to see him at his office. He had screened her Selznick test and was impressed, but he insisted upon making his own test of her at his facilities. Although Virginia now claims, "It wasn't very good," Goldwyn liked it. He negotiated with Selznick, and the latter, via a memo, indicated that Goldwyn was free to hire her. With his productions projected as far ahead as five years, it was Goldwyn's thought to groom Virginia as an eventual co-star for his newly acquired funnyman, Danny Kaye.

Virginia signed a seven-year contract with Goldwyn at a starting salary of $100 per week. When she was whisked off to Hollywood, Mayo and Morton, who wanted to try their luck on the West Coast, went with her. Along with Mayo's wife and child, they rented a house in Hollywood situated just below the famous hillside "Hollywood" sign. Virginia's first task in the movie capital was to aid her ex-partners in finding a girl to replace her in the "Pansy" act. At the Goldwyn studio she located a pretty young woman who became her immediate replacement. The girl was Linda Christian.

It did not take much perception to realize that Virginia would require a good deal of training if she was going to succeed on the screen. Recalling this aspect of her early Goldwyn days, she exclaimed, "My God, it was coming out of my ears—how to speak, how to project my image on the screen, how to act in front of the camera, how to walk— I mean every kind of lesson that I needed for screen work." One of her first coaches was Florence Enright who seemingly never left her side. Others included Gertrude Fogler and Gloria McLean. Goldwyn's plan for Virginia was to star her with Danny Kaye in the comic's first feature, *Up in Arms* (1944). She was tested for the role of Mary Morgan, a girl whom Kaye smuggles aboard his transport ship. However, the comedian did not like her test and felt that she lacked the needed experience. Bowing to Kaye's objections, Goldwyn turned the part over to Constance Dowling, while Virginia was relegated to a temporary spot as one of The Goldwyn Girls. "I resented this bitterly," she says. "All my life I've been plagued by the Goldwyn Girl tag which was not really fair."

Possibly to make amends—but more likely to give her a chance to learn movie techniques at someone else's expense—Goldwyn loaned her to producer Samuel Bronston for *Jack London* (1943), filmed on the Goldwyn lot for release through United Artists (it was released prior to *Up in Arms*). It was at this time that she became acquainted with the film's star, Michael O'Shea, who one day would become her husband.

In the early portions of *Jack London*, Virginia is seen as disarrayed Mamie, a stowaway on a San Francisco-bound oyster ship operated by young London (O'Shea). The fisherman quickly becomes enamored of the selfish girl who later deserts him to pursue her own fantasies. Throughout the remainder of the 94-minute feature his occupations include sailor, writer, and war correspondent, and then he weds Susan Hayward. As Bosley Crowther observed in the *New York Times*, "Frankly, it must be admitted that the proper film biography of London has not yet been made."

Two months after her arrival in California, Virginia was joined by her mother, and they rented an apartment within the Hollywood Towers. Studio press releases of the time divulged that Virginia had never had "a steady beau" and that she collected stray pups. She reportedly liked most sports, ate large meals to keep up her weight, and loved to swim to keep it evenly distributed. It was also written that she had always dreamed of having curly hair and that she enjoyed sketching as a pastime.

Goldwyn loaned her out a second time, this time to producer-director John H. Auer as a San Francisco beauty caught up in the shore-leave adventures of a crew from the merchant marine in RKO's *Seven Days Ashore* (1944). The film, which starred the comedy team of Wally Brown and Alan Carney, with Virginia in sixth billing as Carol, was far from one of RKO's loftier endeavors.

Virginia refers to her next film as her "re-

With Amelita Ward, Gordon Oliver, and Elaine Shepard in *Seven Days Ashore* ('44).

With Walter Brennan and Bob Hope in *The Princess and the Pirate* ('44).

ward" for having been a good girl. Goldwyn tested her ("He wouldn't give you a part unless he tested you") for the part of Princess Margaret in *The Princess and the Pirate* (1944). He decided that she was ready for co-starring status in this Technicolor feature. The pirate of the yarn is Bob Hope, of whom she gratefully says: "He made me feel very much at ease. I was so frightened of the camera. I would become frozen at having this big thing right on top of me. I couldn't seem to overcome it; I held back. But working with Bob gave me a feeling of freedom and I was able to relax."

The film had Hope as Sylvester, a seventeenth-century song-and-dance comic who meets Princess Margaret. She is on the run in order to escape a loveless royal marriage. Captured by a band of buccaneers in quest of a treasure map, they are taken to a place where their captor, La Roche (Walter Slezak), keeps the lovely princess under lock and key for ransom purposes. Sylvester escapes bondage and masks his identity behind a series of outlandish costumes. While his henchmen search for the elusive Sylvester, La Roche attempts to make love to the princess, but she rebuffs him. "I'm willing to wait an hour, a day, even a week," he tells her. "I have infinite patience." With all the firmness that a lady in such circumstances can muster, she tells him, "I assure you, it will be of no avail, no matter how long you wait.... You will find me of strong will, La Roche. You must know I'm not one to be frightened by the threats of such as you." Eventually the two captives manage to escape the despicable La Roche, but not without becoming immersed in several scenes of buffoonery. The film's end has Bing Crosby (unbilled) walking up and claiming the princess for himself.

Virginia "sang" onscreen for the first time in *The Princess and the Pirate,* but the voice heard singing "Kiss Me in the Moonlight" belonged to Louanne Hogan. After the picture's release, Goldwyn must have felt proud of his decision to place Mayo in a co-starring role. Critics such as Bosley Crowther *(New York Times)* admitted that she

The young pin-up queen ('45).

was "a pleasant show in her own right." If Virginia's oncamera histrionics still lacked polish, there was no doubt that she was already a prized piece of curvaceous decoration.

The film earned the actress advantageous coverage in fan magazines and an increase in salary. (Without disclosing actual figures, Miss Mayo merely states that Goldwyn was paying her "thousands" of dollars by the time they parted company.) She adds that the producer was "tight" with money but defends him by saying: "He was the only producer who ever used his own money to finance his films, so you've got to know he was tight." She ignores all the virulence that has been heaped upon the man, for to her way of thinking he was a "darling" altruist. "He and Mrs. Goldwyn were really devoted to developing me as a star; they were like father and mother to me."

She was next cast opposite Danny Kaye—the position for which she was originally taken to Hollywood. With Kaye, it was inevitable that whoever his co-star happened to be, she would be his "fall girl," straight woman," or the less complimentary tag of "stooge." In *Wonder Man* (1945) she is Ellen Shanley, a non-bespectacled librarian whose boyfriend is Edwin Dingle (Kaye). He is a scholarly fellow *with spectacles* whose only claim to fame is having a twin brother named Buzzy Bellew (also Kaye), a nightclub entertainer who is bumped off by unsavory friends. Buzzy's ghost enters Edwin's existence and persuades him to fill in for him. Ellen is naturally bewildered by the erratic change in Edwin and breaks off their relationship when Buzzy's spirit spurs him on to flirt with a nightclub dancer (Vera-Ellen). Edwin ultimately regains his identity, along with Ellen, and it is presumed they will lead the quiet, solemn lives of two bookworms in love.

Virginia did not "sing" in this release, nor did she have the opportunity to wear dressy costumes. A short time after the film's release she told Len Wallace of *Picturegoer*

With Danny Kaye in *Wonder Man* ('45).

magazine, "Playing the straight woman for comedians is great experience for a girl with ambitions—well, let's say of a higher nature. . . . Working with comedians like Kaye and Hope taught me timing, pace, and lots of fine points of acting that I would never have learned otherwise."

Continuing to support the popular Kaye, but at the same time adding to her own growing popularity, Virginia was a singer named Polly Pringle in Goldwyn's *The Kid from Brooklyn* (1946). Also in the cast were two other Goldwyn contractees, Vera-Ellen and Steve Cochran. From the film's title it could be assumed that Kaye is either a baseball player, a gunslinger, a matador, or a prizefighter. It develops that he is the latter, but not by his own design. Polly is the loyal, understanding girlfriend of milkman Burleigh Sullivan (Kaye), and she remains faithful through his misadventures as a champion prizefighter. She is finally able to persuade him to join her in matrimony and face the future together in the dairy business. (If the plotline seems familiar, it had been used before, as Paramount's *The Milky Way* [1936] starring Harold Lloyd and Dorothy Wilson.)

Virginia "sang" two songs in this film (dubbed by Betty Russell), causing Bosley Crowther to agree in his *New York Times* review that she possessed "not unaccelerating charms." She had definitely become Goldwyn's answer to pinup queen Betty Grable, the number one attraction at Twentieth Century-Fox.

Mayo had begun her third Danny Kaye co-starring film, *The Secret Life of Walter Mitty* (1947), based on a James Thurber short story, when she learned that Goldwyn planned to film MacKinlay Kantor's *Glory for Me*. She had read the novel and pictured herself in the role of Marie Derry, a war bride whose promiscuity and love of luxury prevent her from remaining with her G.I. husband when he returns from the war. Anxious to deviate from the "straight woman" mold into which she had been trapped, she asked Goldwyn for the part. He replied sagaciously, "Not a nice girl like you."

Instantly her ambitious nature came to the fore. By recruiting the help of studio workers, she posed for come-hither stills at a neighborhood bar, wearing a tight-fitting, low-bodiced costume with a saucy, feathered hat atop a restyled hairdo. When she placed the revealing stills on Goldwyn's desk, he immediately sent for the film's director, William Wyler. "If she can look like that," he told the director, "I know from her past work and the nerve she's got that she can act the part." Virginia was given the assignment and worked on both pictures simultaneously, with little time left over for anything but eating and sleeping.

The Wyler-directed motion picture, released before the Thurber adaptation, was distributed on November 22, 1946, as *The Best Years of Our Lives* and was to become the number one box-office bonanza of 1947. (It grossed $11.5 million in its first year, according to *Variety*.) For the first time in her movie career, Virginia's name, in fifth billing, appeared above a film's title.

This gripping, bitter-sweet, 172-minute movie relates the story of three World War II servicemen who return to their mid-America homes at war's end and deals with their many adjustments to civilian life. Fredric March stars as Al Stephenson, a former banker, with a wife (Myrna Loy) and two grown children (Teresa Wright and Michael Hall) who find that his attitudes on life have drastically changed. A second returning veteran is an amputee sailor (Harold Russell) who must condition his family to accept him as normal in spite of the mechanical hands the Navy has given him. The third is Air Force captain Fred Derry (Dana Andrews) who had hastily married Marie (Virginia), a pretty but garish showgirl, before he was sent into action. He has a difficult time locating his wife when he returns home, although his father (Roman Bohnen) and stepmother (Gladys George) tell him that she has gone back to work. He covers every nightspot in town (and there are many), but he cannot find her. Meanwhile he gets drunk and runs into the Stephensons who are seeing the town. The daughter Peggy (Wright) takes a

With Vera-Ellen in *The Kid from Brooklyn* ('46).

With Victor Cutler, Teresa Wright, and Dana Andrews in *The Best Years of Our Lives* ('46).

shine to him. The next day he finds Marie who seems genuinely glad to see him, but it soon becomes obvious that she is mostly impressed with his officer's uniform. Once he has discarded that for civvies, her enthusiasm wanes and when his only work opportunity proves to be that of a soda jerk, she finds him disgusting and weak. Insisting that she cannot survive on his meager $65 weekly salary, she continues working (we never see her at her job). There she meets many men and becomes especially interested in a smoothie named Cliff (Steve Cochran). The marriage dissolves when Fred returns home too early one day and finds Marie and Cliff together. She spits out her dissatisfaction with him and voices her intention to obtain a divorce. Fred knew that the breakup was inevitable, but he is heartened now with the realization that he may perhaps have a chance for happiness with Peggy.

The critics unanimously praised the prestige film. James Agee in *The Nation* wrote, "This is one of the very few American studio-made movies in years that seems to me profoundly pleasing, moving and encouraging." *Variety* labeled it "compelling," while Howard Barnes of the *New York Herald-Tribune* found it to be "a work of provocative and moving insistence and beauty." Louella Parsons, in *Cosmopolitan* magazine, praised Goldwyn by ranking the film as "one of his most distinguished productions and definitely one of the best in the matter of production, performance, and direction." Miss Parsons also singled out Virginia's work: "I simply marveled at the brassy effectiveness of [her] work as Dana's cheap, chorus-girl wife. I never dreamed such a pretty creature as Virginia could be that dramatic. I never dreamed either that she could act, but I know now that she can."*

On March 13, 1947, at the Shrine Auditorium in Los Angeles, *The Best Years of Our*

---

*On December 17, 1975, ABC-TV would telecast a modernized version of *The Best Years of Our Lives* called *Returning Home,* with Sherry Jackson in the role created by Virginia and with Tom Selleck as the husband.

With Gordon Jones and Danny Kaye in *The Secret Life of Walter Mitty* ('47).

Lives accumulated seven Academy Awards (out of a total of eight nominations). Although Virginia says that she did not expect a Supporting Actress nomination for her excellent work as Marie, she recalls that John Huston told her that her performance was of "Oscar caliber." In all modesty, she believes that she was overlooked "probably because 'they' figured Wyler was such a great director that he did that for me—I didn't do it; he did it with me."

All during these Goldwyn years of filmmaking, Virginia had been in love with actor Michael O'Shea. Finally he was able to obtain a divorce from his wife Grace (they were the parents of two grown children). On July 5, 1947, Virginia and Mike exchanged wedding vows in a Protestant ceremony at The Little Church of the Flowers at Forest Lawn Cemetery in Glendale, California. She was twenty-six; Mike was forty-one. She wore a street-length gown especially designed for the occasion by costumer Irene Sharaff; it was a pale gray chiffon over pale pink satin. After a reception held at the groom's home on Magnolia Boulevard in Van Nuys, the couple settled down with a honeymoon postponed due to Virginia's busy production schedule. She was at work at the time in the Howard Hawks-directed remake of *Ball of Fire* (1941), entitled *A Song Is Born* (1948). Virginia was not only unable to leave filmmaking for a vacation, but she remembers that Hawks was angry that she had married. The actress recalls that he snorted, "How can she devote her time to the script when she's just gotten married?"

The Secret Life of Walter Mitty was finally released by RKO on July 15, 1947. This time around the credits listed Virginia's name directly below Danny Kaye's and *above* the title. (Previously, in the Kaye pictures, her name was prefaced with the word "with" and appeared beneath the film's title.) In *The Secret Life of Walter Mitty* she is a beauteous creature who appears in all eight of the hero's (Kaye) daydreams, in which he imagines himself in such roles as a Mississippi

With Richard Lane, George Brent, Carole Landis, and Turhan Bey in *Out of the Blue* ('47).

riverboat gambler, an RAF hero, a celebrated surgeon, and a sea captain. She also is seen in a "real" setting when on a commuter train she seeks him out as a protective covering from a spy who is pursuing her. She is Rosalind, the niece of Peter Van Hoorn (Konstantin Shayne), a Dutch immigrant who controls lost art treasures. The gang seeking the booty is headed by Dr. Hollingshead (Boris Karloff) and "The Boot," a notorious Dutch traitor. Mitty falls in love with Rosalind and is unwittingly swept into the mystery. It develops that Rosalind's real uncle has been murdered and that "The Boot" has been impersonating the dead man. In this entry, Virginia modeled the most attractive costumes of her career, outfits designed by Irene Sharaff.

At Eagle-Lion studios, next door to the Goldwyn lot, and operated by a group of independent producers, Virginia co-starred with George Brent in *Out of the Blue* (1947). As Deborah Tyler she creates a supposedly comedic marital situation between a husband (Brent) and his wife (Carole Landis) when she is discovered in an unconscious condition in their Greenwich Village apartment. Cute as the film tries to be, it did nothing to further Virginia's career, nor did it succeed in concealing Brent's progress toward portliness and middle age.

In 1947 a group known as The Affiliated Joneses of Jonesport, Maine, advised Sam Goldwyn that they intended to boycott Virginia's pictures unless she resumed the surname of Jones. Obviously, Goldwyn chose to ignore the threat. That same year she was the recipient of three honors: the Master Hairdressers' Association of Southern California announced that she had a perfect head of hair, while the Whistling Teachers' Institute of America voted her "the girl most likely to be whistled at in 1947." The third distinction was bestowed upon her by the Hosiery Designers of America who placed her at the top of the list of Hollywood girls with the shapeliest legs. That same year it was announced that Virginia would star with

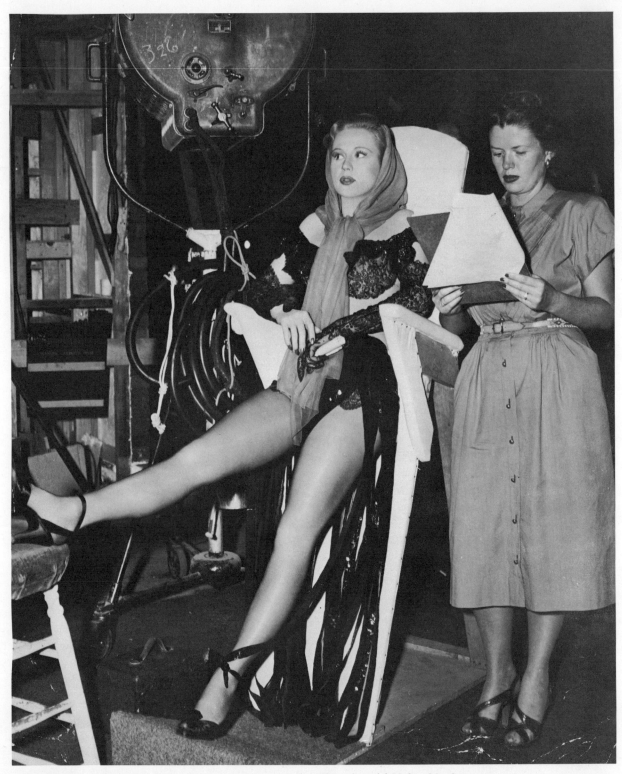

On the set of *A Song Is Born* ('48) with script girl Helen MacSweeney.

Dana Andrews in a loan-out to Warner Bros. for the mystery *The Unsuspected*. The deal did not work out, however, and the suspense film was shot with Joan Caulfield in the feminine lead and with Hurd Hatfield as the romantic interest.

A Song Is Born was not released until August 1948, and it would prove to be Virginia's fifth and final film with Danny Kaye (a situation that pleased Kaye's camp, especially his songwriter wife Sylvia Fine, who felt that too much attention was being paid to Mayo in their joint pictures). Virginia assumed the part played in the 1941 version by Barbara Stanwyck. However, the original character name of Sugarpuss O'Shea now becomes Honey Swanson. This role is pretty much intact from the earlier edition, in that she begins the story as the lady friend of a notorious gambler (Steve Cochran). She is a shapely nightclub singer, filled with woman's intuition and the knowledge of jazz. Because of this latter quality she is employed by Professor Hobart Frisbee (Kaye) and his six sober-faced associates who are anxious to study the evolution of modern jazz. Through the course of their studies they encounter jazz greats like Louis Armstrong, Lionel Hampton, Tommy Dorsey, and Charlie Barnet, and the film dissolves into a succession of specialty acts. Honey Swanson manages to contribute one song ("Daddy-O") to the proceedings (with the soundtrack singing voice of Jeri Sullivan). When it comes time for Honey to return to her boyfriend, she declines, for she has become smitten with the eager-to-learn Frisbee.

In 1948, after five years on Goldwyn's payroll, Virginia was released from her contract. The only official words of explanation from Goldwyn were: "I'm not going to do any more pictures for the next few years that you will be suitable for." While she was unhappy with this decision, she had no option but to abide by it. She free-lanced for one film with producer Saul Elkins in a grade-B melodrama, *Smart Girls Don't Talk* (1948), distributed through Warner Bros. Shot in thirty days and directed by Richard Bare, it tells the story of a beautiful socialite (Virginia) who is intimidated by a racketeer (Bruce Bennett) into joining his ranks. Although effectively photographed by Ted McCord, Virginia's excursion into celluloid crime was hampered by "too much talk of a curiously inept sort" (*Variety*).

Nevertheless, Warner Bros. thought enough of her screen presence to give her a seven-year contract at a time when many of the studio's contract players were being dropped. It was explained to her that revised corporate policy was to include the production of more musicals in which it was calculated that she would prove to be a valuable asset. This interested Virginia, since she was eager to dance onscreen and had not had the opportunity to really do so while under contract to Goldwyn.* With her signing of the contract, it was verbally suggested that she was under consideration for the feminine lead in *The Fountainhead* (1949), but this did not work out for her, and Patricia Neal was the ultimate choice.

Virginia's first Warner Bros. contract film was *Flaxy Martin* (1949), again with the production/direction team of Elkins and Bare. In this gangster film, she had the title role as a moll who hires an attorney (Zachary Scott) earmarked for framing on a gangland murder rap. Both Flaxy and her underworld boyfriend (Douglas Kennedy) are later exposed by the attorney's investigation. *Photoplay*'s Elsa Branden observed, "Apparently it's Virginia Mayo's lot to play dizzy, deceitful dames."

Colorado Territory (1949), her first Western, was filmed near Gallup, New Mexico. It was directed by Raoul Walsh** who had helmed *High Sierra* (1941) with Ida Lupino and Humphrey Bogart, the original version of this remake. Virginia has the role of Colorado Carson, a half-breed gunslinger.

---

*Her comment today regarding this aspect is: "He [Goldwyn] had Vera-Ellen. Who could compare with her—one of the best dancers who ever lived?"

**Joel McCrea would reminisce years later about *Colorado Territory*, Virginia Mayo, and director Raoul Walsh: ". . . [Walsh] got along real well with her. He'd use Mayo when other directors, like Wyler, didn't think she was any good; when she was under contract to Goldwyn, Wyler had to use her in *The Best Years of Our Lives.* Anyway, Walsh liked her. He would do things, like he had a silent shot with her looking after me when I was escaping at the end there, after we had been married in the church. He'd say, 'We'll shoot this silent. . . . All right, Virginia, you see him going. Wes is leaving, you'll never see him again, they may kill him. . . . All right, all right, now take after him, run, get out of there, run, you hear they're serving free drinks around the corner. . . .' She'd be going great and, hell, when she heard 'they're serving free drinks around the corner she fell apart. She'd say, 'Raoul, you break me up, you can't do that. . . .'"

In *A Song Is Born* with Danny Kaye.

With Bruce Bennett in *Smart Girls Don't Talk* ('48).

With Zachary Scott and Douglas Kennedy in *Flaxy Martin* ('49).

With Joel McCrea in *Colorado Territory* ('49).

When train robber Wes McQueen (Joel McCrea) is sprung from prison by confederates, he intends to go straight and return to the arms of his sweetheart (Dorothy Malone). Fate twists his life, however, and he meets Colorado Carson, a tough dame who falls for and protects him. He becomes involved in one final big train robbery with Colorado at his side, but the lawmen have been forewarned by his ex-love and his former confederates, and the train is loaded with deputies. Wes is wounded during the fracas, but Colorado manages to help him climb up a mountainside where they are both shot to death.

Len Wallace reported in *Picturegoer,* "In tackling this wild and woolly part, Virginia follows several notable ladies of the screen, two of whom are Paulette Goddard and the voluptuous Jane Russell. What she now requires is as much subsequent success as Miss Goddard and as little unfortunate publicity as the luckless Jane."

Mayo's next film, *The Girl from Jones Beach* (1949), was critiqued by *Motion Picture* magazine as "light, amusing fare for a summer's evening." It represented Virginia's* first "big" production at Warner Bros., although she was still not asked to dance. Instead she decoratively filled the bathing suits and frocks designed for the black-and-white film by Leah Rhodes. Commercial artist Bob Randolph (Ronald Reagan) is the creator of "The Randolph Girl," who epitomizes all that is lush and lovely in young American pinup girldom. A promoter, Chuck Donovan (Eddie Bracken), would like the model to appear on a television show, and he approaches Randolph with the scheme. As a result, he learns that not one but twelve girls provided the basis for Randolph's sketchboard creation. Undaunted, because the idea means money in his pocket, Donovan hopes to find one young miss who can come

*Lauren Bacall had rejected the role.

With Ronald Reagan, Eddie Bracken, and Dona Drake promoting *The Girl from Jones Beach* ('49).

close to all that the artist has depicted. At Jones Beach, the two fellows spot curvaceous Ruth Wilson (Virginia) who is all they can want. However, she is unimpressed with them and goes about her own business—which is teaching American history to immigrants preparing for citizenship at adult night school. Randolph enrolls in her class as a Czech immigrant (complete with accent), and they eventually fall in love.

This assembly-line film was awarded two and a half stars by *Motion Picture* magazine and criticized by the *New York Times* for its "noticeably low" humor. Two items that might have bolstered the film's success would have been the use of Technicolor and a more original script than the one presented by I. A. L. Diamond.

By mid-1949, along with moviemaking, Michael O'Shea was doing volunteer work as a detective with the sheriff's department of Van Nuys, California. One of his co-workers, and his best friend, was James Dougherty, the first husband of Marilyn Monroe. O'Shea, who had come from a family of policemen, had had the lifelong dream of following in his relatives' footsteps, but his height (5'8") prevented him from doing so.

Virginia was next loaned to Roy Del Ruth for his production of *Red Light* (1949), released through United Artists. She was little more than decoration in this bizarre, religiously oriented tale of revenge and violence, in the role of Carla North, girlfriend to businessman-trucker John Torno (George Raft). When the latter's brother (Arthur Franz) is murdered, she at first tries to persuade strong and stocky Torno to let the police handle the case alone. When he refuses to stay out of the matter, she aids and abets him, mostly by trailing after him throughout much of the film. The picture's title derives from the force that stops him from seeking full revenge—the Bible.

At this low professional juncture, Virginia was fortunately cast opposite James Cagney in a film that has become a classic in the genre of paranoid gangster portraits. In Raoul Walsh's *White Heat* (1949), made at Warner Bros., she gives her best piece of dramatic acting as the cheap, flirting, disloyal Verna Jarrett, wife of the cruel, vile Arthur Cody Jarrett (Cagney). Cody's real love and his inspiration is his aged mother (Margaret Wycherly); his father had gone insane and died in an asylum.

Cody works for the Trader (Fred Clark), a slick San Diego "businessman" who trades the American dollars, stolen by Cody and his gang, to foreign syndicates. When Cody returns home after one job, he is upset because his ma is out shopping. Verna snarls sarcastically, "You like strawberries, don't ya? Well, she just had to get some for *her* boy." Later when the cops close in on Cody, he gives himself up on a lesser heist, one he did not commit, in order to avoid prosecution for the big job. In prison he befriends Vic Pardo (Edmond O'Brien), an undercover Treasury agent assigned to obtain the truth on Cody through their association.

Although Verna informs Cody, "I'll be waitin' for ya, Honey; you can trust me," she soon becomes buddies with Big Ed Somers (Steve Cochran) during Cody's absence. When a pal (Paul Guilfoyle) of Big Ed's foils an attempt to kill Cody in prison, Ma visits her son and tells him that she will put a stop to Verna and Ed's association. Offcamera Verna shoots Ma in the back, and Cody goes mad on learning that his beloved mother is dead. He arranges an escape with Pardo, and they seek out Ed and Verna.

Before his expected arrival, Verna becomes frightened, and she pleads with Ed to run: "I can't stand another night, Ed, listenin', goin' crazy. It ain't just like waitin' for some human bein' who wants t'kill ya. Cody ain't human; fill him full o' lead and he'll still come at ya."

Cody makes his appearance, but he believes Verna's tale that it was Ed who had shot Ma. He in turns kills Ed. Verna saves her own life by vowing love for Cody, thankfully accepting the comic books he supplies for her diversion. The gang's next assigned job is the heist of the $425,000 payroll from a Long Beach chemical plant. During the operation, Vic's real identity as T-Man Hank Fallon is discovered, but he manages to es-

With Lois Wilson on the set of *The Girl from Jones Beach*.

Advertisement for *Red Light* ('49).

214

With Margaret Wycherly and James Cagney in *White Heat* ('49).

cape as hordes of police surround the plant. Verna is apprehended and pleads to no avail with the law to free her. While she is being escorted to jail, Cody is shot by Fallon as he stands high among the chemical tanks which explode and send him skyward.

Bosley Crowther termed Virginia's performance "excellent," while Hedda Hopper commented that through the auspices of *White Heat* Virginia was "uncovered as a real actress." Miss Hopper felt further that she showed "signs of making a serious bid for stardom" in 1950.

Virginia's busiest cinematic year culminated with the release of *Always Leave Them Laughing* (1949), her sixth film of the season. Designed to capitalize on the popularity of television comic Milton Berle, the story is told in flashback of the rise to success of Kip Cooper (Berle), a loud-mouthed barker at Asbury Park. Virginia plays Nancy Egan, a Broadway showgirl whose husband (Bert Lahr) becomes ill and is unable to perform in his show. She dispassionately arranges for Cooper to take his place and imagines that the two of them will become a team. However, he outwits her and goes on to make it to the top on his own. Virginia sang in this movie, her first musical since leaving Goldwyn, but the soundtrack voice was that of Bonnie Lou Williams. Although possessing a cliché-riddled script and lots of corn, the picture was well attended by those Berle fans who were willing to forsake the small screen for their neighborhood movie theatres.

While Doris Day was singing and dancing her way across the Warner Bros. lot, the new decade began inauspiciously for Virginia (although her professional standing was far higher than that of her husband). She was next featured in *Backfire* (1950) with Gordon MacRae and Edmond O'Brien, although Viveca Lindfors had the top-billed spot. Mayo plays nurse Julie Benson who joins her boyfriend Bob Corey (MacRae) in his search for his buddy (O'Brien) who has disappeared and is accused of murdering a gam-

With Milton Berle in *Always Leave Them Laughing* ('49).

With Charles Lane and Gordon MacRae in *Backfire* ('50).

bler (Dane Clark). They engage in various romantic interludes en route, but finally discover that the pal had been kidnapped by the gangster who is now posing as an undertaker. The film did little for anyone's career.

In her first Warner Bros. Technicolor film, *The Flame and the Arrow* (1950), Virginia was asked to do little more than appear absolutely gorgeous, something that required little effort on her part. It is Burt Lancaster who has the athletic focal role in this movie set in medieval Italy. He plays Dardo (also known as The Arrow), a mountaineer who pits his skills and forces against the tyrannical Alessandro (Robert Douglas) and Ulrich (Frank Allenby). The latter, known as The Hawk, hopes to use his Hessians to enslave all of northern Italy. Written by Waldo Salt, the film began on the drawing boards as *The Hawk and the Arrow,* but this title was changed to guarantee recognition for Virginia who was "The Flame."

It was in *The West Point Story* (1950) that Warner Bros. finally allowed Virginia the chance to dance onscreen. The Roy Del Ruth-directed vehicle also reunited her with James Cagney. She plays Eve Dillon, assistant to musical producer Elwin Bixby (Cagney) who adores her. When Bixby accepts the assignment to stage a show at West Point Military Academy, she accompanies him and adds considerably to the revue through song* and dance. For her labors of love, *Time* magazine observed that Virginia "fills her tights admirably."

Her second Western film, described by Bosley Crowther of the *New York Times* as "routine" and "second grade," was *Along the Great Divide* (1951) opposite Kirk Douglas. She is Ann Keith, the daughter of "Pop" (Walter Brennan) who has been falsely accused of murdering the son of a rancher (Morris Ankrum). U.S. Marshal Clint Merrick (Douglas) interrupts the lynching of "Pop" and begins a journey with the old

---

*Her voice was again dubbed by Bonnie Lou Williams who would do all of Virginia's singing in ensuing musicals.

With James Cagney in *The West Point Story* ('50).

217

man to a town where he can receive a fair trial. Along the way they encounter Ann who vainly attempts to rescue her dad. Love develops between the girl and the law enforcer, and the final verdict, after miles of open country tribulations, is that the rancher's son was killed by his own brother (James Anderson). As the picture ends, Ann, Merrick, and "Pop" are seen riding toward a future of unmarried bliss.

"Lux Radio Theatre," sponsored by Lever Brothers, first entered Virginia's career on May 28, 1951, when she was heard in the role of Margaret Jane in an hour's condensation of *Bright Leaf*. Her radio co-stars were Gregory Peck and Ruth Roman. (Patricia Neal had been Margaret Jane in the 1950 Warner Bros. picture.)

Virginia had already been assigned to play the dramatic lead in *Lightning Strikes Twice* (1951) opposite Richard Todd and Zachary Scott, but the studio altered her schedule when a British actress failed to impress the studio in test scenes for *Captain Horatio Hornblower* (1951). Ruth Roman took over for Mayo in *Lightning Strikes Twice,* and Virginia was shipped to Elstree Studios in Britain to play Lady Barbara opposite Gregory Peck, who had the title role in *Captain Horatio Hornblower.* Prior to her arrival in England, and without Virginia's knowledge, British Equity staged a fight to prevent her from gaining a Labour Permit, asserting: "To put U.S. stars in the lead in films which set out to portray the British way of life or have some peculiar British quality destroys such character as our industry still possesses." British Equity further pointed out that Virginia "has a terrific accent." There was no objection to Peck's assignment to portray the C. S. Forester hero due to his "international status and because the film must have at least one American star to give it selling power in the American market." The Ministry of Labour ignored Equity's protest, and a work permit was granted to Warner Bros. on behalf of their blonde star.

Directed by Raoul Walsh, the screen story was adapted by Ivan Goff, Ben Roberts, and Aeneas MacKenzie from Forester's novel bearing the same title. *Captain Horatio Hornblower* is a man's action picture, set during the Napoleonic wars when men of the sea were typically separated from their wives and sweethearts for months—even years—at a stretch. Once it is established in the storyline that the lovely Lady Barbara Wellsley (Virginia) is causing the heart of the man in her life (Dennis O'Dea) to beat faster, he is packed off to engage in lusty sea battles while she waits at home. They are eventually reunited while she is a passenger aboard Hornblower's 38-gun frigate "Lydia." During this traumatic voyage she changes costumes some eighteen times, all of which were designed to enrich the audience's appreciation of cleavage. When her intended, Rear Admiral Sir Rodney Leighton (O'Dea), is killed by French artillery, it is concluded that she is destined to become the Captain's lady.

Look magazine credited Virginia with maneuvering her role "with as much ease and good humor as her less aristocratic movie assignments" (i.e., *White Heat, The West Point Story*). That was quite a compliment, considering the turgid dialogue Mayo had to cope with in this sea epic.

> *Mayo:* How beautiful the stars are tonight. It's as if I were sailing the heavens and not the seas. . . . On a night like this I could forget who I am.
>
> *Mayo (to Gregory Peck):* Is that what you want—a quick passage?
> *Peck:* Every captain wants a quick passage.
> *Mayo:* I don't want a quick [passage]. . . . I don't want the voyage to end.

On the night before the "Lydia" lands at Plymouth, the couple meet and embrace beneath deck.

> *Mayo:* Oh, my love.
> *Peck:* Barbara, Barbara.
> *Mayo:* My dear. . . . my sweet.
> *Peck:* What are we to do.
> *Mayo:* We are lovers and the world's ours.

With Robert Beatty, Gregory Peck, and Terence Morgan in *Captain Horatio Hornblower* ('51).

With Lucille Norman and Virginia Gibson in *Painting the Clouds with Sunshine* ('51).

In 1951 the O'Sheas, with a cowboy partner, purchased a 6,000-acre ranch near Mammoth, Arizona, where they grew cotton in abundance and, among other things, corn. They continued to live in Van Nuys and left the ranch management in the hands of their partner, who was soon more interested in pursuing a rodeo career. (Less than two years later the ranch was sold.) Also in 1951, columnist Sidney Skolsky wisely observed, "Virginia Mayo should be given the Betty Grable treatment. She's pinup bait." In July 1951, Hollywood sculptor Yucca Salamunich claimed that Virginia possessed one of the nation's sexiest pair of shoulder blades. In this distinction she edged out such other Yucca contenders as Jean Wallace, Faye Emerson, Janet Leigh, and the race horse Citation. On the charity circuit, Virginia modeled Don Loper's creation at the Damon Runyon Cancer Fund dinner dance at the Ambassador Hotel and helped net $6,000 for the cause. That same year it was revealed that Virginia could not cook. "No talent in the kitchen," she admitted. "My husband very patiently tries to teach me how to cook."

In *Painting the Clouds with Sunshine* (1951), she danced as never before onscreen. Based on the Avery Hopwood play *Gold Diggers of Broadway*, it is a remake of *Gold Diggers of 1933*, the Warner Bros. musical which starred Joan Blondell, Ruby Keeler, and Aline MacMahon as the three chorines who sought husbands. Virginia, Lucille Norman, and Virginia Gibson took over the characterizations in this Technicolor updated version. Virginia is Carol Dillon (played by Blondell in 1933), the wisecracking member of the sister act. She covets a rich husband and eventually finds him in the person of Tom Conway, the older brother of her dance partner (Gene Nelson). An especially "hot" dance number performed by Virginia and Nelson is "Mambo Man" which involved a combination of rumba and jitterbug to a rhythmic Latin beat. Also in the cast is Dennis Morgan (at the time one of Warner Bros.' highest paid actors) who is Miss Norman's catch as a husband.

Wearing a sarong, Virginia did a languorous South Seas native dance in *Starlift* (1951) as her contribution to the film which was "guested" by such other studio contractees as Doris Day, James Cagney, Gary Cooper, and Jane Wyman. As is customary with these star-drenched revues, the story is shallow, and the only thing that makes the time pass quickly is the appearance of movie favorites in "candid" sequences. Created to tout Hollywood's "Operation Starlift" whose objectives included sending movie stars to entertain troops in Korea, the film was released a month after the ill-funded project folded.

At Hollywood's First Presbyterian Church in May 1952, Virginia participated in a religious play, *Christ on Trial*, in which she played Mary of Bethany. Another glamorous screen actress, Rhonda Fleming, portrayed The Woman of Samaria.

Reunited with Ronald Reagan and Gene Nelson, Virginia was given top billing in *She's Working Her Way Through College* (1952) in the role of "Hot Garters Gertie," a burlesque queen who decides to improve her mind with college courses. Her professor is John Palmer (Reagan) whose wife (Phyllis Thaxter) becomes a mite concerned. Actually all Gertie wants is to learn and to perform in the campus musical, which she does with Gene Nelson. The film was a revamping of the play/movie *The Male Animal*.

After three successive films in which she danced, Virginia was handed a dramatic role in *The Iron Mistress* (1952) as Judalon, a beautiful, fickle, worthless Creole belle. She is adored by Jim Bowie (Alan Ladd) whose enemies are many because of his attachment for her. His love for the woman is manifest when she asks him, "What do you think I am —a Bayou woman to be carried off at the first kiss?" He kisses her and she slaps him. He later tells a friend, "I want her enough to bet the day will come when she wants me." However, he soon tires of her tantrums and moods and treks from New Orleans to Texas where he weds the governor's daughter (Phyllis Kirk) and where he will eventually die at the battle of the Alamo. Although the

With Rhonda Fleming (right) in the play *Christ on Trial* at the Hollywood First Presbyterian Church (May 1952).

With Alan Ladd and Alf Kjellin in *The Iron Mistress* ('52).

film was prefaced with the words "Historical Truth Is Sometimes Stranger Than Fiction," there is a great deal of fiction in Bowie's filmed life story.

With Steve Cochran—who finally had achieved major status—Virginia was co-starred in *She's Back on Broadway* (1953). The film's original title of *Back to Broadway* was altered to include the word "She's" with the hope of inducing Virginia's fans into believing it was a sequel to *She's Working Her Way Through College*. It was not a sequel. Shot in WarnerColor, it was the story of Catherine Terris (Virginia) a one-time Hollywood star who has plummeted on the popularity scale. With the backing of producer John Webber (Frank Lovejoy) she hopes to gain renewed stature through a Broadway musical. The director of the venture is her old flame Rick Sommers (Cochran). It seems that she deserted him some years before when she had the chance for a film career, and he, of course, has never forgiven her. Therefore, he is most reluctant to play the patsy a second time. After several quarrels and walk-outs by both star and director, the show finally gets under way. They fall in love all over again, and she realizes that personal happiness is more important than a show business career. With Gene Nelson she again danced and "sang."

Virginia next was cast opposite Burt Lancaster for a second time in *South Sea Woman* (1953) which provided jobs for a large cast. However, it was a waste of time insofar as both Virginia's and Lancaster's careers were concerned. The story concerned two marines (Lancaster and Chuck Connors) who go AWOL during World War II and land on a South Pacific island with Ginger Martin (Virginia), a showgirl who has gone astray.

In her first loanout in four years, Virginia went to RKO for *Devil's Canyon* (1953), originally entitled *Arizona Outpost*, in which she reverts to dramatics as Abby Nixon, a bandit sent to an all-male prison in the Old West of the 1890s. There she meets fellow convict

Advertisement for *She's Back on Broadway* ('53).

With Burt Lancaster in *South Sea Woman* ('53).

Jesse Gorman (Stephen McNally), a scoundrel whose purpose in life centers upon seeking revenge for the death of his brothers, shot by Billy Reynolds (Dale Robertson), an ex-marshal. She likes Gorman until she is made aware of Billy's charms, and then she assists him in squelching a prison escape led by Gorman.

This film, shot in 3-D, was found by *Photoplay* to contain "some thrills," but "the prison's alleged toughness is never shown convincingly, and Virginia is hampered by over-genteel dialogue."

By mid-1953, movie audiences were often guilty of confusing Virginia with other Hollywood blondes. However, her staunch followers *knew* the difference between her and Marilyn Maxwell, for example, and one movie fan got through the ropes at a Hollywood premiere one night to exude, "You look like a *young* Zsa Zsa Gabor." (Virginia was then thirty-three, while Zsa Zsa was "about" thirty.) Michael O'Shea, always quick with a quip, added, "And whom do I look like—an *old* George Sanders?"

It was during the shooting of *Devil's Canyon* that Virginia learned she was pregnant. After the announcement was made public, O'Shea stated, "Virginia's going to stay home and rest. That's where a pregnant woman belongs. At home. Not working her head off, or chasing all over town. It's dangerous."

On November 12, 1953, at Santa Monica's St. John's Hospital, Mary Catherine O'Shea was born. Weighing seven pounds, three ounces, she seemed a bundle of freckles. Fan magazine writers covered the birth, but O'Shea forbade photographs of the baby, saying: "This is not going to be a three-ring circus. She's going to be treated like any other normal human being."

With Laurence Harvey in *King Richard and the Crusaders* ('54).

With Jack Palance in *The Silver Chalice* ('54).

Virginia returned to the screen after an absence of eleven months as Lady Edith in *King Richard and the Crusaders* (1954). This CinemaScope, color version of Sir Walter Scott's *The Talisman* was a dramatic embarrassment and scarcely sufficed as action fare. In it Mayo is a cousin to King Richard I, the Lionhearted (George Sanders), and betrothed to the Scottish knight Sir Kenneth (Laurence Harvey). However, she is whisked off into the desert by the armies of Italy, France, and Austria which hope to stop Richard's crusading. Meanwhile Richard's life has been threatened by an associate (Robert Douglas), but the blame is focused on Sir Kenneth who must hide in the desert. There he is retrieved by Saladin (Rex Harrison, of all people), the Saracen chief. Eventually Saladin joins Richard's troops in freeing Lady Edith from the evil hordes. The film is talky, flawed, and dull. Mr. Harrison's fear of horses provided several tense moments for Virginia who prayed that the horse he "rode," on which she was carried with tied hands, would not eject its passengers.

Warner Bros. planned to star Virginia in *Helen of Troy,* a story adapted from Homer's *Iliad,* but she recalls that the director (who was ultimately Robert Wise) could not visualize her in the role. *Helen of Troy,* in CinemaScope and WarnerColor, reached motion picture screens ("at a cost of $6,000,000") in 1955, but it starred Rossana Podesta as Helen, supported by an international cast.

Instead, Virginia took the role of Helena in what should have been a good film. However, *The Silver Chalice* (1954), aside from introducing Paul Newman to filmgoers, was a long dragged-out affair (144 minutes). In widescreen and color, it was produced and directed by Victor Saville and loosely derived from Thomas B. Costain's novel. In the would-be epic, Helena (Virginia in exotic eye makeup) is the assistant to Simon the Sorcerer (Jack Palance) who hopes to overthrow the Roman rulers of Jerusalem. Into the biblical scene comes Basil (Newman), a sculptor and childhood friend of Helena's. He has been commissioned to design a chalice for the cup used by Jesus at the Last Supper some twenty years prior. The cup and chalice are later stolen, never to be retrieved. As for Simon, he thinks his magic is so strong that with only a few gimmicks he can pretend to fly, but he plummets to his death from atop a tower. A bewildered Helena is then without an employer, while Basil returns to the solitude of Christianity and the bosom of his wife (Pier Angeli). Otis L. Guernsey, Jr. *(New York Herald-Tribune)* called this meretricious embarrassment "a little theatre production of *Quo Vadis.*"

On loan to RKO for the modestly budgeted *Pearl of the South Pacific* (1955),* Virginia is not a woman named Pearl. The precious item of the title supposedly refers to the black gems existing on a Pacific isle. She is Rita, an adventuress who lures two men (Dennis Morgan and David Farrar) to the island to seek the pearls. There she raises the ardor of a native son (Lance Fuller), confronts an octopus eye-to-eye underwater, and concludes that she loves Morgan who makes an honest woman of her.

Remaining on loan to financially troubled RKO, she next played Ann Alaine, the proprietress of a ladies' dress shop in the Western frontier town of Denver during the Civil War, in *Great Day in the Morning* (1956). (This Jacques Tourneur-directed venture was shot in SuperScope and color.) The town is seemingly inhabited only by ultra-loyal Northerners and Southerners, but Dixie gambler Owen Pentecost (Robert Stack) leads a wagon train to the Confederacy containing two million dollars in gold. Also on hand are Raymond Burr as a gambling hall owner and Ruth Roman as his partner from Boston.

The one advantage *Congo Crossing* (1956) had was Technicolor, and even that was unable to raise the Universal film from adventure yarn mediocrity. A group of fugitives

---

*Years later director Allan Dwan would tell cinema historian/director Peter Bogdanovich, "Oh, that was a terrible picture. It should never have been done.... Everything went wrong on that. It was a mess. But a comedy to me. I was laughing all the way through it, and [producer Benedict] Bogeaus couldn't understand why I was amused, since it was a tragedy."

With Robert Stack and Alex Nicol in *Great Day in the Morning* ('56).

from justice congregate in the West African settlement of Congotanga where extradition laws are not observed. There Louise Whitman (Virginia) finds solace in the arms of David Carr (George Nader) while pint-sized, pudgy Colonel Arragas (Peter Lorre) stalks them.

At Twentieth Century-Fox Virginia starred in a Western when the sagebrush genre was enjoying a brief rejuvenation period. In *The Proud Ones* (1956), lensed in CinemaScope and color, she provides the obligatory love interest to Robert Ryan, a marshal whose life is not very safe.

Back at Warner Bros. where Natalie Wood was the young starlet on the rise, Virginia was in yet another Western, *The Big Land* (1957). As Helen, she says to Alan Ladd, "You're a strange man. Who are you, Morgan?" He drifts into a Kansas town as a cattle driver whose Texas herd gets only $1.50 a head on the market controlled by the evil Brog (Anthony Caruso). By befriending the town drunk, Jagger (Edmond O'Brien), who is also Helen's brother, Morgan plans to build a new town on the prairie. All goes well and the town is constructed. However, while Morgan is in Texas seeking new cattle, Brog threatens to run the cattle buyers out of town and Jagger is killed. When Morgan returns, Helen says, "What's the use? I don't care anymore. It isn't worth it, all the burnings, killings. I'm leaving this town and all its ugly memories." He professes his love for her and dispatches Brog with bullets, thus leaving the way clear for them to live peaceably.

Before Irwin Allen was to produce such money-making bonanzas as *The Poseidon Adventure* (1972) and *The Towering Inferno* (1974), he brought forth *The Story of Mankind* (1957), a jumbled mess featuring a great deal of offbeat casting. It was acceptable for Vincent Price to play the devil denouncing

In *Congo Crossing* ('56).

With Robert Ryan in *The Proud Ones* ('56).

With Helmut Dantine in *The Story of Mankind* ('57).

mankind in a heavenly tribunal and for Ronald Colman to portray the Spirit of Man who defends man's follies. But Groucho Marx as Peter Minuit? Harpo Marx as Isaac Newton? Marie Wilson as Marie Antoinette? Hedy Lamarr as Joan of Arc? Was Allen kidding? Virginia says "No! He was serious." She further admits, "I played, of all things, Cleopatra," and chuckles, "I was so rotten!" Although the film can now be enjoyed as "high camp," at the time of its release the *New York Times* stated: "It is the kind of pontification that any kid who has ever dozed through a history class has learned to see through."

Meanwhile, back in the saddle (at Allied Artists this time) in *The Tall Stranger* (1957), Virginia is aboard a wagon train headed across the Colorado territory when a tall cowboy (Joel McCrea) appears out of the dust to serve as escort and provide romance among the sage.

Virginia's final two jobs under her Warner Bros. pact were undistinguished Westerns. In the first, *Fort Dobbs* (1958), cast opposite Clint Walker (who had developed his physique but not any acting prowess), she is widow Celia Gray who, with her son (Richard Eyer), crosses the prairie to Fort Dobbs. En route they are rescued from a Comanche attack by suspected murderer Gar Davis (Walker). At the fort they find dead soldiers and a living sheriff (Russ Conway). As the Indians prepare to attack the fort again, Davis rides for help and returns in the nick of time to save Celia, her son, and the sheriff. According to polite *Variety,* "Miss Mayo has performed better, but she's still a fine-looking woman."

It was inevitable that Randolph Scott would be Virginia's co-star if she lingered long enough on the cinema Western trail. In *Westbound* (1959) she is Norma, a former girlfriend of John Hayes (Scott) but now married to Clay Putnam (Andrew Duggan). In Colorado during the Civil War, Hayes, a Union officer, reactivates the Overland Stage Lines to transport gold from California to Northern banks. The Confederates, headed by Clay, hope to stop the gold, but he is killed. Norma returns home while Hayes falls in love with Jeannie Miller (Karen Steele).

Virginia, nearly forty years old, was then set at liberty by Warner Bros. and forced to free-lance. She now reflects, "I probably should have had another few years at really gut kind of work at a studio in order to maintain a stronger position as an actress." Without comparing her acting abilities to those of Olivia de Havilland ("I was never the actress she was"), she does cite Olivia's success after leaving Warner Bros. as an example of what can happen if given the proper scripts and exposure, adding: "I do feel that I could have developed a little bit more with a couple more years at a studio, but at that time they started dropping all contracts—times were beginning to change."

Television, the medium partly responsible for the changes in Hollywood, provided work for Virginia in 1958 and 1959 when she guest-starred on "The Loretta Young Show," "Wagon Train," and "Lux Playhouse." In 1959 she and Michael O'Shea made a pilot for an ABC-TV series called "McGary and His Mouse," but the network, influenced by a sponsor, chose "The Donna Reed Show" (which went on to enjoy eight seasons of popularity) as its top situation-comedy presentation.

Smarting from this defeat, the O'Sheas considered the possibility of moving to New England where, as Mike put it, "I want to go into a business where you don't have to knuckle down to anyone and where you can speak the truth. Someplace with lots of cool weather. Everytime I go out into the sun I break out in skin cancer." They did not, however, leave California.

Although cast as a dancer in the low-budget *Jet Over the Atlantic* (1959), Virginia did not dance onscreen. Rather, she and a planeload of passengers have a lot to worry about as a bomb, hidden by George Macready, begins to emit deadly fumes which kill the pilot (Armando Saenz). Her boyfriend (Guy Madison), an escaped convicted murderer who is being returned to the United States from Madrid by an FBI agent (George

With Clint Walker in *Fort Dobbs* ('58).

With Randolph Scott and Andrew Duggan in *Westbound* ('59).

With Argentina Brunetti and Guy Madison in *Jet Over the Atlantic* ('59).

Raft!), is an ex-Air Force pilot. Thus it is he who lands the plane at New York's International Airport without mishap. Once on the ground, the police arrive with word that Madison had been framed on the homicide charge. Finally Virginia and Guy are free. (The "Madrid" scenes were filmed in Mexico City.)

Following the lead suit of many one-time American film names, Virginia next went to Italy and Spain for *La Rivolta Dei Mercenari (Revolt of the Mercenaries)* (1960), playing a duchess. The picture, although shown occasionally on television, was not put into general theatre release in the U.S. Virginia's voice was partially dubbed for this cloak-and-sandal entry because, as she says, "They pushed me back to the United States before I could finish the dubbing; they weren't going to pay my salary anymore."

During the late Fifties and early Sixties Mayo and O'Shea appeared together in several summer stock productions: *The Tunnel of Love, Fiorello,* and *George Washington Slept Here.* The husband-and-wife team proved to be an effective box-office attraction with theatre audiences.

After a period of semi-retirement from the movies, Virginia returned to film in A. C. Lyles' budget Western, *Young Fury* (1965), shot at Paramount. It was a mixed blessing to see Virginia once more onscreen, this time surrounded by other former big names, including Rory Calhoun (as her gunslinger husband), William Bendix (the blacksmith), Richard Arlen (the sheriff), and Lon Chaney, Jr. (the bartender).

The following year she went on location to the Caribbean for *Castle of Evil* (1966), released by United Picture Corporation. It is a lot of hooey about a wealthy eccentric (William Thourlby) who dies and leaves a will which is to be read in the presence of all those who were with him at the time of his death. Following the tried-and-true premise of *The Cat and the Canary*, several of the would-be beneficiaries are killed, including the doctor (David Brian) and the

With husband Michael O'Shea in Hollywood (July 1959).

With William Thourlby in *Castle of Evil* ('66).

housekeeper (Shelley Morrison), and there are attempts made on the life of Sable (Virginia), the dead millionaire's mistress. As it turns out the housekeeper was responsible. She admits before she dies that she programmed an electronic man to kill all the others so that she would inherit the full estate. It is engineer Matt Granger (beefy Scott Brady) who destroys the out-of-whack electronic man with a laser gun. *Variety* noted that Virginia is "excellent and deserves better than her current career in low budgeters."

However, professional luck was not with Virginia. She tested for the feminine lead in the CBS-TV comedy series "Green Acres," but the part went to Eva Gabor, who enjoyed six seasons of prime-time exposure (from its debut in September 1966), not to mention the healthy income from syndicated reruns.

In 1967 A. C. Lyles offered Virginia employment in another of his cheapie oaters, *Fort Utah*. In very lackluster terms the picture focused on the plight of a wagon train heading ever westward. As Linda Lee, Virginia is jaded and hard-bitten, but she possesses the ever-present heart of gold. Her co-"stars" included John Ireland, Scott Brady, James Craig, Richard Arlen, and Jim Davis.

Also in 1967 Virginia performed two weeks of summer stock in Illinois as Dolly Gallagher Levi in *Hello, Dolly!* This established a new career bent for Virginia, and thereafter she starred for eight months at the Thunderbird Hotel in Las Vegas in the musical *That Certain Girl*. From there she went on to star in *Forty Carats* and *Cactus Flower*, as her bookings took her across America. In September 1972, she replaced June Allyson in the San Francisco Civic Light Opera's production of *No, No, Nanette*. As Sue Smith, she played the part made famous in the Broadway revival by Ruby Keeler, and she ably demonstrated that she could still dance. She was then scheduled to

With John Ireland in *Fort Utah* ('67).

make a film—*Starcrossed*—for producer-director John Carr, but the project was abandoned.

In Dallas, Texas, on December 4, 1973, where Virginia was performing in a dinner theatre presentation of *Forty Carats*, Michael O'Shea suffered a fatal heart attack. He was sixty-seven. A year earlier, in Chicago, Virginia had told Mary Daniels of the *Chicago Tribune*, "I think you have to have some kind of partner in life. He's taught me a great deal. We've had a great deal of fun. My God, he's interesting and we get along great."

The University of Southern California's special collection department was the recipient in September 1974 of a collection of memorabilia documenting Virginia's acting career to date. She donated not only newspaper clips but scripts from her film, TV, and stage appearances, along with vintage movie magazines and photographs.

In July 1975 Virginia was offered the title role in Ted V. Mikel's proposed movie *The Mistress of Castle Reigh*, opposite Cesar Romero, but this project did not materialize. Two months later she accepted a spot in Paramount's *Won Ton Ton, the Dog Who Saved Hollywood* (1976). It was one of those ventures which hinged on garnering a lot of publicity by casting one-time name personalities in cameo roles. In support of "Gus," a large German shepherd dog, Virginia played a nondescript secretary to studio mogul Art Carney. Others in the film included Joan Blondell, Rory Calhoun, Yvonne De Carlo, Milton Berle, Dorothy Lamour, Phil Silvers, and Andy Devine. When released in the spring of 1976, the spoof proved to be one of the deadlier bombs from Hollywood. Everyone wondered what the fuss had been about. Virginia, looking rather drab and bewildered, had one of the lengthier guest assignments.

Meanwhile, in November 1975, Virginia guested in a segment of NBC-TV's "Police Story" in a cameo role as a drunk driver.* Here she was not only flashy but excellent in her characterization. It was like a glimpse of the Warner Bros. star of two decades prior. That same month she returned to the road in the new farce, *Move Over, Mrs. Markham*, which premiered at the New Cave Theatre in Vancouver, British Columbia. The tour took her to Florida and to St. Charles, Illinois, in mid-1976.

Suddenly in 1976 Virginia found herself quite preoccupied with filmmaking again. She was in the Superstition Mountains area of Arizona for the shooting of *The Glass Cage*, a low-budget modern Gothic feature costarring Aldo Ray, Ann Michelle, and Jim Negele. The thriller, produced/directed/scripted by Michael de Gaetano, never had official release, but a soundtrack album of the suspense film (with music by Lor Crane) was released by RCA Records in 1977. At least *French Quarter*, shot in New Orleans, did reach distribution in late 1977, a year

In the late Sixties.

---

*She had appeared on an episode of CBS-TV's "Daktari" in 1967 and was on *The Diary* episode of NBC-TV's "Night Gallery" in November 1971. About that time she made a New York City bank commercial for television, one that did not please her at all.

With daughter Mary Catherine and husband Michael O'Shea in 1970.

Advertisement for *French Quarter* ('77).

With Bert Parks (far left) in the stage production of *Good News* (Milburn, New Jersey, June 1977).

and a half after it was lensed. Set at the turn of the century in the Storyville (brothel) section of New Orleans, it featured Virginia with Bruce Davison and Lindsay Bloom.

March 1977 found Mayo guesting on the short-lived teleseries, "Lanigan's Rabbi," an NBC network program starring Art Carney. She portrayed a once famous beauty who returns to the town of Cameron to sit in on the murder trial of a former lover. It was at this time that Virginia told the press, "Producers don't know where to put you. A gap occurs after you are a glamorous leading lady. Shelley Winters, on the other hand, has always had a corner on the market because she's always played character roles." Regarding her guest role on "Lanigan's Rabbi" she explained, "These parts seldom come up and you get impatient with the fact that all the women from my era are competing for the same part.... Men who are older than I and who co-starred with me in films are still working as leading men—only they work with twenty-seven-year-old actresses."

In the summer of 1977 Virginia joined with Bert Parks in a tour of the musical *Good News*. When *Newark Star-Ledger* reporter Bette Spero interviewed Mayo, the columnist noted, "Miss Mayo is still golden-haired, but the once shoulder-length tresses that looked so seductive with the low-cut gowns of the Fifties are now a more manageable medium length. The actress, at fifty-five and a grandmother, is still attractive but is more pleasantly plump than svelte."

Admitted Mayo to Spero: "It's sad but a physical fact of life. Dancing is hard for me now. I used to love to dance. It was so easy and so much fun. After all, I started as a dancer."

Reminiscing about her array of film directors, Virginia singled out Raoul Walsh, a neighbor of hers. "He was a funny but sensitive man who was real gutsy in making movies move, in giving them vitality. But then he was merely considered a good director, nothing more. Today he's getting his just acclaim." (Walsh in recent years told Vir-

The Virginia Mayo of today.

ginia that she should really remake their *White Heat* and this time take on the Cagney role herself!)

Of her leading men, she cited James Cagney and Alan Ladd as two favorites: "Cagney was always very sure of himself in his acting. He was all business on the set, acting very cool and collected. In *White Heat* we were all terribly excited about working with Cagney! Even then he was considered a great talent, and we listened to any little thing he said, hoping some of his talent would infect us. He was certainly the most dynamic talent I ever saw on a screen. His acting was like an explosion.

"Ladd, by contrast, was oblivious of his handsomeness and haunted by the fear that his acting wasn't good enough. Alan was one of the sweetest people who ever lived but he was too ethereal and 'too pretty' for some of the critics' taste. He was not a tough guy, despite what he played onscreen. He was almost frightened of life."

During her East Coast tour of *Good News*

Virginia took time to appear on the "Joe Franklin Show" on New York City's Channel 9. On the air she was the extremely positive, grateful ex-movie queen who "loved" all her past pictures, even the bad ones. One of her interesting anecdotes was her recollection that she had heard that authoress Jacqueline Susann had based the major character of Neeley O'Hara in her novel *Valley of the Dolls* on both Judy Garland and Mayo—"the vaudeville part of my life," she quickly added. "Jackie and I appeared with Eddie Cantor in *Banjo Eyes* on Broadway. I remember I used to catch Jackie staring at me all the time. I wondered what she was up to."

In early February 1979, it was announced that Virginia would join with Gene Barry, Stuart Whitman, Bradford Dillman, John Ireland, and Mel Ferrer in the feature film *Guyana, Crime of the Century*. But when shooting began in Mexico City later that month, under the direction of Rene Cardona, Jr., Yvonne De Carlo had taken over the role. Instead, Virginia went to Las Vegas to star in the stage show *Too Many for the Bed*, a comedy by Ray Cooney and John Chapman. It opened at the Union Plaza Hotel Theatre on April 3rd.

Today, Virginia resides in Thousand Oaks, California, in a home built by her and Michael O'Shea. Sharing the house are daughter Mary Catherine and husband-chef Kent Lee Johnston (married December 17, 1972) and their son Lucas Michael (born July 25, 1975). Mary Catherine has made no bid toward an acting career. "It would have been to my advantage to get into it because of my parents," she says, "but I felt I didn't have the talent so why waste everybody's time."

Virginia does not mind grandmotherhood in the least. "It's just fine with me," she says with a proud smile." Although Mayo was reported "linked" with Hollywood columnist Lee Graham in recent years, it was just a friendship and she has no plans for a second marriage.

In evaluating her film career to date, she insists, "Let's face it. I had to take what I could get and I did the best I could with it.

Onstage in 1979.

I think I was a better actress than I was allowed to be. I wasn't all that beautiful, just photographed well. I always felt Susan [Hayward] was a great actress, but people seemed to single out her beauty instead.

"Time ran out for me because it ran out for everyone. But making movies was a thrilling period in my life. I'd like to do it all over again!"

FILMOGRAPHY

FOLLIES GIRL *(Producers Releasing Corporation, 1943)* 71 min.

Producer, William Rowland; associate producer, Irvin Schapp; director, Rowland; story, Marcy Klauber, Art Jarrett, Stedman Coles; screenplay, Klauber, Charles Robinson; additional dialogue, Pat Flick, Lew Hearn; music director, Ernie Holst; music supervisor, Robert Warren; vocal arranger, Travis Johnson; choreography, Larry Ceballos; songs, Mary Schaeffer; Nick Kenny, Kim Gannon, and Ken Lane; Fred Wise, Buddy Kaye, and Sid Lippman; Nick and Charles Kenny, Sunny Burke, and John Murphy; Robert Warren; Wise, Kaye, and Lippman; dialogue director, Arthur Pierson; assistant director, John Graham; costumes, Mary Grant; camera, George Webber; editors, Samuel Datlowe, Jerome Schnur, G. E. Schweneger.

Wendy Barrie (Anne Merriday); Doris Nolan (Francine La Rue); Gordon Oliver (Private Jerry Hamlin); Anne Barrett (Bunny); Arthur Pierson (Sergeant Bill Perkins); J. C. Nugent (J. B. Hamlin); Cora Witherspoon (Mrs. Hamlin); William Harrigan (Jimmy Dobson); Jay Brennan (Andre Duval); Lew Hearn (Lew); Cliff Hall (Cliff); Marion McGuire (Trixie); Pat C. Flick (Patsy, the Waiter); Anthony Blair (Somers); Jerri Blanchard (Jerri); Serjei Radamsky (Scarini); G. Swayne Gordon (Doorman); Fritzi Scheff (Herself); Johnny Long and His Band, Bobby Byrne and His Band, Ray Heatherton and His Band, Ernie Holst and His Band (Themselves); Virginia Mayo (Model); Tito Vuolo (Mifaldi); Amanda Randolph (Hamlin Maid); Jack Lambert (Man in Phone Booth); Jake Winston, Don Bruce, Ray Melbach (Three Heat Waves).

JACK LONDON *(United Artists, 1943)* 94 min.

Producer Samuel Bronston; associate producer, Joseph K. Nadel; director, Alfred Santell; based on *The Book of Jack London* by Charmian London; screenplay, Ernest Pascal; art director, Bernard Herzbrun; set decorator, Earl Wooden; dialogue director, Edward Padula; assistant director, Sam Nelson; music director, Fred Rich; sound, Ben Winkler; special effects, Harry Redmond; camera, John W. Boyle; editor, William Ziegler.

Michael O'Shea (Jack London); Susan Hayward (Charmian Kittredge); Ona Massen (Freda Maloof); Harry Davenport (Professor Hilliard); Frank Craven (Old Tom); Virginia Mayo (Mamie); Ralph Morgan (George Brett); Louise Beavers (Mammy Jenny); Jonathan Hale (Kerwin Maxwell); Leonard Strong (Captain Tanaka); Paul Hurst ("Lucky Luke" Lanigan); Regis Toomey (Scratch Nelson); Hobart Cavanaugh (Mike); Olin Howlin (Mailman); Albert Van Antwerp (French Frank); Ernie Adams (Whiskey Bob); John Kelly (Red John); Robert Homans (Captain Allen); Morgan Conway (Richard Harding Davis); Edward Earle (James Hare); Arthur Loft (Fred Palmer); Lumsden Hare (English Correspondent); Brooks Benedict (American Correspondent); Mai Lee Foo (Geisha Dancer); Robert Katcher (Hiroshi); Pierre Watkin (American Consul); Paul Fung (Japanese General); Charlie Lung (Interpreter); Bruce Wong (Japanese Official); Eddie Lee (Japanese Sergeant); John Fisher (Spider); Jack Roper (Spider); Sven Hugo Borg (Victor); Sid D'Albrook (Axel); Davison Clark (Commissioner); Harold Minjir, Roy Gordon, Torben Meyer (Literary Guests); Charlene Newman (Child); Edmund Cobb (Father); Wallis Clark (Theodore Roosevelt); Charles Miller (William Loeb); Richard Loo (Japanese Ambassador); Dick Curtis (Cannery Foreman); Sarah Padden (Cannery Woman); Evelyn Finley (Indian Maid); Rose Plummer (Charmian's Secretary).

UP IN ARMS *(RKO, 1944)* C-105 min.

Producer, Samuel Goldwyn; associate producer, Don Hartman; director, Elliott Nugent; based on the play *The Nervous Wreck* by Owen Davis; screenplay, Hartman, Allen Boretz, Robert Pirosh; art directors, Perry Ferguson, Stewart Chaney, McClure Capps; set decorator, Howard Bristol; music arranger, Ray Heindorf; music director, Louis Forbes; songs, Harold Arlen and Ted Koehler; Sylvia Fine and Max Liebman; assistant director, Louis Germonprez; sound, Fred Lau; special camera effects, Clarence Slifer, R. O. Binger; camera, Ray Rennahan; editors, Daniel Mandell, James Newcom.

Danny Kaye (Danny Weems); Constance Dowling (Mary Morgan); Dinah Shore (Virginia); Dana Andrews (Joe); Louis Calhern (Colonel Ashley); George Mathews (Blackie); Benny Baker (Butterball); Elisha Cook, Jr. (Info Jones); Lyle Talbot (Sergeant Gelsey); Walter Catlett (Major Brock); George Meeker (Ashley's Aide); Tom Keene (Captain—Ashley's Aide); Margaret Dumont (Mrs. Willoughby); Edward Earle (Sherwood); Harry Hayden (Dr. Weavermacher); Sig Arno (Waiter); Oliver Blake, Larry Steers (Board Members); Stanley Gilbert (Man in Lobby); Isabel Withers, John Hamilton (Couple); Eddie Kane (Wedding Guest in Dream); Terrance Ray, Matt Willis (Sentries in Hold); June Lang, Virginia Mayo, Dorothy Merritt, Lorraine Miller, Myrna Dell, Audrey Young, Virginia Wicks, Ruth

Valmy, Mary Moore, Kay Morley, Shelby Payne, Lee Nugent (Nurses); Frosty Royce (Bakery Man); Al Benault (Cop).

SEVEN DAYS ASHORE (RKO, 1944) 74 min.

Producer/director, John H. Auer; story, Jacques Duval; screenplay, Edward Verdier, Irving Phillips, Lawrence Kimble; music director, C. Bakaleinikoff; choreography, Charles O'Curran; orchestrator, Gene Rose; songs, Lew Pollack and Mort Greene; Freddie Fisher; art director, Albert S. D'Agostino; set decorators, Darrell Silvera, William Stevens; assistant director, Harry Scott; special effects, Vernon L. Walker; sound, Bailey Fesler; camera, Russell Metty; editor, Harry Marker.

Wally Brown (Monty); Alan Carney (Orval); Marcy McGuire (Dot); Dooley Wilson (Jason); Gordon Oliver (Dan Arland); Virginia Mayo (Carol); Amelita Ward (Lucy); Elaine Shepard (Annabelle); Marjorie Gateson (Mrs. Arland); Alan Dinehart (Mr. Arland); Miriam LaVelle (Hazel); Margaret Dumont (Mrs. Coxton Lynch); Emory Parnell (Captain Harvey); Ian Wolfe (Process Server); Freddie Slack and His Orchestra, Freddie Fisher and His Band (Themselves); Dorothy Malone (Betty); Patti Brill, Daun Kennedy, Elaine Anderson, Elaine Riley, Shirley O'Hara (Girls in Band); William Haade, Charles Cane (Bosun's Mates); Ruth Cherrington, Helen Dickson (Dowagers); Bill Dyer (Soldier); Michael St. Angel (Marine).

THE PRINCESS AND THE PIRATE (RKO, 1944) C-95 min.

Producer, Samuel Goldwyn; associate producer, Don Hartman; director, David Butler; story, Sy Bartlett; adaptors, Allen Boretz, Curtis Kenyon; screenplay, Hartman, Melville Shavelson, Everett Freeman; Technicolor consultant, Natalie Kalmus; music, David Rose; song, Jimmy McHugh and Harold Adamson; art directors, Ernst Fegte, McClure Capps; set decorator, Howard Bristol; art consultant, Hugo Ballin; assistant director, Barton Adams; sound, Fred Lau; special camera effects, R. O. Binger and Clarence Slifer; camera, Victor Milner; editor, Daniel Mandell.

Bob Hope (Sylvester); Virginia Mayo (Princess Margaret); Walter Brennan (Featherhead); Walter Slezak (Governor La Roche); Victor McLaglen (The Hook); Marc Lawrence (Pedro); Hugo Haas (Proprietor of Bucket of Blood Inn); Maude Eburne (Landlady); Adia Kuznetzoff (Don Jose); Brandon Hurst (Mr. Polly); Tom Kennedy (Alonzo); Stanley Andrews (Captain of Mary Ann); Robert Warwick (The King); Tom Tyler (Lieutenant); Ralph Dunn (Murderous Pirate); Weldon Heyburn, Edward Peil (Palace Guards); Alan Bridge, Al Hill, Mike Mazurki (Pirates); Jack Carr (Bartender); Constantine Romanoff, Robert Hale (Citizens); Frank Moran, Oscar Hendrian (Hecklers); Alma Carroll, Ruth Valmy (Handmaidens); Rondo Hatton (Gorilla Man); Richard Alexander (Holdup Man); Sammy Stein (Black Jack Thug); Bing Crosby (Bit).

WONDER MAN (RKO, 1945) C-98 min.

Producer, Samuel Goldwyn; director, Bruce Humberstone; story, Arthur Sheekman; adaptors, Jack Jevne, Eddie Moran; screenplay, Don Hartman, Melville Shavelson, Philip Rapp; choreography, John Wray; special material, Sylvia Fine; music/orchestrator/music director, Ray Heindorf; music director, Louis Forbes; songs, Leo Robin and David Rose; assistant director, William McGarry; art directors, Ernest Fegte, McClure Capps; set decorator, Howard Bristol; Technicolor consultants, Natalie Kalmus, Mitchell Kovaleski; sound, Fred Lau; special camera effects, John Fulton; camera, Victor Milner, William Snyder; editor, Daniel Mandell.

Danny Kaye (Buzzy Bellew/Edwin Dingle); Virginia Mayo (Ellen Shanley); Vera-Ellen (Midge Mallon); Allen Jenkins (Chimp); Edward Brophy (Torso); S. Z. Sakall (Schmidt); Steve Cochran (Ten Grand Jackson); Donald Woods (Monte Rossen); Otto Kruger (District Attorney O'Brien); Richard Lane (Assistant District Attorney Grosset); Natalie Schafer (Mrs. Hume); Alice Mock (The Prima Donna); Virginia Gilmore (Girl on Bench in Park); Ruth Valmy, Alma Carroll, Karen Gaylor, Chili Williams, Gloria Delson, Margie Stewart, Ellen Hall, Mary Jane Woods, Katherine Booth, Phyllis Forbes, Martha Montgomery (Goldwyn Girls); Huntz Hall (Sailor); Jack Norton (Drunk at Table); Cecil Cunningham (Barker); Mary Field (District Attorney's Secretary); Eddie Dunn (Cop); Byron Foulger (Customer); Luis Alberni (Prompter); Noel Cravat, Nick Thompson, Nino Pipitone, Baldo Minuti (Opera Singers); Margie Stewart (Page Girl); Frank Melton (Waiter).

THE KID FROM BROOKLYN (RKO, 1946) C-114 min.

Producer, Sam Goldwyn; director, Norman Z. McLeod; based on the play *The Milky Way* by Lynn Root and Harry Clark; adaptors, Don Hartman and Melville Shavelson; screenplay, Grover Jones, Frank Butler, Richard Connell; Technicolor consultants, Natalie Kalmus, Mitchell Kovaleski; art directors, Perry Ferguson, Stewart Chaney, McClure Capps; set decorators, Howard Bristol, Clifford Porter; choreography, Bernard Pearce; vocal arranger, Kay Thompson; music director, Carmen Dragon; music supervisor, Louis Forbes; songs, Jule Styne and Sammy

Cahn; assistant director, Arthur Black; sound, Fred Lau; camera, Gregg Toland; editor, Daniel Mandell.

Danny Kaye (Burleigh Sullivan); Virginia Mayo (Polly Pringle); Vera-Ellen (Susie Sullivan); Steve Cochran (Speed McFarlane); Eve Arden (Ann Westley); Walter Abel (Gabby Sloan); Lionel Stander (Spider Schultz); Fay Bainter (Mrs. E. Winthrop LeMoyne); Clarence Kolb (Mr. Austin); Victor Cutler (Photographer); Jerome Cowan (Fight Announcer); Don Wilson, Knox Manning (Radio Announcers); Johnny Downs (Master of Ceremonies); Kay Thompson (Matron); Charles Cane (Willard); Karen Gaylord, Ruth Valmy, Virginia Belmont, Jean Cronin, Vonne Lester, Tyra Vaughn, Kismi Stefan, Helen Kimball, Donna Hamilton, Jan Byrant (Goldwyn Girls); Robert Strong, Billy Newell, Tom Quinn (Photographers); Frank Moran (Fight Manager); Billy Wayne, George Chandler (Reporters); Almeda Fowler (Bystander); Betty Blythe, James Carlisle (Mrs. LeMoyne's Friends); Pierre Watkin (Mr. LeMoyne); Snub Pollard (Man Who Reacts to Lion); Gil Dennis (Dancer); Jack Norton (Guest); Robert Wade Chatterton (Man Who Lifts Up Susie).

THE BEST YEARS OF OUR LIVES *(RKO, 1946)* 172 min.

Producer, Samuel Goldwyn; director, William Wyler; based on the novel *Glory for Me* by MacKinlay Kantor; screenplay, Robert E. Sherwood; art directors, Perry Ferguson, George Jenkins; set decorator, Julia Heron; song, Hoagy Carmichael and Sidney Arodin; music, Hugo Friedhofer; music director, Emil Newman; assistant director, Joseph Boyle; sound, Richard De Weese; camera, Gregg Toland; editor, Daniel Mandell.

Myrna Loy (Milly Stephenson); Fredric March (Al Stephenson); Dana Andrews (Fred Derry); Teresa Wright (Peggy Stephenson); Virginia Mayo (Marie Derry); Cathy O'Donnell (Wilma Cameron); Hoagy Carmichael (Butch Engle); Harold Russell (Homer Parrish); Gladys George (Hortense Derry); Roman Bohnen (Pat Derry); Ray Collins (Mr. Milton); Minna Gombell (Mrs. Parrish); Walter Baldwin (Mr. Parrish); Steve Cochran (Cliff); Dorothy Adams (Mrs. Cameron); Don Beddoe (Mr. Cameron); Victor Cutler (Woody); Marlene Aames (Luella Parrish); Charles Halton (Prew); Ray Teal (Mr. Mollett); Howland Chamberlin (Thorpe); Dean White (Novak); Erskine Sanford (Bullard); Michael Hall (Rob Stephenson); Blake Edwards (Corporal); Donald Kerr (Steve, the Bartender); Johnny Tyrrell (Gus, the Waiter); Clancy Cooper (Taxi Driver); Ben Erway (Latham); Heinie Conklin, Billy Engle (Customers); Edward Earle (Steese); John Ince (Ryan); Joyce Compton (Hatcheck Girl); Tom Dugan (Doorman); James Ames (Jackie); Richard Gordon (Maitre d'); Norman Phillips (Merkle).

THE SECRET LIFE OF WALTER MITTY *(RKO, 1947)* C-110 min.

Producer, Samuel Goldwyn; director, Norman Z. McLeod; based on the story by James Thurber; screenplay, Ken Englund, Everett Freeman; Technicolor consultants, Natalie Kalmus, Mitchell Kovaleski; art directors, George Jenkins, Perry Ferguson; set decorator, Casey Roberts; costumes, Irene Sharoff; music, David Raksin; music director, Emil Newman; songs, Sylvia Fine; assistant director, Rollie Asher; sound, Fred Lau; special camera effects, John Fulton; camera, Lee Garmes; editor, Monica Collingwood.

Danny Kaye (Walter Mitty); Virginia Mayo (Rosalind Van Hoorn); Boris Karloff (Dr. Hugo Hollingshead); Fay Bainter (Mrs. Mitty); Ann Rutherford (Gertrude Griswold); Thurston Hall (Bruce Pierce); Gordon Jones (Tubby Wadsworth); Florence Bates (Mrs. Griswold); Konstantin Shayne (Peter Van Hoorn); Reginald Denny (RAF Colonel); Henry Corden (Hendrick); Doris Lloyd (Mrs. Follinsbee); Fritz Feld (Anatole); Frank Reicher (Maasdam); Milton Parsons (Butler); Mary Brewer, Betty Carlyle, Lorraine DeRome, Jackie Jordan, Martha Montgomery, Pat Patrick, Lynn Walker (Goldwyn Girls); Bess Flowers (Illustrator); Donna Dax (Stenographer); John Tyrrell, Raoul Freeman (Department Heads); Sam Ash (Art Editor); Dorothy Granger, Harry L. Woods (Wrong Mr. and Mrs. Follinsbee); Hank Worden (Western Character); Vernon Dent (Bartender); Henry Kolker (Dr. Benbow); Frank LaRue (Conductor); Brick Sullivan (Cop); Minerva Urecal (Woman with Hat); Maude Eburne (Fitter); George Chandler (Mate); Vincent Pelletier (Narrator for Dream Sequence).

OUT OF THE BLUE *(Eagle-Lion, 1947)* 86 min.

Producer, Isadore Goldsmith; director, Leigh Jason; story, Vera Caspary; screenplay, Walter Bullock, Caspary, Edward Eliscu; art director, Edward Jewell; set decorator, Armor Marlowe; music, Carmen Dragon; music director, Irving Friedman; song, Will Jason and Henry Nemo; assistant director, Howard W. Koch; sound, Leon Becker, William H. Lynch; special camera effects, George J. Teague; camera, Jackson Rose; editor, Norman Colbert.

George Brent (Arthur Earthleigh); Virginia Mayo (Deborah Tyler); Turhan Bey (David Galleo); Ann Dvorak (Olive Jensen); Carole Landis (Mae Earthleigh); Elizabeth Patterson (Miss

Spring); Julia Dean (Miss Ritchie); Richard Lane (Detective Noonan); Charles Smith (Elevator Boy); Paul Harvey (Holliston); Alton E. Horton (Detective Dombry); Hadda Brooks (Black Singer); Flame the Dog (Rabelais); Robert Bilder (Milkman); Paul Palmer (Doorman); George Carleton (Veterinarian); Lee Phelps (Motorcycle Cop); Ralph Sanford (Desk Sergeant); Jerry Marlowe (Cop).

A SONG IS BORN (*RKO, 1948*) C-113 min.

Producer, Samuel Goldwyn; director, Howard Hawks; based on the screen story "From A to Z" by Billy Wilder and Thomas Monroe; screenplay, Harry Tugend; Technicolor consultants, Natalie Kalmus, William Fritzsche; art directors, George Jenkins, Perry Ferguson; set decorator, Julia Heron; music director, Emil Newman, Hugo Friedhofer; orchestrator, Sonny Burke; songs, Don Raye, Gene De Paul; assistant director, Joseph Boyle; makeup, Robert Stephanoff; costumes, Irene Sharaff; sound, Fred Lau; special effects, John Fulton; camera, Gregg Toland; editor, Daniel Mandell.

Danny Kaye (Professor Hobart Frisbee); Virginia Mayo (Honey Swanson); Benny Goodman (Professor Magenbruch); Tommy Dorsey and His Orchestra, Louis Armstrong and His Orchestra, Lionel Hampton and His Orchestra, Charlie Barnet and His Orchestra, Mel Powell and His Orchestra (Themselves); Buck & Bubbles, Page Cavanaugh Trio, Golden Gate Quartet, Russo and The Samba Kings (Specialties); Hugh Herbert (Professor Twingle); Steve Cochran (Tony Crow); J. Edward Bromberg (Dr. Elfini); Felix Bressart (Professor Gerkikoff); Ludwig Stossel (Professor Traumer); O. Z. Whitehead (Professor Oddly); Esther Dale (Miss Bragg); Mary Field (Miss Totten); Howland Chamberlin (Mr. Setter); Paul Langton (Joe); Sidney Blackmer (Adams); Ben Welden (Monte); Ben Chasen (Ben); Peter Virgo (Louis); Harry Babasin (Bass); Louie Belson (Drums); Alton Hendrickson (Guitar); Norma Gentner (Girl with Samba King); Will Lee, Muni Seroff (Waiters); Susan George (Cigarette Girl); Jill Meredith, Janie New, Barbara Hamilton, Jeffrey Sayre, Gene Morgan (People at Dorsey Club); Pat Walker (Photographer at Dorsey Club); Lane Chandler (Policeman at Inn); Joe Devlin (Gangster); Robert Dudley (Justice of the Peace); Joseph Crehan (District Attorney); Jack Gargan (Stenotypist).

SMART GIRLS DON'T TALK (*Warner Bros., 1948*) 81 min.

Producer, Saul Elkins; director, Richard Bare; screenplay, William Sackheim; art director, Stanley Fleischer; set decorator, William Wallace; music, David Buttolph; orchestrator, Leonid Raab; makeup, Perc Westmore; assistant director, Elmer Decker; sound, Stanley Jones; special effects, Robert Burks; camera, Ted McCord; editor, Clarence Kolster.

Virginia Mayo (Linda Vickers); Bruce Bennett (Marty Fain); Robert Hutton (Doc Vickers); Tom D'Andrea (Sparky Lynch); Richard Rober (Lieutenant McReady); Helen Westcott (Toni Peters); Richard Benedict (Cliff Saunders); Ben Welden (Nelson Clark); Richard Walsh (Johnny Warjak); Eddie Foster, George Hoagland, Bud Cokes (Gunmen); Phyllis Coates (Cigarette Girl); Creighton Hale (Apartment House Clerk); Leo White (Headwaiter); Edna Harris (Miss Frey); Philo McCullough (Roulette Croupier); Jack Mower (Houseman); Ted Stanhope (Bert).

FLAXY MARTIN (*Warner Bros., 1949*) 89 min.

Producer, Saul Elkins; director, Richard Bare; screenplay, David Lang; art director, Ted Smith; set decorator, Lyle Reifsnider; music, William Lava; orchestrator, Charles Maxwell; assistant director, Elmer Decker; dialogue director, John Maxwell; makeup, Perc Westmore; sound, Everett Brown; special effects, William McGann, Edwin DuPar; camera, Carl Guthrie; editor, Frank Magee.

Virginia Mayo (Flaxy Martin); Zachary Scott (Walter Colby); Dorothy Malone (Nora Carson); Tom D'Andrea (Sam Malko); Helen Westcott (Peggy Farrar); Douglas Kennedy (Hap Richie); Elisha Cook, Jr. (Roper); Douglas Fowley, Buddy Roosevelt (Detectives); Monte Blue (Joe, the Detective); Jack Overman (Caesar); Frances Morris (Woman Witness); Jack Cheatham (Police Operator); George Sherwood (Police Officer); Ed Dearing, Ed Parker (Motorcycle Cops); George Magrill (Court Officer); Rose Plummer (Court Spectator); Fred Kelsey (Watchman); John Elliott (Judge Edward R. McVey); Lee Phelps (Guard); Marjorie Bennett (Neighbor).

COLORADO TERRITORY (*Warner Bros., 1949*) 94 min.

Producer, Anthony Veiller; director, Raoul Walsh; screenplay, John Twist, Edmund H. North; music, David Buttolph; orchestrator, Maurice de Packh; assistant director, Russell Saunders; dialogue director, Eugene Busch; makeup, Perc Westmore; art director, Ted Smith; sound, Leslie G. Hewitt; special effects, H. F. Koenekamp; camera, Sid Hickox; editor, Owen Marks.

Joel McCrea (Wes McQueen); Virginia Mayo (Colorado Carson); Dorothy Malone (Julie Ann Winslow); Henry Hull (Winslow); John Archer (Reno Blake); James Mitchell (Duke Harris);

Morris Ankrum (U.S. Marshal); Basil Ruysdael (Dave Rickard); Frank Puglia (Brother Tomas); Ian Wolfe (Wallace); Harry Woods (Pluthner); Houseley Stevenson (Prospector); Victor Kilian (Sheriff); Oliver Blake (Station Agent); Monte Blue (Another U.S. Marshal); Maude Prickett (Mrs. Wallace); Jack Daley (Fireman); Fred Kelsey (Engineer); Irene Elinor (Amalia, the Mexican Woman); Gray Eyes (Old Indian); Jack Montgomery, Artie Ortego (Deputy Marshals); Glenn Thompson, Charles Horvath (Train Guards); Carl Harbaugh (Brakeman); Hallene Hill (Aunt Georgina).

THE GIRL FROM JONES BEACH *(Warner Bros., 1949)* 78 min.

Producer, Alex Gottlieb; director, Peter Godfrey; story, Allen Boretz; screenplay, I. A. L. Diamond; art director, Stanley Fleischer; set decorator, William Kuehl; music, David Buttolph; orchestrator, Leonid Raab; costumes, Leah Rhodes; makeup, George Bau; assistant director, Art Lueker; sound, Dolph Thomas; special effects, William McGann, Edwin DuPar; camera, Carl Guthrie; editor, Rudi Fehr.

Ronald Reagan [Bob Randolph (Robert Venerik)]; Virginia Mayo (Ruth Wilson); Eddie Bracken [Chuck Donovan (Charles Patrick Donovan)]; Dona Drake (Connie Martin); Henry Travers (Judge John Bullfinch); Lois Wilson (Mrs. Wilson); Florence Bates (Emma Shoemaker); Jerome Cowan (Mr. Graves); Helen Westcott (Miss Brooks); Paul Harvey (Jim Townsend); Lloyd Corrigan (Mr. Evergood); Myrna Dell (Lorraine Scott); William Forrest (Mr. Woody); Gary Gray (Woody Wilson); Mary Stuart (Hazel); Lennie Bremen (News Vendor); Buddy Roosevelt (Conductor); Jeff Richards, Dale Robertson (Lifeguards); Guy Wilkerson (Janitor); Lola Albright (Vickie); Patricia Northrop (Miss Shoemaker as a Girl); Creighton Hale (Waiter); Ray Montgomery (Brooks' Date); Joi Lansing, Betty Underwood, Carol Brewster, Joan Vohs, Karen Gaylord, Alice Wallace (Models); Oliver Blake (Court Clerk).

RED LIGHT *(United Artists, 1949)* 83 min.

Producer/director, Roy Del Ruth; screenplay, George Callahan; music, Dmitri Tiomkin; art director, F. Paul Sylos; camera, Bert Glennon; editor, Richard Heermance.

George Raft (John Torno); Virginia Mayo (Carla North); Gene Lockhart (Warni Hazard); Barton MacLane (Strecker); Henry "Harry" Morgan (Rocky); Raymond Burr (Nick Cherney); Arthur Franz (Jess Torno); Arthur Shields (Father Redmond); Frank Orth (Stoner); Philip Pine (Pablo); Movita Castenada (Trina); Paul Frees (Bellhop); Claire Carleton (Waitress); Edward Gargan (Truck Driver); Soledad Jiminez (Pablo's Mother); Polly Moran (Chambermaid).

WHITE HEAT *(Warner Bros., 1949)* 114 min. (Reissue title: *Sin Street Confidential*)

Producer, Louis F. Edelman; director, Raoul Walsh; suggested by a story by Virginia Kellogg; screenplay, Ivan Goff, Ben Roberts; art director, Edward Carrere; set decorator, Fred M. MacLean; music Max Steiner; orchestrator, Murray Cutter; assistant director, Russell Saunders; makeup, Perc Westmore; costumes, Leah Rhodes; sound, Leslie Hewitt; special effects, Roy Davidson, H. F. Koenekamp; camera, Sid Hickox; editor, Owen Marks.

James Cagney (Arthur Cody Jarrett); Virginia Mayo (Verna Jarrett); Edmond O'Brien (Hank Fallon—alias Vic Pardo); Margaret Wycherly (Ma Jarrett); Steve Cochran (Big Ed Somers); John Archer (Phillip Evans); Wally Cassell (Cotton Valetti); Fred Clark (Daniel Winston, the Trader); Ford Rainey (Zuckie Hommell); Fred Coby (Happy Taylor); G. Pat Collins (Herbert, the Reader); Mickey Knox (Het Kohler); Paul Guilfoyle (Roy Parker); Robert Osterloh (Tommy Ryley); Ian MacDonald (Bo Creel); Ray Montgomery (Ernie Trent); Jim Toney (Brakeman); Leo Cleary (Fireman); Murray Leonard (Engineer); Terry O'Sullivan (Radio Announcer); Marshall Bradford (Chief of Police); Milton Parsons (Willie Rolf, the Stoolie); John Pickard (Government Agent); Bob Foulk (Guard at Plant); Jim Thorpe (Convict); Eddie Foster (Nat Lefeld); Lee Phelps (Tower Guard); Perry Ivins (Simpson, the Prison Doctor); Nolan Leary (Gas Station Owner); Grandon Rhodes, John McGuire (Psychiatrists); Harry Lauter (Radio Patrolman of Car A).

ALWAYS LEAVE THEM LAUGHING *(Warner Bros., 1949)* 116 min.

Producer, Jerry Wald; director, Roy Del Ruth; story, Max Shulman, Richard Mealand; screenplay, Melville Shavelson, Jack Rose; set decorator, William Kuehl; music director, Ray Heindorf; songs and special music, Sammy Cahn; assistant director, Mel Dellar; makeup, Perc Westmore; choreograhy, LeRoy Prinz; costumes, Leah Rhodes; sound, Oliver S. Garretson; camera, Ernest Haller; editor, Clarence Kolster.

Milton Berle (Kip Cooper); Virginia Mayo (Nancy Egan); Ruth Roman (Fay Washburn); Bert Lahr (Eddie Egan); Alan Hale (Mr. Washburn); Grace Hayes (Mrs. Washburn); Jerome Cowan (Elliott Lewis); Lloyd Gough (Monte Wilson); Ransom Sherman (Richards); Iris Adrian (Julie Adams); Wally Vernon (Comic); Cecil Stewart and His Royal Rogues, The Moroccans,

O'Donnell & Blair (Specialties); Max Showalter (Bit).

BACKFIRE *(Warner Bros., 1950)* 91 min.

Producer, Anthony Veiller; director, Vincent Sherman; story, Larry Marcus; screenplay, Marcus, Ivan Goff, Ben Roberts; art director, Anton Grot; music director, Ray Heindorf; camera, Carl Guthrie; editor, Thomas Reilly.

Viveca Lindfors (Lysa Randolph); Dane Clark (Ben Arno); Virginia Mayo (Julie Benson); Edmond O'Brien (Steve Connolly); Gordon MacRae (Bob Corey); Ed Begley (Captain Garcia); Frances Robinson (Mrs. Blayne); Richard Rober (Solly Blayne); Monte Blue (Detective Sergeant Pluthner); David Hoffman (Burns); Sheila MacRae (Bonnie); Ida Moore (Sybil); Leonard Strong (Quong); John Ridgely (Plainclothesman); Ray Montgomery (Attendant); Charles Jordan (Cab Driver); Philo McCullough (Police Car Driver); Helen Westcott (Receptionist); Fred Kelsey (Man); Harry Woods (Guest); Ernie Anderson (James, the Servant); Harry Seymour (Rocky, the Pianist).

THE FLAME AND THE ARROW *(Warner Bros., 1950)* C-88 min.

Producers, Harold Hecht, Frank Ross; director, Jacques Tourneur; story/screenplay, Waldo Salt; art director, Edward Carrere; music, Max Steiner; camera, Ernest Haller; editor, Alan Crosland, Jr.

Burt Lancaster (Dardo); Virginia Mayo (Anne); Robert Douglas (Alessandro); Aline MacMahon (Nonna Batoli); Frank Allenby (Ulrich); Nick Cravat (Piccolo); Lynne Baggett (Francesca); Gordon Gebert (Rudi); Norman Lloyd (Troubadour); Victor Kilian (Apothecary); Francis Pierlot (Papa Pietro); Robin Hughes (Skinner).

THE WEST POINT STORY *(Warner Bros., 1950)* 107 min. (British release title: *Fine and Dandy*)

Producer, Louis F. Edelman; director, Roy Del Ruth; story, Irving Wallace; screenplay, John Monks, Jr., Charles Hoffman, Wallace; art director, Charles H. Clarke; set decorator, Armor E. Marlowe; music director, Ray Heindorf; orchestrator, Frank Perkins; songs, Jule Styne and Sammy Cahn; vocal arranger, Hugh Martin; choreography, LeRoy Prinz; dance stagers, Eddie Prinz, Al White; Mr. Cagney's dances created by Johnny Boyle, Jr.; costumes, Milo Anderson, Marjorie Best; assistant director, Mel Deller; sound, Francis J. Scheid; special effects, Edwin DuPar; camera, Sid Hickox; editor, Owen Marks.

James Cagney (Edwin Bixby); Virginia Mayo (Eve Dillon); Doris Day (Jan Wilson); Gordon MacRae (Tom Fletcher); Gene Nelson (Hal Courtland); Roland Winters (Harry Everhart); Alan Hale (Bull Gilbert); Raymond Roe (Bixby's "Wife"); Wilton Graff (Lieutenant-Colonel Martin); Frank Ferguson (Commandant); Glen Turnbull (Hoofer); Walter Ruick (Piano Player); John Hedloe (Cadet); Jerome Cowan (William Jacelyn); Jack Kelly (Officer-in-Charge); James Young, Don Shartel, Joel Marston, James Dobson (Cadets); Victor Desney (French Attaché); Lute Crockett (Senator); Wheaton Chambers (Secretary).

ALONG THE GREAT DIVIDE *(Warner Bros., 1951)* 88 min.

Producer, Anthony Veiller; director, Raoul Walsh; story/screenplay, Walter Doniger, Lewis Meltzer; music, David Buttolph; art director, Edward Carrere; camera, Sid Hickox; editor, Thomas Reilly.

Kirk Douglas (U.S. Marshal Clint Merrick); Virginia Mayo (Ann Keith); John Agar (Billy Shear); Walter Brennan (Tim "Pop" Keith); Ray Teal (Deputy Lou Gray); Hugh Sanders (Sam Weaver); Morris Ankrum (Ned Roden); James Anderson (Dan Roden); Charles Meredith (Judge); Lane Chandler (Sheriff); Guy Wilkerson (Jury Foreman); Zon Murray (Wilson, the Witness); Al Ferguson (Bailiff); Sam Ash (Defense Counsel).

CAPTAIN HORATIO HORNBLOWER *(Warner Bros., 1951)* C-117 min.

Director, Raoul Walsh; based on the novel by C. S. Forester; screenplay, Ivan Goff, Ben Roberts, Aeneas MacKenzie; art director, Tom Morahan; music, Robert Farnon; music director, Louis Levy; sound, Harold King; camera, Guy Green; editor, Jack Harris.

Gregory Peck (Captain Horatio Hornblower, R.N.); Virginia Mayo (Lady Barbara Wellsley); Robert Beatty (Lieutenant Bush); Moultrie Kelsall (Lieutenant Crystal); Terence Morgan (Second Lieutenant Gerard); James Kenney (Mr. Midshipman Longley); Alec Mango (El Supremo); Dennis O'Dea (Rear Admiral Sir Rodney Leighton); Michael Goodliffe (Colonel Caillard); John Witty (Entenza); James Robertson Justice (Seaman Quist); Michael Dolan (Surgeon Gundarson); Stanley Baker (Bosun's Mate Harrison); Richard Hearne (Polwheal); Alan Tilvern (Hernandez); Christopher Lee (Spanish Captain); Richard Johnson (Macrae); Patrick Young (Lieutenant Radot); Ronald Adam (Admiral Macartney, R.N.); Basil Bartlett (Captain Elliott, R.N.); Robert Cawdron (French Mate on "Witch of Indor"); Jack Stewart, Russell Waters (Seamen); Sam Kydd (Seaman Garvin).

PAINTING THE CLOUDS WITH SUNSHINE *(Warner Bros., 1951)* C-86 min.

Producer, William Jacobs; director, David Butler; based on the play *Gold Diggers of Broadway* by Avery Hopwood; screenplay, Harry Clark, Roland Kibbee, Peter Milne; art director, Edward Carrere; music director, Ray Heindorf; choreography, LeRoy Prinz; camera, Wilfrid M. Cline; editor, Irene Morra.

Dennis Morgan (Vince Nichols); Virginia Mayo (Carol); Gene Nelson (Ted Lansing); S. Z. Sakall (Felix Hoff); Lucille Norman (Abby); Virginia Gibson (Vi); Wallace Ford (Sam Parks); Tom Conway (Bennington); Tom Dugan (Barney); Jack Law (Orchestra Leader); Abe Dinovitch (Busboy); Harry Mendoza (Rolondo); Dolores Castle (Yvette); Tristram Coffin (Manager); Eddie Acuff, Jack Daley (Doormen); Brick Sullivan, Paul Gustine (Housemen); Donald Kerr (Dealer); Garnett Marks (Manager); Joe Recht (Bellboy); Crauford Kent, Frank Dae (Board Members); William Vedder (Cadwalder).

STARLIFT *(Warner Bros., 1951)* 103 min.

Producer, Robert Arthur; director, Roy Del Ruth; story, John Klorer; screenplay, Klorer, Karl Lamb; art director, Charles H. Clarke; music director, Ray Heindorf; songs, Joe Young and Jimmy Monaco; Ira and George Gershwin; Cole Porter; Sammy Cahn and Jule Styne; Irving Kahal and Sammy Fain; Edward Heymann and Dana Suesse; Harry Ruskin and Henry Sullivan; Percy Faith; Ruby Ralesin and Phil Harris; camera, Ted McCord; editor, William Ziegler.

Doris Day, Gordon MacRae, Virginia Mayo, Gene Nelson, Ruth Roman (Themselves); Janice Rule (Nell Wayne); Dick Wesson (Sergeant Mike Nolan); Ron Hagerty (Corporal Rick Williams); Richard Webb (Colonel Callan); Hayden Rorke (Chaplain); Howard St. John (Steve Rogers); Ann Doran (Mrs. Callan); Tommy Farrell (Turner); John Maxwell (George Norris); Don Beddoe (Bob Wayne); Mary Adams (Sue Wayne); Bigelow Sayre (Dr. Williams); Eleanor Audley (Mrs. Williams); James Cagney, Gary Cooper, Virginia Gibson, Phil Harris, Frank Lovejoy, Lucille Norman, Louella Parsons, Randolph Scott, Jane Wyman, Patrice Wymore (Themselves); Pat Henry (Theatre Manager); Gordon Polk (Chief Usher); Joe Turkel (Litter Case); Jill Richards (Flight Nurse); Ray Montgomery (Captain Nelson); Walter Brennan, Jr. (Driver); Eddie Coonz (Reporter); Ezelle Poule (Waitress); Dick Ryan (Doctor); Dolores Castle, Dorothy Kennedy (Nurses); William Hunt (Boy with Cane); Steve Gregory (Boy with Camera); Bill Hudson (Crew Chief); Sarah Spencer (Miss Parsons' Assistant).

SHE'S WORKING HER WAY THROUGH COLLEGE *(Warner Bros., 1952)* C-104 min.

Producer, William Jacobs; director, Bruce Humberstone; based on the play *The Male Animal* by James Thurber and Elliott Nugent; screenplay, Peter Milne; art director, Charles H. Clarke; choreography, LeRoy Prinz; songs, Sammy Cahn and Vernon Duke; assistant director, Don Page; camera, Wilfrid M. Cline; editor, Clarence Kolster.

Virginia Mayo [Angela Gardner (Hot Garters Gertie)]; Ronald Reagan (John Palmer); Gene Nelson (Don Weston); Don DeFore (Shep Slade); Phyllis Thaxter (Helen Palmer); Patrice Wymore (Ivy Williams); Roland Winters (Fred Copeland); Raymond Greenleaf (Dean Rogers); Norman Bartold (Tiny Gordon); Amanda Randolph (Maybelle); Henrietta Taylor (Mrs. Copeland); Hope Sansbury (Mrs. Rogers); George Meader (Professor); Eve Miller (Secretary); The Blackburn Twins (Specialty Number); Dick Reeves (Mike); Patricia Hawks, Donna Ring, Frances Zucco (Coeds); Ray Linn, Jr. (Senator); Betty Arlen, Valerie Vernon, Hazel Shaw, Barbara Ritchi (Chorus Girls); Mark Lowell, Jimmy Ogg (Sailors); Ginger Crowley, Larry Craig (Students).

THE IRON MISTRESS *(Warner Bros., 1952)* C-110 min.

Producer, Henry Blanke; director, Gordon Douglas; story, Paul I. Wellman; screenplay, James R. Webb; art director, John Beckman; set decorator, George James Hopkins; music, Max Steiner; orchestrator, Murray Cutter; camera, John Seitz; editor, Alan Crosland, Jr.

Alan Ladd (Jim Bowie); Virginia Mayo (Judalon); Joseph Calleia (Juan Moreno); Alf Kjellin (Phillipe de Cabanal); Ned Young (Henri Contrecourt); Douglas Dick (Marcisse de Bornay); Phyllis Kirk (Ursula); Tony Caruso (Bloody Jack Sturdevant); George Voskovec (James Audubon); Don Beddoe (General Cuny); Richard Carlyle (Rezin Bowie); Richard Crane (John Bowie); Sarah Selby (Mrs. Bowie); Jay Novello (Judge Crain); Gordon Nelson (Dr. Maddox); George Lewis (Wells); David Wolfe (James Black); Nick Dennis (Nez Coupe); Edward Colmans (Don Juan de Veramendi); Daria Massey (Theresa de Veramendi); Harold Gordon (Andrew Marschalk); Ramsey Hill (Malot); Eugene Borden (Cocquelon); Jean Del Val (St. Sylvain); Amanda Randolph (Maria); Reed Howes, Dick Cogan (Players); Salvador Baguez (Mexican Artist); Madge Blake (Mrs. Cuny).

SHE'S BACK ON BROADWAY *(Warner Bros., 1953)* C-95 min.

Producer, Henry Blanke; director, Gordon Douglas; screenplay, Orin Jannings; music numbers staged by LeRoy Prinz; songs, Bob Hilliard and Carl Sigman; art director, Edward Carrere; camera, Edwin DuPar; editor, Folmar Blangsted.

Virginia Mayo (Catherine Terris); Steve Cochran (Rick Sommers); Gene Nelson (Gordon Evans); Patrice Wymore (Karen Keene); Frank Lovejoy (John Webber); Virginia Gibson (Angela Korinna); Paul Picerni (Jud Kellogg); Ned Young (Rafferty); Larry Keating (Mitchell Parks); Douglas Spencer (Lew Ludlow); Taylor Holmes (Talbot); Condos & Brandow (Specialty Act); Mabel Albertson (Velma Trumbull); Jacqueline De Wit (Lisa Kramer); Paul Bryar (Ned Golby); Harry Tyler (Rhodes); Cliff Ferre (Lyn Humphries); Lenny Sherman (Ernest Tandy); Phyllis Coates (Blonde); Caleen Calder (Val); Howard Price (Sandy); Ray Kyle (Micky); Sy Melano (Baritone); Ray Walker (Guide Bus Driver); Minerva Urecal (Landlady); Harlan Hoagland (Waiter); Jack Kenney (Loader); Kathleen Freeman (Annie); Percy Helton (News Vendor).

SOUTH SEA WOMAN *(Warner Bros., 1953)* 99 min.

Producer, Sam Bischoff; director, Arthur Lubin; based on the play *General Court-Martial* by William N. Rankin; screenplay, Edwin Blum; art director, Edward Carrere; music, David Buttolph; choreography, Lester Horton; camera, Ted McCord; editor, Clarence Kolster.

Burt Lancaster (Sergeant James O'Hearn); Virginia Mayo (Ginger Martin); Chuck Connors (Davey White); Barry Kelley (Colonel Hickman); Hayden Rorke (Lieutenant Fears); Leon Askin (Marchand); Veola Vonn (Madame Duval); Raymond Greenleaf (Captain Peabody); Robert Sweeney (Lieutenant Miller); Paul Burke (Ensign Hoyt); Cliff Clark (Lieutenant Colonel Parker); John Alderson (Fitzroy); Rudolph Anders (Van Dorck); Henri Letondal (Alphonse); Georges Saurel (Jacques); Arthur Shields (Jimmylegs Donovan); William O'Leary (Mr. Smith); John Damler (Lieutenant Kellogg); Alena Awes (Mimi); Jacqueline Duval (Julie); Violet Daniels (Suzette); Paul Bryar (Captain of the Gendarmes); Anthony Radecki (Military Policeman); Keye Luke, Frank Kumagai, Edo Mito, Robert Kino, Rollin Moriyama (Japanese Officers).

DEVIL'S CANYON *(RKO, 1953)* C-92 min.

Producer, Edmund Grainger; director, Alfred Werker; story, Bennett R. Cohen, Norton S. Parker; screenplay, Frederick Hazlitt Brennan; music, Daniele Amfitheatrof; art directors, Albert D'Agostino, Jack Okey; camera, Nicholas Musuraca; editor, Gene Palmer.

Virginia Mayo (Abby Nixon); Dale Robertson (Billy Reynolds); Stephen McNally (Jesse Gorman); Arthur Hunnicutt (Frank Taggert); Robert Keith (Steve Morgan); Jay C. Flippen (Captain Wells); Whit Bissell (Virgil); George J. Lewis (Colonel Gomez); Morris Ankrum (Sheriff); James Bell (Dr. Betts); William Phillips (Red); Earl Holliman (Joe); Irving Bacon (Abby's Guard); Jim Hayward (Man in Saloon); Fred Coby (Cole Gorman); John Cliff (Bud Gorman); Glenn Strange (Marshall, the Wagon Driver); Murray Alper (Driver-Guard); Harold "Stubby" Kruger (Prisoner); Paul Fix (Gatling Guard); Gregg Martell (Tower Guard); Larry Blake (Hysterical Prisoner).

KING RICHARD AND THE CRUSADERS *(Warner Bros., 1954)* C-114 min.

Producer, Henry Blanke; director, David Butler; based on the novel *The Talisman* by Sir Walter Scott; screenplay, John Twist; art director, Bertram Tuttle; music, Max Steiner; assistant director, Oren Haglund; camera, Peverell Marley; editor, Edith Morra.

Rex Harrison (Emir Ilderim); Virginia Mayo (Lady Edith); George Sanders (King Richard III); Laurence Harvey (Sir Kenneth); Robert Douglas (Sir Giles Amaury); Michael Pate (Montferrat); Paula Raymond (Queen Berengaria); Lester Matthews (Archbishop of Tyre); Antony Eustrel (Baron De Vaux); Henry Corden (King Philip of France); Wilton Graff (Duke Leopold of Austria); Nick Cravat (Nectobanus); Leslie Bradley (Castelain Captain); Nejla Ates (Moorish Dancing Girl); Larry Chance (Castelain Bowman); Robin Hughes (King's Guard); Lumsden Hare, Leonard Penn, Leonard Mudie, Gavin Muir (Physicians); Harry Cording (Castelain Spokesman); Herbert Dean (Captain of Royal Guard); Otto Reichow, Rudolph Anders (German Knights); John Alderson (Mob Leader).

THE SILVER CHALICE *(Warner Bros. 1954)* C-144 min.

Producer, Victor Saville; associate producer, Lester Samuels; director, Saville; based on the novel by Thomas B. Costain; screenplay, Samuels; production designer, Rolf Gerard; music, Franz Waxman; assistant directors, Melvin Dellar, Russell Llewellyn; choreography, Stephen Papick; art director, Boris Leven; camera, William V. Skall; editor, George White.

Virginia Mayo (Helena); Jack Palance (Simon); Paul Newman (Basil); Pier Angeli (Deborra); Alexander Scourby (Luke); Joseph Wiseman (Mijamin); E. G. Marshall (Ignatius); Walter Hampden (Joseph); Jacques Aubuchon (Nero); Herbert Rudley (Linus); Albert Dekker (Kester); Michael Pate (Aaron); Lorne Greene (Peter); Terence De Marney (Sosthene); Don Randolph (Selech); David Stewart (Adam); Phillip Tonge (Ohad); Ian Wolfe (Theron); Robert Middleton (Idbash); Mort Marshall (Benjie); Larry Dobkin

(Ephraim); Natalie Wood (Helena as a Girl); Peter Reynolds (Basil as a Boy); Mel Welles (Marcos); Jack Raine (Magistrate); Byrl Machin (Eulalia); John Sheffield, John Marlowe, Paul Power (Witnesses to Adoption); Frank Hagney, Harry Wilson (Ruffians); Charles Bewley (Roman Commander); David Bond (Cameleer); Allen Michaelson (High Priest); Lester Sharpe (Oasis Keeper); Laguna Festival of Art Players (Tableau Performers); Antony Eustral (Maximus, the Ship's Master).

PEARL OF THE SOUTH PACIFIC (RKO, 1955) C-85 min.

Producer, Benedict Bogeaus; director, Allan Dwan; screenplay, Talbot Jennings, Richard Landau, Jesse Lasky, Jr.; music, Lou Forbes; assistant directors, Lew Borzage, Elmer Decker; art director, Van Nest Polglase; camera, John Alton; editor, James Leicester.

Virginia Mayo (Rita); Dennis Morgan (Dan); David Farrar (Bully); Basil Ruysdael (Mr. Michael); Lance Fuller (George); Murvyn Vye (Halemano); Lisa Montell (Momu); Carol Thurston (Mother).

GREAT DAY IN THE MORNING (RKO, 1956) C-92 min.

Producer, Edmund Grainger; director, Jacques Tourneur; based on the novel by Robert Hardy Andrews; screenplay, Lesser Samuels; art directors, Albert D'Agostino, Jack Okey; music director, Constantine Bakaleinikoff; music, Leith Stevens; assistant director, Jimmy Casey; costumes, Gwen Wakeling; camera, William Snyder; editor, Harry Marker.

Virginia Mayo (Ann Alaine); Robert Stack (Owen Pentecost); Ruth Roman (Boston Grant); Alex Nicol (Stephen Kirby); Raymond Burr (Jumbo Means); Leo Gordon (Zeff Masterson); Donald McDonald (Gary Lawford); Regis Toomey (Father Murphy); Peter Whitney (Phil, the Cannibal); Dan White (Rogers).

CONGO CROSSING (Universal, 1956) C-87 min.

Producer, Howard Christie; director, Joseph Pevney; story, Houston Branch; screenplay, Richard Alan Simmons; art directors, Alexander Golitzen, Robert Boyle; assistant directors, Frank Shaw, Terry Nelson; gowns, Bill Thomas; music director, Joseph Gershenson; camera, Russell Metty; editor, Sherman Todd.

Virginia Mayo (Louise Whitman); George Nader (David Carr); Peter Lorre (Colonel Arragas); Michael Pate (Bart O'Connell); Rex Ingram (Dr. Gorman); Tonio Selwart (Carl Rittner); Kathryn Givney (Amelia Abbott); Raymond Bailey (Peter Mannering); George Ramsey (Miguel Diniz); Tudor Owen (Emile Zorfus); Bernard Hamilton (Pompala); Harold Dyrenforth (Steiner); Maurice Doner (Marquette); Ted Hecht (Official); Saul Gorss (Van Meer); Manny Emanuel (Corot); Jules Brock (Native Boy); Marvin Lindsay (Bit).

THE PROUD ONES (Twentieth Century-Fox, 1956) C-94 min.

Producer, Robert L. Jacks; director, Robert D. Webb; based on the novel by Verne Athanas; screenplay, Edmund North, Joseph Petracca; music, Lionel Newman; orchestrator, Maurice de Packh; costumes, Travilla; assistant director, Ad Schaumer; art directors, Lyle Wheeler, Leland Fuller; camera, Lucien Ballard; editor, Hugh S. Fowler.

Robert Ryan (Cass); Virginia Mayo (Sally); Jeffrey Hunter (Thad); Robert Middleton (Honest John Barrett); Walter Brennan (Jake); Arthur O'Connell (Jim Dexter); Ken Clark (Pike); Rodolfo Acosta (Chico); George Mathews (Dillon); Fay Roope (Markham); Edward Platt (Dr. Barlow); Whit Bissell (Mr. Bolton); Paul Burns (Billy Smith); Richard Deacon (Barber); Lois Ray (Belle); Jackie Coogan (Man on Make); Juanita Close (Helen); Harry Carter (Houseman); Steve Darrell (Trail Boss); Mary Thomas, Jonni Paris (Waitresses); I. Stanford Jolley (Crooked Card Player).

THE BIG LAND (Warner Bros., 1957) C-93 min.

Associate producer, George C. Bertholon; director, Gordon Douglas; based on the novel *Buffalo Grass* by Frank Gruber; screenplay, David Dortort, Martin Rackin; art director, Malcolm Bert; music, David Buttolph; orchestrator, Gus Levene; camera, John Seitz; editor, Thomas Reilly.

Alan Ladd (Chad Morgan); Virginia Mayo (Helen); Edmond O'Brien (Jagger); Julie Bishop (Kate Johnson); John Qualen (Sven Johnson); Anthony Caruso (Brog); Don Castle (Draper); David Ladd (David Johnson); George Lewis (Dawson); James Anderson (Cole); Les Johnson (Texan Rider); Don Kelly (Billy); James Seay (Ben); Jack Wrather, Jr. (Olaf Johnson); John McKee (Smoky); Gayle Kellogg (Brog's Gang Member); Steve Darrell (Manager); John Doucette (Hagan); Stacey Keach, Sr. (Man); Paul Bryar (Bartender); Mel Ford (Farmer); Kit Carson (Singer).

THE STORY OF MANKIND (Warner Brothers, 1957) C-100 min.

Producer, Irwin Allen; associate producer, George E. Swink; director, Allen; based on the book by Hendrik van Loon; screenplay, Allen, Charles Bennett; art director, Art Loel; music/

music director, Paul Sawtell; camera, Nick Musuraca; editors, Roland Gross, Gene Palmer.

Ronald Colman (Spirit of Man); Hedy Lamarr (Joan of Arc); Groucho Marx (Peter Minuit); Harpo Marx (Isaac Newton); Chico Marx (Monk); Virginia Mayo (Cleopatra); Agnes Moorehead (Queen Elizabeth); Vincent Price (Devil); Peter Lorre (Nero); Charles Coburn (Hippocrates); Cedric Hardwicke (High Judge); Cesar Romero (Spanish Envoy); John Carradine (Khufu); Dennis Hopper (Napoleon); Marie Wilson (Marie Antoinette); Helmut Dantine (Antony); Edward Everett Horton (Sir Walter Raleigh); Reginald Gardiner (Shakespeare); Marie Windsor (Josephine); Cathy O'Donnell (Early Christian Woman); Franklin Pangborn (Marquis de Varennes); Melville Cooper (Major Domo); Henry Daniell (Bishop of Beauvais); Francis X. Bushman (Moses); Jim Ameche (Alexander Graham Bell); Dani Crayne (Helen of Troy); Anthony Dexter (Columbus); Austin Green (Lincoln); Bobby Watson (Hitler); Reginald Sheffield (Caesar).

THE TALL STRANGER *(Allied Artists, 1957)* C-81 min.

Producer, Walter Mirisch; associate producer, Richard Heermance; director, Thomas Carr; story, Louis L'Amour; screenplay, Christopher Knopf; assistant directors, Austen Jewell, Paul Cameron; music, Hans Salter; art director, David Milton; camera, Wilfrid Cline; editor, William Austin.

Joel McCrea (Ned Bannon); Virginia Mayo (Ellen); Barry Kelley (Hardy Bishop); Michael Ansara (Zarata); Ray Teal (Cap); Whit Bissell (Judson); Michael Pate (Charley); Leo Gordon (Stark); James Dobson (Dud); Robert Foulk (Pagones); Adam Kennedy (Red); George Neise (Harper); George J. Lewis (Chavez); Guy Prescott (Barrett); Mauritz Hugo (Purcell); Ralph Reed (Murray); Ann Morrison (Mrs. Judson); Tom London, Lennie Geer (Workers); Don McGuire, Danny Sands (Settlers); Philip Phillips (Will).

FORT DOBBS *(Warner Bros. 1958)* 90 min.

Producer, Martin Rackin; director, Gordon Douglas; screenplay, Burt Kennedy, George W. George; music, Max Steiner; orchestrator, Murray Cutter; second unit and assistant director, William Kissel; art director, Stanley Fleischer; set decorator, Frank M. Miller; costumes, Marjorie Best; makeup, Gordon Bau; camera, William Clothier; editor, Clarence Kolster.

Clint Walker (Gar Davis); Virginia Mayo (Celia Gray); Brian Keith (Clett); Richard Eyer (Chad Gray); Russ Conway (Sheriff); Michael Dante (Billings).

WESTBOUND *(Warner Bros., 1959)* C-71 min.

Producer, Henry Blanke; director, Budd Boetticher; story, Berne Giler, Albert Shelby; screenplay, Giler; art director, Howard Campbell; set decorator, Gene Redd; costumes, Howard Shoup; makeup, Gordon Bau; assistant director, William Kissel; camera, Peverell Marley; editor, Philip Anderson.

Randolph Scott (John Hayes); Virginia Mayo (Norma Putnam); Karen Steele (Jeannie Miller); Michael Dante (Rod Miller); Andrew Duggan (Clay Putnam); Michael Pate (Mace); Wally Brown (Stubby); John Day (Russ); Walter Barnes (Willis); Fred Sherman (Christy); Mack Williams (Colonel Vance); Ed Prentiss (James Fuller); Jack Perrin (Man); Creighton Hale, Gertrude Keeler (Passengers); Walter Reed (Doctor); Buddy Roosevelt, Charles Morton (Stock Tenders).

JET OVER THE ATLANTIC *(Inter Continent, 1959)* 95 min.

Producer, Benedict Bogeaus; director, Byron Haskin; screenplay, Irving H. Cooper; music, Louis Forbes; songs, Forbes and Jack Hoffman; art directors, John Mansbridge, Ramon Rodriguez Granada; assistant director, Jamie Contreras; sound, Jose Carlos; camera, George Stahl; editor, James Leicester.

Guy Madison (Brett Matoon); Virginia Mayo (Jean Gruney); George Raft (Stafford); Ilona Massey (Mme. Galli-Cazetti); George Macready (Lord Robert Leverett); Anna Lee (Ursula Leverett); Margaret Lindsay (Mrs. Lanyard); Venetia Stevenson (June Elliott); Mary Anderson (Maria); Brett Halsey (Dr. Vanderbird); Argentina Brunetti (Miss Hooten); Frederic Worlock (Dean Halltree); Tudor Owen (Mr. Priestwood); Hilda Moreno (Mrs. Priestwood); John Kelly (Garbotz); Cesar Agarte (Co-Pilot); Armando Saenz (Pilot).

LA RIVOLTA DEI MERCENARI (REVOLT OF THE MERCENARIES) *(Prodas-Chapalo, 1960)* C-100 min.

Producer, Antonio Canelli; director, Piero Costa; screenplay, Vincenzoni, Musso, Falletti, Boccacci, Costa; camera, Godofredo Pacheco.

Virginia Mayo (Duchess de Rivalte); Conrado Sanriartin (Lucio de Rialto); Susanna Canales (Katia); Livio Lorenzon (Keller); Carto Calo (Miriam); and: Tonias Blanco, Franco Fantasia, Alfredo Mayo, John Kitzmiller, Luciano Benetti, Marco Tutti.

YOUNG FURY *(Paramount, 1965)* C-80 min.

Producer, A. C. Lyles; director, Chris Nyby; story, Steve Fisher, Lyles; screenplay, Fisher; art directors, Hal Pereira, Arthur Lonergan; music, Paul Dunlap; camera, Haskell Boggs; editor, Marvin Coll.

Rory Calhoun (Clint McCoy); Virginia Mayo (Sarah McCoy); Lon Chaney, Jr. (Bartender); Richard Arlen (Sheriff Jenkins); John Agar (Dawson); William Bendix (Blacksmith); Preston Pierce (Tige McCoy); Linda Foster (Sally Miller); Robert Biheller (Biff Dane); Rex Bell, Jr. (Farmer); Merry Anders (Alice); Jody McCrea (Stone); Joan Huntington (Kathy); Dave Dunlop (Smith).

CASTLE OF EVIL *(United Picture Corporation, 1966)* C-81 min.

Executive producer, Fred Jordan; producer, Erle Lyon; director, Francis D. Lyons; screenplay, Charles A. Wallace; art director, Paul Sylos, Jr.; music, Paul Dunlap; sound, John Bury; camera, Brick Marquard; editor, Robert S. Eisen.

Scott Brady (Matt Granger); Virginia Mayo (Sable); David Brian (Robert Hawley); Lisa Gaye (Carol Harris); Hugh Marlowe (Dr. Corozal); Shelley Morrison (Lupe); Ernest Sarracino (Tunki); William Thourlby (Electronic Man); Natividad Vacio (Machado).

FORT UTAH *(Paramount, 1967)* C-83 min.

Producer, A. C. Lyles; director, Lesley Selander; screenplay, Steve Fisher, Andrew Craddock; art directors, Hal Pereira, Al Roelofo; set decorators, Robert Benton, John Sturtevant; makeup, Wally Westmore; assistant director, Ralph Axness; music, Jimmie Haskell; sound, John Carter, John Wilkinson; special camera effects, Paul K. Lerpae; camera, Lothrop Worth; editor, John F. Schreyer.

John Ireland (Tom Horn); Virginia Mayo (Linda Lee); Scott Brady (Dajin); John Russell (Eli Jones); Robert Strauss (Ben Stokes); James Craig (Bo Greer); Richard Arlen (Sam Tyler); Jim Davis (Scarecrow); Donald Barry (Harris); Harry Lauter (Britches); Reg Parton (Rafe); Eric Cody (Shirt); Read Morgan (Cavalry Lieutenant).

WON TON TON, THE DOG WHO SAVED HOLLYWOOD *(Paramount, 1976)* C-92 min.

Producers, David V. Picker, Arnold Schulman, Michael Winner; director, Winner; screenplay, Schulman, Cy Howard; art director, Ward Preston; set director, Ned Parsons; assistant director, Charles Okyn; makeup, Philip Rhodes; music, Neal Hefti; dogs trained by Karl Miller; sound, Bob Post; camera, Richard H. Kline; editor, Bernard Gribble.

Dennis Morgan (Tour Guide); Shecky Greene (Tourist); Phil Leeds, Cliff Norton (Dog Catchers); Madeline Kahn (Estie Del Ruth); Teri Garr (Fluffy Peters); Romo Vincent (Short-Order Cook); Bruce Dern (Grayson Potchuck); Sterling Holloway (Old Man on Bus); William Benedict (Man on Bus); Dorothy Gulliver (Old Woman on Bus); William Demarest (Studio Gatekeeper); Art Carney (J.J. Fromberg); Virginia Mayo (Miss Battley); Henny Youngman (Manny Farber); Rory Calhoun (Philip Hart); Billy Barty (Assistant Director); Henry Wilcoxon (Silent Film Director); Richard Arlen, Ricardo Montalban (Silent Film Stars); Johnny Weissmuller, Jackie Coogan (Stage Hands); Jack La Rue (Silent Film Villain); Joan Blondell (Landlady); Yvonne De Carlo (Cleaning Woman); Ethel Merman (Hedda Parsons); Aldo Ray (Stubby Stebbins); Broderick Crawford (Special Effects Man); Dorothy Lamour (Visiting Film Star); Phil Silvers (Murray Fromberg); Nancy Walker (Mrs. Fromberg); Gloria DeHaven, Ann Miller, Janet Blair, Cyd Charisse (President's Girls); Stepin Fetchit (Dancing Butler); Ken Murray (Souvenir Salesman); George Jessel (Awards Announcer); Rudy Vallee (Autograph Hound); Dean Stockwell (Paul Lavell); Dick Haymes (James Crawford); Tab Hunter (David Hamilton); Ron Leibman (Rudy Montague); Fritz Feld (Rudy's Butler); Robert Alda (Richard Entwhistle); Dennis Day (Singing Telegraph Man); The Ritz Brothers (Cleaning Women); Jesse White (Rudy's Agent); Carmel Myers (Woman Journalist); Jack Carter (Male Journalist); Victor Mature (Nick); Barbara Nichols (Nick's Girl); Fernando Lamas, Zsa Zsa Gabor (Stars at Premiere); Huntz Hall (Moving Man); Doodles Weaver (Man in Mexican Film); Edgar Bergen (Professor Quicksand); Peter Lawford (Slapstick Star); Morey Amsterdam, Eddie Foy, Jr. (Custard Pie Stars); Alice Faye (Secretary at Gate); Ann Rutherford (Grayson's Studio Secretary); Milton Berle (Blind Man); Patricia Morison, Guy Madison (Stars at Screening); John Carradine (Drunk); Walter Pidgeon (Grayson's Butler); Keye Luke (Cook in Kitchen); Pedro Gonzales-Gonzales (Mexican Projectionist); Army Archerd (Premiere M.C.).

FRENCH QUARTER *(Crown International, 1977)* C-

Executive producer, Herb Schneiderman; associate producer, Tony Alatis; producer/director, Dennis Kane; screenplay, Barney Cohen, Kane; music, Dick Hyman; camera, Jerry Kalogeratos.

With: Bruce Davison, Virginia Mayo, Lindsay Bloom, Lance Legault, Ann Michelle, Alisha Fontaine.

HAUNTED *(1977)*

Producer/director/screenplay, Michael de Gaetano; music, Lor Crane.

With: Virginia Mayo, Aldo Ray, Jim Negele, Ann Michelle.

The Oomph Girl in 1944.

5

ANN SHERIDAN

> 5' 5½"   118 pounds
> Red hair   Hazel eyes
> Pisces

IN THE FORTIES, the best way a dame could handle a smart guy was with a wise remark. Ann Sheridan knew all the quick remarks and had ready answers to all the wisecracks thrust at her during her Hollywood career. She possessed a certain charm, a subtle knack for being direct, and a fine shapely appearance. She was labeled "The Oomph Girl" by studio publicists, much as in the Twenties Clara Bow had been branded "The It Girl." It helped to build Ann's screen image, but it also caused her to be stereotyped oncamera.

It seemed that no one actress portrayed a struggling working girl better than Miss Sheridan, and at Warner Bros. she had ample opportunity in their output of proletarian dramas. But she was equally at ease in sophisticated comedy, quite capable of delivering brisk dialogue with the proper timing. In many ways she was a unique cinema commodity, never fully exploited for her full array of versatility.

As David Shipman would judge in his admirable book *The Great Movie Stars: The Golden Years*: "She was a good all-rounder but was at her most direct as a Brooklynesque hash-slinger, quick with the wisecracks, slamming back at Cagney (or George Raft or Pat O'Brien). It wasn't a type that was appreciated too much, when great acting was confused with Greer Garson or Norma Shearer; nor was Sheridan in the same league as Betty Grable as a pin-up.... She really was too warm, too lush, and too genuinely glamorous to compete with the other tinny girls. Her singing voice, for instance, a warm contralto, is much more in tune with today's taste. At all events, she never quite received her due."

When she died in January 1967, the *London Times* would sum up: "Without ever quite achieving the mythic status of a super-star, she was always a pleasure to watch, and, as with all true stars, was never quite like anyone else."

Clara Lou Sheridan was born on Sunday, February 21, 1915, in Denton, Texas. She was named after a neighbor, Clara Evans, and her mother, Lula Stewart Warren. Her father, George W. Sheridan, owned both a garage, where he worked as supervisor and mechanic, and a ranch. He was allegedly a direct descendant of the Civil War General Philip Sheridan. Clara Lou was the youngest of six children, one of whom died while still an infant.

Young Clara Lou grew up on the ranch. She acquired all the tomboy traits: whistling through her fingers, bulldogging a steer, making a fire by rubbing two sticks together, and even shooting a pistol with fair accuracy. Always around horses, Clara Lou learned to ride exceptionally well.

She attended Robert E. Lee grade school and then went to Denton Junior High where she achieved high scholastic standing. She later matriculated at North Texas State Teachers College. While enrolled in acting classes there, she became intrigued. ("Secretly I wanted to be a band singer. But that meant I thought I was pretty, and vanity was 'bad.'") Initially she had intended to major in art, but she switched her major to dramatics. She finally found the nerve to audition for a vocalist post with the college band, and nurtured a notion of someday going to New York and joining a chorus line.

It was in 1933, while Clara Lou was still in college, that her sister Kitty, as a lark, entered Clara Lou's photo in Paramount's "Search for Beauty" contest. Shortly afterward the coed was reading the *Dallas News* on campus and, to her astonishment, saw her photograph in the newspaper as one of the contestants. Furious, she drove forty miles to Dallas, stormed into the paper's city room, and began to scold drama editor John Rosenfield for entering her in the contest without permission. Rosenfield eventually was able to explain who the real culprit was.

Months passed, and Clara Lou was about to return to North Texas State for the fall semester. While packing her bags in Waco where she had been visiting relatives during the summer recess, John Rosenfield phoned her and said: "Come on home, Red. You won one of the trips to Hollywood." "You must be nuts!" she exclaimed. "What are you talking about?" Enthused, Rosenfield continued, "I mean it. You won one of the trips. Paramount's going to put you in a movie. You can't get out of it now. You and fourteen other girls won parts in the picture, but you're the only girl from our state. You can't let Texas down."

Not being one to let anyone down, Clara Lou, on Friday, September 15, 1933, accompanied by her mother and father, brother George, and sisters Mabel, Pauline, and Kitty, drove to the railroad station in Dallas for the trip to California.

Paramount did not give its contest winners any acting lessons before putting them before the cameras. Actually, all that was required was that they look pretty and display their well-proportioned curves. Clara Lou was one of six who were given Paramount stock contracts. Another was Gwenllian Gill, while the male counterparts in the contest included Julian Madison, Colin Tapley, and Alfred Delcambre. The film *Search for Beauty* (1934), featuring Larry "Buster" Crabbe and Ida Lupino, was eventually released in Dallas, and the marquee at the local theatre listed Clara Lou Sheridan as the star. Dallas theatregoers, as well as all movie viewers, saw Clara Lou in a most remarkable performance—peeking over the shoulders of two other contest winners and grinning.

Actually, after the making of *Search for Beauty*, Paramount had few if any plans for the contestants signed to contracts. Fortunately for Clara Lou, she had answered "yes" to a particular question on the ques-

Gwenllian Gill, Ann Sheridan, Colin Tapley, Alfred Delcambre, Julian Madison, and Eldred Tidbury—new Paramount contract players ('33)

tionnaire handed to all the contest winners. The reply was to the query "Can you ride a horse?" Thus Clara Lou began her career as a gal in the saddle, a career which saw her gallop through many cowboy films in two years, as well as double for more genteel stars. Often just her hands and/or feet were used in closeups. Frequently the fledgling actress would be escorted to a soundstage, display her hands holding a letter, and, after the sequence was filmed, disappear to her next chore. She often had no idea on which film she was then working.

Clara Lou felt fortunate to be earning $50 weekly—a respectable salary during the Depression years. She had a six-month contract with option clauses that would escalate her salary in $25 steps if the studio continued to use her. She was in no position to ask for a raise, even though she knew of other stock people who started at $150 per week. Clara Lou, like many other stable players at the lot, had a variety of walk-ons and bits in films. While they provided her with little screen exposure (often her footage would be cut from the release print), it did give her the necessary professional experience. In *Kiss and Make Up* (1934), starring Cary Grant and Helen Mack, she was a beauty operator; Jack Oakie's *Shoot the Works* (1934) found her as a secretary; she was a phone operator in Cary Grant's *Ladies Should Listen* (1934); in George Raft's *Limehouse Blues* (1934), Clara Lou can be spotted as the girl with the couples in one crowd scene. By the time of Randolph Scott's *Home on the Range* (1935), one of the studio's Zane Grey Westerns, Clara Lou was playing the role of an entertainer, and in George Raft and Carole Lombard's *Rumba* (1935) she was a dancer.

As a living promotion for *We're Not Dressing* ('34).

Modeling, 1935 style.

If Clara Lou had a long way to go to join the ranks of studio stars Carole Lombard, Claudette Colbert, Mae West, Marlene Dietrich, and Sylvia Sidney, she was certainly industrious. Obligingly she posed for the requisite cheesecake shots, attended studio functions as living set dressing, and participated in the acting school's theatre. In 1935, the stock company was performing a play, *The Milky Way,* in which Clara Lou had the role of Ann. Executives from the front office called her in and told her that Clara Lou Sheridan was too long for the marquee. It was one of her first indications that the company had actual plans for her career. They asked the Texas miss to select a new first name. She chose Lou, but the studio insisted that it would confuse the public since it sounded too much like a man's name. Finally she returned to the play rehearsals and asked her co-players for their help. One said, "Since you're playing the part of Ann in *The Milky Way,* why not Ann?" The front office agreed to the new name, Ann Sheridan.

Behold My Wife! (1935), starring Sylvia Sidney and Gene Raymond, provided Ann with her first chance to use the new name tag. It also allowed her an opportunity to display her rising talent. She was in two scenes, one of them a very dramatic sequence in which she commits suicide. Sheridan herself believed that suicide bit was the main reason why Paramount renewed her option. Also Mitchell Leisen, who directed the film, was a good pal of Ann's, and he pushed the scene on the front office. Years later, Ann would say, "Committing suicide is a great thing, you know, to have in a picture. It's something that draws your eye to the girl."

Her first leading role at Paramount was in a quickie entitled *Car 99* (1935) in which she played opposite Fred MacMurray and Sir Guy Standing. Then there was a Zane Grey Western with Randolph Scott, entitled *Rocky Mountain Mystery* (1935), and *Mississippi* (1935), an A-film with W. C. Fields and Bing Crosby, in which Joan Bennett was the light-haired heroine, while Ann was merely a school girl. In her only loan-out while at

With Randolph Scott in *Rocky Mountain Mystery* ('35).

With J. Carroll Naish (right) in *The Crusades* ('35).

Paramount, Ann went over to Ambassador to join Kermit Maynard in *Red Blood of Courage* (1935) filmed at the Talisman Studio.

Even optimistic Ann realized that her career at Paramount was not progressing as it should. There was just too much stiff competition and no lord protector to promote her status. In George Raft's *The Glass Key* (1935), Ann was merely the nurse who attended to the star's wounds in the hospital scene. For Cecil B. DeMille's *The Crusades* (1935) Ann had one line of dialogue, "The cross, the cross, let me kiss the cross," which she said with a distinctive Texas accent. Then there was a closeup of her weeping face—very unglamorous.* As if to seal Ann's fate at the studio, Paramount released a short subject to promote the DeMille blockbuster. Ann was included in the featurette entitled *The Extra Girl*. The studio then dropped her option.

Anxious for any kind of film work, Ann found a job at Universal in *Off Side*, retitled *Fighting Youth* (1935). Much of the Charles Farrell-Edward Nugent program feature was shot at the Los Angeles Coliseum. Cast as Carol Arlington, Ann was on the project for three weeks at $125 per week. She then had to survive on that accumulated sum for several lean months. She seriously thought of abandoning her career and returning to Texas. Her agent at the time, Bill Meiklejohn, insisted that he would find her some screen work, even if for the time being it had to be extra roles. However, she had learned in Hollywood that if you are not under studio contract and accept extra work, you are branded forever. Thus she scorned all extra jobs and soon dropped Meiklejohn as her representative and signed with Dick Pollimer. Among the new agent's other clients were Ida Lupino, Anita Louise, and Tom Brown. Pollimer finally persuaded Max Arnow, the casting director at Warner Bros. to give Ann a screen test. She tested and received a small part in *Sing Me a Love Song* (1936) featuring James Melton and Patricia Ellis. The director of the modest film was Ray Enright, whom Ann would later declare to be her favorite such craftsman.

Max Arnow was impressed with Ann and her performance as Lola Parker in *Sing Me a Love Song,* even though most critics and reviewers were more intent upon the comedy relief provided by ZaSu Pitts and Allen Jenkins. Arnow persuaded his studio bosses to sign Ann to a six-month contract at $75 a week. She would remain with the studio for twelve years.

Ann was next cast in the powerful social drama *Black Legion* (1936) which focused on a Ku Klux Klan-type organization. Under Archie Mayo's direction, the film featured floggings, burnings, and a climactic shooting. Ann played the role of Betty Grogan, the girlfriend of Dick Foran. Although her part was not major (Humphrey Bogart as the confused ex-factory worker had the lead), it was a bigger assignment than any she had enjoyed at Paramount. As the weepy girl Ann proved that she would fit in well with the Warner Bros. stock company. Offcamera, she became good friends with Bogart who admired her flinty, honest ways.

Meanwhile, she had been dating Philadelphia-born Edward Norris who, after a stage and newspaper career, was making a second try at a film career. By 1936 he was appearing in featured parts at MGM (*Small Town Girl*) and at Universal (*The Magnificent Brute*). He and Ann met in the lobby of the apartment house where they both resided. She felt that the 5'11", dark-haired, brown-eyed actor was the handsomest man she had ever seen and he in turn was attracted by the pert actress. A mutual acquaintance introduced them officially the next day, and he then asked Ann for a date. They went dancing at the Biltmore Bowl and soon agreed that they were in love. One week after they met, on Sunday, August 26, 1936, they were wed in Ensenada, Mexico.

With two friends of Norris, actors Ivan

---

*Ann had hoped that the role would be very chic, and she was greatly disillusioned by the experience. "I thought, 'Oh, how wonderful to wear a black wig.' Well, I didn't know they take 'em out of stock and they slam 'em on your head and it doesn't fit and the hair lace comes loose and they come up and glue it on just before the take and it falls off again—I was so horrible looking! Really, it was awful."

Posing with Humphrey Bogart, Erin O'Brien-Moore, Dickie Jones, and Dick Foran for *Black Legion* ('36).

Lebedeff and Bruce Pierce, in attendance, a Mexican judge performed the marriage ceremony. Ann wore a white slack suit and a paisley scarf, her red hair tied with a white ribbon. The groom and attendants were garbed in sports clothes. The judge read the ritual quickly, the groom kissed the bride, and the wedding party returned to Hollywood.

Warner Bros. then awarded Ann the part of schoolteacher Judy Nolan in *The Great O'Malley* (1936), with Pat O'Brien in the title part. It was a simple story of a tough cop (O'Brien) with a strict regard for the law who is softened by his affection for a crippled little girl (Sybil Jason). Humphrey Bogart was cast as the girl's dad who is caught in the act of robbery by O'Brien and later sentenced to prison. Ann had a sizable role in the proceedings as the love interest of hard-working Officer O'Malley. (Years later Ann would joke of the role, "That was just a schoolteacher who said, 'He's an evil man [Bogart]. They went that way.'")

While her film career was progressing, her marriage was deteriorating. A mere 375 days after she they were wed, Ann and Norris separated. (They would divorce in 1939.) Hollywood observers cited the fact that Ann's career was rising faster than Norris' as a major point of friction between the two. The now single Ann would become a very popular bachelor girl in the movie colony, an asset as anyone's escort.

She next appeared in Warner Bros.' *San Quentin* (1937), which reunited her with Pat O'Brien and Humphrey Bogart, under Lloyd Bacon's direction. The prison drama was filled with studio stock players, including such regulars as Joe Sawyer, Barton MacLane, Veda Ann Borg, and Emmett Vogan. This was one of the company's tough jail pictures on a lesser scale. As cafe singer May Kennedy, Ann had the opportunity to wear Howard Shoup gowns and sing the Harry Warren/Al Dubin tune "How Could You?" Her languorous style as a chanteuse was visually more exciting than her competent

The Warner Bros. contractee in 1936.

With Gordon Oliver, Emmett Vogan, and Pat O'Brien in *San Quentin* ('37).

husky vocals.* It was to Ann's credit that she made her role as the girlfriend of convicted convict Red Kennedy (Bogart) so convincing. Her luminous hazel eyes seemed to have been made for closeups, especially when they were supposed to be filled with tears.

*In a 1966 interview with Ray Hagen for *Screen Facts* magazine, Ann would recall, "It was the first time I sang in a picture.... I went to quite a few voice coaches, but that was through the studio. Nobody can teach me to sing. I haven't got that kind of a voice. It's kind of an odd voice.... To make me a singer would be absolutely impossible. I haven't got the range or anything else, and I know it. But I went to many voice coaches."

Kay Francis, Bette Davis, and Olivia de Havilland were the three most important female contract stars on the Warner Bros. lot in 1937. Wisecracking blonde Joan Blondell would be departing soon for Columbia Pictures, Marion Davies would retire, and Paramount's Claudette Colbert was at the Burbank facilities only on special loan-out for *Tovarich*. Ann Sheridan's rivals for roles at the studio were the like of Jane Bryan, Priscilla Lane, Beverly Roberts, and Jane Wyman. (Newcomer Lana Turner, after making a splash in *They Won't Forget* and a few other bits in 1937, would leave the lot for a long tenure at MGM.) At the time Ann's competition at the studio were receiving such weekly salaries as: Margaret Lindsay, $1,000; Priscilla Lane, $500; Gale Page, $400; Beverly Roberts, $350; Gloria Dickson, $200.

Ann recalls: "I did almost every B-picture that was ever made on the Warner lot." While this was an exaggeration, economy-minded Jack L. Warner did keep his players very busy, moving from one production to another. Other 1937 releases that featured Ann were the low-grade *Wine, Women and Horses* with Barton MacLane and Dick Purcell—a remake of Edward G. Robinson's *Dark Hazard* (1934)—and *The Footloose Heiress* with Craig Reynolds, Anne Nagel, and William Hopper (son of columnist Hedda). Ann hoped that the work would help to lead her career to better things.

However, the year 1938 began no differently than the prior one. For the double-feature market she joined with John Litel, Mary Maguire, and Dick Purcell in *Alcatraz Island* (1938), produced for Bryan Foy's B-unit. This prison fare was followed by *She Loved a Fireman* (1938), of which she says: "God, wouldn't you know I'd do that!" Next came two cheapies derived from Mignon Eberhart mystery novels. *The Patient in Room 18* (1938) was a hospital homicide affair, co-starring Ann with Patric Knowles. *Mystery House* (1938), featuring Ann, Dick Purcell, and Anne Nagel, was extracted from Miss Eberhart's novel *The Mystery of Hunting's End*. Its greatest virtue was that it was only sixty-one minutes long. A step forward was *The Cowboy from Brooklyn* (1938) which presented resident crooner Dick Powell as a radio performer who must prove he is an authentic cowhand. After this lighthearted fluff, Ann did her best to enliven *Little Miss Thoroughbred* (1938), with Janet Kay Chapman as the girl in question.

Years later Ann vividly recalled how her next assignment, a loan-out, came about. "It was on request—an interview with John Stahl, God love him. I went over all dressed up fit to kill. Warner Bros. had fitted me out with a wardrobe; they gave me the fox furs and the hat and all that stuff and sent me over to Mr. Stahl." The picture was Universal's *Letter of Introduction* (1938) in which an aspiring actress (Andrea Leeds) tries to

With Patric Knowles in *The Patient in Room 18* ('38).

With John Litel, Janet Kay Chapman, and Frank McHugh in *Little Miss Thoroughbred* ('38).

achieve theatrical success without the help of famous father Adolphe Menjou. Sheridan, in her five short scenes, portrayed the other woman (Menjou's mistress). Others in the cast included Edgar Bergen (with Charlie McCarthy, of course), smart-mouthed Eve Arden, and smiling hoofer George Murphy. Returning to Warner Bros. Ann joined with Margaret Lindsay and Marie Wilson in *Broadway Musketeers* (1938), a remake of that well-endowed *Three on a Match* (1933) which had starred Ann Dvorak, Bette Davis, and Joan Blondell. The new version, directed by John Farrow, was a pale imitation of its predecessor.

Warner Bros., like the other studios, had the habit of taking enormous numbers of photographs of their stars when they were between pictures. Photographer George Hurrell was a standout cameraman, and he brought expressive qualities to his still work. Hurrell's photographic sophistication did a great deal to aid Ann's career. In fact, his series of glamour shots of the actress might well have influenced her studio bosses in their handling of her career.

During the latter part of 1938, Ann was to obtain her first starring role in an A-picture for the studio. The film was the classic gangster saga of two slum boys growing up together, one turning out good, the other bad (along the same plotline as MGM's *Manhattan Melodrama* in 1934). *Angels with Dirty Faces* would prove to be the start of Ann's rise in the film world. She co-starred opposite James Cagney, Pat O'Brien, the Dead End Kids, and Humphrey Bogart. Directed by the workhorse of Warner Bros., Michael Curtiz, this excellent tale of the streets skyrocketed the career of B-picture Sheridan into a more highly favored cinema commodity. She portrayed Laury Ferguson, a former childhood playmate of Rocky Sullivan (Cagney) and Jerry Connelly (O'Brien). In a rut —running a boarding house and helping Father Connelly to regenerate a gang of slum kids—she encounters ex-convict Sullivan. He is a man with big ideas, and she envisions herself as the flashy and glamorous girl she has always wanted to be.

Viewing this 97-minute feature is sheer bliss. The combination of Cagney, Sheridan, and O'Brien in well-polished performances could not be better. Ann plays the role of a Depression child who wants more out of life than grime and purity. When Cagney hires her for his club, she has her big chance to parade in luxurious gowns and to be the center of attention for the customers.

The genius of Ann's screen performance is that she could be so believable. At times she is tough and smart-mouthed; at others she is teary and soulful as she weighs the moral value between ill-gotten wealth and honest, untinseled happiness. She is the link between bad guy Cagney and the voice of conscience, Father Connelly.

Pugnacious Cagney, like all of Ann's leading men, found her to be a delightful and willing performer who had no artificial airs and refused to play games on or off the set. As it turned out, Cagney became her first real acting teacher. Just before each scene was shot, Cagney would take her off to a quiet corner of the set and say, "Look, kid, this is the way to play this. See, you. . . ." Sheridan once described her co-star's personality: "Cagney off the screen is exactly like Cagney on it. It was always 'Hi ya, baby,' or 'How are ya, sweetheart?' He's a great guy. He didn't smoke or drink. He could get drunk on two drinks of liquor. And he never made the party scene."

After her success in *Angels with Dirty Faces*, Ann was tagged as an important personage in the film industry. Long out of her apprentice period, she was now an established personality. However, it might have taken her longer to achieve stardom had not a fluke of publicity gimmickry skyrocketed her to national fame. As it happened, the series of George Hurrell still shots of Ann made the rounds of columnists and magazine reporters. Famed journalist Walter Winchell, commenting on one of her photos, wrote, "Ann Sheridan in this film has plenty of Umph!" The studio stole the idea, changed the spelling to "Oomph," and set up a contest to name Hollywood's "Oomph Girl," really the most glamorous actress in the business.

The publicity stunt was engineered to obtain column space for Warner Bros. and for Ann Sheridan. The non-Warner glamour gals entered in the judging were Dolores Del Rio, Marlene Dietrich, Alice Faye, Hedy Lamarr, Carole Lombard, and Norma Shearer. Each contestant was to have a photo submitted to the committee so that the judges could assess the subjects in their best pose. The shot of Ann was one taken by Hurrell showing her lying on a leopard skin, wearing a crepe negligee, with a roll-back collar and long sleeves.

Ace publicist Bob Taplinger arranged an award dinner at the Los Angeles Town House to name the "Oomph Girl." The thirteen arbiters who convened that evening included Rudy Vallee, Earl Carroll, Busby Berkeley, David Niven, Orry-Kelly, Dudley Field Malone, the Earl of Warwick, and, of course, George Hurrell. "I can't remember that evening too well," Ann would say decades later. "It was one of those nerve-racking things and I actually can't remember very much of it." Ann, putting on her best smile, accepted the accolade of "The Oomph Girl" when her name was announced as the winner.

The next day, someone in the publicity department at Warner Bros. walked up to studio boss Jack L. Warner and showed him the layout in the paper and the sizable publicity on the contest. Warner said, "Aah, she'll be dead in six months," and then threw the newspaper back at him.

Publicity worked for her even further. It was written that Ann said, "Oomph is the sound a fat man makes when he bends over to tie his shoelace in a telephone booth." She did not actually say this, for it was a press agent's invention, but she adopted it wholeheartedly. "Oomph" did for Ann's career what the sarong had done for Dorothy Lamour and the "peek-a-boo" low-slung hair style would do for Veronica Lake.

After the Oomph campaign, Ann was sent on a personal appearance tour to promote herself and the studio product. Her stops included Washington, D.C. and a stay at the Warner Bros. flagship theatre, The Strand, in New York. For her act she sang a medley of old songs and spoke about some of her

With Guinn "Big Boy" Williams, Victor Jory, and Ward Bond in *Dodge City* ('39).

company's upcoming pictures. Because of the tour, Ann missed out on the role of Joyce Conover in the James Cagney/George Raft film *Each Dawn I Die* (1939). Jane Bryan was substituted. Sheridan was also scheduled to portray Panama in the Cagney gangster film *The Roaring Twenties* (1939). Gladys George replaced Sheridan who replaced Lee Patrick who replaced Glenda Farrell. Plans for Columbia to borrow Ann to co-star in *Golden Boy* (1939) did not come about; Barbara Stanwyck was given the important role opposite newcomer William Holden.

When she returned to Hollywood, Ann found herself in a special category as a very marketable property. Warner Bros. suddenly was anxious to capitalize on her Oomph Girl popularity and rushed her into *They Made Me a Criminal* (1939), a Busby Berkeley-directed remake of *The Life of Jimmy Dolan* (1933). John Garfield was starred as a boxer on the lam who takes refuge on a farm out west. The love and affection of the people who live there—especially Gramma (May Robson) and heroine Peggy (Gloria Dickson)—reform him and cause him to change his bitter, anti-establishment ways. It is an enjoyable feature, with fine support from the Dead End Kids, and especially from Claude Rains as a Dick Tracy-type detective. Ann had a relatively short role as Goldie, the gold-digging hussy who runs after Garfield. Despite her brief part, Warner Bros. gave Ann prominent billing in the feature, at the expense of Gloria Dickson who actually had the female leading role.*

The same situation occurred in Ann's next assignment, *Dodge City* (1939), a sprawling, brawling, slam-bang super-Western directed by Michael Curtiz. It was the fifth co-starring vehicle for the screen love team of Errol Flynn and Olivia de Havilland, and it was Warner Bros.' major entry in the year of the big sagebrush movie cycle. Flynn, in his first Western, was cast as devil-may-care Wade Hatton, the man hired to clean up the town. Bruce Cabot was villainous Jeff Sur-

---

*Ann fondly recalled making *They Made Me a Criminal* in her interview with Ray Hagen in 1966: "John Garfield was a dear man. He was like the little guy who brought the apple for the teacher, and here I was, this hussy with the fuzzy hair and the décolletage dress. I was supposed to kiss John, but Buz [Berkeley] said: 'Hold it until I say cut. Just keep kissing him.' Well of course he wouldn't say it, and I had John around the neck and on the floor—he was absolutely red."

rett, with Alan Hale and Guinn "Big Boy" Williams as Flynn's sidekicks. Among the supporting cast were such on-lot regulars as John Litel, Ward Bond, Henry Travers, Henry O'Neill, Victor Jory, Douglas Fowley, and Monte Blue. Miss de Havilland was the demure miss who initially despises Flynn for having shot her brother; later they fall in love. As a focal point of contrast, Ann was Ruby Gilman, the reigning singer at the Gay Lady Saloon. Although Ann's character loses Flynn's love in the plotline, she received special billing in the advertisement, promoting her appearance as the risqué showgirl. It was Ann's first feature in color, and she says: "Almost made me blind, that incredible color lighting!"

Naughty But Nice (1939) had been sitting on the shelf for many months before Warner Bros. decided to release it, taking advantage of Ann's growing popularity with the public. Actually it is a rather breezy comedy which cast Sheridan opposite Dick Powell. The story centers on a stuffy music professor (Powell) who unwittingly composes a popular hit tune. His fame turns him into a different person, and other complications ensue. The rest of the cast under Ray Enright's direction included Gale Page, Ronald Reagan, Allen Jenkins, Helen Broderick, ZaSu Pitts, and Jerry Colonna. This musical comedy contained various compositions by Bach, Mozart, Liszt, and Wagner, and enabled Ann to start another close friendship. She and co-star Gale Page became very good friends, and Ann used to refer to her as "my favorite Cherokee girl friend."

About this time, Ann, gaining further popularity on as well as off the set, was interviewed by director George Cukor for the part of Scarlett O'Hara in the pending David O. Selznick production of *Gone with the Wind*. Warner Bros. had no objection to the interview, for it only further proved the industry interest in Ann Sheridan. As is well known, Vivien Leigh eventually played the Academy

With Morton Lowry and Helen Parrish in *Winter Carnival* ('39).

With costume designer Howard Shoup at Warner Bros. in 1939.

Award-winning role in the MGM Civil War epic.

Losing out on that important loan-out, Ann instead went to United Artists for *Winter Carnival* (1939), set at Dartmouth College during a snow holiday weekend. Ann portrayed divorcée Jill Baxter in love with a college professor (Richard Carlson). A pleasant but forgettable romantic drama, the film holds some interest in cinema history as being another instance of writer F. Scott Fitzgerald's attempting to conform to the Hollywood production line scenario system and failing.

One of the more positive professional steps for Ann occurred at a chance meeting in the studio commissary with good friend and fellow Warner Bros. employee Paul Muni. The distinguished actor advised her to use the "Oomph" exposure to her advantage. He told her that the publicity had made her a valuable commodity and that she could therefore pressure the studio into giving her worthwhile parts.

However, more celluloid fodder was her immediate fate. In the remake of *The Crowd Roars* (1932), entitled *Indianapolis Speedway* (1939), Ann joined with Pat O'Brien, John Payne, Gale Page, and Frank McHugh. Once again Sheridan inherited an old Joan Blondell role. The tattered story focused on two brothers in the speedway racing business, the older one (O'Brien) trying futilely to keep the younger one (Payne) out of the sport. Ann played Frankie Merrick, one of the film's two love interests. The austere *New York Times* was not very enthused about the rehashed story or Ann. "We won't say any more about the story except to deny stoutly the Warner advertisements that this is the picture that gives their 'oomph girl,' Ann Sheridan, the 'big part you've wanted to see her play.' It isn't a big part and, so far as we are concerned, we don't remember wanting to see her play it. So there! Besides, she doesn't play it any too well, seeming to mistake sulkiness for sultryness and being of much less service to the melodrama than Gale Page who isn't an 'oomph girl' but knows what to do when the camera's looking." Nevertheless, the public had more confidence in Ann than the *Times'* Frank S. Nugent, and she continued to gain in popularity at the box office.

Ann's sixth and final 1939 release was *Angels Wash Their Faces,* the studio's attempt to cash in on the previous year's winner, *Angels with Dirty Faces.* However, this would-be sequel directed by Ray Enright could not stand up to the forerunner, no matter how the routine plot tried to capture some of the spunk of the Cagney/O'Brien/Sheridan classic. Here Ann plays Joy Ryan, a protective sister trying to clear the police record of her younger delinquent brother (Frankie Thomas). Despite her efforts he takes up with the local gang of juvenile no-gooders and becomes involved in more scrapes. Ronald Reagan was on hand as Ann's love interest, and the Dead End Kids were their usual mischievous yet sensitive selves.

Besides the public, Ann had her champions in the media field. One fan magazine article of the time bemoaned, "Ann is more often than most miscast and her beauty and talent are wasted. Lovely, luscious, soft, purring, she is the dream of every good and bad man; she makes our hearts beat properly, with all their force and vigor, with what the doctor calls palpitation, but which is the way every heart beats when it really has something to beat for."

Hollywood was also purring with the alleged romance of Sheridan and eligible playboy actor Cesar Romero. They met during her separation from Eddie Norris. During the separation Norris was rumored to be engaged to another, while Ann was seen frequently with Romero. Now being referred to as the "Texas Bombshell," Miss Sheridan was touted as the girl most likely to snag bachelor Romero. However, their "romance," though not their friendship, soon became a thing of the past. Another of her real romantic interests of the period was singer Allan Jones.

Ann moved into the new decade with a dubious award from *The Harvard Lampoon.* The undergraduate journal voted her as the actress least likely to succeed. Countering

In 1939.

this was Harvard's rival campus journal, Yale's *The Record*. The latter's editor, Roy S. Fox, Jr., defending Miss Sheridan, challenged *Lampoon* editor J. Russell Bowie to a duel.

Regarding the situation, Ann was quoted as saying, "I wonder what those bozos think is success. I don't mind criticism, but I hate to have it come from Harvard." At the time, Ann, Olivia de Havilland, Miriam Hopkins, Priscilla Lane, and new contractee Ida Lupino, along with Queen of the Lot Bette Davis, were the most important female attractions at the Burbank facilities. Sheridan was earning a $600 weekly salary.

However, the good roles were yet to be earmarked for Ann. She was seen in still another remake, this time a new version of *20,000 Years in Sing Sing* (1933) that had starred Bette Davis and Spencer Tracy. The new edition, entitled *Castle on the Hudson* (1940), featured Ann in tandem with Pat O'Brien (as the warden) and John Garfield (as the tough convict). Although the overall film is not up to the original, the characterizations here are more powerful. Sheridan offered a sound portrayal as Kay Manners, the faithful, tough, and vulnerable songstress.

Ann's love life was taking a very interesting turn at this juncture. Back in 1939—November 1, to be exact—Warner Bros. arranged a date between Ann and the studio's handsome leading actor George Brent.* It was purely a publicity stunt, but suddenly Ann and George started to take a keen interest in one another. Within six months of their meeting, they were dating each other steadily.

Following *Castle on the Hudson,* Jack L. Warner finally decided to allow Ann a starring vehicle of her own. Writer Louis Bromfield was paid $50,000 for his story "Better than Life." At first the part of the leading lady was offered to Bette Davis, but she rejected it. Associate producer Mark Hellinger then suggested that the studio allow Ann to have the lead because she had been working so hard for the company. Director Lewis Seiler and executive producer Hal B. Wallis agreed. Upon her return to Hollywood from a personal appearance tour and modeling assignment in Manhattan, Ann was informed that Hellinger wanted her in the film and that it would truly be a starring part for her. She gladly accepted and co-starred with good friend Humphrey Bogart, with Jeffrey Lynn, ZaSu Pitts, and John Litel also in the cast.

The amusing tale, retitled *It All Came True* (1940), dealt with former club singer Sarah Jane Ryan (Ann) and struggling song writer Tommy Taylor (Lynn) returning home to a boarding house presided over by their mothers (Una O'Connor and Jessie Busley). With him, Tommy brings "Mr. Grasselli," actually a fugitive gangster (Bogart). Grasselli killed a policeman with Tommy's gun, and now Tommy must hide him to protect himself. Eventually, through the kindness shown him by Sarah Jane, Tommy, and their mothers, Grasselli breaks down and clears Tommy, enabling the young lovers to wed. In the course of the feature, Ann sang "Angel in Disguise" and "The Gaucho Serenade," wore Howard Shoup gowns, and played her role with enthusiasm and spunk.

At this time Ann was dating several eligible men. Her beaus included actor David Niven, directors Jean Negulesco and Anatole Litvak, Cesar Romero occasionally, Pat DeCicco, and, most frequently, George Brent. She was also seen on the club circuit with Dr. Charles M. "Spud" Taylor, a Los Angeles specialist in rare diseases.

Again Warner Bros.' Mark Hellinger had his casting eye out for Ann whom he admired and was growing to love. He began pre-production on his next project, *Torrid Zone* (1940). George Raft was scheduled to star in the feature, but he balked and was replaced by James Cagney. Helen Vinson replaced Astrid Allwyn as the fast-talking other dame, and Pat O'Brien, Andy Devine, and Jerome Cowan were scheduled to co-star. With the part of Lee Donley still open, Cagney suggested that Ann test for the part.

---

*For a detailed study of the life and career of Galway, Ireland-born (March 15, 1899 or 1904) Brent, see *The Debonairs* (Arlington House, 1975).

With Humphrey Bogart in *It All Came True* ('40).

With James Cagney in *Torrid Zone* ('40).

Hellinger agreed, the studio heads approved, and she got the assignment.

Director William Keighley selected the locale, the Warner Bros. thirty-acre annex backlot. Here they planted 950 banana trees in a make-believe grove that was part of the Central America setting. *Torrid Zone* with its rugged action, racy romance, and zesty dialogue (delivered by the principals at breakneck speed) was the perfect picture for Ann. As the chanteuse with a shady past and an unpromising future, she worked wonderfully with co-leads O'Brien (a banana plantation boss) and Cagney (the ex-foreman). She was most alluring in a black-sequined gown singing a hot rendition of "Mi Caballero." The film finally gave Ann an excellent chance to display her brittle style. Audiences found that she had a fine knack for comedy and fast dialogue.

The critics took note of Ann. "Miss Sheridan is entirely at ease as the hardboiled torch singer, and when the occasion demands sentiment and simplicity, that, too, is at her command" *(New York World-Telegram)*. "Ann Sheridan steps up a notch or two in our estimation as the femme fatale of the piece" *(New York Times)*. "Oomph Girl Sheridan is never affected by the heat. She hops on and off moving banana trains, gets thrown in and out of jail, never even needs to change her one immaculate dress" *(Time* magazine).

The studio had kept Ann busy as a contract player, and, now that she had strong marquee appeal, it intended to profit by the situation as much as possible. She went from one film to another, with hardly a break in between. She had not yet learned to say no to her studio bosses. (And when she was not busy onscreen or undertaking publicity photo sessions, she could be heard on such radio programs as "Screen Guild Theatre" —in April 1940 she appeared with Bob Hope in a version of *Elmer the Great.*)

Warner Bros. had purchased the screen rights to A. I. Bezzerides' novel *Long Haul*, the story of truck drivers and the rough lives they lead. Mark Hellinger was to be the associate producer of the film, with Hal B. Wallis as executive producer. Action director Raoul Walsh was to direct this brisk tale of the reckless trucking world. George Raft was cast as the lead, along with Ida Lupino, Humphrey Bogart, Alan Hale, Gale Page, and a batch of contract supporting players (including John Litel, Henry O'Neill, George Tobias, and Roscoe Karns). With Sheridan's popularity now at an unbelievable height, and with the help of Hellinger, she was given the lead in this working man's film, entitled *They Drive by Night* (1940).

The true highlight of this action-packed, rough-and-tumble tale is the razor-sharp dialogue by Jerry Wald and Richard Macaulay (the team responsible for *Torrid Zone*'s punchy lines). Here Ann's lines are excellent and very spicy. She is first seen in Barney's Diner as a knowing hash-house waitress. Barney's eatery is the spot where all the truckers gather to have "java" and "shoot the breeze." As Cassie Hartley, Ann confronts all the guys, fending off their wise remarks with retorts of her own.

1st Player: Hey Red, this steak's tough.
Ann: Well you can't send it back now, you bent it!
2nd Player: I'll be back this way tonight, Red.
Ann: Thanks for the warning.
Karns: Another cup of java!
Tobias: You must like our coffee.
Karns: It stinks.
Ann: I notice you're drinking your seventh cup.
Karns: I like your sugar.
[Enters George Raft]
Raft: Gimme a cup of coffee.
Ann: Anything else?
Raft: Yeah, what else you got that ain't poisonous?
Ann: I don't know—I never eat here.
Litel: How 'bout takin' my order, Red?
Ann: How 'bout takin' your time?
Raft: Nice fixture, Barney.

Tobias: Yeah, she'll do. Not a bad thing to know.
3rd Player: Nice chassis, huh, Joe?
Raft: Classy chassis.
Ann: Yes, and it's all mine too. I don't owe any payments on it!
3rd Player: I'd be glad to finance it, baby.
Ann: Who do you think you're kidding? You couldn't pay for the headlights. (To Raft) Anything else?
Raft: Yeah, but it ain't on the menu.
Ann: And it ain't gonna be. You'd better settle for a hamburger.
Raft: Okay. With onions.

They Drive by Night is a fine blend of a message picture with action, romance, and risqué dialogue. Yet the film's real highlight is the bravura performance of Ida Lupino as the woman consumed by passion. In her seductive style, she added a flamboyant dimension to the film, emphasized by her mad scene in the courtroom.

During the filming of *They Drive by Night*, Ann had been dating her co-star George Raft. Despite their dates being another studio publicity stunt, George Brent became enraged at this coupling. (The situation also disturbed widow Norma Shearer who had been romancing with Raft.)

Warner Bros. was planning another tough film of the struggling proletarians, based on Aben Kandel's novel *City for Conquest*. The studio scheduled Raoul Walsh to direct this 1940 release, but Walsh was replaced by Anatole Litvak who served as producer/director of the feature, and James Cagney was signed to star. The studio wanted Ginger Rogers to co-star, but Sylvia Sidney was actually signed for the female lead. Yet when Litvak and Cagney began pre-production work, it was decided that Ann would be a more appropriate choice for the role of Peggy Nash. Surrounding Cagney and Sheridan would be such veteran performers as Donald Crisp, Frank McHugh, George Tobias, and Frank Craven. Newcomer Arthur Kennedy was signed for his film debut in the role of Cagney's younger brother.

City for Conquest is a tale of New York City,

With Humphrey Bogart and George Raft in *They Drive by Night* ('40).

With James Cagney in *City for Conquest* ('40).

its working people, its dreamers, and its sheer magic. The story focuses on East Side truck driver Danny Kenny (Cagney) who is a prizefighter on the side, punching his way in the ring to earn money for his kid brother's (Kennedy) music education. Cagney's girl Peggy (Ann) is tired of the tenement life and yearns for glamour and success. She teams with dancing gigolo Murray Burns (Anthony Quinn), while Cagney turns professional fighter. Later Cagney is nearly blinded in the ring and must retire. At the finale, with brother Eddie conducting his own symphony at Carnegie Hall, Cagney and Ann are reunited for a tearful climax.

Ann and fellow ex-Paramount player Quinn performed their own dance routines under the direction of choreographer Robert Vreeland. Ann received solid reviews for her performance. "Miss Sheridan is excellent as the girl, displaying dancing abilities in several ballroom numbers with Quinn" (*Variety*). "Any picture that has Mr. Cagney and Miss Sheridan is bound to be tough and salty, right off the city's streets. And this one is. Miss Sheridan waxes quite emotional, and Mr. Cagney, as usual, gives the story the old one-two punch" (*New York Times*). "The forceful personalities of James Cagney and Ann Sheridan are more than enough to make up for the deficiencies of *City for Conquest,* and whatever success the picture enjoys, which should be considerable, may be laid to the presence of these two stars in the cast, rather than to any ingenuity in plot, characterization or development. Miss Sheridan turns on her celebrated 'oomph' at every given opportunity, and, on occasion, even does some fine acting on her own behalf, which is more than you'd expect" (*New York Morning Telegraph*).

Ann enjoyed her role as Peggy Nash and

she appreciated the chance of working with Cagney. "It was a very good part, and of course it was Cagney again. He sold like wildfire. To be in a picture with him was just the greatest."

Ann's popularity (if not her salary) was rising weekly, and she was dating Brent regularly, even though George was seen occasionally in public with Bette Davis (who had a strong fondness for her favorite oncamera leading man). Most of the media publicity about Ann stated that she was playing the field and dating a variety of Hollywood's most eligible bachelors. She was still active in modeling between film assignments.

Warner Bros. again went on the move to cash in on her popularity. Her first picture in 1941 was a simple comedy entitled *Honeymoon for Three,* directed by Lloyd Bacon. The studio thought that the teaming of Ann with her offscreen romantic interest would generate plenty of attention from the public. George Brent co-starred with Ann in this remake of *Goodbye Again* (1933), with Sheridan again interpreting a role once performed onscreen by Joan Blondell. Others in the cast were Charles Ruggles, Osa Massen, Jane Wyman, and Walter Catlett. It was just another breezy comedy in which novelist Brent, on tour in Cleveland, is saved by his secretary (Ann) from the clutches of an old flame (Massen). In the 77-minute picture, Brent kisses Ann for approximately 56.2 seconds of screen time. Realistically the only chance of success for the picture was Ann's charm and lure. William Boehnel *(New York World-Telegram)* noted, "It takes more oomph—even the fourteen carat variety—to keep a comedy, especially one as porous-knit as this, bubbling on its merry way for 80 to 90 minutes [sic]. It takes invention, wit, and humor, and *Honeymoon for Three* is lacking all three."

After *Honeymoon for Three,* Ann followed the path of Bette Davis, Olivia de Havilland, and Ida Lupino by contesting her contract with the top brass at Warner Bros. Her major fight concerned a salary raise. The studio balked at giving her the $2,000 a week she wanted (and deserved). As a result

With George Brent in *Honeymoon for Three* ('41).

With Claire James, Peggy Diggins, Leslie Brooks, Georgia Carroll, Marguerite Chapman, and Katherine Aldridge in *Navy Blues* ('41).

she was suspended for three months without pay. (While she was away from the lot she lost out on joining James Cagney and Olivia de Havilland in *The Strawberry Blonde* (1941); Rita Hayworth replaced Ann in this superior study of nostalgic romance.)

It was during this period that Sheridan came to learn that Warner Bros. was thinking of filming Henry Bellamann's bestseller, *Kings Row*, a forerunner of *Peyton Place*, set around the year 1910. Scuttlebutt insisted that the prime role of Randy Monoghan would go to Bette Davis, who was given first choice of any property purchased by the company. Ann wanted the part, nevertheless, and pressured the studio with this additional demand besides the push for a salary increase. Finally the clawing and tugging was settled. She did not get the full salary increase she had wanted, but she did obtain a pay raise as well as retroactive compensation for the time she was suspended. She was also given the female lead in *Kings Row* (1941).

Humphrey Bogart was instrumental in Ann's winning the Randy Monoghan part, encouraging her to fight for it. He told her: "I think you ought to have it. I think you'd be wonderful as Randy Monoghan. Read it, fight for it, do anything you can." Ann went out and purchased the book, and the rest is history.

As part of the deal, Ann agreed to do a comedy for the studio, and with most of the world at war, it obviously was to be a military comedy. Lloyd Bacon was to direct this farce, entitled *Navy Blues* (1941). The cast included Ann, Martha Raye, Jack Oakie, Jack Haley, and Jack Carson, and in the chorus line was the "Navy Blues Sextette," which consisted of Marguerite Chapman, Leslie Brooks, Peggy Diggins, Georgia Carroll, Katharine (Kay) Aldridge, and Claire James. (These girls would be sent on an extensive promotional tour much as the "Search for Beauty" contest winners had years before when Ann first came to Paramount.)

Ex-Paramount star Martha Raye shone as the big-mouthed, big-hearted Lillibelle, while the rest of the cast seemed to fade into the background. The picture, to many, was a low point in the history of Warner Bros. musicals, unsalvaged by the noisy, brassy proceedings. For some unexplained reason, Ann's singing voice was dubbed in the film, one of the few times this occurred in her movie career. At least her publicity photos for the picture were excellent. She had several shots taken in a short skirt designed with stripes and stars, a sailor's top (with bare middle), and a sailor's hat. One of the ad lines for *Navy Blues* read, "Sailor, beware! Sheridan at work."

While most of Europe was at war, Warner Bros.' backlot was being transformed into pre-World War I middle America, the setting for *Kings Row,* which was directed by Sam Wood. Casey Robinson wrote the scenario for a cast that included Ann, Robert Cummings, Ronald Reagan, Claude Rains, Charles Coburn, Betty Field, Judith Anderson, Maria Ouspenskaya, and Nancy Coleman. In the course of this 130-minute entry, one discovers that this seemingly idyllic midwestern town is host to sadistic doctors and greedy businessmen, all horrifying in their own ways. As Randy Monoghan, the railroad worker's daughter from the wrong part of town, Ann eventually weds Drake McHugh (Reagan), the town's former wild playboy now reduced to humility through impoverishment and an accident, as a result of which his legs are amputated by sadistic Dr. Henry Gordon (Charles Coburn). Meanwhile, one of the couple's childhood friends, Parris Mitchell (Cummings), has become a doctor and gone off to Vienna to study modern medical methods, coming under the influence of Sigmund Freud. Mitchell returns to Kings Row and helps Drake find the strength to adapt to his misfortunes. The youngish doctor also falls in love with a new resident (Kaaren Verne), and everything ends on a positive note.

Many knowledgeable people consider this film Ann's finest, and her portrayal the best she has given. She offers a fully shaded performance, avoiding the glib sassiness that

With Pat Moriarity, Ernest Cossart, Nancy Coleman, and Robert Cummings in *Kings Row* ('41).

had been her prior trademark. In the period wardrobe she was at her most fetching, almost wholesome—something one had never associated with "The Oomph Girl."

During the filming of *Kings Row,* Ann found herself in a trying professional position. Hal B. Wallis, production supervisor at the studio, decided that he wanted Ann to bolster the box-office potential of his project, *The Man Who Came to Dinner* (1941). She had tested for the picture, and he liked her interpretation of Lorraine Sheldon, the worldly actress (patterned, allegedly, after Gertrude Lawrence). What Sheridan did not know was that Wallis and director William Keighley planned to film their brittle, wacky comedy at the same time that *Kings Row* was being shot. Thus Ann found herself in two major films at the same time and working doubly hard. As she would recall, "I didn't care about playing Lorraine Sheldon. I used to work, say, one day on *Kings Row* and the next day on *The Man Who Came to Dinner,* or one morning I'd work as Lorraine Sheldon and that afternoon I was Randy Monoghan. . . . Well, it was horrible! And more than that, the makeup, hair-do, everything. Awful thing to have to go through."

Adding to Ann's confusion at the time was the presence of Bette Davis as the leading female in *The Man Who Came to Dinner.* Sheridan would remember, "She wasn't happy about a lot of things, there's no doubt about that. . . . I think she was conditioned at the time to remain angry at Miriam Hopkins and think that anybody on the set was going to fight with her. I wouldn't fight with her at all. I agreed with her, with everything she said. Then she got very nice and today [1966] we're very friendly. She was just—temperamental? Who isn't temperamental? I'm as temperamental as all get-out if I feel I have to be. Maybe she had a headache, maybe she didn't feel well. Maybe she wasn't satisfied with her part or her clothes or the way the director was doing a scene—many things can enter into it."

The Man Who Came to Dinner is a really funny piece of work. Monty Woolley as the pompous, irascible columnist is riveting in his performance, as are Ann as the glamorous star, Jimmy Durante as the wild song-and-dance man, Mary Wickes as the beleaguered Nurse Preen, and Reginald Gardiner as the playwright Beverly Carlton. The most distracting element in the feature is the built-up, out-of-whack romance between Woolley's patient secretary (Davis) and the local newspaperman (Richard Travis).

While making both *Kings Row* and *The Man Who Came to Dinner* Ann was paid for one film while doing the two. That was the rule on the Warner Bros. lot, and anyone who didn't like it took a suspension.

There were rumors that Ann and Ronald Reagan would be teamed in *Casablanca* as a follow-up to *Kings Row,* but this never came to pass, and the parts went to Ingrid Bergman and Humphrey Bogart. There was also another project in the air, but it was all in the mind of ace prankster Humphrey Bogart. As Ann would remember for *Screen Facts* magazine in 1966: "I loved Bogart, but he was a monster. He was always teasing everybody. After he touted me for *Kings Row,* and it worked out so well, he came down to the set of something I was doing and said, 'Annie, the front office has bought the greatest story under the sun, and you've got to do it.' . . . And I said, 'Oh Bogie, God love you for *Kings Row*; that was the greatest part I ever had. Thank you for touting me on it and tipping me off on this one. I'll get in touch with them [the front office] right away.

"Well, this monster went to Lupino and pulled the same thing, and a couple of other actresses on the lot, and if I hadn't had to go right into a scene, I would have been on the telephone too. I understand that the front office—I think it was Steve Trilling at the time—was deluged with actresses wanting to get a copy of this script. I said to the fashion editor of Warners in my dressing room, 'Oh, God love that Bogie, he's just tipped me off on another thing to do,' and I told her the title and I saw a strange look come over her face.

"She said, 'Oh well, yeah, that's wonderful,' and let it go. Mark Hellinger came in a few minutes later, and when I told him he

With Monty Woolley in *The Man Who Came to Dinner* ('41).

asked me what it was, and I said, *The Story of Fanny Hill.* Well, Mark got hysterical with laughter and said, 'Don't you know who Fanny Hill was?' And I said no, and I didn't. Ida Lupino didn't know either. . . . all of us stupid dames not knowing. And I swear I would have been on the phone to try and get it. But Hellinger was rolling on the floor, telling me she was the greatest known madam in England. . . . These are the kind of gags Bogart pulled on everybody! We all had laughs about it, and afterwards of course I threatened to kill him."

Between the chaos, frolicking, and hard work on the sound stages, Ann took a giant step in her personal life when she and George Brent decided to elope. They both thought that starting 1942 as Mr. and Mrs. Brent would be a good omen. To shy away from the expected publicity, they decided to rendezvous away from Hollywood. Brent would leave the film capital after completing *In This Our Life,* and Ann, slightly disguised, would be waiting for him in El Paso, Texas, in an airport waiting room. Brent went to the appointed place where he was greeted by Ann dressed in a black coat (collar turned up) and a black slouched hat. Glasses covered her eyes, and she said: "Mr. Watson, I believe?"

The couple then proceeded to Florida, only to be grounded en route in Memphis because of a blizzard. Ann retained her disguise, but Brent was ever fearful that he would be recognized lounging about the airport terminal.

Finally they arrived in Palm Beach, Florida, and went to the home of George's sister, the widowed Mrs. Sam Harris. (She was called China because someone had once remarked that she looked Oriental.) Ann had counted on time in Palm Beach to purchase a wedding gown, but the delay erased all extra time: China had the guests already at the house (for security purposes), and Ann decided to wear the champagne tulle outfit she had packed. Over the dress she draped a mantilla of ivory chantilly lace.

The screen star came down the short aisle on the arm of lawyer William Q. Cain, China's attorney (his wife was also present at the ceremony). George Brent, dressed in a white dinner jacket and black dress trousers, and with his nephew Pat Watson as best man, began to exchange the marital vows with Clara Lou Sheridan. The ceremony was performed by Judge Richard P. Robbins. The only other guest present was Mrs. Walter Giblin, the former actress Constance Talmadge, who was China Harris' close friend. Somehow two photographers showed up on the scene, but no one had the heart to eject them from the proceedings. Thereafter Brent carried the new Mrs. Brent across the threshold of the cottage that China had prepared for them. The date was Monday, January 5, 1942.

The couple spent their first days of honeymooning at the cottage (it rained heavily for two and a half days after the wedding). They finally left for La Quinta for three days and wired the studio to inform the brass of their whereabouts and to learn about their pending work schedules. Brent called Ann "Red," "Tex," or "Piyute," while she acknowledged him as "Keoki" (Hawaiian for George) and "Brenty."

When they returned to Hollywood they set up headquarters at George's apartment. The first day back from their honeymoon they rushed to their respective film assignments and plunged into work. Brent went to United Artists to make *Twin Beds* with Joan Bennett, while Ann, back at Warner Bros., was replacing Ida Lupino as the star of *Juke Girl* (1942), co-starring Ronald Reagan, Richard Whorf, and Alan Hale. The rough-and-tumble tale of crop pickers and farmers in Florida was another of the Warner sagas of the working class, but it did not gel into a manageable property. In fact, it was a professional step backward for Ann, and she always detested the picture.

As part of its contribution to the effort to sell war bonds, Warner Bros. turned out *Wings for the Eagle* (1942) starring Ann with that recurring buddy screen team of Dennis Morgan and Jack Carson. Lloyd Bacon directed this story about defense workers in a bomber plant, with the plotline being sub-

With Dennis Morgan and Jack Carson in *Wings for the Eagle* ('42).

With Jack Benny and Charles Coburn in *George Washington Slept Here* ('42).

merged in the message to promote defense bonds. The cast even went out to the Lockheed factory and made speeches to induce the workers there to purchase war bonds. The ads for *Wings for the Eagle* announced, "Ann's carrying a new torch . . . an acetylene torch in a plane plant! She's working on the bomber-line and has the boys doing tailspins."

The studio brass soon discovered that curvaceous Ann, with her husky voice and sincere look, was perfect for the role of bond saleswoman. They encouraged her to make personal appearances with co-worker Ronald Reagan in assorted war bond drives—in between pictures, of course.

Having proved that she was a natural for comedy, Ann was told to report to the sound stages to replace Olivia de Havilland and co-star with Jack Benny in *George Washington Slept Here*, a very loosely derived screen rendition of the George S. Kaufman-Moss Hart Broadway play.* Foreshadowing *The Egg and I* (1947) which had a theme of city folk trying to adjust to farm life, here Ann's Connie Fuller was the insistent wife who decides that she and Bill (Benny) must return to Mother Nature in Bucks County, Pennsylvania.

To bolster the rather undisciplined proceedings, there was nasal Percy Kilbride (from the stage version), Charles Coburn, Lee Patrick, Hattie McDaniel, and Franklin Pangborn for comedy relief, but it was all played on a very unsubtle level. Surprisingly, the *New York Times* thought that Ann handled her acting chores quite capably.

At this time Ann and Brent were moving emotionally farther and farther apart.* It seemed that domestically restless Brent was losing interest in The Oomph Girl and vice versa. They were seeing less and less of one another, especially because of Ann's tough filming schedule and promotion of war bond sales. Meanwhile, Brent was preparing to enter the Army as a civilian flight instructor, since he was too old for actual combat duty. After less than a year of marriage, the couple separated. She moved to her own ranch house in Reseda, California, taking along a donkey which Brent had given her as a Valentine gift.

Exactly one year from the day of their marriage, the Brents were divorced. Ann left the set of *Thank Your Lucky Stars* to fly to Mexico to file for the decree. On Tuesday, January 5, 1943, she was granted her decree from the First Circuit Court of the First Judicial District of Morelos. Explanations for the breakup were vague, although it was rumored that Brent had his romantic eye on Hungarian film star Ilona Massey, his co-star of *International Lady* (1941). Years later, Ann would say to *TV Guide* in regard to her first two marriages, "With both men, there was no honesty between us. And if two people living together can't be honest, then I don't want it."

Ann had a particular affinity for prank-loving, roguish Errol Flynn, and he admired the no-nonsense attitude of this fun-loving actress. He liked the fact that her dressing room was closed to no one, and that she could pal about with all ranks and types of people. Thus when Warner Bros. announced that Flynn would star in the major

---

*In the late seventies, after her husband's death, widow Mary Livingstone would detail in her book account of the legendary Jack Benny that he may have had an affair with Ann Sheridan. As Livingstone wrote, "I could tell from things Jack said that he liked Ann. . . . It upset me. Then George Brent called to say he knew Jack had sent Ann flowers." Livingstone recalls that at a dinner party she walked up to her rival and said, "Miss Sheridan, I don't know whether you like Jack or he likes you, but you are making a picture together and I wanted to remind you of something. Jack wouldn't give my little finger for your whole body." According to Livingstone, after Sheridan had left the social function, Benny said to Mary, "Well, you were right, doll. You never have to worry about me."

*One of the joyous moments together occurred while Brent was filming *The Gay Sisters* (1942) with Barbara Stanwyck. "On one set," Ann would recall, "we had rigged up a whole thing for Brent. They had a wedding scene, and I left the picture I was on and put on her wedding gown. George and I had just been married, two or three months. And when 'Here Comes the Bride' was played, I walked down the aisle and stood beside him. You know what? I could have killed him. He didn't even break up. He out-deadpanned every one of us. I finally said, 'You're supposed to laugh,' and he grinned! But Stanwyck is so tiny and I'm so broad-shouldered, her wedding dress stayed open all the way down my back. They had to pull it across and pin it. She was such a tiny thing."

resistance drama, *Edge of Darkness* (1943), Ann readily agreed to be his co-star.* Under Lewis Milestone's direction, the studio assembled quite a diverse cast: Flynn, Ann, Walter Huston, Ruth Gordon, Judith Anderson, Nancy Coleman, Helmut Dantine, and Morris Carnovsky. Set in the occupied Norwegian town of Trollness, the film told of the brave defense of democracy by the inhabitants.

As operations leader Gunnar Brogge, Flynn was a rather unbelievable Scandinavian, but neither was Ann a likely choice for Karen Stensgard, the girl educated at college in Oslo. However, this was Hollywood in the 1940s. World War II was raging, and moviegoers wanted patriotic, escapist entertainment, so nearly anything was acceptable. Comparatively, Ann had little to do in *Edge of Darkness,* but to her relatively few scenes she brought her usual honesty. She was a most fetching distraction as the machine gun-toting patriot aiding her countrymen in battling the oppressive Nazis. The feature concludes with a voice-over of President Roosevelt commending the Scandinavians for their bravery in his "Look to Norway" speech.

Olivia de Havilland, Ida Lupino, and Bette Davis continued to balk at projects submitted by the front office, but Ann was always much more compliant. Her demands were far less, but of course her victories far more minor at the studio.

Since all the studios were turning out all-star variety revue films, Warner Bros. decided to do its own, with Mark Hellinger producing the venture. Meanwhile, Ann had been hoping to embark on a U.S.O. tour, but there was always "just one more film" to be made. Hellinger asked her to appear in *Thank Your Lucky Stars* (1943), and she loved the man too much to refuse him. The entire Warner Bros. stock company was on hand for the project (except for James Cagney who was about to depart the studio). The cast included Dennis Morgan (as an undiscovered crooner), Joan Leslie (as an undiscovered songwriter), and Eddie Cantor in a dual role as Old Banjo Eyes himself and as tour guide Joe Simpson. Playing themselves were such favorites as Bogart, Lupino, Davis, de Havilland, Garfield, Flynn, Dinah Shore, Alexis Smith, Jack Carson, and of course "Annie" Sheridan.

Since Ann was anxious to fly off to Mexico for her divorce from Brent (a matter she kept from the studio), she pressured Hellinger to complete her sequence in as few days as possible. She sang one song, "Love Isn't Born, It's Made" by Arthur Schwartz and Frank Loesser. It was a saucy tune and Sheridan delivered it well.

Patriotic Ann still wanted to undertake a major U.S.O. tour. She had performed a short jaunt of military camps in Wyoming, Kansas, and Missouri just after her marriage to Brent, and the G.I.'s had gone wild over her. She was elected "Queen Jeep" by the American doughboys at a fort in Wyoming, and fourteen Coast Guard artillerymen made her an honorary commander. She was a popular pinup girl along with Betty Grable, Rita Hayworth, and Maria Montez. However, the studio held her for one more picture before they allowed her to go on tour.

That picture was *The Doughgirls* (1944), produced by Mark Hellinger. As Ann said about it later, "I hated it. I was in New York at the time it was chosen for me, or I was chosen for it, whichever you want to call it. I went to see the play and notified the studio that there wasn't one single part that I could play with any honesty, and that I didn't think

---

*In regard to working with Flynn, Ann would relate years later, "Oh, that was a wonderful time. He was going through the Satterly rape trial. He used to go to court in the morning and come back and report to us on the set what had happened. Milestone and all of us used to just gather around and start gurgling from the toes up at the reports of Old Dad Flynn. It was absolutely fascinating, the things this idiot child accused him of.... Flynn was always strictly fun. Never any trouble. I adored him. I never had trouble with any leading men. Really, I always got along well with everybody. You see, all of us were covered. If we were in a scene—well, take Flynn, for instance—and it was his scene, I knew that the scene was going to be played mostly on Flynn. I could only play my part to the best of my ability. I knew that I would be protected because I was also a studio property. If the scene was mine and they wanted it to go to me, they would cut to me. I had nothing to do with the cutting or any of that. I've known other people to go in and beef at the cuttings of pictures, but I never did."

At the height of her screen allure in the early Forties.

With Alexis Smith, Jane Wyman, Eve Arden, and Francis Pierlot in *The Doughgirls* ('44).

it was a good play. I figured that unless you could use the dirt of the play, which they certainly couldn't do on the screen with the Johnston Office, it would lose all its color—which it did. But oh, there was a big knockdown, drag-out fight over that, threatening me with suspension. If it hadn't been for Mark, I wouldn't have taken it."

There was quite a diverse quintet of leading ladies for *The Doughgirls* which comically dealt with the crowded wartime situation in Washington, D.C. Besides Ann, there were Alexis Smith, Jane Wyman, Irene Manning, and Eve Arden. The latter (in Arlene Francis' stage role) played distinguished Russian sniper Natalia Moskoroff who shoots pigeons from her hotel terrace, adores double-feature movies, and enjoys long hikes to Baltimore. Aiding and abetting this watered-down version of a hilarious plotline were Jack "Double Take" Carson and Charlie "Bumbling" Ruggles.

In mid-1943, Ann finally left on the C.B.I. (China, Burma, and India) Tour, which lasted four months. She traveled with comedian Ben Blue, and dancers Ruth Enasl and Jackie Miles. Mary Linda, an accordionist, was also part of the troupe. Sheridan sang a few songs and played the straight girl in Blue's crazy act. The G.I.'s adored her, and she took to them equally. The officers tried to monopolize her time, but she was interested only in the enlisted men.

While on tour, Ann won the heart of many a serviceman. A whole campful of Canadian soldiers elected her as their choice to be "the party of the second part in a blood transfusion." A shipful of British sailors wrote that if she would adopt them they would be the "envy of His Majesty's Navy." Other titles bestowed on her were "The Modern Venus" and "Major Menace to Men."

Ann was not immune to exhaustion, and the tough schedule and life had its effect as she went from 128 to 112 pounds. She had been existing on K-rations and sleeping on the floors of planes and occasionally in the bucket seats of cars or jeeps. Before she left on tour, Ann had rejected the lead in another of Warner Bros.' all-star productions. The film was *Hollywood Canteen* (1944) and detailed the life at the servicemen's hangout founded by Bette Davis and John Garfield. The thin plotline (between specialty routines) told of a G.I. who wants to date the darling of the screen and eventually falls in love with her. Sheridan read the script and refused it, insisting that the premise was an insult to every G.I. She felt that this film might lead every serviceman into believing he could marry a movie queen. Joan Leslie was given the part. Some time before, in late 1942, Ann had tested for the lead in *Saratoga Trunk*, which would not be released until 1945. She wanted the part, but she did not photograph well in a blonde wig, and her attempts at a French accent clashed with her Texas diction. Ingrid Bergman was eventually picked as Gary Cooper's co-star.

Back home from her C.B.I. tour, Ann began another romance. For many, this was one of the more beautiful relationships of recent times. Ann had met press agent Steve Hanagan at a Christmas get-together. It was love at first sight for each party. Ann was particularly attracted to his affable, sincere ways, a mirror of her own best qualities.

Notwithstanding her personal happiness, Ann was having problems at the studio. Immediately on returning to the Burbank lot, she went to work on a remake of *The Animal Kingdom*, entitled *One More Tomorrow*. Her co-stars were Dennis Morgan, Jack Carson, Alexis Smith, and Jane Wyman. A few weeks into filming, it was discovered that producer Benjamin Glazer had not received a Production Code approval from the Johnston Office. The front office immediately closed down the picture, because without the Johnston Seal the film could not be released. While this problem was being ironed out, Ann was cast in *Shine On Harvest Moon* (1944), a fictionalized biography of singing performer Nora Bayes. Strangely, except for the finale, the film was shot in black-and-white, showing a peculiar lack of faith in Ann's box-office magnetism, even granting

With dancer Ruth Enasl, comedian Ben Blue, dancer J. Miles, and accordionist Mary Linda at LaGuardia Airport (New York) returning from a USO tour from Africa to China in 1943.

the wartime restrictions on color stock. This David Butler-directed musical was to be Ann's bid to enter the ranks of Alice Faye, Betty Grable, Judy Garland, and Rita Hayworth, the queens of Hollywood nostalgia musicals. Ann's singing was dubbed by Lynn Martin.

Sheridan's co-stars in *Shine On Harvest Moon* were Dennis Morgan, Jack Carson, Irene Manning, S. Z. Sakall, and Marie Wilson. Perhaps Howard Barnes *(New York Herald-Tribune)* best summed up why the picture was not the vehicle Ann had anticipated: "The truth is that even so resourceful a player as Ann Sheridan is behind the eight ball throughout most of the film. As a honky-tonk entertainer who incurs the wrath of a Milwaukee big shot and teams up with a renowned songwriter only to become blacklisted by her former associates, she gives a lusty and appealing portrayal. The continuity lets her down on more than one occasion. When she walks out on Jack Norworth (Morgan) under the delusion that he will immediately team up with her rival, it is impossible for her to give the scene any trace of credibility."

Regarding the multi-hued finale, John McManus *(PM)* observed: "Just for bad measure, there is a Technicolor insert at the end in which for some inexplicable reason everyone turns up decorated as some kind of truck-garden vegetable. As a certain other critic remarked: 'At this point Warners must have traded in the script for a seed catalog.'"

With *Shine On Harvest Moon* completed, Ann shuttled back to *One More Tomorrow*. Producer Benjamin Glazer had been dismissed and shipped off to South America for a rest; director Peter Godfrey replaced Irving Rapper; and a revamped scenario skirted around the confines of the Production Code. (The character played by Dane

With Johnnie Berkes in *Shine On Harvest Moon* ('44).

With Dennis Morgan in *One More Tomorrow* ('46).

Clark in the original plot was eliminated.) Although completed in November 1943, it would not be released until May 1946. At that time it was passed off by critics as just another casualty of Hollywood's trying to "improve upon" a Broadway original, and certainly not living up to the film original released by RKO in 1932 and starring Ann Harding, Leslie Howard, Myrna Loy, Neil Hamilton, and William Gargan.

Ann was on suspension for eighteen months after completing *One More Tomorrow*. The fight was more over stories than salary, but she was hoping to get a "pay raise and a picture deal." As she would recall, "My option was coming up, which put me in a good position." The net result of Ann vs. Warner Bros. was that she obtained a six-film deal, to be made over a period of three years, with a higher stipulated salary than before and script approval.

Among the projects Ann rejected was *Mildred Pierce* (1945) which eventually was turned over to ex-MGM star Joan Crawford as a comeback vehicle. It won Miss Crawford an Academy Award. Another project which never materialized was a film biography of composer Vincent Youmans to be called *Sometimes (Un)Happy*.

During much of the period away from filmmaking, Ann was on trips with Steve Hanagan. He constantly tried to persuade her to give up the movies, believing that only then could he possibly ask her to wed him. However, Ann was too career oriented, which eventually led to the severance of her relationship with Hanagan.

As her return vehicle for Warner Bros., Ann accepted *Nora Prentiss,* which was completed in late April 1946 and released in late February 1947. It was the slick story of a physician (Kent Smith) who leaves his drab life when he falls in love with a nightclub singer (Ann). The functional melodrama served its purpose in the woman's market, as did *The Unfaithful* (1947), also directed by Vincent Sherman. This was an unofficial remake of *The Letter,* filmed in 1929 with Jeanne Eagels and again in 1940 with Bette Davis. Ann's co-stars here were Lew Ayres, Zachary Scott, and Eve Arden.

In 1948 jokester Ann and director John Huston whipped up a little scheme to play on Humphrey Bogart while filming *The Trea-*

With Lew Ayres, John Hoyt, and Zachary Scott in *The Unfaithful* ('47).

sure of the Sierra Madre. As a lark, she dressed in a padded black satin dress and sashayed by Bogart as he came out of a Mexican bar. It was really a gag to see if Bogart would recognize her. He did not. Huston himself appeared in the picture as the "Man in White."

After this cameo Ann accepted the co-lead in a Western called *Silver River* (1948). Sheridan hoped that working with Flynn would be fun again, but he was already on the downhill slide and the project was fraught with problems. The studio wasted little budget on this Raoul Walsh-directed feature, lensing it in black and white and using other telltale economy measures. At the time no one, least of all Ann, realized that this would be her last film on the home lot.

The studio, already reducing its roster in the post-World War II changeover, tried to get Ann to do another picture, but no project was suitable to her tastes. (Among those she rejected was *Caged* in 1950 which even-tually went to Eleanor Parker.) However, the studio could not suspend her because she had a picture deal. Instead she went on loan-out to RKO for *Good Sam* (1948) with Gary Cooper. Directed by Leo McCarey, the story premise concerns a good-natured guy who just cannot say no, and then when he needs help, the townsfolk let him down (initially). Even the usually antagonistic Bosley Crowther *(New York Times)* had pleasant words to write about Ann's performance: "Ann Sheridan gives a thoroughly amusing look at a woman who accepts her husband's bigness of heart with bitter and candid distaste. As a matter of fact, it is the lovely and willful sarcasm in her approach—the non-Pollyannaism—that keys the whole purpose of the film." Nevertheless, there was not the necessary chemistry between Sheridan and Cooper to give this low-key comedy the proper box-office appeal.

Rather than return to Warner Bros. and wait in hopes of getting a suitable vehicle, Ann negotiated to buy out her remaining six months of contract time with the studio. For $35,000, Jack L. Warner agreed to let Ann become a free-lance artist. While Ann did not admire her former boss professionally, she held no grudges against him socially. Even in 1966 she could admit, "I adore Jack socially. He's a lot of fun." Her biggest regret about her tenure at Warner Bros. was: "They always thought of me as The Oomph Girl, never as an actress. I could never convince them that I could act." (Among the projects for which Ann had begged the studio to loan her out was the Texas Guinan biography, filmed at Paramount in 1945 with Betty Hutton, entitled *The Incendiary Blonde*.)

Ann, the critics, and the public were quite enthusiastic about her next project, *I Was a Male War Bride* (1949), shot at Twentieth Century-Fox by director Howard Hawks. Dapper Cary Grant was her co-star in this hilarious account of a French military captain and an American WAC. When they wed, the only way he can enter the United States is to pose as "a war bride." Ann and Grant hoped to make follow-ups to this delightful entry, but, as she said, "We just never found another good comedy, that's all. It's a sin and a shame too, because I think we should have done two or three."

I Was a Male War Bride had been filmed over a ten-month period in Germany, England, and the United States, but Ann's next —also at Twentieth Century-Fox (as part of a package deal)—was all shot on the back lot. *Stella* (1950) co-starred Ann with Victor Mature, David Wayne, and Frank Fontaine. It was one of those wacky comedies that just did not seem funny onscreen. Worst of all, Ann, continuing to wear her closer-cropped hair-do, no longer had the glamorous Oomph Look of her Warner Bros. days. She was thirty-five years old and her career was sliding.

Stella quite naturally led to no more Twentieth Century-Fox film ventures, and she agreed to a multi-picture deal at Universal. The first was *Woman on the Run* (1950) directed by Norman Foster. It was definitely a B-picture and had Ann as Eleanor Johnson trying to find her husband, a witness to a gangland slaying. In its low-keyed métier, Ann is quite effective. The next three at Uni-

With Gary Cooper in *Good Sam* ('48).

293

With Cary Grant and William Pullen in *I Was a Male War Bride* ('49).

With Frank Jenks and Dennis O'Keefe in *Woman on the Run* ('50).

versal (where Francis the Talking Mule and Ma and Pa Kettle films were the breadwinners) were pleasant but very forgettable. They were produced by Leonard Goldstein and his then associate-assistant, Ross Hunter, the latter a good pal of Ann's. The most intriguing of the trio was *Take Me to Town* (1953), shot in color and directed by Douglas Sirk. It featured Ann as Vermilion O'Toole. Just as in the old Warner Bros. days, Ann was a saloon singer on the lam who finds love with a widowed preacher (Sterling Hayden) and his three children. Thanks to fine work in front of and behind the cameras, the picture is a satisfying bit of Americana. Producer Ross Hunter later hoped to make a Broadway musical of the property and wanted Ann to recreate her role, but the project never came to fruition.

Now that her film career was grinding to a slow halt, it seemed likely that Ann and her on-again, off-again beau Steve Hanagan would finally wed. However, in February 1953, while he was in Nairobi on business, he died of a heart attack. When his estate was settled, Ann received a bequest of $218,399. Among the assets of the late publicist/businessman was a gold wristwatch inscribed "Steve, Love Annie, 1949." This was valued at $75. A distraught Ann went to Mexico, hoping that travel would help her to forget.

About this time Ann was involved in a lawsuit with movie mogul Howard Hughes. He had signed her to do the film *Carriage Entrance*. She wanted Robert Mitchum as her leading man, but Hughes insisted on contractee Mel Ferrer. The picture was made in 1949 with Ava Gardner in Ann's role, and with Mitchum and Melvyn Douglas as the leading men. Mercurial Hughes did not release the film until 1951 and then under the title *My Forbidden Past.* It proved to be a box-office dud. To settle the contract litigation between them, Ann agreed to make *Appointment in Honduras* (1953) for Hughes' RKO studio. Jacques Tourneur directed, and her co-stars were Glenn Ford and Zachary Scott. Regarding this waste of color celluloid, Ann would say, "I was tired of fighting and thought it was just about time to call everything off and say oh, to hell with it. So I consulted the lawyer and he told me to do it if I thought the script was worth it, and I said, 'Oh well, it may be, I don't know.' So, I accepted it. Never saw it. I heard it was an absolute horror."

Having become passé in the film medium,

With Howard Duff and William Harrigan in *Steel Town* ('52).

Ann turned her attention to television where her name still had marketable value. She debuted on NBC-TV's "Ford Theatre" on June 18, 1953, in an episode entitled *Malaya Incident,* and in the next few years she guest-starred on "Lux Video Theatre," "Schlitz Playhouse of Stars," "U.S. Steel Hour," and "Playhouse 90." She even made a pilot for an unsold series entitled "Calling Terry Conway" which got a screening on NBC-TV during its summer rerun season (August 14, 1956).

There were no major film offers in the mid-1950s, but she did manage to garner two big screen roles for the 1956 season. She made a beautiful picture for Republic called *Come Next Spring.* Directed by R. G. Springsteen on location in Sacramento, and co-starring Steve Cochran (who packaged the production), it was a wonderfully low-keyed study of rural life. It concerned a family overcoming nature and the prejudices of the townsfolk (they have a mute son) in making a go of their farm. Had the film received a more intelligent releasing campaign, it would not have suffered such a bad case of box-office anemia.

The role of Bess Ballot in *Come Next Spring* found Ann dressed in simple farm outfits and with scant makeup. In contrast, her part as Amanda in MGM's musical remake of *The Women* allowed her to dress in high fashion and sport chic dialogue. Unfortunately *The Opposite Sex* was such an outdated, diluted rendition of the Broadway and film original that it failed to please many viewers. June Allyson had the lead in the tame proceedings, while Ann, along with another ex-Warner Bros. star, Joan Blondell, was reduced to a near cameo part.

In this period Ann purchased a home in the San Fernando Valley. Only later did she learn why she had obtained such a bargain. She was informed at the title closing that the house was definitely inhabited by a Chinese ghost. The caretaker insisted that the previous owners frequently heard clop-clop sounds of sandals running over tiles. How-

With Lee Aaker, Harvey Grant, and Dusty Henley in *Take Me to Town* ('53).

With Zachary Scott in *Appointment in Honduras* ('53).

ever, Ann, who held no belief in apparitions, had no intention of moving.

On paper a good many projects seem more viable than when scrutinized as finished film projects. What attracted Ann most about *The Woman and the Hunter* (1957) was the chance to travel to Africa. It was, according to Ann, "really an interesting script originally—a silly thing about a woman who wants to marry a guy—she's his secretary and she kills him and then takes on his son, and she takes on the white hunter. It made sense in the script, but the way they cut it, it made no sense whatsoever. It's the damnedest thing I've ever seen in my life. And not even in color, which was very horrible, what with the color makeup. Very black and very white, and all that." Ann participated in the venture on a percentage deal (and never made any profit on the venture), co-starring with David Farrar and John Loder. It was never shown theatrically in the United States, instead being sold directly to television.

In 1948 when she was preparing to make *I Was a Male War Bride,* Ann told the press, "There have been three phases in my career —and the present one, playing comedy and to hell with the oomph, is by far the most satisfying." In 1958 she added another facet to her show business work—the stage. She joined Dan Dailey and Franchot Tone in a version of William Saroyan's *The Time of Your Life* which was performed in Brussels at the time of the 1958 Exposition. Late in the summer of 1958 she tried her luck on the straw-hat circuit in the United States, opening in Norman Krasna's *Kind Sir.** Under Gus Schirmer's direction the show opened

---

*Reviewing the Chicago sojourn of *Kind Sir,* Claudia Cassidy *(Chicago Tribune)* observed, "As the actress, Ann Sheridan is a handsome redhead with a figure so fine she even looks attractive when she sits down in a short, tight dress. Her wardrobe is extensive, an entrance in white satin drew a hand, and she sounds like Tallulah Bankhead if Miss Bankhead had been born in Texas." Herman Kogan *(Chicago Sun-Times)* reported, "In looks, flaming-haired Ann Sheridan is more of a dazzler on a stage than in any movie in which this admirer has ever seen her. . . . But in acting ability before a live audience—even as wild-to-clap a group as witnessed her theatre debut in *Kind Sir* at the Edgewater Beach Playhouse Monday night—she is lamentably limited."

Cheesecake, 1957 style.

at the theatre in East Hampton, Long Island. The show was edited and updated from the script that had been used for the 1953 Broadway version starring Charles Boyer and Mary Martin. "We didn't play it straight," Ann would recall. "It was strictly for comedy." Her co-star was Scott McKay who would soon become her constant escort in private life.

Ann's only TV work in 1958 was a December 31 episode *(The Dark Cloud)* of the CBS series "Pursuit." Then came a pre-Broadway tour of *Odd Man In,* adapted from a French play by Robin Long. It was a grueling, unpleasant experience, as she recalled it: "We played it for five months, but they [the producers] never intended to rewrite, or to bring it to Broadway. They only intended to make as much money as they could, and they did, from the outlying districts of the country. . . . We played sixty-nine cities in five months. . . . [It was] the hard way to learn about the theatre. Very hard. And with a sinus infection, I was back down to 112 pounds again."

Of the opening engagement Ann stated: "We opened in—let me see, where did I have my first coughing fit?—Philadelphia. Opening night. The critics said the best thing about the play was Miss Sheridan's coughing fit when she had to leave the stage. And I did, because by that time I had an infected sinus. Well, we got through the play. Usually the actors got pretty good reviews. The play, never."

Thereafter, Ann became a peripheral figure in show business. Occasionally she would appear on a TV variety show, such as Perry Como's (where she sang "Guess Who I Saw Today"), or be the guest star on a TV series ("U.S. Steel Hour" in 1960, "Wagon Train" in 1962), but generally she remained in the background. Often she would accompany Scott McKay on his acting jaunts—for example, during the summer of 1961 when he was touring with Susan Oliver and William Redfield in *Under the Yum Yum Tree.* Plans for Ann and Scott to wed were constantly postponed because of his prior matrimonial situation.

In 1964 there was a stir of publicity when it was announced that Ann would star in a Broadway musical version of the life story of evangelist Aimee Semple McPherson, a project that had long interested Rosalind Russell and her producer husband, Frederick Brisson. However the press release was premature, since neither a script nor backing had been obtained, and there were still rights to be cleared with the subject's heirs.

Throughout the early Sixties Ann had been based in Manhattan, occasionally appearing as a guest panelist on quiz shows—just enough to provide some fresh income and keep her name professionally alive. Occasionally she would undertake a brief summer stock tour. One vivid episode on a tour of the Midwest remained fresh in Ann's mind. While performing in Detroit, she said, "a car manufacturer's wife invited me to a party. She put me at the end of the pool and, I swear, turned *spotlights* on me. I felt like an ape in a cage. . . . I fought too long—and hard—for my dignity, to be treated like a freak. . . . That broad doesn't know how close she came to being knocked cold."

Ann had not given up hope of returning to her career in a more substantial way, but she joked of picture-making, 1960s style, "Today it's all 'Singing in the Surf' pictures. If you can't ride a surfboard, you're out of work. There are a few good parts being written for women my age, but Roz Russell gets those. The rest of us stand in line."

Then in the fall of 1965, Ann, an ardent soap opera enthusiast, joined the cast of NBC-TV's "Another World," playing the role of Katherine Corning. The schedule was rough, since she had to rise at 4 A.M. to prepare for the trek to the Brooklyn television studio, the rehearsals, and then the 3:00–3:30 telecast. Ann was not sure how long the part would last, but she enjoyed the activity and renewed status immensely. She also appeared on such game shows as "The Price Is Right," "To Tell the Truth," and "The Match Game."

Back in the limelight, Ann was suddenly worthy of reporters' interest. In early 1966 *TV Guide* interviewed the "Tabasco-tongued

In a publicity pose for *The Opposite Sex* ('56).

With future husband Scott McKay in 1964.

With Douglas Fowley and Ruth McDevitt in the CBS-TV series "Pistols 'n' Petticoats" ('66).

Texan" and elicited the following quotes.

On integrity: "You're going to find that I'm honest. To a fault, people tell me. But I tell them, 'What the blazes. Life is too short to go pussyfooting around.'"

On leaving the studio in a chauffeur-driven limousine as soon as her acting is completed for the day's episode: "I get paid to act, not socialize. So I act and go home. In comfort, too. Friends say, 'Isn't it nice of NBC to get you a limousine?' NBC, hell! I pay for this. I'm too old to have my teeth shaken out in a bus."

On her soap opera assignment: "I took the job because people were saying I was lazy. 'Sheridan doesn't want to work anymore,' they said. So I decided to do a soap. That's 9,000 *new* words a day. Let them say I'm lazy *now*. . . . On heavy days, it's murder. What I do is visualize the script. Picture the page. When the other actors stop talking, I talk."

On the golden age of Hollywood: "People think that because a few actors out there were nuts, we *all* were. Nothing but wild parties. What wild parties? We all went to bed at eleven. I've seen parties in New York that make Hollywood look like the A & P."

On the new Hollywood: "What have they done to the place? I don't know it anymore. The lots are chaotic. TV has turned everything into big ugly factories. . . . I'm indignant!"

In 1965 Ann had made a pilot for a teleseries entitled "Pistols 'n' Petticoats." Cast as Henrietta Hanks of Wretched, Colorado, her role was that of a quick-drawing, gun-toting member of the fastest guns in the West. Early in 1966 the pilot was sold as a Fall 1966 series, and she gave her notice to the soap opera. She arrived in Hollywood in February to begin shooting the first thirteen episodes, with fellow series regulars Ruth McDevitt and Douglas Fowley.

The show debuted on Saturday night, September 17, 1966, and it received acceptable reviews from the critics and a sufficiently strong audience interest to keep the series running for at least a season. However, ironically and sadly, Ann could not enjoy her new-found fame. She had been finding it difficult to swallow and had consulted several physicians. At first it was diagnosed as an ulcer, but she knew better. She went to other doctors, and a biopsy report revealed the presence of an inoperable, very advanced cancer in the esophagus and liver. Nevertheless, Ann refused to concede defeat. More importantly, she refused to withdraw from the series, fearing that her absence would cause the show to be canceled and put a lot of people out of work.

Meanwhile she and Scott McKay decided to marry. On Sunday, June 5, 1966, fifty-one-year-old Ann and forty-nine-year-old McKay were wed in Los Angeles. Her business manager Bart Hackley and his wife were the attendants. The newlyweds went to Hawaii for a two-week honeymoon.

Sheridan then returned to the set of "Pistols 'n' Petticoats." With its *Cat Ballou-*type wacky humor it was gaining popularity with the public. Ann signed for an additional thirteen weeks of episodes, but she began to lose weight rapidly, and she would often stagger across the set helplessly. Some unknowing observers thought she was drunk. She was down to eighty-five pounds and was taking cancer treatments once a week at Cedars of Lebanon Hospital in Los Angeles. As Ann confided to one sympathetic acquaintance, "I'm going . . . [to] perform just as long as I'm able. I've tried all my life to entertain the public and I'm not going to let them down now." She vowed never to tell the cast of her series about her plight. Sometimes due to weakness, she would have to be carried off the set. She was a gallant trouper in every sense of the word.

On Saturday, January 21, 1967, Ann died in her San Fernando Valley home. Her last words were, "I'm going to be all right." Scott McKay had canceled his road tour of *Luv* to be near her during this critical period. "Pistols 'n' Petticoats" played out its 26-week run, and in late 1967 Universal spliced together episodes from the series and released it as a feature entitled *The Far Out West.*

In her last years, Ann was asked to evaluate her position in film history. She replied, candidly as always, "There's no position, really. It'll be just one of those things that's written off, for heaven's sake. It won't mean anything."

Regarding her method of acting: "Be as honest as you can. That's the only approach. . . . Hard work and honesty."

In reviewing her career with cinema writer Ray Hagen, Miss Sheridan summed up, "Some people have such interesting things happen to them during the knock-down, drag-out try for a career. Others, it just seems to drag along, and mine sounds so boring. If something exciting had happened I could understand, but it was just hard work, that's all."

FILMOGRAPHY

As Clara Lou Sheridan:

SEARCH FOR BEAUTY *(Paramount, 1934)* 78 min.

Director, Erle Kenton; based on the play *Love Your Body* by Schuyler E. Grey and Paul R. Milton; screen story, David Boehm, Maurice Watkins; screenplay, Frank Butler, Claude Binyon, Sam Hellman; songs, Ralph Rainger and Leo Robin; sound, Joel Butler; camera, Harry Fischbeck; editor, James Smith.

Larry "Buster" Crabbe (Don Jackson); Ida Lupino (Barbara Hilton); Toby Wing (Sally); James Gleason (Dan Healey); Robert Armstrong (Larry Williams); Gertrude Michael (Jean Strange); Roscoe Karns (Newspaper Reporter); Verna Hillie (Susie); Pop Kenton (Caretaker); Frank McGlynn, Sr. (Reverend Rankin); Clara Lou Sheridan (Beauty Contestant).

BOLERO *(Paramount, 1934)* 80 min.

Associate producer, Benjamin Glazer; director, Wesley Ruggles; story, Carey Wilson, Kubec Glasmon, Ruth Ridenour; screenplay, Horace Jackson; composition "Bolero" by Maurice Ravel; new music, Ralph Rainger; sound, Earl Hayman; camera, Leo Tover; editor, Hugh Bennett.

George Raft (Raoul DeBaere); Carole Lombard (Helen Hathaway); Sally Rand (Annette); Frances Drake (Leona); William Frawley (Mike DeBaere); Ray Milland (Lord Robert Coray); Gloria Shea (Lucy); Gertrude Michael (Lady Claire D'Argon); Dell Henderson (Theatre Manager); Frank G. Dunn (Hotel Manager); Martha Bamattre (Belgian Landlady); Paul Panzer (Bailiff); Adolph Millar (German Beer Garden Manager); Anne Shaw (Young Matron); Phillips Smalley (Leona's Angel); John Irwin (Porter); Gregory Golubeff (Orchestra Leader); Clara Lou Sheridan (Bit);

COLLEGE RHYTHM *(Paramount, 1934)* 83 min.

Director, Norman Taurog; story, George Marion, Jr.; screenplay, Walter DeLeon, John McDermott, Francis Martin; songs, Mack Gordon and Harry Revel; choreography, LeRoy Prinz; camera, Leo Tover, Ted Tetzlaff; editor, LeRoy Stone, Edward Dmytryk.

Joe Penner (Joe); Jack Oakie (Francis J. "Love and Kisses" Finnegan); Lanny Ross (Larry Stacey); Lyda Roberti (Mimi); Helen Mack (June Cort); George Barbier (John P. Stacey); Mary Brian (Gloria Van Dayham); Franklin Pangborn (Peabody); Robert McWade (Herman Whimple); Harold Minjir (Witherspoon); Joe Sawyer (Spud Miller); Julian Madison (Jimmy Poole); Mary Wallace (Peggy Small); Dutch Hendrian (Taylor, the Captain of Whimple Team); Bradley Metcalfe (Sonny Whimple); Dean Jagger (Coach); Eric Alden (Stacey Quarterback); Lee Phelps (Timekeeper); Gilbert Wilson (Whimple Quarterback); Douglas Wood (Tramp); Harry Strang (Taxi Driver); Clara Lou Sheridan (Glove Counter Salesgirl); Herbert Evans (Evans, the Whimple Butler); Dennis O'Keefe (Store Doorman); Kenny Baker (Chorus Boy, Cheerleader in "Take a Number From 1 to 10" Routine); Sarah Jane Fulks [Jane Wyman] (Girl).

COME ON MARINES! *(Paramount, 1934)* 68 min.

Director, Henry Hathaway; story, Philip Wylie; screenplay, Byron Morgan, Joel Sayre; music, Ralph Rainger; song, Rainger and Leo Robin; art directors, Hans Dreier, Earl Hedrick; sound, Jack Goodrich; camera, Ben Reynolds; editor, James Smith.

Richard Arlen (Lucky Davis); Ida Lupino (Esther Smith-Hamilton); Roscoe Karns (Terence V. "Spud" McGurk); Grace Bradley (Jo-Jo LaVerne); Edmund Breese (General Cabot); Monte Blue (Lieutenant Allen); Virginia Hammond (Susie Raybourn); Roger Gray (Celano); Julian Madison (Brick); Emile Chautard (Priest); Clara Lou Sheridan (Shirley); Toby Wing [Dolly (Dorothy Barclay)]; Lona Andre (Loretta); Leo Chalzel (Bumpy); Pat Flaherty (Peewee Martin); Fuzzy Knight (Mike); Jean Chatburn, Jenifer Gray, Kay McCoy, Mary Blackwood (Girls); Brooks Benedict (Marine Orderly); Harry Strang (Radio Operator); Kit Guard (Cook); Jack Pennick (Corporal Spike); James Bradbury, Jr., Harry Tenbrook, Charles Sullivan, Eddie Baker (Marines); Colin Tapley, Yancey Lane, Eldred Tidbury (Bits); Anna Demetrio (Fat Cantina Woman); Billy Franey (Henderson, the Street Cleaner); Boyd Irwin (Officer).

MURDER AT THE VANITIES *(Paramount, 1934)* 89 min.

Producer, E. Lloyd Sheldon; director, Mitchell Leisen; based on the play by Earl Carroll and Rufus King; screenplay, Carey Wilson, Joseph Gollomb; dialogue, Sam Hellman; songs, Leo Robin and Ralph Rainger; camera, Leo Tover; editor, Billy Shea.

Carl Brisson (Eric Lander); Victor McLaglen (Bill Murdock); Jack Oakie (Jack Ellery); Kitty Carlisle (Ann Ware); Dorothy Stickney (Norma Watson); Gertrude Michael (Rita Ross); Jessie Ralph (Mrs. Helene Smith); Charles Middleton

(Homer Boothby); Gail Patrick (Sadie Evans); Donald Meek (Dr. Saunders); Otto Hoffman (Walsh); Charles McAvoy (Ben); Beryl Wallace (Beryl); Barbara Fritchie (Vivien); Toby Wing (Nancy); Lona Andre (Lona); Colin Tapley (Stage Manager); William Arnold (Treasurer); Cecil Weston (Miss Bernstein); Hal Greene (Call Boy); Stanley Blystone (Policeman); Betty Bethune (Fat Charwoman); Clara Lou Sheridan (Lou); Gwenllian Gill (Gwen); Duke Ellington and His Orchestra (Themselves); Leda Necova, Anya Taranda, Wanda Perry, Evelyn Kelly, Dorothy Dawes, Ernestine Anderson, Laurie Shevlin, Ruth Hilliard, Constance Jordan, Marion Callahan (Earl Carroll Girls).

KISS AND MAKE UP (*Paramount, 1934*) 80 min.

Producer, B. P. Schulberg; directors, Harlan Thompson, Jean Negulesco; based on the play by Stephen Bekeffi; adaptor, Jane Hinton; screenplay, Harlan Thompson, George Marion, Jr.; songs, Ralph Rainger and Leo Robin; art directors, Hans Dreier, Ernst Fegte; sound, Jack Goodrich; camera, Leon Shamroy.

Cary Grant (Dr. Maurice Lamar); Helen Mack (Anne); Genevieve Tobin (Eve Caron); Edward Everett Horton (Marcel Caron); Lucien Littlefield (Max Pascal); Mona Maris (Countess Rita); Kay Williams (Vilma); Lucille Lund (Magda); Rafael Storm (Rolando); Mme. Bonita Weber (Mme. Severac); Sam Ash (Plumber); Toby Wing (Consuelo Claghorne); Henry Armetta (Chairman of Banquet); Chick Collins, John Sinclair (Taxi Drivers); Rita Gould (Mme. Dupont); Dorothy Christy (Cheta); Clara Lou Sheridan (Beauty Operator); Judith Arlen, Jean Gale, Hazel Hayes, Lu-Anne Meredith (Beauty Clinic Nurses); Dorothy Drake (Bit); Gigi Parrish (Radio Listener); Jean Carmen (Maharajah's Wife); Julie Bishop, Betty Bryson (Beauty Clinic Patients).

SHOOT THE WORKS (*Paramount, 1934*) 82 min.

Director, Wesley Ruggles; based on the play *The Great Magoo* by Ben Hecht and Gene Fowler; screenplay, Howard J. Green; songs, Mack Gordon and Harry Revel; Leo Robin and Ralph Rainger; art directors, Hans Dreier, Robert Usher; camera, Leo Tover.

Jack Oakie (Nicky); Ben Bernie (Joe David); Dorothy Dell (Lily Raquel); Arline Judge (Jackie); Alison Skipworth (Countess); Roscoe Karns (Sailor Burke); William Frawley (Larry Hale); Paul Cavanagh (Bill Ritchie); Lew Cody (Axel Hanratty); Monte Vandergrift (Man from Board of Health); Jill Dennett (Wanda); Lee Kohlmar (Professor Jonas); Tony Merlo (Headwaiter); Ben Taggart (Detective); Charles McAvoy (Cop); Frank Prince (Crooner); Clara Lou Sheridan (Secretary).

THE NOTORIOUS SOPHIE LANG (*Paramount, 1934*) 64 min.

Producer, Bayard Veiller; director, Ralph Murphy; based on stories by Frederick Irving Anderson; screenplay, Anthony Veiller; art directors, Hans Dreier, Robert Odell; camera, Al Gilks.

Gertrude Michael [Sophie Lang (Elisa Morgan)]; Paul Cavanagh [Max Bernard (Sir Nigel Crane)]; Arthur Byron (Inspector Stone); Alison Skipworth (Aunt Nellis); Leon Errol (Stubbs); Ben Taggart (Captain Thompson); Norman Ainslie (Robin); Arthur Hoyt, Edward McWade (Jewelers); Madame Jacoby (Countess Dineski); Ferdinand Gottschalk (Augustus Telfmen); Dell Henderson (House Detective); Stanhope Wheatcroft (Floor Walker); William Jeffries, Jack Mulhall, Perry Ivins, Alphonse Martell (Clerks); Joe Sawyer (Building Guard); Adrian Rosley (Oscar); Clara Lou Sheridan (Extra); Jack Pennick (Bystander).

LADIES SHOULD LISTEN (*Paramount, 1934*) 62 min.

Producer, Douglas MacLean; director, Frank Tuttle; story, Alfred Savoir, Guy Bolton; adaptor, Bolton; screenplay, Claude Binyon, Frank Butler; art directors, Hans Dreier, Ernst Fegte; sound, Earl Hayman; camera, Harry Sharp.

Cary Grant (Julian de Lussac); Frances Drake (Anna Mirelle); Edward Everett Horton (Paul Vernet); Rosita Moreno (Marguerite Cintos); George Barbier (Joseph Flamberg); Nydia Westman (Susie Flamberg); Charles Ray (Henri, the Porter); Charles Arnt (Albert, the Manservant); Rafael Corio (Ramon Cintos); Clara Lou Sheridan (Adele, the Operator); Henrietta Burnside (Operator); Joe North (Butler).

YOU BELONG TO ME (*Paramount, 1934*) 66 min.

Director, Alfred Werker; story, Elizabeth Alexander; screenplay, Grover Jones, William Slavens McNutt, Walter DeLeon; songs Leo Robin and Sam Coslow; Milan Roder and Coslow; art directors, Hans Dreier, Robert Usher; camera, Leo Tover.

Lee Tracy (Bud Hannigan); Helen Mack (Florence Faxon); Helen Morgan (Madame Alva); David Jack Holt (Jimmy Faxon); Arthur Pierson (Hap Stanley); Lynne Overman (Brown); Dean Jagger (Instructor); Edwin Stanley (School Principal); Irene Ware (Lita Lacey); Hugh McCormick (Ventriloquist); Lou Cass (Joe Mantell); Max Mack (Jack Mandell); Mary Owen (Maisie Kelly); Reverend Neal Dodd (Minister); Irving Bacon (Stage Manager); Allen Fox (Usher); Eddie Borden (Poker Player); Willie Fung (Waiter); Jerry Tucker, Wally Albright, Jr. (Schoolboys); Bernard Suss (The Doctor); Frank Rice (Stagehand); Clara Lou Sheridan, Gwenllian Gill (Girls at Wedding); Charles Dorety (Loud Voice); Billy Bletcher (Man with Comb).

WAGON WHEELS (*Paramount, 1934*) 56 min. (TV title: *Caravans West*)

Director, Charles Barton; based on the novel *Fighting Caravans* by Zane Grey; screenplay, Jack Cunningham, Charles Logan, Carl A. Buss; art director, Earl Hedricks; camera, William Mellor; editor, Jack Dennis.

Randolph Scott (Clint Belmet); Gail Patrick (Nancy Wellington); Billy Lee (Sonny Wellington); Monte Blue (Murdock); Raymond Hatton (Jim Burch); Jan Duggan (Abby Masters); Leila Bennett (Hetty Masters); Olin Howland (Bill O'Meary); J. P. McGowan (Couch); James Marcus (Jed); Helen Hunt (Mrs. Jed); James B. "Pop" Kenton (Masters); Alfred Delcambre (Ebe); John Marston (Orator); Sam McDaniel (Black Coachman); Howard Wilson (Permit Officer); Michael Visaroff (Russian); E. Alyn Warren (The Factor); Fern Emmett (Settler); Clara Lou Sheridan (Extra); Harold Goodwin (Nancy's Brother); Lew Meehan (Listener); Eldred Tilbury (Chauncey).

MRS. WIGGS OF THE CABBAGE PATCH (*Paramount, 1934*) 80 min.

Producer, Douglas MacLean; director, Norman Taurog; story, Alice Hegan Rice, Anne Crawford Flexner; screenplay, William Slavens McNutt, Jane Storm; art directors, Hans Dreier, Robert Odell; camera, Charles Lang.

Pauline Lord (Mrs. Wiggs); W. C. Fields (Mr. Stubbins); ZaSu Pitts (Miss Hazy); Evelyn Venable (Lucy Olcott); Kent Taylor (Bob Redding); Charles Middleton (Mr. Bagby); Donald Meek (Mr. Wiggs); Jimmy Butler (Bill Wiggs); George Breakston (Jimmy Wiggs); Edith Fellows (Australia Wiggs); Virginia Weidler (Europena Wiggs); Carmencita Johnson (Asia Wiggs); George Reed (Julius); Mildred Gover (Priscilla); Arthur Housman (Dick Harris); Sam Flint (Agent Jenkins); James Robinson (Mose); Bentley Hewlett (Box-Office Man); Edward Tamblyn (Usher); Clara Lou Sheridan (Girl); Lillian Elliott (Mrs. Bagby); Earl Pingree (Brakeman); George Pearce (Minister); Dell Henderson (House Manager); Al Shaw, Sam Lee (Comedians).

LIMEHOUSE BLUES (*Paramount, 1934*) 66 min.

Director, Alexander Hall; story, Arthur Phillips; screenplay, Phillips, Cyril Hume, Grover Jones; song, Sam Coslow; art directors, Hans Dreier, Robert Usher; camera, Harry Fischbeck.

George Raft (Harry Young); Jean Parker (Toni); Anna May Wong (Tu Tuan); Kent Taylor (Eric Benton); Montagu Love (Pug Talbot); Billy Bevan (Herb); John Rogers (Smokey); Robert Lorraine (Inspector Sheridan); E. Alyn Warren (Ching Lee); Wyndham Standing (Assistant Commissioner Kenyon); Louis Vincenot (Rhama); Eily Malyon (Woman Who Finds Pug); Forrester Harvey (McDonald); Robert "Bob" Adair (Policeman in Pug's House); Elsie Prescott (Woman Employment Agent); James May (Taxi Driver); Colin Kenny (Davis); Eric Blore (Man Slummer); Colin Tapley (Man Fighting with Wife); Rita Carlyle (His Wife); Desmond Roberts (Constable); Tempe Pigott (Maggie); Otto Yamaoka (Chinese Waiter on Boat); Dora Mayfield (Flower Woman); Clara Lou Sheridan (Girl with Couples).

ENTER MADAM (*Paramount, 1934*) 82 min.

Producer, A. Benjamin Gilbert; director, Elliot Nugent; based on the play *Enter Madame* by Gilda Varesi Archibald and Dorothea Donn-Byrne; screenplay, Charles Brackett, Gladys Lehman; art directors, Hans Dreier, Ernst Fegte; costumes, Travis Banton; sound, M. M. Paggi; camera, Theodor Sparkuhl, William Mellor.

Elissa Landi (Lisa Della Robbia); Cary Grant (Gerald Fitzgerald); Lynne Overman (Mr. Farnum); Sharon Lynne (Flora Preston); Michelette Burani (Bice); Paul Porcasi (Archimede); Adrian Rosley (Doctor); Cecilia Parker (Aline Chalmers); Frank Albertson (John Fitzgerald); Wilfred Hari (Tamamoto); Torben Meyer (Carlson); Harold Berquist (Bjorgenson); Diana Lewis (Operator); Richard Bonelli (Scarpia on Stage); Dick Kline (Stage Manager); Gino Corrado (Waiter); Matt McHugh (Reporter); Mildred Boothe (Trixie, the Reporter); Lorimer Johnston (Bit); Clara Lou Sheridan (Extra); Los Angeles Opera Company (Themselves).

HOME ON THE RANGE (*Paramount, 1935*) 54 min.

Producer, Harold Hurley; director, Arthur Jacobson; based on the novel *Code of the West* by Zane Grey; screenplay, Ethel Doherty, Grant Garrett, Charles Logue; camera, William Mellor; editor, Jack Dennis.

Jackie Coogan (Jack); Randolph Scott (Tom Hatfield); Evelyn Brent (Georgie); Dean Jagger (Thurman); Addison Richards (Beady); Fuzzy

Knight (Cracker); Howard Wilson (Bill Morris); Phillip Morris (Benson); Albert Hart (Undertaker); Allen Wood (Flash); Richard Carle (Butts); Ralph Remley (Brown); C. L. Sherwood (Shorty); Clara Lou Sheridan (Girl Entertainer); Francis Sayles (Hotel Clerk); Jack Clark (Sheriff); Joe Morrison (Nightclub Singer); Alfred Delcambre (Bit).

RUMBA *(Paramount, 1935)* 71 min.

Producer, William LeBaron; director, Marion Gering; idea, Guy Endore, Seena Owen; screenplay, Howard J. Green; additional dialogue, Harry Ruskin, Frank Partos; songs, Ralph Rainger; Spanish lyrics, Francois B. de Valdes; choreography, LeRoy Prinz; George Raft/Carole Lombard specialty number created and staged by Veloz and Yolanda; art directors, Hans Dreier, Robert Usher; costumes, Travis Banton; sound, J. A. Goodrich; camera, Ted Tetzlaff; editor, Hugh Bennett.

George Raft (Joe Martin); Carole Lombard (Diane Harrison); Margo (Carmelita); Lynne Overman (Flash); Monroe Owsley (Hobart Fletcher); Iris Adrian (Goldie Allen); Gail Patrick (Patsy Fletcher); Samuel S. Hinds (Henry B. Harrison); Virginia Hammond (Mrs. Harrison); Jameson Thomas (Jack Solanger); Soledad Jimenez (Maria); Paul Porcasi (Carlos); Raymond McKee (Dance Director); Akim Tamiroff (Tony); Mack Gray (Assistant Dance Instructor); Dennis O'Keefe (Man in Diane's Party at Theatre); Eldred Tidbury (Watkins); Bruce Warren (Dean); Hugh Enfield [Craig Reynolds] (Bromley); Rafael Corio (Alfredo); Rafael Storm (Cashier); James Burke, Eddie Dunn, James P. Burtis (Reporters); Dick Rush (Policeman); E. H. Calvert (Police Captain); Hooper Atchley (Doctor); Clara Lou Sheridan (Dance Girl); Brooks Benedict (Extra in Audience); Olga Barrancos, Luis Barrancos, Lara Puente, the Pimento Twins (Rumba Dancers); Zora (Specialty Dancer); Jane Wyman (Chorus Girl).

As Ann Sheridan:
BEHOLD MY WIFE! *(Paramount, 1935)* 79 min.

Producer, B. P. Schulberg; director, Mitchell Leisen; based on the novel *The Translation of a Savage* by Sir Gilbert Parker; screenplay, Vincent Lawrence, Grover Jones; adaptors, William R. Lipman, Oliver La Garge; camera, Leon Shamroy.

Sylvia Sidney (Tonita Stormcloud); Gene Raymond (Michael Carter); Juliette Compton (Diana Carter-Curson); Laura Hope Crews (Mrs. Carter); H. B. Warner (Hubert Carter); Monroe Owsley (Bob Prentice); Kenneth Thomson (Jim Curson); Ann Sheridan (Mary White); Charlotte Granville (Mrs. Sykes); Dean Jagger (Pete); Charles Middleton (Juan Stormcloud); Eric Blore (Benson, the Butler); Ralph Remley (Jenkins); Cecil Weston (Gibson); Dewey Robinson (Bryan, the Detective); Charles C. Wilson (Police Captain); Edward Gargan (Connolly, the Detective); Olin Howland (Mattingly); Gregory Whitespear (Medicine Man); Jim Thorpe (Indian Chief); Otto Hoffman (Minister); Evelyn Selbie (Neighbor Woman); Nella Walker (Mrs. Copperwaithe); Jack Mulhall, Martin Malone, Neal Burns (Reporters at Train); Mabel Forrest (Society Dowager); Rafael Storm, Phil Tead, Eddie "Rochester" Anderson, Matt McHugh (Chauffeurs); Joe Sawyer (Morton—Michael's Chauffeur); Kate Price (Mrs. McGregor, the Cook).

CAR 99 *(Paramount, 1935)* 75 min.

Presenter, Adolph Zukor; producer, Bayard Veiller; director, Charlie Barton; based on stories by Karl Detzer; screenplay, Detzer, C. Gardner Sullivan; art directors, Hans Dreier, Robert Usher; camera, William C. Mellor.

Fred MacMurray (Ross Martin); Ann Sheridan (Mary Adams); Sir Guy Standing [Professor Anthony (John Viken)]; Frank Craven (Sheriff Pete Arnot); William Frawley (Sergeant Barrel); Marina Schubert (Nan Anthony); Dean Jagger (Jim Burton); John Howard (Recruit Carney); Robert Kent (Recruit Blatsky); Del Cambre (Recruit Jamison); Nora Cecil (Granny); Joe Sawyer (Whitey); Mack Gray (Smoke); Eddie Dunn (Mac, the Servant); Peter Hancock (Eddie); Howard Wilson (Dutch); Al Hill (Hawkeye, the Hood); Eddy Chandler (Recruit Haynes); John Sinclair (Crook in Sedan); Russell Hopton (Operator Harper); Charles Wilson (Police Captain Ryan); Jack Cheatham (Radio Sergeant Meyers); Duke York (Cop); Malcolm McGregor (Pilot); Charles Sullivan (Green Gang Hood).

ROCKY MOUNTAIN MYSTERY *(Paramount, 1935)* 63 min. (Reissue title: *The Fighting Westerner*)

Director, Charles Barton; based on the novel *Golden Dreams* by Zane Grey; screenplay, Edward E. Paramore, Jr., Ethel Doherty; camera, Archie Stout; editor, Jack Dennis.

Randolph Scott (Larry Sutton); Charles "Chic" Sale (Tex Murdock); Mrs. Leslie Carter (Mrs. Berg); Kathleen Burke (Flora); George Marion, Sr. (Ballard); Ann Sheridan (Rita Ballard); James C. Eagles (John Berg); Howard Wilson (Fritz Ballard); Willie Fung (Ling Yat); Florence Roberts (Mrs. Ballard).

MISSISSIPPI *(Paramount, 1935)* 80 min.

Producer, Arthur Hornblow, Jr.; director, A. Edward Sutherland; based on the play by Booth Tarkington; adaptors, Herbert Fields, Claude

Binyon; screenplay, Francis Martin, Jack Cunningham; songs, Richard Rodgers and Lorenz Hart; art directors, Hans Dreier, Bernard Herzbrun; sound, Eugene Merritt; camera, Charles Lang; editor, Chandler House.

Bing Crosby (Tom Grayson); W. C. Fields (Commodore Jackson); Joan Bennett (Lucy Rumford); Queenie Smith (Alabam); Gail Patrick (Elvira Rumford); Claude Gillingwater (General Rumford); John Miljan (Major Patterson); Ed Pawley (Joe Patterson); Fred Kohler, Sr. (Captain Blackie); John Larkin (Rumba); Libby Taylor (Lavinia); Harry Myers (Stage Manager); Paul Hurst (Hefty); Theresa Maxwell Conover (Miss Markham); King Baggott, Mahlon Hamilton, Al Richmond, Francis McDonald, Stanley Andrews, Eddie Sturgis, George Lloyd (Gamblers); Jules Cowles, Harry Cody (Bartenders); Forrest Taylor, Warner Richmond, Lew Kelly, Matthew Betz (Men at Bar); Jack Mulhall (Duelist); Bill Howard (Man in Auditorium); Victor Potel, Dennis O'Keefe (Guests); Helene Chadwick, Jerome Storm (Extras at Opening); The Cabin Kids, Molasses, and January (Themselves); Ann Sheridan (Schoolgirl).

RED BLOOD OF COURAGE *(Ambassador, 1935)* 55 min.

Producers, Maurice Cohn, Sig Neufeld; director, Jack English; based on the novel by James Oliver Curwood; screenplay, Barry Barringer; camera, Arthur Reed; editor, Richard G. Wray.

Kermit Maynard [Jim Sullivan (James Anderson)]; Ann Sheridan (Beth Henry); Reginald Barlow (Mark Henry/Pete Drago); Ben Hendricks, Jr. (Bart Slager); George Regas (Frenchy); Nat Carr (Meyer); Charles King (Joe); Rocky the Horse (Himself); Carl Mathews (Indian in Store/Mountie); Milt Morante (Gunman); Art Dillard (Henchman).

THE GLASS KEY *(Paramount, 1935)* 80 min.

Producer, E. Lloyd Sheldon; director, Frank Tuttle; based on the novel by Dashiell Hammett; screenplay, Kathryn Scola, Kubec Glasmon, Harry Ruskin; camera, Henry Sharp; editor, Hugh Bennett.

George Raft (Ed Beaumont); Edward Arnold (Paul Madvig); Claire Dodd (Janet Henry); Rosalind Keith (Opal Madvig); Charles Richman (Senator Henry); Robert Gleckler (Shad O'Rory); Guinn "Big Boy" Williams (Jeff); Ray Milland (Taylor Henry); Tammany Young (Clarkie); Harry Tyler (Henry Sloss); Charles C. Wilson (Farr); Emma Dunn (Mom); Matt McHugh (Puggy); Patrick Moriarty (Mulrooney); Mack Gray (Duke); Frank Marlowe (Walter Ivans); Herbert Evans (Senator's Butler); George H. Reed (Black Serving Man); Percy Morris (Bartender); Irving Bacon (Waiter); Ann Sheridan (Nurse); Henry Roquemore (Hinkle); Frank O'Connor (McLaughlin); Michael Mark (Swartz); Del Cambre (Reporter); Veda Buckland (Landlady); George Ernest (Boy).

THE CRUSADES *(Paramount, 1935)* 123 min.

Producer/director, Cecil B. DeMille; story/screenplay, Harold Lamb, Waldemar Young, Dudley Nichols; song, Leo Robin, Richard Whiting, and Rudolph Kopp; camera, Victor Milner.

Loretta Young (Berangaria, Princess of Navarre); Henry Wilcoxon (Richard, King of England); Ian Keith (Saladin, Sultan of Islam); C. Aubrey Smith (The Hermit); Katherine DeMille (Alice, Princess of France); Joseph Schildkraut (Conrad, Marquis of Montferrat); Alan Hale (Blondel); C. Henry Gordon (Philip II, King of France); George Barbier (Sancho, King of Navarre); Montagu Love (Blacksmith); Lumsden Hare (Robert, Earl of Leicester); William Farnum (Hugo, Duke of Burgundy); Hobart Bosworth (Frederick, Duke of the Germans); Pedro de Cordoba (Karakush); Ramsay Hill (John, Prince of England); Mischa Auer (Monk); Maurice Murphy (Alan, Richard's Squire); Paul Sotoff (Michael, Prince of Russia); Sven Hugo Borg (Sverro, the Norse King); Anna Demetrio (Duenna); Fred Malatosta (William, King of Sicily); Hans Von Twardowski (Nicholas, Count of Hungary); Perry Askam (Soldier); Jason Robards (Amir Slave in Saladin's Garden); J. Carroll Naish (Arab Slave Seller); Georgia Caine (Nun); Pat Moore (Leicester's Squire); Ann Sheridan, Jean Fenwick (Christian Girls); John Carradine (Bit); Guy Usher (Grey Beard); Boyd Irwin, Sr. (Templar); Harry Cording, Stanley Andrews, Maurice Black, William B. Davidson (Amirs).

FIGHTING YOUTH *(Universal, 1935)* 66 min.

Producer, Fred S. Meyer; associate producer, Ansel Friedberger; director, Hamilton MacFadden; story, Stanley Meyer; screenplay, Henry Johnson, Florabel Muir, MacFadden; art director, Ralph Berger; camera, Eddie Snyder; editor, Bernard Burton.

Charles Farrell (Larry Davis); Edward J. Nugent (Tony Tonnetti); June Martel (Betty Wilson); Ann Sheridan (Carol Arlington); Andy Devine (Cy Kipp); Glen Boles (Paul); Stephen Alden Chase (Louis Markoff); Phyllis Fraser (Dodo Gates); Herman Bing (Herman); J. Farrell MacDonald (Coach Nat Parker); Murray Kinnell (Dean James Churchill); David Worth (Captain Blake); Dutch Fehring (Bit); Frank Baker (Baker); Jeff Cravath (Assistant Coach); Frank Sully, Howard "Red" Christie, Nick Lukats, Leslie Cooper (Football Players); Jim Thorpe, Jim

Purvis, Paul Schwegler, Dale Van Sickel, Larry "Moon" Mullins (Old Graduates); Mickey Bennett (Newsboy); David O'Brien (Rooter for Manchester); Hamilton MacFadden (Doctor); Russell Wade (Buck's Roommate); Walter A. Johnson (Buck); Edmund Cobb, Dell Henderson (Detectives); Tiny Sandford (Truck Driver); Clara Kimball Young (Housemother); John King (Tim, a Student); Jean Rogers (Coed at Game).

SING ME A LOVE SONG (*First National, 1936*) 79 min.

Director, Ray Enright; story, Harry Sauber; screenplay, Sig Herzig, Jerry Wald; camera, Arthur Todd; editor, Terry Morse.

James Melton (Jerry Haynes); Patricia Ellis (Jean Martin); Hugh Herbert (Sigfried Hammerschlog); ZaSu Pitts (Gwen); Allen Jenkins (Christopher Cross); Nat Pendleton (Red); Walter Catlett (Sprague); Ann Sheridan (Lola Parker); Georgia Caine (Mrs. Parker); Dennis Moore (Ronald Blakeley); Charles Halton (Willard); Hobart Cavanaugh (Berton); Charles Richman (Goodrich); Granville Bates (Malcolm); Billy Arnold (Waiter); Lyle Moraine (Bellboy); George Guhl (Cop); Betty Farrington (Customer); George Sorel (Headwaiter); Adrian Rosley (Waiter); Linda Perry (Miss Joyce, the Secretary); Gordon Hart (Caldwell); Robert Emmett O'Connor, Harry Hollingsworth (Detectives); Emmett Vogan (Floorwalker).

BLACK LEGION (*Warner Bros., 1936*) 83 min.

Associate producer, Robert Lord; director, Archie Mayo; story, Lord; screenplay, Abem Finkel, William Wister Haines; music, Bernhard Kaun; art director, Robert Haas; gowns, Milo Anderson; assistant director, Jack Sullivan; sound, C. A. Riggs; special effects, Fred Jackman, Jr., H. F. Koenekamp; camera, George Barnes; editor, Owen Marks.

Humphrey Bogart (Frank Taylor); Dick Foran (Ed Jackson); Erin O'Brien-Moore (Ruth Taylor); Ann Sheridan (Betty Grogan); Robert Barrat (Brown); Helen Flint (Pearl Davis); Joe Sawyer (Cliff Moore); Addison Richards (Prosecuting Attorney); Eddie Acuff (Metcalf); Clifford Soubier (Mike Grogan); Paul Harvey (Billings); Samuel S. Hinds (Judge); John Litel (Tommy Smith); Alonzo Price (Alexander Hargrave); Dickie Jones (Buddy Taylor); Dorothy Vaughan (Mrs. Grogan); Henry Brandon (Joe Dombrowski); Charles Halton (Osgood); Pat C. Flick (Nick Strumpas); Francis Sayles (Charlie); Paul Stanton (Dr. Barham); Harry Hayden (Jones); Egon Brecher (Old Man Dombrowski); Dennis Moore, Carlyle Moore, Jr., Milton Kibbee (Reporters); Max Wagner (Truck Driver); Eddy Chandler, Robert E. Homans (Cops); Fredrich Lindsley (*March of Time* Voice); John Hallam Hiestand, Ted Bliss, Frank Nelson, Fredric MacKaye (Radio Announcers and Actors).

THE GREAT O'MALLEY (*Warner Bros., 1936*) 71 min.

Associate producer, Harry Joe Brown; director, William Dieterle; based on the story "The Making of O'Malley" by Gerald Beaumont; screenplay, Milton Krims, Tom Reed; music, Heinz Roemheld; gowns, Milo Anderson; art director, Hugh Reticker; assistant director, Frank Shaw; dialogue director, Irving Rapper; sound, Francis J. Scheid; special effects, James Gibbons, Fred Jackman, Jr., H. F. Koenekamp; camera, Ernest Haller; editor, Warren Low.

Pat O'Brien (James Aloysius O'Malley); Sybil Jason (Barbara Phillips); Humphrey Bogart (John Phillips); Ann Sheridan (Judy Nolan); Frieda Inescort (Mrs. Phillips); Donald Crisp (Captain Cromwell); Henry O'Neill (Defense Attorney); Craig Reynolds (Motorist); Hobart Cavanaugh (Pinky Holden); Gordon Hart (Doctor); Mary Gordon (Mrs. O'Malley); Mabel Colcord (Mrs. Flaherty); Frank Sheridan (Father Patrick); Lillian Harmer (Miss Taylor); Delmar Watson (Tubby); Frank Reicher (Dr. Larson); Bob Perry (Man Getting Shine); Charles Wilson (Cop); Max Wagner (Bus Driver); Jack Mower, Arthur Millett (Detectives).

SAN QUENTIN (*Warner Bros., 1937*) 70 min.

Associate producer, Samuel Bischoff; director, Lloyd Bacon; story, Robert Tasker, John Bright; screenplay, Peter Milne, Humphrey Cobb; music, Heinz Roemheld, Charles Maxwell, David Raksin; orchestrators, Joseph Nussbaum, Ray Heindorf; song, Harry Warren and Al Dubin; assistant director, Dick Mayberry; art director, Esdras Hartley; gowns, Howard Shoup; sound, Everett A. Brown; special effects, James Gibbons, H. F. Koenekamp; camera, Sid Hickox; editor, William Holmes.

Pat O'Brien (Captain Stephen Jameson); Humphrey Bogart (Red Kennedy); Ann Sheridan (May Kennedy); Barton MacLane (Lieutenant Druggin); Joe Sawyer ("Sailor Boy" Hansen); James Robbins (Mickey Callahan); Veda Ann Borg (Helen); Joseph King (Warden Taylor); Gordon Oliver (Lieutenant); Emmett Vogan (Captain); Garry Owen (Dopey); Marc Lawrence (Venetti); Max Wagner (Prison Runner); William Pawley, George Lloyd, Frank Faylen, Al Hill (Convicts); Raymond Hatton (Pawnbroker); Hal Neiman (Convict #38216); William Williams (Convict Conklin); Glen Cavender (Convict Hastings); Lane Chandler (Guard); Dennis Moore (Convict Simpson); Ralph Dunn (Head Guard); Ralph Byrd (Cop on Phone); John Ince

(Old Convict); Bob Wilkie (Young Convict in Riot); Frank Fanning (Cop in Radio Car); Jack Mower, Claire White (Couple in Car).

WINE, WOMEN AND HORSES (Warner Bros., 1937) 64 min.

Supervisor, Bryan Foy; director, Louis King; story, W. R. Burnett; screenplay, Roy Chanslor; art director, Esdras Hartley; gowns, Howard Shoup; dialogue director, Reggie Hammerstein; camera, James Van Trees, Sr.; editor, Jack Saper.

Barton MacLane (Jim Turner); Ann Sheridan (Valerie); Dick Purcell (George Mayhew); Peggy Bates (Marjorie Mayhew); Walter Cassell (Pres Barrow); Lottie Williams (Mrs. Mayhew); Kenneth Harlan (Jed Bright); Eugene Jackson (Eight Ball); Charles Foy (Broadway); James Robbins (Joe); Nita (Lady Luck); Addison Richards (Bit).

THE FOOTLOOSE HEIRESS (Warner Bros., 1937) 59 min.

Director, William Clemens; story/screenplay, Robert White; camera, Arthur Edeson; editor, Lou Hesse.

Craig Reynolds (Bruce "Butch" Baeder); Ann Sheridan (Kay Allyn); Anne Nagel (Linda Pierson); William Hopper (Jack Pierson); Hugh O'Connell (John C. Allyn); Teddy Hart (Charlie McCarthy); Hal Neiman (Luke Peaneather); Frank Orth (Justice Cuttler); William Eberhardt (Wilbur Frost); Loia Cheaney (Sarah Cutter).

ALCATRAZ ISLAND (Warner Bros., 1938) 61 min.

Supervisor, Bryan Foy; based on the story "Alcatraz" by Crane Wilbur; screenplay, Wilbur; art director, Esdras Hartley; gowns, Howard Shoup; camera, L. William O'Connell; editor, Frank Dewar.

John Litel (Gat Brower); Mary Maguire (Ann); Ann Sheridan (Flo Allen); Gordon Oliver (George Drake); Dick Purcell (Harp Santell); Ben Welden ("Red" Carroll); Addison Richards (Fred MacLane); George E. Stone (Tough Tony Burke); Vladimir Sokoloff (Flying Dutchman); Peggy Bates (Miss Toliver); Charles Trowbridge (Warden Jackson); Janet Shaw (Sally Carruthers); Doris Lloyd (Miss Marquand); Matty Fain (Butch); Anderson Lawler (Whitey Edwards); Ed Keane (Crandall); Walter Young (Federal Judge); Ed Stanley (U.S. Attorney); Granville Owen (Gat's Secretary); Sol Gorss (Gat's Bodyguard); Sam Cohen (Maury Schwartz); Milton Kibbee, Perc Teeple (Court Clerks); Myrtle Stedman (Woman); Mike Lally, Al Herman, Jack Gardner, Alan Davis (Convicts); Guy Usher (Principal Keeper); Cliff Saum, Henry Otho, Pat O'Malley, Ralph Dunn, Galan Galt, Ted Oliver (Guards); Francis Sayles (Bailiff); Earl Dwire (Judge).

SHE LOVED A FIREMAN (Warner Bros., 1938) 57 min.

Producer, Bryan Foy; director, John Farrow; story, Carlton C. Sand; screenplay, Sand, Morton Grant; camera, Lon O'Connell; editor, Tommy Pratt.

Dick Foran (Red); Ann Sheridan (Margie); Robert Armstrong (Smokey Shannon); Eddie Acuff (Skillet); Veda Ann Borg (Betty); May Beatty (Mrs. Michaels); Eddy Chandler (Callahan); Lane Chandler (Patton); Ted Oliver (Lieutenant Grimes); Pat Flaherty (Duggan); Leo White (Barber); Kathrin Clare Ward (Mrs. Murphy); Myrtle Stedman (Mrs. Brown); Brick Sullivan (Man at Dance); Janet Shaw (Girl at Dance); Fred "Snowflake" Toones (Joe); Minerva Urecal (Nurse Purdy); Huey White (Turtle); Allen Mathews (Junior Officer); Wilfred Lucas (Captain); Eddie Hart (McDermott).

THE PATIENT IN ROOM 18 (Warner Bros., 1938) 60 min.

Associate producer, Bryan Foy; directors, Bobby Connolly, Crane Wilbur; based on the novel by Mignon Eberhart; screenplay, Eugene Solow, Robertson White; camera, James Van Trees; editor, Lou Hesse.

Patric Knowles (Lance O'Leary); Ann Sheridan (Sarah Keate); Eric Stanley (Bentley); John Ridgely (Jim Warren); Roselle Towne (Maida Day); Jean Benedict (Carol Lethany); Harland Tucker (Dr. Arthur Lethany); Edward Raquelo (Dr. Fred Hajek); Charles Trowbridge (Dr. Balman); Vicki Lester (Nurse); Cliff Clark (Inspector Foley); Ralph Sanford (Donahue); Frank Orth (John Higgins); Greta Meyer (Hilda); Walter Young (Coroner); Ralph Dunn (Hotel Clerk); George Offerman, Jr. (Newsboy); Glen Cavender (Doorman); Jack Richardson (Cabby); Cliff Saum, Jack Mower (Policemen); Spec O'Donnell (Elevator Operator); William Hopper (Grabshot); Owen King (Day Clerk).

MYSTERY HOUSE (Warner Bros., 1938) 61 min.

Associate producer, Bryan Foy; director, Noel Smith; based on the novel *The Mystery of Hunting's End* by Mignon Eberhart; screenplay, Sherman Lowe, Robertson White; camera, L. William O'Connell; editor, Frank Magee.

Ann Sheridan (Sarah Keate); Dick Purcell (Lance O'Leary); Anne Nagel (Gwen Kingery); William Hopper (Lal Killian); Anthony Averill (Julian Barre); Hugh O'Connell (Newell Morse); Ben Welden (Gerald Frawley); Sheila Bromley

(Terice Von Elm); Elspeth Dudgeon (Lucy Kingery); Anderson Lawler (Joe Paggi); Trevor Bardette (Bruker); Eric Stanley (Huber Kingery); Jean Benedict (Helen Page); Jack Mower (Coroner); Stuart Holmes (Jury Foreman); Loia Cheaney (Secretary); John Harron (Director).

THE COWBOY FROM BROOKLYN (*Warner Bros., 1938*) 77 min.

Producer, Hal B. Wallis; associate producer, Lou Edelman; director, Lloyd Bacon; based on the play *Howdy, Stranger* by Robert Sloan and Louis Peletier, Jr.; screenplay, Earl Baldwin; art director, Esdras Hartley; music director, Leo F. Forbstein; songs, Richard Whiting, Johnny Mercer, and Harry Warren; camera, Arthur Edeson; editor, James Gibbon.

Dick Powell (Elly Jordan); Pat O'Brien (Roy Chadwick); Priscilla Lane (Jane Hardy); Dick Foran (Sam Thorne); Ann Sheridan (Maxine Chadwick); Johnnie Davis (Jeff Hardy); Ronald Reagan (Pat Dunn); Emma Dunn (Ma Hardy); Granville Bates (Pop Hardy); James Stephenson (Professor Landis); Hobart Cavanaugh (Mr. Jordan); Elisabeth Risdon (Mrs. Jordan); Dennie Moore (Abby Pitts); Rosella Towne (Panthea); May Boley (Mrs. Kirnkenheim); Harry Barris (Louie); Candy Candido (Spec); Donald Briggs (*Star* Reporter); Jeffrey Lynn (*Chronicle* Reporter); John Ridgely (*Beacon* Reporter); William B. Davidson (Mr. Alvey); Mary Field (Myrtle Semple); Monte Vandergrift, Eddy Chandler (Brakemen); Cliff Saum (Conductor); Sam Hayes (News Commentator); Jack Wise, Eddie Graham (Reporters); Dorothy Vaughan (Fat Woman); Jack Moore (Timekeeper); Ben Hendricks (Judge); Emmett Vogan (Loudspeaker Announcer).

LITTLE MISS THOROUGHBRED (*Warner Bros., 1938*) 65 min.

Director, John Farrow; story, Albert DeMond; screenplay, DeMond, George Bricker; camera, L. William O'Connell; editor, Everett Dodd.

John Litel (Nails Morgan); Ann Sheridan (Madge Perry); Frank McHugh (Tom Harrington); Janet Kay Chapman (Mary Jane); Eric Stanley (Colonel Whitcomb); Robert Homans (Officer O'Reilly); Charles Wilson (Dutch Fultz); John Ridgely (Slug); Dorothy Vaughan (Mrs. O'Reilly); Cy Kendall (District Attorney Sheridan); Paul Everton (Judge Stanhope); Jean Benedict (Sister Margaret); Maureen Ryan (Sister Patricia); Lottie Williams (Mother Superior); Frank Orth (Marriage Clerk); James Nolan (Interne); Loia Cheaney (Apartment House Manager); Marianne Edwards (Elsie); Jimmy Fox (Pawnbroker); Vera Lewis, Fern Berry (Women Spectators); Laura Jean Williams (Mary O'Reilly); Gerianne Raphael (Kathleen O'Reilly); Spec O'Donnell (Jockey); Stuart Holmes, Walter Murray (Judges); Gordon Hart (Defense Attorney); Harry Weil (Jury Foreman).

LETTER OF INTRODUCTION (*Universal, 1938*) 103 min.

Producer/director, John M. Stahl; screenplay, Sheridan Gibney, Leonard Spigelgass; camera, Karl Freund; editor, Ted J. Kent.

Adolphe Menjou (John Mannering); Edgar Bergen and Charlie McCarthy (Themselves); Andrea Leeds (Kay Martin); George Murphy (Barry Paige); Eve Arden (Cora); Rita Johnson (Honey); Ernest Cossart (Andrews); Ann Sheridan (Lydia); Jonathan Hale (Woodstock); Frank Jenks (Joe); Walter Perry (Backstage Doorman); Frances Robinson (Hatcheck Girl); Eleanor Hansen (Stagestruck Girl); Constance Moore (Autograph Hunter); Russell Hopton (Process Server); Esther Ralston (Mrs. Sinclair); Doris Lloyd (Charlotte); Irving Bacon, Ray Walker (Reporters); Natalie Moorhead (Mrs. Raleigh); Crauford Kent (Mr. Sinclair); Gordon "Bill" Elliott (Backgammon); Donald Barry, Philip Trent (Men at Party); Dorothy Granger (Woman at Party); Kane Richmond (Man); John Archer, Allen Fox (Photographers); Alphonse Martell (Maitre d').

BROADWAY MUSKETEERS (*Warner Bros., 1938*) 62 min.

Director, John Farrow; new screen story/screenplay, Don Ryan, Kenneth Gamet; camera, L. William O'Connell.

Margaret Lindsay (Isabel Dowling); Ann Sheridan (Fay Reynolds); Marie Wilson (Connie Todd); John Litel (Stanley Dowling); Janet Chapman (Judy Dowling); Dick Purcell (Vince Morrell); Richard Bond (Phil Peyton); Anthony Averill (Nick); Horace McMahon (Gurk); Dewey Robinson (Milt); Dorothy Adams (Anna); Jimmy Conlin (Skinner); John Ridgely (M.C.); Howard Mitchell, Ted Oliver, Eddy Chandler, Charles Hickman (Detectives); Marian Alden (Floor Nurse); Stuart Holmes (Bartender); Myra Marsh (Matron); Dudley Dickerson (Porter); Sol Gorss (Driver); Hal Craig, Claud Payton, Francis Sayles, Cliff Saum, Ralph Sanford (Policemen); Jan Holm (Teacher); Vera Lewis (Landlady); John Hiestand (News Announcer).

ANGELS WITH DIRTY FACES (*Warner Bros., 1938*) 97 min.

Producer, Sam Bischoff; director, Michael Curtiz; story, Rowland Brown; screenplay, John Wexley, Warren Duff; art director, Robert Haas; assistant director, Sherry Shourds; technical advisor, Father J. J. Devlin; music, Max Steiner;

orchestrator, Hugo Friedhofer; song, Fred Fisher and Maurice Spitalny; costumes, Orry-Kelly; dialogue director, Jo Graham; makeup, Perc Westmore; sound, Everett A. Brown; camera, Sol Polito; editor, Owen Marks.

James Cagney (Rocky Sullivan); Pat O'Brien (Father Jerry Connelly); Humphrey Bogart (James Frazier); Ann Sheridan (Laury Martin); George Bancroft (Mac Keefer); Billy Halop (Soapy); Bobby Jordan (Swing); Leo Gorcey (Bim); Bernard Punsley (Hunky); Gabriel Dell (Pasty); Huntz Hall (Crab); Frankie Burke (Rocky as a Boy); William Tracy (Jerry as a Boy); Marilyn Knowlden (Laury as a Girl); Joe Downing (Steve); Adrian Morris (Blackie); Oscar O'Shea (Guard Kennedy); Edward Pawley (Guard Edwards); William Pawley (Bugs, the Gunman); Charles Sullivan, Theodore Rand (Gunmen); John Hamilton (Police Captain); Earl Dwire (Priest); The St. Brendan's Church Choir (Themselves); William Worthington (Warden); James Farley (Railroad Yard Watchman); Pat O'Malley, Jack C. Smith (Railroad Guards); Roger McGee, Vince Lombardi, Sonny Bupp (Boys); Chuck Stubbs (Red); Eddie Syracuse (Maggione Boy); George Sorel (Headwaiter); Harry Hayden (Pharmacist); Dick Rich, Steven Darrell, Joe Devlin (Gangsters); Donald Kerr, Jack Goodrich, Al Lloyd, Jeffrey Sayre, Charles Marsh, Alexander Lockwood, Earl Gunn, Carlyle Moore (Reporters); Vera Lewis (Soapy's Mother); Frank Coghlan, Jr., David Durand (Boys in Poolroom); Mary Gordon (Mrs. Patrick McGee); Charles Trowbridge (Norton J. White, the *Press* Editor); William Crowell (Whimpering Convict); Poppy Wilde (Girl at Gaming Table); Jack Perrin (Guard on Death Row).

THEY MADE ME A CRIMINAL *(Warner Bros., 1939)* 92 min.

Producers, Jack L. Warner, Hal B. Wallis; associate producer, Benjamin Glazer; director, Busby Berkeley; based on the play by Bertram Millhauser and Beulah Marie Dix; screenplay, Sid Herzig; music, Max Steiner; camera, James Wong Howe; editor, Jack Killifer.

John Garfield (Johnnie Burns); Gloria Dickson (Peggy); Claude Rains (Detective Phelan); Ann Sheridan (Goldie); May Robson (Gramma); Billy Halop (Tommy); Bobby Jordan (Angel); Leo Gorcey (Spit); Huntz Hall (Dippy); Gabriel Dell (T. B.); Robert Gleckler (Doc Ward); John Ridgely (Magee); Barbara Pepper (Budgie); William Davidson (Ennis); Ward Bond (Lenihan); Robert Strange (Melvin); Louis Jean Heydt (Smith); Ronald Sinclair (J. Douglas Williamson); Frank Riggu (Rutchek); Cliff Clark (Manager); Dick Wessel (Collucci); Raymond Brown (Sheriff); Sam Hayes (Fight Announcer); Irving Bacon (Speed, the Gas Station Attendant); Sam McDaniel (Splash); Bert Roach (Hendricks); Dorothy Varden (Woman); Eddy Chandler, Hal Craig (Detectives); Jack Austin, Frank Meredith (Cops); Richard Bond, Nat Carr (Reporters); Elliott Sullivan (Hoodlum); Tom Dugan, Frank Mayo, Cliff Saum, Al Lloyd, Arthur Housman, John Sheehan (Men); Leyland Hodgson (Mr. Williamson); Doris Lloyd (Mrs. Williamson); Stuart Holmes (Timekeeper); Bob Perry (Cawley); Nat Carr (Haskell); Clem Bevans (Ticket Taker); Jack Wise (Ticketman).

DODGE CITY *(Warner Bros., 1939)* C-105 min.

Executive producer, Hal B. Wallis; associate producer, Robert Lord; director, Michael Curtiz; screenplay, Robert Buckner; music, Max Steiner; orchestrator, Hugo Friedhofer; assistant director, Sherry Shourds; color consultant, Morgan Padelford; art director, Ted Smith; costumes, Milo Anderson; makeup, Perc Westmore; dialogue director, Jo Graham; sound, Oliver S. Garretson; special effects, Byron Haskin, Rex Wimpy; camera, Sol Polito; associate Technicolor camera, Ray Rennahan; editor, George Amy.

Errol Flynn (Wade Hatton); Olivia de Havilland (Abbie Irving); Ann Sheridan (Ruby Gilman); Bruce Cabot (Jeff Surrett); Frank McHugh (Joe Clemens); Alan Hale (Rusty Hart); John Litel (Matt Cole); Victor Jory (Yancy); Henry Travers (Dr. Irving); Henry O'Neill (Colonel Dodge); Guinn "Big Boy" Williams (Tex Baird); Gloria Holden (Mrs. Cole); Douglas Fowley (Munger); William Lundigan (Lee Irving); Georgia Caine (Mrs. Irving); Charles Halton (Surrett's Lawyer); Ward Bond (Bud Taylor); Bobby Watson (Harry Cole); Nat Carr (Crocker); Russell Simpson (Orth); Clem Bevans (Charlie, the Barber); Cora Witherspoon (Mrs. McCoy); Joe Crehan (Hammond); Thurston Hall (Twitchell); Chester Clute (Coggins); Monte Blue (Barlow, the Indian Agent); James Burke (Cattle Auctioneer); Robert Homans (Mail Clerk); George Guhl (Jason, the Marshal); Spencer Charters (Clergyman); Ralph Sanford (Brawler); Bud Osborne (Stagecoach Driver/Waiter); Vera Lewis (Woman); Pat O'Malley (Conductor).

NAUGHTY BUT NICE *(Warner Bros., 1939)* 90 min.

Associate producer, Sam Bischoff; director, Ray Enright; screenplay, Richard Macaulay, Jerry Wald; songs, Harry Warren and Johnny Mercer; camera, Arthur L. Todd; editor, Thomas Richards.

Dick Powell (Professor Hardwick); Gale Page (Linda McKay); Ann Sheridan (Zelda Manion);

Helen Broderick (Aunt Martha); Allen Jenkins (Joe Dirk); ZaSu Pitts (Aunt Penelope); Ronald Reagan (Ed Clark); Maxie Rosenbloom (Killer); Jerry Colonna (Allie Gray); Vera Lewis (Aunt Annabella); Elizabeth Dunne (Aunt Henrietta); Luis Alberni (Stanislaus Pysinski); Bill Davidson (Sam Hudson); Granville Bates (Judge); Halliwell Hobbes (Dean Burton); Peter Lind Hayes (Band Leader); Bert Hanlon (Johnny Collins); John Ridgely (Hudson's Assistant); Herbert Rawlinson (Plaintiff's Attorney); Selmer Jackson (Defense Attorney); Hobart Cavanaugh (Piano Tuner); Grady Sutton (Markton).

WINTER CARNIVAL *(United Artists, 1939)* 105 min.

Producer, Walter Wanger; director, Charles F. Reisner; based on the story "Echoes That Old Refrain" by Corey Ford; screenplay, Lester Cole, Budd Schulberg, Maurice Rapf (uncredited, F. Scott Fitzgerald); song, L. Wolfe Gilbert and Werner Janssen; camera, Merritt Gerstad; editor, Dorothy Spencer.

Ann Sheridan (Jill Baxter); Richard Carlson (John Weldon); Helen Parrish (Anne Baxter); James Corner (Mickey Allen); Robert Armstrong (Tiger Reynolds); Alan Baldwin (Dan Reynolds); Joan Leslie (Betsy); Virginia Gilmore (Margie Stafford); Cecil Cunningham (Miss Ainsley); Robert Allen (Rocky Morgan); Marsha Hunt (Lucy Morgan); Susan and Molly McCash (The Twins); Morton Lowry (Count Von Lundborg); Jimmy Butler (Larry Grey); Kenneth Stevens (Male Soloist); Benny Drohan (Bartender); Martin Turner (Pullman Porter); Robert E. Homans (Conductor); John Wray (Poultry Truck Driver); Emory Parnell (Williams, the *New York Mercury* Editor); Al Hill, George Magrill (*Mercury* Reporters); Robert Walker (Wes); Cyril Ring, John Berkes (Reporters at Terminal).

INDIANAPOLIS SPEEDWAY *(Warner Bros., 1939)* 85 min. (British release title: *Devil on Wheels*)

Associate producer, Max Siegel; director, Lloyd Bacon; original screen idea, Howard and William Hawks; screenplay, Sig Herzig, Wally Klein; camera, Sid Hickox; editor, William Holmes.

Pat O'Brien (Joe Greer); John Payne (Eddie Greer); Ann Sheridan (Frankie Merrick); Gale Page (Lee Mason); Frank McHugh (Spud Connors); Grace Stafford (Mrs. Martha Connors); Granville Bates (Mr. Greer); Regis Toomey (Wilbur Shaw); John Ridgely (Ted Horn); John Harron (Red); William Davidson (Duncan Martin); Ed McWade (Tom Dugan); Irving Bacon (Fred Haskill); Tommy Bupp (Haskill's Son); Robert Middlemass (Edward Hart); Charles Halton (Mayor); Sam Hayes, John Conte, Wendell Niles, Reid Kilpatrick (Announcers); Patsy O'Byrne (Vinegary Female); Creighton Hale (Official); Ed Parker (Man); Evelyn Mulhall (Mrs. Martin); George Renavent (Headwaiter); Billy Wayne (Stubby); Monroe Lee (Baby).

ANGELS WASH THEIR FACES *(Warner Bros., 1939)* 76 min.

Associate producer, Max Siegel; director, Ray Enright; story, Jonathan Finn; screenplay, Michael Fessier, Niven Busch, Robert Buckner; camera, Arthur L. Todd; editor, James Gibbon.

Ann Sheridan (Joy Ryan); Ronald Reagan (Pat Remson); Billy Halop (Billy Shafter); Bonita Granville (Peggy Finnegan); Frankie Thomas (Gabe Ryan); Bobby Jordan (Bernie); Bernard Punsley (Sleepy Arkelian); Leo Gorcey (Lee Finnegan); Huntz Hall (Huntz); Gabriel Dell (Luigi); Henry O'Neill (Remsen, Sr.); Berton Churchill (Mayor Dooley); Minor Watson (Maloney); Margaret Hamilton (Miss Hannaberry); Jackie Searle (Alfred Goonplatz); Bernard Nedell (Kroner); Dick Rich (Shuffle); Cy Kendall (Hynes); Grady Sutton (Gildersleeve); Aldrich Bowker (Turnkey); Marjorie Main (Mrs. Arkelian); Robert Strange (Simpkins); Egon Brecher (Mr. Smith); Sibyl Harris (Mrs. Smith); Frank Coghlan, Jr. (Boy); William Hopper (Photographer); Wes Niles (Announcer); Tom Wilson, Jack Mower, Eddy Chandler, Jack Clifford (Cops).

CASTLE ON THE HUDSON *(Warner Bros., 1940)* 77 min. (British release title: *Years Without Days*)

Associate producer, Samuel Bischoff; director, Anatole Litvak; based on the book *20,000 Years in Sing Sing* by Warden Lewis E. Lawes; screenplay, Seton I. Miller, Brown Holmes, Courtenay Terrett; camera, Arthur Edeson; editor, Thomas Richards.

John Garfield (Tommy Gordon); Ann Sheridan (Kay Manners); Pat O'Brien (Warden Walter Long); Burgess Meredith (Steven Rockford); Jerome Cowan (Ed Crowley); Henry O'Neill (District Attorney); Guinn "Big Boy" Williams (Mike Cagle); John Litel (Prison Chaplain); Edward Pawley (Black Jack); Grant Mitchell (Dr. Ames); Margot Stevenson (Ann Rockford); Willard Robertson (Ragan); Robert Homans (Clyde Burton); Nedda Harrigan (Mrs. Long); Wade Boteler (Mac, the Principal Keeper); Billy Wayne (Pete); Joseph Downing, Sol Gorss (Gangsters); Barbara Pepper (Goldie); Robert Strange (Joe Harris); Charles Sherlock, Mike Lally, Jack Mower, Frank Mayo, Pat O'Malley, Walter Miller (Guards); Pat Flaherty (Stretcher Attendant); Ed Kane (Club Manager); Claude Wisberg, Michael

Conroy (Newsboys); Frank Faylen (Guard Who Is Slugged); Nat Carr, William Telark, Bill Hopper (Reporters); Lee Phelps (Guard in Visitor's Room); James Flavin (Guard in Death Row).

IT ALL CAME TRUE *(Warner Bros., 1940)* 97 min.

Executive producer, Hal B. Wallis; associate producer, Mark Hellinger; director, Lewis Seiler; based on the story "Better Than Life" by Louis Bromfield; screenplay, Michael Fessier, Lawrence Kimble; assistant director, Russ Saunders; art director, Max Parker; gowns, Howard Shoup; music, Heinz Roemheld; orchestrators, Ray Heindorf, Frank Perkins; songs, Kim Gannon, Stephan Weiss, and Paul Mann; James Cavanaugh, John Redmond, and Nat Simon; makeup, Perc Westmore; dialogue director, Robert Foulk; choreography, Dave Gould; sound, Dolph Thomas; special effects, Byron Haskin, Edwin B. DuPar; camera, Ernest Haller; editor, Thomas Richards.

Ann Sheridan (Sarah Jane Ryan); Jeffrey Lynn (Tommy Taylor); Humphrey Bogart [Grasselli (Chips Maguire)]; ZaSu Pitts (Miss Flint); Una O'Connor (Maggie Ryan); Jessie Busley (Nora Taylor); John Litel (Mr. Roberts); Grant Mitchell (Mr. Salmon); Felix Bressart (Mr. Boldinin); Charles Judels (Leantopopulos); Brandon Tynan (Mr. Van Diver); Howard Hickman (Mr. Prendergast); Herbert Vigran (Monks).

TORRID ZONE *(Warner Bros., 1940)* 88 min.

Producer, Mark Hellinger; director, William Keighley; screenplay, Richard Macaulay, Jerry Wald; art director, Ted Smith; set decorator, Edward Thorne; music, Adolph Deutsch; music director, Leo F. Forbstein; song, M. K. Jerome and Jack Scholl; costumes, Howard Shoup; technical advisor, John Mari; makeup, Perc Westmore; sound, Oliver S. Garretson; special effects, Byron Haskin, H. F. Koenekamp; camera, James Wong Howe; editor, Jack Killifer.

James Cagney (Nick Butler); Pat O'Brien (Steve Case); Ann Sheridan (Lee Donley); Andy Devine (Wally Davis); Helen Vinson (Gloria Anderson); George Tobias (Rosario); Jerome Cowan (Bob Anderson); George Reeves (Sancho); Victor Kilian (Carlos); Frank Puglia (Rodriguez); John Ridgely (Gardiner); Grady Sutton (Sam, the Secretary); George Humbert (Hotel Manager); Paul Porcasi (Garcia, the Hotel Bar Proprietor); Frank Yaconelli (Lopez); Paul Hurst (Daniels); Jack Mower (Schaeffer); Frank Mayo (McNamara); Dick Botiller (Hernandez); Elvira Sanchez (Rita); Paul Renay (Jose); Rafael Corio (Man); George Regas (Sergeant); Trevor Bardette, Ernesto Piedra (Policemen); Don Orlando (Employee); Manuel Lopez (Chico); Joe Dominguez (Manuel); Joe Molinas (Native); Tony Paton (Charley).

THEY DRIVE BY NIGHT *(Warner Bros., 1940)* 93 min.

Executive producer, Hal B. Wallis; associate producer, Mark Hellinger; director, Raoul Walsh; based on the novel *Long Haul* by A. I. Bezzerides; screenplay, Jerry Wald, Richard Macaulay; music, Adolph Deutsch; orchestrator, Arthur Lange; dialogue director, Hugh MacMullen; assistant director, Elmer Decker; art director, John Hughes; gowns, Milo Anderson; makeup, Perc Westmore; sound, Oliver S. Garretson; special effects, Byron Haskin, H. F. Koenekamp, James Gibbons, John Holden, Edwin B. DuPar; camera, Arthur Edeson; editor, Thomas Richards.

George Raft (Joe Fabrini); Ann Sheridan (Cassie Hartley); Ida Lupino (Lana Carlsen); Humphrey Bogart (Paul Fabrini); Gale Page (Pearl Fabrini); Alan Hale (Ed J. Carlsen); Roscoe Karns (Irish McGurn); John Litel (Harry McNamara); Henry O'Neill (District Attorney); George Tobias (George Rondolos); Charles Halton (Farnsworth); Joyce Compton (Sue Carter); John Ridgely (Hank Dawson); Paul Hurst (Pete Haig); Charles Wilson (Mike Williams); Norman Willis (Neves); George Lloyd (Barney); Lillian Yarbo (Chloe); Eddy Chandler, Frank Faylen, Ralph Sanford, Sol Gorss, Michael Harvey, Eddie Fetherston, Alan Davis, Dick Wessel, Al Hill, Charles Sullivan, Eddie Acuff, Pat Flaherty, Mike Lally, Dutch Hendrian, Frank Mayo, Charles Sherlock, Don Turner, Ralph Lynn (Drivers); Marie Blake (Waitress); Frank Wilcox, J. Anthony Hughes (Reporters); Mack Gray (Mike); Demetris Emanuel (Waiter); Brenda Fowler, Dorothy Vaughan (Matrons); Howard Hickman (Judge); John Hamilton (Defense Attorney); William Haade (Tough Driver); Joe Devlin (Fatso); Phyllis Hamilton (Stenographer).

CITY FOR CONQUEST *(Warner Bros., 1940)* 101 min.

Producer, Anatole Litvak; associate producer, William Cagney; director, Litvak; based on the novel by Aben Kandel; screenplay, John Wexley; art director, Robert Haas; music, Max Steiner; orchestrator, Hugo Friedhofer; music director, Leo F. Forbstein; choreography, Robert Vreeland; costumes, Howard Shoup; makeup, Perc Westmore; dialogue director, Irving Rapper; assistant director, Chuck Hansen; sound, E. A. Brown; special effects, Byron Haskin, Rex Wimpy; camera, Sol Polito, James Wong Howe; editor, William Holmes.

James Cagney (Danny Kenny); Ann Sheridan

(Peggy Nash); Frank Craven (Old-Timer); Donald Crisp (Scotty McPherson); Arthur Kennedy (Eddie Kenny); Frank McHugh (Mutt); George Tobias (Pinky); Jerome Cowan (Dutch Schultz); Anthony Quinn (Murray Burns); Lee Patrick (Gladys); Blanche Yurka (Mrs. Nash); Elia Kazan (Googi); George Lloyd (Goldie); Joyce Compton (Lilly); Thurston Hall (Max Leonard); Ben Welden (Cobb); John Arledge (Salesman); Ed Keane (Gaul); Selmer Jackson, Joseph Crehan (Doctors); Bob Steele (Callahan); Billy Wayne (Henchman); Pat Flaherty (Floor Guard); Sidney Miller (M.C.); Ethelreda Leopold (Dressing Room Blonde); and: Lee Phelps, Howard Hickman, Ed Gargan, Ed Pawley, Margaret Hayes, Murray Alper, Bernice Pilot, and Lucia Carroll.

HONEYMOON FOR THREE *(Warner Bros., 1941)* 77 min.

Associate producer, Henry Blanke; director, Lloyd Bacon; based on the play *Goodbye Again* by Alan Scott and George Haight; screenplay, Earl Baldwin; camera, Ernest Haller; editor, Rudi Fehr.

Ann Sheridan (Anne Rogers); George Brent (Kenneth Bixby); Charles Ruggles (Harvey Wilson); Osa Massen (Julie Wilson); Jane Wyman (Elizabeth Clochessy); William T. Orr (Arthur Westlake); Lee Patrick (Mrs. Pettijohn); Walter Catlett (Waiter); Herbert Anderson (Floyd T. Ingram); Johnny Downs (Chester T. Farrington III).

NAVY BLUES *(Warner Bros., 1941)* 108 min.

Producer, Hal B. Wallis; associate producers, Jerry Wald, Jack Saper; director, Lloyd Bacon; story, Arthur T. Horman; screenplay, Wald, Richard Macaulay, Horman; choreography, Seymour Felix; songs, Arthur Schwartz and Johnny Mercer; camera, Tony Gaudio; dance camera, Sol Polito, James Wong Howe; editor, Rudi Fehr.

Ann Sheridan (Margie Jordan); Jack Oakie (Cake O'Hara); Martha Raye (Lillibelle); Jack Haley (Powerhouse Bolton); Herbert Anderson (Homer Mathews); Jack Carson (Buttons Johnson); Richard Lane (Rocky Anderson); William T. Orr (Mac); Jackie Gleason (Tubby); John Ridgely (Jersey); Howard da Silva (Petty Officer); Frank Wilcox, Hardie Albright (Officers); Ray Cooke (Lucky); Bill Hopper (Ensign Walters); Marguerite Chapman, Leslie Brooks, Peggy Diggins, Georgia Carroll, Katharine [Kay] Aldridge, Claire James (Navy Blues Sextette); Ralph Byrd (Lieutenant); Gig Young, Murray Alper, Will Morgan, Garland Smith, George O'Hanlon, Arthur Gardner (Sailors); Selmer Jackson (Captain Willard); Gaylord [Steve] Pendleton, Pat McVeigh, Don Rowan, Walter Sande (Marines).

THE MAN WHO CAME TO DINNER *(Warner Bros., 1941)* 112 min.

Executive producer, Hal B. Wallis; associate producers, Jerry Wald, Jack Saper; director, William Keighley; based on the play by George S. Kaufman and Moss Hart; screenplay, Julius J. and Philip G. Epstein; music, Frederick Hollander; music director, Leo F. Forbstein; art director, Robert Haas; gowns, Orry-Kelly; assistant director, Dick Mayberry; sound, Charles Lang; camera, Tony Gaudio; editor, Jack Killifer.

Monty Woolley (Sheridan Whiteside); Bette Davis (Maggie Cutler); Ann Sheridan (Lorraine Sheldon); Richard Travis (Bert Jefferson); Jimmy Durante (Banjo); Reginald Gardiner (Beverly Carlton); Billie Burke (Mrs. Stanley); Elisabeth Fraser (June Stanley); Grant Mitchell (Ernest Stanley); George Barbier (Dr. Bradley); Mary Wickes (Miss Preen); Russell Arms (Richard Stanley); Ruth Vivian (Harriett Stanley); Edwin Stanley (John); Betty Roadman (Sarah); Laura Hope Crews (Mrs. Gibbons); Chester Clute (Mr. Gibbons); Charles Drake (Sandy); Nanette Vallon (Cosette); John Ridgely (Radio Man); Pat McVey (Harry); Frank Coghlan, Jr. (Telegraph Boy); Roland Drew (Newspaperman); Sam Hayes (Announcer); Ernie Adams (Haggerty); Dudley Dickerson (Porter); Georgia Carroll, Leslie Brooks, Peggy Diggins, Alix Talton (Girls).

KINGS ROW *(Warner Bros., 1941)* 130 min.

Producer, Hal B. Wallis; associate producer, David Lewis; director, Sam Wood; based on the novel by Henry Bellamann; screenplay, Casey Robinson; music, Erich Wolfgang Korngold; art director, Carl Jules Weyl; camera, James Wong Howe; editor, Ralph Dawson.

Ann Sheridan (Randy Monoghan); Robert Cummings (Parris Mitchell); Ronald Reagan (Drake McHugh); Betty Field (Cassandra Tower); Charles Coburn (Dr. Henry Gordon); Claude Rains (Dr. Alexander Tower); Judith Anderson (Mrs. Harriet Gordon); Nancy Coleman (Louise Gordon); Kaaren Verne (Elisa Sandor); Maria Ouspenskaya (Madame Von Eln); Harry Davenport (Colonel Skeffington); Ernest Cossart (Pa Monoghan); Pat Moriarity (Tom Monoghan); Ilka Gruning (Ann, the Maid); Minor Watson (Sam Winters); Ludwig Stossel (Dr. Berdoff); Erwin Kalser (Mr. Sandor); Egon Brecher (Dr. Candell); Ann Todd (Randy as a Child); Scotty Beckett (Parris as a Child); Douglas Croft (Drake as a Child); Mary Thomas (Cassandra as a Child); Joan Du Valle (Louise as a Child); Danny Jackson (Benny Singer); Henry Blair (Willie); Leah Baird (Aunt Mamie); Eden Gray (Mrs. Tower); Julie Warren (Poppy Ross); Mary Scott (Ginny Ross); Bertha Powell (Esther); Walter Baldwin (Deputy Constable); Frank Milan (Teller); Hank Mann (Livery Stable Keeper); Hermione Sterler (Secretary); Hattie Noel (Gordons' Maid); Emory Parnell (Harley Davis).

JUKE GIRL *(Warner Bros., 1942)* 90 min.

Executive producer, Hal B. Wallis; associate producers, Jerry Wald, Jack Saper; director, Curtis Bernhardt; story, Theodore Pratt; adaptor, Kenneth Gamet; screenplay, A. I. Bezzerides; art director, Robert Haas; camera, Bert Glennon; editor, Warren Low.

Ann Sheridan (Lola Mears); Ronald Reagan (Steve Talbot); Richard Whorf (Danny Frazier); George Tobias (Nick Garcos); Gene Lockhart (Henry Madden); Alan Hale (Yippee); Betty Brewer (Skeeter); Howard da Silva (Cully); Donald MacBride (Muckeye John); Willard Robertson (Mister Just); Faye Emerson (Violet Murphy); Willie Best (Jo-Mo); Fuzzy Knight (Ike Harper); Spencer Charters (Keane); William Davidson (Paley); Frank Wilcox (Truck Driver); William Haade (Watchman); Eddy Waller (Man in Car); Alan Bridge, Milton Kibbee, Glen Strange, Jack Gardner, Fred Kelsey, Frank Pharr (Men); Bill Hopper (Clerk); Frank Mayo (Detective); Dewey Robinson, Kenneth Harlan (Dealers); Pat Flaherty (Mike); Forrest Taylor, Pat McVey (Farmers).

WINGS FOR THE EAGLE *(Warner Bros., 1942)* 85 min.

Producer, Robert Lord; director, Lloyd Bacon; screenplay, Byron Morgan, B. H. Orkow; additional dialogue, Richard Macaulay; art director, Max Parker; music, Frederick Hollander; music director, Leo F. Forbstein; special effects, Byron Haskin, H. F. Koenekamp; camera, Tony Gaudio; editor, Owen Marks.

Ann Sheridan (Roma Maple); Dennis Morgan (Corky Jones); Jack Carson (Brad Maple); George Tobias (Jake Hanso); Russell Arms (Pete Hanso); Don DeFore (Gil Borden); Tom Fadden (Tom "Cyclone" Shaw); John Ridgely (Johnson); Frank Wilcox (Stark); George Meeker (Personnel Man); Fay Helm (Miss Baxter); Billy Curtis (Midget); Emory Parnell (Policeman); Edgar Dearing (Motorcycle Officer).

GEORGE WASHINGTON SLEPT HERE *(Warner Bros., 1942)* 93 min.

Producer, Jerry Wald; director, William Keighley; based on the play by George S. Kaufman and Moss Hart; screenplay, Everett Freeman; art director, Max Parker; camera, Ernest Haller; editor, Ralph Dawson.

Jack Benny (Bill Fuller); Ann Sheridan (Connie Fuller); Charles Coburn (Uncle Stanley); Percy Kilbride (Mr. Kimber); Hattie McDaniel (Hester); William Tracy (Steve Eldridge); Joyce Reynolds (Madge); Lee Patrick (Rena Leslie); Charles Dingle (Mr. Prescott); John Emery (Clayton Evans); Douglas Croft (Raymond); Harvey Stephens (Jeff Douglas); Franklin Pangborn (Mr. Gibney); Chester Clute (Man); Isabel Withers (Woman); Hank Mann, Cliff Saum (Moving Men); Sol Gorss, Glenn Cavender (Well Diggers); Dudley Dickerson (Porter); Jack Mower (Passenger); Gertrude Carr (Wife).

EDGE OF DARKNESS *(Warner Bros., 1943)* 120 min.

Producer, Henry Blanke; director, Lewis Milestone; based on the novel by William Woods; screenplay, Robert Rossen; dialogue director, Herschel Daugherty; technical advisors, Frank U. Peter Pohlenz, E. Wessel Klausen, Gerard Lambert; assistant directors, Sherry Shourds, James McMahon; art director, Robert Haas; set decorator, Julia Heron; gowns, Orry-Kelly; makeup, Perc Westmore; music, Franz Waxman; orchestrator, Leonid Raab; sound, Everett A. Brown; special effects, Lawrence Butler, Willard Van Enger; montages, Don Siegel, James Leicester; camera, Sid Hickox; editor, David Weisbart.

Errol Flynn (Gunnar Brogge); Ann Sheridan (Karen Stensgard); Walter Huston (Dr. Martin Stensgard); Nancy Coleman (Katja); Helmut Dantine (Captain Koenig); Judith Anderson (Gerd Bjarnesen); Ruth Gordon (Anna Stensgard); John Beal (Johann Stensgard); Morris Carnovsky (Sixtus Andersen); Charles Dingle (Kaspar Torgersen); Roman Bohnen (Lars Malken); Richard Fraser (Pastor Aalesen); Art Smith (Knut Osterholm); Tom Fadden (Hammer); Henry Brandon (Major Ruck); Dorothy Tree (Solveig Brategaard); Frank Wilcox (Jensen); Francis Pierlot (Mortensen); Monte Blue (Petersen); Helene Thimig (Frieda); Tonio Selwart (Paul); Henry Rowland (Helmut); Virginia Christine (Hulda); Torben Meyer (Clerk); Fred Giermann, Rolf Lindau, Peter Michael, Peter Van Eyck (Soldiers); Vic Potel, Richard Kipling (Men); Kurt Kreuger (Blond Soldier); William Edmunds (Elderly Sailor); Kurt Katch (German Captain); Vera Lewis (Woman); Walt LaRue (Villager—Patriot).

THANK YOUR LUCKY STARS *(Warner Bros., 1943)* 127 min.

Producer, Mark Hellinger; director, David Butler; story, Everett Freeman, Arthur Schwartz; screenplay, Norman Panama, Melvin Frank, James V. Kern; songs, Schwartz and Frank Loesser; vocal arranger, Dudley Chambers; orchestral arrangements, Ray Heindorf; music adaptor, Heinz Roemheld; orchestrator, Maurice de Packh; choreography/dance stager, LeRoy Prinz; dialogue director, Herbert Farjean; art directors, Anton Grot, Leo K. Kuter; set decorator, Walter F. Tilford; gowns, Milo Anderson; makeup, Perc Westmore; assistant director, Phil Quinn; sound, Francis J. Scheid, Charles David Forrest; special effects, H. F. Koenekamp; camera, Arthur Edeson; editor, Irene Morra.

Eddie Cantor (Joe Simpson/Himself); Joan Leslie (Pat Dixon); Dennis Morgan (Tommy Randolph); Dinah Shore (Herself); S. Z. Sakall (Dr. Schlenna); Edward Everett Horton (Farnsworth); Ruth Donnelly (Nurse Hamilton); Joyce Reynolds (Girl with Book); Richard Lane (Barney Jackson); Don Wilson (Himself); Henry Armetta (Angelo); Willie Best (Soldier); Humphrey Bogart, Jack Carson, Bette Davis, Olivia de Havilland, Errol Flynn, John Garfield, Alan Hale, Ida Lupino, Ann Sheridan, Alexis Smith, George Tobias, Spike Jones and His City Slickers (Specialties); Jack Mower, Creighton Hale (Engineers); Don Barclay (Pete); Stanley Clements, James Copedge (Boys); Leah Baird, Joan Matthews, Phyllis Godfrey, Lillian West, Morgan Brown, George French (Bus Passengers); Joe DeRita (Milquetoast Type); Frank Faylen (Sailor); Eleanor Counts (Sailor's Girlfriend); Charles Soldani, J. W. Cody (Indians); Noble Johnson (Charlie, the Indian); Harry Pilcer (Man in Broadcasting Station); Mike Mazurki (Olaf); Bennie Bartlett (Page Boy); Marjorie Hoshelle, Anne O'Neal (Maids); Jerry Mandy (Chef); Betty Farrington (Assistant Chef); William Haade (Butler); Lou Marcelle (Commentator); Mary Treen (Fan); Ed Gargan (Doorman); Billy Benedict (Busboy); Juanita Stark (Secretary); *Ice Cold Katie Number:* Hattie McDaniel (Gossip); Rita Christiani (Ice Cold Katie); Jess Lee Brooks (Justice); Ford, Harris, and Jones (Trio); Matthew Jones (Gambler); *Errol Flynn Number:* Monte Blue, Art Foster, Fred Kelsey, Elmer Ballard, Buster Wiles, Howard Davies, Tudor Williams, Alan Cook, Fred McEvoy, Bobby Hale, Will Stanton, Charles Irwin, David Thursby, Henry Ibling, Earl Hunsaker, Hubert Hand, Dudley Kuzelle, Ted Billings (Pub Characters); *Bette Davis Number:* Jack Norton (Drunk); Henri DeSoto (Maitre d'); Dick Elliott, Dick Earle (Customers); Harry Adams (Doorman); Sam Adams (Bartender); Conrad Widell (Jitterbug); Charles Francis, Harry Bailey (Bald Men); Joan Winfield (Cigarette Girl); Sylvia Opert, Nancy Worth (Hatcheck Girls); *The Lucky Stars:* Harriette Haddon, Harriett Olsen, Nancy Worth, Joy Barlowe, Janet Barrett, Dorothy Schoemer, Dorothy Dayton, Lucille LaMarr, Sylvia Opert, Mary Landa; *Humphrey Bogart Sequence:* Matt McHugh (Fireman); *Ann Sheridan Number:* Georgia Lee Settle, Virginia Patton (Girls); *Good Night, Good Neighbor Number:* Igor DeNavrotsky (Dancer); Brandon Hurst (Cab Driver); Angelita Mari (Duenna); Lynne Baggett (Miss Latin America); Mary Landa (Miss Spain).

THE DOUGHGIRLS *(Warner Bros., 1944)* 102 min.

Producer, Mark Hellinger; director, James V. Kern; based on the play by Joseph A. Fields; screenplay, Kern, Sam Hellman; additional dialogue, Wilkie Mahoney; assistant director, Phil Quinn; art director, Hugh Reticker; set decorator, Clarence Steensen; music director, Leo F. Forbstein; sound, Stanley Jones; special effects, William McGann; montages, James Leicester; camera, Ernest Haller; editor, Folmer Blangsted.

Ann Sheridan (Edna); Alexis Smith (Nan); Jack Carson (Arthur); Jane Wyman (Vivian); Irene Manning (Mrs. Cadman); Charlie Ruggles (Stanley Slade); Eve Arden (Natalia Moskoroff); John Ridgely (Julius Cadman); Alan Mowbray (Brackenridge Drake); John Alexander (Warren Buckley); Craig Stevens (Tom Dillon); Barbara Brown (Mrs. Cartwright); Francis Pierlot (Mr. Jordan); Donald MacBride (Judge Franklin); Mark Stevens (Lieutenant Harry Keary); Joe DeRita (Stranger); Regis Toomey (Timothy Walsh); Walter DePalma (Justice of the Peace); John Walsh (Bellhop); Grandon Rhodes, Tom Quinn (Clerks); John Hamilton (Businessman); Harry Tyler (Angular Man); Minerva Urecal, Almira Sessions (Hatchet-Faced Women); Oliver Blake (Porter); Lou Marcelle (Announcer's Voice); Ralph Sanford (Workman); Nick Kobliansky (Father Nicholai); Will Fowler (Lieutenant).

SHINE ON HARVEST MOON *(Warner Bros., 1944)* 112 min.*

Producer, William Jacobs; director, David Butler; story, Richard Well; screenplay, Sam Hellman, Well, Francis Swann, James Kern; dialogue director, Hugh Cummings; assistant director, Jesse Hibbs; art director, Charles Novi; set decorator, Jack McConaghy; choreography, LeRoy Prinz; songs, M. K. Jerome and Kim Gannon; Cliff Friend and Charles Tobias; vocal arranger, Dudley Chambers; music adaptor, Heinz Roemheld; music director, Leo F. Forbstein; sound, Dolph Thomas, David Forrest; special effects, Edwin A. DuPar; montages, James Leicester; camera, Arthur Edeson; editor, Irene Morra.

Ann Sheridan (Nora Bayes); Dennis Morgan (Jack Norwood); Jack Carson (Great Georgetti); Irene Manning (Blanche Mallory); S. Z. Sakall (Poppa Karl); Marie Wilson (Margie); Robert Shayne (Dan Costello); Bob Murphy (Desk Sergeant); Will Stanton (Drunk Civilian); The Ashburns, The Four Step Brothers (Specialty Numbers); Paul Panzer (Doorman); Al Hill (Captain

*Technicolor sequence

of Waiters); Mike Mazurki, Frank Hagney (Bouncers); Jack Norton, Bert Roach (Drunks); Nestor Paiva (Romero, the Chef); Charles Marsh, Tom Quinn, Jack Boyle, Duke Johnson, Billy Bletcher, Peggy Carson, Anita Pike, Doria Caron (Vaudevillians); Gino Corrado (Cook); Brandon Hurst (Watchman); *My Own United States Number:* Johnnie Berkes, Bill Young (Tramp Ambassadors); Betty Bryson (Soubrette); *It Looks to Me Like a Big Night Number:* Jack Daley, Mike Donovan, Frank McCarroll, Charles McAvoy, Kernan Cripps, Thomas Murray, George McDonald, Bob Reeves, Bill O'Leary, Charles McMurphy, Allen D. Sewell (Policemen).

ONE MORE TOMORROW *(Warner Bros., 1946)* 88 min.

Producer, Benjamin Glazer; director, Peter Godfrey; based on the play *The Animal Kingdom* by Philip Barry; screenplay, Charles Hoffman, Catherine Turney; additional dialogue, Julius J. and Philip G. Epstein; art director, Anton Grot; set decorator, George James Hopkins; music, Max Steiner; music director, Leo F. Forbstein; assistant director, Jesse Hibbs; sound, Dolph Thomas; camera, Bert Glennon; editor, David Weisbart.

Dennis Morgan (Tom Collier); Ann Sheridan (Christie Sage); Jack Carson (Pat Regan); Alexis Smith (Cecilia Henry); Jane Wyman (Franc Connors); Reginald Gardiner (Jim Fisk); John Loder (Owen Arthur); Thurston Hall (Rufus Collier); Marjorie Gateson (Edna); John Abbott (Joseph Baronova); Marjorie Hoshelle (Illa Baronova); Sig Arno (Poppa); Lynne Baggett, Joan Winfield, Juanita Stark, Robert Hutton, Gertrude Carr, Lottie Williams (Party Guests); William Benedict (Office Boy); John Alvin (Announcer); Henri DeSoto (Headwaiter); Hal K. Dawson (Guest); Otto Hoffman (Stationmaster); Mary Field (Maude Miller); Frances Morris (Young Woman); Fred Essler (Picard); Danny Jackson (Orson Curry); Frank Coghlan, Jr. (Telegraph Boy).

NORA PRENTISS *(Warner Bros., 1947)* 111 min.

Producer, William Jacobs; director, Vincent Sherman; story, Paul Webster, Jack Sobell; screenplay, N. Richard Nash; art director, Anton Grot; set decorator, Walter Tilford; assistant director, Jim McMahon; music, Franz Waxman; music director, Leo F. Forbstein; songs, Jack Scholl, Eddie Cherkose, and M. K. Jerome; sound, Charles Lang; montage, James Leicester; special effects, Harry Barndollar, Edwin DuPar; camera, James Wong Howe; editor, Owen Marks.

Ann Sheridan (Nora Prentiss); Kent Smith (Dr. Richard Talbot); Bruce Bennett (Dr. Joel Merriam); Robert Alda (Phil McDade); Rosemary DeCamp (Lucy Talbot); John Ridgely (Walter Bailey); Robert Arthur (Gregory Talbot); Wanda Hendrix (Bonita Talbot); Helen Brown (Miss Judson); Rory Mallinson (Fleming); Harry Shannon (Police Lieutenant); James Flavin (District Attorney); Douglas Kennedy (Doctor); Don McGuire (Truck Driver); Clifton Young (Policeman); John Newland, John Compton, Ramon Ros (Reporters); Matt McHugh, Wallace Scott (Drunks); Ralph Dunn, Eddy Chandler (Detectives); Clancy Cooper, Alan Bridge (Cops); Creighton Hale (Captain of Waiters); Lee Phelps (Doorman); Fred Kelsey (Turnkey); Philo McCullough (Warden); Gertrude Carr (Mrs. Dobie); Richard Walsh (Bystander); Tiny Jones (Flower Woman); Georgia Caine (Mrs. Sterritt).

THE UNFAITHFUL *(Warner Bros., 1947)* 109 min.

Producer, Jerry Wald; director, Vincent Sherman; screenplay, David Goodis, James Gunn; art director, Leo K. Kuter; set decorator, William Wallace; music, Max Steiner; music director, Leo F. Forbstein; orchestrator, Murray Cutter; assistant director, James McMahon; sound, Francis Scheid; special effects, William McGann, Robert Burks; camera, Ernest Haller; editor, Alan Crosland, Jr.

Ann Sheridan (Chris Hunter); Lew Ayres (Larry Hannaford); Zachary Scott (Bob Hunter); Eve Arden (Paula); Jerome Cowan (Prosecuting Attorney); Steven Geray (Martin Barrow); John Hoyt (Detective Lieutenant Reynolds); Marta Mitrovich (Mrs. Tanner); Douglas Kennedy (Roger); Claire Meade (Martha); Frances Morris (Agnes); Jane Harker (Joan); Joan Winfield (Girl); Maud Fealy (Old Maid); Cary Harrison (Seedy Man); Betty Hill, Charles Marsh, Bob Lowell (Reporters); John Elliott (Judge); George Hickman, Bob Alden (Newsboys); Paul Bradley (Mr. Tanner); Ray Montgomery (Secretary); Mary Field (Receptionist); Monte Blue (Businessman).

THE TREASURE OF THE SIERRA MADRE *(Warner Bros., 1948)* 126 min.

Producer, Henry Blanke; director, John Huston; based on the novel by B. Traven; screenplay, Huston; music, Max Steiner; orchestrator, Murray Cutter; art director, John Hughes; set decorator, Fred M. MacLean; makeup, Perc Westmore; assistant director, Dick Mayberry; sound, Robert B. Lee; special effects, William McGann, H. F. Koenekamp; camera, Ted McCord; editor, Owen Marks.

Humphrey Bogart (Fred C. Dobbs); Walter

Huston (Howard); Tim Holt (Curtin); Bruce Bennett (Cody); Barton MacLane (McCormick); Alfonso Bedoya (Gold Hat); A. Soto Rangel (Presidente); Manuel Donde (El Jefe); Jose Torvay (Pablo); Margarito Luna (Pancho); Jacqueline Dalya (Flashy Girl); Bobby Blake (Mexican Boy); Spencer Chan (Proprietor); Julian Rivero (Barber); John Huston (White Suit); Harry Vejar (Bartender); Pat Flaherty (Customer); Clifton Young, Jack Holt (Flophouse Men); Guillermo Calleo (Mexican Storekeeper); Manuel Donde, Ildefonso Vega, Francisco Islas, Alberto Valdespino (Indians); Mario Mancilla (Youth); Ann Sheridan (Streetwalker); Martin Garralaga (Railroad Conductor).

SILVER RIVER *(Warner Bros., 1948)* 110 min.

Producer, Owen Crump; director, Raoul Walsh; based on an unpublished novel by Stephen Longstreet; screenplay, Longstreet, Harriet Frank, Jr.; art director, Ted Smith; set decorator, William G. Wallace; Miss Sheridan's wardrobe, Travilla; men's wardrobe, Marjorie Best; music, Max Steiner; orchestrator, Murray Cutter; dialogue director, Maurice Murphy; assistant director, Russell Saunders; technical advisor on Civil War sequences, Colonel J. G. Taylor; sound, Francis J. Scheid; montages, James Leicester; special effects, William McGann, Edwin Du Par; camera, Sid Hickox; editor, Alan Crosland, Jr.

Errol Flynn (Captain Mike McComb); Ann Sheridan (Georgia Moore); Thomas Mitchell (John Plato Beck); Bruce Bennett (Stanley Moore); Tom D'Andrea (Pistol Porter); Barton MacLane (Banjo Sweeney); Monte Blue (Buck Chevigee); Jonathan Hale (Major Spencer); Alan Bridge (Sam Slade); Arthur Space (Major Rose); Art Baker (Major Wilson); Joseph Crehan (President Grant); Norman Jolley (Scout); Norman Willis (Honest Harry); Ed Parker (Bugler); Harry Strang, Jerry Jerome, Frank McCarroll, James H. Harrison, Bob Stephenson, Ross Ford (Soldiers); Henry "Harry" Morgan (Tailor); Ian Wolfe (Deputy); Harry Woods (Card Player); Marjorie Bennett (Large Woman); Franklyn Farnum (Officer); Ben Corbett (Henchman); Fred Kelsey (Townsmen); Bud Osborne (Posseman); Russell Hicks (Edwards, the Architect); Dan White, Otto Reichow (Miners).

GOOD SAM *(RKO, 1948)* 113 min.

Producer/director, Leo McCarey; story, McCarey, John Klorer, screenplay, Ken Englund; art director, John B. Goodman; set decorators, Darrell Silvera, Jacques Mapes; music, Robert Emmett Dolan; assistant director, Jesse Hibbs; costumes, William Travilla; sound, John L. Cass, Clem Portman; special effects, Russell Cully; camera, George Barnes; editor, James McKay.

Gary Cooper (Sam Clayton); Ann Sheridan (Lu Clayton); Ray Collins (Reverend Daniels); Edmund Lowe (H. C. Borden); Joan Lorring (Shirley Mae); Clinton Sundberg (Nelson); Minerva Urecal (Mrs. Nelson); Louise Beavers (Chloe); Dick Ross (Claude); Lora Lee Michel (Lulu); Bobby Dolan, Jr. (Butch); Matt Moore (Mr. Butler); Netta Packer (Mrs. Butler); Ruth Roman (Ruthie); Carol Stevens (Mrs. Adams); Todd Karns (Joe Adams); Irving Bacon (Tramp); William Frawley (Tom); Harry Hayden (Banker); Ida Moore (Old Lady); Marta Mitrovich (Mysterious Woman); Sedal Bennett (Woman Chasing Bus); Florence Auer (Woman on Bus); Cliff Clark (Probation Officer); Jack Gargan, Bess Flowers (Parents); Almira Sessions (Landlady); Effie Laird (Mrs. Duffield); Louis Mason (Mr. Duffield); William Haade (Taxi Driver); Dick Elliott, Bert Roach (Politicians); Bert Moorehouse (Man).

I WAS A MALE WAR BRIDE *(Twentieth Century-Fox, 1949)* 105 min. (British release title: *You Can't Sleep Here*)

Producer, Sol C. Siegel; director, Howard Hawks; based on the novel by Henri Rochard; screenplay, Charles Lederer, Leonard Spigelgass, Hagar Wilde; art directors, Lyle Wheeler, Albert Hogsett; set decorators, Thomas Little, Walter M. Scott; music, Cyril J. Mockridge; music director, Lionel Newman; orchestrator, Herbert Spencer; sound, George Leverett, Roger Heman; special camera effects, Fred Sersen; camera, Norbert Brodine, O. H. Borradaile; editor, James B. Clark.

Cary Grant (Henri Rochard); Ann Sheridan (Lieutenant Catherine Gates); Marion Marshall, Randy Stuart (WACS); William Neff (Captain Jack Rumsey); Eugene Gericke (Tony Jowitt); Ruben Wendorf (Innkeeper's Assistant); Lester Sharpe (Waiter); John Whitney (Trumble); Ken Tobey (Seaman); Joe Haworth (Shore Patrol); William Pullen, William Self, Bill Murphy (Sergeants); Otto Reichow, William Yetter (German Policemen); Barbara Perry (Tall WAC); Harry Lauter, Robert Stevenson (Lieutenants); Patricia Curts (Girl in Door); John Serrett (French Notary); Paul Hardmuth (Burghermeister); Martin Milner (Schindler).

STELLA *(Twentieth Century-Fox, 1950)* 83 min.

Producer, Sol C. Siegel; director, Claude Binyon; based on the novel *Family Skeleton* by Doris Miles Disney; screenplay, Binyon; music director, Lionel Newman; art directors, Lyle Wheeler, Mark-Lee Kirk; camera, Joe MacDonald; editor, Harmon Jones.

Ann Sheridan (Stella); Victor Mature (Jeff

DeMarco); David Wayne (Carl Granger); Randy Stuart (Claire); Marion Marshall (Mary); Frank Fontaine (Don); Leif Erickson (Fred); Evelyn Varden (Flora); Lea Penman (Mrs. Calhoun); Joyce MacKenzie (Peggy Denny); Hobart Cavanaugh (Tim Gross); Charles Halton (Mr. Becker); Walter Baldwin (Farmer); Larry Keating (Gil Wright); Lorelie Vitek (Cigarette Girl); Chill Wills (Officer).

WOMAN ON THE RUN (*Universal, 1950*) 77 min.

Producer, Howard Welsch; director, Norman Foster; story, Sylvia Tate; screenplay, Alan Campbell, Foster; art director, Boris Leven; music, Emil Newman and Arthur Lange; camera, Hal Mohr; editor, Otto Ludwig.

Ann Sheridan (Eleanor Johnson); Dennis O'Keefe (Danny Leggett); Robert Keith (Inspector Ferris); Ross Elliott (Frank Johnson); Frank Jenks (Detective Shaw); J. Farrell McDonald (Sea Captain); Thomas Dillon (Joe Gordon); Steven Geray (Dr. Hobler); Reiko Sato (Susie); Victor Sen Yung (Sammy).

STEEL TOWN (*Universal, 1952*) C-85 min.

Producer, Leonard Goldstein; associate producer, Ross Hunter; director, George Sherman; story, Leonard Freeman; screenplay, Gerald Drayson Adams, Lou Breslow; art directors, Bernard Herzbrun, Robert Clatworthy; camera, Charles P. Boyle; editor, Ted J. Kent.

Ann Sheridan ("Red" McNamara); John Lund (Steve Kostane); Howard Duff (Jim Denko); William Harrigan (John McNamara); Eileen Crowe (Millie McNamara); Chick Chandler (Ernie); James Best (Joe Rakich); Nancy Kulp (Dolores); Tudor Owen (McIntosh); Elaine Riley (Valerie); Herbert Lytton (Doctor); Robert Karnes (Interne); Frank Marlowe (Taxi Driver); Lorin Raker (Milquetoasty Man); Lois Wilde (Nurse); James McLaughlin (Helper).

JUST ACROSS THE STREET (*Universal, 1952*) 78 min.

Producer, Leonard Goldstein; associate producer, Ross Hunter; director, Joseph Pevney; story/screenplay, Roswell Rogers, Joel Malone; art directors, Bernard Herzbrun, Emrich Nicholson; music director, Joseph Gershenson; camera, Maury Gertsman; editor, Virgil Vogel.

Ann Sheridan (Henrietta Smith); John Lund (Fred Newcombe); Robert Keith (Walter Medford); Cecil Kellaway (Pop Smith); Harvey Lembeck (Al); Natalie Schafer (Gertrude Medford); Alan Mowbray (Davis); Billie Bird (Pearl); George Eldredge (John Ballinger); Lou Lubin (Man in Trouble); Jack Kruschen (Character); Herbert Vigran (Liquor Salesman); Steve Roberts (C. L.); Fritzi Dugan (Woman in House); George "Shorty" Chirello (Flower Vendor); Miles Shepard, Wally Walker (Cab Drivers).

TAKE ME TO TOWN (*Universal, 1953*) C-81 min.

Producer, Ross Hunter; co-producer, Leonard Goldstein; director, Douglas Sirk; story/screenplay, Richard Morris; art directors, Alexander Golitzen, Hilyard Brown; set decorators, Russel Gauzan, Julia Heron; assistant director, Joseph E. Kenny; music, Joseph Gershenson; choreography, Hal Belfer; sound Leslie Carey; camera, Russell Metty; editor, Milton Carruth.

Ann Sheridan (Vermilion O'Toole); Sterling Hayden (Will Hall); Philip Reed (Newton Cole); Lee Patrick (Rose); Phyllis Stanley (Mrs. Stoffer); Lee Aaker (Corney); Harvey Grant (Petey); Dusty Henley (Bucket); Larry Gates (Ed Daggett); Forrest Lewis (Ed Higgins); Dorothy Neumann (Felice Pickett); Ann Tyrell (Louise Pickett); Robert Anderson (Chuck); Frank Sully (Sammy); Lane Chandler (Mike); Guy Williams (Hero); Alice Kelley (Heroine); Ruth Hampton, Jackie Loughery, Valerie Jackson, Anita Ekberg (Dancehall Girls); Fess Parker (Long John); Dusty Walker (Singer); Mickey Little, Jimmy Karath, Jerry Wayne (Boys).

APPOINTMENT IN HONDURAS (*RKO, 1953*) C-79 min.

Producer, Benedict Bogeaus; director, Jacques Tourneur; screenplay, Karen DeWolfe; art director, Danny Hall; camera, Joseph Biroc; editor, James Leicester.

Glenn Ford (Steve Corbett); Ann Sheridan (Sylvia Sheppard); Zachary Scott (Harry Sheppard); Rodolfo Acosta (Reyes); Jack Elam (Castro); Ric Roman (Jiminez); Rico Alaniz (Bermudez); Paul Zaramba (Luis); Stanley Andrews (Captain McTaggert).

COME NEXT SPRING (*Republic, 1956*) C-92 min.

Producer, Herbert J. Yates; director, R. G. Springsteen; screenplay, Montgomery Pittman; music, Max Steiner; song, Steiner and Adelson; assistant director, Herb Mendelson; costumes, Adele Palmer; art director, Frank Arrigo; camera, Jack Marta; editor, Tony Martinelli.

Ann Sheridan (Bess Ballot); Steve Cochran (Matt Ballot); Walter Brennan (Jeff Storys); Sherry Jackson (Annie Ballot); Richard Eyer (Abraham Ballot); Edgar Buchanan (Mr. Canary); Sonny Tufts (Leroy Hytower); Harry Shannon (Mr. Totter); Rad Fulton (Bob Storys); Mae Clarke (Myrtle); Roscoe Ates (Shorty Wilkins); Wade Ruby (Delbert Meaner); James Best

(Bill Jackson); Dorothy Bernard (Aunt Bessie); Joan Woodbury (Melinda Little); Bill Kendis (Greek Attendant); Gail Bonney (Mrs. Totter); Norma Done (Lovey Crockett).

THE OPPOSITE SEX *(MGM, 1956)* C-117 min.

Producer, Joe Pasternak; director, David Miller; based on the play *The Women* by Clare Boothe; screenplay, Fay and Michael Kanin; art directors, Cedric Gibbons, Daniel B. Cathcart; music supervisor, George Stoll; songs, Nicholas Brodszky and Sammy Cahn; orchestrators, Albert Sendrey, Skip Martin; choreography and music numbers staged by Robert Sidney; assistant director, George Rhein; costumes, Helen Rose; camera, Robert Bronner; editor, John McSweeney, Jr.

June Allyson (Kay); Joan Collins (Crystal); Dolores Gray (Sylvia); Ann Sheridan (Amanda); Ann Miller (Gloria); Leslie Nielsen (Steve Hilliard); Jeff Richards (Buck Winston); Charlotte Greenwood (Lucy); Agnes Moorehead (Countess); Joan Blondell (Edith); Sam Levene (Mike Pearl); Bill Goodwin (Howard Fowler); Alice Pearce (Olga); Barbara Jo Allen [Vera Vague] (Dolly); Sandy Descher (Debbie); Carolyn Jones (Pat); Alan Marshal (Ted); Jonathan Hale (Phelps Potter); Jerry Antea (Leading Male Dancer); Harry James, Art Mooney (Themselves); Dick Shawn (Singer); Jim Backus (Psychiatrist); Celia Lovsky (Lutsi); Harry McKenna (Hughie); Ann Morriss (Receptionist); Dean Jones (Assistant Stage Manager); Kay English (Aristocratic Woman); Gordon Richards (Butler); Barrie Chase, Ellen Ray (Specialty Dancers); Gail Bonney, Maxine Semon, Jean Andren (Gossips); Bob Hopkins (Drunk in 21 Club).

THE WOMAN AND THE HUNTER *(Gross-Krasne-Phoenix, 1957)* 78 min.

Director, George Breakston.

With: Ann Sheridan, David Farrar, John Loder, Jan Merlin.

THE FAR OUT WEST *(Universal, 1967)* C-87 min.

Associate producer, Irving Paley; producer/director, Joe Connelly; teleplay, George Tibbles; music, Jack Elliott; makeup, Bud Westmore.

Ann Sheridan (Henrietta "Hank" Hanks); Ruth McDevitt (Grandma Hanks); Douglas V. Fowley (Grandpa Hanks); Gary Vinson (Sheriff Harold Sykes); Carole Wells (Lucy Hanks); Robert Lowery (Bernard "Buzz" Courtney); Morgan Woodward (Mark Hangman); Lon Chaney (Chief Eagle Shadow); Mark Cavel (Grey Hawk); Leo Gordon (Cyrus Breech); Jay Silverheels (Great Bear); Alec Henteloff (Little Bear); Stanley Adams (Jed Timmons); Lee Patrick (Mrs. Paisley); Charles Meredith (Doctor); with: Gil Lamb, Quinn O'Hara, Fred Williams.

The MGM star in the late Forties.

6

ESTHER WILLIAMS

> 5′ 7″   123 pounds
> Brown hair   Hazel eyes
> Leo

AS *VARIETY* APTLY phrased it, Esther Williams was ". . . pulled to stardom by her swim-suit straps." She was a phenomenon in the Hollywood of the Forties. Undaunted by any serious cinema competition, she was the queen of the aquatic musicals—and at what better studio to be such a novelty star than MGM where there were lavish budgets, top-name supporting casts, and superior technical crews to aid her.

There were many who insisted that Esther's success was all the more remarkable because she could not really sing (she was often dubbed in her films), act, or dance. Ace comedienne Fanny Brice once cracked, "Wet she's a star. Dry she ain't."

William Pratt reasoned in a 1968 *Screen Facts* career study: "Ask a person under twenty-five who Esther Williams is and his only answer will probably be 'the swimmer!' But request the title of one of her films—from almost anyone for that matter—and he'll be hard put for an answer.

"But the very fact that she is well remembered for something after such a long period of career inactivity indicates a certain amount of immortality. . . . Thinking back on her films, there is little outside her presence to make them memorable. Even the titles are hard to distinguish for the uninitiated. For example, who can differentiate between *Easy to Wed* and *Easy to Love* or *Neptune's Daughter* and *Jupiter's Darling*? Most employed the familiar mistaken identity plot which dates back to Astaire and Rogers. . . . That Esther was able to remain a Hollywood Superstar for more than fifteen years, despite so many nonsense movies, is a tribute not only to her swimming prowess but also to her determination to improve and do her best in whatever capacity assigned."

Esther Jane Williams was born on Tuesday, August 8, 1922, in the Los Angeles suburb of Inglewood. She was the fifth and last child born to Lou and Bula G. Williams. (She was preceded by brothers Stanton and David and by sisters Maureen and June.) Lou Williams, of Welsh and Scotch-Irish descent, was a master sign painter and commercial artist. Bula Williams, a school teacher before her marriage, was of Dutch-English extraction, and she remained active in community education affairs. Esther would confide to columnist Louella Parsons in 1950 that her family had been quite poor, adding: "But my mother was so wonderful and we had such a large, happy family that I never felt we didn't have what other children had." For a time, the Williams' economy was aided by Stanton's appearance in silent movies as a child actor, but he died while Esther was still a young child.

One of life's diversions that cost nearly nothing is swimming and frolicking at the various Pacific Ocean beaches. This the Williams family did often. Maureen taught Esther to swim when the latter was about four years old. The child possessed an innate talent for water athletics which her parents heartily encouraged. When Esther was eight, the city of Inglewood constructed a swimming pool on the grounds of the local elementary school, which was handily situated across the street from the Williams' home. Nothing could have been more advantageous for a little girl who loved to swim, and Esther's mother arranged for her to work at the poolhouse. In exchange for keeping count of the bath towels, she was given swimming privileges along with coaching from the lifeguards.

At the age of nine Esther witnessed the 1932 Olympic swimming competition at the Olympic Stadium in Los Angeles where she cheered on Georgia Coleman, the American swimmer who scored an impressive victory. Esther entered her first school swimming meet when she was thirteen and came in second. A few years later she reminisced to Los Angeles newsman Arthur Whitney about her defeat, saying, "I was so discouraged, I cried all the way home. I told my mother I'd never swim again. She told me it was no disgrace to get beaten by somebody better, but it was a disgrace to quit. So I decided I'd have to get better myself."

With her family urging her onward, Esther developed enormous self-confidence in her swimming abilities, and at the age of fifteen she was invited to join the Los Angeles Athletic Club. There she received further training and encouragement from Aileen Allen, a former Olympic champion who was the club's director and swimming coach. Miss Allen predicted that, with hard work, Esther would be a champion within four years. A year later, in 1938, before graduating from Inglewood High School, Esther won the 100-meter free style championship at the Women's AAU Outdoor Nationals held at Des Moines, Iowa. In the same meet she was also a member of the relay teams that won the 300-meter, the 300-yard, and the 800-yard relay championships.

Her mother once said, "She wanted to win because it was fun." Esther went on to garner awards in Miami and Seattle swimming competitions and was named the Pacific Coast champion. Her training and recognition paid off well when she was selected to represent the United States at the Olympics, scheduled to be held at Helsinki, Finland, in 1940. The dream of her young life was soon shattered, however, when the Nazis invaded Poland in September 1939. It was a military move that precipitated the start of World War II, and the Olympic events were canceled.

Esther then enrolled at Los Angeles City College, but she quit after only a few months because of boredom. While attending the college she met a University of Southern California medical student named Leonard W. Kovner who was to become her major romantic interest.

Early in 1940, at the age of eighteen, she went to work at I. Magnin's in Hollywood as a stock clerk and part-time model. She later revealed to Hedda Hopper that she had been promised the chance to become a buyer if she would stick with the business.

However, her modeling days were destined to be short-lived. A short time later she was contacted by master showman Billy Rose who hoped to acquire her services for the West Coast edition of his Aquacade which had been so popular at the New York World's Fair (1939).

The Golden Gate International Exposition was due to reopen on Treasure Island in San Francisco Bay on May 25, 1940. (The first phase of the Exposition ran from February 18, 1939, through October 29, 1939, when it closed at a $4,166,000 deficit.) It was the hope of all concerned that the Rose water spectacle would generate additional interest in the Exposition.

Rose's first offer was for $40 a week, which Esther rejected. As she would recall, "I told him I wasn't interested. It would mean the loss of my amateur standing as a swimmer, and I didn't care about show business." Rose was persistent, and she relented when his price reached $110 a week.*

After quitting her job at Magnin's, Esther went to San Francisco where she swam in three shows daily (four on Saturdays and Sundays) in a specially built, 200-foot-long, 60-foot-wide indoor pool containing 50,000 gallons of water. Her co-star was Johnny Weissmuller, called the "Number One Aquadonis" by San Francisco news people. An estimated 25,000 people paid admissions to see the Aquacade on opening day, with Esther and Johnny swimming to the accompanying singing of Morton Downey. *Time* magazine referred to Esther as a "shapely Aquabelle," while Hollywood's Louella Parsons, after viewing the show, wrote: "Johnny Weissmuller, Esther Williams, and Morton Downey are the biggest forty-cents worth of entertainment I ever saw." The San Francisco press labeled Esther a "prima swimeuse." The Aquacade's publicity department described her as a "typically healthy, alert, vibrant, cultured girl." San Francisco historian Richard Reinhardt (who saw Esther perform) recorded in his *Treasure Island* book, "Miss Williams dove without splashing, swam without snorting, and smiled angelically even under water."

During her early period of employment as a star of Rose's Aquacade, Esther was visited each weekend by student Leonard Kovner. On Thursday, June 27, 1940 (evidently between shows), Esther and Kovner were married in the San Francisco suburb of Los Gatos. She was eighteen; he was twenty-two.

MGM producer Jack Cummings (*Broadway Melody of 1940, Go West, Two Girls on Broadway,* etc.) witnessed Esther's water show and was so impressed that he made an appointment to talk with her. "Mr. Cummings said he thought I could have a movie career," she told Hollywood newsman Arthur Whitney in 1942. "He was really very enthusiastic. I think he was under the impression that I was ready to go to work. I thanked him and said I was really very flattered, but that I couldn't sign a contract because my husband objected to my going into pictures."

The Golden Gate Exposition closed on September 29, 1940, and Esther returned to Los Angeles to begin housekeeping as Mrs. Leonard Kovner. To help with household expenses, she returned to her job at Magnin's. Meanwhile MGM had not given up on signing Esther. Since Sonja Henie on skates was earning big box-office dollars at Twentieth Century-Fox, it was felt that a beautiful swimming star could do the same for MGM. Producer Cummings turned over the persuasion campaign to an agency which sought to break down the Williams-Kovner resistance. A year was to pass before this happened.

According to Esther in a 1948 interview with Hedda Hopper, one rainy day the agency called her at Magnin's. To relieve the boredom of the day she jokingly agreed to a meeting with Louis B. Mayer but *only* if he would send a chauffeured limousine to fetch her. "You see, I just wanted to get into that snazzy car and wave back to my pals," she explained to Hopper. "Before I could wink an eye, however, the agency told me to get ready immediately."

---

*Eleanor Holm was reputedly paid $2,000 weekly for starring in the New York version of the Aquacade.

She recalled that Mayer's first words to her were "You're mighty tall" (5'7"), which she assumed was the end of that professional affair. However, the mogul quickly interjected, "I didn't say you were *too* tall. Sit down and let's talk this matter over." She soon found out that Mayer possessed what she considered to be "a most powerful gift of persuasion." Esther went home to discuss with Kovner the offer of a six-month contract. He reluctantly agreed to her career chance, but it was his conservative belief that any publicity that would be attached to a screen actress wife would not be advantageous to the budding career of a young physician (he was then an interne at Los Angeles General Hospital).

In October 1941, the brown-haired, hazel-eyed Esther signed an MGM contract. The studio publicity department threw a tape around her vital physical areas and told the Hollywood press that she was a delightful 38-27-34. As a homey note, it was revealed that she loved to cook and that she washed and set her own hair.

For the first few months of her contract period Esther faced no cameras. Instead she was enrolled in the studio classrooms where diction and drama were taught. Easily discouraged through boredom, she asked Mayer to release her from the contract, but he refused. The mogul informed her that he had a big part lined up for her in a pending Clark Gable film. (The truth was that he intended using her as a threat to Lana Turner who had gone against studio dictates by wedding Stephen Crane in New York.) Esther was tested with Gable in a scene for *Somewhere I'll Find You* (1942). She looked good in the footage, but the scene revealed

With Mickey Rooney in a publicity pose for *Andy Hardy's Double Life* ('42).

her lack of dramatic training. Although Gable was agreeable to having her as a co-star in this wartime love story, the role went to the erring Miss Turner.

As Esther's debut feature film, MGM chose *Andy Hardy's Double Life* (1942), the thirteenth in the series of Andy Hardy films. Known as a showcase to lend proper exposure to contract starlets, the series had previously displayed the beauty and various talents of Lana Turner, Ruth Hussey, Marsha Hunt, Diana Lewis, Kathryn Grayson, and Donna Reed. In this George Seitz-directed entry, Esther is seventh billed as Sheila Brooks, a girl who temporarily diverts the romantic attentions of Andy Hardy (Mickey Rooney) away from his perennial Carver hometown girlfriend Polly Benedict (Ann Rutherford). Esther, of course, had a swimming scene* in the feature, which prompted Bosley Crowther *(New York Times)* to comment: "[She] is refreshingly pretty." Crowther also noted: "She still has to learn about acting." For their togetherness scenes, since Esther stood a good four inches taller than Rooney, he was placed on an out-of-camera-range stool. In his autobiography, Rooney wrote, "Esther was pleasant to work with and utterly unprofessional. If someone flubbed a line she went to pieces, even if it wasn't she who flubbed it, which it usually was." On another occasion Rooney, reminiscing about the spectacular Miss Williams, noted, "I can't honestly say that Esther Williams ever acted in an Andy Hardy picture, but she swam in one."

With the film's release, MGM launched a widespread publicity campaign on behalf of their new starlet. It was said that the Culver City studio heads found it unbelievable that she had never acted before and considered her the most promising ex-swimming champ to ever appear on screen. The world—anxious for any diversion from the grim World War II battle news—was told that she swam daily at the studio or in the ocean. "Lifeguards hate to see her come to the beach," it was said. "She swims out three miles and they feel they have to watch her."

Early in 1943 Esther signed a seven-year pact with MGM, but she was not to be seen in another feature film until December of that year, and then it was in a brief part as Ellen Bright, a girlfriend of Van Johnson's in *A Guy Named Joe* (1943). The film's star, Spencer Tracy, is an Air Force pilot who is killed but returns to earth in spirit form to give courage to his sweetheart (Irene Dunne) and to train a neophyte flyer (Johnson). Esther's character disappears from the plotline when Johnson sets his cap for Dunne.

Her first starring role was as Caroline Brooks in *Bathing Beauty,* completed on January 10, 1944, and released that July. Originally entitled *Mr. Co-Ed,* the color feature was retitled to shift the focal point from Red Skelton (in top billing) to Esther. Nevertheless, it was still essentially Skelton's picture. Named Steve Elliott, he and Caroline are secretly married. She is a swimming teacher at a girls' school where he enrolls so that he may be closer to her. While Skelton tears through various comic routines as the only male student, Esther swims her way into the audience's affections. A colorful water carnival was incorporated into the plot to better show off her swimming and diving talents. Photographed in Technicolor, the 101-minute film also had the bands of Harry James and Xavier Cugat, along with organist Ethel Smith and decorous singing stars Helen Forrest and Lina Romay. For the aquatic ballet scenes, the studio built a ninety-foot square pool and pumped a million gallons of warm water into it. (So much for wartime restrictions!)

Producer Jack Cummings' faith in Esther paid rich dividends when *Bathing Beauty* was unveiled. Bosley Crowther *(New York Times)* took Esther to his heart by writing, "When she eels through the crystal blue water in a rosy-red bathing suit or splashes in limpid magnificence . . . she's a bathing beauty for our money." According to *The Family Circle* magazine, ". . . her Venus-like limbs have

---

*Esther's swimming pool scene was shown in *Andy Hardy Comes Home* (1958), an unsuccessful attempt to revive the series with Andy very matured and with a son of his own.

With Spencer Tracy, Barry Nelson, and Van Johnson in *A Guy Named Joe* ('43).

With Red Skelton in *Bathing Beauty* ('44).

With Van Johnson and Frances Gifford in *Thrill of a Romance* ('45).

never shone to brighter advantage—in color, under water or over water. For the rest, if you happen to notice, she has pert facile features and personality—enough to get by on, all in all, for quite a spell."

On July 16, 1944, the expected happened when Esther walked out on her husband Leonard Kovner. She applied for a divorce in August, and the decree was granted by Los Angeles Superior Court Judge Stanley Mosk on September 12, 1944, when Esther told the court, "He objected to my career. When I had the opportunity to go into pictures, for several weeks he made it so difficult for me that I became ill. Constant arguments made ours a very unhappy home." Esther's mother testified that Kovner had declared his stand against having children with the assertion: "There won't be another Williams kid brought into the world if I can prevent it."

Esther was reteamed (this time in a co-starring status) with Van Johnson in the Technicolor *Thrill of a Romance* (1945). According to *Time* magazine, the film was as "screwily wholesome as ice cream and toothpaste." In this Joe Pasternak production Esther plays Cynthia Glenn who weds Robert Delbar (Carleton G. Young), a fast-rising economist. They are honeymooning at a resort hotel in the Sierra Nevada mountains which (fortuitously) has a nice swimming pool and a large dance floor. Soon after their arrival, Robert is called away on business. Cynthia bides her time by swimming and dancing until she meets Major Thomas Milvaine (Johnson), a convalescing war hero. She volunteers to teach him to swim, a move that soon leads to love. Robert returns and asks for an annulment which paves the way for the in-love couple to plan their future together. Esther and Johnson were frequently relieved of making oncamera romance by the singing of Metropolitan Opera star Lauritz Melchior and the playing of Tommy Dorsey and his orchestra. Although Esther performed her own singing of the song "I Should Care," backed by the Dorsey band, her diving scenes were doubled by Ruth Nurmi.

In reporting on *Thrill of a Romance*, *Time* magazine discovered that Esther "has the kind of body—displayed in a protean series of bathing suits—which you may dream of but aren't inclined to talk about at the breakfast table, and a nice, easy, assured personality to match." MGM knew that it had the proper formula for forthcoming Williams pictures when *Thrill of a Romance* grossed $4.5 million in U.S. and Canadian rentals alone.

Photoplay magazine's editor, Fred R. Sammis, picked Esther as one of "Ten New Faces to Make Movie History in 1945." (The other nine were: June Haver, William Eythe, Richard Crane, Gloria DeHaven, Diana Lynn, Lauren Bacall, Jeanne Crain, Turhan Bey, and Van Johnson.) Sammis wrote, "Today a studio knows it is smart box office to co-star a boy and a girl whose unknown names on a marquee wink out at moviegoers." In choosing Esther for stardom, Sammis further wrote, "Esther Williams is common clay, uncommonly molded into a perfection of beauty, with a showgirl's height and the figure of a dream, and with only a sure instinct for survival (and a heart) to guide her on her star's road."

Early in 1945, while selling cigarettes for charity at Earl Carroll's restaurant in Hollywood, Esther was introduced to U.S. Army Sergeant Benjamin Gage. The 6'5"-tall Gage had been a radio announcer in civilian life (on Bob Hope's show) and had also gained a certain amount of fame as a singer of popular melodies. On Sunday, November 25, 1945, at Westwood Hills Congregational Church, Esther and Ben were pronounced husband and wife by the Reverend F. Mark Hoag.

For the double-ring ceremony, Esther wore a street-length gown of pale pink crepe with long sleeves and a halo hat of matching pink lace. She carried a prayer book and a small bouquet of white orchids. New MGM star Jane Powell sang "Because" and "I Love You" before the exchange of nuptials. Esther's matron-of-honor was Mrs. J. K. McEldowney, and the guests included Lana Turner, Sonny Tufts, Alan Ladd, Gene Kelly, and Jean-Pierre Aumont. The newlyweds honeymooned at Acapulco, Mexico, where their hotel room overlooked the famous and beautiful harbor. On their return to California, they purchased an English-style cottage of redwood in Pacific Palisades.

In March 1946, MGM released its first postwar, all-star entertainment package, called *The Ziegfeld Follies* (1946). (The film, or portions thereof, had been completed more than a year earlier, but the final product was held up in release because the studio was fearful that the public might think they were not wartime cost conscious.) It is a 110-minute fantasy with William Powell repeating his role as Florenz Ziegfeld, the Broadway producer, who has now died and gone to heaven. From his celestial perch he considers the talent below and magically creates a modern Follies. From then on the picture becomes an elongated series of revue sketches. Esther is the centerpiece of a water ballet for which she wears a skintight, one-piece bathing suit. (Deleted from the final

With groom Benjamin Gage (December 29, 1945).

Advertisement for *Ziegfeld Follies* ('46).

film version was a song number with Esther and James Melton in which he sang "We Will Meet Again," while she bubbled up from the sea.)

The Hoodlum Saint (1946) provided two firsts for Esther. It was the first time since achieving cinema stardom that she was filmed in black-and-white, and it was her first all-dramatic role. Both were mistakes. As May Lorrison, a newswoman who tires of waiting for her man (William Powell) to find his niche in post-World War I America, she did not photograph to best advantage. She sticks by him when he turns from a newspaper career to finance, but when he begins wheeling and dealing indiscriminately, she walks away. When he loses his bankroll in the Wall Street crash of 1929, he returns to journalism, and it is then that Esther's heroine returns to him. Angela Lansbury as chanteuse Dusty Millard garnered more favorable critical and viewer attention than did Esther.

As part of her professional activities, Esther remained very busy when not on the soundstages. There were cheesecake publicity pose sessions, promotional public appearances, and, on occasion, some radio performances. For example, on April 26, 1946, Esther joined the cast of "Duffy's Tavern" playing in a skit about Archie's fashion show.

Wisely, *Easy to Wed* (1946) returned Esther to Technicolor and a bathing suit. Its box-office popularity ($4.5 million in distributors' domestic grosses) helped to raise her studio and industry status. It is a pleasing remake of Metro's *Libeled Lady* (1936) which had starred Spencer Tracy, Myrna Loy, Jean Harlow, and William Powell. The newer rendition was far splashier, with Latin music, dancing, and swimming. Esther is heiress Connie Allenbury (played by Loy in 1936) who sues a newspaper for libel. The editor (Keenan Wynn) hires Bill Chandler (Van Johnson) to enchant her into giving up the case. Connie has no idea what freckled Mr. Chandler is up to, but she does fall in love with him. To make him more attractive, the editor has Bill wed his (the editor's) own girl (Lucille Ball). Ultimately Connie and Bill find love with each other, but not before a number of farcical scenes are recorded. (When *Easy to Wed* had been planned in 1944, MGM originally intended casting Lana Turner in the female lead.)

In a publicity shot with William Powell and Angela Lansbury for *The Hoodlum Saint* ('46).

With Keenan Wynn, Lucille Ball, Cecil Kellaway, and Van Johnson in *Easy to Wed* ('46).

MGM next found it necessary to employ Esther (in top billing for the first time) in one of the most improbable plots ever conceived, for the movie *Fiesta* (1947). In Mexico, where it was filmed, she is Maria Morales, the twin sister to Mario (Ricardo Montalban in his American movie debut). Their papa (Fortunio Bonanova) is a very rich ex-matador who expects Mario to carry on the family profession. However, the son prefers a life of music, and in order to keep peace, Maria masquerades in the bullring as her brother. Incredibly, no one suspects that it is really Maria as she staggers the bulls around the ring. (It is very odd that Papa and Mama [Mary Astor] did not notice her absence while the brother was supposedly dodging the bulls in the ring.) In keeping with her stock-in-trade, Esther was given one swimming scene in the palatial pool. Of course Papa eventually learns the truth, but since his daughter has done such a good job the son is forgiven. John Carroll made a handsome romantic partner for Esther, while Cyd Charisse was paired with Ricardo. In the estimation of the august *New York Times*, the film was "more often conducive to siesta than fiesta."

This Time for Keeps, completed in mid-December 1946 and released in the fall of 1947, is one of those colorful but flimsy screen musicals which the studio assembled hastily in order to showcase some of its contracted musical talents (Lauritz Melchior, Johnny Johnston, Xavier Cugat) and a comedian (Jimmy Durante), with Esther in top billing to insure box-office success. Filmed at Mackinac Island, Saginaw, Michigan, the story traces a year in the lives of Nora (Esther) and Dick (Johnston) whose romance is fraught with continual misunderstandings. The plot, such as it is, is generously interspersed with Melchior's operatic presence, Johnston's popular-song offerings, and Esther's water ballets. With a trio, beauteous Esther did her own singing of "No Wonder They Fell in Love." These days, when *This Time for Keeps* is shown on television, *TV Guide* describes the picture thusly, "Esther Williams swims, Lauritz Melchior and Johnny Johnston sing, Jimmy Durante clowns, Xavier Cugat and band play."

With Cyd Charisse, Ricardo Montalban, and John Carroll in *Fiesta* ('47).

With Jimmy Durante and Dick Simmons in *This Time for Keeps* ('47).

334

In 1947 Hedda Hopper referred to Esther as "Miss Moneybags" because of "the terrific salary raise she's getting from her studio." Miss Hopper also pointed out Esther's interest in handicapped children and her work with the Visually Handicapped Children's Hospital in Los Angeles. Sidney Skolsky described Esther as loving orange juice, preferring to ride with the top of her convertible down, and wearing "a black panty girdle, always." Skolsky invariably ended his columns with the stars' preferences for sleeping, and he told his readers that Esther slept in a large bed because she liked plenty of room. In winter she slept in a flannel nightgown and during the summer in a thin negligee.

Esther revealed to Hedda Hopper that Ben Gage had "gone out of his way to keep out of pictures. He's sensitive about having anyone think that I might help him in the film business. He's done all right in his own field, radio."

In 1947 Esther suffered a miscarriage. It was initially diagnosed by her doctors that she might never have children, but this prognosis was later changed, and Esther said, "We plan to have at least three. I hope my work can be arranged so I can have my career and kids too. If not, I'll have the children anyhow."

In the spring of 1948 Esther announced that she was working on a book called *Or Would You Rather Be a Fish?* in which she would answer all the questions put to her by fans about swimming. She said that her mother, "my closest friend," helped her to reply to letters from fans in which "we even give advice to the lovelorn." It was further announced that Esther was taking voice lessons, because, as she said, "If someone else had to dub my voice, I'd feel like I was cheating the public."

Esther and an MGM company went to Hawaii for location shooting of *On an Island with You* (1948). Her leading man was trim and muscular Peter Lawford, with Ricardo Montalban in the second male lead. With the production team of producer Joseph Pasternak and Richard Thorpe again repeating their chores, it was another Technicolor romp of young love, its mixups, and the resolutions thereof. This time she is Rosalind Reynolds, a movie swimming star in Honolulu to make a motion picture. Her fiancé (Montalban) is along for the joyride, but he is unintentionally dumped when an ex-Air Force flyer (Lawford), now a movie technical advisor, flies her to a remote island. There they fall in love, while Montalban consoles himself with Cyd Charisse back in Honolulu. Also on hand were the ubiquitous Xavier Cugat and Jimmy Durante. In this film, Esther sang "Takin' Miss Mary to the Ball," but it is believed that most of her warbling was dubbed here. While the public enthusiastically endorsed the colorful pap, critical sources such as the *New York Times* chided, "It is a pity that anyone as handsome and expressive as Esther Williams in the water should be permitted the time she does mouthing banalities on dry land."

On Esther's return to Hollywood, columnist Sheilah Graham informed fan magazine readers of what she had heard regarding Esther's alleged unpopularity* during the Hawaiian trek. "I understand they don't drool over there [for her], although I can't understand why. She's always so gracious when I talk with her, and when I see her at premieres she is always signing autographs for fans." As if to prove Miss Graham's point, Esther was named "Miss Newsprint of 1948" by the National Publishers Association, and she reigned as the Queen of Newspaper Week from October 1 to 8, 1948.

Esther received second billing (following Frank Sinatra) for *Take Me Out to the Ball Game* (1949), a Busby Berkeley-directed Technicolor musical in which she replaced an ailing Judy Garland. Although she is K. C. Higgins, the manager of a baseball team called The Wolves, an enterprise far removed from a swimming pool, she is nevertheless given one in-water scene which also allows Sinatra to croon a tune to her.

---

*There were rumors that ever since MGM had built a permanent swimming pool set for Esther's aquatic capers on celluloid, she had become very demanding oncamera and offcamera as well.

With Ricardo Montalban in *On an Island with You* ('48).

With Tom Dugan, Gene Kelly, and Richard Lane in *Take Me Out to the Ball Game* ('49).

Set at the turn of the century, the plot required her bathing costume to be a billowing 1890s model with bloomers. In the story, concocted by Gene Kelly and Stanley Donen, Dennis Ryan (Sinatra) and Eddie O'Brien (Kelly) are vaudevillians whose summers are spent playing baseball as members of The Wolves. Esther as the new owner presents romantic problems since both boys seek her attentions. It is fast-talking O'Brien who wins her over while Ryan takes Shirley (vivacious Betty Garrett) as his gal. Esther sings along with the gang in this Arthur Freed production, but she has no solo numbers.

Based upon her increased audience appeal, Esther was reunited (in top billing this time) with Red Skelton, along with Ricardo Montalban and Betty Garrett, for *Neptune's Daughter* (1949). The ninety-three minutes are a display of MGM's Technicolor opulence in its best form. In this tale of romantic complications, a polo club masseur (Skelton) is mistaken for a renowned polo player (Montalban) by Betty Barrett (Garrett). Esther is her sister who assumes that Montalban is a phony, although she is attracted to him in spite of the presence of her jealous boyfriend (Keenan Wynn). Xavier Cugat is on hand with Latin musical diversions whenever the plot becomes too heavy. Herein Esther and Montalban introduce the Frank Loesser song, "Baby, It's Cold Outside," which would win the Oscar as Best Song of 1949. Skelton and Garrett clearly stole the comedic aspects of the film, but Esther garnered the limelight in her increasingly elaborate swimming scene contributions (even though Montalban swam along with her in one sequence). Critic Bosley Crowther found her to be "lovelier than ever," while the *New York Herald-Tribune* felt obliged to reiterate, "Miss Williams is no actress, but she is extraordinarily graceful when she gets in the drink."

Esther's films were grossing hefty box-office dollars which was just cause for her to be named by *Motion Picture Herald* as one of

America's favorite swimmer in the Forties.

With Keenan Wynn and Betty Garrett in *Neptune's Daughter* ('49).

the top ten stars of 1949. The only other lady on that year's list was Twentieth Century-Fox's Betty Grable. Nevertheless, Esther was not content with the stories she had been asked to do, and she said, "There must be a writer somewhere with a legitimate idea for a swimmer. Everything I've done has been stereotyped."

On Saturday, August 6, 1949, after careful attention to the physician's orders, Esther gave birth to a seven-pound, eight-and-a-half-ounce baby boy at Santa Monica Hospital. The baby was named Benjamin Stanton Gage. Returning home following a five-day hospitalization period, Esther started an exercise routine to lose the twenty-five pounds she had gained during her pregnancy. Within three weeks she was able to get back into the pool, and when she reported to MGM three weeks thereafter, she found that she was down to 128 pounds and that (so the publicity claims) she even had lost one inch off her hips.

Her screen return, after a year, was in *Duchess of Idaho* (1950) which reteamed her for a fourth time with Van Johnson. The plot is much the same as several of her previous

Advertisement for *Duchess of Idaho* ('50).

films: romantic confusion, but with each star eventually being paired with the partner of his or her and the audience's choice. This time it is Paula Raymond and John Lund who are involved in the subordinate love machinations. In the Sun Valley, Idaho, setting, Esther not only swims, but skis, golfs, plays tennis, and ice skates. Highlights of the film are "guest" appearances by dancing Eleanor Powell, singing Lena Horne, and comedic Red Skelton.

In August 1950, Esther signed a new MGM contract which guaranteed her $1,300,000. It was a ten-year pact with no options at $2,500 a week for fifty-two weeks a year. It also provided for a twelve-week vacation each year at full salary, as well as some artistic control over the fate of her starring vehicles.

Her doctor had told Esther to wait two years before planning another child, but she discovered that she was pregnant while in Hawaii for *Pagan Love Song* (1950).* She and

With John Lund in *Duchess of Idaho*.

her husband agreed to keep it quiet for a while, but super-scooper Louella Parsons released the news in her daily column: "Ben and Esther are expecting a little brother for Benjie." The prospective parents were forced to admit that they were expecting another child in December 1950. (Other MGM stars who were pregnant at the same time were June Allyson, Cyd Charisse, and Jane Powell.) On Monday, October 30, 1950, however, Esther began experiencing labor pains, and she checked into Santa Monica Hospital at 10:15 P.M. At 10:46 P.M., a five-pound, six-ounce boy was born prematurely and was placed in an incubator. He was named Kimball Austin Gage.

Pagan Love Song was released in December 1950, at which time the *New York Times* complained, "Presumably there is a story somewhere in the picture, but all we can recollect is a series of incidents, some eye-filling and slightly amusing, others rather pointless and tedious." Set in Tahiti, Esther is a "haole"— half-white, half-native. An Ohio school teacher (Howard Keel) arrives and suspects that she is a full-bloom native, a suspicion which the very tanned Esther does not alter until they fall in love. Again, Esther is seen in well-mounted swim scenes and she sings two songs, both dubbed by Betty Wand.

If audience attendance dipped for *Pagan Love Song* (the film still grossed over $3.2 million!), it did more so for *Texas Carnival*

---

*The filming of *Pagan Love Song* was a saga unto itself. Originally Stanley Donen was selected to direct the musical (very loosely paralleling the then Broadway hit *South Pacific*). However, Esther stated flatly, "I will not do this picture if Stanley is going to direct it. . . . It is as simple as that." Williams believed that Donen (in conjunction with her co-star Gene Kelly) had not responded to her properly in *Take Me Out to the Ball Game*. Acceding to her wishes, executive producer Arthur Freed replaced Donen with choreographer Robert Alton, who to that date had directed only one film, *Merton of the Movies* (1946).

When onlocation filming in Tahiti proved to be out of the question, the company was redirected to Kauai, one of the then less commercialized Hawaiian Islands. The logistics of flying the crew and cast to the Islands were astounding, but eventually the troupe arrived safely, if distraught. The facilities on Kauai were primitive at best; there was one mailboat to the island paradise once every four weeks. For the initial week of scheduled filming the weather was so inclement that nothing was accomplished. Then co-star Howard Keel broke his arm, but with a towel tossed over the injured limb his solo song "Singing in the Sun" was finally shot.

According to Hugh Fordin in his book *The World of Entertainment:* director Alton suffered beginners' jitters; Williams had no particular enthusiasm for her co-lead (Keel); and the Tahitian youths imported for the water ballet number were unattractive, overamorous, and general cutups. Then it was discovered that Esther was pregnant, a condition growing increasingly obvious when she donned her oncamera sarong. Williams communicated the news to her husband on the mainland via a ham radio hookup provided by a local Japanese schoolteacher.

Filming finally concluded on the island by late May and the production was completed at the studio by early July 1950. The shooting totaled nearly $2 million; some $400,000 over budget.

Advertisement for *Pagan Love Song* ('50).

With Howard Keel in *Pagan Love Song*.

With Paula Raymond and Howard Keel in *Texas Carnival* ('51).

(1951) in which Red Skelton walked off with what honors this attenuated Esther Williams picture offered. Mistaken identity—standard operation procedure for the MGM cutie films—was also incorporated into this one. Skelton, a carnival man, is believed to be a Texan with large holdings in oil and cattle. Esther, as his carnival assistant, is mistaken for his sister. Howard Keel (a fast-rising MGM contractee) arrives on the Lone Star terrain to fall in love with Esther. Her appearance in the film is brief in comparison with her other major pictures, but she presents an aquatic scene wherein she is a gossamer vision for Keel. She also sings "Deep in the Heart of Texas," using her own voice.

In 1951 Esther and Ben Gage became the owners of a restaurant named The Trails located in Westchester at 6501 Sepulveda Boulevard. (The venture proved amazingly profitable.) They would later own a second California restaurant, this one located in Culver City.

On October 31, 1951, the Gages officially became foster parents to an eight-year-old Italian boy who lived in Naples with his mother. Through Foster Parents Plan for War Children they provided for the boy's care by contributing fifteen dollars a month for one year. The boy, named Giuseppe Sebastianelli, had lost his home and father during World War II air raids on Naples.

In other charity endeavors, Esther continued her support of the Visually Handicapped Children's Hospital by devoting many hours to teaching children to swim in the pool which she had donated to the cause. The children ranged in age from newly born to nine years. "I cannot tell you," she said, "the importance of making these handicapped children realize they can help themselves and what it does for them."

Esther next did a guest stint in MGM's *Callaway Went Thataway* (1951), which starred Howard Keel as a lookalike for a former movie cowboy hero. In Esther's single scene she played herself asking the cowpoke for autographs for her sons. Under the new

With Joan Evans and Vivian Blaine in *Skirts Ahoy!* ('52).

MGM's prime water splasher at work.

Dore Schary regime at MGM, things were gradually changing. It would take a few years before Esther or the general public realized that she was not to be part of the long-range new order.

Meanwhile the swimming star increased her non-acting interests by arranging with Cole-of-California for endorsement of their bathing suits and by the purchase of a service station and a metal-products plant. She also gifted her mother with the funding to open a counseling office.

Esther was frequently caught in the middle of studio political battles, a natural situation since she was still making such a potent contribution to the company's financial welfare. When Arthur Freed was producing his musical *The Band Wagon* (1952) there was a cameo role for a great movie star, to be seen briefly in a train station sequence with Fred Astaire. Freed intended the "walk-on" for Ava Gardner; studio head Dore Schary did not like Ava and wanted Esther to perform the part. Eventually Schary bowed to Freed's wishes and Gardner was the onfilm cinema beauty in *The Band Wagon*.

Skirts Ahoy! (1952), the next Williams entry, was described by the *New York World-Telegram and Sun* as "flimsy and incredible." It is the tale of three girls (Esther, Vivian Blaine, and Joan Evans) who join the Waves where they find fun and love. Esther, as the film's star, had vetoed the cast presence of originally scheduled Sally Forrest, who was then replaced by Miss Evans. It really did not make much difference because the picture was far from being noteworthy. Esther, of course, managed a swimming scene, this time with two children (Russell and Kathy Tongay).

The most lavish Esther Williams film came next, based on the life of Australian-born swimmer Annette Kellerman. *Million Dollar Mermaid* (1952) is perhaps the best remembered of her twenty-five screen endeavors. Mervyn LeRoy, who directed the expensive production, relates in his autobiography *Take One* (1974): "There was a

Performing for the cameras at MGM.

In a production number for *Million Dollar Mermaid* ('52).

With Creighton Hale, Lillian Culver, and Victor Mature in *Million Dollar Mermaid*.

problem of what to do with a swimmer. The studio had tried several different approaches that had worked, in varying degrees. Mostly they were far-fetched, and the way they got Esther into the water (where she was unsurpassed) had all the subtlety of a kick in the head. It seemed to me that something more appropriate could be found for her." LeRoy says that the story of Annette Kellerman, adapted for the screen by Everett Freeman, was "essentially" true.

The chronicle begins in 1900 at Sydney Harbor, Australia, where ten-year-old Annette (Donna Corcoran) is unable to dance or play with other children because she wears leg braces as a result of polio. She sneaks down to the river to swim, intuitively knowing that the exercise will be beneficial to her weak limbs. Her father Frederick (Walter Pidgeon), a music teacher, is horrified at discovering her swimming habit, but he soon agrees that it is good for her legs and encourages the sport. The years pass and she grows up to become Australia's most famous swimmer with shelves of silver cups. A chance meeting with vaudeville act promoter James Sullivan (Victor Mature) leads London-based Annette to new fame. Later in America, to garner further publicity for her, he has her parade on the beach in a "scanty" new-style bathing suit. She is arrested—and later acquitted—on the charge of indecent exposure. Although her romance with Sullivan falters, she becomes a headlining act at the New York Hippodrome Theatre. Later in Hollywood she is injured during the making of a film. However, Sullivan is on hand to inspire her to recovery.

When out of the water in *Million Dollar Mermaid*, Esther enhanced the Walter Plunkett-designed costumes, but the in-water segments, directed by Busby Berkeley, were the most elaborate ever devised. One, featuring fountains, smoke, and sparklers, is still fondly remembered today. (It was included in MGM's 1974 film *That's Entertainment*.) The film debuted at New York's Radio City Music Hall on December 5, 1952, where it remained for eight weeks. For the picture's finale water ballet, a wide screen was used for spectacular effect.

The Foreign Press Association voted

With Jack Carson and Fernando Lamas in *Dangerous When Wet* ('53).

Esther as the most popular feminine movie player in fifty countries and awarded her the "Henrietta" statuette in January 1953. (This award is now known as the Golden Globe Award.*) In March 1953 it was announced by MGM that Esther's next picture would be *Athena,* in which she would portray the "ugly duckling" of five sisters. However, when *Athena* emerged in 1954, it was with just two onscreen sisters, Jane Powell and Debbie Reynolds.

Esther's cool-off movie for the summer of 1953 was *Dangerous When Wet,* opposite the debonair actor from Argentina, Fernando Lamas. Esther plays Katy Higgins who trains expressly for the purpose of swimming the English Channel. She is abetted by her mother (Charlotte Greenwood), father (William Demarest), manager (Jack Carson), and admirer (Lamas). Barbara Whiting is her teenaged sister who sings (a part originally slated for Debbie Reynolds until she became a star). An underwater sequence has Esther swimming (superimposed) with the popular MGM cartoon characters Tom and Jerry. (Segments such as this proved that the studio was indeed running out of ideas of how to showcase Esther for the public.) Prophetically,** Wanda Hale of the *New York Daily News* decided that, with Lamas, Esther "responds more charmingly and readily than to her past film sweethearts."

On Thursday, October 1, 1953, at Santa Monica Hospital, Esther became a mother for the third time when seven-pound, fifteen-ounce Susan Tenney Gage was born. Thus the hopes that Esther had expressed in 1947 about wanting three children had come true. Susan's godfather was Walter Kohler, the governor of Wisconsin.

---

*Ironically, in 1952 and 1953 Esther was voted "the least cooperative actress" by the Hollywood Women's Press Club. Williams said of this distinction to columnist Louella Parsons, "I was out of the state of California for two months of '53 and in a state of pregnancy for nine months. At least my husband found me cooperative!" On another occasion she noted of her "award," "At least they voted me an actress! That's something!"

**Lamas was then newly divorced from his wife Lydia whom he had wed in 1946. In 1953 it was rumored about Hollywood that he might marry Lana Turner, but on June 25, 1954, he married Arlene Dahl.

The Christmas 1953 offering from MGM was *Easy to Love* starring Esther opposite Van Johnson (their fifth and final screen appearance together). Cypress Gardens, Florida, was easily the highlight of the film. Here she plays Julie Hallerton, a Cypress Gardens aquamaid whose boss Ray Lloyd (Johnson) does not realize that he is in love with her. He is too busy working to take time out for romance. However, when she goes to New York to be crowned "The Citrus Queen," she meets singer Barry Gordon (Tony Martin) and Lloyd promptly becomes jealous. As in most of the Williams films, the plot is naively predictable, and it is the colorful water scenes that appeal most to the public. In this one, her finale number is done on water skis (a sport which she learned in a few days) directed by Busby Berkeley. Through lanes of Cypress Gardens trees she leads twelve boys in V-formation who are picked up by a line of water skiing girls with flying banners attached to their skis. The scene was photographed from overhead by a camera-carrying helicopter. (This scene was featured in 1976's *That's Entertainment, Part II.*) Again, Esther's singing voice was dubbed by Betty Wand.

The Gages celebrated their eighth wedding anniversary on November 25, 1953, with an intimate soiree of cocktails and dinner for guests Marie McDonald, Harry Karl, Denise Darcel, Jeff Donnell, Aldo Ray, Jim Backus, and Dick Wesson. The following month Esther was elected Honorable Mayor of Westchester by the Chamber of Commerce. She defeated actress Joan Shawlee, the candidate backed by the Westchester Kiwanis.

Late in 1953, Esther was reportedly set to open an aquacade at the Sahara Hotel in Las Vegas in July 1954, at a salary of $25,000 weekly. However, in February 1954 these plans were canceled because, it was announced, "Too many parents and their youngsters complained that a nightclub appearance would prohibit children from attending the show." Esther was named Hollywood Mother of the Year on November 28, 1954, by the City of Hope. The citation was

In *Easy to Love* ('53).

In *Easy to Love*.

With new MGM star Grace Kelly in 1954.

In *Jupiter's Darling* ('55).

in recognition of her work on behalf of sick and needy children. (Meanwhile Ben Gage was garnering rave reviews for his singing act at the Sahara Hotel in Las Vegas.)

After an absence of more than a year from screen work, Esther bounced back as Amytis, a vestal virgin engaged to marry Fabius Maximus (George Sanders), the emperor of Rome, in *Jupiter's Darling* (1955). The Technicolor, CinemaScope costume film was based on Robert E. Sherwood's 1927 Broadway comedy *The Road to Rome* which had starred Jane Cowl. The celluloid version is a combination of comedy and dramatics set to music and swimming. The plot has Hannibal (Howard Keel) on the verge of routing Rome, but Amytis enters his camp and manages to change his mind (while falling in love with him).

MGM's advertisements for *Jupiter's Darling* proclaimed: "It's a Wonderful Idea for a Gigantic and Joyous Musical," but despite the use of widescreen and lush color (each of Hannibal's elephants was dyed a brilliant hue), the film was not a success. The *New York Times* pointed out, "The spirit of jest is indicated but barely perceptible in this musical film. Miss Williams had better get back in that water* and start blowing bubbles again."

In the mid-Fifties, there were rumors that Esther might not make another aquatic film because her doctor had forbidden it. This speculation was further emphasized when Esther's MGM contract, which had four years remaining, was nullified by mutual consent in 1955, although MGM circulated the word that she would continue to make a movie a year for them. On the discontinuance of the pact, Esther said, "All they ever did for me at MGM was to change my leading man and the water in the pool."** When she finally checked out of the Metro lot, there was no executive on hand to bid her even a courtesy farewell. Only the long-time studio gateman bothered to wish her a fond goodbye. It was a disappointment that Esther would never forget.

Like so many other at-liberty movie stars, Esther decided to try her luck in television. She entered the small-screen medium on "What's My Line?" with a "mystery" guest appearance, and, in February 1955, with her husband and children, she was interviewed by Edward R. Murrow on "Person to Person."†

There was talk that Esther would star in a film version of the life of athlete Babe Didrikson, but that project did not materialize. Instead, as her first free-lance movie acting job, Esther went to Universal-International for an original story by Rosalind Russell (written under the pseudonym of C. A. McKnight) called "The Gentle Web." The product was released in 1956 as *The Unguarded Moment.* In her first "straight dramatic characterization," she plays Lois Conway, a pretty high school teacher who is nearly sexually attacked by a handsome student (John Saxon). She placates his physical desires by helping him to overcome his mental disturbances, but their association is accompanied by parental and faculty disapproval. Universal's then current male heart-throb, George Nader, was Esther's co-star in the role of a police inspector who becomes interested in her.

For her dramatic role, Esther was congratulated by the *New York Daily News:* "Esther Williams, playing her first [sic] role minus swimsuit, disproves what a wag once said about her, 'Wet she is great, dry she isn't,' or words to that effect. In *The Unguarded Moment,* Esther has full command of the character she impersonates, a school teacher with an embarrassing problem, and she gives a performance of excellent timing and dramatic conviction."

Esther and Ben Gage increased their business acquisitions with a swimming pool construction firm dealing in a variety of backyard above-ground pool models. Their advertisements read, "Esther Williams' all aluminum pools are electrostatically painted and are completely maintenance free."

In the summer of 1956 the couple packaged a touring Aqua Spectacle which opened in London on August 9. Esther starred in this splashtacular, of course. However, her opening at Wembley Pool proved embarrassing when her special rhinestone bathing suit broke its straps and she lost it at the bottom of the pool after her initial dive. The next day she purchased a new and tighter suit. The Aqua Spectacle was televised in America over NBC-TV on September 29, 1956. The ninety-minute program featured both "wet" and "dry" entertainment around a four foot deep, seventy foot long pool designed by Gage. The show then embarked on a six-month tour of the United States and Canada.

---

*In a Roman pool, Esther swam underwater around chalky male statues that came to life, and she later swam through underwater canyons with vengeful warriors in hot pursuit. Her singing voice in this film was dubbed by Jo Ann Greer.

**The standing Esther Williams pool set was covered over for Lana Turner's *The Prodigal* (1955), where it became the basis for the love goddess' temple.

†Esther provided a rather peculiar and too candid appearance on the Murrow outing. She completely ignored Murrow's repeated requests to see the family swimming pool (she instead insisted upon showing the custom-built laundry room), and in a moment of pique called for the governess to carry away baby Susan who had begun babbling oncamera while mother was talking. Husband Ben Gage "apologized" oncamera: "Esther hates to be interrupted when she begins to talk."

In a promotional pose with columnist Vernon Scott in Hollywood (June 1956).

With John Saxon in *The Unguarded Moment* ('56).

In *Raw Wind in Eden* ('58).

Esther next signed an exclusive pact with NBC-TV for a dramatic role on "Lux Video Theatre" in the episode *The Armed Venus*. It was telecast on May 23, 1957.

Later in 1957 she went to Tuscany to star for director Richard Wilson and Universal-International in *Raw Wind in Eden* (1958). Her co-star was Jeff Chandler with whom she became romantically involved. (Chandler was then in the process of obtaining a divorce from Marjorie Hoshelle Chandler, his wife of eleven years.)

On her return to California, Esther told interviewer Art Buchwald of the *Beverly Hills Citizen*, "For the last two years I've been independent, and I assure you I'm far happier. Every time I wanted to do something different at MGM they would pat me on the head and tell me to get back to the pool." In November 1957 she became even more independent when she separated from Ben Gage. (This was their third recorded separation during a twelve-month period.) When Gage moved out of their home, Esther told the press, "We are hoping this is not the end of our marriage, but it is very important while we are trying to solve our trouble not to have these arguments and discussions under the same roof with the children." Esther obtained an interlocutory divorce decree on March 8, 1958, and became Jeff Chandler's great and best friend.

According to *Variety, Raw Wind in Eden* was "seldom exciting or even convincing." It was an inauspicious return to the screen after two years, as Esther on film plays a fashion model who sashays between Chandler and Carlos Thompson, the pair of international playboys who vie for her attentions. With Thompson, she is forced by weather conditions to land on a remote Italian island where Chandler is the master of all he surveys. Esther donned a bathing suit for a pointless scene where she swam off the island shoreline.

Her final divorce decree was issued in a Santa Monica courtroom on Monday, April 20, 1959. Esther insisted that Gage's late hours made her nervous and disrupted her life as a mother. The divorce was granted on a charge of mental cruelty. Esther received custody of the couple's three children, their home at 2077 Mandeville Canyon Road in West Los Angeles, and one dollar a month alimony payments.*

Her second television special was aired in color over NBC-TV on August 8, 1960, as *Esther Williams at Cypress Gardens*. Described by her before showtime as a "wet book musical," the hour-long show featured her as a movie celebrity in Cypress Gardens to film a video special. During rehearsals she is informed by her press agent (Joey Bishop)

---

*Gage would die on April 28, 1978, in Los Angeles at the age of sixty-three.

With Carlos Thompson in *Raw Wind in Eden*.

that the Prince of Persia (Fernando Lamas) and his harem have arrived. Naturally the prince gets in her way and vice versa. At a cost of some $500,000 a "wet sound stage" was constructed for Esther's swim scenes. The pool measured 165 by 80 feet and contained 870,000 gallons of warm water.

During 1960 Esther was a member of President Eisenhower's Council on Youth Fitness and continued to devote time to the Visually Handicapped Children's Hospital. After her Cypress Gardens show, it was rumored that she and Jeff Chandler, her "boyfriend of three years," had parted ways. Further gossip romantically linked her with Fernando Lamas, but no one took the pairing too seriously until Lamas was divorced by Arlene Dahl in August 1960 on the customary Hollywood grounds of "mental cruelty." Louella Parsons reported, "Whether this romance will continue no one can say, but as this is being written, the Latin lover seems to have fallen hard for the Movie Mermaid."

Esther once again journeyed to Europe for the making of a film—this time to Munich, Germany. The picture was Twentieth Century-Fox's *The Big Show* (1961), a third version of the Jerome Weidman novel *I'll Never Go There Anymore*. (In 1949 it was called *House of Strangers* with Susan Hayward; in 1954 it reappeared as the Western *Broken Lance* with Jean Peters.) The best element of the new version was the CinemaScope, color filming by Otto Heller who captured the ambiance of The Krone Circus of Germany. The plot, on the other hand, is very heavy-handed. Esther is Hillary Allen, a wealthy American who enters the lives of the Everard circus family. She falls in love with Josef Everard (Cliff Robertson), but he is under the domination of his aging father (Nehemiah Persoff). In the course of the melodrama Esther was permitted one swim scene

With Cliff Robertson in *The Big Show* ('61).

at a Scandinavian resort pool. Her role, although it afforded her top-billing, was actually secondary to the storyline. The *New York Times* labeled Esther "starry-eyed," while *Variety* merely referred to her as "decorative."

Fernando Lamas trekked to Europe to visit Esther on and off the set of *The Big Show*. The pair lingered on the continent where he directed and co-starred with Esther in *La Fuente Magica (The Magic Fountain)* (1961). In the Spanish-made film which has not seen U.S. distribution, she is an American on tour in Spain where she meets a wealthy Spaniard (Lamas). They are brought together in love when a village fountain which had been dry for years suddenly spurts to life. It is an omen considered to be auspicious for lovers.

That undistinguished film brought to a conclusion (to date) the movie career of Esther Williams, the one-time MGM superstar whose twenty-two features for that studio had grossed a reported $90 million. Throughout her film career at MGM she appeared in more color productions than any other major contract player. (Of her twenty-five feature releases, only three were in black and white.)

It was reported that Esther intended to star in a television series, beginning in September 1961, but those plans never materialized.

Items about Esther and her family continued to make news in spite of her self-enforced retirement. On November 29, 1964, her sister June was killed in a freeway accident near Yucca Valley, California; in 1966 her sixteen-year-old son Benjie was the number one freestyle swimmer at Santa Monica High School, while that same year her son Kimball (6'7") underwent five surgery sessions at Santa Monica Hospital after his legs were fractured in seventeen places in a motorcycle accident.

In 1967 Esther (whose weight had been fluctuating over the recent years) and Fernando Lamas went to Fort Lauderdale, Florida, where she was inducted into the Swimming Hall of Fame.

Rumors persisted about the status of the Williams-Lamas relationship. Some writers

The aquatic star in December 1962.

declared that they had been married in Rome as early as February 27, 1963. On February 11, 1969, columnist Earl Wilson revealed, "Esther Williams and long-time friend Fernando Lamas report they got married a week ago," but this has not been substantiated. Other sources insist they were secretly and officially joined in matrimony on December 31, 1969, at the Founders' Church of Religious Science in Hollywood.

On December 29, 1971, Esther's mother died at Capistrano Beach, California. As for Esther, she seemed content to "sit in my Santa Monica home watching my kids grow up," but she did a Kellogg cereal TV commercial in 1972 with a swimming pool as a prop. During the next two years she gained considerable weight, and on December 26, 1974, she made the nation's newspapers when she was arrested by the California Highway Patrol for speeding while intoxicated on the Ventura Freeway in southern California. Lamas bailed her out of jail by paying the state-required $300 fine.

In August 1975 Helen Ives (Burl Ives' ex-wife), the owner of the Australian television rights to "This Is Your Life," asked Esther to appear as a guest (along with Walter Pidgeon) when the show honored Annette Kellerman. The two ex-MGM players did so.

When *That's Entertainment, Part I* (1974) and *Part II* (1976) were released, many onetime MGM stars were recruited for national and international publicity junkets to promote the films. Esther was not part of the contingent. Some insisted that she had never forgiven MGM for their curt dismissal of her; others suggested that her untrim figure was the central reason for her nonparticipation. At any event, Esther became further annoyed with her onetime employer and in September 1976 sued MGM for $1 million in breach of contract and invasion of privacy damages. As detailed in *The Hollywood Reporter:* "She said sequences from her Forties and Fifties films were used in the musical documentaries without her consent and in violation of a 1951 agreement.

"That agreement, modified in 1955, gave MGM exclusive rights to all proceeds from the showing of the movies, including *Million Dollar Mermaid, Dangerous When Wet, Pagan Love Song,* and *Bathing Beauty* among others.

"But Williams contended in her superior court suit that the fact does not allow the studios to use sequences of her films in an entirely different picture without consulting her or sharing the profits of its release. She said *That's Entertainment* and its sequel were 'unwarranted exploitations' of her and 'an invasion of privacy.'"

Evidently the opponents made their peace out of court, because the clips remained in the compilation features.

In the late Seventies, Esther's public appearances, such as attending a 1978 televised tribute to Elizabeth Taylor, have all been made in conjunction with spouse Fernando Lamas. She remains firm on the subject of retirement. "I am very happy and will not change my present life for all the movie glory in the world," she insisted to the *National Enquirer*'s Henry Gris. "People repeatedly ask me if I don't miss the movies. The truth of the matter is that I never get bored." As she answered one Hollywood columnist who queried her about the possibility of a return to show business, "No. I've had that splash."

According to Lamas, Esther told him when they were wed, "I am going to quit because if we are going to be together, you are the kind of man who needs his woman there." Lamas insists that Williams refuses these days to give any TV interviews because if she did one, she would have to do them all.

According to Gris of the *Enquirer,* Esther still has a sense of humor. Regarding the fans who still recognize her, Williams explains, "When they look at me inquisitively, I pull out this little card and hand it to them. And we have a good laugh." The card is light blue, and contains the printed words (above a sketch of ocean waves), "Yes, I Still Swim!"

FILMOGRAPHY

ANDY HARDY'S DOUBLE LIFE (*MGM, 1942*) 92 min.

Director, George B. Seitz; based on characters created by Aurania Rouverol; screenplay, Agnes Christine Johnston; music, Daniele Amfitheatrof; art director, Cedric Gibbons; camera, George Folsey, John Mescall; editor, Gene Ruggiero.

Mickey Rooney (Andrew Hardy); Lewis Stone (Judge James Hardy); Fay Holden (Mrs. Emily Hardy); Cecilia Parker (Marion Hardy); Ann Rutherford (Polly Benedict); Sara Haden (Aunt Milly); Esther Williams (Sheila Brooks); William Lundigan (Jeff Willis); Susan Peters (Wainwright College Girl); Robert Pittard (Botsy); Arthur Space (Stedman's Lawyer); Howard Hickman (Lincoln's Lawyer); Mary Currier (Mrs. Stedman); Erville Alderson (Bailiff); Mickey Martin (Bud); John Walsh (Harry); Charles Peck (Jack); Frank Chalfant (Kirk); Frank Coghlan, Jr. (Red); David McKim (Nelson); Mantan Moreland (Prentiss); Bobby Blake (Tooky); Addison Richards (George Benedict); Roger Moore (Court Clerk); Robert Emmett O'Connor (Conductor).

A GUY NAMED JOE (*MGM, 1943*) 118 min.

Producer, Everett Riskin; director, Victor Fleming; story, Chandler Sprague, David Boehm; adaptor, Frederick Hazlitt Brennan; screenplay, Dalton Trumbo; music, Herbert Stothart; art directors, Cedric Gibbons, Lyle Wheeler; set decorators, Edwin B. Willis, Ralph Hurst; assistant director, Horace Hough; sound, Charles E. Wallace; special effects, Arnold Gillespie, Donald Jahraus, Warren Newcombe; camera, George Folsey, Karl Freund; editor, Frank Sullivan.

Spencer Tracy (Pete Sandidge); Irene Dunne (Dorinda Durston); Van Johnson (Ted Randall); Ward Bond (Al Yackey); James Gleason ("Nails" Kilpatrick); Lionel Barrymore (The General); Barry Nelson (Dick Rumney); Don DeFore ("Powerhouse" O'Rourke); Henry O'Neill (Colonel Hendricks); Addison Richards (Major Corbett); Charles Smith (Sanderson); Mary Elliott (Dancehall Girl); Earl Schenck (Colonel Sykes); Bill Arthur, John Bogden, Harold S. Landon (Cadets); Elizabeth Valentine (Washerwoman's Child); Arthur Stenning, George Kirby (Fishermen); Maurice Murphy (Captain Robertson); William Bishop (Ray); Esther Williams (Ellen Bright); Gibson Gowland (Bartender); Mary McLeod, Aileen Haley (Hostesses); Oliver Cross (American Major); Wyndham Standing (English Colonel); Violet Seton (Bartender's Wife); Kirk Alyn (Officer Flyer in Heaven); Frank Faylen, Phil Van Zandt (Majors); Blake Edwards, Marshall Reed, Robert Lowell, Michael Owen, Stephen Barclay, Neyle Morrow (Flyers); Charles King III (Radio Operator); Jacqueline White (Helen); Arthur Space (San Francisco Airport Captain).

BATHING BEAUTY (*MGM, 1944*) C-101 min.

Producer, Jack Cummings; director, George Sidney; based on the screen story "Mr. Co-Ed" by Kenneth Earl, M. M. Musselman, and Curtis Kenyon; screenplay, Dorothy Kingsley, Allen Boretz, Frank Waldman; Technicolor consultant, Natalie Kalmus; music supervisor/director, Johnny Green; orchestrators, Ted Duncan, Calvin Jackson, Johnny Thompson; choreography, Jack Donahue, Robert Alton; art directors, Stephen Goosson, Merrill Pye; set decorators, Edwin B. Willis, McLean Nisbet; water ballet staged by John Murray Anderson; songs, Green; assistant director, George Ryan; sound, Frank B. MacKenzie, Ralph A. Shugart, William R. Edmondson; camera, Harry Stradling; editor, Blanche Sewell.

Red Skelton (Steve Elliott); Esther Williams (Caroline Brooks); Basil Rathbone (George Adams); Jean Porter (Jean Allenwood); Jacqueline Dalya (Maria Dorango); Bill Goodwin (Willis Evans); Donald Meek (Chester Klazenfrantz); Nana Bryant (Dean Clinton); Harry James (Harry); Buddy Moreno (Buddy); Helen Forrest (Helen); Carlos Ramirez (Specialty); Ethel Smith (Organist); Harry James' Music Makers, Xavier Cugat and His Orchestra with Lina Romay (Themselves); William Hayden (Bit); Sarah Edwards (Miss Phillips); Almira Sessions (Miss Kern); Elspeth Dudgeon (Miss Travers); Ann Codee (Mme. Zarka, the Ballet Teacher); Francis Pierlot (Professor Hendricks); Earl Schenck (Professor Nichols); Dorothy Adams (Miss Hanney); Shelby Payne (Cigarette Girl); Margaret Dumont (Mrs. Allenwood); Russell Hicks (Mr. Allenwood); Joe Yule (Bartender); Mary Ann Hawkins (Specialty Swimmer); Bertha Priestley (Fat Girl); Janis Paige (Janis); Noreen Nash (Noreen); Dorothy Ford (Dorothy); Vicky Lane, Margaret Adams, Margaret Adden, Katharine Book, Beverly Tyler, Ann Lundeen, Beryl McCutcheon, Gloria Lake, Betty Jaynes, Mary Perine (Coeds); Mildred Riley, Aina Constant, Sarah Wallace (Showgirls); Fidel Castro (Bit).

THRILL OF A ROMANCE (*MGM, 1945*) C-105 min.

Producer, Joe Pasternak; director, Richard Thorpe; screenplay, Richard Connell, Gladys Lehman; Technicolor consultants, Natalie Kalmus, Henri Jaffa; art directors, Cedric Gibbons, Hans Peters; set decorators, Edwin B. Willis, Jack Bonar; music/music director, Georgie Stoll; orchestrators, Calvin Jackson, Ted Duncan, Joseph Nussbaum, Hugo Winterhalter, Fred Norman; songs, Ralph Freed and Sammy Fain; Sammy Cahn, Alex Stordahl, and Paul Weston; Stoll and Richard Connell; Stoll, Ralph Blane, and Kay Thompson; Jack Meskill and Earl Brent; assistant director, Marvin Stuart; sound, Joe Edmondson; camera, Harry Stradling; editor, George Boemler.

Esther Williams (Cynthia Glenn); Van Johnson (Major Thomas Milvaine); Frances Gifford (Maude Bancroft); Henry Travers (Robert Glenn); Spring Byington (Nona Glenn); Lauritz Melchior (Mr. Nils Knudsen); Tommy Dorsey (Orchestra Leader); Carleton G. Young (Robert G. Delbar); Helene Stanley (Susan); Donald Curtis (K. I. Karny); Jerry Scott (Lyonel); Billy House (Dr. Tove); Ethel Griffies (Mrs. Fenway); Vince Barnett (Oscar); Fernando Alvarado (Julio); Joan Fay Macoboy (Betty); Carli Elinor (Gypsy Orchestra Leader); Thurston Hall (J. P. Bancroft); King Sisters (Specialty); Stuart Holmes, Alex Novinsky (Chess Players); Art Buehler (Chauffeur); Arno Frey (Headwaiter); Jack Baxley (Detective); Virginia Brissac (Secretary); Dick Earle (Mr. Carker); Pierre Watkin (Stout Tycoon); Henry Daniels, Jr., Douglas Cowan, Fulton Burley, Wally Boag, Phil Hanna, Joe Sullivan (Canadian Flyers); Ray Goulding (Dance Extra); Jack Shea (Donald Curtis' Diving Double); Ruth Nurmi (Esther Williams' Diving Double); Tony Coppalla (Waiter); Selmer Jackson (Hotel Clerk); Robert Emmett O'Connor (Mr. Vemmering); Jean Porter (Brick).

THE ZIEGFELD FOLLIES *(MGM, 1946)* C-110 min.

Producer, Arthur Freed; director, Vincente Minnelli (uncredited: George Sidney, Norman Taurog, Merrill Pye); screenplay, E. Y. Harburg, Jack McGowan, Guy Bolton, Frank Sullivan, John Murray Anderson, Lemuel Ayers, Don Loper, Kay Thompson, Roger Edens, Hugh Martin, Ralph Blane, William Noble, Wilkie Mahoney, Cal Howard, Erick Charell, Max Liebman, Bill Schorr, Harry Crane, Lou Holtz, Eddie Cantor, Allen Boretz, Edgar Allan Woolf, Phil Rapp, Al Lewis, Joseph Schrank, Robert Alton, Eugene Loring, Robert Lewis, Charles Walters, James O'Hanlon, David Freedman, Joseph Erons, Irving Brecher, Samson Raphaelson, Everett and Devery Freeman; choreography, Robert Alton; songs, George and Ira Gershwin; Harry Warren and Freed; Roger Edens and Kay Thompson; Edens, Hugh Martin, and Blane; music director, Lennie Hayton; orchestrators, Conrad Salinger, Wally Heglin; vocal arranger, Thompson; Technicolor consultants, Natalie Kalmus, Henri Jaffa; art directors, Cedric Gibbons, Jack Martin Smith, Merrill Pye, Lemuel Ayers; set decorators, Edwin B. Willis, Mac Alper; puppet costumes, Florence Bunin; costume supervisor, Irene; costume designers, Irene, Helen Rose; makeup, Jack Dawn; sound, Douglas Shearer; camera, George Folsey, Charles Rosher; puppetoon sequence camera, William Ferrari; editor, Albert Akst.

William Powell (Florenz Ziegfeld); *Here's to the Ladies*: Fred Astaire, Lucille Ball, Cyd Charisse; *A Water Ballet*: Esther Williams; *Number, Please*: Keenan Wynn; Kay Williams (On Phone); Peter Lawford (Phone Voice); Audrey Totter (Voice of Telephone Operator); *Traviata*: James Melton, Marion Bell; *Pay the Two Dollars*: Victor Moore, Edward Arnold (Themselves); Ray Teal (Special Officer); Joseph Crehan (Judge); William B. Davidson (Presiding Judge); Eddie Dunn, Garry Owens (Officers); Harry Hayden (Warden); *This Heart of Mine*: Fred Astaire (The Impostor); Lucille Bremer (The Princess); Count Stefenelli (The Duke); Naomi Childers (The Duchess); Helen Boice (The Countess); Charles Coleman (The Major); Robert Wayne (Retired Dyspeptic); Feodor Chaliapin (Lieutenant); Sam Flint (The Flunky); Shirlee Howard, Natalie Draper, Noreen Roth [Nash], Dorothy Van Nuys, Katherine [Karin] Booth, Lucille Casey, Eve Whitney, Elaine Shepard, Frances Donelan, Helen O'Hara, Aina Constant, Aileen Haley (Showgirls); *A Sweepstakes Ticket*: Fanny Brice (Norma); Hume Cronyn (Monty); William Frawley (Martin); Arthur Walsh (Telegraph Boy); *Love*: Lena Horne; *When Television Comes*: Red Skelton; *Limehouse Blues*: Fred Astaire (Tai Long); Lucille Bremer (Moy Ling); Robert Lewis (Chinese Gentleman); Charles Lunard, Robert Ames, Jack Regas, Sidney Gordon (Four Men with Masks); Cyd Charisse (Chicken); James King (Rooster); Eugene Loring (Costermonger); Harriet Lee (Singer in Dive); *A Great Lady Has an Interview*: Judy Garland (The Star); Rex Evans (The Butler); *The Babbitt and the Bromide*: Fred Astaire, Gene Kelly; *Beauty*: Kathryn Grayson, the Ziegfeld Girls.

THE HOODLUM SAINT *(MGM, 1946)* 93 min.

Producer, Cliff Reid; director, Norman Taurog; screenplay, Frank Wead, James Hill; art directors, Cedric Gibbons, Harry McAffee; set decorator, Edwin B. Willis; assistant director, Horace Hough; music, Nathaniel Shilkret; sound, Douglas Shearer; special effects, Warren Newcombe; camera, Ray June; editor, Ferris Webster.

William Powell (Terry Ellerton O'Neill); Esther Williams (Kay Lorrison); Angela Lansbury (Dusty Millard); James Gleason (Snarp); Lewis Stone (Father Nolan); Rags Ragland (Fishface); Frank McHugh (Three-Fingers); Slim Summerville (Eel); Roman Bohnen (Father O'Doul); Charles Arnt (Cy Nolan); Louis Jean Heydt (Mike Flaherty); Charles Trowbridge (Uncle Joe Lorrison); Henry O'Neill (Lewis J. Malbery); Matt Moore (Father Duffy); Trevor Bardette (Rabbi Meyerberg); Addison Richards (Reverend Miller); Tom Dugan (Bugsy); Emma Dunn (Maggie); Mary Gordon (Trina); Ernest Anderson (Sam); Charles D. Brown (Ed Collner); Paul Langton (Burton Kinston); Al Murphy (Benny); Jack Davis, Garry Owen (Cops); Byron Foulger (J. Cornwall Travers); Will Wright (Allan Smith); Mary Lord (Mary); Sam Finn, William Janssen, Harry Tenbrook, Sol Davis, Phil Friedman, John George, Captain Fred Somers, Billy Engle, Al Thompson, Heinie Conklin (Mugs); Aileen Haley, Alice Wallace, Marilyn Kinsley, Beryl McCutcheon, Frances Donelan (Bridesmaids); Jean Thorsen, Lucille Casey, Mary Jane French, Ethel Tobin (Second Group of Bridesmaids); Connie Weiler, Peggy O'Neill (Cigarette Girls); Tom Dillon, Chester Conklin (Cops); Robert Emmett O'Connor (Conductor); Fred "Snowflake" Toone (Pullman Porter); Sarah Edwards, Betty Blythe (Women); Russell Hicks (Marty Martindale); Forbes Murray (Prosperous Man); Harry Hayden (Mr. Samuels); Katherine [Karin] Booth (Bride); Tim Murdock (Groom).

EASY TO WED *(MGM, 1946)* C-110 min.

Producer, Jack Cummings; director, Edward Buzzell; based on the screenplay *Libeled Lady* by Maurine Watkins, Howard Emmett Rogers, and George Oppenheimer; adaptor, Dorothy Kingsley; Technicolor consultants, Natalie Kalmus, Henri Jaffa; art directors, Cedric Gibbons, Hans Peters; set decorators, Edwin B. Willis, Jack Bonar; choreography, Jack Donahue; music, Johnny Green; orchestrator, Ted Duncan; songs, Ted Duncan and Green; Robert Franklin and Green; Ralph Blane and Green; Osvaldo Farres; assistant director, Herman Webber; sound, Douglas Shearer; camera, Harry Stradling; editor, Blanche Sewell.

Van Johnson (Bill Chandler); Esther Williams (Connie Allenbury); Lucille Ball (Gladys Benton); Keenan Wynn (Warren Haggerty); Cecil Kellaway (J. B. Allenbury); Carlos Ramirez (Carlos); Ben Blue (Spike Dolan); Ethel Smith (Ethel); June Lockhart (Babs Norvell); Grant Mitchell (Homer Henshaw); Josephine Whittell (Mrs. Burns Norvell); Jean Porter (Frances); Paul Harvey (Farwood); Jonathan Hale (Boswell); James Flavin (Joe); Colin Travers (Sherwood's Secretary); Robert Emmett O'Connor (Taxi Driver); Sybil Merritt (Receptionist); Katherine [Karin] Booth (Clerk); Dick Winslow (Orchestra Leader); George Calliga (Headwaiter); Tom Dugan (Waiter); Chavo de Leon, Nina Bara (Rumba Dancers); Mitzie Uehlein, Mildred Sellers, Phyllis Graffeo, Kanza Omar, Louise Burnette, Patricia Denise (Girls at Pool); Charles Knight, Guy Bates Post, John Valentine (Butlers); Walter Soderling, Sarah Edwards (Mr. and Mrs. Dibson).

FIESTA *(MGM, 1947)* C-104 min.

Producer, Jack Cummings; director, Richard Thorpe; screenplay, George Bruce, Lester Cole; Technicolor consultants, Natalie Kalmus, Henri Jaffa; art directors, Cedric Gibbons, William Ferrari; set decorators, Edwin B. Willis, Thomas Theuerkauf; assistant director, Al Jennings; music, Johnny Green; original suite, Aaron Copeland; additional orchestrations, Ted Duncan; choreography, Eugene Loring; sound, Douglas Shearer; camera, Sidney Wagner, Charles Rosher, Wilfrid M. Cline; editor, Blanche Sewell.

Esther Williams (Maria Morales); Akim Tamiroff (Chato Vasquez); Ricardo Montalban (Mario Morales); John Carroll (Jose "Pepe" Ortega); Mary Astor (Senora Morales); Cyd Charisse (Conchita); Fortunio Bonanova (Antonio Morales); Hugo Haas (Maximino Contreras); Jean Van (Maria Morales as a Child); Joey Preston (Mario Morales as a Child); Frank Puglia (Doctor); Los Bocheros (The Basque Singers); Alan Napier (Middle-Aged American); Alex Montoya (Vaquero); Rosa Rey (Housekeeper); Nacho Galindo (Proprietor); Robert Emmett O'Connor (Bus Driver); Soledad Jimenez (Nurse); Rudy Rama (Photographer); Jose Portugal (Reporter); Ben Welden, Dewey Robinson (Cops).

THIS TIME FOR KEEPS *(MGM, 1947)* C-105 min.

Producer, Joe Pasternak; director, Richard Thorpe; story, Erwin Gelsey, Lorraine Fielding; screenplay, Gladys Lehman; art directors, Cedric Gibbons, Randall Duell; set decorators, Edwin B. Willis, Henry W. Grace; Technicolor consultants, Natalie Kalmus, Henri Jaffa; choreography, Stanley Donen; music director, Georgie Stoll; songs, Ralph Freed and Sammy Fain; Jimmy Durante; Benny Davis and Harry Akst; Freed and Burton Lane; Leslie Kirk; assistant director, Al Jennings; special effects, A. Arnold Gillespie; camera, Karl Freund; editor, John Dunning.

Esther Williams (Nora Cambaretti); Lauritz

Melchior (Hans Herald); Jimmy Durante (Ferdi Farro); Johnny Johnston (Dick Johnson); Xavier Cugat (Himself); Dame May Whitty (Grandma); Sharon McManus (Deborah); Richard Simmons (Gordon Coome); Mary Stuart (Frances); Ludwig Stossel (Peter); Nella Walker (Mrs. Allenbury); William Tannen, Robert Strickland, Kenneth Tobey, Don Garner (Soldiers); Herbert Heywood (Doorman); Holmes Herbert (Norman); Nan Bennett (Luci LeRoy); Esther Dale (Mrs. Fields); Duncan Richardson (Duncan); Chris Drake (Soldier at Pool); Anne Francis, Richard Terry (Bobby-Soxers); Dorothy Porter (Singer with Cugat's Maid); Harry Tyler (Bartender).

ON AN ISLAND WITH YOU *(MGM, 1948)* C-107 min.

Producer, Joe Pasternak; director, Richard Thorpe; story, Charles Martin, Hans Wilhelm; screenplay, Dorothy Kingsley, Dorothy Cooper, Martin, Wilhelm; Technicolor consultants, Natalie Kalmus, Henri Jaffa; art directors, Cedric Gibbons, Edward Carfagno; set decorators, Edwin B. Willis, Richard A. Pefferie; music director, Georgie Stoll; songs, Nacio Herb Brown and Edward Heyman; choreography, Jack Donahue; assistant director, Al Jennings; makeup, Jack Dawn; costumes, Irene; sound, Douglas Shearer, James K. Brock; special effects, Arnold Gillespie; camera, Charles Rosher; editors, Douglas Biggs, Ferris Webster.

Esther Williams (Rosalind Reynolds); Peter Lawford (Lieutenant Lawrence Y. Kingslee); Ricardo Montalban (Ricardo Montez); Jimmy Durante (Buckley); Cyd Charisse (Yvonne Torro); Xavier Cugat (Himself); Leon Ames (Commander Harrison); Kathryn Beaumont (Penelope Peabody); Dick Simmons (George Blaine); Marie Windsor (Jane); Arthur Walsh (Second Assistant Director); Nina Ross (Mrs. Peabody); Betty Reilly (Vocalist); Kay Norton (Martha, the Hairdresser); Nolan Leary (Cameraman); Chester Clute (Tommy, the Waiter); Carl Leviness (Desk Clerk); Cosmo Sardo (Barber); Dick Winslow (Bald Radio Operator); Jimmy Dale (Navigator); Sam Tubuo (Native Chief); Lester Dorr (Photographer); Franklin Parker (Lieutenant—Technical Advisor); Emelia Leovalli (Grandmother); Uluao Letuli (Sword Dancer).

TAKE ME OUT TO THE BALL GAME *(MGM, 1949)* C-93 min. (British release title: *Everybody's Cheering*)

Producer, Arthur Freed; associate producer, Roger Edens; director, Busby Berkeley; story, Gene Kelly, Stanley Donen; screenplay, Harry Tugend, George Wells, (uncredited) Harry Crane; songs, Betty Comden, Adolph Green, and Edens; vocal arranger, Robert Tucker; music director, Adolph Deutsch; music numbers staged by Kelly and Donen; Technicolor consultants, Natalie Kalmus, James Gooch; art directors, Cedric Gibbons, Daniel B. Cathcart; set decorators, Edwin B. Willis, Henry W. Grace; women's costumes, Helen Rose; men's costumes, Valles; makeup, Jack Dawn; sound, Douglas Shearer; special effects, Warren Newcombe; montage, Peter Ballbusch; camera, George Folsey; editor, Blanche Sewell.

Frank Sinatra (Dennis Ryan); Esther Williams (K. C. Higgins); Gene Kelly (Eddie O'Brien); Betty Garrett (Shirley Delwyn); Edward Arnold (Joe Lorgan); Jules Munshin (Nat Goldberg); Richard Lane (Michael Gilhuly); Tom Dugan (Slappy Burke); Murray Alper (Zalinka); Wilton Graff (Nick Donford); Mack Gray, Charles Regan (Henchmen); Saul Gorss (Steve); Douglas Fowley (Karl); Eddie Parkes (Dr. Winston); James Burke (Cop in Park); The Blackburn Twins (Specialty); Gordon Jones (Senator Catcher); Jack Bruce, John "Red" Burger, Aaron Phillips, Edward Cutler, Ellsworth Blake, Harry Allen, Joseph Roach, Hubert Kerns, Pete Kooy, Robert Simpson, Richard Landry, Jack Boyle, Richard Beavers (Wolves' Team); Virginia Bates, Joi Lansing (Girls on Train); Mitchell Lewis (Fisherman); Esther Michaelson (Fisherman's Wife); Almira Sessions, Isabel O'Madigan, Gil Perkins, Robert Stephenson, Charles Sullivan, Edna Harris (Fans).

NEPTUNE'S DAUGHTER *(MGM, 1949)* C-93 min.

Producer, Jack Cummings; director, Edward Buzzell; screenplay, Dorothy Kingsley; additional dialogue, Ray Singer, Dick Chevillat; Technicolor consultants, Natalie Kalmus, Henri Jaffa; art directors, Cedric Gibbons, Edward Carfagno; set decorators, Edwin B. Willis, Arthur Krams; songs, Frank Loesser; orchestrator, Leo Arnaud; music director, Georgie Stoll; choreography, Jack Donahue; makeup, Jack Dawn; costumes, Irene; sound, Douglas Shearer, Ralph Pender; camera, Charles Rosher; editor, Irvine Warburton.

Esther Williams (Eve Barrett); Red Skelton (Jack Spratt); Ricardo Montalban (Jose O'Rourke); Betty Garrett (Betty Barrett); Keenan Wynn (Joe Beckett); Xavier Cugat (Himself); Ted de Corsia (Lukie Luzette); Mike Mazurki (Mac Mazolla); Mel Blanc (Julio); Juan Duval (Groom); George Mann (Tall Wrangler); Frank Mitchell (Little Wrangler); William Lewin (Official); Harold S. Kruger (Coach); Joi Lansing (Linda); Danilo Valente (South American Player); Theresa Harris (Matilda); Bette Arlen,

Jonnie Pierce, Dorothy Abbott, Sue Casey, Diane Gump, Jackie Hammette (Models); Roque Ybarra, Heinie Conklin (Grooms); Pierre Watkin (Mr. Canford); Clarence Hennecke (Gardner).

DUCHESS OF IDAHO (MGM, 1950) C-98 min.

Producer, Joe Pasternak; director, Robert Z. Leonard; story/screenplay, Dorothy Cooper, Jerry Davis; art directors, Cedric Gibbons, Malcolm Brown; music director, Georgie Stoll; songs, Al Rinker and Floyd Huddlestone; G. M. Beilenson and M. Beelby; Lee Pearl and Henry Nemo; Kermit Goell and Fred Spielman; camera, Charles Schoenbaum; editor, Adrienne Fazan.

Esther Williams (Christine Riverton Duncan); Van Johnson (Dick Layne); John Lund (Douglas J. Morrisson); Paula Raymond (Ellen Hallet); Clinton Sundberg (Matson); Connie Haines (Peggy Elliott); Mel Torme (Cyril); Amanda Blake (Linda Kinston); Tommy Farrell (Chuck); Sig Arno (Monsieur Le Blanche); Dick Simmons (Alex I. Collins); Charles Smith (Johnny); John Louis Johnson (Pullman Porter); Red Skelton (Guest Master of Ceremonies); Eleanor Powell, Lena Horne (Themselves); Roger Moore (Escort); Bunny Waters (Marsha); Dorothy Douglas (Eleanor); Mae Clarke (Betty, the Flower Girl); Johnny Trebach (Waiter); Suzanne Ridgeway (Cleo); Larry Steers, Harold Miller (Men at Table); Allen Ray (Elevator Man).

PAGAN LOVE SONG (MGM, 1950) C-76 min.

Producer, Arthur Freed; director, Robert Alton; based on the novel *Tahiti Landfall* by William S. Stone; screenplay, Robert Nathan, Jerry Davis, (uncredited) Ivan Tors; technical advisor, Stone; songs, Harry Warren and Freed; music director, Adolph Deutsch; vocal arranger, Robert Tucker; orchestrator, Conrad Salinger; Technicolor consultants, Henri Jaffa, James Gooch; art directors, Cedric Gibbons, Randall Duell; set decorators, Edwin B. Willis, Jack D. Moore; costumes, Helen Rose; makeup, William Tuttle; sound, Douglas Shearer; special effects, A. Arnold Gillespie, Warren Newcombe; camera, Charles Rosher; editor, Adrienne Fazan.

Esther Williams (Mimi Bennett); Howard Keel (Hazard Endicott); Minna Gombell (Kate Bennett); Charles Mauu (Tavae); Rita Moreno (Teuru); Philip Costa (Manu); Dione Leillani (Tani); Charles Freund (Papera); Marcelle Corday (Countess Marianai); Sam Maikai (Tua); Helen Rapoza (Angela); Birdie DeBolt (Mama Ruau); Bill Kaliloa (Mara); Carlo Cook (Monsieur Bouchet).

TEXAS CARNIVAL (MGM, 1951) C-77 min.

Producer, Jack Cummings; director, Charles Walters; story, George Wells, Dorothy Kingsley; screenplay, Kingsley; music director, David Rose; songs, Dorothy Fields and Harry Warren; David Rose and Earl K. Brent; choreography, Hermes Pan; art directors, Cedric Gibbons, William Ferrari; camera, Robert Planck; editor, Adrienne Fazan.

Esther Williams (Debbie Telford); Red Skelton (Cornie Quinell); Howard Keel (Slim Shelby); Paula Raymond (Marilla Sabinas); Ann Miller (Sunshine Jackson); Keenan Wynn (Dan Sabinas); Tom Tully (Sheriff Jackson); Glenn Strange (Tex Hodgkins); Dick Wessel, Donald MacBride (Pitchmen); Marjorie Wood (Mrs. Gaytes); Hans Conried (Hotel Clerk); Thurston Hall (Mr. Gaytes); Duke Johnson (Juggler); Foy Willing and His Orchestra (Themselves); Red Norvo Trio (Themselves); Michael Dugan (Card Player); Doug Carter (Cab Driver); Earle Hodgins (Doorman); Gil Patrick (Assistant Clerk); Rhea Mitchell (Dealer); Emmett Lynn (Cook); Bess Flowers, Jack Daley, Fred Santley (Bits in Lobby); Joe Roach, Manuel Petroff, Robert Fortier, William Lundy, Alex Goudovitch (Specialty Dancers).

CALLAWAY WENT THATAWAY (MGM, 1951) 81 min. (British release title: *The Star Said No*)

Producers/directors/story/screenplay, Norman Panama, Melvin Frank; art directors, Cedric Gibbons, Eddie Imazu; music, Marlin Skiles; camera, Ray June; editor, Cotton Warburton.

Fred MacMurray (Mike Frye); Dorothy McGuire (Deborah Patterson); Howard Keel (Stretch Barnes/Smoky Callaway); Jesse White (Georgie Markham); Fay Roope (Tom Lorrison); Natalie Schafer (Martha Lorrison); Douglas Kennedy (Drunk); Elisabeth Fraser (Marie); Johnny Indrisano (Johnny Tarranto); Stan Freberg (Marvin); Don Haggerty (Director); June Allyson, Clark Gable, Dick Powell, Elizabeth Taylor, Esther Williams (Guest Stars); Dorothy Andre (Girl); Kay Scott, Margie Liszt (Phone Girls); Glenn Strange (Black Norton); Mae Clarke (Mother); Hugh Beaumont (Mr. Adkins); Earle Hodgins (Doorman).

SKIRTS AHOY! (MGM, 1952) C-109 min.

Producer, Joe Pasternak; director, Sidney Lanfield; story/screenplay, Isobel Lennart; music director, Georgie Stoll; songs, Harry Warren and Ralph Blane; music numbers created and staged by Nick Castle; art directors, Cedric Gibbons, Daniel B. Cathcart; camera, William Mellor; editor, Cotton Warburton.

Esther Williams (Whitney Young); Joan Evans (Mary Kate Yarbrough); Vivian Blaine (Una Yancy); Barry Sullivan (Lieutenant Commander

Paul Elcott); Keefe Brasselle (Dick Hallson); Billy Eckstine (Himself); Dean Miller (Archie O'Conovan); Margalo Gillmore (Lieutenant Commander Stauton); The DeMarco Sisters (The William Sisters); Jeff Donnell (Lieutenant Giff); Thurston Hall (Thatcher Kinston); Russell Tongay (Little Boy); Kathy Tongay (Little Girl); Marimba Merrymakers (Specialty); Roy Roberts (Captain Graymont); Emmett Lynn (Plumber); Hayden Rorke (Doctor); Debbie Reynolds, Bobby Van (Guest Stars); Paul Harvey (Old Naval Officer); Ruth Lee (Mrs. Yarbrough); Whit Bissell (Mr. Yarbrough); Rudy Lee (Randy); Madge Blake (Mrs. Vance); Mae Clarke (Miss La Valle); Byron Foulger (Tea Room Manager); Juanita Moore, Millie Bruce, Suzette Harbin (Black Drill Team); Henny Backus (Nurse); Robert Board (Young Sailor); Mary Foran (Fat Girl); William Haade (Bosun's Mate).

MILLION DOLLAR MERMAID *(MGM, 1952)* C-115 min. (British release title: *The One-Piece Bathing Suit*)

Producer, Arthur Hornblow, Jr.; director, Mervyn LeRoy; screenplay, Everett Freeman; music director, Adolph Deutsch; orchestrator, Alexander Courage; production numbers staged by Busby Berkeley; underwater choreography, Audrene Brier; art director, Cedric Gibbons; set decorators, Edwin B. Willis, Richard Pefferle; camera, George J. Folsey; editor, John McSweeney, Jr.

Esther Williams (Annette Kellerman); Victor Mature (James Sullivan); Walter Pidgeon (Frederick Kellerman); David Brian (Alfred Harper); Donna Corcoran (Annette at Ten); Jesse White (Doc Cronnel); Maria Tallchief (Pavlova); Howard Freeman (Aldrich); Charles Watts (Policeman); Wilton Graff (Garvey); Frank Ferguson (Prosecutor); James Bell (Judge); James Flavin (Conductor); Willis Bouchey (Director); Adrienne D'Ambricourt (Marie, the Housekeeper); Charles Heard (Official); Clive Morgan (Judge); Queenie Leonard (Mrs. Graves); Stuart Torres (Son); Leslie Denison (Purser); Wilson Benge (Caretaker); Elisabeth Slifer (Soprano); Al Ferguson (London Bobby); Vernon Downing (Newspaper Man); Creighton Hale (Husband); George Wallace (Bud Williams); Tiny Kelly, Pat Flaherty (Cops); Paul Bradley (Defense Attorney); Louis Manley (Fire-eater); Edward Clark (Elderly Man); Gail Bonney (Woman).

DANGEROUS WHEN WET *(MGM, 1953)* C-95 min.

Producer, George Wells; director, Charles Walters; story/screenplay, Dorothy Kingsley; art directors, Cedric Gibbons, Jack Martin Smith; songs, Arthur Schwartz and Johnny Mercer; music numbers staged by Walters, Billy Daniel; montage, Peter Ballabusch; camera, Harold Rosson; editor, John McSweeney.

Esther Williams (Katy Higgins); Fernando Lamas (Andre Lanet); Jack Carson (Windy Webbe); Charlotte Greenwood (Ma Higgins); Denise Darcel (Gigi Mignon); William Demarest (Pa Higgins); Donna Corcoran ("Junior" Higgins); Barbara Whiting (Susie Higgins); Bunny Waters (Greta); Henri Letondal (Joubert); Paul Bryar (Pierre); Jack Raine (Stuart Frye); Richard Alexander (Egyptian Channel Swimmer); Tudor Owen (Old Salt); Ann Codee (Mrs. Lanet); Michael Dugan (Ad Lib); Roger Moore, Reginald Simpson (Reporters); John McKee (Photographer); Arthur Gould-Porter (English Steward); Aminta Dyne (English Woman Guest); James Fairfax (English Cab Driver); Molly Glessing (English Waitress); Eugene Borden (French Mayor); Pat O'Moore (Bob Gerrard); Jimmy Aubrey (Bartender).

EASY TO LOVE *(MGM, 1953)* C-96 min.

Producer, Joe Pasternak; director, Charles Walters; story, Laslo Vadnay; screenplay, Vadnay, William Roberts; art directors, Cedric Gibbons, Jack Martin Smith; musical numbers created and staged by Busby Berkeley; songs, Mann Curtis and Vic Mizzy; Cole Porter; Johnny Green; music directors, Lennie Hayton, Georgie Stoll; camera, Ray June; editor, Gene Ruggiero.

Esther Williams (Julie Hallerton); Van Johnson (Ray Lloyd); Tony Martin (Barry Gordon); John Bromfield (Hank); Edna Skinner (Nancy); King Donovan (Ben); Paul Bryar (Mr. Barnes); Carroll Baker (Clarice); Eddie Oliver (Bandleader); Benny Rubin (Oscar Levenson); Harriett Brest, Helen Dickson, Ann Luther, Maude Erickson, Peggy Remington, Violet Seton, Dorothy Vernon (Women Guests in Lobby); Edward Clark (Gardener); June Whitley (Costume Designer); Richard Downing Pope, Bud Gaines (Tourists); Byron Kane, Reginald Simpson (Photographers); Joe Mell (Sleepy Waiter); Hal Berns (Melvin, the Pianist); Margaret Bert (Mrs. Huffnagel); Emory Parnell (Mr. Huffnagel); David Newell (Makeup Man); Sondra Gould (Ben's Wife); Lillian Culver (Flora); Fenton Hamilton (Fat Man).

JUPITER'S DARLING *(MGM, 1955)* C-96 min.

Producer, George Wells; director, George Sidney; based on the play *The Road to Rome* by Robert E. Sherwood; screenplay, Dorothy Kingsley; art directors, Cedric Gibbons, Urie McCleary; music director, David Rose; songs, Burton Lane and Harold Adamson; choreography, Hermes Pan; costumes, Helen Rose, Walter Plunkett; assistant director, George Rheim; camera, Paul C.

Vogel, Charles Rosher; editor, Ralph E. Winters.

Esther Williams (Amytis); Howard Keel (Hannibal); Marge Champion (Meta); Gower Champion (Varius); George Sanders (Fabius Maximus); Richard Haydn (Horatio); William Demarest (Mago); Norma Varden (Fabia); Douglass Dumbrille (Scipio); Henry Corden (Carthalo); Michael Ansara (Maharbal); Martha Wentworth (Widow Titus); John Olszweski (Principal Swimming Statue); Chris Alcaide (Ballo); Tom Monroe (Outrider); Mort Mills, Gene Roth, Michael Dugan (Guards); Frank Radcliffe (Specialty); Bruno VeSota (Bystander); Paul Maxey (Lucullus); William Tannen (Roman Courier); Alberto Morin (Arrow Maker); Richard Hale (Auctioneer); Frank Jacquet (Senator); Paul Newland (Roman Captain); Jack Shea (Drunken Guard); Mitchell Kowal (Sentry).

THE UNGUARDED MOMENT (*Universal, 1956*) 95 min.

Producer, Gordon Kay; director, Harry Keller; based on the story "The Gentle Web" by Rosalind Russell and Larry Marcus; screenplay, Herb Meadow, Marcus; art directors, Alexander Golitzen, Alfred Sweeney; music director, Joseph Gershenson; music, Herman Stein; assistant directors, Joseph E. Kenny, Terry Nelson; camera, William Daniels; editor, Edward Curtiss.

Esther Williams (Lois Conway); George Nader (Harry Graham); Edward Andrews (Mr. Bennett); John Saxon (Leonard Bennett); Les Tremayne (Mr. Pendleton); Jack Albertson (Prof); Dani Crayne (Josie Warren); John Wilder (Sandy); Edward Platt (Attorney Briggs); Robert Williams (Detective); Eleanor Audley (Secretary).

RAW WIND IN EDEN (*Universal, 1958*) C-93 min.

Producer, William Alland; director, Richard Wilson; story, Dan Lundberg, Elizabeth Wilson; screenplay, the Wilsons; art directors, Alexander Golitzen, Alfred Ybarra; set decorator, Russell A. Gausman; music, Hans J. Salter; music supervisor, Joseph Gershenson; song, Jay Livingston and Ray Evans; makeup, Bud Westmore; assistant director, Terence Nelson; sound, Leslie I. Carey, Umberto Picistrelli; editor, Russell F. Schoengarth.

Esther Williams (Laura); Jeff Chandler [Mark Moore (Scott Moorehouse)]; Rossana Podesta (Costanza); Carlos Thompson (Wally Tucker); Rik Battaglia (Gavino); Eduardo de Filippo (Urbano).

THE BIG SHOW (*Twentieth Century-Fox, 1961*) C-113 min.

Producers, Ted Sherdeman, James B. Clark; director, Clark; screenplay, Sherdeman; music, Paul Sawtell and Bert Shefter; art director, Ludwig Reiber; makeup, Josef Coesfeld, Klara Kraft; assistant director, Herman Goebel; costumes, Teddy Turai-Rossi; sound, Walter Ruhland, Don McKay; camera, Otto Heller; editor, Benjamin Laird.

Esther Williams (Hillary Allen); Cliff Robertson (Josef Everard); Nehemiah Persoff (Bruno Everard); Robert Vaughn (Klaus Everard); Margia Dean (Carlotta Martinez); David Nelson (Eric Solden); Carol Christensen (Garda Everard); Kurt Pecher (Hans Everard); Renata Mannhardt (Teresa Vizzini); Franco Andrei (Fredrik Everard); Peter Capell (Vizzini); Stephen Schnabel (Lawyer); Carleton Young (Judge Richter); Philo Hauser (Ringmaster); Mariza Tomic (Frau Stein); Gerd Vespermann (Prosecutor); The Krone Circus (Themselves).

LA FUENTE MAGICA (*THE MAGIC FOUNTAIN*) (*Spanish, 1961*) C-90 min.

Director, Fernando Lamas.

With: Esther Williams, Fernando Lamas, Marta Reeves, Angel Ortiz, Fernando Sanchu, Elena Barrios.

With Claude Jarman, Jr., in *The Yearling* ('46).

7

JANE WYMAN

> 5′ 5″   110 pounds
> Chestnut brown hair   Brown eyes
> Capricorn

FEW OTHER PERFORMERS have so successfully risen from bit player to star as has Jane Wyman, an actress with an interesting but not conventionally pretty face. Who could have predicted that the brash, bleached blonde who paraded through a series of walk-ons in Warner Bros. features of the mid-Thirties would become an Academy Award winner for that studio's *Johnny Belinda* (1949)? It certainly demonstrated that in tinseltown, if one had a high degree of individuality and a burning drive to succeed, then a range of versatile talent might someday count for something.

By the Fifties, when Wyman was riding the crest of a wave as a tearjerker heroine, *Coronet* magazine would observe that in Hollywood she was "... regarded with a respect that would amount almost to veneration if she were not so easygoing." How had this amazing transformation from untutored chorine to major box-office attraction happened. In a 1948 magazine piece, Wyman related the inner change that had occurred: "By nature I have always been a very serious-minded person.... There were many times when I felt I was ready to do serious roles. But invariably, when a dumb-bunny role came along, I was elected. I realize now, if they had given me a chance at serious drama, I wouldn't have been ready. But, of course, then I could think of only one thing—they'll *never* accept this turned-up nose for anything but comedy.... This 'change' in me began when I was borrowed by MGM for the role of Ma Baxter in *The Yearling*. There are many who will understand my great feeling of release. There are those who won't understand and who can't understand. For the first time in my life, I was no longer shy, or afraid of being ridiculed about my ambitions. From that moment my turned-up nose became something that nature placed in the center of my face. Period."

Later, when the spunky motion picture celebrity realized that her film career was waning, she astutely turned to television, following in the footsteps of her pal Loretta Young. Like the latter, she developed a successful video anthology drama series in the Fifties. As she gradually drifted away from show business, Jane devoted her energies to charity work, displaying the same tenacity that won her stardom. It is this enduring feisty quality that typifies her as a prime "Forties Gal."

Sarah Jane Fulks was born on January 4, 1914, in St. Joseph, Missouri. She was the youngest of three children, her brother and sister already being in high school when she was born, and her parents well into middle age. Her father, identified only as R. D. Fulks (one source lists him as "Richard Dick Fulks"), reportedly took an active interest in the civic affairs of St. Joseph, serving at various times as mayor, chief of detectives, and county collector. (Jane, in recent years, is the first to admit that a good many of the "facts" concerning her early years were total studio fabrication.) Her mother, the former Emma Reise, born in Saarbrucken, Germany, had no vocation of her own in St. Joseph. However, from the first she wanted Sarah Jane to become a movie star. In preparation for that future, the child was given dancing lessons from an early age. Supposedly she studied with choreographer LeRoy Prinz's father, a connection which would be of use to her later in Hollywood.

When Sarah Jane was eight years old, her mother took her to Hollywood, ostensibly to visit relatives. The real purpose of the journey was to display the talents of this would-be moppet star to various Hollywood producers. To Mrs. Fulks' surprise and dismay, they were generally unimpressed. Sarah Jane, however, continued with her training and in 1929, after her father died, she and her mother once again ventured west to Hollywood. This time they settled down for a long stay.

According to the garbled chronology of the teenager's life, she attended Los Angeles High School and appeared in an assortment of community play offerings such as *Joan of Arc* and *Father Returns*. Wherever the future star may have been on a certain date in her teen years or whatever she was then doing, she had unpleasant memories of those times.

On one occasion she revealed: "I was reared under such strict discipline that it was years before I could reason myself out of the bitterness that I had brought from a childhood hemmed in by rigid rules, many of which I broke without knowing it and was punished long afterward by being denied something I had joyously anticipated."

At another time, Miss Wyman would admit: "I was never allowed [in high school] to see one of the football games.... It wasn't malice on the part of my family. It was thoughtlessness. I was told to be home at a certain hour each day and there were to be no excuses of any sort for not being there. ... It was a routine that they thought was good for me and believed was right. I thought and I still think that I missed something important, something that would have been good for me, in my school days. Maybe it was because there was so much difference in age between my mother and me. Perhaps it was because my sister was older and was able, somehow, to accommodate herself to mother's standards more easily than I did. Mother and I were . . . and still are . . . friends. We've never had a mother-and-daughter relationship.... I went to work to support myself while I was still in my early teens.... I am aware that I loathed school as I grew older."

When not making the rounds of studios after school or on days she missed classes, Sarah Jane had an assortment of odd jobs.

One of her brief careers, supposedly, was as a waitress, but it was short-lived, for the owner of the downtown Los Angeles coffee shop fired her because she could not cut the pie into six geometrically even wedges.

As far as can be determined, her first screen assignment was in Eddie Cantor's *The Kid from Spain* (1932) at United Artists. Along with Betty Grable, Paulette Goddard, and Toby Wing, she was a chorine for this Samuel Goldwyn production.

Later studio publicity would have the public believe that in 1933 the would-be actress returned to her home state where she registered at the University of Missouri to study music. As the fiction continues, before the end of the first semester, while singing at a party, she was heard by a fellow partygoer and signed to a contract as a radio singer. For the next year Sarah Jane, now known under the name Jane Durrell, *allegedly* toured the Midwest, South, and West, singing the blues on radio stations in such cities as New Orleans. However, on a recent TV talk show, Jane claimed that the "facts" about her blues singing tour were fabricated by the Warner Bros. publicity department.

Rumors—not studio-concocted—continue to circulate that in 1933 Jane was still in Hollywood and that in that year the teenager, who reduced from 135 to 110 pounds, was briefly wed. However, this possible turn of domestic events has yet to be documented.

It is known that in 1933 she appeared—very briefly—in the Joe E. Brown/First National comedy *Elmer the Great*, a fun-laden excursion into the world of baseball. By this point in her life, Sarah Jane Fulks strongly identified herself with the world of chorines. Without realizing it, and having no one to correct her, she was a parody of the gum-chewing leg kicker à la Veda Ann Borg or Iris Adrian. In the early days of her stay in Hollywood, she wore long artificial eyelashes glued to her own, one at a time. This makeup looked adequate at first, but soon resembled jackstraws, which she had to separate in order to see. With $70 she had managed to save, Sarah Jane purchased a glamorous black and red gown and a skimpy fox jacket that barely reached across her shoulders. She would shift the jacket when passing someone she wanted to impress, to make them think that it reached all around her. She wore excessive makeup until one of her chorine co-workers slipped her a note which read, "Powder is powder and paint is paint. But we like a girl that these things ain't." Thereafter she mended her ways and began to wear makeup sensibly.

Her one documented film appearance in 1934 is a walk-on bit in *College Rhythm* at Paramount starring Joe "Want a Duck" Penner, Jack Oakie, and Lyda Roberti. Another future Forties star, Clara Lou (later Ann) Sheridan, played a glove saleslady in this musical entry. By this period, Sarah Jane, who sported an inordinate amount of flashy fake jewelry, had changed the color of her hair from its natural chestnut brown to ash blonde.*

In 1935 Sarah Jane appeared in three screen musicals at Paramount. She was in the chorus of *Rumba,* which had George Raft and Carole Lombard as stars. That movie was followed by *All the King's Horses,* in which Carl Brisson was a Hollywood musical star who is the double of a Ruritanian monarch. Finally, *Stolen Harmony* was a bizarre George Raft vehicle following the adventures of a band aboard a live-in bus.

The next year did not start out much better. At Twentieth Century-Fox she was nearly invisible in the Alice Faye-Warner Baxter musical extravaganza, *King of Burlesque*. At Paramount she was in the background of the Bing Crosby-Ethel Merman-Ida Lupino version of Cole Porter's *Anything Goes.*

It was allegedly at this time that Jane secured an interview with top choreographer LeRoy Prinz. According to which story is believed, the big meeting occurred through chance because William Demarest

---

*Over the next decade, the actress' hair color underwent several changes. For *Smart Blonde* (1936) she was back to her natural color; then in 1938 for *Brother Rat* she dyed it blonde again, and in 1943 for *Princess O'Rourke* she again returned to her chestnut brown hue.

(then an agent, later an actor) took an interest in her, or because Sarah Jane's mother suggested a logical introduction through the girl's dance studies with Prinz' father. In any event, she was told by Prinz: "Your face doesn't go with your voice." (In the chorus, she was reportedly nicknamed "Dog Puss" because of her unusual pug nose and high cheek-boned face.) Therefore Jane continued for a time to accept any bit parts in the chorus she could obtain.

Finally she did get a break when she was cast in Universal's *My Man Godfrey* (1936), the impeccable screwball comedy starring Carole Lombard and William Powell. As Jane would later recall, "It was just a bit part in the scavenger hunt, and, believe me, you had to have a telephoto lens to tell me from Madame Schumann-Heink. I didn't know that this part was in the nature of a screen test." Although the few lines she spoke to Carole Lombard were later cut, she says: "I'm still in the picture next to the monkey and the organ grinder, but you have to look fast to see me. That monkey bit me, too."

Whatever her fate in that film, Warner Bros. found something about Sarah Jane that they liked, and they signed her to a contract in 1936. She changed her screen name to Jane Wyman. Even then her determination to scale the heights was apparent. Hollywood columnist Sidney Skolsky would report that, on her first Warner Bros. questionnaire, in answer to the query "What is your present ambition?" she wrote: "Not to be just an actress, but *the* actress at the studio."

As a fledgling at Warner Bros. where Kay Francis, Bette Davis, and Joan Blondell were the stellar female attractions, contractee Jane Wyman did all the conventional things to get her *new* name known: "I posed in bathing suits with Santa Claus, the Easter bunny, and the Thanksgiving turkey." She also made appearances at exhibitors' conventions and premieres and recalls that she did a "lot of photo layouts with other people's clothing."

The studio gave her acting lessons because her voice was still odd and untrained.

Jane herself eagerly sought to learn her craft from the stars who were on the lot. "I was always being invited over to her [Kay Francis'] house. It was like a big family rather than a studio. Jimmy Cagney was a strict disciplinarian, although I never appeared in his films. Pat O'Brien was always teaching me the tricks of the business. Even Bette Davis was kind and encouraging to 'the kids,' as we were called."

Then came the film that helped to launch the chorine onto the path of an Academy Award. The picture was Busby Berkeley's *Stage Struck* (1936), starring Dick Powell, Joan Blondell, and Warren William. At one point in the 86-minute proceedings, Jane steps forward and says to Powell, "My name is Bessie Fuffnick. I swim, dive, imitate wild birds, and play the trombone." She had broken the cinema's sound barrier. Jane's lines are reported to have broken up Dick Powell several times, necessitating over $2,000 in retakes.

Meanwhile, Jane continued her apprenticeship with unbilled roles at Warner Bros. She was in *Cain and Mabel* (1936), a Clark Gable-Marion Davies musical about a boxer and a Broadway star, and *Polo Joe* (1936), Joe E. Brown's last comedy at Warner Bros. For the latter film, Jane was still wearing pronounced makeup, having very long black eyelashes and very thinly penciled arching eyebrows.

In *Smart Blonde* (1936) Jane finally received screen billing. In this first entry of the Torchy Blane detective series, she was eighth-billed as Dixie, the hatcheck girl who is the pal of wisecracking Glenda Farrell. When the feature was ready for release, Miss Farrell is reputed to have approached Jane in the studio cafeteria and said, "We ran *Smart Blonde*, Janie. With you in the same studio, I'll have to watch my step." Those proved to be prophetic words.

Ready, Willing and Able (1937) had Jane eleventh-billed as a dumb bunny named Dot in this Ruby Keeler musical. In *The King and the Chorus Girl* (1937), loosely based on the story of Edward VIII, with a scenario by Norman Krasna and Groucho Marx, Jane was a Folies Bergère chorus girl named Babette. According to *Silver Screen* magazine, French-accented Jane "out-Simoned Simone Simon as Babette." *Slim* (1937), starring Henry Fonda, Margaret Lindsay, and Pat O'Brien, was the story of a "grunt" or apprentice telephone lineman, and had Jane as Stuart Erwin's girl.

By the time *Slim* was released in late June 1937, Jane had married. Her groom was Myron Futterman, a New Orleans dress manufacturer. The marriage to Futterman would not fare well. In fact, on Friday, November 11, 1938, Jane would sue for divorce. The *New York Daily News* would report, "Because her manufacturer-husband, Myron Futterman, constantly praised his first wife and compared Jane Wyman, his current spouse, unfavorably with her, the film actress today sued for divorce."

In the meantime, Jane, like Warner Bros. newcomer Ann Sheridan, continued to grind out films for the home lot. *The Singing Marine* (1937), another Dick Powell musical comedy, featured the crooner as a private who wins an amateur singing contest. Jane played Joan, Doris Weston's friend, and one of Powell's many admirers. There was much more footage for Jane in *Mr. Dodd Takes the Air* (1937) which introduced Kenny Baker as an electrician's helper who wants to be a radio baritone. Jane played Marjorie Day, the romantic lead. Although the film received mixed reviews, Jane earned generally favorable notices. "Jane Wyman plays the romantic lead nicely" *(Variety).* "[She is] an attractive little gal" *(New York World-Telegram).* "A pretty girl named Jane Wyman capably dulls the silly edge of her role as the ingenue" *(Brooklyn Eagle).* She was "decorative," according to the *New York Journal,* while *Silver Screen* magazine called her "enchanting with her rather flip acting and her eyes that would charm the sphinx."

Apparently ambitious Jane was overly excited by *Mr. Dodd Takes the Air,* a remake of *The Crooner* (1932) which starred David Manners and Ann Dvorak. If reports in the *New York Mirror* and the *New York Daily News* can be believed, she collapsed in the screening room while viewing the rushes. The studio, too, was beginning its buildup of her, appreciating her onscreen daffiness. The film's pressbook termed her a "pretty little starlet who is going places in the movies and is being groomed for stardom by her studio."

Her final 1937 release was *Public Wedding,* the first B-picture to top-bill Jane. In it she played Flip Lane, the stepdaughter of the owner of a carnival. She agrees to marry the partner, complete with a stunt-laden wedding to promote the carnival, but she later falls in love with an artist (William Hopper). Of this minor fluff, *Variety* noted, "Jane Wyman has plenty to do but isn't overboard on acting."

Warner Bros. was finding that Jane was slowly but surely becoming a marketable commodity. There were even requests for loan-outs of her screen services. She went to Universal for the low-budget *The Spy Ring* (1938). The film's ad line was: "A death-dealing plot—and a girl who saw through make-believe love to foil it." However, she was almost eliminated from the release print of Warner Bros.' solidly budgeted *Fools for Scandal* (1938) starring Carole Lombard and Fernand Gravet in a weak bid to sustain the screwball comedy cycle.

He Couldn't Say No (1938) starred Frank McHugh as a man in love with a statue that turns out to have been posed for by a senator's daughter. In *Wide Open Faces* (1938), made for Columbia, Jane renewed her working association with wide-mouthed comedian Joe E. Brown, playing his girlfriend Betty Martin. The *New York Herald-Tribune* summed up this bit of celluloid nonsense by deciding, "There is nothing else to do but focus one's eyes again on Mr. Brown, a pretty young actress named Jane Wyman, and the reliable Alison Skipworth."

It was while working on this comedy that Jane indulged in one of her early practical jokes. While in the wardrobe department, she noticed two starlets come in for costumes they would require for their Scarlett O'Hara/*Gone with the Wind* screen tests. The contest for the plum part was then in full swing. Jane went over to them and advised

With Joe E. Brown in *Wide Open Faces* ('38).

the girls that they need not bother since she had already been signed for the role. She may have derived some small amusement from their crestfallen looks, but the joke backfired. When word circulated of her stunt, she was called "Scarlett" by cast and crew of the Columbia picture.

Jane next went to work for MGM in a boxing story, *The Crowd Roars* (1938), which rematched the stars of *A Yank at Oxford* (1938), Robert Taylor and Maureen O'Sullivan, and also sought to steer Taylor away from his pretty boy image. Wyman was again cast in a subordinate role, this time as a gal named Vivian.

By now Warner Bros. was beginning to ponder whether Jane could and/or should play only fast-talking, wise-cracking roles. As she would later complain, "I've played more chorus girls of the kind who never were except on the screen than almost any girl in Hollywood. I was a chorus girl myself for quite a long time, and I never once met a girl like those I played in pictures." The studio next gave her a meatier role, one with some dimension, in *Brother Rat* (1938). This adaptation of the successful John Monks, Jr./Fred Finklehoffe Broadway hit was intended as a showcase for such contract players as Priscilla Lane, Eddie Albert, Jane Bryan, and Wayne Morris. Jane and Ronald Reagan* (then still a studio utility per-

---

*Reagan was born on February 6, 1911, in Tampio, Illinois. He lived a "Tom Sawyer" boyhood, played sports enthusiastically, and read voraciously. He worked his way through Eureka College, studying dramatics among other subjects, and graduated in 1932. He became a radio sports announcer in Iowa, eventually met an actor's agent, took a Warner Bros. screen test, and was signed to a seven-year pact. His first film was *Love Is on the Air* (1937). He continued in B-pictures until he got a break with *Brother Rat*. His performance in that movie led Warner Bros. to put him in Bette Davis' *Dark Victory* (1939). For a detailed study of Mr. Reagan's career, see *The All-Americans* (Arlington House, 1977).

former) were paired as one of the three couples around whose antics at the Virginia Military Academy the film focused. The three prime cadets (Morris, Albert, and Reagan) drift into all sorts of troubles involving girls, classes, faculty, money, and a baby biology experiment. As Claire Adams, Jane wore oversized glasses and had a blonde-colored hair-do. The reviews of the amusing comedy were all glowing. The *New York Times* refused to single out any performer other than Eddie Albert as best.

In her star years, Jane would reminisce about her film days in the late Thirties: "[I was earning] $68 a week after taxes and scared each time my contract came up for renewal that I'd be dropped. I didn't blame anybody but myself for my slow progress. I thank Bryan Foy, who was in charge of the B-unit [at Warner Bros.], for keeping me busy." It seemed at the time that the only voice of true encouragement came from *Silver Screen* magazine. In its November 1937 issue dealing with "Which Will Win the Golden Apple of Success?" and discussing Jane, Olympe Bradna, and Jane Bryan, the journal had perceived about Miss Wyman: "Slender, sophisticated in bearing and in speech, and excitingly attractive. . . . More the comedienne, smart, flashy, with an ocean of personality to project her along the path of success. Were she cast in a deeply dramatic role, though, I believe she would fulfill the task satisfactorily."

In *Tail Spin* (1939) made at Twentieth Century-Fox, Jane appeared in goggles and flying togs as a smart-mouthed flyer named Alabama. Alice Faye and Constance Bennett shared the honors in what the *New York Herald-Tribune* critic called "as bad an aviation photoplay as I can remember." Warner Bros.' *Private Detective* (1939) had Jane playing the lead role in a film that closely paralleled the studio's Torchy Blane series. With the help of policeman Dick Foran, Jane's Myrna Winslow tracks down a murderer

With John Payne and Walter Catlett in *Kid Nightingale* ('39).

while suffering through a harrowing series of escapades. *The Kid from Kokomo* (1939) offered Jane in yet another girlfriend role, playing subordinate to dumb but mother-loving boxer Wayne Morris and enterprising but thoughtful manager Pat O'Brien. May Robson as the old vagrant O'Brien hires to impersonate Morris' mom carried the film along with her humorous portrayal. The film was co-scripted by Jerry Wald, who was later to play an important role in Jane's life as a friend and as the producer of *Johnny Belinda* (1948), *The Glass Menagerie* (1950), and *The Blue Veil* (1951).

The pressbook to *The Kid from Kokomo* alleges: "Warner Brothers decided that after her three-year probationary period Jane should be groomed for real stardom." Her next picture seemed to be a promotion of sorts. She was made the star of the Torchy Blane series, inheriting the role from Glenda Farrell and Lola Lane (who had appeared in one of the entries). *Torchy Plays with Dynamite* (1939) followed the usual pattern for the property: girl reporter Torchy tracks down killer Eddie (Eddie Marr) by befriending his moll in a San Francisco jail. In this quickie, Jane's heroine was aided by police lieutenant Allen Jenkins. The *New York Post* advised, "Little Miss Wyman performs as though she had closely followed Glenda Farrell's actions and mannerisms." After this picture Jane was made an honorary member of the Los Angeles Policewoman's Division.

Jane next had the honor of appearing in her third boxing feature in two years. *Kid Nightingale* (1939) was the narrative of an aspiring opera singer, played by John Payne, who trains to fight in the ring in order to develop his breathing power. A shady promoter corrals him and pits him against a series of phony opponents, allowing him to warble to the accompaniment of a band after each knockout. Jane's Judy Craig was judged "cute" by the *New York Daily News*.

Despite the poor quality of her 1939 releases, Jane had progressed career-wise during the year. The columnists had begun taking notice of her. An especially important development was the interest taken in her by Louella Parsons. In Louella's own words, "I first met Jane in 1939 when she was one of a group of little known but most promising young Hollywood players I took on a vaudeville tour of the country. In our 'act' I did my column and my radio show from the stage of the various motion picture theatres, and then introduced the young players as 'The Stars of Tomorrow.' . . . How well I remember the Jane Wyman of that tour. . . . Her choice of clothes left much to be desired, and she was mad about jewelry, 'junk' and otherwise. The more she could pile on, in fact, the better, and what she couldn't wear, she carried. You could hear Jane coming a block away."*

One of the other "stars of tomorrow" on the tour was Ronald Reagan, whom Jane had met on the set of *Brother Rat*. Even then, according to Eddie Albert, "Ronald Reagan began squiring her around." However, it was on the Parsons tour that the relationship developed** and reached its first highly serious moment. In Louella's words: "Life was very much the way Jane wanted it on a certain day our vaudeville tour took us to Philadelphia. Her brown eyes were sparkling and her voice was bubbling with happiness as she told me: 'Have I got a scoop for you! Ronnie and I are engaged!' I had known that Janie worshiped Ronnie, but I hadn't realized he was falling seriously in love with her. I announced the engagement that night from the stage and in the newspapers."

Not every columnist who dealt with Jane was as captivated by her as was Louella. Hy Gardner, apparently snubbed by Jane, pub-

---

*On another occasion Louella would describe the early Jane and her career: "That girl was very blonde; she usually played meanie [sic] roles that were not terribly important to the story. She chafed at the bit, but she was so busy having a good time that her career didn't matter the way it does today [1950]; of course she was very young then."

**One *Photoplay* magazine article stated of their romance, "Long before Ronald was aware of Janie's existence, she knew *he was there*. But Ronnie had had his heart bashed in once and wouldn't look Janie's way for a long time. When he did, it was all over but the wedding." On the Parsons vaudeville tour, according to *Photoplay*, "in every city they toured, Ronnie and Jane would seek out Italian restaurants" for the spaghetti he craved.

lished a sarcastic newspaper piece in which he stated: "The Wyman woman, unlike the genuine cream of the cinema crop whose names are box-office magic, seems to consider the approach of a reporter as an irksome intrusion upon the privacy of a high-priced public goldfish." Casting aspersions upon her knitting a pair of socks for Ronald Reagan that looked like "a navy hammock," he stated that the "Wyman-about-town . . . used to weigh 146 pounds and likes to box. . . . She sings the 'St. Louis Blues' in six different languages and accompanies herself at the piano—which obviously assures Miss Wyman at least that she's in good company."

While Jane was busy on the tour and romancing Ronald, Warner Bros. announced that it had agreed to loan her to Columbia for the female lead opposite Joe E. Brown in *Beware, Spooks!* (1939), but it would be Mary Carlisle who was assigned the heroine role in the comedy.

Once back in Hollywood, Jane attempted to divide her time between a film career and being an engaged woman. Reagan gave her a large amethyst ring to celebrate their new status. After the announcement of their engagement, the couple were offered a paid elopement to Honolulu by a publication if they would allow a cameraman to go along and take candid pictures of the wedding and honeymoon. Needless to say, they refused.

Jane found time to tell the press about how she had changed: "I used to be the kind of person who sat around swank nightclubs with a big fuzz on my head and a long cigarette holder sticking out of my face. Athletics held no charm for me. First I was too lazy, and then what for? Till along came Reagan and all I heard was football and track and swimming and golf. The only way I could get to see him was out on a golf course. So where do you think I went? Out on a golf course."

As the new decade began, Jane's film career seemed to be stagnating, but there were still staunch endorsers of her potential. *Photoplay* called her "a blond cyclone on two small feet" and nicknamed her "Dynamite."

The article linked her professionally with Burgess Meredith, Raymond Massey, Dennis Morgan, Ida Lupino, John Carroll, and a few others, and explained, "Here they come, those familiar faces of the screen, those steadfast people who are slowly rising to new heights and new places. We've watched them rise from tiniest bits to meatier roles and on and on up the road to fame."

Warner Bros., attempting to follow up on the popularity of *Brother Rat,* made a sequel entitled *Brother Rat and a Baby* (1940). Although the starring players were the same, the feature was a disappointment as it traced the three cadets through their lives in the outer world after graduation. The ads stressed the presence of the plotline baby in the follow-up: "Call out the Marines!!! Call out the Militia!!! The 'Brother Rats' have a BABY . . . and *Boy,* what a BABY!" Bosley Crowther *(New York Times)* countered, stating that the film "demonstrates how horrible dormitory fun can be when carried over, inexcusably, into an adult world," while the *New York Herald-Tribune* complained that it was "a far-fetched and not very funny script."

Much of the same cast was in the sequel, including Eddie Albert, Wayne Morris, and Ronald Reagan. To stretch the point, many of the same performers, plus a Lane sister (Rosemary), were assigned to *An Angel from Texas* (1940). It was yet another rendition of George S. Kaufman's play *The Butter and Egg Man. Flight Angels* (1940) found Jane in a picture about stewardesses. One above-par scene found Wyman and Margot Stevenson in a knock-down, drag-out fight. It culminates with Jane throwing cold cream at her adversary, and Margot countering with a statue base. The *New York Herald-Tribune* took notice of Jane: "Miss Jane Wyman has the only well-written part in the film, and she plays it with spitfire vigor. As the blonde hostess, who is either chasing her man in the face of stiff competition from planes in which he seems to have more interest, or swapping screams and kicks with a disagreeable hostess, she has good lines and uses them well."

With Olivia de Havilland and Eddie Albert in *My Love Came Back* ('40).

With Ronald Reagan in *Tugboat Annie Sails Again* ('40).

While Ronald Reagan was gaining attention in such films as *Knute Rockne—All American* (1940), Jane had an occasional A-picture to her credit, but it was usually in a subordinate role, as was true in *My Love Came Back* (1940). This time she is the pal to Olivia de Havilland, the latter playing a concert violinist trying to find a husband. Eddie Albert played Jane's zany beau, an intermittently suicidal young man. *Tugboat Annie Sails Again* (1940) paired Jane and Ronald Reagan in a disappointing sequel that starred Marjorie Rambeau and Alan Hale in the roles performed at MGM in 1933 by Marie Dressler and Wallace Beery. The *New York Times* noted: "Ronald Reagan and Jane Wyman make a pleasant pair of incidental lovebirds amid so many gulls." *Gambling on the High Seas* (1940) featured Jane as Laurie Ogden, the secretary to a gang boss who runs a gambling ship. In the course of the proceedings, she falls for Wayne Morris and helps him to capture the hoodlums.

The year 1940 may not have been a good one for Jane's professional status (she was earning $200 weekly), but her personal life took a decided turn for the happier when she wed Ronald Reagan on Friday, January 26, 1940. The couple were married* in the Wee Kirk o' the Heather at Forest Lawn. (*Photoplay* magazine claimed that the newlyweds had neglected to kiss while sitting in the wishing chair at Forest Lawn after the ceremony.) A reception was given for the Reagans at the home of Louella Parsons and her doctor husband. Every year, starting with the first Valentine's Day after they were married, Reagan would send Jane a nosegay of red and white roses with the note, "Happy, Happy Valentine's Day . . . From Me."

In 1941 Jane and Reagan appeared in a short subject *How to Improve Your Golf*. Her feature film roles were not much more imaginative at this time. *Honeymoon for Three* (1941) was a weak comedy remake of *Goodbye Again* which relied on the presence of Ann "The Oomph Girl" Sheridan and her real-life husband-to-be, George Brent, for its box-office mileage. Jane was Sheridan's understanding friend. The *New York Times* acknowledged of Wyman's appearance in the Western *Bad Men of Missouri* (1941): "[She] apparently is a very pretty girl, but she has what must be one of the shortest romantic roles in the history of horse opera." Dennis Morgan, Wayne Morris, and Arthur Kennedy had the leading roles in this fictional account of the Younger brothers. *You're in the Army Now* (1941) was outright but impoverished slapstick that caught Jane in the midst of labored antics by Jimmy Durante and Phil Silvers. She also played opposite Edward Everett Horton and Jeffrey Lynn in *The Body Disappears* (1941), a sketchy blend of comedy, science fiction, and suspense.

While the Warner Bros. casting department was not favoring Jane, the publicity division was working energetically to promote her. They saw to it that she was (finally) among those selected by exhibitors in a *Motion Picture Herald-Fame* poll as likely to become a star. On Thanksgiving Eve in 1941, she ate dinner with a troop of Army men. In December of that year, she was made an honorary top sergeant of Battery F of the Third Coast Artillery.

Meanwhile Jane was constantly quoted on her marriage to popular leading man Ronald Reagan. She admitted, "When we were married, neither Ronnie nor I was a star. We were both featured players, making $500 a week. I wasn't a glamour queen and he wasn't a matinee idol. We were just two kids trying to get the breaks in pictures. . . . But look at Ronnie now. He's gone leaps and bounds ahead of me. But I'm terribly proud of him all the same."

On another occasion she revealed, "Marrying Ronnie worked a miracle for me. It changed a dull, suspicious, anxious woman into someone I am proud and happy to be.

---

*For their wedding ceremony, Jane indulged in another of her practical jokes. She sent Reagan an envelope of Carnation Instant Milk with the inscription, "Ronald, my love—I could find no rice to prepare for the happy celebration. All I can offer are these happy white flakes to shower upon you forever. Your Jane." Reagan counted this as one of his favorite Jane Wyman pranks.

Modeling for the press in 1941.

With William T. Orr, Charlie Ruggles, Ann Sheridan, and George Brent in *Honeymoon for Three* ('41).

Someone at ease, relaxed, receptive to good and lovely things. . . . [On the set of *Brother Rat*] I was drawn to him at once. . . . He was such a sunny person. . . . I never felt free to talk to anyone until I met Ronnie."

There was another new aspect of the Reagans' life for the couple to discuss with the press. On Monday, January 27, 1941—Jane's twenty-seventh birthday—their daughter Maureen Elizabeth was born. Reagan confided, "I think Jane started talking about a baby the day after we were married. I wanted one, too, but I used all my male logic to persuade her that every young couple ought to wait a year. She agreed I was right as usual and she was wrong. So we had a baby."

At the hospital when Jane was told it was a girl, she turned her head away and said, "Oh, don't talk about it. . . . Oh, Ronnie, it took so long, and it's *still* only a girl." However, later she "argued him" into believing she wanted a girl.

During this period the Reagans were living in a penthouse apartment in the Hollywood area, furnished inexpensively, in anticipation of saving money for an actual house. Jane would recall: "Instead of nightclubbing, we've spent most of our free time looking for a lot—looking at model homes. . . . One night we went to see Rosalind Russell in *This Thing Called Love* [1941]. As soon as her house flashed on the screen, both Ronnie and I said at once, 'That's it!' Next morning we dashed over to Columbia and got the plans. We had a miniature house made. It became a regular plaything, with us deciding little changes here and there and how we'd arrange our furniture to fit."

In 1942 Ronald Reagan gained a tremen-

With Regis Toomey and Donald MacBride in *You're in the Army Now* ('41).

dous career boost with his role of Drake McHugh, the tragic ex-playboy in *Kings Row*. That same year the Reagans purchased their "dream" house and he enlisted in the army where he would remain until January 1946. Reagan was assigned to the motion picture unit of the Army Air Corps at Culver City, California, but he was able to live at home, since his post provided no living quarters for officers. While Reagan was away for long stretches of time during the war, Jane would complain to Louella Parsons, "Now I'm carrying the ball financially." She also helped to carry the ball for the country, performing regularly during the war for Camp Shows, Inc., and selling bonds. By late 1943 she had sold some $7.5 million worth of defense bonds.

Jane the actress and breadwinner had some candid comments on her vocation: "Ronnie and I look on our careers as business propositions and not as anything glamorous or out of the ordinary. . . . Our Maureen has given us a new perspective, and certainly she has given us both the inspiration to be doubly successful in our business and to plan for the future. . . . And what marriage can go on the rocks when plans are always being made for tomorrow and next year and the years after that?"

Larceny, Inc. (1942) marked a milestone of sorts for Jane. The film, which featured Edward G. Robinson, Broderick Crawford, and Edward Brophy as ex-convicts pretending to go straight in order to rob a bank, had Anthony Quinn as a villain who tries to muscle in on the crooked proceedings. What was memorable about this picture for Jane, despite the minor role she had, was that it was the first of a string of features in which she would appear with Jack Carson. On loan to RKO for *My Favorite Spy* (1942), Jane played a counterespionage agent who joins bandleader Kay Kyser in corralling a group of enemy operatives. Ellen Drew played Kyser's frustrated bride, longing to spend the night with him but always finding him preoccupied with Jane.

With husband Lieutenant Ronald Reagan at the California State Military Guard Ball ('42).

With Edward G. Robinson in *Larceny, Inc.* ('42).

With Jack Carson, Robert Cummings, Olivia de Havilland, Charles Coburn, and Minor Watson in *Princess O'Rourke* ('43).

With Jack Carson in *Make Your Own Bed* ('44).

With Cy Kendall, Stuart Crawford, and Jerome Cowan in *Crime by Night* ('44).

With Craig Stevens, Alexis Smith, John Ridgely, Ann Sheridan, Jack Carson, Eve Arden, and Nick Kobliansky in *The Doughgirls* ('44).

At one point in the early Forties, Jane fretted, "I'm queen of the sub-plots. I'm the girl who's the second romantic lead. I always get a man, too, but the customers worry about the star first, then about me. For seven years I've been the leading lady's confidante, advisor, pal, sister, severest critic." Such was the case with Twentieth Century-Fox's *Footlight Serenade* (1942) in which she was Betty Grable's friend and roommate. The *New York Times* admitted that Jane and Cobina Wright, Jr., had "paper-doll roles."

In 1943 Jane found time to substitute host for an ailing Jack Benny on his radio show, alternating the chore with Robert Taylor and Orson Welles. She had only one film in release that year, but it was an important assignment in terms of her career. *Princess O'Rourke* starred Olivia de Havilland as an exiled princess, Charles Coburn as her uncle, and Robert Cummings as the pilot who mistakes her for an exiled waif. It was the first project in which Jane (now a brunette again) and Jack Carson (as Cummings' co-pilot) were paired importantly. As a married couple who befriend the top-billed stars, they help steer the focal romance to an amusing conclusion in President Roosevelt's White House study. As one reviewer admitted: "Jack Carson and Jane Wyman draw rich humor and honest sentiment from the roles of two friends." The scenario won an Oscar for Norman Krasna.

Jane's performance in this film, particularly in a scene with Carson in a Chinese restaurant, was instrumental in launching her into major stardom. Unfortunately, Warner Bros. at the time failed to grasp her newly revealed ability and nearly buried her in several trivial roles. There was one major project along the way, *One More Tomorrow*. However, this remake of *The Animal Kingdom* ran into production code problems, and, although finally completed in November 1943, it would not be released until early 1946.

A dim B-picture entitled *Make Your Own Bed* (1944) top-billed Jack Carson and Jane as a private detective and his girlfriend. It was a forced comedy in which the two pose as servants to foil and capture Nazi saboteurs. *Crime by Night* (1944) had actually been completed in February 1942 but had sat on the shelf. It cast Jane once more as a private eye, this time assisting detective Jerome Cowan who has walked into a murder trap.

Jane next played Jack Carson's newlywed bride in a mad if forced farce set in wartime Washington, D.C., entitled *The Doughgirls* (1944).* She was billed below Ann Sheridan and Alexis Smith, but above another Warner Bros. workhorse, Eve Arden (the best element in the picture). With much of the frantic action taking place in a crowded hotel suite, the pace was furious. Jane played a "priceless nitwit who is a great admirer of President Roosevelt because of his fine acting in *Yankee Doodle Dandy*" (*New York Times*).

Hollywood Canteen (1944) was one of those oversized enterprises in which Hollywood patted itself on the back. There was a loose story line about a G.I. (Robert Hutton) wanting to date Joan Leslie, but for the most part the film is a series of short guest appearances by a bevy of Warner stars, including an explanation of the Canteen by its co-founder, Bette Davis. Jane sang "What Are You Doing the Rest of Your Life?" with perennial co-star Jack Carson.

In 1945 came the turning point in Jane's cinema career. Producer Charles Brackett, as well as director/writer Billy Wilder, had viewed Jane's performance in *Princess O'Rourke*, and they wanted her to have an important role in Paramount's screen version of *The Lost Weekend* (1945). The film was to be based on Charles Jackson's harrowing novel of an alcoholic. Brackett would later explain, "We wanted to get away from the suffering type. We wanted a girl with a gift for life. We needed some gusto in the picture." Jane was startled that they had considered her. "I was in New York on a publicity tour when Wilder phoned me and asked me to read the book. I couldn't for the life

---

*Maureen, on seeing her mother in a film for the first time, in *The Doughgirls*, ran down the aisle and shrieked "You can't do that to my mommy" when she saw Jack Carson pick Jane up and drop her on the floor.

With Barbara Stanwyck and Robert Hutton in *Hollywood Canteen* ('44).

of me find any part for me to play; I was so conditioned to think of myself as a comedienne. I was completely floored when Billy [Wilder] said he wanted me for the part of the girlfriend to the hero." On another occasion, she added, "There's no use my trying to talk about the girl's part. I don't know a thing about it. You see, they've had to write it in. The girl in the book is just a bit. The picture will make her part equal with the man's. Barbara Stanwyck was first reported to have the part. But, I don't know why, now they've got me for it. All I'm sure about is that the girl is not a drunkard."

The Lost Weekend, the penetrating account of a five-day bender, featured an Academy Award-winning performance by Ray Milland as the alcoholic writer Don Birnam. In the course of the black-and-white film, Birnam maneuvers his brother (Phillip Terry) and Jane, as his girl, out of his desperate way so that he can embark on a binge. He is seen in Nat's, a dingy Third Avenue bar designed by Paramount to resemble P. J. Clarke's; in the dipsomaniac ward at Bellevue; on Third Avenue trying to pawn his typewriter for a drink; in a posh restaurant stealing a woman's purse to pay for his drinks; and at his brother's apartment, which he tears apart in his desperate search for a hidden bottle of alcohol.

In her co-starring role, Jane portrayed Helen St. James, a loyal, level-headed, tenacious woman who is in love with Birnam despite his alcoholism, and who believes in him enough to stick with him through several years of torment. She takes care of him on occasion, sleeps on his doorstep one night waiting in vain for him to come home, and at the finale prevents his suicide by infusing him with new hope. At this point she delivers an inspirational speech when his typewriter is fortuitously returned by bartender Nat (Howard da Silva).

The Lost Weekend garnered four Oscars, a New York Film Critics Award for Best Film of 1945, and a whole slew of commendations for Milland himself. Jane did not go unnoticed. The *New York World-Telegram* stated that she had revealed "unsuspected power," while the *New York Times* offered: "Jane Wyman assumes with quiet authority a difficult role." The *New York Herald-Tribune* agreed that she was "properly restrained as the fiancée."

As Jane's career picked up long overdue momentum, there were changes in her domestic life. When rumors of problems between her and Reagan began to surface, Louella Parsons printed their denials. Said Jane, "I swore I was not even going to deny this silly talk, but you're different. . . . Ronnie and I haven't had even a good old-fashioned family argument. Of course, I have a hot temper . . . but Ronnie, who has the disposition of an angel, just lets me blow off steam until I get my mad out of my system. He never fights back." Miss Parsons editorialized that the couple were bad newspaper copy because they were just "Mr. and Mrs. Average Citizen of any good-sized town."

Yet a little later in the year Reagan admitted, "True, Jane wasn't satisfied with the way her own career was going along. But she would say, 'I have so much of everything I won't be unhappy because I'm not getting the pictures I want.'" For her part, Jane explained that Reagan was "restless" after just having been assigned back to a military home base, frustrated that he not been at the front because of his poor eyesight. The couple claimed to Miss Parsons, "Everything is just right now, Louella. Ronnie and I have our lovely home, Maureen, our duties and our careers. We are far luckier than most young couples in that even the war hasn't parted us. We have so much. Can't gossips let us keep our happiness?"

Still later in 1945, sharp-eyed columnists noted that Jane had taken a mysterious trip out of town alone and that Reagan was seen driving about Hollywood alone. Reporters drew the too obvious conclusion that the couple had finally separated. However, soon

With Ray Milland and Phillip Terry in *The Lost Weekend* ('45).

With Ann Sheridan in *One More Tomorrow* ('46).

With Monty Woolley, Alexis Smith, Dorothy Malone, and Donald Woods in *Night and Day* ('46).

Jane returned home with an adopted baby boy, whom the couple named Michael Edward Reagan. The movie actors had feared that any initial publicity on the matter might have ruined the chances for his adoption.

Jane's two Warner Bros. films for 1946 did not reflect her post-*Lost Weekend* importance, for each project had long been in the works. The ill-fated *One More Tomorrow* had a May 1946 release, and the best the *New York Herald-Tribune* could say of the venture was that it had "a sorry script." As Franc Connors, Ann Sheridan's assistant who was a photographer for a magazine called *The Bantam,* Jane was fifth-billed and had little to do. Once again beefy, double-take Jack Carson was her romantic interest.

Night and Day (1946) was the Hollywood version of the life of playboy composer Cole Porter. The film was "selected by Warner Bros. as the symbol of progress made in twenty years of talkies." It starred Cary Grant, Alexis Smith, and Monty Woolley (playing himself). The well-executed musical numbers were the saving grace of this 128-minute color feature directed by Michael Curtiz. In the lead, Grant was pallid and ill at ease, and Miss Smith's role as his society wife was far from multi-dimensional. Jane played—what else but?—a blonde showgirl named Gracie Harris. This was one of her least favorite assignments. In response to an interviewer's question, "When did you dislike yourself on the screen?" she replied, "In *Night and Day.* I don't like that addle-pated type of comedy role. It's mostly a fill-in, contributing nothing but a few vaudeville laughs." Despite her small role, the reviewers did notice Jane's presence. "Jane Wyman, as a showgirl, and Eve Arden, who plays a French songstress in broad burlesque, are both very amusing," reported the *New York Times.* The *New York Herald-Tribune* noted Jane's "doing a minor and rather tough job with éclat."

If *The Lost Weekend* was the turning point in Jane's career, her next feature, done on loan-out to MGM, was the highpoint of her lengthy and often backtracking road to success. *The Yearling* (1946) was an adaptation of Marjorie Kinnan Rawlings' Pulitzer Prize-winning novel, and Jane's characterization of Ma Baxter in the film would win her an Academy Award nomination. She had clearly progressed a long way from her days as a Samuel Goldwyn chorus kicker.

The filming of *The Yearling* had been planned since 1939, the year that actual preparations began. Starting in early 1941, with Victor Fleming as director, Spencer Tracy as Pa Baxter, Anne Revere as Ma Baxter, and a youth named Gene Eckman as Jody, shooting began on location in the Florida backwoods. By May 1941 there were unspecified production difficulties, including rumors of a disagreement between Fleming and producer Sidney Franklin. There were also complications with the unpredictable weather and with the animals used in the picture. (The focal fawn was growing too quickly and the pigs were unruly.) King Vidor was next hired to direct, but he found that he had insufficient time to become properly familiar with the script. By the summer of 1941, the production, which had already cost $500,000, was shelved.

There were revival plans in 1942 and 1944, with Roddy McDowall tested in 1942 for the part of Jody, but nothing materialized. Then in 1946 MGM assigned director Clarence Brown to make another try. Brown recalled Jane's *Lost Weekend* performance and requested her for the production. Gregory Peck was cast in the role of Pa Baxter. After a well-publicized national search, a Tennessee lad named Claude Jarman, Jr., was signed to play Jody. Shooting went on for nine and a half months, mostly on Florida location. Once more there were problems with heat and humidity, with the corn fields which had to look a certain way for particular scenes in the chronology, and with the fawns. Sixteen animals were actually used to represent the film's own fawn, "Flag."

In the color feature Jane plays the embittered, patient spouse of Peck, he being the head of a Florida backwoods family. She is lovingly severe with their son Jody, a gentle, blond-haired boy who approaches the first stage of maturity within the story when he becomes attached to "Flag," the pet fawn. In time the animal begins destroying the Baxters' corn crop, and Jane is finally forced to shoot it. However, she merely wounds the fawn and it is Jody who must track after the pet and end its life. Later he runs away, but eventually returns home. He is no longer the carefree young boy he once was.

The movie has several exciting and touching episodes: the bear hunt where Jody and Peck corner "Slewfoot" only to see him escape, the snake bite scene where Peck kills the fawn's mother to use the doe's heart and liver as medicine, a fight with the neighboring Forrester boys, the death of Jody's young friend, and the climactic shooting of the fawn. (This incident made a great impression on Maureen Reagan. Reported Jane, "My child wouldn't speak to me for two weeks because I shot the deer.")

All three of the major performers in *The Yearling* won accolades for their work. Jane, who in the picture had to milk cows, weed, feed chickens and hogs, chop wood, cook, sew, and scrub, received high praise from the *New York Times:* "Jane Wyman, while she does not have the physical characteristics of the original 'Ma,' compels credulity and sympathy for a woman of stern and spartan stripe."

At the premiere* of *The Yearling*, Jane received much notice from fashion columnists. One of them, Edith Gwynn, described her outfit. "Jane Wyman's white lace gown and white evening wrap came in for its share of attention.... But the really knockout part of her costume consisted of the unusual earring and ring set. The ring was a highly polished saucerish disc of platinum. And set low in the center was a huge pearl. The earrings, of course, matched the ring, though much smaller. The effect created by the reflection of the pearl on the polished metal

---

*When producer Sidney Franklin screened a rough cut of *The Yearling* for the Reagans, the Pecks, the Jarmans, and Clarence Brown, everyone sat in stony silence at the conclusion. Brown pleaded, "Will somebody kindly say something?" Reagan blinked and came to: "There's nothing to say. I can't figure if I've just been to church or ought to go there."

and vice versa was really something."

Jane's nomination for the Academy Award as Best Actress was met with stiff competition. Olivia de Havilland, who actually won the Oscar that year, was nominated for her role in *To Each His Own*. The other rivals were Celia Johnson *(Brief Encounter)*, Jennifer Jones *(Duel in the Sun)*, and Rosalind Russell *(Sister Kenny)*.

Following her new success, Jane negotiated a new pact with Warner Bros. Although the legal limit on such contracts was seven years, in the heady flush of popularity her agreement was for ten years. Effective as of January 1, 1948, the contract included a clause allowing Jane permission to appear on television. This privilege, which demonstrated great foresight, would not be exercised by her until early in 1955. The contract also gave her the right to make one outside picture a year. Jane has stated that she signed again with Warner Bros. partly out of gratitude for all the years the studio had supported her.

When Reagan was finally discharged from military service and he reported back to Warner Bros. to complete his contract, he discovered that his career was on the wane, and it did not help matters that his wife was doing so well in the industry. It did not take a marriage counselor to read between the lines when he complained to columnist Hedda Hopper, "I think Jane takes her work too seriously for one thing." Jane highlighted another difference between herself and her husband when she stated in 1946, "They wanted him to run for Congress. He's very politically-minded. I'm not."

While Reagan was grinding out two box-office duds *(Stallion Road* and *That Hagen Girl)* and one success *(The Voice of the Turtle)*, Jane was at work on a neighboring Warner Bros. soundstage in *Cheyenne* (1947). While she was making the latter, playing dark-haired Ann Kincaid, there were some retakes required for *The Yearling* in which she was light-haired, and she had to "dig up" a blonde wig for the retakes at MGM. *Cheyenne* starred Dennis Morgan as a gambler who becomes a range detective for

With husband Ronald Reagan and children Michael and Maureen in 1946.

With Bruce Bennett and Janis Paige in *Cheyenne* ('47).

Wells Fargo, with Jane as the wife of badman Bruce Bennett. By the end of the Western, she has fallen in love with heroic Morgan. This film was by no means a step in the right direction for Jane.

In RKO's *Magic Town* (1947), Jane played a small-town newspaper editor to James Stewart's slick poll-taker.* The premise revolves about Stewart's discovery that the town of Grandview perfectly represents the whole nation in miniature—its opinions mirror the country's to the last percentage point. When Jane learns and publishes all, the citizens of Grandview become self-conscious and attempt to capitalize on their good fortune. Stewart eventually rises from disgrace and redeems the town and his love affair with Jane.

Magic Town represented an early example of the acting of the "new" Jane Wyman. Now she was less frenetic on camera, amusing but not broad, able to work with an established star and to convey true dramatic nuances. Her high point in the film was in a classroom scene in which she recites "Hiawatha" as a counterpoint to Stewart's "The Charge of the Light Brigade," both of them getting louder and louder, but ending together.

During the making of *Magic Town*, *The Yearling* had had its triumphant premiere. After that, Jane found a sign on the door of her *Magic Town* dressing room: "The Queen —Merry Christmas and Happy Yearling." Thereafter, there were more concrete acts of praise. Jane was selected as one of the five leading film players in the 1946–47 *Film Daily* poll. In 1946 Jane had been voted the ideal working mother by the North Hollywood Women's Professional Club. Jane said about this, "And *that* was a surprise. The publicity department didn't have anything to do with it." In 1947 she was named "Hollywood's most attractive mother."

---

*Years later director William Wellman would remember, "I was in on that thing from the beginning, and I wish I never started it. It stunk! Frank [Capra] and Bob [Riskin] had a big argument about the picture and Riskin asked me to do it. I told him this is the kind of picture only Capra could do. It's not my kind of film."

The Reagans now owned a ranch in the San Fernando Valley which they called "Yearling Row" and where they bred horses, one of which appeared in Reagan's *Stallion Road* (1947). On Thursday, June 26, 1947, a baby girl was born to Jane. The birth was four months premature, and the infant died the next day. Reagan was in the hospital at the same time with viral pneumonia.

When Jane recovered from her personal tragedy, there was some question as to what her next property would be. She was still not in the rank of the studio's Bette Davis, Joan Crawford, or Barbara Stanwyck, but Warner Bros. was trying to find tailor-made vehicles for her. There were rumors that she might star in *Earth and High Heaven,* and actual location footage was shot for another proposed vehicle, *Ethan Frome,* before that was abandoned. Meanwhile, Jane had set her heart on playing the title role in *Johnny Belinda,* based on the Elmer Harris play that had starred Helen Craig.

It was with this film—completed in November 1947, but not released until October 1948—that Jane finally made her indelible mark on the Hollywood world. Accounts of how she became involved in the Jean Negulesco-directed project vary. She has been quoted as saying, "It took two years before I could get anyone interested in *Johnny Belinda*. I had seen the play in New York and thought it was a wonderful characterization, but who wants a leading lady in an expensive picture who doesn't say a word! But I just wouldn't give up!" Another account was offered by the producer Jerry Wald who had watched her rising career with interest. He thought that she would be perfect for the lead, despite the fact that she was nearly fifteen years too old for the part.

The plot of *Johnny Belinda* is that of a pathetic teenage deaf-mute living in a bleak Nova Scotia fishing village with her overworked father (Charles Bickford). He is a man embittered by the early death of his wife and his daughter's handicap. Sharing their home is her sharp-tongued aunt (Agnes Moorehead). The girl is treated like a brute and uncomprehending animal, given

With Lew Ayres in *Johnny Belinda* ('48).

menial tasks, and understood by no one. With the arrival in town of a youngish doctor (Lew Ayres), a change takes place in her existence. He takes a kindly interest in her, teaches her sign language and lip reading, and awakens her spirit. The picture then takes a sharp melodramatic turn as the girl is raped by the local lothario (Stephen McNally, who had played the doctor in the stage version). In time she gives birth to a child, and the villagers suspect the doctor of being the father. Later McNally and Bickford clash in a violent argument, and the father is pushed off a cliff. In a poignant scene, Wyman says the Lord's Prayer in sign language over the body of her father. When McNally comes to the girl's room against her wishes, she shoots him. At her trial, with Ayres standing by her steadfastly, all the tragic elements are untangled. The film concludes with Jane and Ayres facing a happier future together.

Quite obviously, the role she played in *Johnny Belinda* required a good deal of preparation. As she recalled: "It's an absorbing characterization, an emotional challenge to any actress. There were many obstacles to overcome. Illness and other work delayed the start of the picture, so I had a whole year in which to study the script, to learn to know Belinda. Elizabeth Gesner, who has devoted years to working with the deaf, was engaged as technical advisor. She taught Lew and me sign language and lip reading. As my model for emotion, Mrs. Gesner found a young Mexican girl who had been born deaf. The girl was brought to my home and to the studio often so that I could study her, and we made innumerable tests of her in 16 and 35 millimeter film. I spent many hours with the cheerful youngster, watching her every reaction."

Jane also explained: "What I am trying hardest to get into my characterization is a certain quality that I saw in her eyes. I can describe it only as an 'anticipation light,' the look of one who wants so eagerly to share in things. All deaf people have that inquiring, interested, alive look. They must be keener, more alert than the rest of us. [But] even after weeks of tests, my tests, something was missing. Suddenly I realized what was wrong. I could hear. I could act deaf, but it lacked a realistic feeling, and that showed on my face. So I had plastic, wax and cotton ear stops made to block out all sounds, and I wore them throughout actual shooting, to give me the necessary faltering indecision."

The director, cast, and crew developed a set of signals which they employed when they had to give Jane her instructions about timing, keeping within camera lines, and so on. Jane also made sure that she reacted a beat late to lines and cues, adding to the realism of her portrayal. She would walk starting with her left foot, and often used her left hand instead of her usual right. She worked closely with the wardrobe department, choosing materials and clothes that would give her just the right pathetic appeal.

The point of these meticulous preparations was to convey the spirit of the deaf girl, the timidity and suppressed silence broken only by the expressiveness of her eyes and at times her smile. Director Negulesco has stated that the picture was made with great love, and Jane adds, "If, by *Johnny Belinda*, the deaf are more compassionately understood by those who have the blessing of hearing, then I think all of us concerned will have accomplished our purpose."

Some of the details involved with the location work in Mendocino, California, reveal the feelings that blended into the project. As Jane related, "We spent six weeks in a hamlet on the northern California coast where the countryside closely resembles the Nova Scotia landscape. The population consisted of the innkeeper and the postmaster who served the people in outlying sections. In the evenings we made our own fun, formed a community sing among our company—hymns and folk songs. We felt so isolated, yet oddly at peace, that no one wanted to play cards or dance. It was as though the spirit of the simple people of Belinda's remote world hung over and around us."

Critics were unanimous in their praise of *Johnny Belinda* and of Jane in particular. Many gave her much of the credit for preventing the film from becoming a mawkish tearjerker, instead making it a poignant and sincere effort. These are some representative comments: "It is the girl about whom the whole story revolves, who gives a performance surpassingly beautiful in its slow, luminous awakening of joy and understanding. It is all the more beautiful in its accomplishment without words, perhaps *because* it is so wordlessly expressive" (Archer Winsten, *New York Post*). "Miss Wyman brings superior insight and tenderness to the role. Not once does she speak throughout the picture. Her face is the mirror of her thoughts. Yet she makes this pathetic young woman glow with emotional warmth" (Bosley Crowther, *New York Times*). "Miss Jane Wyman . . . gives an amazingly expressive and sensitive performance—the finest of her

With Loretta Young (the 1947 winner) at the 1948 Oscar Awards.

career" (*Cue* magazine). "Her performance is a personal success, a socko demonstration that an artist can shape a mood and sway an audience through projected emotions without a spoken word" *(Variety)*. "A complete departure from the wise-cracking comedy roles usually associated with Miss Wyman. . . . She establishes herself as one of Hollywood's foremost dramatic actresses" *(New York Enquirer)*.

Jane received many awards and citations for her performance in *Johnny Belinda*. Most notable among these was the Academy Award for Best Actress of 1948. She was competing against Ingrid Bergman *(Joan of Arc)*, Olivia de Havilland *(The Snake Pit)*, Irene Dunne *(I Remember Mama)*, and Barbara Stanwyck *(Sorry, Wrong Number)*.

On Thursday, March 24, 1949, Jane was announced as the winner. She remembers the Award ceremony vividly: "I was sitting with the Jerry Walds, who are old buddies, just two rows behind Irene [Dunne]. There was something about the line of her neck that convinced me she was going to get the prize. I was slumped low in my seat (I've often been told that I don't know how to sit like a lady), sort of trying to hide so that I could sneak out. My purse was open on my lap, and when they started reading off the names I began wiping my nose with a handkerchief. It wasn't running; it's just a nervous habit, I guess. When my name was called I had to push myself forward to get up; the bag fell and baubles started rolling down the aisle. I must have been quite a sight trying to pick up things and get to the stage at the same time. I was so excited I didn't know what to say (Bob Montgomery, standing in the wings, grinned at me and said 'You're on your own, honey; I can't help you now'), so I just blurted out something. You always think of something to say, so I didn't prepare anything in advance, just in case I didn't win."

What Jane "blurted out" is regarded as a classic in brevity for an acceptance speech at the Academy Awards. "I accept this award very gratefully for keeping my mouth shut once. I think I'll do it again."

In addition to the Academy Award, Jane received a citation from the Latin American Consular Association for her work, and a plaque and a silver compact box as best actress from the Osaka Film Festival in 1950. She also received the *Picturegoer* magazine Gold Medal. The *London Daily Express* awarded her a prize of 1,000 pounds as "actress of the year." (Jane donated this prize to the Royal Academy of Dramatic Arts to create a scholarship, receiving a gracious letter of thanks from the Queen of England.) The publicity generated in Britain by this award and the subsequent donation served to pack London's Warner Theatre in Leicester Square, prompting Warner Bros. to announce that Jane was "now to be considered right up in the Bette Davis-Joan Crawford class."

One of the few people who did *not* like *Johnny Belinda* was Jack L. Warner who complained when he saw the daily rushes that the picture was about nothing but rolling fog and shots of sea gulls. When he viewed the completed picture, Warner disliked it so much that Jean Negulesco was fired from the lot and the picture was shelved. Fortunately, Jack's brother in New York saw the film and liked it so much that he insisted it be released. After the critical and popular acclaim for the picture was apparent, Jane made Jack L. Warner pay for a large trade ad apologizing to and thanking the entire cast and crew.

Jane had been escorted to the Academy Award ceremony by Lew Ayres, while Ronald Reagan had come to the festivities alone, for by March 1949 the Reagans were in the process of being divorced. When they separated in January 1948, Reagan told columnist Gladys Hall: "It's a strange character I'm married to, but—I love her. . . . Please remember that Jane went through a very bad time when, after the strain of waiting for another baby, she lost it. Then, perhaps, before she was strong enough, she went into *Johnny Belinda*. It was a taxing, difficult role. Perhaps, too, my seriousness about public affairs has bored Jane."

Louella Parsons was typically more dramatic: "No marital separation since I broke the story that Mary Pickford, America's sweetheart, was leaving Douglas Fairbanks has had the effect of the parting of the Reagans. Just as Mary and Doug stood for all that is best in this town, so have Ronnie and Jane. . . . To those of us who are close friends, they were an ideal Mr. and Mrs. . . . When he was ill, six months ago, she was almost out of her mind with worry. . . . Jane, who was expecting a baby at the time, was so distraught that she gave birth prematurely. The baby did not live."

According to Miss Parsons, Reagan said: "Right now, Jane needs very much to have a fling and I intend to let her have it. She is sick and nervous and not herself. . . . Jane says she loves me, but is no longer 'in love' with me, and points out that this is a fine distinction. That, I don't believe. I think she is nervous, despondent, and because of this she feels our life together has become humdrum."

Louella ended her piece with an observation, Parsons-style. "He's trying so hard—almost courting the wife he loves back to him."

In his book *They Call Me the Show Business Priest* (1973), Father Robert Perrella, a friend of Wyman, relates, "She admits it was exasperating to awake in the middle of the night, prepare for work, and have someone at the breakfast table, newspaper in hand, expounding on the far right, far left, the conservative right, the conservative left, the middle-of-the-roader. She harbors no ill feeling toward him."

One fan magazine of the day reported: "It is no secret Lew Ayres is responsible for the breakup." However, according to United Press International, Jane testified that she and Ronnie had "differences over politics" and that his being president of the Screen Actors Guild caused them to argue and him to have little time for her.

After her separation, Jane moved to an eight-room house in Bel Air, designed by architect Paul Williams. She took up residence with Maureen, Michael, and three servants. Of the domestics, she said, "These girls are my friends and the friends of my children. They live here with us; it's their home; they're just as important to the running of it as I am. Every kind of work has dignity if you put it there."

On Thursday, May 6, 1948, Jane filed for divorce from Reagan. The interlocutory decree was granted on Monday, June 28, 1948, and the final decree would be issued on Monday, July 18, 1949. As settlement in the divorce, Jane received custody of the two children and $500 a month for their support, and Reagan had to maintain $25,000 insurance policies on both himself and Jane and keep up their jointly owned home. Jane retained the right to ride horseback at their ranch. In June 1947, plans had been announced for a "Wyman-Reagan School of Speech and Dramatic Arts" at Eureka College in Illinois, Ronald's alma mater. The Reagans were contributing half the cost of the $150,000 building which was to serve as a chapel and theatre, with motion picture facilities. Plans for the construction went ahead despite the divorce.

Commenting at the time on the divorce, Reagan told Hedda Hopper that he should have named *Johnny Belinda* as co-respondent: "If I've had any competition it's been only in the roles she played on the screen."

Before *Johnny Belinda* became such a surprise hit, aided by Jane's cross-country promotional tour, Warner Bros. was not thinking very highly of its dramatic actress. The studio blithely cast her in a silly comedy with David Niven entitled *A Kiss in the Dark* (1949). She prances about in shorts and a Turkish towel while she both loves and fights with concert pianist Niven. The *New York Herald-Tribune* would chide: "It is luckless timing that finds Jane Wyman, winner of an Academy Award, appearing in a shabby and ridiculous film. . . . The actress gives no hint of the artistry that distinguished *Johnny Belinda*. She parades her gams with an almost exhibitionistic fervor. . . . Altogether, hers is a woefully inept performance. She should turn the face of her Oscar to the wall." Jane would later comment, "I used to do nothing but comedy, and then I stopped

With David Niven, Broderick Crawford, and Victor Moore in *A Kiss in the Dark* ('49).

With Dennis Morgan in *The Lady Takes a Sailor* ('49).

it and went into serious drama. When I returned to it recently in *A Kiss in the Dark*, I found my timing had slipped somewhat. I'd been away from it too long. Comedy is very tricky. And I take my hat off to anyone who can play it well. The two best comediennes on the screen, at least in my opinion, are Betty Hutton and Jean Arthur."

The Lady Takes a Sailor (1949)—first titled *The Octopus and Miss Smith*—presents Jane as the businesslike head of the Buyers' Research Institute which gives its seal of approval to consumer products. Dennis Morgan is the captain of a one-man underwater tractor-tank. Eve Arden was notable as an acid-witted career girl. The plot was too absurd and the comedy too forced to merit much audience enthusiasm, but Jane's Oscar gave the film some box-office appeal.

Warner Bros. next made a light-hearted effort to lampoon its stars, directors, producers, and publicity men in *It's a Great Feeling* (1949), a color comedy whose plot concerned Jack Carson's effort to direct himself, Dennis Morgan, and Doris Day (as a movie-struck commissary waitress). Directors Raoul Walsh, Michael Curtiz, King Vidor, and David Butler (who actually directed) are all seen heatedly refusing to direct the hammy Carson. Cameo appearances were made by Edward G. Robinson, Joan Crawford, Gary Cooper, Errol Flynn, and a host of others. Jane had a bit as herself, fainting when she hears she is wanted to co-star again with Carson. Daughter Maureen appeared in the slapstick bit.

After Jane's *Johnny Belinda* Oscar, there was talk of co-starring Jane and Lew Ayres in the Henry and Phoebe Ephron comedy *Career Girl*, but the project did not materialize. There were also rumors that Jane might play the female lead in *A Streetcar Named Desire*, but the part would eventually go to Vivien Leigh. Jane herself wanted now to concentrate on good character roles. She informed the press that she was not terribly concerned if the roles she accepted were not of star calibre, just as long as they were interesting. On the Warner Bros. lot she had by now acquired prestige status. When Bette Davis, among others, left the studio in the 1948–49 changeover of talent, she left behind her huge dressing room trailer which would not fit through the main gates, and Jane inherited the vehicle. (Years later it would be dismantled and carted off to the San Fernando Valley where it became the office for a real estate man.)

Columnist Sheilah Graham around that time wrote an article on Jane, naming her as one of "Hollywood's Dangerous Women." As she explained, "I mean those women who are dangerous to you if you are a producer, if you are a bachelor, of if you are another star who wants the same wonderful part in some new production . . . [the women whose] wits, courage, determination and sex appeal give them the highest potential for succeeding in whatever they make up their minds to get. . . . They say that the number one reason why Jane Wyman divorced Ronald Reagan was because she was bored with him. I don't know about that, but Jane *does* like to gadabout and she does like to have fun. She likes to dance. She likes to dress up. She likes men. And they find her dangerously desirable. She has a clean look that seems to arouse them. She's smart, emotional, ambitious. . . . This, added to everything else, makes her someone to be reckoned with."

Early in April of 1949 Jane left for England to work in *Stage Fright* (1950), an adaptation of Selwyn Jepson's novel *Man Running*. Her director was to be the prestigious Alfred Hitchcock. In this suspense tale, Jane plays a Royal Academy of Dramatic Arts student in love with a young man (Richard Todd) who is sought by the police for homicide. Jane suspects that entertainer Marlene Dietrich is the real killer. Thus Wyman and her father (Alastair Sim in a wonderfully droll performance) set about to establish Dietrich's guilt. In the course of the film, Jane falls in love with police inspector Michael Wilding.

There has been some controversy about Jane's attitude toward her role in *Stage Fright*. Hitchcock has said, "I ran into great difficulties with Jane. In her disguise as a

Seen off at Southampton, England, by director Alfred Hitchcock after completing *Stage Fright* (September 22, 1949).

lady's maid [as part of the plot to trap Dietrich], she should have been rather unglamorous; after all, she was supposed to be impersonating an unattractive maid. But every time she saw the rushes and how she looked alongside Marlene Dietrich, she would burst into tears. She couldn't accept the idea of her face being in character, while Dietrich looked so great. She kept improving her appearance every day and that's how she failed to maintain the character." But Jane denies this, recalling that she said to Dietrich, "Well, Marlene, I'll leave the glamour to you." In fact, Jane publicly had fine things to say of the legendary Dietrich: "The most fascinating person I've ever met. On days when she had no studio call she would come on the set just the same. She'd fix my dress, make suggestions about my hair and makeup, and help me in many ways." About her director, she would comment, "He looks like a little tubby pixie."

While in England, Jane was overly sensitive about how she should behave, now that she was a famous star. As she told Louella Parsons, "I realize the press was very good to me in England. We had one big meeting, but I watched myself to see that I wouldn't make any mistakes because, as I said, I felt I was not only acting for myself, but for all of Hollywood, and I didn't want to disillusion any of the reporters. Art and politics, you know, should never be mixed—so I feel that actresses who go to a foreign country should try to talk about the things they know . . . the theatre, motion pictures, books, plays, etc."

Jane picked up her cockney accent for *Stage Fright* in this way: "The girl [Kay Walsh] who played Nellie in the picture is one of England's best character actresses, and I lived with her for a week while she taught me. I was very pleased when one of the men in the crew who is a cockney said, 'Miss Wyman, you've got just the right inflection in your voice.' You know, I fell in love with the character I played in *Stage Fright* just the way I did the deaf girl in *Johnny Belinda*. I like to play people who have problems and to solve them if possible."

Stage Fright, despite the hoopla of Hitchcock returning to England for the filming, actually has had little impact in the director's canon of films. It had an important cast and received good bookings, but it was an implausible, heavy-handed mystery that did little to advance the careers of any of its participants. Miss Dietrich and Alastair Sim received the best notices, while Jane was criticized by some for her unconvincing love scenes.

Yet her private life proved quite the contrary. Columnist Ruth Waterbury reported that Jane will tell anyone who will listen, " 'Lew Ayres is the love of my life.' Ayres says nothing, puffs contentedly on his pipe, holds Jane's hand during their many nights out. At her divorce hearing, Jane said, 'I know I'm going to look like the heavy, divorcing the All-American boy. I'm in a situation lots of women are in. I don't know whether it is better for the children's sakes to hold an empty marriage together, or to start afresh and hope for future happiness.' " Miss Waterbury added, "And this is no whitewash—they never had a date of any sort together until well after Jane and Ronnie had separated. They probably will be married this summer when Jane's divorce becomes final. Lew has had Jane down to meet his family. They now are going openly everywhere together, and exclusively with one another. Yet most of the time, no one sees them because they are alone together, talking, reading, studying, painting." (Ironically Ayres had been against having Jane as his *Johnny Belinda* co-star. He thought Jane was a "cutie" and that Teresa Wright would be more appropriate for the deaf mute role.)

However, the Wyman/Ayres alliance cooled, and Jane, one of the most popular and in-demand persons in Hollywood, was suddenly lonely. "I thought when my divorce was final, the telephone would ring itself right off the table. Well, it has. The vet has called to say we could take the dog home. The dentist has called about the children's teeth. The dressmaker has called, the hairdresser has called, even the radio survey people have called. But after six o'clock, things quiet down considerably."

Newspaperman Sidney Skolsky reported that Jane and Reagan continued to be good friends. "Jane has a painting of him in her dressing room. He often visits and watches her when she is working on a picture. She doesn't visit him on his set." Jane and Ronnie alternated on Sundays taking the children to Sunday school. On Friday nights, Ronald would try to take Maureen to some cultural event. On Saturday, Mike went to Ronald's ranch. When Jane was in London making *Stage Fright*, Ronald stayed at her house to supervise the children. There were even rumors circulating that Jane was pregnant and was going to remarry Reagan to save her name. The gossip, so legend has it, started when Reagan was overheard at lunch at The Players discussing a film role and saying: "In the picture I discover my divorced wife is pregnant and I have to come home and remarry her."

Jane was continually pestered about two subjects. The first was her ex-spouse. She has said, "It's bad taste to talk about ex-husbands and ex-wives, that's all." On another occasion she added cryptically, "Not *one* of those stories about Ronnie and me *ever touched* the truth! They were so unkind." The second subject was about remarriage, and in regard to this she answered Louella Parsons rather heatedly: "Oh dear, do you, of all people, have to ask me that? How can I say? There is no one now. My career and my children keep me very busy. I know you love Ronnie, and I know you love me, but can't we just once have an interview and not talk about my broken marriage and what caused it? Let's just say I still think Ronnie is a fine man and a wonderful father."

Warner Bros. mentioned that Jane would probably star in the long-postponed version of James Cain's *Serenade*, but it was not until 1956 that the project reached the screen, and then with Joan Fontaine and Sarita Montiel in the female roles opposite Mario Lanza. Jack L. Warner also insisted that Ring Lardner's story "Haircut" was being adapted for Jane, but that project disintegrated.

However, she did star in Warner Bros.' *The Glass Menagerie* (1950), based on Tennessee Williams' Broadway drama. It is the well-known story of crippled young Laura Wingfield (played by Jane at the age of thirty-five), her illusion-dominated mother (Gertrude Lawrence), her dreamy brother (Arthur Kennedy), and the "gentleman caller" (Kirk Douglas). Jane offered a sensitively interpreted performance as the shy and fragile young woman living in a world of her own dominated by a collection of small glass animals. To add realism to the part, she wore a special shoe which made her limp. (Plans for her to wear a heavy leg brace were canceled when it proved a distraction during rehearsals.) Her scene by candlelight with Douglas was singled out by astute critics as the best moment in the film. The *New York Herald-Tribune* commented: "Of the four principals, Jane Wyman as Laura is the most convincing.... She duplicates much of the same fragile sweetness which she displayed in *Johnny Belinda*."

Producer Jerry Wald supervised this major project, and he had his own insights about her talents: "She isn't fresh anymore. She's mellowed, but not marshmallowed. In the old days, she'd read a script and ten minutes later be in the picture; a script was a script and to hell with it. Now she reads a script, studies the character for weeks and months, discusses it thoroughly, and has a deep and perfect understanding of the part before she goes before the cameras. Jane should never do comedies again. Comediennes in this town are a dime a dozen. She is a great dramatic actress.... The remarkable thing about Jane is that she has grown up. Most actresses never do."

Evidently Hollywood filmmakers did not heed Wald's sage advice. She went over to MGM for *Three Guys Named Mike* (1951), a witless if congenial comedy billed as "a non-stop flight into funland." (It was a project planned by Metro in 1948 for Lana Turner.) *Three Guys* was the account of an airline stewardess (Jane) who is romantically pursued by three Mikes—Van Johnson as a research scientist, Howard Keel as a pilot, and Barry

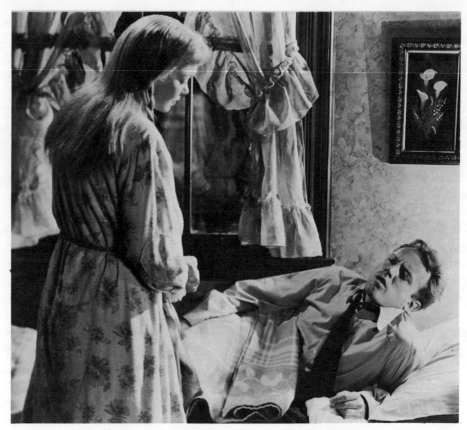

With Arthur Kennedy in *The Glass Menagerie* ('50).

Sullivan as an advertising executive. It was pretty much the type of vehicle that Esther Williams handled at Metro. For the picture's finale, Jane jumps into a sarong and the boys clash in a fight. It would be unfair to reveal who wins.

Paramount's *Here Comes the Groom* (1951), directed by Frank Capra, starred Jane and Bing Crosby in a romantic farce. He is a newsman who has brought two French orphans back to the United States with him and has five days to get married. Jane is Emmadel Jones, a fisherman's daughter who was a childhood sweetheart of his but who is now engaged to a Boston millionaire (Franchot Tone). Alexis Smith, who once outshone Jane at Warner Bros. and was now freelancing, played the other woman. The *New York Times* found: "Jane Wyman can still scamper, and she does plenty of it here." Jane and Bing sing the hit tune "In the Cool, Cool, Cool of the Evening," which won an Academy Award as Best Song, and the film helped to introduce the young songstress Anna Maria Alberghetti. Jane said of this venture, "It was a holiday doing this picture with Bing."

According to Louella Parsons, Jane was concerned that she had been doing too many dramatic parts: "All those roles without any glamour are getting me down. It's bad for my morale, too. I need a change, and so do my fans." Louella commented, "She got her wish in *Here Comes the Groom* with Bing Crosby, and set the town on its ear with her unexpected talent. . . . 'If you can hold your own with Crosby, you've hit the top' is an old saying in Hollywood. . . . Jane fairly sparkled through songs and dances, and looked cute as a button doing it."

Not only that, but she impressed a variety of important people with her singing. The London Palladium offered her a singing engagement, but she rejected it. Yet she did sign a contract with Decca Records. She recorded "In the Cool, Cool, Cool of the Eve-

402

ning" with Crosby, with the couple dueting "Misto Cristofo Columbo" on the other side of the single. In ensuing years she would cut singles of "Blow Out the Candle," "I Love That Feelin'," "It Was Nice While the Money Rolled In," and "Why Didn't I?" She would duet "No Two People" with Danny Kaye, and with Kaye, Jimmy Durante, and Groucho Marx she would sing "Black Strap Molasses" and "How D'ye Do and Shake Hands."

In typical Hollywood fashion, her home lot, Warner Bros., still could not decide how best to exploit Jane. They ordered her to co-star with Kirk Douglas in a Western— *Along the Great Divide* (1951). She refused and Virginia Mayo replaced her. Instead Jane relocated to RKO for *The Blue Veil* (1951), a remake of the well-regarded 1942 French film which had starred Gaby Morlay. This RKO assignment (previously offered to an unimpressed Greta Garbo and Ingrid Bergman) proved to be one of the most taxing in Jane's entire career, especially in terms of makeup. It was the first independent production of Jerry Wald and Norman Krasna at that studio. In this "four hanky" picture, Jane plays Louise Mason, a World War I widow who becomes a children's nurse after losing her only child. The 113-minute feature traces her life for thirty years as she cares for a succession of charges, spurning her own chance for personal happiness in favor of offering tender devotion to her children. She refuses the love of aging Charles Laughton and fit Richard Carlson, self-sacrificingly shames Joan Blondell into leaving show business to care for her daughter (Natalie Wood), loses a court custody case to an irresponsible couple who have suddenly decided they want their son back from adoption, and finally grows too old to be hired as a nursemaid. She decides to take "anything near children" and becomes a public school janitress. However, one of her "children," now a doctor, finds her, gives her a surprise

With Reverend Neal Dodd, Charles Lane, Bing Crosby, Beverly Washburn, and Jack Gencel in *Here Comes the Groom* ('51).

party which many of her former charges attend, and offers her a permanent post in his house caring for his two children.

The ad line for the film asked "Who is the *real* mother of this child?" and pictured Jane tenderly clutching a slightly cross-eyed infant. The *New York Times* offered, "Miss Wyman—the whole thing, naturally—has little to do herself except to age daintily," and it labeled the product "a whoppingly banal tear-jerker." *Variety*, however, countered, "It was a personal triumph that ranks with, if not surpassing, any for which she has previously been kudoed."

Jane's complex makeup was created and executed by Perc Westmore. Apparently they formed a close professional relationship on the sound stage, for years later (in 1957) it would be reported: "[Westmore] got out of a hospital bed at Hollywood Presbyterian to cut Jane Wyman's hair. She has her glamour look back, and the bangs she wore which were so cute." In any case, during the making of *The Blue Veil*, Wyman spent as many as fourteen hours a day in the thick latex masking necessary to give her the aged look.

As she did with several previous roles, Jane sought to understand as much as possible about her characterization. "Well, honey," she told one reporter, "I put a lot of research in it. First of all, I started studying old people—at the club, on the lot or in restaurants. I know a lot of them must have thought me crazy. I would just sit and stare. Then, I went to the library and read up on the subject. It was an education, honey. I found out that as people age, their bone structure changes. That's why they stoop and walk the way they do. Next, Perc Westmore and I spent many nights right here in this den until one or two o'clock sketching the various postures of old people."

Jane was also coached in her role aging by Laughton on the set, and she said about him: "He has a phenomenal brain. He is the most learned man I have ever met. To sit and talk with him is an intellectual bath. I

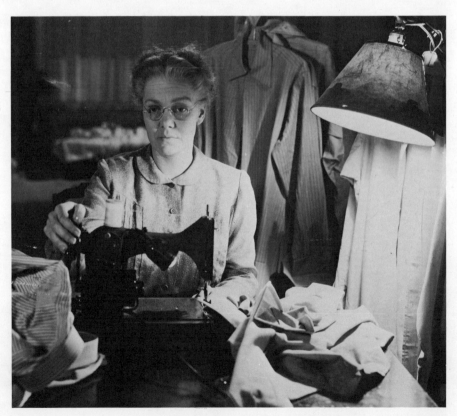

In *The Blue Veil* ('51).

learned more about acting from him in ten days than I could have learned in ten years knocking my own blundering head against walls. He makes me *feel* old."

Maureen Reagan saw the film at its premiere, accompanying her mother. The eleven-year-old cried through three handkerchiefs. When she was asked how Jane felt about the film, she responded, "My mother? Well, I want you to know she was sitting right next to me, and she wasn't moved at *all*. I don't believe my mother *understands* drama!"

Jane received her third Oscar nomination for *The Blue Veil*. Her rivals were Katharine Hepburn *(The African Queen)*, Vivien Leigh, who won *(A Streetcar Named Desire)*, Eleanor Parker *(Detective Story)*, and Shelley Winters *(A Place in the Sun)*. Jane did, however, win a Foreign Correspondents' Golden Globe Award for the Best Performance of the Year.

Her fourth and final 1951 release was a cameo in Warner Bros.' all-star extravaganza entitled *Starlift* (1951). It dealt with the implementation of the idea (dreamed up by a soldier in love with a starlet) of screen celebrities visiting Travis Air Force Base, the take-off point for Korea, in an air shuttle of entertainers from Hollywood. Jane did her bit by singing "I May Be Wrong" during a personal appearance at an Army hospital.

In the years after her divorce from Reagan and before she eventually remarried, there was much notice taken of the men Jane dated. She was reported as "seeing" costumer Milo Anderson who escorted her to the premiere of Reagan's *The Hasty Heart* (1949), Peter Lawford, Cedric Hardwicke, and Gregson Bautzer, a handsome lawyer who had "eluded almost every belle in Hollywood." The latter was spotted with Jane on various occasions during 1950, and in 1951 he escorted her and Maureen to the premiere of *The Blue Veil*. According to *Photoplay* magazine, Jane and Greg Bautzer were so close to marrying that they had Wasserman tests (required by California law) at the office of the Reagan children's pediatrician (in order to avoid publicity), but the affair drifted into nothingness. Lana Turner, who should know, once termed Bautzer "the greatest escape artist in town."

A more serious romance for Jane occurred early in 1952 when, after only ten weeks of acquaintance, Jane (age thirty-eight) and Travis Kleefeld (age twenty-six), heir to a vast building enterprise, announced their engagement. Even Jane's closest friends were surprised. The couple planned a June 1952 wedding, with a real trousseau, a European honeymoon, and Edith Head designing Jane's travel wardrobe. The engagement lasted three weeks before Jane called it off. She insisted that pressures from the press and from friends had forced both the engagement and the disengagement. It all seemed like a real-life rehearsal for Jane's future film *All That Heaven Allows* (1955).

Meanwhile, in 1952, Ronald Reagan made his final Warner Bros. film (*The Winning Team* with Doris Day) and married starlet Nancy Davis.

In 1951, according to a *New York Times'* report of a three and a half month poll in some fifty countries by newspapers, radio stations, and magazines sampling one million people, Gregory Peck and Jane were voted "the world's favorite screen actor and actress." Runners-up were Alan Ladd and Ingrid Bergman. Nevertheless, for some bizarre reason, Warner Bros. chose to sandwich Wyman into *The Story of Will Rogers* (1952), a very standard biography that offered her little chance to exhibit her money-earning talents.* Will Rogers, Jr., portrayed his father, and Jane enacted his wife. The Michael Curtiz-directed film was overly maudlin and lackluster and it failed at the box office. Even so, on the strength of her previous year's picture grosses, Jane was named second at the box office by *Film Daily* newspaper, right behind Gary Cooper, and ahead of Susan Hayward, Bing Crosby, June

---

*Warner Bros. had been planning to film *The Story of Will Rogers* since early 1944. At one point in the fall of that year Joel McCrea was announced to star in the project, with Mark Hellinger producing and Michael Curtiz directing. When McCrea maneuvered out of the production, the studio tested Bing Crosby, John Wayne, Stuart Erwin, *et al.* to portray the great comedian, finally shelving the concept till the early Fifties.

With Dick Wesson and Janice Rule in *Starlift* ('51).

Jane Wyman's "Church Scene" painting used for a Hallmark greeting card ('52).

Publicity pose for *Just for You* ('52).

Allyson, Doris Day, Gregory Peck, Esther Williams, Cary Grant, and John Wayne.

Bing Crosby was so taken with Jane in his previous film excursion with her that he obtained her services for Paramount's *Just for You* (1952). In it, Jane played Carolina Hill, a zesty Broadway star who is more or less engaged to Crosby, a writer of musicals who has no time for his offspring. Crosby's son (Robert Arthur) falls in love with Wyman. By the end of the film, Bing and Jane are happily together singing* "Zing a Little Zong," the son is reconciled to the situation, and Crosby's daughter (Natalie Wood) has been accepted at the exclusive girls' school she longs to attend. An amusing bit of dialogue within the film occurs when Arthur introduces Wyman to his friends on the beach. After naming each boy and following that with a "Yale '53" or a "Harvard '54," Jane counters with "And I'm Regent 5-3098." The boys boggle.

Columbia's *Let's Do It Again* (1953) was the first of Jane's appearances as the remake queen of the Fifties. (Her nearest rival was June Allyson.) The classic talkie version of the story, *The Awful Truth* (1937), had Irene Dunne, Cary Grant, and Ralph Bellamy in the roles now played in this musical revamping by Jane, Ray Milland, and Aldo Ray. Jane is singer Constance Stuart and Milland is her composer husband. Each suspects the other of marital infidelity, and they file for divorce. By the end of their sixty-day divorce decree period, each has frightened off a potential new spouse for the other and the two realize they are still in love. Jane, to scare off Milland's very proper fiancée and her family, poses as his floozie sister and dances the "Ambesi puberty ritual—a dance designed to separate the men from the boys" and sings about wanting to make love "the jungle way." While this retread—the fourth edition of the tale—was not up to the wit and bite of its predecessors, it had an appeal all its own.

Jane met her third (also to be her fourth) husband on the set of *Let's Do It Again*. Freddie Karger was a Columbia Pictures associate music director at the time. After a whirlwind one-month courtship—although they had known each casually for a long time before—they eloped and married on Saturday, November 1, 1952, at the El Montecito Presbyterian Church in Santa Barbara. Karger's closest friend, actor-director Richard Quine, and his wife were in attendance. It was Karger's second marriage, and he had a daughter Terry from that union. The couple spent their one-day honeymoon at a ranch in San Ysidro.

So Big (1953) was the third version of the Edna Ferber novel which had previously showcased Colleen Moore (1925) and Barbara Stanwyck (1932). In effect it was a rural soap opera, the first in a string of soapers that would close out another phase of Jane's show-business career. In it she plays an idealistic young school teacher named Selina who believes that the world's people are wheat (tillers of the soil) or emeralds (artists). Widowed soon after wedding a truck farmer, she continues his work and

With Walter Coy in *So Big* ('53).

---
*Jane and Crosby recorded their songs from this film for Decca Records.

brings up their son, nicknamed "So Big," to be an architect. Although he rebels for a spell, everything turns out properly for Selina, the dignified and wise philosopher of rural life. Despite its homespun and teary nature, *So Big* was still an engrossing vehicle. The *New York Times* reported, "Miss Wyman, whose acting of drudges has become a virtual standard on the screen, is remarkably strong and effective."

During this period of star vehicles, Jane was undergoing many transitions. In the early fifties she became a Roman Catholic. (In early 1955 she would have her two children baptized in the faith, inviting Reagan and his wife to attend, and Sheilah Graham described Jane as never before looking "so peaceful.")

Of her star power, one columnist reported, "Until eight years ago she was no money-draw and there were no problems. When she became an important star, she and Jack Warner sat down together and talked for six hours.... It was not a question of whether Jane would do comedy or drama; it was a matter of general principles."

Jane said of her relations with Jack Warner, "We have a mutual respect. If one of us says "It's raining," the other doesn't bother looking out the window to see."

Despite her celebrity position, Jane had fixed ideas about her right to privacy: "I feel an obligation to the public that is twofold—to make good pictures and to lead the best possible life. Outside of that, what else can there be? You can't take the public into your home; there isn't room. If you open that front door and let the world in, if you open your heart and let the world in, how do you maintain an intimate relationship with your husband, with your children? It's as simple as this—would the public rather live in my house or see me on the screen?"

On Sunday, January 3, 1954, Jane and Karger separated, after hardly more than fourteen months of marriage. A petition for divorce was filed by Jane on January 8 in the Superior Court of Santa Monica and a hearing set for January 26. However, on January 25, Jane was reported to have contracted a virus, and the hearing was delayed. In May the couple were reported still to be negotiating. They separated finally on November 7, and the interlocutory decree was granted on December 7. The testimony included Jane's affirmation that Karger had stated, "I'm sorry that I married you." The final decree was granted on December 30, 1955. The petition for the divorce stated there was no community property and no joint children, and that each party relinquished all claims to the earnings and holdings of the other forevermore. Jane also requested the legal right to resume her former name of Wyman.

The exclusive phase of Jane's Warner Bros. contract, which paid her $3,500 weekly, ended in 1953. After that, she received $200,000 per film. Universal met that fee for its remake of *Magnificent Obsession* (1954), a sudsy melodrama directed in fine style by Douglas Sirk. She and Rock Hudson repeated the roles once handled by Irene Dunne and Robert Taylor. Hudson plays Bob Merrick, the rich playboy indirectly responsible for the death of Jane's doctor husband.

Later, attempting to apologize for his part in her widowhood, he inadvertently causes an accident which leaves her blind. In time he becomes privy to the mystical secret (doing random good without hope of reward) that made her husband such a good individual. Eventually he goes back to medical school and becomes a sterling surgeon. He operates on Wyman and cures her blindness. Throughout all this, swelling Frank Skinner music and tearjerking dialogue add to the appeal of this woman's picture. The *New York Times* championed, "In appealing contrast to Miss Dunne's pristine languor, Miss Wyman is, as usual, refreshingly believable throughout."

As with the other handicapped roles she had interpreted in the past, Jane strove for complete authenticity here: "I discovered from a blind companion, who assisted me with technical advice on *Magnificent Obsession,* that my greatest problem would be the tendency to overact. The blind do not careen around rooms knocking over vases and

With Rock Hudson in *Magnificent Obsession* ('54).

lamps, nor do they grope wildly at the air in front of them. With this type of handicap as with all the others, I learned the importance of knowing how blind persons feel inside. In transmitting that sense of blindness and emotion, the problem, as with all acting, is to make the audience emote for you."

Hollywood frequently responds to a real tear-duct opener, and so Jane received her fourth Academy Award nomination. In the running with her were Dorothy Dandridge *(Carmen Jones)*, Judy Garland *(A Star Is Born)*, Audrey Hepburn *(Sabrina)*, and Grace Kelly, the winner *(The Country Girl)*. This was the third of Jane's Oscar nominations for films made away from Warner Bros.

Paramount's *Lucy Gallant* (1955), which pitted Jane romantically against Charlton Heston,* was another woman-oriented feature, this time set in an oil boom town in Texas. Jane plays a youngish bride-to-be who is disappointed and goes west to forget her jilted lover. On a stopover in an oil town she sells her wedding trousseau for ready cash and decides to remain there, opening a department store. Later on in the 104-minute film, the store burns down, Jane rejects Heston's amorous advances, there are backyard barbecues and a fashion show introduced by Texas' then governor Allan Shivers and narrated by Edith Head, and other assorted catastrophes and adventures before Jane settles down with her ex-farmer millionaire (Heston). The film was generally panned, but Jane's performance was regarded as serviceable, while Claire Trevor (as the good-hearted prostitute) and Thelma Ritter (as the yokel who becomes rich overnight) were credited with infusing some life into the tame happenings.

Producer Ross Hunter and director Douglas Sirk reteamed with Jane for Universal's *All That Heaven Allows* (1955), and for good

---

*During the making of *Lucy Gallant*, outspoken Wyman advised Heston to "lose that fat rear you're carrying around." Candid Jane also had advice for her other co-stars, including Rock Hudson, as to how to improve their box-office standing.

With Ethel Merman and Fred Karger in June 1954.

With Charlton Heston in *Lucy Gallant* ('55).

luck at the box office Rock Hudson and Barbara Rush, also of *Magnificent Obsession*, were joined in the package. As Cary Scott, Jane was a not very merry widow who allows her gardener (Hudson) to romance her. However, his life-style and his age are far below Jane's. Her children advise her against seeing Hudson, but eventually they are reunited to find happiness on their own terms. While the color film is well crafted and sensibly acted (save for stilted Hudson), it retains a ludicrous melodramatic air that undercuts its theme of individualism and spiritual freedom. Shortcomings and all, the picture found its audience, and Jane made the *Film Daily*'s annual poll as one of the top ten box-office stars of the year.

Miracle in the Rain (1956) was anything but that. It had been previously done as a CBS-TV drama in 1953 with Phyllis Thaxter and William Prince. Warner Bros. hired Ben Hecht to expand the storyline and cast Jane opposite Van Johnson, under Rudolph Maté's direction. It was shot largely on location in New York, with a World War II background. Its fanciful theme has timid, homely secretary (Jane) falling in love with soldier Johnson. When he goes off to war and is killed in action, he miraculously comes back to life to return to her the Roman coin she had given him as a good-luck keepsake. A voiceover narrator at the finale asserts, "Thus a story of New York and of an antique Roman coin. That's the way we heard it. We'd like to believe it's true." Giving the demented film some credit, there were occasional touching moments and superior performances by Eileen Heckart (as Jane's best friend), Josephine Hutchinson (her mother), and William Gargan (her errant father).

Although Jane reportedly said that thereafter she would only do comedies on the big screen, it was to television that she next turned. One major reason was that Jack Warner had ignored *Miracle in the Rain* because he had *Giant* in release at the same time. As she said: "I realized that the time for my kind of film was passing, that the blockbuster was now in. So I got out while the going was good." When Jane left Warner Bros. she had been on suspension only three times during her entire twenty-year career with the studio. As she put it, "While Bette [Davis] and Cagney were battling, I went on working. I was a team player. And if I ever had a problem, I went to the top man. Since I was usually right, he had to give in."

Jane had made her first television appearance* on Sunday, January 2, 1955, on the "G.E. Theatre" in a half-hour segment entitled *Amelia*. Explaining why she had waited so long to make her video bow, she stated about TV in the late Forties, "In those days everything was live, and I knew this wasn't for me. I'm strictly a movie actress—this is a profession all by itself, completely distinct from the theatre, and I knew that I wouldn't and couldn't go in and compete with the Broadway actresses who easily adapted themselves to this new medium. I had to wait until film became acceptable to the networks and the sponsors."

Jane did not want to play the same character week after week in a series, so her "Fireside Theatre" anthology series was born. She debuted on Tuesday, August 30, 1955, over NBC-TV, following in the pattern that had made Loretta Young so successful in the medium. (In fact, in later years, Loretta and Jane would often swap episode scripts.) She contracted to star in twenty of the thirty-six half-hour shows, with reruns filling out the season. In addition to acting, she was also the hostess. The series was budgeted at $4.5 million, with Jane as head of Lewman, Ltd., which was producing the series at Republic Studios. Procter and Gamble's Duz, Ivory Soap, and Crisco were the sponsoring products.

Jane's anthology series—later called "The Jane Wyman Theatre"—ran for three TV seasons, from the early fall of 1955 to the spring of 1958. In the course of the series, Jane played such diverse characters as

---

*In the late Forties and early Fifties, Jane had frequently been heard on radio in anthology series, recreating the roles made famous by others in film versions.

412

On "The Jane Wyman Theatre" with Penny Santon in the episode *The Thread* (NBC-TV, January 22, 1956).

With Eileen Heckart and Van Johnson in *Miracle in the Rain* ('56).

With Clifton Webb, Carol Lynley, and Jill St. John in *Holiday for Lovers* ('59).

an Air Force censorship officer, an irresponsible socialite, an embittered spinster, a circus trapeze artist, and a nurse in a mental hospital.* Almost all the plots were melodramatic, with murders, frame-ups, mysteries, and grief-crazed threats uppermost. Jane was twice Emmy-nominated but lost on each occasion to Loretta Young. When Jane's three seasons on TV were completed, she sold the package to be shown in rerun syndication. As late as the 1962–63 TV season her show was being telecast five afternoons a week.

In 1959, Jane, who made occasional appearances on TV, came out of semi-retirement to serve as a last-minute replacement for Gene Tierney in Twentieth Century-Fox's film *Holiday for Lovers*. She played Clifton Webb's wife in this mildly amusing comedy. The next year she was Aunt Polly in *Pollyanna* (1960), the first of two Walt Disney films in which she appeared. The ads described her thusly, "She could open up her pocketbook—but not her heart." Although overshadowed by the effervescent Hayley Mills in the title role, Jane was noted as "properly prim and correct" *(New York Times)*.

Since their divorce, Jane and Freddie Karger had continued to meet. On Saturday, March 11, 1961, they were rewed by a priest in a quiet ceremony in Newport Beach, California.

In 1961, Jane made guest appearances on three TV shows ("Rawhide," "The Investigators," and "G.E. Theatre"—the latter hosted by Ronald Reagan), and the next

---

*According to the book *They Call Me the Show Business Priest*, once, "while filming a segment of her TV series, she and an actor enacted a tender love scene. When he placed his lips upon hers, she realized he attempted to soul-kiss her. She gave no reaction, spoke no words. The segment completed, she fired him. And she thundered—sturdy, straight, and strong: 'The son of a bitch hasn't gotten a job since.' "

year she returned to Walt Disney's film studio to join with Fred MacMurray in *Bon Voyage* (1962). It carefully followed the Disney style of family entertainment as it detailed the misadventures of Fred and Jane leading their brood on a continental trek. Thanks to the Disney promotional backing, the feature grossed $5 million in the United States and Canada.

Jane was featured in an episode of "Wagon Train" in 1962 and in a segment of "Naked City" in 1963, and then she was inactive in show business until the end of the decade. However, she still had professional ambitions. In June 1964 it was announced that she would make her Broadway bow in *Not in Her Stars,* a romantic comedy by George Baxt. Jane was to play a widow who finds it difficult to make a new life for herself. Anita Louise was to co-star and Nancy Walker was to direct, but the project never came to fruition.

On Tuesday, March 9, 1965, Jane was divorced by Freddie Karger. He told the court that she had walked out on him; she charged "grievous mental cruelty" and said that he had an "uncontrollable temper."

A year later, in May 1966, it was reported Jane would appear on Broadway in *Wonderful Us,* a drama by Reginald Denham and Mary Orr. The play, based on an actual case, concerned two fifteen-year-old girls who develop a close friendship and then kill the girl's mother when she attempts to smash their camaraderie. Jane was to play a reporter/friend of the dead woman who sets out to discover the murderers. Jane did not ultimately appear in this play, either. That September she was scheduled to make her nightclub debut with Donald O'Connor at Harrah's in Lake Tahoe, but, after rehearsing, a week before the opening she was rushed to Cedars of Lebanon Hospital in Hollywood with acute pancreatitis, and she had to cancel the engagement.

Since her divorce from Karger and the near halt of her career, Jane has focused her activities on golf, fishing, and painting. She first started painting during the filming of *Johnny Belinda.* "When the fog [on location north of San Francisco] was thick, we'd put up our easels and have a ball painting." In 1952 one of Jane's paintings, entitled "Church Scene," was used for a Hallmark Christmas card in a series of stars' paintings cards. (She presented the canvas original to Lew Ayres.) The Jane of recent years says, "I take painting seriously. And I don't want people to think I'm just an aging actress filling in free time with a paintbrush."

Jane's last feature film to date was *How to Commit Marriage* (1969) with Bob Hope and Jackie Gleason. She has said of the misadventure: "[It was] a Mickey Mouse job. It was dated stuff about gurus." She again played a nice mother, this time about to be divorced by Hope, who at times in the dim picture disguises himself as a mod playboy and as a Hindu mystic. The *New York Times* reported, "Time seems to have had a stop. I don't know what kind of magic camera filters were used, but Miss Wyman, whose first movie this is in seven years, Gleason, who loves the good life, and particularly Hope, who is on the far side of 65, all look remarkably fit for people who could be physical ruins." That same year Jane appeared on a Bob Hope TV special.

Chipper Jane has been an occasional guest star on television in the Seventies. She starred with Dean Stockwell and Dana Andrews on the telefeature *The Failing of Raymond* (1971) about a school teacher terrorized by a schizoid former student; guested on "The Bold Ones" (as a projected pilot for a distaff "Marcus Welby, M.D." series) and "Sixth Sense" in 1972; and more recently was segment star for the *The Desertion of Keith Ryder* episode (1974) on "Owen Marshall, Counselor at Large." Since then she has appeared infrequently on talk shows and charity marathon outings.

Beginning in 1967, Jane has devoted a significant amount of time and energy to working for the Arthritis Foundation. In that year, she was a guest on the Annual Arthritis Telethon. In February 1968 Jane hostessed the Southern California telethon for the same disease, and she continues to do so yearly. In July 1968 she was elected to the

With Fred MacMurray in *Bon Voyage* ('62).

With Bob Hope, Tim Matthieson, and Joanna Cameron in *How to Commit Marriage* ('69).

In the *When Hell Froze* episode (NBC-TV, February 2, 1966) of "The Bob Hope Chrysler Theatre."

Board of Governors of the chapter, and she still serves in that capacity. In 1972 Jane was elected to the Executive Committee of the National Board of Directors for the Arthritis Foundation, and in 1973 she served on the Board's Public Education Committee. In both 1973 and 1974 Jane was National Campaign Chairman for the Foundation's fund-raising drives, traveling extensively, making speeches, and attending meetings. In 1975 she and Allen Ludden co-hosted the twentieth annual "Stop Arthritis Telethon." Also in that year, the National Governing Members elected her a Lifetime Honorary Director of the Arthritis Foundation. (In recent years, Jane often substituted for the ailing and now deceased spokeswoman Rosalind Russell, a sufferer of arthritis and a major supporter of its charity drives.)

During the years of Ronald Reagan's governorship of California and his more recent bids for the Republican presidential nomination, Jane remained discreetly out of the political scene. Her two children by Reagan continue to be a major interest. Maureen, twice wed and divorced, has been an actress and a TV/radio commentator, and she has held a variety of other jobs, most recently campaigning for women's liberation and for her father. (She has also stated, "I have a career of my own and I'm getting awfully sick of being known as somebody's kid.") Son Michael, who went to Valley State College in preparation for law school, is now a boat dealer.

In 1975 Jane sold her Los Angeles home and moved to Carmel, where she concentrated on charity work, painting, and her standby sports, golf and fishing.

It would be two years before Jane would make prominent public appearances again. She, along with Esther Williams and other stars of the Forties and Fifties, was present at the March 1, 1977, American Film Institute tribute to Bette Davis. On June 25, 1977, at the St. Francis Hotel in San Francisco, Wyman was presented with the annual Charles B. Harding Award for Distinguished Service on behalf of the Arthritis Foundation at ceremonies held during the annual meeting of the Foundation. The Oscar-winning star received a gold medallion for volunteer service. When the Directors Guild of America saluted director Clarence Brown on July 16, 1978, in Hollywood, Jane was among the many celebrities to reminisce on the rostrum about the filmmaker. At the benefit premiere for Gregory Peck's *MacArthur,* Jane was much in evidence, and at the post-screening party at the Beverly Wilshire Hotel, she sat with such stars as Loretta Young and Irene Dunne.

In early 1978 Jane joined with Anson "Happy Days" Williams and others on the "Stop Arthritis Telethon" on KTLA-TV in Los Angeles. The March 14, 1978, telecast of the "Dinah" show found Jane guesting with Shirley MacLaine, Robert Conrad, Cheryl Tiegs, and director Herbert Ross. Jane, in fine shape, except for her unflattering white hair color, retold the story of the night she won her Oscar. At one point in the familiar narration she had to "shush" puckish MacLaine who tried to interject a few remarks.

When asked that perennial question about one day returning to filmmaking, Jane responded a few years ago, "I won't lower myself to act in the type of films that are selling these days. I simply refuse to play a prostitute, a dope addict, or a murderess. . . . I don't like all the sick pictures being made. There is too much of it going on. Why should we put the seamy side of life up there on the screen when we're supposed to be entertainers? . . . Sometimes non-exposure is better than appearing in the wrong thing." Then she added: "I'm just not that ambitious anymore. I'm through clawing after parts. I've got other things going."

However, Jane had a change of heart in mid-1978. Executive producer Ron Samuels signed Wyman to guest-star in *The Incredible Journey of Doctor Meg Laurel.* It featured Lindsay Wagner as a Harvard-trained doctor who returns to the Appalachian hills of Kentucky in the early Thirties to start a clinic. Billed as "Miss Jane Wyman," the former Warner Bros. star was cast as a colorful local character who practices folk medicine. The

With daughter Maureen Reagan in Las Vegas (February 1970).

With director Clarence Brown at the Directors Guild of America Tribute to Brown on July 16, 1977 in Hollywood.

With director Alfred Hitchcock, restaurateur Maude Chasen (center), and George Burns for the NBC-TV special *The Pursuit of Youth* ('77).

Advertisement for *The Incredible Journey of Doctor Meg Laurel* (CBS-TV, January 2, 1979).

three-hour CBS-TV color movie was aired on Tuesday, January 2, 1979. The reviews for the show — a potential series — were tepid, but Jane received plaudits: "What could have been a routine Wagner-Wyman confrontation and eventual joining of forces was upgraded by a very professional reading of the healer's part by Wyman....Wyman's underplaying defanged some terrible cornpone dialogue and some folkhealing methods..." (*Variety*). "The most appeal is that of Granny Arrowroot as played by Jane Wyman, although this is not the most demanding role of her career" (*New York Daily News*). "Jane Wyman, as the local medicine-woman, is simply first-rate" (*TV Guide*). "Jane Wyman as a backwoods 'Granny doctor,' manifests a credible sturdiness and wisdom..." (*Hollywood Reporter*).

When asked if her performance could be interpreted as the start of a "second acting career," she cagily replied, "I haven't the faintest idea. Let's see how it goes." Evidently the thrill of being in front of the cameras again appealed to Jane, for she has since signed to appear in an episode of ABC-TV's "The Love Boat" series.

FILMOGRAPHY

As Sarah Jane Fulks:

THE KID FROM SPAIN *(United Artists, 1932)* 90 min.

Producer, Samuel Goldwyn; director, Leo McCarey; story/screenplay, William Anthony McGuire, Bert Kalmar, Harry Ruby; songs, Kalmar and Ruby; Kalmar, Ruby, and Harry Akst; music numbers staged by Busby Berkeley; sound, Vinton Vernon; camera, Gregg Toland; editor, Stuart Heisler.

Eddie Cantor (Eddie Williams); Lyda Roberti (Rosalie); Robert Young (Ricardo); Ruth Hall (Anita Gomez); John Miljan (Pancho); Noah Beery (Alonzo Gomez); J. Carroll Naish (Pedro); Robert Emmett O'Connor (Crawford); Stanley Fields (Jose); Paul Porcasi (Gonzales, the Border Guard); Julian Rivero (Dalmores); Theresa Maxwell Conover (Martha Oliver); Walter Walker (Dean); Ben Hendricks, Jr. (Red); Sidney Franklin (Bit); Betty Grable, Paulette Goddard, Toby Wing, Sarah Jane Fulks (Goldwyn Girls); Edgar Connor (Black Bull Handler); Harry C. Bradley (Man on Line); Harry Gribbon (Traffic Cop); Leo Willis (Robber); Eddie Foster (Patron).

ELMER THE GREAT *(First National, 1933)* 64 min.

Director, Mervyn LeRoy; based on the play by Ring Lardner, George M. Cohan; adaptor, Tom Geraghty; camera, Arthur Todd; editor, Thomas Pratt.

Joe E. Brown (Elmer Kane); Patricia Ellis (Nellie Poole); Frank McHugh (High-Hips Healy); Claire Dodd (Evelyn); Preston Foster (Walker); Russell Hopton (Whitey); Sterling Holloway (Nick); Emma Dunn (Mrs. Kane); Charles Wilson (Bull McWade); Jessie Ralph (Sarah Crosby); Douglass Dumbrille (Stillman); Charles Delaney (Johnny Abbott); Berton Churchill (Colonel Moffitt); J. Carroll Naish (Jerry); Gene Morgan (Noonan); Sarah Jane Fulks (Bit).

COLLEGE RHYTHM *(Paramount, 1934)* 83 min.

Director, Norman Taurog; story, George Marion, Jr.; screenplay, Walter DeLeon, John McDermott, Francis Martin; songs, Mack Gordon and Harry Revel; choreography, LeRoy Prinz; camera, Leo Tover, Ted Tetzlaff; editor, LeRoy Stone, Edward Dmytryk.

Joe Penner (Joe); Jack Oakie (Francis J. "Love and Kisses" Finnegan); Lanny Ross (Larry Stacey); Lyda Roberti (Mimi); Helen Mack (June Cort); George Barbier (John P. Stacey); Mary Brian (Gloria Van Dayham); Franklin Pangborn (Peabody); Robert McWade (Herman Whimple); Harold Minjir (Witherspoon); Joe Sawyer (Spud Miller); Julian Madison (Jimmy Poole); Mary Wallace (Peggy Small); Dutch Hendrian (Taylor—Captain of Whimple Team); Bradley Metcalfe (Sonny Whimple); Dean Jagger (Coach); Eric Alden (Stacey Quarterback); Lee Phelps (Timekeeper); Gilbert Wilson (Whimple Quarterback); Douglas Wood (Tramp); Harry Strang (Taxi Driver); Clara Lou Sheridan [Ann Sheridan] (Glove Salesgirl); Herbert Evans (Evans—Whimple Butler); Dennis O'Keefe (Store Doorman); Kenny Baker (Chorus Boy—Cheerleader "Take a Number from 1 to 10 Routine"); Sarah Jane Fulks (Girl).

RUMBA *(Paramount, 1935)* 71 min.

Producer, William LeBaron; director, Marion Gering; idea, Guy Endore, Seena Owen; screenplay, Howard J. Green; additional dialogue, Harry Ruskin, Frank Partos; songs, Ralph Rainger; Spanish lyrics, Francois B. de Valdes; choreography, LeRoy Prinz; George Raft/Carole Lombard specialty number created and staged by Veloz and Yolanda; art directors, Hans Dreier, Robert Usher; costumes, Travis Banton; sound, J. A. Goodrich; camera, Ted Tetzlaff; editor, Hugh Bennett.

George Raft (Joe Martin); Carole Lombard (Diane Harrison); Margo (Carmelita); Lynne Overman (Flash); Monroe Owsley (Hobart Fletcher); Iris Adrian (Goldie Allen); Gail Patrick (Patsy Fletcher); Samuel S. Hinds (Henry B. Harrison); Virginia Hammond (Mrs. Harrison); Jameson Thomas (Jack Solanger); Soledad Jimenez (Maria); Paul Porcasi (Carlos); Raymond McKee (Dance Director); Akim Tamiroff (Tony); Mack Gray (Assistant Dance Instructor); Dennis O'Keefe (Man in Diane's Party at Theatre); Eldred Tidbury (Watkins); Bruce Warren (Dean); Hugh Enfield [Craig Reynolds] (Bromley); Rafael Corio (Alfredo); Rafael Storm (Cashier); James Burke, Eddie Dunn, James P. Burtis (Reporters); Dick Rush (Policeman); E. H. Calvert (Police Captain); Hooper Atchley (Doctor); Clara Lou Sheridan [Ann Sheridan] (Dance Girl); Brooks Benedict (Extra in Audience); Olga Barrancos, Luis Barrancos, Lara Fuento, Pimento Twins (Rumba Dancers); Zora (Specialty Dancer); Sarah Jane Fulks (Chorus Girl).

ALL THE KING'S HORSES *(Paramount, 1935)* 86 min.

Producer, William LeBaron; director, Frank Tuttle; based on the play *Carlo Rocco* by Laurence Clark, Max Giersberg, Frederik Herendeen, and Edward Horan; screenplay, Tuttle, Frederick Stephani; songs, Sam Coslow; camera, Henry Sharp; editor, Richard Currier.

Carl Brisson (King Rudolph/Carlo Rocco); Mary Ellis (Elaine, the Queen); Edward Everett Horton (Peppi); Eugene Pallette ("Con" Conley); Katherine DeMille (Mimi); Rosita (Ilonka); Arnold Korff (Baron Kraemer); Marina Schubert (Steffi); Stanley Andrews (Count Batthy); Edwin Maxwell, Richard Barbee (Gentlemen); Eric Mayne (Minister of Finance); Phillips Smalley (Count Blotenheim); Michael Mark (Clerk); Walter McGrail (Baron Kurt Chizlinska); George MacQuarrie (Prince Rumpfoffer); Arthur Hoyt (Henpecked Husband); Grace Hayle (Wife of Henpecked Husband); Dina Smirnova (Woman Crook); Leo White (Hotel Manager); Rolfe Sedan (Orchestra Leader); Sarah Jane Fulks (Girl).

STOLEN HARMONY (*Paramount, 1935*) 77 min.

Producer, Albert Lewis; director, Alfred Werker; story, Leon Gordon; screenplay, Gordon, Harry Ruskin, Claude Binyon, Lewis Foster; songs, Harry Revel and Mack Gordon; choreography, LeRoy Prinz; art directors, Hans Dreier, Bernard Herzbrun; camera, Harry Fischbeck; editor, Otho Lovering.

George Raft (Ray Angelo, alias Ray Ferraro); Ben Bernie (Jack Conrad); Grace Bradley (Jean Loring); Goodee Montgomery (Lil Davis); Lloyd Nolan (Chesty Burrage); Ralf Harolde (Dude Williams); William Cagney (Schoolboy Howe); William Pawley (Turk Connors); Charles E. Arnt (Clem Walters); Cully Richards (Pete, the Cabby); Jack Norton (Dick Phillips); Christian Rub (Mathew Huxley); Leslie Fenton (Joe Harris); Fred "Snowflake" Toones (Henry, the Bartender on the Bus); Frank Prince (Hero in "Fagin, Youse Is a Viper"); Ruth Clifford (Nurse); Carol Holloway (Mother of Six Kids); Robert Emmett O'Connor (Warden Clark); Eddie McGill, Jack Perry, Jack Herrick (Prison Trio); John Kelly (Bates, the Prison Bandleader); James Mack (Pop, the Elderly Doorman); Lois January, Ada Ince, Margaret Nearing, Adele Jerome (Girls in Sextet); Sarah Jane Fulks (Girl); Ben Taggart (Police Sergeant at Hotel).

KING OF BURLESQUE (*Twentieth Century-Fox, 1936*) 88 min.

Producer, Darryl F. Zanuck; associate producer, Kenneth Macgowan; director, Sidney Lanfield; story, Vina Delmar; adaptor, James Seymour; screenplay, Gene Markey, Harry Tugend; choreography, Sammy Lee; songs, Jimmy McHugh and Ted Koehler; Jack Yellen and Lew Pollack; music director, Victor Baravalle; assistant director, A. F. Erickson; costumes, Gwen Wakeling; art director, Hans Peters; set decorator, Thomas Little; sound, E. Clayton Ward, Roger Heman; camera, Peverell Marley; editor, Ralph Dietrich.

Warner Baxter (Kerry Bolton); Alice Faye (Pat Doran); Jack Oakie (Joe Cooney); Arline Judge (Connie); Mona Barrie (Rosalind Cleve); Gregory Ratoff (Kolpolpeck); Dixie Dunbar (Maria); Fats Waller (Ben); Nick Long, Jr. (Anthony Lamb); Kenny Baker (Arthur); Charles Quigley (Stanley Drake); Keye Luke (Wong); Gareth Joplin (Bootblack); Harry Welch (Spud La Rue); Claudia Coleman (Belle Weaver); Sarah Jane Fulks (Girl).

ANYTHING GOES (*Paramount, 1936*) 97 min. (TV title: *Tops Is the Limit*)

Producer, Benjamin Glazer; director, Lewis Milestone; based on the play by Howard Lindsay and Russel Crouse; songs, Cole Porter; additional songs, Leo Robin and Richard A. Whiting; Frederick Hollander; Hoagy Carmichael and Edward Heyman; camera, Karl Struss; editor, Eda Warren.

Bing Crosby (Billy Crocker); Ethel Merman (Reno Sweeney); Charles Ruggles (Reverend Dr. Moon); Ida Lupino (Hope Harcourt); Grace Bradley (Bonnie Le Tour); Arthur Treacher (Sir Evelyn Oakleigh); Robert McWade (Elisha J. Whitney); Richard Carle (Bishop Dobson); Margaret Dumont (Mrs. Wentworth); Jerry Tucker (Junior); Edward Gargan (Detective); Matt Moore (Ship's Captain); Rolfe Sedan (Bearded Man); G. Pat Collins (Purser); Harry Wilson, Bud Fine, Matt McHugh (Pug Uglies); Billy Dooley (Ship's Photographer); Sarah Jane Fulks (Bit).

MY MAN GODFREY (*Universal, 1936*) 93 min.

Producer/director, Gregory La Cava; based on the novel by Eric Hatch; screenplay, Morrie Ryskind, Hatch, La Cava; music, Charles Previn; assistant director, Scott R. Beal; art director, Charles D. Hall; camera, Ted Tetzlaff; editor, Ted Kent.

William Powell (Godfrey Parke); Carole Lombard (Irene Bullock); Alice Brady (Angelica Bullock); Gail Patrick (Cornelia Bullock); Jean Dixon (Molly); Eugene Pallette (Alexander Bullock); Alan Mowbray (Tommy Gray); Mischa Auer (Carlo); Robert Light (Faithful George); Pat Flaherty (Mike); Franklin Pangborn (Score Keeper); Robert Perry (Bob, the Hobo); Selmer Jackson (Blake, the Guest); Grace Field, Kathryn Perry, Harley Wood, Elaine Cochrane, David Horsley, Philip Merrick (Socialites); Ernie Adams (Forgotten Man); Phyllis Crane (Party Guest); Grady Sutton (Von Rumple); Jack Chefe (Road Waiter); Eddie Fetherston (Process Server); Edward Gargan, James Flavin (Detectives); Arthur Wanzer (Man); Art Singley (Chauffeur); Reginald Mason (Mayor); Bess Flowers (Guest); Sarah Jane Fulks (Girl at Party).

As Jane Wyman:

STAGE STRUCK (*First National, 1936*) 86 min.

Director, Busby Berkeley; story, Robert Lord; contributor, Warren Duff; screenplay, Tom Buckingham, Pat C. Flick; songs, E. Y. Harburg and Harold Arlen; music director, Leo F. Forbstein; camera, Byron Haskin; editor, Tom Richards.

Dick Powell (George Randall); Joan Blondell (Peggy Revere); Warren William (Harris); Jean Madden (Ruth Williams); Frank McHugh (Sid); Carol Hughes (Grace Randall); Hobart Cavanaugh (Wayne); Spring Byington (Mrs. Randall); Johnny Arthur (Oscar Freud); Craig Reynolds (Gilmore Frost); Andrew Tombes (Burns Heywood); Lulu McConnell ("Toots" O'Connor); Ed Gargan (Riordan); Eddy Chandler (Heney); Thomas Pogue (Dr. Stanley); Libby Taylor (Yvonne); George Offerman, Jr. (Wilbur); Irene Coleman (Brunette); Henry Martin (Black Chauffeur); Herbert Ashley (Bartender); George Riley (Drunk); Leo White (Waiter); Iris Adrian (Miss DeRue); Rosalind Marquis (Miss LaReno); Jane Wyman (Bessie Fuffnick); Val and Ernie Stanton (Marley and Cooper); Charles Croker King (Alexander, the Critic); Mary Gordon (Mrs. Cassidy); Sarah Edwards (Spinster School Marm in Aquarium).

CAIN AND MABEL (*Warner Bros., 1936*) 90 min.

Supervisor, Sam Bischoff; director, Lloyd Bacon; story, Earl Baldwin, H. C. Witwer; screenplay, Laird Doyle; songs, Harry Warren and Al Dubin; choreography, Bobby Connolly; music director, Leo F. Forbstein; art director, Robert Haas; music arranger, Ray Heindorf; gowns, Orry-Kelly; camera, George Barnes; editor, William Holmes.

Marion Davies (Mabel O'Dare); Clark Gable (Larry Cain); Allen Jenkins (Dodo Mullens); Roscoe Karns (Aloysius K. Reilly); Ruth Donnelly (Aunt Mimi); Walter Catlett (Jake Sherman); William Collier, Sr. (Pop Harrison); Pert Kelton (Teddy Williams); David Carlyle (Ronny Caldwell); E. E. Clive (Charles Fenwick); Hobart Cavenaugh (Milo); Joseph Crehan (Reed's Manager); Perc Teeple (Man); Mary Treen (Cashier); Leona McGenty (Fat Waitress); Eily Malyon (Old Maid); Robert Middlemass (Manager); Marie Prevost (Receptionist); Al Williams (Call Boy); Bert Moorhouse (Desk Clerk); George Ovey (Stage Door Man); Dick French, William R. Arnold, Earl Tree (Cameramen); Milton Kibbee (Cab Driver); Emmett Vogan (Athletic Club Clerk); Lee Phelps (Announcer); George Turner (Double for Gable); Jane Wyman (Bit); *Coney Island Number:* Rosalind Marquis (Cinderella); Hal Nieman (Napoleon); Rose Terrell (Delilah); Earl Askam (Samson); Robert Eberhardt (Popeye); Delos Jewkes, Jack Bergman (Smith Brothers); George Bruggerman (Caesar); Arthur Thalasso (Nero); Leo White (Man at Deauville); Georgie Billing (Boy); John Lince (Old Man); Josephine Allen (Old Lady).

POLO JOE (*Warner Bros., 1936*) 62 min.

Director, William McGann; screenplay, Peter Milne, Hugh Cummings; camera, L. William O'Connell; editor, Clarence Kolster.

Joe E. Brown (Joe Bolton); Carol Hughes (Mary Hilton); Richard "Skeets" Gallagher (Heywood); Joseph King (Colonel Hilton); Fay Holden (Aunt Minnie); Olive Tell (Mrs. Hilton); Gordon Elliott (Don Trumbeau); George E. Stone (Loafer); David Newell (Jack Hilton); Frank Orth (Bert); John Kelly (Rusty); Milton Kibbee (Marker); Charles Foy (Loafer); Dudley Dickerson (Porter); Stuart Holmes (Conductor); Wayne Morris (Boy); Perc Teeple, Sam Rice (Men); Jacqueline Saunders (Woman); Frank Darien (Baggage Man); Anne Nagel, Marjorie Weaver, Shirley Lloyd, Louise Bates, Ed Mortimer, Elsa Peterson, William J. Worthington, Dick French, Bess Flowers (Guests); John Alexander (William, the Waiter); Sam McDaniel (Harvey, the Waiter); Muriel Kearney (Girls at Polo Field); Eddy Chandler, Harry Hollingsworth (Detectives); James P. Burtis, Max Hoffman, Jr. (Cops); Guy Kingsford, Marc Kramer, Leo McCabe, Bruce Warren (Polo Players); Jane Wyman, Victoria Vinton (Girls at Polo Field); Cyril Ring, David Worth, Ted A. Thompson, Maxine Anderson, Thomas Curran, Myrtle Stedman (Spectators).

SMART BLONDE (*Warner Bros., 1936*) 65 min.

Associate producer, Bryan Foy; director, Frank McDonald; story, Frederick Nebel; screenplay, Don Ryan, Kenneth Gamet; songs, M. K. Jerome and Jack Scholl; camera, Warren Lynch; editor, Frank Magee.

Glenda Farrell (Torchy Blane); Barton MacLane (Steve McBride); Winifred Shaw (Dolly Ireland); Addison Richards (Fitz Mularkey); David Carlyle [Robert Paige] (Lewis Friel); Charlotte Wynters (Marcia Friel); Craig Reynolds (Tom Carney); Jane Wyman (Dixie); Joseph Crehan (Tiny Torgenson); George Lloyd (Pickney Sax); Max Wagner (Butch Cannon); Tom Kennedy (Gahagan); John Sheehan (Blyfuss); Allen Pomeroy (Taxi Driver); Cliff Saum (Conductor); Paul Panzer (Blind Beggar); Al Hill (Taxi Driver); Joseph Cunningham (City Editor); Jack H. Richardson (Murphy); Chic Bruno (Bozo); Frank Faylen (Ambulance Driver); Wayne Morris (Information Clerk); Dennis Moore (Interne); Milton Kibbee (Harms, the Ballistics Expert);

Fred "Snowflake" Toones, Martin Turner (Red Caps).

GOLD DIGGERS OF 1937 *(First National, 1936)* 100 min.

Producer, Hal B. Wallis; associate producer, Earl Baldwin; director, Lloyd Bacon; story, Richard Maibaum, Michael Wallach, George Haight; screenplay, Warren Duff; music director, Leo F. Forbstein; songs, Harry Warren and Al Dubin; Harold Arlen and E. Y. Harburg; music numbers staged by Busby Berkeley; camera, Arthur Edeson; editor, Thomas Richards.

Dick Powell (Rosmer Peek); Joan Blondell (Norma Perry); Glenda Farrell (Genevieve Larkin); Victor Moore (J. J. Hobart); Lee Dixon (Boop Oglethorpe); Osgood Perkins (Morty Wethered); Charles D. Brown (John Hugo); Rosalind Marquis (Sally); Irene Ware (Irene); William B. Davidson (Andy Callahan); Joseph Crehan (Chairman of Insurance Convention); Susan Fleming (Lucille Bailey); Charles Halton (Dr. Warshoff); Olin Howland (Dr. McDuffy); Paul Irving (Dr. Henry); Harry C. Bradley (Dr. Bell); Fred "Snowflake" Toones (Snowflake); Pat West (Drunken Salesman); Iris Adrian (Verna); Cliff Saum (Conductor); Tom Wilson (Baggage Man); Frank Faylen (Man in Washroom); Jack Norton (Drunk); Marjorie Weaver, Lucille Keeling (Girls); Selmer Jackson (Speculator); Jane Wyman (Chorus Girl in "Love and War" Number).

READY, WILLING AND ABLE *(Warner Bros., 1937)* 93 min.

Director, Ray Enright; story, Richard Macaulay; screenplay, Jerry Wald, Sig Herzig, Warren Duff; songs, Johnny Mercer and Richard Whiting; choreography, Bobby Connolly; camera, Sol Polito; editor, Doug Gould.

Ruby Keeler (Jane Clarke); Ross Alexander (Barry Granville); Allen Jenkins (Jay Van Cortland); Lee Dixon (Pinky Blair); Louise Fazenda (Mrs. Clara Heingman); Carol Hughes (Angie); Winifred Shaw (English Jane Clarke); Hugh O'Connell (Truman Hardy); Addison Richards (Ed McNeil); Teddy Hart (Yip Nolan); Jane Wyman (Dot); Adrian Rosley (Tailor); E. E. Clive (Lord Samuel Buffington); Lillian Kemble-Cooper (Lady Buffington); Shaw and Lee (Piano Movers); Barnett Parker (Reginald Fortescue, the British Waiter); May Boley (Mrs. Boadle); Charles Halton (Brockman); James Newill (Singing Voice of Ross Alexander); Dickie Jones (Kid); Milton Kibbee (Steward); Carlyle Moore, Jr., Dennis Moore (Reporters); Saul Gorss (Cameraman); Gertrude Pedlar, William Worthington (Elderly Couple); Elsa Buchanan (Maid); Cliff Saum (Yip's Assistant).

THE KING AND THE CHORUS GIRL *(Warner Bros., 1937)* 94 min.

Producer/director, Mervyn LeRoy; story/screenplay, Norman Krasna, Groucho Marx; songs, Werner Richard Heymann, Ted Koehler; music director, Leo F. Forbstein; choreography, Bobby Connolly; camera, Tony Gaudio; editor, Thomas Richards.

Fernand Gravet (Alfred); Joan Blondell (Dorothy); Edward Everett Horton (Count Humbert); Alan Mowbray (Duchess Anna); Jane Wyman (Babette); Luis Alberni (Gaston); Kenny Baker (Singer); Shaw & Lee (Specialty Performers); Ben Welden (Waiter); Adrian Rosley (Concierge) Lionel Pape (Professor Kornish); Leonard Mudie (Footman); Ferdinand Schumann-Heink (Chauffeur); Torben Meyer (Eric); Armand Kaliz (Theatre Manager); Georgette Rhodes (Hatcheck Girl); George Sorel, Alphonse Martell (Servants); Sam Ash, Lee Kohlmar (Violinists); Carlos San Martin (Cop); Gaston Glass (Junior Officer); Robert Graves (Captain of Ocean Liner).

SLIM *(Warner Bros., 1937)* 80 min.

Producer, Hal B. Wallis; associate producer, Sam Bischoff; director, Ray Enright; story/screenplay, William Wister Haines; dialogue director, Gene Lewis; art director, Ted Smith; music director, Leo F. Forbstein; special camera effects, Byron Haskin; camera, Sid Hickox; editor, Owen Marks.

Pat O'Brien (Red Blayd); Henry Fonda (Slim); Margaret Lindsay (Cally); Stuart Erwin (Stumpy); J. Farrell MacDonald (Pop Traver); Craig Reynolds, Alonzo Price, Douglas Williams (Gamblers); Harland Tucker (Garretson); John Litel (Wyatt Ranstead); James Robbins (Braithwaite); Jane Wyman (Stumpy's Girl Friend); Richard Purcell (Tom); Joe Sawyer (Wilcox); Carlyle Moore (Grunt); Maidel Turner (Mrs. Johnson); Max Wagner (Griff); Walter Miller (Jim Vincent); Ben Hendricks (Kelly); Dick Wessel (Al); Cliff Saum (Reel Boss); Herbert Heywood (Timekeeper); Edwin Maxwell (Corton); Ferdinand Schumann-Heink (Waiter); John Harron, Henry Otho (Workmen); Brenda Fowler (Miss Ferredice).

THE SINGING MARINE *(Warner Bros., 1937)* 105 min.

Director, Ray Enright; screenplay, Delmer Daves; songs, Harry Warren and Al Lewis; music numbers staged by Busby Berkeley; camera, Arthur Todd.

Dick Powell (Robert Brent); Doris Weston (Peggy Randall); Hugh Herbert (Aeneas Phinney/Mrs. Fowler); Lee Dixon (Slim Baxter); Allen Jenkins (Sergeant Mike Kelly); Jane Darwell (Ma Marine); Marcia Ralston (Helen Young); George "Doc" Rockwell (Doc Rockwell); Larry Adler (Larry); Berton Churchill (J. Montgomery Madison); Addison Richards (Fowler); Jane Wyman (Joan); Guinn "Big Boy" Williams (Dopey); Eddie Acuff (Sam); Veda Ann Borg (Diane); James Robbins (Sammy); Henry O'Neill (Captain Skinner); Tetsu Komai (Chang); Miki Morita (Ah Ling); Rose King (Fanny Hatteras); Edward Price (Travel Information Clerk); Walter Miller, Ward Bond (First Sergeants); Lane Chandler, Hal Craig (Squad Leaders); John Hamilton (Colonel); Lucille Osborne (Soubrette); Sam McDaniel (Black Man); Murray Alper (Marine); Jane Weir, Trudy Marson, Frances Morris, Patsy "Babe" Kane (Girls at Phone); *Night over Shanghai Number:* Eric Portman (Derelict); Valerie Bergere (Chinese Madame); Suzanne Kim (Chinese Dancer).

MR. DODD TAKES THE AIR *(Warner Bros., 1937)* 86 min.

Producer, Mervyn LeRoy; director, Alfred E. Green; based on the story "The Great Crooner" by Clarence Budington Kelland; screenplay, William Wister Haines, Elaine Ryan; songs, Harry Warren and Al Dubin; music director, Leo F. Forbstein; music arranger, Adolph Deutsch; art director, Robert Haas; camera, Arthur Edeson; editor, Thomas Richards.

Kenny Baker (Claude Dodd); Alice Brady (Mme. Sonia Moro); Gertrude Michael (Jessica Stafford); Jane Wyman (Marjorie Day); Frank McHugh (Sniffer Sears); John Eldredge (Jim Lidin); Ferris Taylor (Hiram Doremus); Maidel Turner (Lil Doremus); Henry O'Neill (Gateway); Addison Richards (Doctor); Clifford Soubier (Ben Kidder); Sibyl Harris (Mrs. Kidder); Harry Davenport (Doc Quinn); Florence Gill (Miss Carrie Bowers); Anderson Lawler (Production Manager); Linda Perry (Information Desk Girl); Claudia Simmons (Phone Girl); Paul Regan Maxey (Fred, the Substitute Singer); James Ford (Guest); Frank Faylen (Reporter); Eric Wilton (Butler); John Spacey (Headwaiter); Elliott Sullivan (Taxi Driver); Owen King (Announcer); William Hopper (Production Manager).

PUBLIC WEDDING *(Warner Bros., 1937)* 58 min.

Director, Nick Grinde; story, Houston Branch; screenplay, Roy Chanslor, Branch; camera, L. W. O'Connell; editor, Frank DeWar.

Jane Wyman (Flip Lane); William Hopper (Tony Burke); Richard Purcell (Joe Taylor); Marie Wilson (Tessie); Berton Churchill (Pop Lane); James Robbins (Nick); Raymond Hatton (Deacon); Veda Ann Borg (Bernice); Zeni Vatori (Gus); Curtis Karpe (Pete); Jimmy Fox (Jeremiah Boggs); George Guhl (Sheriff); Eddie Anderson (Porter); Frank Faylen (Trainman); James Burtis, Eddy Chandler (Detectives); Milton Kibbee (Jailer); Cy Kendall (Police Captain); Sarah Edwards (Mrs. Van Drexel); Frank Hammond (Harrison, the Banker).

THE SPY RING *(Universal, 1938)* 61 min.

Producer, Trem Carr; associate producer, Paul Malvern; director, Joseph H. Lewis; based on a story by Frank Van Wyck Mason; screenplay, George Waggner; assistant director, Glenn Cook; music director, Charles Previn; camera, Harry Neumann.

William Hall (Captain Tod Hayden); Jane Wyman (Elaine Burdette); Esther Ralston [billed as Jane Carlaton] (Jean Bruce); Robert Warwick (Colonel Burdette); Leon Ames (Frank Denton); Don Barclay (Timothy O'Reilly); Ben Alexander (Captain Don Mayhew); Egon Brecher (Brigadier General A. R. Bowen); Paul Sutton (Charley, the Chauffeur); Jack Mulhall (Captain Tex Randolph); LeRoy Mason (Paul Douglas); Phillip Trent (Captain Robert Scott); Harry Woods (Captain Holden); Harry Harvey, Pat Gleason, Eddie Parker (Reporters); Eddie Gribbon, Forrest Taylor (Sergeants).

FOOLS FOR SCANDAL *(Warner Bros., 1938)* 81 min.

Producer/director, Mervyn LeRoy; based on the play *Return Engagement* by Nancy Hamilton, James Shute, and Rosemary Casey; screenplay, Herbert and Joseph Fields; additional dialogue, Irving Beecher; music director, Leo F. Forbstein; songs, Richard Rodgers and Lorenz Hart; orchestrator, Adolph Deutsch; choreography, Bobby Connolly; art director, Anton Grot; gowns, Milo Anderson; Miss Lombard's gown, Travis Banton; sound, E. A. Brown, David Forrest; camera, Ted Tetzlaff; editor, William Holmes.

Carole Lombard (Kay Winters); Fernand Gravet (Rene); Ralph Bellamy (Phillip Chester); Allen Jenkins (Dewey Gibson); Isabel Jeans (Lady Paula Malveston); Marie Wilson (Myrtle); Marcia Ralston (Jill); Tola Nesmith (Agnes); Heather Thatcher (Lady Potter-Porter); Jacques Lory (Papa); Tempe Piggott (Bessie); Michellette Burani (Mme. Brioche); Jeni LeGon (Specialty); Andre Marsaudon, Albert Petit (Gendarmes); Louis Durat, Hugh McArthur (Young Men); Elizabeth Dunne, Sarah Edwards (Tourists); Isabelle La Mal (Chambermaid); Michael Romanoff, Leon Lasky (Party Guests); Rochelle Hall (Phyllis); Elspeth Dudgeon (Cynthia); Rosella Towne (Diana); Peter Hobbes (Reporter); Jane Wyman (Bit).

SHE COULDN'T SAY NO (Warner Bros., 1938) 57 min.

Director, Lewis Seiler; screenplay, Robertson White, Joseph Schrank, Ben Grauman Kohn; camera, Arthur Todd; editor, Frank Dewar.

With: Frank McHugh, Jane Wyman, Cora Witherspoon.

WIDE OPEN FACES (Columbia, 1938) 67 min.

Producer, David Loew; director, Kurt Neumann; story, Richard Flournoy; screenplay, Earle Snell, Clarence Marks, Joe Bigelow; additional dialogue, Pat C. Flick; camera, James Wilson; editor, Jack Ogilvie.

Joe E. Brown (Wilbur Meeks); Jane Wyman (Betty Martin); Alison Skipworth (Auntie); Lyda Roberti (Kitty); Alan Baxter (Tony); Lucien Littlefield (P. T. "Doc" Williams); Sidney Toler (Sheriff); Berton Churchill (Mr. Crawford); Barbara Pepper (Belle); Joseph Downing (Stretch); Stanley Fields (Duke); Horace Murphy (Mr. Schultz).

THE CROWD ROARS (MGM, 1938) 92 min.

Producer, Sam Zimbalist; director, Richard Thorpe; story, George Bruce; screenplay, Thomas Lennon, Bruce, George Oppenheimer; sound, Douglas Shearer; camera, John Seitz; editor, Conrad A. Nervig.

Robert Taylor (Tommy McCoy); Edward Arnold (Jim Cain); Maureen O'Sullivan (Sheila Carson); Frank Morgan (Brian McCoy); William Gargan (Johnny Martin); Nat Pendleton (Pug Welsh); Lionel Stander (Happy); Jane Wyman (Vivian); Leona Roberts (Laura McCoy); Charles D. Brown (Bill Thorne); Donald Barry (Pete Mariola); Dick Rich (Mariola's Assistant); Elspeth Dudgeon (Agatha DeHaven); Gwendolyn Logan (Margaret DeHaven); Hudson Shotwell (Boy Bryerson); Isabel Jewell (Mrs. Martin); Donald Douglas (Murray); Roy Barcroft (Photographer); Hal LeSeur (Usher); Brent Sargent (Metcalf); William Norton Bailey (Ticket Collector); Jack Pennick, Joe Caits (Bits).

BROTHER RAT (Warner Bros., 1938) 90 min.

Producer, Hal B. Wallis; associate producer, Robert Lord; director, William Keighley; based on the play by John Monks, Jr. and Fred B. Finklehoffe; screenplay, Richard Macaulay, Jerry Wald; art director, Max Parker; music director, Leo F. Forbstein; camera, Ernest Haller; editor, William Holmes.

Wayne Morris (Billy Randolph); Priscilla Lane (Joyce Winfree); Eddie Albert (Bing Edwards); Ronald Reagan (Dan Crawford); Jane Wyman (Claire Adams); Jane Bryan (Kate Rice); Johnnie Davis (A. Furman Townsend, Jr.); Henry O'Neill (Colonel Ramm); William Tracy ("Mistol" Bottom); Larry Williams (Harley Harrington); Gordon Oliver (Captain "Lacedrawers" Rogers); Jessie Busley (Mrs. Brooks); Louise Beavers (Jenny); Robert Scott ("Tripod" Andrews); Fred Hamilton ("Newsreel" Scott); Oscar Hendrian (Coach); Isabel Withers (Nurse); Junior Coghlan (Fourth Classman); Don DeFore (Catcher); Wilfred Lucas (Doctor).

TAIL SPIN (Twentieth Century-Fox, 1939) 84 min.

Producer, Darryl F. Zanuck; associate producer, Harry Joe Brown; director, Roy Del Ruth; screenplay, Frank Wead; art director, Bernard Herzbrun, Rudolph Sternad; set decorator, Thomas Little; costumes, Gwen Wakeling; technical directors, Paul Mantz, Clifford W. Henderson; music director, Louis Silvers; song, Mack Gordon and Harry Revel; sound, Eugene Grossman, Roger Heman; camera, Karl Freund; editor, Allen McNeil.

Alice Faye (Trixie Lee); Constance Bennett (Gerry Lester); Nancy Kelly (Lois Allen); Joan Davis (Babe Dugan); Charles Farrell (Bud); Jane Wyman (Alabama); Kane Richmond (Dick "Tex" Price); Wally Vernon (Chick); Joan Valerie (Sunny); Edward Norris (Speed Allen); J. Anthony Hughes (Al Moore); Harry Davenport (T.P. Lester); Mary Gordon (Mrs. Lee); Harry Rosenthal (Cafe Manager); Irving Bacon (Storekeeper); Sam Hayes (Announcer).

PRIVATE DETECTIVE (Warner Bros., 1939) 55 min.

Director, Noel Smith; story, Kay Krausse; screenplay, Earle Snell, Raymond Schrock; camera, Ted McCord; editor, Harold McLernon.

Jane Wyman (Myrna Winslow); Dick Foran (Jim Rickey); Gloria Dickson (Mona Lannon); Maxie Rosenbloom (Brody); John Ridgely (Donald Norton); Morgan Conway (Nat Flavin); John Eldredge (Millard Bannon); Joseph Crehan (Murphy); Dick Rich (Chick Jerome); Henry Blair (Bobby Lannon); Julie Stevens (Mona's Maid); William Davidson (Evans); Selmer Jackson (Sanger); Vera Lewis (Mrs. Widner); Willie Best (Valet); Creighton Hale (Coroner); Leo Gorcey (Newsboy); Maris Wrixon (Telephone Operator); Sol Gorss (Taxi Driver); Lottie Williams (Mrs. Smith); Earl Dwire (Justice of Peace); Frank Dae (Judge).

THE KID FROM KOKOMO (Warner Bros., 1939) 95 min.

Director, Lewis Seiler; story, Dalton Trumbo; screenplay, Jerry Wald, Richard Macaulay; camera, Sid Hickox; editor, Jack Killifer.

Pat O'Brien (Bill Murphy); Wayne Morris (Homer Baston); Joan Blondell (Doris Harvey); Jane Wyman (Miss Bronson); May Robson (Ma

"Maggie" Martin); Maxie Rosenbloom (Curly Bender); Ed Brophy (Eddie Black); Stanley Fields (Muscles); Sidney Toler (Judge Bronson); Winifred Harris (Mrs. Bronson); Morgan Conway (Louie); John Ridgely (Sam); Frank Mayo (Durb); Ward Bond (Klewicke); Clem Bevans (Jim); Olin Howland (Stan); Paul Hurst, Tom Wilson, Frank Hagney, Bob Perry (Old Men); Jack Mower (Hotel Clerk); Nat Carr (Court Clerk); Emmett Vogan (Fight Announcer); Charles Randolph (Referee).

TORCHY PLAYS WITH DYNAMITE *(Warner Bros., 1939)* 59 min.

Director, Noel Smith; based on characters created by Frederick Nebel; screen story, Scott Littleton; screenplay, Charles Belden, Earle Snell; camera, Arthur L. Todd; editor, Harold McLernon.

Jane Wyman (Torchy Blane); Allen Jenkins (Lieutenant Steve McBride); Tom Kennedy (Gahagan); Joe Cunningham (Maxie); Sheila Bromley ("Jackie" McGuire); Eddie Marr (Denver Eddie); Edgar Dearing (Jim Simmons); Frank Shannon (Inspector McTavish); Bruce MacFarlane (Bugsie); George Lloyd (Harp); Aldrich Bowker (Police Court Judge); John Ridgely, Larry Williams (Reporters); John Harron (Motorcycle Cop); Cliff Clark (Kelly); Tiny Roebuck ("Bone Crusher"); Ruth Robinson (Head Matron); Kate Lawson (Guard); Frank Moran (Handler); John "Skins" Miller (Taxi Driver); John Sheehan (Desk Sergeant O'Toole).

KID NIGHTINGALE *(Warner Bros., 1939)* 57 min.

Director, George Amy; story, Lee Katz; screenplay, Charles Belden, Raymond Schrock; camera, Arthur Edeson; editor, Frederick Richards.

John Payne (Steve Nelson); Jane Wyman (Judy Craig); Walter Catlett (Skip Davis); Ed Brophy (Mike Jordan); Charles D. Brown (Charles Paxton); John Ridgely (Whitey); Max Hoffman, Jr. (Fitts); Harry Burns (Strangler Columbo/Rudolfo Terrassi); William Haade (Rocky); Winifred Harris (Mrs. Reynolds); Helen Troy (Marge); Steve Mason (Fighter); Claude Wisberg (Messenger); Nat Carr, Frank Mayo (Men); Creighton Hale (Boxing Commission Representative); Pat Flaherty (Soxey); Jerry Mandy (Orchestra Leader); Constantine Romanoff, Mike Tellegen (Wrestlers).

BROTHER RAT AND A BABY *(Warner Bros., 1940)* 87 min.

Producers, Jack L. Warner, Hal B. Wallis; associate producer, Robert Lord; director, Ray Enright; screen story, Fred F. Finklehoffe, John Monks, Jr.; screenplay, Jerry Wald, Richard Macaulay; camera, Charles Rosher; editor, Clarence Kolster.

Wayne Morris (Billy Randolph); Priscilla Lane (Joyce Winfree); Eddie Albert ("Bing" Edwards); Jane Bryan (Kate); Ronald Reagan (Dan Crawford); Jane Wyman (Claire Ramm); Peter Good ("Commencement"); Larry Williams (Harley Harrington); Arthur Treacher (McGregor); Moroni Olsen (Colonel); Jessie Busley (Mrs. Brooks); Paul Harvey (Sterling Randolph); Berton Churchill (Mr. Harper); Nana Bryant (Mrs. Harper); Mayo Methot (Girl in Bus); Ed Gargan (Cab Driver); Billy Wayne (Expressman); Irving Bacon (Man in Hospital); Carlyle Moore, Jr. (Lieutenant); Richard Clayton, Alan Ladd, David Willock (Cadets); Douglas Meins (Western Union Boy); Ed Parker (Fireman); John Hamilton (Judge); Cliff Clark (Police Captain); John Dilson (Pawnbroker).

AN ANGEL FROM TEXAS *(Warner Bros., 1940)* 69 min.

Associate producer, Robert Fellows; director, Ray Enright; based on the play *The Butter and Egg Man* by George S. Kaufman; screenplay, Fred Niblo, Jr., Bertram Millhauser; camera, Arthur L. Todd; editor, Clarence Kolster.

Eddie Albert (Peter Coleman); Wayne Morris (Mr. McClure); Rosemary Lane (Lydia Weston); Jane Wyman (Marge Allen); Ronald Reagan (Mr. Allen); Ruth Terry (Valerie Blayne); John Litel (Quigley); Hobart Cavanaugh (Mr. Robelink); Ann Shoemaker (Addie Lou Coleman); Tom Kennedy (Chopper); Milburn Stone (Pooch Davis); Elliott Sullivan (Garvey); Paul Phillips (Louis); Emmett Vogan (Bonham); Ferris Taylor (Mayor O'Dempsey); George Irving (Actor); Lottie Williams (Aunt Minnie); Mira McKinney (Mrs. Mills); Vera Lewis (Mrs. Gates); Jack Kennedy (Stationmaster); Ed Gargan (Cop); Eddie Acuff, Jimmy Fox (Stagehands); Al Stedman (Stage Manager); Ralph Dunn (General); Joe Levine (Small Boy).

FLIGHT ANGELS *(Warner Bros., 1940)* 74 min.

Producer, Jack L. Warner; associate producer, Edmund Grainger; director, Lewis Seiler; story, Jerry Wald, Richard Macaulay; screenplay, Maurice Leo; camera, L. W. O'Connell; editor, James Gibbon.

Virginia Bruce (Mary Norvell); Dennis Morgan (Chick Farber); Wayne Morris (Artie Dixon); Jane Wyman (Nan Hudson); Ralph Bellamy (Bill Graves); John Litel (Dr. Barlett); Margot Stevenson (Rita); Dorothea Kent (Mabel); John Ridgely (Lieutenant Parsons); Maris Wrixon (Bonnie); Lucille Fairbanks (Thelma); Jan Clayton (Jane Morrow); Marilyn [Lynn] Merrick (Peggy); William Hopper (Lefty); Phyllis Hamilton (Phyllis); Nell O'Day (Sue); Elizabeth Sifton (Dora); Mary Anderson (Daisy Lou); Carol Hughes (Texas); Ferris Taylor (Mr. Kimball); Richard Elliott (Mr. Rutledge); Natalie Moorhead (Miss Mason); Leona Roberts (Mrs. Hutchinson); John Arledge (Mr. Perry); Janet Shaw (Mrs. Perry); Grace Stafford (Buxton); Victor Zimmerman (Captain Brady); Jean O'Donnell (Grace); Peter Ashley (Joe); Peggy Keyes (Stewardess); Creighton Hale (Attendant); Dutch Hendrian (Mechanic); Addison Richards, Tony Hughes (Officers); Rosella Towne (Student).

MY LOVE CAME BACK (Warner Bros., 1940) 81 min.

Producers, Jack L. Warner, Hal B. Wallis; associate producer, Wolfgang Reinhardt; director, Kurt Bernhardt; story, Walter Reisch; screenplay, Ivan Goff, Robert Buckner, Earl Baldwin; art director, Max Parker; music, Heinz Roemheld; orchestrator, Ray Heindorf; music director, Leo F. Forbstein; camera, Charles Rosher; editor, Rudi Fehr.

Olivia de Havilland (Amelia Cullen); Jeffrey Lynn (Tony Baldwin); Eddie Albert (Dusty Rhodes); Jane Wyman (Joy O'Keefe); Charles Winninger (Julius Malette); Spring Byington (Mrs. Malette); Ann Gillis (Valerie Malette); William Orr (Paul Malette); S. Z. Sakall (Ludwig); Grant Mitchell (Dr. Kobbe); Charles Trowbridge (Dr. Downey); Mabel Taliaferro (Dowager); Sidney Bracy (Butler); Nanette Vallon (Sophie); William Davidson (Agent); Tommy Baker (Boy); Creighton Hale (Clerk); Jack Mower, Richard Kipling (Executives); Richard Clayton (Valerie's Escort); John Dilson (Cashier).

TUGBOAT ANNIE SAILS AGAIN (Warner Bros., 1940) 77 min.

Director, Lewis Seiler; based on characters created by Norman Reilly Raine; screenplay, Walter DeLeon; music, Max Steiner; camera, Arthur Edeson.

Marjorie Rambeau (Tugboat Annie); Jane Wyman (Peggy Armstrong); Ronald Reagan (Eddie Kent); Alan Hale (Captain Bullwinkle); Charles Halton (Alec Severn); Clarence Kolb (J. B. Armstrong); Paul Hurst (Pete); Victor Kilian (Sam); Chill Wills (Shiftless); Harry Shannon (Captain Mahoney); John Hamilton (Captain Broad); Sidney Bracy (Limey); Jack Mower (Johnson); Dana Dale (Rosie); Josephine Whittell (Miss Morgan); Neil Reagan (Rex Olcott); George Meader (Bradley); Don Turner, Glen Cavender (Men); Al Lloyd (Little Guy); Creighton Hale (Chauffeur); George Campeau (Olcott's Announcer).

GAMBLING ON THE HIGH SEAS (Warner Bros., 1940) 56 min.

Director, George Amy; based on an idea by Martin Mooney; screenplay, Robert E. Kent; camera, Arthur Todd.

Wayne Morris (Jim Carver); Jane Wyman (Laurie Ogden); Gilbert Roland (Greg Morella); John Litel (U.S. District Attorney); Roger Pryor (Max Gates); Frank Wilcox (Stone); Robert Strange (Larry Brill); John Gallaudet (Steve Sterling); Frank Ferguson (City District Attorney); Harry Shannon (Chief of Police); George Reeves (Reporter); George Meader (Secretary); William Pawley (Frank); Murray Alper (Louie); Gus Glassmire (Editor); Creighton Hale (Nelson); Maude Allen (Matron); Frank Mayo (Cop); Cliff Saum (Henchman); Dutch Hendrian, Alan Pomeroy (Federal Men); William Hopper (Station Operator); Jack Mower, John Harron (Coast Guard Officers); Walter Wilson (Judge).

HONEYMOON FOR THREE (Warner Bros., 1941) 77 min.

Associate producer, Henry Blanke; director, Lloyd Bacon; based on the play *Goodbye Again* by Alan Scott and George Haight; screenplay, Earl Baldwin; camera, Ernest Haller; editor, Rudi Fehr.

Ann Sheridan (Anne Rogers); George Brent (Kenneth Bixby); Charles Ruggles (Harvey Wilson); Osa Massen (Julie Wilson); Jane Wyman (Elizabeth Clochessy); William T. Orr (Arthur Westlake); Lee Patrick (Mrs. Pettijohn); Walter Catlett (Waiter); Herbert Anderson (Floyd T. Ingram); Johnny Downs (Chester T. Farrington III).

BAD MEN OF MISSOURI (Warner Bros., 1941) 74 min.

Director, Ray Enright; story, Robert E. Kent; screenplay, Charles Grayson; art director, Ted Smith; camera, Arthur Todd; editor, Clarence Kolster.

Dennis Morgan (Cole Younger); Wayne Morris (Bob Younger); Jane Wyman (Mary Hathaway); Arthur Kennedy (Jim Younger); Victor Jory (William Merrick); Howard da Silva (Greg Bilson); Walter Catlett (Mr. Pettibone); Alan Baxter (Jesse James); Faye Emerson (Martha Adams); Frank Wilcox (Minister); Russell Simpson (Hank Younger); Virginia Brissac (Mrs. Hathaway); Erville Alderson (Mr. Adams); Spencer Charters (Clem); Dorothy Vaughan (Mrs. Dalton); Hugh Sothern (Robinson); Sam McDaniel (Wash); Robert Winkler (Willie Younger); Ann E. Todd (Amy Younger); Roscoe Ates (Lafe); Duncan Renaldo, Frank Mayo, Jack Mower (Henchmen); Tom Tyler (Deputy Sheriff); Creighton Hale (Bank Representative); Leah

Baird (Miss Brooks); Dix Davis (Bob Dalton); Sonny Bupp (Grat Dalton); Henry Blair (Tod Dalton); John Beck (Preacher); Ed Stanley (Prison Doctor); Charles Middleton (Porterville Sheriff); Milton Kibbee (Man); Vera Lewis (Woman).

YOU'RE IN THE ARMY NOW (*Warner Bros., 1941*) 79 min.

Associate producer, Ben Stoloff; director, Lewis Seiler; screenplay, Paul Gerard Smith, George Beatty; camera, Arthur Todd.

Jimmy Durante (Jeeper Smith); Phil Silvers (Breezy Jones); Jane Wyman (Bliss Dobson); Regis Toomey (Joe Radcliffe); Donald MacBride (Colonel Dobson); Joe Sawyer (Sergeant Madden); Clarence Kolb (General Winthrop); Paul Harvey (General Philpott); George Meeker (Captain Austin); Paul Stanton (Colonel Rogers); William Haade (Sergeant Thorpe); Etta McDaniel (Della); Marguerite Chapman, Georgia Carroll, Peggy Diggins, Alice Talton, Kay Aldridge, Leslie Brooks (Navy Blues Sextette); Matty Malneck and His Orchestra (Themselves); Murray Alper (Supply Sergeant); Charles Drake, Harry Lewis (Recruits); Gig Young, Jack Gardner, Arthur Gardner (Men); Dick French (Captain Plant); Sally Loomis (Drum Majorette); Armando & Lita (Dance Team); David Newell (Staff Sergeant); Weldon Heyburn (Sergeant of the Guard).

THE BODY DISAPPEARS (*Warner Bros., 1941*) 72 min.

Associate producer, Ben Stoloff, director, D. Ross Lederman; based on the story *Black Widow* by Scott Darling, Erna Lazarus; screenplay, Darling, Lazarus; special camera effects, Edwin A. DuPar; camera, Allen G. Siegler, editor, Frederick Richards.

Jeffrey Lynn (Peter DeHaven); Jane Wyman (Lynn Shotesbury); Edward Everett Horton (Professor Shotesbury); Marguerite Chapman (Christine Lunceford); Herbert Anderson (George "Doc" Appleby); Davie Bruce (Jimmy Barbour); Craig Stevens (Robert Struck); Willie Best (Willie); Natalie Schafer (Mrs. Lunceford); Tod Andrews (Bill); William Hopper (Terrence Abbott); Ivan Simpson (Dean Claxton); Charles Halton (Professor Mogg); Wade Boteler (Inspector Deming); Frank Ferguson (Professor McAuley); Romaine Callender (Professor Barkley); Vera Lewis (Mrs. Mogg); Leslie Brooks, Peggy Diggins (Bridesmaids); Charles Drake (Arthur); Stuart Holmes (Waiter); Sol Gorss, Frank Sully (Attendants); Eddy Chandler (Desk Sergeant); Leah Baird (Nurse); Thornton Edwards (Motorcycle Cop); Eddie Kane (Stage Manager); Jimmy Fox (Clerk); Mary Brodel (Nora); Harry Lewis (Elevator Boy); Wedgwood Nowell, Houseley Stevenson, Sr. (Professors); Georgia Carroll (Phone Girl); Ann Edmonds, Juanita Stark, Paula Francis (Coeds).

LARCENY, INC. (*Warner Bros., 1942*) 95 min.

Producer, Hal B. Wallis; associate producers, Jack Saper, Jerry Wald; director, Lloyd Bacon; based on the play *The Night Before Christmas* by Laura and S. J. Perelman; screenplay, Everett Freeman, Edwin Gilbert; camera, Tony Gaudio; editor, Ralph Dawson.

Edward G. Robinson (Pressure Maxwell); Jane Wyman (Denny Costello); Broderick Crawford (Jug Martin); Jack Carson (Jeff Randolph); Anthony Quinn (Leo Dexter); Edward S. Brophy (Weepy Davis); Harry Davenport (Homer Bigelow); Vera Vague (Mademoiselle Gloria); John Qualen (Sam Bachrach); Grant Mitchell (Aspinwall); Jack C. [Jackie] Gleason (Hobart); Andrew Tombes (Oscar Engelhart); Joseph Downing (Smitty); George Meeker (Mr. Jackson); Fortunio Bonanova (Anton Copoulos); Joseph Crehan (Warden); Jean Ames (Florence); William Davidson (McCarthy); Chester Clute (Buchanan); Creighton Hale (Mr. Carmichael); Emory Parnell (Officer O'Casey); Joe Devlin (Umpire); Jimmy O'Gatty (Convict); Charles Drake (Auto Driver); Grace Stafford (Secretary); Pat O'Malley, Ted Oliver, Harry Strang (Cops); Philo Reh, Fred Walburn (Urchins); Don Barclay (Drunk); Kitty Kelly (Woman); Wallace Scott (Sandwich Man); Fred Kelsey (Bronson); William Hopper, Jack Mower (Customers); Bill Phillips (Muggsy); James Flavin (Guard); Arthur Q. Bryan (Stout Man).

MY FAVORITE SPY (*RKO, 1942*) 87 min.

Producer, Harold Lloyd; director, Tay Garnett; story, M. Coates Webster; screenplay, Sig Herzig, William Bowers; music, Roy Webb; music arranger, George Duning; assistant director, James A. Anderson; music director, C. Bakaleinikoff; art directors, Albert S. D'Agostino, Carroll Clark; special effects, Vernon Walker; camera, Robert de Grasse; editor, Desmond Marquette.

Kay Kyser (Himself); Ellen Drew (Terry Kyser); Jane Wyman (Connie); Robert Armstrong (Harry Robinson); Helen Westley (Aunt Jessie); Ish Kabibble (Ish); William Demarest (Flower Pot Cop); Una O'Connor (Cora, the Maid); Lionel Royce (Winters); Moroni Olsen (Major Allen); George Cleveland (Gus); Vaughan Glaser (Colonel Moffett); Hobart Cavanaugh (Jules); Teddy Hart (Soldier); Kay Kyser's Band Featuring Sully Mason, Dorothy Dunn, Trudy Irwin, and the Music Maids (Themselves); Edmund Glover (Spelvin); Ralph Sanford (Theatre Cop); Murray

Alper (Kay's Driver); Barbara Pepper ("B" Girl); Bert Roach (Park Bit); Bud Geary, Fred Graham (Marines); Jack Norton (Drunk); Kit Guard (Henchman); Bobby Barber (Man in Park); Pat Flaherty (Recruit).

FOOTLIGHT SERENADE *(Twentieth Century-Fox, 1942)* 80 min.

Producer, William LeBaron; director, Gregory Ratoff; based on the story "Dynamite" by Fidel La Barba and Kenneth Earl; screenplay, Robert Ellis, Helen Logan, Lynn Starling; art directors, Richard Day, Roger Heman; music director, Charles Henderson; choreography, Hermes Pan; songs, Leo Robin and Ralph Rainger; costumes, Earl Luick; camera, Leo Garmes; editor, Robert Simpson.

John Payne (Bill Smith); Betty Grable (Pat Lambert); Victor Mature (Tommy Lundy); Jane Wyman (Flo La Verne); James Gleason (Bruce McKay); Phil Silvers (Slap); Cobina Wright, Jr. (Estelle Evans); June Lang (June); Frank Orth (Doorman); Manton Moreland (Dresser); Irving Bacon (Porter); Charles Tannen (Stage Director); George Dobbs (Dance Director); Billy Newell (Writer); Harry Barris (Composer); Sheila Ryan, George Holmes (Bits); Trudy Marshall (Secretary); Frank Coghlan, Jr. (Usher); Russ Clark, Frankie Van (Referees); Bud and Jim Mercer (Dance Specialty); Pat McKee (Pug); Wilbur Mack (Boxing Commissioner).

PRINCESS O'ROURKE *(Warner Bros., 1943)* 94 min.

Producer, Hal B. Wallis; director/screenplay, Norman Krasna; art director, Max Parker; set decorator, George James Hopkins; music, Frederick Hollander; music director, Leo F. Forbstein; songs, Ira Gershwin, E. Y. Harburg, and Arthur Schwartz; assistant director, Frank Heath; sound, Stanley Jones; camera, Ernest Haller; editor, Warren Low.

Olivia de Havilland (Maria); Robert Cummings (Eddie O'Rourke); Jack Carson (Dave); Jane Wyman (Jean); Charles Coburn (Uncle); Gladys Cooper (Miss Haskell); Harry Davenport (Supreme Court Justice); Minor Watson (Washburn); Ray Walker (G-Man); Nana Bryant (Mrs. Mulvaney); Nydia Westman (Mrs. Bowers); Curt Bois (Count Peter DeChendome); Dave Willock (Delivery Boy); Julie Bishop (Stewardess); Mary Field (Clara Stilwell); Jody Gilbert (Truck Driver Woman); Katherine Price (Housekeeper); Bill Edwards (Switchboard Operator); Nan Wynn (Singer); Christian Rub (Janitor).

MAKE YOUR OWN BED *(Warner Bros., 1944)* 82 min.

Producer, Alex Gottlieb; director, Peter Godfrey; based on the play by Harvey J. O'Higgins and Harriet Ford; adaptor, Richard Weil; screenplay, Francis Swann, Edmund Joseph; art director, Stanley Fleischer; set decorator, Clarence Steensen; music, Hugo Roemheld; music director, Leo F. Forbstein; assistant director, Les Guthrie; sound, Charles Lang; special effects, Willard Van Enger; camera, Robert Burks; editor, Clarence Kolster.

Jack Carson (Jerry Curtis); Jane Wyman (Susan Courtney); Irene Manning (Vivian Whirtle); Alan Hale (Walter Whirtle); George Tobias (Boris Murphy); Robert Shayne (Lester Knight); Tala Birell (Marie Gruber); Ricardo Cortez (Fritz Alten); Marjorie Hoshelle (Elsa Wehmer); Kurt Katch (Paul Hassan); Harry Bradley (Mr. Brookin); William Kennedy (F.B.I. Man); Jack Mower (Chauffeur); Leah Baird (John's Wife); Ernest Hilliard, George Kirby (Men in Waiting Room); Jack Norton (Drunk); Joan Winfield (Whirtle's Secretary); Marie Blake (Woman).

CRIME BY NIGHT *(Warner Bros., 1944)* 72 min.

Associate producer, William Jacobs; director, William Clemens; based on the novel *Forty Whacks* by Geoffrey Homes; screenplay, Richard Weil, Homes; art director, Charles Novi; set decorator, Julie Heron, Casey Roberts; assistant director, Don Page; dialogue director, Harry Seymour; sound, Robert B. Lee; special effects, Lawrence Butler, Edwin Linden; camera, Henry Sharp; editor, Douglas Gould.

Jane Wyman (Robbie Vance); Jerome Cowan (Sam Campbell); Faye Emerson (Ann Marlowe); Charles Lang (Paul Goff); Eleanor Parker (Irene Carr); Stuart Crawford (Larry Perden); Cy Kendall (Sheriff Ambers); Charles Wilson (District Attorney Hyatt); Juanita Stark (Maisie); George Guhl (Dick Blake); Dick Wessel (Man); Creighton Hale (Grayson); Ed Parker, Jack Stoney, Jack Cheatham, Frank Mayo (Deputies); Hank Mann (Mr. Dinwiddie); Dick Rich (Fred, the Chauffeur); Bud Messinger (Bellboy); Roy Brant (Roy, the Waiter); Jack Mower (Tenant).

THE DOUGHGIRLS *(Warner Bros., 1944)* 102 min.

Producer, Mark Hellinger; director, James V. Kern; based on the play by Joseph A. Fields; screenplay, Kern, Sam Hellman; additional dialogue, Wilkie Mahoney; assistant director, Phil Quinn; art director, Hugh Reticker; set decorator, Clarence Steensen; music director, Leo F. Forbstein; sound, Stanley Jones; special effects, William McGann; montages, James Leicester; camera, Ernest Haller; editor, Folmer Blangsted.

Ann Sheridan (Edna); Alexis Smith (Nan); Jack Carson (Arthur); Jane Wyman (Vivian); Irene Manning (Mrs. Cadman); Charlie Ruggles (Stanley Slade); Eve Arden (Natalia Moskoroff); John Ridgely (Julius Cadman); Alan Mowbray (Brackenridge Drake); John Alexander (Warren Buckley); Craig Stevens (Tom Dillon); Barbara Brown (Mrs. Cartwright); Francis Pierlot (Mr. Jordan); Donald MacBride (Judge Franklin); Mark Stevens (Lieutenant Harry Keary); Joe DeRita (Stranger); Regis Toomey (Timothy Walsh); Walter DePalma (Justice of the Peace); John Walsh (Bellhop); Grandon Rhodes, Tom Quinn (Clerks); John Hamilton (Businessman); Harry Tyler (Angular Man); Minerva Urecal, Almira Sessions (Hatchet-Faced Women); Oliver Blake (Porter); Lou Marcelle (Announcer's Voice); Ralph Sanford (Workman); Nick Kobliansky (Father Nicholai); Will Fowler (Lieutenant).

HOLLYWOOD CANTEEN (*Warner Bros., 1944*) 124 min.

Producer, Alex Gottlieb; director/screenplay, Delmer Daves; music numbers staged by LeRoy Prinz; art director, Leo Kuter; set decorator, Casey Roberts; assistant director, Art Lucker; makeup, Perc Westmore; wardrobe, Milo Anderson; music director, Leo F. Forbstein; music adaptor, Ray Heindorf; songs, Cole Porter, E. Y. Harburg, and Burton Lane; Ted Koehler and Lane; Harold Adamson and Vernon Duke; Koehler and M. K. Jerome; Marian Sunshine, Julio Blanco, and Obdulio Morales; Larry Neal and Jimmy Mundy; Bob Nolan; Heindorf; Koehler, Heindorf, and Jerome; Jean Barry, Leah Worth, and Dick Charles; camera, Bert Glennon; editor, Christian Nyby.

Joan Leslie (Herself); Robert Hutton (Slim); Dane Clark (Sergeant); Janis Paige (Angela); Andrews Sisters, Jack Benny, Joe E. Brown, Eddie Cantor, Kitty Carlisle, Jack Carson, Joan Crawford, Helmut Dantine, Bette Davis, Faye Emerson, Victor Francen, John Garfield, Sydney Greenstreet, Alan Hale, Paul Henreid, Andrea King, Peter Lorre, Ida Lupino, Irene Manning, Nora Martin, Joan McCracken, Dolores Moran, Dennis Morgan, Eleanor Parker, William Prince, Joyce Reynolds, John Ridgely, Roy Rogers and Trigger, S. Z. Sakall, Alexis Smith, Zachary Scott, Barbara Stanwyck, Craig Stevens, Joseph Szigeti, Donald Woods, Jane Wyman, Jimmy Dorsey and His Band, Carmen Cavallaro and His Orchestra, Golden Gate Quartet, Rosario & Antonio, Sons of the Pioneers, Virginia Patton, Lynne Baggett, Betty Alexander, Julie Bishop, Robert Shayne, Johnny Mitchell, John Sheridan, Colleen Townsend, Angela Green, Paul Brooke, Marianne O'Brien, Dorothy Malone, Bill Kennedy, Mary Gordon, Chef Joseph Milani (Themselves); Jonathan Hale (Mr. Brodel); Barbara Brown (Mrs. Brodel); Betty Brodel (Herself); Steve Richards [Mark Stevens], Dick Erdman (Soldiers on Deck); James Flavin (Marine Sergeant); Eddie Marr (Dance Director); Ray Teal (Captain); Rudolph Friml, Jr. (Orchestra Leader); George Turner (Tough Marine); Betty Bryson, Willard Van Simons, William Alcorn, Jack Mattis, Jack Coffey (Dance Specialty).

THE LOST WEEKEND (*Paramount, 1945*) 101 min.

Producer, Charles Brackett; director, Billy Wilder; based on the novel by Charles R. Jackson; screenplay, Brackett, Wilder; art directors, Hans Dreier, Earl Hedrick; set decorator, Bertram Granger; assistant director, C. C. Coleman; music, Miklos Rozsa; sound, Stanley Colley; special camera effects, Gordon Jennings; process camera, Farciot Edouart; camera, John F. Seitz; editor, Doane Harrison.

Ray Milland (Don Birnam); Jane Wyman (Helen St. James); Phillip Terry (Nick Birnam); Howard da Silva (Nat, the Bartender); Doris Dowling (Gloria); Frank Faylen (Bim); Mary Young (Mrs. Deveridge); Anita Bolster (Mrs. Foley); Lilian Fontaine (Mrs. St. James); Lewis L. Russell (Charles St. James); Frank Orth (Opera Attendant); Gisela Werbiseck (Mrs. Wertheim); Eddie Laughton (Mr. Brophy); Harry Barris (Piano Player); Craig Reynolds (M.M.'s Escort); Jayne Hazard (M.M.); Walter Baldwin (Albany); Fred "Snowflake" Toones, Clarence Muse (Washroom Attendants); Bertram Marburgh, Lester Sharpe (Jewish Men); Byron Foulger (Shopkeeper); Gene Ashley, Jerry James, William Meader (Male Nurses); Emmett Vogan (Doctor).

ONE MORE TOMORROW (*Warner Bros., 1946*) 88 min.

Producer, Benjamin Glazer; director, Peter Godfrey; based on the play *The Animal Kingdom* by Philip Barry; screenplay, Charles Hoffman, Catherine Turney; additional dialogue, Julius J. and Philip G. Epstein; art director, Anton Grot; set decorator, George James Hopkins; music, Max Steiner; music director, Leo F. Forbstein; assistant director, Jesse Hibbs; sound, Dolph Thomas; camera, Bert Glennon; editor, David Weisbart.

Dennis Morgan (Tom Collier); Ann Sheridan (Christie Sage); Jack Carson (Pat Regan); Alexis Smith (Cecilia Henry); Jane Wyman (Franc Connors); Reginald Gardiner (Jim Fisk); John Loder (Owen Arthur); Thurston Hall (Rufus Collier); Marjorie Gateson (Edna); John Abbott (Joseph Baronova); Marjorie Hoshelle (Illa Baronova); Sig Arno (Poppa); Lynne Baggett, Joan Winfield, Juanita Stark, Robert Hutton, Gertrude Carr, Lottie Williams (Party Guests); William Benedict (Office Boy); John Alvin (Announcer); Henri

DeSoto (Headwaiter); Hal K. Dawson (Guest); Otto Hoffman (Stationmaster); Mary Field (Maude Miller); Frances Morris (Young Woman); Fred Essler (Picard); Danny Jackson (Orson Curry); Frank Coghlan, Jr. (Telegraph Boy).

NIGHT AND DAY (*Warner Bros., 1946*) C-128 min.

Producer, Arthur Schwartz; director, Michael Curtiz; based on the career of Cole Porter; adaptor, Jack Moffitt; screenplay, Charles Hoffman, Leo Townsend, William Bowers; Technicolor consultants, Natalie Kalmus, Leonard Doss; art director, John Hughes; set decorator, Armor Marlowe; music director, Leo F. Forbstein; music and songs, Cole Porter; additional music/adaptor, Max Steiner; vocal arranger, Dudley Chambers; production numbers' orchestrator/conductor, Ray Heindorf; choreography, LeRoy Prinz; dialogue director, Herschel Daugherty; sound, Everett A. Brown, David Forrest; montages, James Leicester; special effects, Robert Burks; camera, Peverell Marley, William V. Skall; editor, David Weisbart.

Cary Grant (Cole Porter); Alexis Smith (Linda Lee Porter); Monty Woolley (Himself); Ginny Simms (Carole Hills); Jane Wyman (Gracie Harris); Eve Arden (Gabrielle); Victor Francen (Anatole Giron); Alan Hale (Leon Dowling); Dorothy Malone (Nancy); Tom D'Andrea (Bernie); Selena Royle (Kate Porter); Donald Woods (Ward Blackburn); Henry Stephenson (Omer Cole); Sig Ruman (Wilowsky); Paul Cavanagh (Bart McClelland); Carlos Ramirez (Specialty Singer); Milada Mladova, George Zoritch, Estelle Sloan (Specialty Dancers); Adam & Jayne DeGatano (Specialty Team); Mary Martin (Guest Appearance); James Dobbs, John Compton (Students); John Alvin (Petey); Clarence Muse (Cadet); George Meader (Minister); Virginia Sale (Minister's Wife); Creighton Hale, Paul Gustine (Men in Theatre); George Riley (O'Halloran); Laura Treadwell (Woman in Theatre); Howard Freeman (Producer); John "Red" Pierson ("Peaches"); Joyce Compton (Chorine); Herman Bing (Second "Peaches"); Elizabeth Valentine (Hospital Matron); Eva Novak, Paula Rae (Nurses); Almira Sessions, Hobart Cavanaugh (Couple in Hospital Corridor); Cyril Ring, Vivian Oakland (Married Couple); Joe Kirkwood, Jr., Gene Stanley (Classmates of Cole Porter); Mel Torme (Drummer).

THE YEARLING (*MGM, 1946*) C-134 min.

Producer, Sidney Franklin; director, Clarence Brown; based on the novel by Marjorie Rawlings; screenplay, Paul Osborn; second unit director, Chester M. Franklin; Technicolor consultants, Natalie Kalmus, Henri Jaffa; art directors, Cedric Gibbons, Paul Groesse; set decorator, Ed Willis; music, Herbert Stothart; assistant director, Joe Boyle; sound, Douglas Shearer; special effects, Warren Newcombe; camera, Charles Rosher, Leonard Smith, Arthur Arling; editor, Harold F. Kress.

Gregory Peck (Pa Baxter); Jane Wyman (Ma Baxter); Claude Jarman, Jr. (Joe Baxter); Chill Wills (Buck Forrester); Clem Bevans (Pa Forrester); Margaret Wycherly (Ma Forrester); Forrest Tucker (Lem Forrester); Henry Travers (Mr. Boyles); Donn Gift (Fodderwing); Daniel White (Millwheel); Matt Willis (Gabby); George Mann (Pack); Arthur Hohl (Arch); June Lockhart (Twink Weatherby); Joan Wells (Eulalie); Jeff York (Oliver); B. H. Chick York (Doc Wilson); Victor Kilian (Captain); Frank Eldredge (Dockhand); Jane Green (Mrs. Saunders); Houseley Stevenson (Mr. Ranger).

CHEYENNE (*Warner Bros., 1947*) 100 min. (TV title: *Wyoming Kid*)

Producer, Robert Buckner; director, Raoul Walsh; story, Paul I. Wellman; screenplay, Alan LeMay, Thames Williamson; art director, Ted Smith; set decorator, Jack McConaghy; music, Max Steiner; orchestrator, Hugo Friedhofer; music director, Leo F. Forbstein; assistant director, Reggie Callow; dialogue director, John Maxwell; special effects, William McGann, H. F. Koenekamp; camera, Sid Hickox; editor, Christian Nyby.

Dennis Morgan (James Wylie); Jane Wyman (Ann Kincaid); Janis Paige (Emily Carson); Bruce Bennett (Ed Landers); Alan Hale (Fred Durkin); Arthur Kennedy (Sundance Kid); Barton MacLane (Webb Yancey); Tom Tyler (Pecos); Bob Steele (Bucky); John Compton (Limpy Bill); John Alvin (Single Jack); Monte Blue (Timberline); Anne O'Neal (Mrs. Kittredge); Tom Fadden (Charlie, the Stage Driver); Britt Wood (Swamper); Norman Willis, Ray Teal, Kenneth MacDonald, Robert Filmer (Gamblers); Lee ["Lasses"] White (Charlie, the Hotelkeeper); Snub Pollard, Ethan Laidlaw (Barflies); Jack Mower (Deputy).

MAGIC TOWN (*RKO, 1947*) 103 min.

Producer, Robert Riskin; director, William Wellman; screenplay, Riskin; art director, Lionel Banks; set decorator, George Sawley; music, Roy Webb; music director, C. Bakaleinikoff; songs, Mel Torme and Bob Wells; assistant director, Arthur S. Black; sound, John Tribby, Terry Kellum; camera, Joseph F. Biroc; editor, Sherman Todd.

James Stewart (Lawrence "Rip" Smith); Jane Wyman (Mary Peterman); Kent Smith (Hoopendecker); Ned Sparks (Ike Sloan); Wallace Ford (Lou Dicketts); Regis Toomey (Ed Weaver); Ann Doran (Mrs. Weaver); Donald Meek (Mr. Twiddle); E. J. Ballantine (Moody); Ann Shoemaker (Ma Peterman); Mickey Kuhn (Hank Nickleby); Howard Freeman (Richard Nickleby); Harry Holman (Mayor); Mary Currier (Mrs. Frisby); Mickey Roth (Bob Peterman); Frank Fenton (Birch); George Irving (Senator Wilton); Selmer Jackson (Charlie Stringer); Julia Dean (Mrs. Wilton); George Chandler (Bus Driver); Danny Mummert (Benny); Griff Barnett (Henry); William Haade, Dick Wessel (Moving Men); John Ince (Postman); Edgar Dearing (Gray-Haired Man); Snub Pollard (Townsman).

JOHNNY BELINDA (*Warner Bros., 1948*) 101 min.

Producer, Jerry Wald; director, Jean Negulesco; based on the play by Elmer Harris; screenplay, Irmgard von Cube, Allen Vincent; art director, Robert Haas; set decorator, William Wallace; music, Max Steiner; orchestrator, Murray Cutter; music director, Leo F. Forbstein; assistant director, Mel Dellar; makeup, Perc Westmore; costumes, Milo Anderson; sound, Charles Lang; special effects, William McGann, Edwin DuPar; camera, Ted McCord; editor, David Weisbart.

Jane Wyman (Belinda McDonald); Lew Ayres (Dr. Robert Richardson); Charles Bickford (Black McDonald); Agnes Moorehead (Aggie McDonald); Stephen McNally (Locky McCormick); Jan Sterling (Stella Maguire); Rosalind Ivan (Mrs. Peggety); Dan Seymour (Pacquet); Mabel Paige (Mrs. Lutz); Ida Moore (Mrs. McKee); Alan Napier (Defense Attorney); Monte Blue (Ben); Douglas Kennedy (Interpreter); James Craven (Floyd McQuiggen); Jeff Richards (Fergus McQuiggen); Joan Winfield (Mrs. Tim Moore); Ian Wolfe (Rector); Holmes Herbert (Judge); Ray Montgomery (Tim Moore); Jonathan Hale (Dr. Gray); Creighton Hale (Bailiff); Charles Horvath (Churchgoer); Snub Pollard, Franklyn Farnum (Jurymen).

A KISS IN THE DARK (*Warner Bros., 1949*) 87 min.

Producer, Harry Kurnitz; director, Delmer Daves; story, Everett and Devery Freeman; screenplay, Kurnitz; art director, Stanley Fleischer; set decorator, William Huehl; music, Max Steiner; music director, Ray Heindorf; orchestrator, Murray Cutter; assistant director, William Kissel; makeup, Ed Voigt; costumes, Milo Anderson; sound, Charles Lang; camera, Robert Burks; editor, David Weisbart.

David Niven (Eric Phillips); Jane Wyman (Polly Haines); Victor Moore (Horace Willoughby); Wayne Morris (Bruce Arnold); Broderick Crawford (Mr. Botts); Joseph Buloff (Peter Canilo); Maria Ouspenskaya (Madame Karina); Curt Bois (Schloss); Percival Vivian (Benton); Raymond Greenleaf (Martin Soames); Parker Eggleston (Willie); Norman Ollestad (Freddie); Frank Dae (Hiram Knale); Joe Devlin (Electrician); Claire Meade (Anna, the Cook); Creighton Hale, Bess Myers, Paulette Evans, Paul Panzer, Jack Wise, Fred Marlow (Tenants); Phyllis Coates (Mrs. Hale); Jimmy Dodd (Stuffy Nelson); Larry Rio (Taxi Driver); Stuart Holmes (Stage Manager).

THE LADY TAKES A SAILOR (*Warner Bros., 1949*) 99 min.

Producer, Harry Kurnitz; director, Michael Curtiz; story, Jerry Gruskin; screenplay, Everett Freeman; assistant director, Sherry Shourds; art director, Edward Carrere; set decorator, George James Hopkins; music, Max Steiner; orchestrator, Murray Cutter; makeup, Perc Westmore, Al Greenway; costumes, Milo Anderson; sound, Everett A. Brown; special effects, Roy Davidson, H. F. Koenekamp; camera, Ted McCord; editor, David Weisbart.

Jane Wyman (Jennifer Smith); Dennis Morgan (Bill Craig); Eve Arden (Susan Wayne); Robert Douglas (John Tyson); Allyn Joslyn (Ralph Whitcomb); Tom Tully (Henry Duckworth); Lina Romay (Raquel Riviera); William Frawley (Oliver Harker); Fred Clark (Victor Sangell); Charles Meredith (Dr. McKewen); Craig Stevens (Danvers); Tom Stevenson (Institute Guide); Ray Montgomery (Lab Man); Ruth Lewis (Miss Clark); Ruth Lee (Miss Brand); Sonia Bryden (Arlette); Walter Shumway (Dr. Coombs); Olan Soule (Secretary); Emil Rameau (Dr. Mittenwald); Russ Conway (Constable); Bridget Brown (Hatcheck Girl); George Spaulding (Admiral Morell); Nina Prescott (Tyson's Secretary).

IT'S A GREAT FEELING (*Warner Bros., 1949*) C-84 min.

Producer, Alex Gottlieb; director, David Butler; story, I. A. L. Diamond; screenplay, Jack Rose, Melville Shavelson; art director, Stanley Fleischer; set decorator, Lyle B. Reifsnider; assistant director, Phil Quinn; music number staged by LeRoy Prinz; music, Ray Heindorf; songs, Jule Styne and Sammy Cahn; costumes, Milo Anderson; makeup, Perc Westmore; Technicolor consultants, Natalie Kalmus, Mitchell Kovaleski; sound, Dolph Thomas, David Forrest; special effects, William McGann, H. F. Koenekamp; camera, Wilfrid M. Cline; editor, Irene Morra.

Dennis Morgan (Himself); Doris Day (Judy Adams); Jack Carson (Himself); Bill Goodwin (Arthur Trent); Irving Bacon (Information

Clerk); Claire Carleton (Grace); Harlan Warde (Publicity Man); Jacqueline DeWit (Trent's Secretary); The Mazzone-Abbott Dancers (Themselves); Wilfred Lucas (Mr. Adams); Pat Flaherty (Gate Guard); Wendy Lee (Manicurist); Nita Talbot, Joan Vohs, Sue Casey, Eve Whitney, Carol Brewster (Models); Lois Austin (Saleslady); Tom Dugan (Wrestling Fan in Bar); James Holden (Soda Jerk); Dudley Dickerson (Porter); Sandra Gould (Train Passenger in Upper Berth); Errol Flynn (Jeffrey Bushdinkle, the Groom); Gary Cooper, Joan Crawford, Sydney Greenstreet, Danny Kaye, Patricia Neal, Eleanor Parker, Ronald Reagan, Edward G. Robinson, Jane Wyman, Maureen Reagan, David Butler, Michael Curtiz, King Vidor, Raoul Walsh (Themselves).

STAGE FRIGHT *(Warner Bros., 1950)* 110 min.

Producer/director, Alfred Hitchcock; based on the novel *Man Running* by Selwyn Jepson; screenplay, Whitfield Cook; adaptor, Alma Reville; additional dialogue, James Bridie; music director, Louis Levy; music, Leighton Lucas; song, Cole Porter; Miss Wyman's wardrobe, Milo Anderson; Miss Dietrich's wardrobe, Christian Dior; makeup, Colin Guarde; sound, Harold King; camera, Wilkie Cooper; editor, Edward Jarvis.

Jane Wyman (Eve Gill); Marlene Dietrich (Charlotte Inwood); Michael Wilding (Smith); Richard Todd (Jonathan Cooper); Alastair Sim (Commodore Gill); Kay Walsh (Nellie); Dame Sybil Thorndike (Mrs. Gill); Miles Malleson (Bibulous Gentleman); Hector MacGregor (Freddie); Joyce Grenfell (Shooting Gallery Attendant); Andre Morell (Inspector Byard); Patricia Hitchcock (Chubby); Alfred Hitchcock (Passerby); and Irene Handl, Arthur Howard, Everley Gregg, Cyril Chamberlain, and Helen Goss.

THE GLASS MENAGERIE *(Warner Bros., 1950)* 106 min.

Producers, Jerry Wald, Charles K. Feldman; director, Irving Rapper; based on the play by Tennessee Williams; screenplay, Williams, Peter Berneis; art director, Robert Haas; music, Max Steiner; camera, Robert Burks; editor, David Weisbart.

Jane Wyman (Laura Wingfield); Kirk Douglas (Jim O'Connor); Gertrude Lawrence (Amanda Wingfield); Arthur Kennedy (Tom Wingfield); Ralph Sanford (Mendoza); Gertrude Graner (Woman Instructor); Ann Tyrell (Department Store Clerk); Perdita Chandler (Girl in Bar); Louise Lorrimer (Miss Porter); Sean McClory (Richard); James Horn, Marshall Romer (Callers); Sarah Edwards (Mrs. Miller).

THREE GUYS NAMED MIKE *(MGM, 1951)* 90 min.

Producer, Armand Deutsch; director, Charles Walters; story, Ruth Brooke Flippen; screenplay, Sidney Shelton; art directors, Cedric Gibbons, William Ferrari; music, Bronislau Kaper; camera, Paul C. Vogel; editor, Irvine Warburton.

Jane Wyman (Marcy Lewis); Van Johnson (Michael Lawrence); Howard Keel (Mike Jamison); Barry Sullivan (Mike Tracy); Phyllis Kirk (Kathy Hunter); Anne Sargent (Jan Baler); Jeff Donnell (Alice Raymond); Herbert Heyes (Scott Bellamy); Robert Sherwood (Benson); Don McGuire (MacWade Parker); Barbara Billingsley (Ann White); Hugh Sanders (Mr. Williams); John Maxwell (Dr. Matthew Hardy); Lewis Martin (C. R. Smith); Ethel "Pug" Wells (Herself); Sydney Mason (Osgood); Percy Helton (Hawkins); Dan Foster (Rogers); Jack Shea (Nashville Passenger Agent); King Mojave (Passenger Agent); Arthur Space (Clerk); Matt Moore (Mr. Tannen); Mae Clarke (Convair Passenger); Jack Gargan (Mr. Rogers).

HERE COMES THE GROOM *(Paramount, 1951)* 113 min.

Producer/director, Frank Capra; story, Robert Riskin, Liam O'Brien; screenplay, Virginia Van Upp, O'Brien, Myles Connolly; art directors, Hal Pereira, Earl Hedrick, music director, Joseph J. Lilley; songs, Jay Livingston and Ray Evans; Hoagy Carmichael and Johnny Mercer; camera, George Barnes; editor, Ellsworth Hoagland.

Bing Crosby (Pete); Jane Wyman (Emmadel Jones); Alexis Smith (Winifred Stanley); Franchot Tone (Wilbur Stanley); James Barton (Pa Jones); Robert Keith (George Degnan); Jacques Gencel (Bobby); Beverly Washburn (Suzi); Connie Gilchrist (Ma Jones); Walter Catlett (McGonigle); Alan Reed (Mr. Godfrey); Minna Gombel (Mrs. Godfrey); Howard Freeman (Governor); Maidel Turner (Aunt Abby); H. B. Warner (Uncle Elihu); Nicholas Joy (Uncle Prentiss); Ian Wolfe (Uncle Adam); Ellen Corby (Mrs. McGonigle); James Burke (Policeman); Irving Bacon (Baines); Ted Thorpe (Paul Pippitt); Art Baker (Radio Announcer); Anna Maria Alberghetti (Theresa); Dorothy Lamour, Frank Fontaine, Louis Armstrong, Phil Harris, Cass Daley (Themselves); Franklyn Farnum, J. Farrell MacDonald (Men); Carl Switzer (Messenger); Almira Sessions (Woman); Charles Lane (Detective).

THE BLUE VEIL *(RKO, 1951)* 113 min.

Producers, Jerry Wald, Norman Krasna; director, Curtis Bernhardt; story, Francois Campaux; screenplay, Norman Corwin; art directors, Albert S. D'Agostino, Carroll Clark; music director, C. Bakaleinikoff; camera, Franz Planer; editor, George Amy.

Jane Wyman (Louise Mason); Charles Laughton (Fred K. Begley); Joan Blondell (Annie Rawlins); Richard Carlson (Gerald Kean); Agnes Moorehead (Mrs. Palfrey); Don Taylor (Dr. Robert Palfrey); Cyril Cusack (Frank Hutchins); Everett Sloane (District Attorney); Natalie Wood (Stephanie Rawlins); Vivian Vance (Alicia); Carleton Young (Mr. Palfrey); Alan Napier (Professor Carter); Warner Anderson (Bill); Les Tremayne (Joplin); Dan Seymour (Pelt); Dan O'Herlihy (Hugh Williams); Gary Jackson (Robert Palfrey as a Boy); Gregory Marshall (Harrison Palfrey); Dee Pollack (Tony).

STARLIFT (*Warner Bros., 1951*) 103 min.

Producer, Robert Arthur; director, Roy Del Ruth; story, John Klorer; screenplay, Klorer, Karl Lamb; art director, Charles H. Clarke; music director, Ray Heindorf; songs, Joe Young and Jimmy Monaco; Ira and George Gershwin; Cole Porter; Sammy Cahn and Jule Styne; Irving Kahal and Sammy Fain; Edward Heyman and Dana Suesse; Harry Ruskin and Henry Sullivan; Percy Faith; Ruby Ralesin and Phil Harris; camera, Ted McCord; editor, William Ziegler.

Doris Day, Gordon MacRae, Virginia Mayo, Gene Nelson, Ruth Roman (Themselves); Janice Rule (Nell Wayne); Dick Wesson (Sergeant Mike Nolan); Ron Hagerthy (Corporal Rick Williams); Richard Webb (Colonel Callan); Hayden Rorke (Chaplain); Howard St. John (Steve Rogers); Ann Doran (Mrs. Callan); Tommy Farrell (Turner); John Maxwell (George Norris); Don Beddoe (Bob Wayne); Mary Adams (Sue Wayne); Bigelow Sayre (Dr. Williams); Eleanor Audley (Mrs. Williams); James Cagney, Gary Cooper, Virginia Gibson, Phil Harris, Frank Lovejoy, Lucille Norman, Louella Parsons, Randolph Scott, Jane Wyman, Patrice Wymore (Themselves); Pat Henry (Theatre Manager); Gordon Polk (Chief Usher); Joe Turkel (Litter Case); Jill Richards (Flight Nurse); Ray Montgomery (Captain Nelson); Walter Brennan, Jr. (Driver); Eddie Coonz (Reporter); Ezelle Poule (Waitress); Dick Ryan (Doctor); Dolores Castle, Dorothy Kennedy (Nurses); William Hunt (Boy with Cane); Steve Gregory (Boy with Camera); Bill Hudson (Crew Chief); Sarah Spencer (Louella Parsons' Assistant).

THE STORY OF WILL ROGERS (*Warner Bros., 1952*) C-109 min.

Producer, Robert Arthur; director, Michael Curtiz; based on the story "Uncle Clem's Boy" by Mrs. Will Rogers; screenplay, Stanley Roberts, Frank Davis; adaptor, John C. Moffitt; music, Victor Young; assistant director, Sherry Shourds; art director, Edward Carrere; camera, Wilfrid M. Cline; editor, Folmer Blangsted.

Will Rogers, Jr. (Will Rogers); Jane Wyman (Betty Rogers); Carl Benton Reid (Clem Rogers); Slim Pickens (Dusty Donovan); Eve Miller (Cora Marshall); Noah Beery, Jr. (Wiley Post); James Gleason (Bert Lynn); Margaret Field (Sally Rogers); Brian Daly (Tom McSpadden); Steve Brodie (Dave Marshall); Jay Silverheels (Joe Arrow); Pinky Tomlin (Orville); Mary Wickes (Mrs. Foster); Richard Kean (Mr. Cavendish); Earl Lee (President Wilson); William Forrest (Flo Ziegfeld); Slats Taylor (Art Fraser); Eddie Cantor (Himself); Robert Scott Correll (Younger Will, Jr.); Carol Ann Gainey (Younger Mary); Michael Gainey (Younger Jimmy/Young Will); Carol Nugent (Young Mary); Jack Burnette (Young Jimmy); Paul McWilliam (Dead-Eye Dick); Dub Taylor (Actor); Olan Soule (Secretary); Madge Journeay (Honey Girl Kate); Denver Dixon, Bob Rose (Bits); Monte Blue (Delegate).

JUST FOR YOU (*Paramount, 1952*) C-104 min.

Producer, Pat Duggan; director, Elliott Nugent; based on the story "Famous" by Stephen Vincent Benet; screenplay, Robert Carson; art directors, Hal Pereira, Roland Anderson; set decorators, Sam Comer, Rad Moyer; music director, Emil Newman; songs, Harry Warren and Leo Robin; choreography, Helen Tamiris; camera, George Barnes; editor, Doane Harrison.

Bing Crosby (Jordan Blake); Jane Wyman (Carolina Hill); Ethel Barrymore (Allida de Bronkhart); Robert Arthur (Jerry Blake); Natalie Wood (Barbara Blake); Cora Witherspoon (Mrs. Angevine); Ben Lessy (Georgie Polansky); Regis Toomey (Hodges); Art Smith (Leo); Leon Tyler (David McKenzie); Willis Bouchey (Hank Ross); Herbert Vigran (George); Irene Martin (Member of U.S.O. Troupe); Nancy Hale (Guest); Daniel Nagrin, Miriam Pandor, Florence Lessing (Specialty Dancers); Franklyn Farnum (Cook); Brick Sullivan (Policeman); Buck Harrington (Police Sergeant); Bess Flowers, Mary Bayless (Women); Jack Mulhall (Major); Max Keith (Stage Manager); Robert S. Scott (Lieutenant).

LET'S DO IT AGAIN (*Columbia, 1953*) C-95 min.

Producer, Oscar Saul; director, Alexander Hall; based on the play by Arthur Richman; screenplay, Mary Loos, Richard Sale; songs, Lester Lee, Ned Washington; choreography, Lee Scott, Valerie Bettis; music director, Morris Stoloff; art director, Walter Holscher; camera, Charles Lawton, Jr.; editor, Charles Nelson.

Jane Wyman (Constance Stuart); Ray Milland (Gary Stuart); Aldo Ray (Frank McGraw); Leon Ames (Chet Stuart); Valerie Bettis (Lilly Adair); Tom Helmore (Courtney Craig); Karin Booth

(Deborah Randolph); Mary Treen (Nelly); Richard Wessel (Mover); Kathryn Givney (Mrs. Randolph); Herbert Heyes (Mr. Randolph); Maurice Stein (Willie); Frank Remley (Pete); Don Rice (Hal); Don Gibson (Gas Station Attendant); Bob Hopkins (Another Mover); Major Sam Harris (Bit); Howard Negley (Charlie, the Cop); Robert Williams (Bartender); Douglas Evans (Manager of Black Cat); Herb Vigran (Charlie, the Theatre Manager).

SO BIG *(Warner Bros., 1953)* 101 min.

Producer, Henry Blanke; director, Robert Wise; based on the novel by Edna Ferber; screenplay, John Twist; art director, John Beckman; music, Max Steiner; camera, Ellsworth Fredericks; editor, Thomas Reilly.

Jane Wyman (Selina Dejong); Sterling Hayden (Pervus Dejong); Dick Beymer (Roelf at Age Twelve); Ruth Swanson (Maartje Pool); Roland Winters (Klaas Pool); Tommy Rettig (Dirk at Eight); Steve Forrest (Dirk at Twenty-Five); Dorothy Christy (Widow Paarlenberg); Jacques Aubuchon (August Hempel); Elisabeth Fraser (Julie Hempel); Nancy Olson (Dallas O'Mara); Martha Hyer (Paula Hempel); Walter Coy (Roelf at Forty); Noralee Norman (Geertje Pool); Jill Janssen (Jozina Pool); Kerry Donnelly (Paul at Eight); Kenneth Osmond (Eugene at Nine); Lotte Stein (Meena); Vera Miles, Evan Loew, Frances Osborne, Jean Garvin, Carol Grel (Girls); Lily Kemble Cooper (Miss Fister); Grandon Rhodes (Bainbridge); Bud Osborne (Wagon Driver); Dorothy Granger, Elizabeth Russell (Ladies); Dick Alexander (Bidder); David McMahon (Cop); Kenner G. Kemp (Hempel's Chauffeur).

MAGNIFICENT OBSESSION *(Universal, 1954)* C-108 min.

Producer, Ross Hunter; director, Douglas Sirk; based on the novel by Lloyd C. Douglas and the screenplay by Sarah Y. Mason and Victor Heerman; adaptor, Wells Root; new screenplay, Robert Blees; color consultant, William Fitzche; art directors, Bernard Herzbrun, Emrich Nicholson; set decorators, Russell A. Gausman, Ruby R. Levitt; costumes, Bill Thomas; music, Frank Skinner; special effects, David Harsley; camera, Russell Metty; editor, Milton Carruth.

Jane Wyman (Helen Phillips); Rock Hudson (Bob Merrick); Agnes Moorehead (Nancy Ashford); Barbara Rush (Joyce Phillips); Gregg Palmer (Tom Masterson); Otto Kruger (Randolph); Paul Cavanagh (Dr. Giraud); Sara Shane (Valerie); Richard H. Cutting (Dr. Dodge); Judy Nugent (Judy); Helen Kleeb (Mrs. Eden); Robert B. Williams (Sergeant Burnham); Will White (Sergeant Ames); George Lynn (Williams); Jack Kelly (Mechanic); Lisa Gaye (Switchboard Girl); Mae Clarke (Mrs. Miller); Lucille Lamar (Nurse); Frederick Stevens (Cafe Owner); Helen Winston (Receptionist); Gail Bonney (Phyllis); Norbert Schiller (Mr. Long); Harold Dyrenforth (Mr. Jouvet); Alexander Campbell (Dr. Allan); Rudolph Anders (Dr. Fuss); Myrna Hansen (Customer).

LUCY GALLANT *(Paramount, 1955)* C-104 min.

Producers, William H. Pine, William C. Thomas; director, Robert Parrish; based on the novel *The Life of Lucy Gallant* by Margaret Cousins; screenplay, John Lee Mahin, Winston Miller; art directors, Hal Pereira, Henry Bumstead; music director, Van Cleave; song, Jay Livingston and Ray Evans; costumes, Edith Head; assistant director, William McGarry; camera, Lionel Lindon; editor, Howard Smith.

Jane Wyman (Lucy Gallant); Charlton Heston (Casey Cole); Claire Trevor (Lady MacBeth); Thelma Ritter (Molly Basserman); William Demarest (Charles Madden); Wallace Ford (Gus Basserman); Gloria Talbott (Laura Wilson); Tom Helmore (Jim Wardman); James Westerfield (Frank Wilson); Mary Field (Irma Wilson); Governor Allan Shivers of Texas (Himself); Edith Head (Herself); Joel Fluellen (Summertime); Louise Arthur (Sal); Jay Adler (Stationmaster); Frank Marlowe (Nolan); Roscoe Ates (Anderson); Jack Pepper, Edmund Cobb, Frank Hagney, Fern Burry, Mary Boyd (Bits); Gene Roth (Oil Man).

ALL THAT HEAVEN ALLOWS *(Universal, 1955)* C-89 min.

Producer, Ross Hunter; director, Douglas Sirk; story, Edna Lee, Harry Lee; screenplay, Peg Fenwick; dialogue director, Jack Daniels; color consultant, William Fritzche; art directors, Alexander Golitzen, Eric Orbom; set decorators, Russell A. Gausman, Julia Heron; music, Frank Skinner; music supervisor, Joseph Gershenson; costumes, Bill Thomas; assistant directors, Joseph Kenny, George Lollier; camera, Russell Metty; editor, Frank Gross.

Jane Wyman (Cary Scott); Rock Hudson (Ron Kirby); Agnes Moorehead (Sara Warren); Conrad Nagel (Harvey); Gloria Talbott (Fay); William Reynolds (Ned); Virginia Grey (Alida); Charles Drake (Nick Anderson); Hayden Rorke (Dr. Hennessy); Jacqueline de Wit (Nona Plash); Donald Curtis (Howard Hoffer); Nestor Paiva (Manuel); Leigh Snowden (Jo-Ann); Forrest Lewis (Mr. Macks); Tol Avery (Tom Allenby); Merry Anders (Mary Ann); Paul Keast (Mark Plash); David Janssen (Reddie Norton); Gia Scala (Manuel's Daughter); Eleanor Audley (Mrs. Humphrey); Edna Smith, Jack Davidson (Bits); Helen Mayon (Nurse).

MIRACLE IN THE RAIN (*Warner Bros., 1956*) 107 min.

Producer, Frank P. Rosenberg; director, Rudolph Maté; story/screenplay, Ben Hecht; art director, Leo K. Kuter; music/music director, Franz Waxman; orchestrator, Leonid Raab; song, Ray Heindorf, M. K. Jerome, Ned Washington; costumes, Milo Anderson; assistant directors, Mel Dellar, Lee White; camera, Russell Metty; editor, Thomas Reilly.

Jane Wyman (Ruth Wood); Van Johnson (Arthur Hugenon); Peggie Castle (Millie Kranz); Fred Clark (Stephen Jalonik); Eileen Heckart (Grace Ullman); Josephine Hutchinson (Agnes Wood); William Gargan (Harry Wood); Marcel Dalio (Waiter); George Givot (Headwaiter); Barbara Nichols (Arleene Witchy); Halliwell Hobbes (Eli B. Windgate); Paul Picerni (Young Priest); Alan King (Sergeant Gil Parker); Irene Seidner (Mrs. Hamer); Arte Johnson (Monty); Marian Holmes (Mrs. Rickles); Minerva Urecal (Mrs. Canelli); Frank Scannell (Auctioneer); Walter Kingson (Narrator); Anna Dewey (Elderly Woman); Lucita (Accordionist); Rose Allen (Elderly Woman); Jess Kirkpatrick (Andy, the Bartender); Allen Ray (Forty-Year-Old Man); Diana Dawson (Twenty-Five-Year-Old Woman).

HOLIDAY FOR LOVERS (*Twentieth Century-Fox, 1959*) C-102 min.

Producer, David Weisbart; director, Henry Levin; based on the play by Ronald Alexander; screenplay, Luther Davis; music, Leigh Harline; music director, Lionel Newman; title song, Sammy Cahn and James Van Heusen; art directors, Lyle Wheeler, Herman Blumenthal; set decorators, Walter M. Scott, Paul S. Fox; wardrobe designer, Charles LeMaire; makeup, Ben Nye; color consultant, Leonard Doss; assistant director, Eli Dunn; sound, Alfred Bruzlin, Harry M. Leonard; special camera effects, L. B. Abbott, James Gordon; camera, Charles G. Clarke; editor, Stuart Gilmore.

Clifton Webb (Robert Dean); Jane Wyman (Mary Dean); Jill St. John (Meg Dean); Carol Lynley (Betsy Dean); Paul Henreid (Eduardo Barroso); Gary Crosby (Paul Gattling); Nico Minardos (Carlos); Wally Brown (Joe); Henny Backus (Connie); Nora O'Mahoney (Mrs. Murphy); Buck Class (Staff Sergeant); Al Austin (Technical Sergeant); Nester Amaral and His Orchestra (Themselves); Jose Greco (Himself); Eric Morris (Air Policeman); Gardner McKay (Airman First Class); Manuel Paris (Beaming Peruvian); Anna Kareen (Latin Stewardess); Angelo De Meo, Anthony Ross (Matadors); David Ahdar (Brazilian Cab Driver); Peter Helm (Tragic Young Man); Ingrid Goude (Receptionist); Wendy Wilde (American Stewardess).

POLLYANNA (*Buena Vista, 1960*) C-134 min.

Producer, Walt Disney; director, David Swift; based on the novel by Eleanor H. Porter; screenplay, Swift; music, Paul Smith; orchestrator, Franklyn Marks; makeup, Pat McNally; costumes, Walter Plunkett, Chuck Keehne, Gertrude Casey; art directors, Carroll Clark, Robert Clatworthy; set decorators, Emile Kuri, Fred MacLean; assistant director, Joseph Behm; sound, Robert O. Cook, Dean Thomas; special effects, Ub Iwerks; camera, Russell Harlan; editor, Frank Gross.

Hayley Mills (Pollyanna); Jane Wyman (Aunt Polly); Richard Egan (Dr. Edmund Chilton); Karl Malden (Reverend Paul Ford); Nancy Olson (Nancy Furman); Adolphe Menjou (Mr. Pendergast); Donald Crisp (Mayor Karl Warren); Agnes Moorehead (Mrs. Snow); Kevin Corcoran (Jimmy Bean); James Drury (George Dodds); Reta Shaw (Tillie Lagerlof); Leora Dana (Mrs. Paul Ford); Anne Seymour (Mrs. Amelia Tarbell); Edward Platt (Ben Tarbell); Mary Grace Canfield (Angelica); Jenny Egan (Mildred Snow); Gage Clarke (Mr. Murg); Ian Wolfe (Mr. Neely); Nolan Leary (Mr. Thomas); Edgar Dearing (Mr. Gorman).

BON VOYAGE (*Buena Vista, 1962*) C-130 min.

Producer, Walt Disney; associate producers, Bill Walsh, Ron Miller; director, James Neilson; based on the book by Marrijane and Joseph Hayes; screenplay, Walsh; assistant director, Joseph L. McEveety; art directors, Carroll Clark, Marvin Aubrey Davis; set decorators, Emile Kuri, Hal Gausman; special titles, Bill Justice, Xavier Atencio; costumes, Bill Thomas; costumers, Chuck Keehne, Gertrude Casey; makeup, Pat McNally; music, Paul Smith; song, Richard M. and Robert B. Sherman; sound, Robert O. Cook, Dean Thomas; special effects, Eustace Lycett; camera, William Snyder; editor, Cotton Warburton.

Fred MacMurray (Harry Willard); Jane Wyman (Katie Willard); Michael Callan (Nick O'Mara); Deborah Walley (Amy Willard); Tommy Kirk (Elliott Willard); Kevin Corcoran (Skipper Willard); Jessie Royce Landis (La Contessa); Georgette Anys (Madame Clebert); Ivan Desny (Rudolph); Francoise Prevost (Girl); Carol White (Penelope); Howard I. Smith (Judge Henderson); Casey Adams (Tight Suit); James Milhollin (Librarian); Marcel Hillaire (Sewer Guide); Richard Wattis (Englishman); Hassan Khayyam (Shamra's Father); Ana Maria Majalca (Shamra).

HOW TO COMMIT MARRIAGE (*Cinerama, 1969*) C-98 min.

Executive producer, Bob Hope; producer, Bill Lawrence; director, Norman Panama; screenplay, Ben Starr, Michael Kanin; music/music director, Joseph J. Lilley; additional music, The Comfortable Chair; choreography, Jack Baker; art director, Edward Engoron; set decorator, John Lamphear; titles/montage, Wayne Fitzgerald; costumes, Nolan Miller; sound, Glen Glenn; special effects, Justus Gibbs; camera, Charles Lang; editor, Ronald Sinclair.

Bob Hope (Frank Benson); Jackie Gleason (Oliver Poe); Jane Wyman (Elaine Benson); Maureen Arthur (Lois Grey); Leslie Nielsen (Phil Fletcher); Tina Louise (LaVerne Baker); Paul Stewart (Attorney); Irwin Corey (The Baba Ziba); Joanna Cameron (Nancy Benson); Tim Matthieson (David Poe); The Comfortable Chair (Themselves).

THE FAILING OF RAYMOND *(ABC-TV, 1971)* C-73 min.

Producer, George Eckstein; director, Boris Sagal; teleplay, Adrian Spies; music, Pat Williams; camera, Ben Colman; editor, John Kaufman, Jr.

Jane Wyman (Mary Bloomquist); Dean Stockwell (Raymond); Dana Andrews (Allan MacDonald); Paul Henreid (Dr. Abel); Murray Hamilton (Sergeant Manzak); Tim O'Connor (Cliff Roeder); Priscilla Pointer (History Teacher); Mary Jackson (Latin Teacher); Adrienne Marden (Librarian); Catherine Louise Sagal (Girl Patient); Robert Karnes (City Editor); Ray Ballard (Store Owner).

THE INCREDIBLE JOURNEY OF DOCTOR MEG LAUREL *(CBS-TV, 1979)* C-131 min.

Executive producer, Ron Samuels; producer, Paul Radin; director, Guy Green; teleplay, Michael Berk, Douglas Schwartz, Joseph Fineman; music, Gerald Fried; art director, Jack DeShields; sound, Richard Wagner; camera, Al Francis; editor, Gloryette Clark.

Lindsay Wagner (Meg Laurel); Jane Wyman (Granny Arrowroot); Dorothy McGuire (Effie Web); Andrew Duggan (Judge Adamson); Gary Lockwood (Harley Moon); Brock Peters (Joe); John Reilly (Thom Laurel); Charles Tyner (Doug Slocumb); James Woods (Sin Eater); Woodrow Parfrey (Messerschmidt); Peggy Walton (Mrs. Slocumb); Kathi Soucie (Becca); Tracey Gold (Laurie Mae Moon); Cherilyn Parsons (Sophie Pride); Gary Graham (Jacob Barth); Ray Young (Joel); Tom Spratley (Dentist); Gloria Stuart (Rose Hooper); Meegan King (Willis); David Gregory (Herm); Dee Croxton (Mildred Koch); Hazel Johnson (Vryle Macy); Pauline McFadgen (Corra Macy); Carolyn Jane Reed (Mrs. Pride); Sam Jones (Roy); Philip G. Schultz (Butler); Sharon McGrath (Twelve Year Old); Cathy Carriacaburu (Evelyn); Marta Nichols (Seven Year Old).

ABOUT THE STAFF

JAMES ROBERT PARISH, Los Angeles-based writer, was born in Cambridge, Massachusetts. He attended the University of Pennsylvania and graduated as a Phi Beta Kappa with an honors degree in English. A graduate of the University of Pennsylvania Law School, he is a member of the New York Bar. As president of Entertainment Copyright Research Co., Inc., he headed a major research facility for the media industries. Later he was a film interviewer with film trade papers. He is the author of many books, including *The Fox Girls, The RKO Gals, Actors TV Credits, 1952–72* (and Supplement), *The Tough Guys, The Jeanette MacDonald Story, The Elvis Presley Scrapbook,* and *The Hollywood Beauties*. Among those he has co-authored are *The MGM Stock Company, The Debonairs, Liza!, The Leading Ladies, Hollywood Character Actors, The Great Science Fiction Pictures,* and the *Funsters*.

DON E. STANKE in recent years has interviewed more than forty personalities of American film and cinema and has had career articles published on most of them in assorted film journals. Interviewing and writing is avocational, since Stanke is a full-time administrative manager with a San Francisco-based corporation. With Mr. Parish, he is the co-author of *The Glamour Girls, The Swashbucklers, The Debonairs, The All-Americans,* and *The Leading Ladies.* He has contributed to the books *The Real Star #2, The Tough Guys, Hollywood Players: The Thirties, Hollywood Beauties,* and *The Hollywood Kids.*

ROGER GREENE received a B.A. from St. John's College, Annapolis, and an M.F.A. from Columbia University in New York City. He has worked as an editorial assistant on the staff of Collier's Encyclopedia, taught filmmaking to children, done freelance photo research, and now prepares scripts for armed forces training pictures. He currently resides in Manhattan.

THOMAS NOCERINO, a graduate of the John Jay College of Criminal Justice, works in New York City where he fosters his interest in cinema history. Recently married, he resides in Brooklyn.

Brooklyn-born JOHN ROBERT COCCHI has been viewing and collating data on motion pictures since an early age. He is now regarded as one of America's most thorough film researchers. He was research associate on *The American Movies Reference Book: The Sound Era* (and Supplement), *The Fox Girls, Good Dames, The MGM Stock Company: The Golden Era, The Hollywood Beauties,* and *The Funsters,* among others, and a contributing editor to *The Films of Jeanette MacDonald and Nelson Eddy*. He has written cinema history articles for such journals as *Film Fan Monthly* and *Screen Facts,* and is the author of *The Westerns: A Picture Quiz Book*. He is co-founder of one of New York City's leading film societies.

New York-born FLORENCE SOLOMON attended Hunter College and then joined Ligon Johnson's copyright research office. Later, she was appointed director for research at Entertainment Copyright Research Co., Inc., and is presently a reference supervisor at ASCAP's Index Division in New York City. Miss Solomon has collaborated on such volumes as *The American Movies Reference Book: The Sound Era, TV Movies, The Great Movie Series, Vincent Price Unmasked, Film Directors Guide: Western Europe,* and several others. She is a niece of the noted sculptor, the late Sir Jacob Epstein.

Index

Numbers in italics indicate pages showing photographs of the individuals and movies mentioned. If the letter "n" follows a page number, the reference is to a footnote on the indicated page.

Aaker, Lee, *296*
Academy Award, 33, 55, 56, 82, 85, 88, 92, 98, 99, *101*, 102, 112, 132, 151, 153, 206, 291, 337, 370, 385, 386, 389, *394*, 395, 396, 398, 402, 410, 418
Actor's Cues, 14
Ada, 104, *104*, 105
Adam Had Four Sons, 72, 73
Adams, Edie, 108, 179
Adams, Lee, 48
Adler, Luther, 88
Adrian, Iris, 369
Adventures of Sherlock Holmes, The, 142, 155
Affiliated Joneses, 207
African Queen, The, 32, 405
"Again," 160
Agee, James, 12, 18, 21, 80, 84, 155, 205
Aherne, Brian, 142, 153
"Aladdin's Lamp," 139
Alberghetti, Anna Maria, 402
Albert, Eddie, 82, 96, *96*, 145, 147, 176, 372, 373, 374, 375, *376*, 377
Alcatraz Island, 265
Alcoholics Anonymous, 96
Alda, Robert, 156
Aldrich, Robert, 168
Aldridge, Katharine (Kay), 279, *279*
"Alfred Hitchcock Presents," 169
Alice in Wonderland, 135
All About Eve, 48, 67
All Americans, The, 372 n
Allen, Aileen, 324
Allen, Irwin, 227, 230
Allenby, Frank, 217
Allied Artists, 166, 230
All That Heaven Allows, 405, 410
All the King's Horses, 369
All the President's Men, 52
Allwyn, Astrid, 273

Allyson, June, 95, 234, 296, 340, 408
Along the Great Divide, 217, 403
Altman, Robert, 58
Alton, Robert, 340 n
Always Leave Them Laughing, 215, *216*
Ambassador, 261
Amelia, 412
American Academy of Dramatic Arts, 12, 14
"American Film Institute 10th Anniversary," 55
American Repertory Theatre, 82
"Am I Blue?" 16
Among the Living, 73
Anderson, James, 218
Anderson, John Murray, 198
Anderson, Judith, 280, 286
Anderson, Maxwell, 28
Anderson, Milo, 28, 405
"And Her Tears Flowed Like Wine," 22
And Now Tomorrow, 80, *81*
Andrews, Dana, *66*, 82, 88, 168, 203, *205*, 415
Andy Hardy's Double Life, *326*, 327
Andy Warhol's Interview, 134
Angel from Texas, An, 375
Angeli, Pier, 226
"Angel in Disguise," 273
Angels Wash Their Faces, 271
Angels with Dirty Faces, 266, 267, 271
Animal Kingdom, The, 289, 385
Ankrum, Morris, 217
Anna Lucasta, 98 n
"Another World," 299
Answer, The, 179
Antoinette Perry Award. *See* Tony Award
Anything Goes, 138, 369
Applause! 11, 48, 49, *50*, 55
Appointment in Honduras, 295, *297*
Aquacade, 325
Aqua Spectacle, 352

441

Arden, Eve, 55, 76, *77*, 266, 288, *288*, 291, *384*, 385, 389, 398
Arkin, Alan, 171
Arlen, Richard, 76, 136, 141, 234
Armed Venus, The, 354
Armstrong, Louis, 141, 209
Arnow, Max, 70 n, 261
Arthritis Foundation, 415, 418
Arthur, Jean, 69, 398
Arthur, Robert, 408
Artistry in Cinema Award, 180 n
Artists and Models, 141, *141*
Aspern Papers, The, 82, 84
Astaire, Fred, 323, 345
Astor, Mary, 333
Athena, 348
Auer, John H., 199
Aumont, Jean-Pierre, 330
Auntie Mame, 102 n
Awful Truth, The, 408
Axelrod, George, 41
Ayres, Lew, 291, *292*, 393, *393*, 395, 396, 398, 400, 415

"Baby, It's Cold Outside," 88, 337
Bacal, Natalie, 12
Bacall, Betty, *See* Bacall, Lauren
Bacall, Lauren, 11–59, 98, 131, 212 n, 330
Bach (composer), 269
Backfire, 215, *216*
Back Street, 104–5, *105*
Backtrack, 171, *176*
Backus, Jim, 348
Bacon, Lloyd, 262, 278, 279, 283
Bad Men of Missouri, 377
Bagai, Ram, *163*
Bainter, Fay, 142, *143*, 156
Baker, Dorothy, 28
Baker, Joe Don, 171
Baker, Kenny, 371
Baker, Mary, 24
Ball, Lucille, 331, *333*
Ball of Fire, 206
Balsam, Martin, *51*, 52, *104*
Band of Angels, 98 n
Band Wagon, The, 345
Banjo Eyes, 197–98, 241
Bankhead, Tallulah, 12, 297 n
Bantam, 389
Bara, Theda, 141 n
Bare, Richard, 109
Bari, Lynn, 88
Barker, Gregory, 80, *81*, 112–13, 113 n
Barker, Jeffrey "Jess," 77, 80, *81*, 82, 91, 93, 94
Barker, Lex, 77 n
Barker, Timothy, 80, *81*, 113

Barnes, George, 132, 148
Barnes, Howard, 73, 144, 148, 205, 290
Barnet, Charlie, 209
Barrett, Edith, 149, *149*
Barrie, Wendy, 198
Barry, Don "Red," 95, *96*
Barry, Gene, 94, 241
Barrymore, Dolores Costello, 139
Barrymore, John, Jr., 168
Barrymore, Lionel, *26*, 28
Bathing Beauty, 327, *328*, 358
Bautzer, Gregson, 405
Baxt, George, 415
Baxter, Anne, 48, 49, 87
Baxter, Warner, 73, 369
Beatty, Mrs. Charles, 164
Beatty, Robert, *219*
Beau Geste, 70, 72, 73
"Because," 330
Beck, John, 98
Beery, Wallace, 377
Behold My Wife! 259
Bellamann, Henry, 279
Bellamy, Ralph, 139, *140*, 408
Bendix, William, 79, 80
Bennett, Bruce, 156, *157*, 209, *210*, *391*, 392
Bennett, Constance, 373
Bennett, Joan, 20 n, 69, 259, 283
Benny, Jack, 141, *141*, *284*, 285, 385
Bergen, Edgar, 82, 266
Bergman, Ingrid, 45 n, 52, 73, 98 n, 289, 395, 403, 405
Bergner, Elisabeth, 159
Berkeley, Busby, 267, 268, 335, 347, 348, 370
Berkes, Johnnie, *290*
Berle, Milton, 215, *216*, 236
Bernhardt, Curtis, 155
Bernhardt, Sarah, 67
Bernstein, Carl, 52
Best Actor, 32. *See also* Academy Award
Best Actress, 85, 88, 98, 390, 395. *See also* Academy Award
Best Supporting Actress, 28, 33. *See also* Academy Award
Best Years of Our Lives, The, 195, 203, *205*, 205–6, 209 n
"Better than Life," 273
Beverly Hills Citizen, 354
Beware, My Lovely, 165, *165*
Beware, Spooks! 375
Bey, Turhan, 18, *207*, 330
Bezzerides, A. I., 275
Bickford, Charles, 392, *393*
Bigamist, The, 166, *167*, 168
Big Event, 53
Big Knife, The, *167*, 168

442

Big Land, The, 227
Big Show, The, 88 n, 355–56, *356*
Big Sleep, The, 10, 22, 24 n
"Bill," 156 n
Bill, Tony, 174
Bishop, Joey, 354
Bishop Misbehaves, The, 137
Black Legion, 261, *262*
"Black Strap Molasses," 403
Blaine, Vivian, *343,* 345
Blakely, James, 136
Blithe Spirit, 33, *36*
Blockade, 178
Blondell, Joan, 220, 236, 264, 266, 271, 278, 296, 370, 403
Blood Alley, 33, *34*
Bloom, Lindsay, 239
Blowing Wild, 32
"Blow Out the Candle," 403
Blue, Ben, 288, *289*
Blue, Monte, 269
Blue Veil, The, 374, 403–5, *404*
Blumenfeld, Ralph, 48
Blyth, Ann, 91
"Bob Hope Chrysler Theatre, The," 44, *417*
"Body and Soul," 156 n
Body Disappears, The, 377
Boehnel, William, 278
Bogart, Daletrend Gemelle, 59 n
Bogart, Humphrey, *10,* 11, 16, *17,* 18, *20,* 21, 22, *24, 25,* 26, *26, 27,* 28, 30, 32, 33, *35, 37, 37,* 45, 46, 52, 53, 55, 56, 98, 145, *146,* 147, 148, 209, 261, 262, *262,* 264, 266, 273, *274,* 275, *276,* 279, 281, 286, 291, 292
Bogart, James Stephen Humphrey, 59 n
Bogart, Leslie Howard, 30, *35,* 59 n
Bogart, Stephen Humphrey, 28, *35, 37,* 59 n
Bohnen, Roman, 151, 203
"Bold Ones, The," 415
"Bold Venture," 30
Boles, John, 141, 142
Bonanova, Fortunio, 333
"Bonanza," 169
Bond, Anson, 160
Bond, Ward, 86, *268,* 269
Bondi, Beulah, *81,* 179
Bon Voyage, 415, *416*
Book of Jack London, The, 79
Booth, Shirley, 92
Bordertown, 145
Borg, Veda Ann, 262, 369
Borgnine, Ernest, 176
Boswell, Connie, 141
Bow, Clara, 255
Bowie, J. Russell, 273
Bowman, Lee, 82, *83,* 142

Boyd, Stephen, 102
Boyer, Charles, 20, *21,* 73, 102, 137, 150, 168, 299
Bracken, Eddie, 77, 212, *212*
Brackett, Charles, 385
Bradlee, Ben, 52
Bradley, Lovyss, *84*
Bradna, Olympe, 373
Brady, Scott, 234
Brand, Neville, *176*
Brandon, Elsa, 209
Brasselle, Keefe, 160, 163
Brennan, Walter, 16, *200,* 217
Brent, George, 145, 207, *207,* 273, 276, 278, *278,* 283, 285, 286, 377, *379*
Brian, David, 232
Brice, Fanny, 323
Brief Encounter, 390
Bright Leaf, 29, 30, 218
Brisson, Carl, 135, 369
Brisson, Frederick, 299
British Equity, 218
British International Studios, 133
Britton, Barbara, 77
Broadway Melody of 1940, 325
Broadway Musketeers, 266
Broderick, Helen, 269
Broken Lance, 88 n, 355
Bromfield, Louis, 18, 28, 273
Bronston, Samuel, 77, 199
Brontë, Anne, 155
Brontë, Branwell, 155
Brontë, Charlotte, 155
Brontë, Emily, 155
Brooklyn Eagle, 68, 371
Brooks, Leslie, 279, *279*
Brophy, Edward, 380
Brother Rat, 369 n, 372, 374, 375, 379
Brother Rat and a Baby, 375
Brown, Clarence, 389, 390 n, 418, *420*
Brown, Helen Gurley, 43
Brown, James, 77
Brown, Joe E., 73, 369, 370, 371, *372,* 375
Brown, Katharine, 69
Brown, Peter, *176*
Brown, Rowland, 14
Brown, Tom, 261
Brown, Wally, 199
Bruce, Nigel, 142
Brunetti, Argentina, 232
Bryan, Jane, 70, *71,* 145, 264, 268, 372, 373
Buchwald, Art, 354
Buckner, Robert, 21
"Burke's Law," 169
Burnett, Carol, 55
Burns, Bob, 73

Burns, George, *420*
Burr, Raymond, 226
Burrows, Abe, 43
Busley, Jessie, 273
Butler, David, 290, 398
Butter and Egg Man, The, 375
Butterworth, Charles, 73

Cabot, Bruce, 268
Cactus Flower, 11, 43, 45, *46, 49*, 55, 234
Caged, 168, 292
Cagney, James, 102, 145, 195, 213, *215*, 217, *217*, 220, 240, 255, 266, 267, 268, 271, 273, 274, 275, 276, 277, *277*, 278, 279, 286, 370, 412
Cain, James, 401
Cain, William Q., 283
Cain and Mabel, 370
Caits, Joseph, *143*
Calhoun, Rory, 91, 236
California State Military Guard Ball, *381*
Callaway Went Thataway, 343
"Calling Terry Conway," 296
Call of the Wild, The, 79
Cameron, Joanna, *416*
Cameron, Kate, 22
Campbell, Pat, 174
Campus Cinderella, 70, *71*
Can-Can, 98
Cannes Festival, 98
Canova, Judy, 73, 141
Cantor, Eddie, 12, 154, 197, 198, 241, 286, 369
Cantor, Marilyn, 12
Canyon Passage, 82
Capra, Frank, 392 n, 402
Captain Horatio Hornblower, 218, *219*
Captain's Paradise, The, 168 n
Capucine, 108
Cardona, Rene, Jr., 241
Career Girl, 398
Carlisle, Mary, 375
Carlson, Richard, 271, 403
Carmen Jones, 410
Carmichael, Hoagy, 16, 28
Carminati, Tullio, 136, *136*
Carney, Alan, 199
Carney, Art, 236, 239
Car 99, 259
Carnovsky, Morris, 286
Carr, John, 236
Carriage Entrance, 295
Carrillo, Leo, 139
Carroll, Earl, 267, 330
Carroll, Georgia, 279, *279*
Carroll, John, 76, 333, *334*, 375
Carroll, Kathleen, 171

Carroll, Lewis, 135
Carroll, Madeleine, 142
Carson, Jack, *29*, 30, 151, 279, 283, *284*, 286, 288, 289, 290, *347*, 348, 380, *382, 383, 384*, 385, 389, 398
Carson, Robert, 70
Caruso, Anthony, 227
Casablanca, 281
"Casey at the Bat," 32
Cash, Johnny, 180
Cassel, Jean-Pierre, 52
Cassidy, Claudia, 297 n
Castle of Evil, 232, *234*
Castle on the Hudson, 273
Cat and the Canary, The, 232
Catlett, Walter, 278, *373*
Cat on a Hot Tin Roof, 102 n
Caulfield, Joan, 208
Cavett, Frank, 82
Chalkley, Floyd Eaton, 98, 99, 102, *103*, 105, 106, 108, 109
Chandler, Jeff, 94, 102, *103*, 142, 354
Chandler, Marjorie Hoshelle, 354
Chandler, Raymond, 22
Chaney, Lon, 41 n
Chapman, Janet Kay, 265, *266*
Chapman, John, 241
Chapman, Marguerite, 279, *279*
Charisse, Cyd, 333, *334*, 335, 340
Charles B. Harding Award, 418
"Charlie's Angels," 180
Chasen, Meg, *420*
Chatterton, Ruth, 151
Cheyenne, 390, *391*
Chicago Sun-Times, 297 n
Chicago Tribune, 236, 297 n
Christian, Linda, 198
Christie, Agatha, 49
Christ on Trial, 220, *221*
"Church Scene," *406*, 415
City for Conquest, 276–77, *277*
Clarence House, 132
Clark, Dane, 156, *157*, 217, 290–91
Clark, Fred, 213
Claudia, 14, 15
Cleopatra, 102, 135
Coburn, Charles, 280, *284*, 285, *382*, 385
Cobweb, The, 32, 33, 41
Cochran, Steve, 168, 203, 205, 209, 213, 222, 296
Coco, 48
Coe, Richard L., 45
Cohn, Harry, 148
Colbert, Claudette, 33, *36*, 102, 135, 259, 264
Cole, Jack, 37
Coleman, Georgia, 324

Coleman, Nancy, 154, 155, *156*, 280, *280*, 286
College Rhythm, 369
Collier's, 133
Colman, Ronald, 142–43, *144*
Colonna, Jerry, 269
Colorado Territory, 209, *211*
Columbia Pictures, 15, 24, 45 n, 73, 77, 139, 142, 148, 159, 160, 168, 171, 264, 268, 375, 379, 408
"Columbo," 180
Comden, Betty, 30, 48
Come Back, Little Sheba, 92
Come Next Spring, 296
Come On Marines! 136
Come to the Stable, 88
Comet over Broadway, 70
Comingore, Dorothy, *71*
Commercial Break, A, 52
Como, Perry, 299
Confidential Agent, 20, 21, *21*, 22
Congo Crossing, 226, *228*
Connery, Sean, *51*, 52
Connolly, Mike, 94, 95
Connolly, Walter, 139
Connor, Whitfield, 86, *86*, 92
Connors, Chuck, 222
Connors, Franc, 389
Connors, Michael, 106
Conqueror, The, 97, 98, 112 n
Conrad, Robert, 418
Conte, Richard, 26, 88, 96
Convy, Bert, 55
Conway, Russ, 230
Conway, Tom, 220
Cook, Alton, 32
Coombes, Al, 174
Cooney, Ray, 241
Cooper, Gary, 30, 32, 70, *72*, 93, 137, 220, 289, 292, *293*, 398, 405
Corcoran, Donna, 347
Corey, Wendell, 168
Cornell, Katharine, 12
Coronet, 367
Cosmopolitan, 205
Cossart, Ernest, *280*
Costain, Thomas B., 226
Cotton, Joseph, 169
Council on Youth Fitness, 355
Count Dracula Society, 176
Country Girl, The, 410
Cover Girl, 15
Cowan, Jerome, 273, *384*, 385
Cowan, Lester, 148
Coward, Noël, 33, *36*, 39
Cowboy from Brooklyn, The, 265
Cowl, Jane, 12, 351

Coy, Walter, *408*
Crabbe, Larry "Buster," 135, 139, 256
Craig, David, 48
Craig, Helen, 392
Craig, James, *170*, 234
Craig, Michael, 106, *106*
Crain, Jeanne, 18, 87, 88, 330
Crane, Lor, 236
Crane, Richard, 18, 330
Crane, Stephen, 326
Craven, Frank, 276
Crawford, Broderick, 380, *397*
Crawford, Joan, 91, 150 n, 291, 392, 395, 398
Crawford, Stuart, *384*
Crehan, Joseph, *71*
Crenna, Richard, 55
Crichton, Kyle, 133
Crime by Night, 384, 385
Crisp, Donald, 276
Crist, Judith, 43
Crooner, The, 371
Crosby, Bing, 30, 138, 155, 201, 259, 369, 402, 403, *403*, 405, 408
Crosby, Bob, *74*
Crowd Roars, The, 271, 372
Crowther, Bosley, 21, 22, 79, 93, 148, 152, 153, 154, 155, 159, 171, 199, 201, 203, 215, 217, 292, 327, 337, 375, 394
Crusades, The, 260, 261
Cue, 395
Cugat, Xavier, 327, 333, 335, 337
Cukor, George, 269
Culver, Lillian, *346*
Cummings, Jack, 325, 327
Cummings, Robert, 85, 280, *280*, *382*, 385
Curtis, Tony, 43
Curtiz, Michael, 147, 266, 268, 389, 398, 405
Curzon, George, 133
Cutler, Victor, *205*

Dahl, Arlene, 91, 348 n, 355
Dahl-Wolfe, Louise, 14
Dailey, Dan, 90, 297
"Daktari," 236 n
Daley, Cass, 154
Dallas News, 256
Dandridge, Dorothy, 410
Dangerous When Wet, 347, 348, 358
Danielovitch, Issur. *See* Douglas, Kirk
Daniels, Mary, 236
Danner, Blythe, 179
Dantine, Helmut, *229*, 286
Darcel, Denise, 348
Dark Cloud, The, 299
Dark Hazard, 265
Dark Passage, 24, *24*, 25

445

Dark Victory, 106, 372 n
Dark Waters, 80
Darnell, Linda, 87, 91, 98 n
Da Silva, Howard, 386
David and Bathsheba, 90, *90*
Davies, Marion, 264, 370
Davis, Bette, 12, 33, 48, 49, 70, 106, *107,* 131, 132, 144, 145, 151, 153, 159, 195, 264, 266, 273, 278, 279, 281, 286, 289, 291, 370, 372 n, 385, 392, 395, 398, 412, 418
Davis, Jim, 234
Davis, Johnnie, *71*
Davis, Nancy, 405
Davison, Bruce, 239
Day, Doris, 28, 215, 220, 398, 408
Dead End Kids, 266, 268, 271
Deadhead Miles, 171
Deadline at Dawn, 82
Dead Reckoning, 24
"Dear John," 163
De Carlo, Yvonne, 98 n, 168 n, 236, 241
DeCicco, Pat, 273
"Deep in the Heart of Texas," 343
Deep Valley, 156, *157*
de Gaetano, Michael, 236
de Gunzberg, Niki, 14
DeHaven, Gloria, 18, 330
de Havilland, Olivia, 87, 88, 98 n, 131, 145, 153, 155, *156,* 230, 264, 268, 269, 273, 278, 279, 285, 286, *376,* 377, *382,* 385, 390, 395
Dekker, Albert, 73
Delcambre, Alfred, 256, *257*
Delmont, Betty Lou, 28
Del Rio, Dolores, 267
Demarest, William, 348, 369
de Maigret, Liev, 139
Demetrius and the Gladiators, 93
DeMille, Cecil B., 74, 142, 261
Denham, Reginald, 148, 415
Denning, Richard, *72,* 73
Dennis, Ruth, 288
Dennis, Sandy, 55
Denny, Reginald, 139
Desertion of Keith Ryder, The, 415
Designing Woman, 37, *38*
Desperate Hours, The, 36
DeSylva, Buddy, 80
Detective Story, 405
Devil's Canyon, 222, 224
Devil's Rain, The, 176, *179*
Devine, Andy, 236, 273
Devotion, 131, 155, *156*
Diamond, I. A. L., 213
Diary, The, 236 n
Dickson, Gloria, 145, 265, 268
Didrikson, Babe, 352

Dietrich, Marlene, 18, 28, 91, 259, 267, 398, 400
Diggins, Peggy, 279, *279*
Dillman, Bradford, 241
Dinelli, Mel, 165
Directors Guild of America, 418, 420
Disney, Walt, 414, 415
Distant Fury, A, 175
Dodd, Neal, *403*
Dodge City, 268, *268*
Donen, Stanley, 337, 340
Donlevy, Brian, 82
"Donna Reed Show, The," *173,* 230
Donnell, Jeff, 348
Dorsey, Tommy, 209, 329
Double Indemnity, 80
Double Jeopardy, 44
Dougherty, James, 213
Doughgirls, The, 286, 288, *288, 384,* 385
Douglas, Kirk, 14, 28, *29,* 33, 99, *99,* 217, 401, 403
Douglas, Melvyn, 295
Douglas, Robert, 217, 226
Dowling, Constance, 198
Downey, Morton, 325
Downs, Johnny, 73
Doyle, Arthur Conan, 142
Drake, Dona, *212*
"Dreamer, The," 153
Dressler, Marie, 377
Drew, Ellen, 380
Dubin, Al, 261
Duchess of Idaho, 339, *339, 340*
Duchin, Eddie, 155
Duel in the Sun, 98 n, 390
Duff, Bridget, 166, *172,* 180
Duff, Howard, *162,* 163, 165, 166, 168, 169, 171, *171, 172,* 174, *175,* 180, *295*
"Duffy's Tavern," 154, 331
Dugan, Tom, *143, 337*
Duggan, Andrew, 230, *231*
Duke, Patty, 109
du Maurier, George, 137
Dunn, Emma, 149
Dunn, Judy Ann, 90
Dunne, Irene, 327, 395, 408, 409, 418
Duprez, June, 82
Durante, Jimmy, 281, 333, *334,* 335, 377, 403
Durrell, Jane. *See* Wyman, Jane
Dvorak, Ann, 266, 371
Dwan, Allan, 133

Each Dawn I Die, 268
Eagels, Jeanne, 291
Eagle-Lion, 207
Earth and High Heaven, 392
Easy to Love, 323, 348, *349*

Easy to Wed, 323, 331, *333*
Eberhart, Mignon, 265
Eccentricities of a Nightingale, 179
Eckman, Gene, 389
Edge of Darkness, 286
Edward, My Son, 88
Edward VIII, 370
Egan, Richard, 94
Egg and I, The, 285
Elam, Jack, 90
Elephant Hill, 102
Elkins, Saul, 209
"Ellery Queen," 179
Ellis, Mary, 136
Ellis, Patricia, 261
Elmer the Great, 275, 369
Elsom, Isobel, 149
Elstree Studios, 218
Emerald Productions. *See* Filmmakers
Emerson, Faye, 220
Emmy Award, 169
Enasl, Ruth, *289*
Enright, Florence, 198
Enright, Ray, 261, 269, 271
Ephron, Henry, 398
Ephron, Phoebe, 398
Erasmus Hall High School, 68
Erwin, Stuart, 371, 405 n
Escape Me Never, *158*, 159
Esmond, Carl, 102
Esquire, 14
Esther Williams at Cypress Gardens, 354
Ethan Frome, 392
Eureka College, 372 n, 396
Evans, Clara, 256
Evans, Joan, *343*, 345
Evans, Linda, 178
Extra Girl, The, 261
Eyer, Robert, 105, 230
Eythe, William, 18, 330

Failing of Raymond, The, 415
Fairbanks, Douglas, 396
Falcon Maltese, The, 22
Family Circle, 327
Fan, The, 56
Farmer, Frances, 70, 176
Farmer's Daughter, The, 85
Far Out West, The, 302
Farrar, David, 226, 297
Farrell, Charles, 261
Farrell, Glenda, 268, 370, 374
Farrow, John, 266
"Father Knows Best," 169
Father Returns, 368
Faulkner, William, 16, 55

Faye, Alice, 91, 267, 290, 369, 373
Feagan Drama School, 69
Feldman, Charles, 15, 164 n
Female Artillery, 174, *178*
Fenton, Joseph, 196
Ferber, Edna, 408
Ferrer, Mel, 241, 295
Field, Betty, 280
Field, Ron, 48
Fields, W. C., 259
Fiesta, 333, *334*
Fight for Your Lady, 141
Fighting Seabees, The, 79
Fighting Youth, 261
Film Daily, 392, 405, 412
Film Fan Monthly, 132
Film Festival, 53
Filmgoer's Companion, The, 195
Filmmakers, 160, 163, 165, 166, 168
Films and Filming, 52
Films in Review, 37
Finch, Peter, 105
Fine, Sylvia, 209
Finklehoffe, Fred, 372
Finney, Albert, 52
Fiorello, 232
"Fireside Theatre," 412
First National, 134, 369
Fitzgerald, F. Scott, 33, 271
Fitzgerald, Geraldine, 142
Flame and the Arrow, The, *194*, 217
Flame over India, 40, 41
Flaxy Martin, 209, *211*
Fleming, Rhonda, 168, 220, *221*
Fleming, Victor, 389
Flight Angels, 375
Flynn, Errol, 70, 145, 153, 159, 268, 269, 285, 286, 292, 398
Foch, Nina, *178*
Fogler, Gertrude, 198
Foley, Tom, 174
Follies Girl, 198
Fonda, Henry, 33, 43, 52, 371
Fontaine, Frank, 293
Fontaine, Joan, 166, 168, 401
Fontanne, Lynn, 55
Food of the Gods, The, 179
Fools for Scandal, 371
Footlight Serenade, 385
Footloose Heiress, The, 265
Foran, Dick, 261, *262*, 373
Ford, Glenn, 160, 179, 180 n, 295
Fordin, Hugh, 340 n
"Ford Theatre," 296
Foreign Press Association, 92
Forester, C. S., 218

Forest Rangers, The, 76
Forever Amber, 98 n
Forever and a Day, 152
Forrest, Helen, 327
Forrest, Sally, 160, 163, 164, 168, 345
Fort Dobbs, 230, *231*
Fort Utah, 234, *235*
Forty Carats, 234, 236
For Whom the Bell Tolls, 98 n, 153
Foster, Norman, 293
Foster, Preston, 139, *140*
Fountainhead, The, 209
Four Star Productions, 168
"Four Star Theatre," 168
Fowley, Douglas, 269, *301,* 302
Fox, Roy S., Jr., 273
Foy, Bryan, 265
Francen, Victor, 154, 155
Francis, Arlene, 288
Francis, Kay, 12, 70, 131, 264, 370
Frank, Gerold, 95
Franklin, Sidney, 389, 390 n
Franklin Street, 14
Franz, Arthur, 213
Freed, Arthur, 337, 340 n, 345
Freeman, Everett, 347
Freeman, Mona, 91
French Quarter, 236, *238*
Froman, Jane, 91
Frye, William, 171
Fuchs, Daniel, 151
Fulks, Emma Reise, 368
Fulks, R. D., 368
Fulks, Sara Jane. *See* Wyman, Jane
Fuller, Lance, 226
Furthman, Jules, 16
Futterman, Myron, 371

Gabel, Martin, 85
Gabin, Jean, 150, *150*
Gable, Clark, 30, 86, 94, 150 n, 326, 327, 370
Gabor, Eva, 234
Gabor, Zsa Zsa, 224
Gage, Benjamin (Ben), 330, *330,* 335, 339, 340, 343, 351, 352, 354
Gage, Benjamin Stanton (Benjie), 339, 340, 356
Gage, Kimball Austin, 340, 356
Gage, Susan Tenney, 348
Galligan, David, 134
Gambling on the High Seas, 377
Garbo, Greta, 67, 112, 403
Gardella, Kay, 52
Garden of Evil, 93
Gardiner, Reginald, 281
Gardner, Ava, 91, 98 n, 295, 345
Gardner, Hy, 374

Garfield, John, 145, 147, 148, *148,* 268, 273, 286, 289
Gargan, William, 291, 412
Garland, Judy, 20 n, 30, 109, 241, 290, 335, 410
Garner, James, 56
Garrett, Betty, 337, *339*
Garson, Greer, 255
"Gaucho Serenade, The," 273
Gavin, John, 104
Gay Desperado, The, 139
Gaynor, Janet, 133, 134
Gaynor, Mitzi, 99
Gay Sisters, The, 285 n
Gencel, Jack, *403*
"General Electric Theatre, The," *174,* 412, 414
Gentle People, The, 147
"Gentle Web, The," 352
George, Gladys, 203, 268
George Washington Slept Here, 232, 284, 285
Gesner, Elizabeth, 393
Ghost Camera, The, 134
Giant, 412
Gibson, Virginia, *219,* 220
Gielgud, John, 39
Gifford, Frances, *329*
Gift of Love, The, 37, *39*
Gilbert and Sullivan, 14
Gill, Gwenllian, 256, *257*
Girl from Jones Beach, The, 26, 212, *212, 214*
Girls Commercial High School, 68
Girls in Their Summer Dresses, The, 33 n
Girls on Probation, 70, *71*
Gish, Dorothy, 165
Glass Cage, The, 236
Glass Key, The, 261
Glass Menagerie, The, 374, 401, *402*
Glazer, Benjamin, 289, 290
Gleason, Jackie, 415
Gleason, James, 139
Glory for Me, 203
Goddard, Paulette, 69, 73, 76, 98 n, 212, 369
Godfrey, Peter, 290
Goetz, Ruth, 14
Goff, Ivan, 218
Gold Diggers in Paris, 98 n
Gold Diggers of Broadway, 220
Gold Diggers of 1933, 220
Golden Boy, 268
Golden Gate International Exposition, 325
Golden Globe Award, 405. *See also* Henrietta Award
Golden Scroll Award, 176
Gold Medal, 395
Goldstein, Leonard, 295
Goldwyn, Samuel, 88, 195, 198, 202, 203, 205, 207, 209, 369, 389

Gone with the Wind, 69, 74, 86, 269, 371
Goodbye Again, 278
Goodbye Charlie, 11, *40,* 41
Good News, 239, *239,* 241
Good Sam, 292, *293*
Gordon, Bert I., 179
Gordon, Max, 14
Gordon, Ruth, 55, 286
Gould, Elliott, 90
Go West, 325
Grable, Betty, 32, 87, 91, 203, 220, 255, 286, 290, 339, 369, 385
Graham, Barbara, 99, 102
Graham, Billy, 94
Graham, Katherine, 52
Graham, Lee, 241
Graham, Sheilah, 335, 398, 409
Grant, Cary, 55, 155, 257, 293, *294,* 389, 408
Grant, Harvey, *296*
Grauman's Chinese Theatre, *89*
Gravet, Fernand, 371
Grayson, Kathryn, 327
Great Day in the Morning, 226, *227*
Great Movie Stars: The Golden Years, The, 255
Great O'Malley, The, 262
Green, Adolph, 30, 48
"Green Acres," 234
Greene, Graham, 20, 21
Greenwood, Charlotte, 348
Greer, Jane, 168
Greer, Jo Ann, 352 n
Grey, Virginia, 105
Griffith, Andy, 174, *177*
Griffith, Edward H., 77
Gris, Henry, 358
Guernsey, Otis L., Jr., 226
"Guess Who I Saw Today," 299
Guilfoyle, Paul, 213
Guinan, Texas, 293
Guinness, Alec, 168 n
Guyana, Crime of the Century, 241
Guy Named Joe, A, 327, *328*
Gwenn, Edmund, 168
Gwynn, Edith, 390

Hackley, Bart, 302
Hagen, Jean, 168
Hagen, Ray, 264 n, 268 n, 303
"Haircut," 401
Hairy Ape, The, 79, 80
Hale, Alan, 144, 269, 275, 283, 377
Hale, Creighton, *346*
Hale, Wanda, 348
Haley, Jack, 279
Hall, Michael, 203

Haller, Ernest, 155
Halliday, John, 137
Halliwell, Leslie, 195
Hamilton, Neil, 291
Hampton, Lionel, 209
Hanagan, Steve, 289, 291, 295
Hanalis, Blanche, 171
Hanmer, Don, 165
Happy Endings, *51,* 52
Hard, Fast and Beautiful, 164
Harding, Ann, 137, *170,* 291
Hard Way, The, 131, 150–51, *151,* 152, 153, 160
Hardwicke, Cedric, 405
Harlow, Jean, 134, 331
Harper, 45, 47
Harper's Bazaar, 14, 15
Harrigan, Kate, 68
Harrigan, William, *295*
Harris, Elmer, 392
Harris, Julie, 47
Harris, Mrs. Sam, 283
Harrison, Joan, 82
Harrison, Rex, 108, 226
Hart, Moss, 285
Harvard Lampoon, 105, 271, 273
Harvey, Laurence, *225,* 226
Hasty Heart, The, 405
Hatfield, Hurd, 208
Hathaway, Henry, 92, 137
"Have Gun, Will Travel," 169
Haver, June, 18, 87, 330
Havoc, June, 26
Hawks, Howard, 15, 16, 22, 53, 206, 293
Hayden, Sterling, 295
Hayes, Helen, 12
Hayward, Leland, 39
Hayward, Louis, 142, 149, *149,* 150, 152, 155, 159
Hayward, Susan, 37, 67–113, 160, 199, 241, 355, 405
Hayworth, Rita, 18, 49, 69 n, 91, 142, 279, 286, 290
Head, Edith, 88, 405, 410
Health, 57
Heat of Anger, 109, *112*
Hecht, Ben, 412
Heckart, Eileen, 412, *413*
He Couldn't Say No, 371
Heflin, Van, 33, 86
Heiress, The, 88
Heisler, Stuart, 82
Helen of Troy, 226
Heller, Otto, 355
Hellinger, Mark, 273, 275, 281, 282, 286, 288, 405 n
Hello, Dolly! 234

Hemingway, Ernest, 15, 91
Henie, Sonja, 325
Henley, Dusty, *296*
Henreid, Paul, 26, 154, *154,* 155, *156*
Henrietta Award, 93, 348. *See also* Golden Globe Award
Henry, Charlotte, 135
Hepburn, Audrey, 410
Hepburn, Katharine, 18, 32, 37, 48, 69, 98, 112, 405
Here Comes the Groom, 402, *403*
Here Comes the Navy, 139
Here's Looking at You, Kid, 145 n, 159
Her First Affaire, 133, *134*
Herridge, Frances, 176
Herrmann, Bernard, 93
Herschel, 87
Heston, Charlton, 92, *92,* 112, 410, *411*
High Finance, 134
High Sierra, 145, *146,* 147, 148, 160, 209
Hilda Crane, 98
Hiller, Wendy, *51,* 52
Hipp, Edward Sothern, 48
Hitchcock, Alfred, 398, *399,* 400, *420*
Hitch-Hiker, The, 166
Hit Parade of 1943, 76, 77
Hoag, F. Mark, 330
Hoffman, Charles, 155
Hogan, Louanne, 201
Hold Back the Dawn, 73
Holden, William, 77, 109, *111,* 268
Holiday for Lovers, 414, *414*
Hollywood Canteen, 77
Hollywood Canteen, 154, 288, 385, *386*
Hollywood Hotel, 69
Hollywood Reporter, 55, 94, 98, 137, 358, 421
Hollywood Women's Press Club, 348 n
Holm, Celeste, 109, 159
Holm, Eleanor, 325 n
Holmes, Dennis, 102
Home on the Range, 257
Homer, 226
Honeymoon for Three, 278, *278,* 377, *379*
Honey Pot, The, 106, 108
Hoodlum Saint, The, 331, *332*
Hope, Bob, 195, *200,* 201, 275, 330, 415, *416*
Hopkins, Miriam, 145, 273, 281
Hopper, Hedda, 88, 141, 215, 324, 325, 335, 390, 396
Hopper, William, 265, 371
Hopwood, Avery, 220
Horne, Lena, 340
Horner, Harry, 166
Horton, Edward Everett, 377
Hosiery Designers of America, 207
Hoskins, Basil, 52

House Committee on Un-American Activities, 26
House of Strangers, 87, 88 n, 355
Howard, Leslie, 291
"How Could You?" 262
"How D'ye Do and Shake Hands," 403
Howes, Sally Anne, *178*
"How Little We Know," 16
How to Commit Marriage, 415, *416*
How to Improve Your Golf, 377
How to Marry a Millionaire, 31, 32
Hoyt, John, *292*
Huber, Harold, *143*
Hudson, Rock, 33, 409, 410 n, *410,* 412
Hughes, Howard, 98, 135, 164, 165, 295
Hull, Henry, 156
Hunt, Marsha, 82, 327
Hunter, Ross, 104, 295, 410
Hurrell, George, 266, 267
Hussey, Ruth, 327
Huston, John, 26, 28, 32, 206, 286, 291, 292
Hutchinson, Josephine, 412
Hutton, Betty, 79, 293, 398
Hutton, Robert, 385, *386*
Hyde-White, Wilfrid, 104, *104*
Hyer, Martha, 20 n
Hymer, Warren, *143*

I Can Get It for You Wholesale, 90
Ida Lupino, 131
I'd Climb the Highest Mountain, 88, *89*
I Died a Thousand Times, 147
Iliad, 226
I Lived with You, 134, 135
I'll Cry Tomorrow, 95, 96, *96,* 97, 98
I'll Never Go There Anymore, 88, 355
I Love a Mystery, 174
"I Love That Feelin'," 403
"I Love You," 330
Image of a Doctor, 174
I Married a Witch, 76
"I May Be Wrong," 405
Incendiary Blonde, The, 293
Incredible Journey of Doctor Meg Laurel, The, 418, *421*
Indianapolis Speedway, 271
In Our Time, 154, *154*
International Lady, 285
Interrupted Melody, 98
"In the Cool, Cool, Cool of the Evening," 402
In This Our Life, 283
Ireland, John, 234, *235,* 241
I Remember Mama, 395
Iron Mistress, The, 220, *222*
"I Should Care," 329
It All Came True, 273, *274*

I Thank a Fool, 105
It's a Great Feeling, 398
"It Was Nice While the Money Rolled In," 403
Ives, Burl, 358
Ives, Helen, 358
I Want to Live! 67, *100, 101,* 102
I Was a Male War Bride, 293, *294,* 297
I Will Be Remembered, 180

Jack London, 77, 199
Jackson, Andrew, 92
Jackson, Charles, 385
Jackson, Glenda, 55
Jackson, Selmer, *92*
Jackson, Sherry, 205 n
Jacobs, Artie, 70
Jaffe, Sam, 24
James, Claire, 279, *279*
James, Harry, 327
James, Henry, 82, 84
"Jane Wyman Theatre, The," 412, *413*
Janis, Elsie, 91
Jarman, Claude, Jr., *366,* 389
Jarmyn, Jill, 95
Jason, Sybil, 262
Jeans, Ursula, *40,* 135
Jenkins, Allen, 269, 374
Jenks, Frank, *294*
Jennifer, 166, *166*
Jepson, Selwyn, 398
Jet over the Atlantic, 230, *232*
Joan of Arc, 368, 395
"Joe Franklin Show," 241
Johnny Belinda, 367, 374, 392–95, *393,* 396, 398, 400, 401, 415
Johnny Two by Four, 14
Johnson, Celia, 168 n, 390
Johnson, Erskine, 94
Johnson, Nunnally, 30
Johnson, Rita, 84
Johnson, Van, 18, 327, *328,* 329, *329,* 330, 331, *333,* 339, 348, 401, 412, *413*
Johnston, Johnny, 333
Johnston, Kent Lee, 241
Johnston, Lucas Michael, 241
Johnston Office, 288, 289
Jones, Allan, 271
Jones, Barry, 93
Jones, Dickie, *262*
Jones, Gordon, *206*
Jones, Jennifer, 98, 98 n, 153, 390
Jones, Lee Lake, 196, *196*
Jones, Luke Ward, 196
Jones, Martha Henrietta Rautenstrauch, 196
Jones, Virginia Clara. *See* Mayo, Virginia
Jonson, Ben, 106

Jory, Victor, *268,* 269
Juke Girl, 283
Julia Richman High School, 12
Julius Caesar, 133
Junior Bonner, 171
Jupiter's Darling, 323, 351, *351*
Just for You, 407, 408
Justice, James Robertson, *90*
Justin, John, 94, *95*

Kandel, Aben, 276
Kantor, MacKinlay, 203
Karger, Freddie, 408, 409, *411,* 414, 415
Karger, Terry, 408
Karl, Harry, 348
Karloff, Boris, 207
Karns, Roscoe, 275
Kasha, Lawrence, 48
Kaufman, George S., 14, 285, 375
Kaye, Danny, 30, 195, 198, 202, *202,* 203, 206, *206,* 209, *210,* 403
Keel, Howard, 340, 340 n, *342,* 343, 351, 401
Keeler, Ruby, 220, 234, 370
Keighley, William, 275, 281
Kellaway, Cecil, 333
Kellerman, Annette, 345, 347, 358
Kelly, Gene, 330, 337, *337,* 340 n
Kelly, Grace, 37, 94, *350,* 410
Kendall, Cy, *384*
Kennedy, Arthur, 92, 155, 276, 277, 377, 401, 402
Kennedy, Douglas, 209, *211*
Kennedy, Edgar, 139
Kerr, Deborah, 88, 91, 102 n
Keyes, Evelyn, 26, 149
Key Largo, 26, 28
Kid from Brooklyn, The, 203, *204*
Kid from Kokomo, The, 374
Kid from Spain, The, 369
Kid Nightingale, 373, 374
Kid Stuff. See My Boys Are Good Boys
Kilbride, Percy, 285
Kind Sir, 297
King, Andrea, 156
King, Henry, 94
King and the Chorus Girl, The, 370
King of Burlesque, 369
King Richard and the Crusaders, 225, 226
Kings Row, 279, *280,* 280–81, 380
Kipling, Rudyard, 142, 144
Kipness, Joseph, 48
Kirk, Phyllis, 220
Kiss and Make Up, 257
Kiss in the Dark, A, 396, *397,* 398
"Kiss Me in the Moonlight," 201
Kjellin, Alf, *222*

Kleefeld, Travis, 405
Knowles, Patric, 265, *265*
Knox, Alexander, 147
Knute Rockne—All American, 377
Kobliansky, Nick, *384*
Koch, Howard, 154
Kogan, Herman, 297 n
Kohler, Walter, 348
Kohn, Rose Simon, 155
Korngold, Erich Wolfgang, 147, 155, 159
Kostelanetz, Andre, 141
Kovner, Leonard W., 324, 325, 329
Krasna, Norman, 297, 370, 385, 403
Krasner, Milton, 88
Krone Circus, 355
Kyser, Kay, 380

LaCentra, Peg, 82, 156 n, 159
Ladd, Alan, 79, 80, 220, *222,* 227, 240, 330, 405
Ladies in Retirement, 148–49, *149,* 179
Ladies Should Listen, 257
Lady and the Mob, The, 142, *143*
Lady Takes a Sailor, The, *397,* 398
La Fuente Magica, 356
Lahr, Bert, 215
Lake, Veronica, 18, 24, 76, 267
Lamarr, Hedy, 230, 267
Lamas, Fernando, *347,* 348, 355, 356, 358
Lamas, Lydia, 348 n
Lamour, Dorothy, 236, 267
Lancaster, Burt, *194,* 217, 222, *224*
Lanchester, Elsa, 149, *149*
Landa, Mary, 288, *289*
Landis, Carole, 207, *207*
Lane, Charles, *216,* 403
Lane, Lola, 374
Lane, Lupino, 133
Lane, Priscilla, 12, 98 n, 145, 264, 265, 273, 372
Lane, Richard, *207, 337*
Lane, Rosemary, 98 n, 375
Langella, Frank, 179
"Lanigan's Rabbi," 239
Lansbury, Angela, 331, *332*
Lanza, Mario, 401
Larceny, Inc., 380, *382*
Lardner, Ring, 401
"Laredo," 171
La Rivolta Dei Mercenari, 232
Lasky, Jesse, 138, 139
Last Tycoon, The, 33
Latin American Consular Association, 395
Laughton, Charles, 403, 404
Lauren Bacall—By Myself, 57, *58*
Lawford, Peter, 335, 405
Lawrence, Gertrude, 281, 401
Lawson, John Howard, 82

Lazar, "Swifty," 30
LeBaron, William, 74
Lebedeff, Ivan, 261–62
Lederer, Francis, *138,* 139
Leeds, Andrea, 265
Leeds, Peter, *96*
Left Hand of God, The, 35
LeGallienne, Eva, 82
Leigh, Janet, 180 n, 220
Leigh, Vivien, 39, 143, 269, 398, 405
Leisen, Mitchell, 259
Le Maire, Charles, 88, 91
LeMay, Alan, 86
Leonard, Queenie, 149
Leonard, Sheldon, 16, *17*
LeRoy, Mervyn, 345, 347
Leslie, Joan, 131, 145, 147, 151, 154, 286, 289, 385
Let's Do It Again, 408
Let's Get Married, 139, *140*
Letter, The, 291
Letter from Bataan, A, 76
Letter of Introduction, 265
Letters, The, 176
Lewis, Diana, 327
Lewman, Ltd., 412
Libeled Lady, 331
Liberty, 70
Life, 18
Life Begins at 8:30, 152, *152*
Life of Jimmy Dolan, The, 268
Life with Mother Superior, 171
Lightning Strikes Twice, 218
Light of Heart, The, 152
Light's Diamond Jubilee, 33 n
Light That Failed, The, 142–44, *144,* 145 n
Limehouse Blues, 257
Lindfors, Viveca, 215
Lindsay, Margaret, 265, 266, 371
Liszt (composer), 269
Litel, John, 265, *266,* 269, 273, 275
Little Foxes, The, 151
Little Miss Thoroughbred, 165, *266*
Litvak, Anatole, 273, 276
Livingston, Mary, 285 n
Lloyd, Harold, 203
Loder, John, 297
Loesser, Frank, 88, 286, 337
Logan, Joshua, 99
Lombard, Carole, 137, 257, 259, 267, 369, 370, 371
London, Charmian Kittredge, 79
London, Jack, 147
London, Julie, 86
London Daily Express, 395
London Times, 256

Lone Wolf Spy Hunt, The, 142
Long, Richard, 86
Long, Robin, 299
Long Haul, 275
Look, 88, 218
Loper, Don, 220
"Loretta Young Show, The," 230
Lorre, Peter, 21, 227
Los Angeles Athletic Club, 324
Los Angeles City College, 324
Los Angeles High School, 368
Los Angeles Philharmonic, 139
Los Angeles Times, 12 n
Lost Love, The. See *Lost Moment, The*
Lost Moment, The, 84, *85*
Lost Weekend, The, 82, 385–86, *387,* 389
Louise, Anita, 261, 415
Love, Montagu, 155
"Love Boat, The," 421
"Love for Love," 159
Love Is a Many Splendored Thing, 98
"Love Isn't Born, It's Made," 286
Love Is on the Air, 372 n
Lovejoy, Frank, 166, 222
Love Your Body, 135
Lowry, Morton, *269*
Loy, Myrna, 203, 291, 331
Luce, Clare Booth, 99
Lucy Gallant, 410, *411*
Ludden, Allen, 418
Luft, Sid, 20 n
Lukas, Paul, 82
Lumet, Sam, 52
Lund, John, 340, *340*
Lundigan, William, 88, *89*
Lunt, Alfred, 55
Lupino, Alfredo, 132
Lupino, Connie Emerald (Weenie), 132, 133, 135
Lupino, George, 132
Lupino, Harry, 132
Lupino, Ida, 131–80, 209, 256, 261, 273, 275, 276, 278, 281, 283, 286, 369, 375
Lupino, Mark, 132
Lupino, Rita, 132, 135, 142
Lupino, Stanley, 132, 133, 135, 138, 142, 150
Lust for Gold, 160, *161*
Lusty Men, The, 91
Luv, 302
"Lux Playhouse," 230
"Lux Radio Theatre," 142, 218
"Lux Video Theatre," 296, 354
Lydia, 53
Lyles, A. C., 232, 234
Lynley, Carol, *414*
Lynn, Diana, 18, 330
Lynn, Jeffrey, 145, 273, 377

MacArthur, 418
Macaulay, Richard, 275
MacBride, Donald, 147, *380*
McCall's, 39
McCarey, Leo, 292
McClelland, Doug, 67, 95
McCord, Ted, 209
McCrea, Joel, 147, 209 n, *211,* 212, 230, 405 n
McDaniel, Hattie, 285
McDevitt, Ruth, *301,* 302
McDonald, Marie, 348
MacDougall, Ranald, 30
McDowall, Roddy, 41, *44,* 389
McEldowney, Mrs. J. K., 330
McGavin, Darren, *111*
McGillivray, David, 52
"McGory and His Mouse," 230
McGuire, Daniel J., 108
McGuire, Don, 156
McGuire, Dorothy, 14
McHugh, Frank, *266,* 271, 276, 371
Mack, Helen, 257
Mack, Tommy, *143*
McKay, Scott, 299, *301,* 302
MacKenzie, Aeneas, 218
McLaglen, Cyril, 134
McLaglen, Victor, 139
McLain, Johnny, 155
MacLaine, Shirley, 98, 102 n, 418
MacLane, Barton, 262, 265
McLean, Gloria, 198
MacMahon, Aline, 220
McManus, John, 290
MacMurray, Fred, *31,* 33, 76, 259, 415, *416*
McNally, Stephen, 163, 224, 393
McPherson, Aimee Semple, 299
McQueen, Steve, 171
MacRae, Gordon, 215, *216*
Macready, George, 230
MacSweeney, Helen, 208
Mademoiselle, 132
Madison, Guy, 230, 232, *232*
Madison, Julian, 256, *257*
Magic Town, 392
Magnani, Anna, 98
Magnificent Brute, The, 261
Magnificent Obsession, 409–10, *410,* 412
Maguire, Mary, 265
Mainbocher, 41
Make Up Your Mind, 154
Make Your Own Bed, 383, 385
Malaya Incident, 296
Male Animal, The, 220
Malloy, Gert, 139
Malone, Dorothy, 33, *388*
Malone, Dudley Field, 267

Mame, 109, *110*
Mamoulian, Rouben, 139
Man, The, 165
Manhattan Melodrama, 266
"Man I Love, The," 156 n
Man I Love, The, 156, *157*, 160
Mankiewicz, Joseph L., 106
Mann, Daniel, 96, 109
Manners, David, 371
Manning, Irene, 288, 290
Man Running, 398
Mansfield, Jayne, 98 n
Man Who Came to Dinner, The, 281, *282*
Man with the Golden Arm, The, 37 n
March, Fredric, 76, 203
"March of Dimes Special," 154
"Marcus Welby, M.D.," 415
Marihugh, Tammy, 105
Marked Woman, 18
Marlowe, Hugh, 93
Marquand, John P., 33, 98
Marr, Eddie, 374
Marrener, Edith. *See* Hayward, Susan
Marrener, Edythe. *See* Hayward, Susan
Marrener, Ellen, 68
Marrener, Florence, 68, 69, 113
Marrener, Walter, 68, 112
Marrener, Walter, Jr., 68
Marriage-Go-Round, The, 102
Marshal, Alan, 69, 142
Marshall, Brenda, 145
Marshall, George, 86
Martin, Dean, 104, *104*
Martin, Lynn, 290
Martin, Mary, 299
Martin, Tony, 348
Martini, Nino, 139
Marx, Barbara, 52
Marx, Groucho, 230, 370, 403
Marx, Harpo, 230
Mason, James, 104
Massen, Osa, 278
Massey, Ilona, 285
Massey, Raymond, 76, 375
Master Hairdressers' Association of Southern California, 207
Match Game, The, 299
Matthieson, Tim, *416*
Mature, Victor, 93, 293, *346*, 347
Maxwell, John, 168
Maxwell, Marilyn, 224
Mayer, Louis B., 325, 326
Maynard, Kermit, 261
Mayo, Andy, 197
Mayo, Archie, 261
Mayo, Virginia, 26, 131, 147, 195–241, 403

Mazurki, Mike, *34*
Meadows, Jayne, *90*
Medford, Benny, 69, 80
Meehan, Thomas, 12
Meeker, Ralph, 179, 180
Meiklejohn, Bill, 261
Melchior, Lauritz, 329, 333
Melford, George, *92*
Melton, James, 261, 331
Melville Goodwin, U.S.A., 33, 98
Mencken, Helen, 18
Menjou, Adolphe, 266
Meredith, Burgess, 375
Merman, Ethel, 138, 369, *411*
Merry Wives of Windsor, The, 197
Merton of the Movies, 340 n
Methot, Mayo, 18
MGM, 37, 88, 95, 150 n, 265, 271, 296, 323, 325, 326, 327, 330, 331, 333, 335, 343, 345, *346*, 347, 348, *350*, 352, 356, 358, 367, 377, 380, 401, 402
"Mi Caballero," 275
Michelle, Ann, 236
Midsummer Night's Dream, A, 197
Mikel, Ted V., 236
Mildred Pierce, 291
Miles, Jackie, 288, *289*
Miles, Sarah, 24 n
Miles, Vera, 104
Milestone, Lewis, 136, 286
Milkman, The, 91
Milky Way, The, 203, 259
Milland, Ray, 70, *72*, 76, 82, 386, 387, *387*, 408
Miller, John J., 174
Million Dollar Mermaid, *344*, 345, 347, 358
Mills, Hayley, 171, 414
Mills, John, 134
Miracle in the Rain, 412, *413*
Mississippi, 259
Missouri, University of, 369
"Misto Cristofo Columbo," 403
Mistress of Castle Reigh, The, 236
Mitchell, Cameron, 32, 93
Mitchell, Grant, *81*
Mitchell, Margaret, 86
Mitchell, Thomas, 147, 150, 168, *170*
Mitchum, Robert, 24 n, 33, 92, 94, 295
Molière, 86
Molnar, Walter, 16
Money for Speed, 134, 135
Monks, John, 372
Monroe, Marilyn, 32, 93, 213
"Monsieur Sans Gene," 138
Montalban, Ricardo, 333, *334*, 335, *336*, 337
Montez, Maria, 286

Montgomery, Ed, 99, 102
Montgomery, Elizabeth, 106
Montgomery, Lee H., *178*
Montgomery, Robert, 86, 142, 395
Montiel, Sarita, 401
Moontide, 149, *150*
Moore, Cleo, *169*
Moore, Colleen, 408
Moore, Mary Tyler, 55
Moore, Victor, *397*
Moorehead, Agnes, 26, 84, 112 n, 392
Moran, Dolores, 16, 156
Moran, Peggy, *71*
Morgan, Dennis, 21, 145, 151, 220, 226, 283, *284*, 286, 289, 290, *291*, 375, 377, 392, *397*, 398
Morgan, Ralph, 142
Morgan, Terence, *219*
Moriarity, Pat, *280*
Morlay, Gaby, 403
Morris, Wayne, 145, 372, 373, 374, 375, 377
Morrison, Shelley, 234
Morton, Nomi, 197, 198
Mosk, Stanley, 329
Motion Picture, 28, 212, 213
Motion Picture Herald, 337
Mourning Becomes Electra, 85
Move Over, Mrs. Markham, 236
Mozart (composer), 269
"Mr. Adams and Eve," *171*
Mr. Dodd Takes the Air, 371
Muni, Paul, 145, 271
Murder, He Says, 98 n
Murder on the Orient Express, 49, *51*
Murphy, George, 266
Murrow, Edward R., 33 n, 39, 352
My Boys Are Good Boys, 179–80, *180*
My Cousin Rachel, 98 n
My Favorite Spy, 380
My Foolish Heart, 66, 88
My Forbidden Past, 295
My Love Came Back, *376*, 377
My Man Godfrey, 370
My Sister Eileen, 14
Mystery House, 265
Mystery of Hunting's End, The, 265

Nader, George, 227, 352
Nagel, Anne, 265
Naish, J. Carroll, *260*
"Naked City," 415
Naldi, Aldo, *17*
Nathan, George Jean, 14
Nation, 18, 21, 80, 205
National Academy of Vocal Arts, 28
National Enquirer, 174, 358

National Film Society, 180 n
Natwick, Mildred, *36*
Naughty But Nice, 269
Navaroo, Anne, *178*
Navy Blues, 279, 279–80
"Navy Blues Sextette," 279
Nazimova, 154, *154*
Neal, Patricia, 30, 52, 209, 218
Negele, Jim, 236
Negulesco, Jean, 273, 392, 394, 395
Neilson, James, 171
Nelson, Barry, 45, *328*
Nelson, Gene, 220, 222
Nelson, Kay, 160
Nelson, Ron, 108
Neptune's Daughter, 88, 323, 337, *339*
Never Fear, 163
Newark Evening News, 48
Newark Star-Ledger, 239
Newman, Paul, 45, 47, 226
Newmar, Julie, 104
Newsweek, 28, 73, 82, 145, 155, 165, 169
New York Daily News, 22, 52, 171, 348, 352, 371, 374, 421
New York Enquirer, 395
New York Film Critics' Award, 153, 386
New York Herald-Tribune, 73, 139, 144, 148, 151, 205, 226, 290, 337, 371, 373, 375, 387, 389, 396, 401
New York Journal, 371
New York Journal-American, 41 n
New York Mirror, 371
New York Post, 48, 176, 374, 394
New York Times, 21, 22, 24 n, 41 n, 49, 52, 73, 79, 84, 85, 86, 93, 135, 138, 139, 144, 148, 149, 152, 153, 155, 156, 159, 171, 199, 201, 203, 213, 217, 230, 271, 275, 277, 285, 292, 327, 333, 340, 351, 356, 373, 375, 377, 385, 389, 390, 394, 402, 404, 409, 414, 415
New York World-Telegram, 32, 151, 275, 371, 387
New York World-Telegram and Sun, 345
Nicol, Alex, *227*
Night and Day, *388*, 389
"Night Episode," 236
Night of the Iguana, 98 n
Niven, David, 30, 33 n, 168, 267, 273, 396, *397*
Nolan, Doris, 198
Nolan, Jack Edmund, 132
Nolan, Lloyd, 180
No, No, Nanette, 234
Nora Prentiss, 291
Norman, Lucille, *219*, 220
Norris, Edward, 261, 262, 271
North Texas State Teachers College, 256
North West Frontier, 39

Not in Her Stars, 415
Not Wanted, 160
"No Two People," 403
Novak, Kim, *36*, 102
Novello, Ivor, 134
"No Wonder They Fell in Love," 333
Nugent, Edward, 261
Nugent, Frank S., 139, 144, 271
Nurmi, Ruth, 329

Oakie, Jack, 141–42, 257, 279, 369
Oberon, Merle, 80
O'Brian, Hugh, 163
O'Brien, Edmond, 166, 213, 215, 227
O'Brien, Pat, 145, 255, 262, *264*, 266, 267, 271, 273, 275, 370, 371, 374
O'Brien-Moore, Erin, *262*
O'Connor, Donald, 415
O'Connor, John J., 49
O'Connor, Una, 273
Odd Man In, 299
O'Dea, Dennis, 218
Odets, Clifford, 168
O'Driscoll, Martha, 77
Office of War Information, 79
Off Side, 261
O'Keefe, Dennis, 79, *294*
Oliver, Gordon, *199*, *264*
Oliver, Susan, 299
Olivier, Laurence, 39
Olympics, 324
On an Island with You, 335, *336*
On Dangerous Ground, 165
O'Neill, Eugene, 80
O'Neill, Henry, 145, 269, 275
One More Tomorrow, 289, 290–91, *291*, 385, *388*, 389
One Rainy Afternoon, *138*, 139
$1,000 a Touchdown, 73
"On Trial," 169
Opposite Sex, The, 296, *300*
Orr, Mary, 415
Orr, William T., *379*
Orry-Kelly, 267
Or Would You Rather Be a Fish? 335
Osaka Film Festival, 395
Oscar. *See* Academy Award
O'Shea, Grace, 206
O'Shea, Kevin, 198
O'Shea, Mary Catherine, 224, *237*, 241
O'Shea, Michael, 79, 199, 206, 213, 220, 224, 230, 232, *233*, 236, *237*, 241
O'Sullivan, Maureen, 137, 372
Our Leading Citizen, 73
Ouspenskaya, Maria, 280
Out of the Blue, 207, *207*

Out of the Fog, 147, 148
Outrage, 164
Overman, Lynn, 139
Owen, Reginald, 139
"Owen Marshall, Counselor at Large," 415

Pagan Love Song, 340, *341*, *342*, 358
Page, Gale, 145, 265, 269, 271, 275
Page, Geraldine, 98 n
Paget, Debra, 88
Paige, Janis, 26, *391*
Painted Veil, The, 98 n
Painting the Clouds with Sunshine, 219, 220
Palance, Jack, 147, *167*, 168, *225*, 226
Pangborn, Franklin, 285
Paramount Pictures, 49, 70, 73, 74, 79, 80, 102, 135, 136, 137, 138, 141, 142, 143 n, 171, 203, 256, *257*, 259, 261, 264, 277, 279, 293, 369, 386, 402
Paris in Spring, 136, *136*
Parker, Dorothy, 82
Parker, Eleanor, 98, 98 n, 131, *158*, 159, 292, 405
Parkins, Barbara, *108*, 109
Parks, Bert, 239, *239*
Parrish, Helen, *269*
Parsons, Louella, 37, 69, 70, 205, 324, 325, 340, 348 n, 355, 374, 377, 380, 387, 395–96, 400, 401, 402
Passionate Witch, The, 76
Pasternak, Joseph, 329, 335
Patient in Room 18, The, 265, *265*
Patrick, Gail, *137*
Patrick, Lee, 268, 285
Paxinou, Katina, 21, 153
Payne, John, 86, 271, *373*, 374
Pearl of the South Pacific, 226
Peck, Gregory, 37, *38*, 90, *90*, 91, 218, *219*, 389, 390, 405, 408, 418
Peckinpah, Sam, 171
Pedelty, Donovan, 135
Pelikan, Lisa, 55
Penner, Joe, 369
Percy, Edward, 148
Perfect Gentlemen, 55, *55*
"Perfect Legs Institute of America," 73
Perkins, Anthony (Tony), *51*, 52
Perreau, Gigi, 88
Perrella, Robert, 396
Perry, Sandra, 155
Perske, Betty Joan. *See* Bacall, Lauren
Perske, Natalie Weinstein. *See* Bacal, Natalie
Perske, Sally, 12 n
Perske, William, 12
Persoff, Nehemiah, 355
"Person to Person," 33 n, 352

"Pete and Mac," 179
Peter Ibbetson, 137–38
Peter Perry Pictures, 180
Peters, Jean, 88 n, 355
Petrified Forest, The, 33
Pettebone, Jean, 80
Peyton Place, 99, 279
Philadelphia Bulletin, 53
Philadelphia Story, The, 197
Phillips, Mary, 18
Photoplay, 18, 24, 91, 152, 168, 209, 224, 330, 374 n, 375, 377, 405
Picasso, 49
Pickford, Mary, 138, 139, 396
Picturegoer, 33, 134, 135, 202, 212, 395
Pidgeon, Walter, 347, 358
Pierce, Bruce, 262
Pierlot, Francis, *288*
Piggott, James, 196
Pillow to Post, 131, 155
Pinky, 88
"Pistols 'n' Petticoats," *301*, 302
Pitts, ZaSu, 261, 269, 273
Place in the Sun, A, 405
"Playhouse 90," 296
Plunkett, Walter, 347
PM, 145, 290
Podesta, Rossana, 226
"Police Story," 236
Polier, Rex, 53
Polito, Sol, 147
Pollard, Alexander, *141*
Pollimer, Dick, 261
Pollyanna, 414
Polo Joe, 370
Porter, Cole, 98, 138, 369, 389
Poseidon Adventure, The, 227
Powell, Dick, 98, 112 n, 154, 168, 265, 269, 370, 371
Powell, Eleanor, 340
Powell, Jane, 330, 340, 348
Powell, William, 330, 331, *332*, 370
Power, Tyrone, 90, 94
Powers, Mala, 164
Pratt, William, 323
President's Lady, The, 92, *92*
Pressburger, Arnold, 138
Preston, Robert, *51*, 52, 70, *72*, 76, 87, 171
Price, Vincent, 168, *170*, 227
"Price Is Right, The," 299
Prince, William, 155, 412
Prince of Arcadia, 135
Princess and the Pirate, The, 195, *200*, 201
Princess O'Rourke, 369 n, *382*, 385
Prinz, LeRoy, 368, 369–70
Private Detective, 373

Private Hell 36, 168
Prodigal, The, 352 n
Producers Releasing Corporation, 198
"Producers Showcase," 33
Production Code, 289, 290
Proud Ones, The, 227, *229*
Public Wedding, 371
Pujal, Rene, 138
Pullen, William, *294*
Purcell, Dick, 265
Purdom, Edmund, 169, *170*
"Pursuit," 299
Pursuit of Youth, The, 420
Pygmalion, 133

Quine, Richard, 408
Quinn, Anthony, 277, 380
Quo Vadis, 226

Rackin, Martin, 109
Raft, George, 139, 144, 145, 147, 171, 213, 232, 255, 257, 261, 268, 273, 275, 276, *276*, 369
Rains, Claude, 268, 280
Rambeau, Marjorie, 377
Raphael, John Nathaniel, 137
Rapper, Irene, 290
Rathbone, Basil, 142
Ratoff, Gregory, 73
Rat Pack, Holmby Hills, 30
Rawhide, 90
"Rawhide," 414
Rawlings, Marjorie Kinnan, 389
Raw Wind in Eden, 354, *354*, 355
Ray, Aldo, 236, 348, 408
Ray, Ida. *See* Lupino, Ida
Ray, Nicholas, 92, 165
Raye, Martha, 73, 141, 279
Raymond, Gene, 259
Raymond, Paula, 340, *342*
Ready for Love, 136
Ready, Willing and Able, 370
Reagan, Maureen Elizabeth, 379, 380, 385 n, 387, 390, *391*, 396, 398, 401, 405, 418, *419*
Reagan, Michael Edward, 389, *391*, 396, 401, 418
Reagan, Ronald, 21, 69, 70, *71*, 145, 163, 212, *212*, 220, 269, 271, 280, 281, 283, 285, 372, 374, 375, *376*, 377, 379–80, *381*, 387, 389, 390, *391*, 392, 395, 396, 398, 400, 405, 409, 414, 418
Reams, Lee Roy, *50*
Reap the Wild Wind, 74, *75*
Record, The, 273
Red Blood of Courage, 261
Redding, Margaret. *See* Hayward, Susan
Redfield, William, 299

Redgrave, Vanessa, 52
Red Light, 213, *214*
Reed, Donna, *173*, 327
Reed, Ralph, *31*
Reeves, Theodore, 155
Reinhardt, Richard, 325
Reisfeld, Bert, *163*
Republic, 73, 76, 78, 296
Returning Home, 205 n
Revengers, The, 109, *111*
Revere, Anne, 389
Reynolds, Craig, 265
Reynolds, Debbie, 41, 348
Rhodes, Erik, *138*, 142
Rhodes, Grandon, *77*, 160
Rhodes, Leah, 212
Ridgely, John, 22, *384*
Ridges, Stanley, 82
Riskin, Bob, 392 n
Ritter, Thelma, 91, 410
RKO, 82, 84, 91, 98, 139, 141, 152, 164, 165, 168, 199, 206, 222, 226, 292, 295, 380, 403
Road House, 159, 160, *161*
Road to Rome, The, 351
Roaring Twenties, The, 268
Robards, Jason, Jr., 41, *42*, *43*, 47, 52
Robards, Sam Prideaux, 41, *43*, 59 n
Robbins, Harold, 106
Robbins, Richard P., 283
Robe, The, 93
Roberti, Lyda, 369
Roberts, Ben, 218
Roberts, Beverly, 264, 265
Roberts, Casey, 155
Roberts, Rachel, *51*, 52
Robertson, Cliff, 108, 355, *356*
Robertson, Dale, 224
Robinson, Casey, 280
Robinson, Edward G., 28, 88, 145, 147, *148*, 154, 265, 380, *382*, 398
Robson, Flora, 148, 149
Robson, Mark, 88
Robson, May, 268, 374
Rockettes, 197
"Rockford Files, The," 56
Rocky Mountain Mystery, 259, *260*
Rogers, Ginger, 28, 276, 323
Rogers, Henry, 80
Rogers, Will, Jr., 405
"Rogues, The," 169
Roman, Ruth, 30, 218, 226
Romance on the High Seas, 26
Romanoff, Mike, 30
Romay, Lina, 327
Romero, Cesar, 236, 271, 273
Rooney, Mickey, *326*

Roosevelt, 286
Rose, Billy, 198, 325
Rose Bowl, 139
Rosenfield, John, 256
Rose Tattoo, The, 98
Ross, Herbert, 418
Rossen, Robert, 147
Roth, Lillian, 95, 96, *97*
Royal Academy of Dramatic Arts, 132, 133, 395, 398
Rubene, Maury, 139
Rudie, Evelyn, 37, *39*
Ruggles, Charles, 138, 278, 288, *379*
Rule, Janice, *406*
Rumba, 257, 369
Rush, Barbara, 412
Russell, Betty, 203
Russell, Harold, 203
Russell, Jane, 95, 212
Russell, Rosalind, 85, 102 n, 171, 299, 352, 379, 390, 418
Ruth, Roy Del, 213, 217
Rutherford, Ann, *173*, 327
Ryan, Robert, 165, *165*, 227, *229*

Sabrina, 410
Saenz, Armando, 230
St. Amand, Joseph, 73
St. John, Jill, 414
St. Joseph, Ellis, 154
St. Louis Globe-Democrat, 196
St. Louis Municipal Opera, 197
Sakall, S. Z., 290
Salamunich, Yucca, 220
Salinger, J. D., 88
Salt, Waldo, 217
"Sam Benedict," 169
Sammis, Fred R., 18, 330
"Sam Spade," 163
Samuels, Ron, 418
Sanders, George, 90, 168, 224, 226, 351
San Francisco Civic Light Opera, 234
San Francisco Examiner, 99, 176
San Quentin, 262, *264*
Santana Pictures Corporation, 24
Santell, Alfred, 77
Santon, Penny, *413*
Saratoga Trunk, 289
Saroyan, William, 297
Satterly trial, 286 n
Saturday Evening Post, 12, 15, 45, 69, 75
Saturday Review, 166
Saville, Victor, 226
Sawyer, Joseph, *143*, 262
Saxon, John, 352, *353*
Saxon Charm, The, 86

Say Goodbye, Maggie Cole, 109, *111*
Schary, Dore, 37, 95, 345
Schettler, Herb, *20*
Schirmer, Gus, 297
"Schlitz Playhouse of Stars," 296
Schwartz, Arthur, 286
Scott, Adrian, 82
Scott, Lizabeth, 24, 49
Scott, Randolph, 230, *231,* 257, 259, *260*
Scott, Vernon, *353*
Scott, Walter, 226
Scott, Zachary, 209, *211,* 218, 291, *292,* 295, 297
Scotti, Tony, *108*
Screen Actors Guild, 396
Screen Facts, 264 n, 281, 323
"Screen Guild Theatre," 275
Sea Devils, 139, *140*
Search for Beauty, 135, 256
Sea Wolf, The, 147, *148*
Sebastianelli, Giuseppe, 343
Secret Life of Walter Mitty, The, 195, 203, 206, *206*
Seiler, Lewis, 273
Seitz, George, 327
Selleck, Tom, 205
Selznick, David O., 33 n, 69, 86, 198
Sennwald, Andre, 138
Sentimental Journey, 37
Separate Tables, 102 n
Serenade, 401
Seven Days Ashore, 199, *199*
Seven Faces of Dr. Lao, The, 41
Seven Year Itch, The, 41
Sex and the Single Girl, 43, *45*
Seymour, Dan, 16, *17*
Shakespeare, 133, 196
Shanghai, 137
Shannon, Harry, 87
Sharaff, Irene, 206
Shatner, William, 176
Shaw, George Bernard, 135
Shaw, Irwin, 33 n, 147
Shawlee, Joan, 348
Shayne, Konstantin, 207
Shearer, Norma, 255, 267, 276
She Loved a Fireman, 265
Shepard, Elaine, *199*
Sheridan, Ann, 18, 88, 131, 135–36, 144, 145, 255–303, 369, 371, 377, *379,* *384,* 385, *388,* 389
Sheridan, Clara Lou. *See* Sheridan, Ann
Sheridan, George, 256
Sheridan, George W., 256
Sheridan, Kitty, 256
Sheridan, Lula Stewart Warren, 256
Sheridan, Mabel, 256

Sheridan, Pauline, 256
Sheridan, Philip, 256
Sherman, Vincent, 154, 155, 291
Sherwood, Robert E., 351
She's Back on Broadway, 222, *223*
She's Working Her Way Through College, 220, 222
Shine On Harvest Moon, 289–90, *290*
Shipman, David, 255
Shipp, Mary, 166
Shivers, Allan, 410
Shock Treatment, 41, *44*
Shootist, The, 52, *53*
Shoot the Works, 257
Shore, Dinah, 286
Shoup, Howard, 262, *270,* 273
Show Business Priest, The. See They Call Me the Show Business Priest
Sidney, Sylvia, 147, 259, 276
Siegel, Don, 52, 168
Siegel, Sol C., 88
Silke, James R., 145 n, 159
Silver Chalice, The, 225, 226
Silver River, 292
Silvers, Phil, 236, 377
Silver Screen, 371, 373
Sim, Alastair, 398, 400
Simmons, Dick, *334*
Simmons, Jean, 98
Sinatra, Frank, 30, *36,* 37, 52, 335, 337
Sinclair, Hugh, 159
Singing Marine, The, 371
Singleton, Penny, 70
Sing Me a Love Song, 261
Sirk, Douglas, 33, 295, 409, 410
Sis Hopkins, 73, *74*
Sister Kenny, 390
Sisters, The, 70, 106
Sistrom, Joseph, 86
"Sixth Sense," 415
Skelton, Red, 327, *328,* 337, 340, 343
Skinner, Frank, 409
Skipworth, Alison, 371
Skirmish on the Home Front, 79
Skirts Ahoy! 343, 345
Skolsky, Sidney, 220, 335, 370, 400
Slezak, Walter, 201
Slim, 371
Sloane, Everett, 168
Small, Edward, 139
Small Town Girl, 261
"Small World," 39
Smart Blonde, 369 n, 370
Smart Girl, 137, *137*
Smart Girls Don't Talk, 209, *210*
Smash-Up, The Story of a Woman, 82, *83,* 85
Smight, Jack, 47

Smith, Alexis, 21, 286, 288, *288*, 289, *384*, 385, *388*, 389, 402
Smith, C. Aubrey, 152
Smith, Charles Martin, *178*
Smith, Ethel, 327
Smith, Kent, 88, 291
Smith, Thorne, 76
Snake Pit, The, 87, 395
Snows of Kilimanjaro, The, 91
So Big, *408*, 408–9
Soldan High School, 197
Soldier of Fortune, 94
Some Came Running, 102 n
Sometimes (Un)Happy, 291
Somewhere I'll Find You, 326
Song Is Born, A, 206, *208*, 208–9, *210*
Song of Bernadette, The, 153
Sorry, Wrong Number, 395
Southern California, University of, 236
South Pacific, 99
South Sea Woman, 222, *224*
Spero, Bette, 239
Springsteen, R. G., 296
Spy Ring, The, 371
Stack, Robert, 33, 37, *39*, 226, *227*
Stacy, James, 109, *112*
Stage Door Canteen, 14
Stage Fright, 398, *399*, 400, 401
Stage Struck, 370
Stahl, John, 265
Stallion Road, 21, 390, 392
Standing, Guy, 259
Stanwyck, Barbara, 67, 80, 109, 112, 142, 209, 268, 285 n, 386, *386*, 392, 395, 408
Starcrossed, 236
Star Is Born, A, 410
Stark, John, 176
Starlift, 220, 405, *406*
"Star Spangled Hollywood" revue, 176
Star Spangled Rhythm, 76
Steele, Karen, 230
Steel Town, 295
Steiger, Rod, 168
Stella, 88, 293
Stephenson, James, 145
Sterling, Jan, *169*
Sterling Films, 133
Stevens, Craig, *384*
Stevenson, Adlai, 43
Stevenson, Margot, 375
Stewart, Henry, 52
Stewart, James, 52, 155, 392
Stigwood, Robert, 56
Stockwell, Dean, 415
Stolen Harmony, 369
Stolen Hours, 106, *106*

Stoltz, Myrl, 30
Stompanato, Johnny, 106
Stone, Peter, 52
"Stop Arthritis Telethon," 418
Storm Warning, 28
Story of Fanny Hill, The, 283
Story of Mankind, The, 227, *229*
Story of Will Rogers, The, 405
Strange Intruder, 169, *170*
Strangers in 7A, 174, *177*
Strasberg, Lee, 41
Strawberry Blonde, The, 279
Street, James, 85
Streetcar Named Desire, A, 398, 405
"Streets of San Francisco, The," *178*
Strouse, Charles, 48
Sullivan, Barry, 80, *81*, 401–2
Sullivan, Ed, 32
Sullivan, Jeri, 209
Summertime, 98
Sun Also Rises, The, 98 n
Susann, Jacqueline, 109, 241
Swanson, Gloria, 30
"Swan Song, The," 180
Sweet Bird of Youth, 98 n
Swimming Hall of Fame, 356

Tail Spin, 373
Take Me Out to the Ball Game, 335, *337*, 340 n
Take Me to Town, 295, *296*
"Takin' Miss Mary to the Ball," 335
Talisman, The, 226
Talisman Studio, 261
Tall Stranger, The, 230
Talmadge, Constance, 283
Talman, William, 166
Tapley, Colin, 256, *257*
Taplinger, Bob, 267
Tap Roots, 85, 86, *86*
Tate, Harry, *134*
Tate, Sharon, 109
Taylor, Charles M. "Spud," 273
Taylor, Don, 96
Taylor, Elizabeth, 91, 102, 102 n, 358
Taylor, Kent, 137, *137*
Taylor, Rachel, 41
Taylor, Robert, 372, 385, 409
Tell It to Louella, 37
Terry, Phillip, 386, *387*
Texas Carnival, 340, *342*
Thank Your Lucky Stars, 131, 153, *153*, 285, 286
That Certain Girl, 234
Thatcher, Heather, 70
That Hagen Girl, 390
That's Entertainment, Part I, 347, 358
That's Entertainment, Part II, 348, 358

Thaxter, Phyllis, 168, 220, 412
Thayer, Lorna, *100*
They Call Me the Show Business Priest, 396, 414 n
They Drive by Night, 144–45, 147, 148, 174, 275, 276, *276*
They Made Me a Criminal, 268
"They're Either Too Young or Too Old," 153
They Won't Believe Me, 84, *84*
They Won't Forget, 264
Think 20th, 109
Thirty-Nine Steps, The, 142
"This Is Your Life," 358
This Thing Called Love, 379
This Time for Keeps, 333, *334*
Thomas, Frankie, 271
Thompson, Carlos, 354, *355*
Thompson, Howard, 43
Thompson, J. Lee, 39
Thorpe, Richard, 335
Thourlby, William, 232, *234*
Thread, The, 413
Three Cheers for the Irish, 98 n
Three Faces of Eve, 98
Three Guys Named Mike, 401
Three on a Match, 266
Thrill of a Romance, 329, 329–30
Thunder in the Sun, 102, *103*
Thurber, James, 203
Tidbury, Eldred, *257*
Tiegs, Cheryl, 418
Tierney, Gene, 87, 414
Time, 11, *47*, 49, 73, 80, 84, 151, 155, 217, 275, 325, 329
Time of Your Life, The, 297
"Toast of the Town," 32
Tobias, George, 153, 275, 276
Todd, Richard, 218, 398
Todd, Thelma, 138
To Each His Own, 155, 390
To Have and Have Not, 15, 16, *17*, 18, 20, 30, 53
Tone, Franchot, 147, 297, 402
Toney, Jim, *143*
Tongay, Kathy, 345
Tongay, Russell, 345
Tony Award, 48, 56
Too Many for the Bed, 241
Toomey, Regis, *380*
Top Secret Affair, 98, *99*
Torchy Plays with Dynamite, 374
Torrid Zone, 273, *274*, 275
"To Tell the Truth," 299
Totter, Audrey, 168
Tourneur, Jacques, 82, 295
Tovarich, 264

Towering Inferno, The, 227
Toys in the Attic, 41
Tracy, Spencer, 37, 273, 327, *328*, 331, 389
Trahey, Jane, 171
Travers, Henry, 269
Travis, Richard, 281
Travolta, John, 176
Treasure Island (Reinhardt), 325
Treasure of the Sierra Madre, The, 291–92
Trevor, Claire, 28, 164, 410
Trial of Mary Surratt, The, 169
Trilling, Steve, 281
Trouble with Angelo, The, 171
Truex, Ernest, 76
Truman, Harry S., 18
Tucker, Bobby, 99
Tufts, Sonny, 330
Tugboat Annie Sails Again, 376, 377
Tulsa, 87, *87*
Tunnel of Love, The, 232
Turner, Cheryl, 106
Turner, Lana, 33, 77 n, 99, 106, 150 n, 264, 326, 327, 330, 331, 348 n, 352 n, 401, 405
TV Guide, 109, 285, 299, 333, 421
Twentieth Century–Fox, 15, 32, 34, 37, 41, *42*, 87, 90, 91, 92, 93, 94, 98, 99, 102, 109, 142, 149, 159, 227, 293, 325, 339, 355, 369, 385, 414
20,000 Years in Sing Sing, 273
Twin Beds, 283
Two Girls on Broadway, 325
Two Guys from Milwaukee, 21, 22

"Uncle Wiggily in Connecticut," 88
Under the Yum Yum Tree, 299
Unfaithful, The, 291, *292*
Ungaro, 52
Unguarded Moment, The, 352, *353*
United Artists, 24 n, 76, 77, 80, 134, 142, 213, 283, 369
United Picture Corporation, 232
United Press International, 396
Universal, 33, 82, 104, 166, 226, 261, 265, 293, 302, 352, 371, 409, 410
Unsuspected, The, 208
Untamed, 94, *95*
"Untouchables, The," 169
Up in Arms, 198, 199
Ure, Mary, 109
"U.S. Steel Hour," 296, 299

Valentine, Paul, 88
Vallee, Rudy, 197, 267
Valley of the Dolls, 68, *108,* 109, 109 n, 241
Van Fleet, Jo, 95, *96*
Van Heusen, Jimmy, 30

Van Upp, Virginia, 77
Variety, 18, 24 n, 88, 109, 136, 142, 179, 203, 205, 209, 230, 234, 323, 354, 356, 371, 395, 404, 421
Venice Film Festival, 168
Vera-Ellen, 202, 203, *204,* 209 n
Vermilye, Jerry, 131
Verne, Kaaren, 280
Vickers, Martha, 22, 156
Vidor, Charles, 148
Vidor, King, 389, 398
Viertel, Peter, 151
Vinson, Helen, 273
"Virginian, The," 169, 171, *175*
Visart, Natalie, 76
Vitaphone, 69
Vogan, Emmett, 262, *264*
Voice of the Turtle, The, 390
Volpone, 106
Von Eltz, Theodore, 22
Von Zell, Harry, 154
Vorhaus, Bernard, 134
Vreeland, Diana, 14
Vreeland, Robert, 277

Wagner (composer), 269
Wagner, Lindsay, 418, 421
Wagner, Robert, 47
"Wagon Train," 230, 299, 415
Wald, Jerry, 28, 92, 150, 275, 374, 392, 395, 401, 403
Waldron, Charles, 22
Walker, Clint, 230, *231*
Walker, Helen, 98 n
Walker, Nancy, 415
Wallace, Jean, 220
Wallace, Len, 202, 212
Wallis, Hal B., 20 n, 28, 159, 273, 275, 281
Walsh, Kay, 400
Walsh, Raoul, 141, 144, 145, 209, 213, 218, 239, 276, 292, 398
Walter Thornton Agency, 69
Walton, Tony, 52
Wand, Betty, 340, 348
Wanger, Walter, 82, 85, 86, 87, 102
Ward, Amelita, *199*
Warner, Jack L., 15, 18, 21, 22, 30, 159, 195, 265, 267, 273, 293, 395, 409, 412
Warner Bros., 15, 16, 18, 20, 21, 24, 28, 30, 33, 45, 69, 70, 98, 131, 132, 144, 145, 147, 148, 150, 153, 154, 155, 159, 168, 195, 208, 209, 212, 213, 215, 217, 218, 220, 227, 230, 236, 261, 262, *263,* 264, 265, 266, 267, 268, 269, *270,* 271, 273, 275, 276, 278, 279, 280, 281, 283, 285, 286, 291, 292, 293, 369, 370, 371, 372, 373, 374, 375, 377, 385, 389, 390, 392, 395, 396, 397, 398, 401, 402, 403, 405, 409, 410, 412
Warren, Harry, 262
Warwick, Earl of, 267
Washburn, Beverly, *403*
Washington (General), 196
Washington, Ned, 88
Washington Post, 45
Waterbury, Ruth, 400
Watson, Minor, *382*
Watson, Pat, 283
Wayne, David, 91, 293
Wayne, John, 33, *34,* 52, *53, 75,* 76, 79, 93, *97,* 98, 112 n, 405, 408
Wayward Bus, The, 98 n
Weaver, Dennis, 174, *178*
Webb, Clifton, 33, 414, *414*
Weidler, Virginia, 142
Weidman, Jerome, 88, 90, 355
Weingarten, Lawrence, *97*
Weissmuller, Johnny, 325
Welles, Orson, 385
Wellman, William, 143, 143 n, 392 n
Wells, H. G., 179
We're Not Dressing, 137, *258*
Wesson, Dick, 348, *406*
West, Mae, 41 n, 259
West, Roland, 138
Westbound, 230, *231*
Westmore, Perc, 404
Weston, Doris, 371
West Point Story, The, 217, *217,* 218
"We Will Meet Again," 331
Wexler, Norman, 56
"What Are You Doing the Rest of Your Life?" 385
What Price Glory, 139
"What's My Line?" 352
Wheeler, Lois, 88
When Hell Froze, 417
Where Angels Go . . . Trouble Follows, 171
Where Love Has Gone, 106, *107*
While the City Sleeps, 168, *170*
Whistling Teachers' Institute of America, 207
Whitcomb, Jon, 73
White Heat, 195, 213, 215, *215,* 218, 240
White Witch Doctor, 92
Whiting, Barbara, 348
Whitley, Crane, *166*
Whitman, Stuart, 41, *44,* 241
Whitney, Arthur, 324
Whitney, Eleanore, 139
Whorf, Richard, 283
"Why Didn't I?" 403
"Why Was I Born?" 156
Wickes, Mary, 281

Wide Open Faces, 371, *372*
"Wide World of Entertainment," 52
Widmark, Richard, 33, 52, 93, 159, *161*
Wientge, Alice, 196, 197
Wiggam, Lionel, 86
Wilde, Cornel, 152, 159
Wilder, Billy, 385, 386
Wilding, Michael, 398
Wildwood Productions, 52
Wilhelm (Kaiser), 132
William, Warren, 142, 370
Williams, Andy, 16, 22
Williams, Anson, 418
Williams, Bill, 82
Williams, Bonnie Lou, 215, 217 n
Williams, Bula G., 324
Williams, David, 324
Williams, Emlyn, 152
Williams, Esther, 18, 88 n, 323–58, 402, 408, 418
Williams, Guinn "Big Boy," *268*, 269
Williams, June, 324, 356
Williams, Lou, 324
Williams, Maureen, 324
Williams, Paul, 396
Williams, Stanton, 324
Williams, Sumner, 165
Williams, Tennessee, 179, 401
Wills, Chill, *87*
Wills, Mary, 88
Will Success Spoil Rock Hunter? 41
Will There Really Be a Morning? 176
Wilson, Dorothy, 203
Wilson, Earl, 48, 358
Wilson, Eileen, 109
Wilson, Lois, *214*
Wilson, Marie, 230, 266, 290
Wilson, Richard, 354
Winchell, Walter, 18, 267
Wine, Women and Horses, 265
Wing, Toby, 369
Wings for the Eagle, 283, *284*, 285
Winning Team, The, 405
Winsten, Archer, 394
Winter, Keith, 155
Winter Carnival, 269, 271
Winters, Shelley, 47, 147, 168, 239, 405
Wise, Robert, 67, 226
With a Song in My Heart, 91, 92, 95
Woman and the Hunter, The, 297
Woman in Hiding, 162, 163
Woman Obsessed, 102
Woman of the Year, 37
Woman on the Run, 293, *294*
Woman's World, 31, 33
Women, The, 296
Women in Chains, 174

Women's AAU Outdoor Nationals, 324
Women's Prison, 168, *169*
Wonderful Town, 53, *54*
Wonderful Us, 415
Wonder Man, 195, 202, *202*
Won Ton Ton, the Dog Who Saved Hollywood, 236
Wood, Natalie, 43, *45*, 227, 403, 408
Wood, Sam, 280
Wood, Yvonne, 86
Woods, Donald, *388*
Woodward, Bob, 52
Woodward, Joanne, 98
Woolley, Monty, 152, *152*, 154, 281, *282*, *388*, 389
World of Entertainment, The, 340 n
Wren, P. C., 70
Wright, Cobina, Jr., 385
Wright, Teresa, 203, *205*, 400
Written on the Wind, 33
Wuthering Heights, 142
Wyatt, Jane, 169
Wycherly, Margaret, 213, *215*
Wyler, William, 26, 203, 209 n
Wyman, Jane, 70, 131, 145, *163*, 220, 264, 278, 288, *288*, 289, 367–421
Wynn, Keenan, 331, *333*, 337, *339*

Yacht Club Boys, *141*
Yank at Oxford, A, 372
Yankee Doodle Dandy, 385
Yearling, The, 366, 367, 389–90, 392
York, Cal, 94, 155
York, Michael, 52
You Can't Take It with You, 77
You Made Me Love You, 138
Youmans, Vincent, 291
Young, Carleton G., 329
Young, Collier H., 159, 160, *160*, 163, 164, *164*, 166
Young, Gig, 159, *161*
Young, Loretta, 80, *81*, 85, 88, 91, 137, 368, *394*, 412, 414, 418
Young, Robert, 84, *84*
Young, Victor, 88
Young and Willing, 77
Young Fury, 232
Young Man with a Horn, 28, *29*
You're in the Army Now, 377, *380*
Yours for the Asking, 139

Zanuck, Darryl F., 87
Zimbalist, Efrem, Jr., 88
Ziegfeld, Florenz, 330
Ziegfeld Follies, The, 330, *331*
"Zing a Little Zong," 408
Zucco, George, 142